ALSO BY CAROLINE WEBER

Terror and Its Discontents:
Suspect Words in Revolutionary France

QUEEN OF FASHION

QUEEN OF

FASHION

WHAT MARIE ANTOINETTE WORE
TO THE REVOLUTION

CAROLINE WEBER

HENRY HOLT AND COMPANY   NEW YORK

Henry Holt and Company, LLC
Publishers since 1866
175 Fifth Avenue
New York, New York 10010
www.henryholt.com

Henry Holt® and 🞝® are registered trademarks of
Henry Holt and Company, LLC.

Distributed in Canada by H. B. Fenn and Company Ltd.

Library of Congress Cataloging-in-Publication Data
Weber, Caroline, [date]
    Queen of fashion : what Marie Antoinette wore to the Revolution /
Caroline Weber.—1st ed.
        p.   cm.
    Includes bibliographical references and index.
    ISBN-13: 978-0-8050-7949-4
    ISBN-10: 0-8050-7949-1
    1. Marie Antoinette, Queen, consort of Louis XVI, King of France,
1775–1793—Clothing.   2. Fashion—France—History—18th century.
3. France–Courts and courtiers—Clothing—History—18th century.
4. France—History—Louis XVI, 1774–1793.   I. Title.
GT865.W37 2006
391.00944—dc22   2006041234

Henry Holt books are available for special promotions and premiums.
For details contact: Director, Special Markets.

First Edition 2006

Designed by Kelly Too

Printed in the United States of America
1 3 5 7 9 10 8 6 4 2

For Tom, as always

To be the most *à la mode* woman alive seemed to [Marie Antoinette] the most desirable thing imaginable; and this foible, unworthy of a great sovereign, has been the sole cause of all the exaggerated faults that people have so cruelly ascribed to her.

—THE COMTESSE DE BOIGNE

These fashions are symbolic and women of quality will know perfectly well how to interpret them.

—*LE JOURNAL DE LA MODE ET DU GOÛT*

· CONTENTS ·

QUEEN OF FASHION

INTRODUCTION

Designed for his 2000 Christian Dior "Masquerade and Bondage" collection, John Galliano's "Marie Antoinette" dress tells an unexpected story. True to the architecture of eighteenth-century court costume, the gown features tantalizing décolletage, a rigidly corseted waist, a ladder or *échelle* of flirty bows on the bodice, and a froth of flounced skirts inflated by petticoats and hoops. Its splendid excess evokes France's most colorful queen . . . even before one notices the embroidered portraits of the lady herself that adorn each of its hoop-skirted hip panels. (Plate 1.)

But the two portraits deserve a closer look, for it is they that tell the story. On the gown's left hip panel the designer has placed an image of Marie Antoinette in her notorious faux shepherdess's garb—a frilly little apron tied over a pastel frock, a decorative staff wound with streaming pink ribbons, and a mile-high hairdo obviously ill suited to the tending of livestock. In keeping with the Queen's frivolous reputation, the embroidered ensemble is more suggestive of Little Bo Peep than of lofty monarchical grandeur. On the right hip panel, Galliano offers a depiction of the same woman, also devoid of royal attributes, but this time in a mode more gruesome than whimsical. Here, she wears a markedly plain, utilitarian dress, with a simple white kerchief knotted around her throat and a drooping red "liberty bonnet"—the emblem of her revolutionary persecutors—clamped onto her brutally shorn head. This image portrays the consort trudging toward the guillotine, to lay her neck beneath its waiting blade.

Galliano's opposing vignettes elegantly express the French queen's well-known trajectory from glamour to tragedy, from extravagant privilege to utter defeat. Yet the juxtaposition does more still. Weaving the arc of her roller-coaster existence into the very fabric of a dress, the designer posits what appears to be a direct relationship between Marie Antoinette's frippery and her demise. He seems to imply that her destiny as an icon both of *ancien régime* frivolity and of revolutionary vengeance—of capricious, entitled masquerade and deadly political bondage—is closely intertwined with the history of her apparel. This is a formulation that I find revelatory indeed, for, like Galliano, I have scrutinized Marie Antoinette's fashion statements. And I have discovered that they were, in every sense, accessories to the campaign she waged against the oppressive cultural strictures and harsh political animosities that beset her throughout her twenty-three-year tenure in France.

This is a work about the role of fashion in the life of Marie Antoinette, whose clothing choices—so influential in the last decades of the eighteenth century—played a part in determining both her own fate and that of the *ancien régime* as a whole. This is not a tale that other biographers have chosen to recount. From Edmund Burke in the eighteenth century to Stefan Zweig in the twentieth, many chroniclers of her life and times have cast Marie Antoinette as the icon of an exquisite but doomed social order, and not without reason.[1] Indeed, her very presence in Galliano's collection and in a host of other contemporary cultural media—from the fashion press to popular film, and from Madonna's performances and posters to a Swiss watch company's recent advertising campaign—confirms her undiminished ability to conjure up both the flamboyance and the folly of a vanished aristocratic world.[2]

But I think there is more to consider about this icon. In charting Marie Antoinette's fateful course from the gilded halls of Versailles to the blood-splashed steps of the guillotine, historians rarely emphasize the tremendous importance that her public attached to what she was wearing at each step along the way. In a recent anthology edited by Dena Goodman, a group of contemporary scholars explores how "crucial political and cultural contests were enacted on the very body of the Queen."[3] In these analyses, Marie Antoinette's sexuality, fertility, and other physical characteristics are shown to have been both pretexts and catalysts for the fierce debates about gender, class, and power that rocked the *ancien régime* and fueled the Revolution. Yet, curiously, Marie Antoinette's costumes—and what they meant to the people around her—receive little extensive notice in Goodman's volume, except in a few brilliant passages by Pierre Saint-Amand (who rightly suggests that "the story of Marie Antoinette can be read as a series of costumed events") and Mary Sheriff (who analyzes a portrait of the Queen dressed in a particularly unusual ensemble).[4] Apart from these two scholars, Chantal Thomas, whose superb book *The Wicked Queen* identifies Marie Antoinette's modishness as one of the many reasons the French public turned against her, has stood virtually alone in considering "the crucial political and cultural contests" sparked by the Queen's daring fashions.[5]

It is time for a still more detailed treatment of this issue, because a thorough reexamination of Marie Antoinette's biography reveals the startling consistency and force with which her costumes triggered severe sociopolitical disorder. As Galliano's gown suggests, the interplay between the consort and her public was an incendiary, ultimately fatal one. By examining the sartorial politics that informed her rise and fall, I hope to cast new light on this endlessly analyzed, inexhaustibly fascinating historical figure.

FROM THE MOMENT THE FOURTEEN-YEAR-OLD AUSTRIAN-BORN ARCHduchess Maria Antonia arrived in France to marry the heir to the Bourbon throne, matters of clothing and appearance proved central to her existence. For the future and, later, reigning queen, a rigid protocol governed much of what she wore, how she wore it, when she wore it, and even who put it on her person. Designed to showcase and affirm the magnificence of the Bourbon dynasty, this protocol had been imposed by French monarchs on their courtiers, and on their consorts, for generations.

Even before she left her native Vienna for the court of France in the spring of 1770, the young princess received an intensive crash course in the Bourbon approach to looks, dress, and public image. She was redesigned from tooth to coif, and a renowned French dance instructor trained her to move gracefully while wearing high heels, hoopskirts, and a hefty, cumbersome train. Her appearance, her elders ceaselessly reminded her, would make or break her success as a French royal wife.

Yet from her earliest days at Versailles, Marie Antoinette staged a revolt against entrenched court etiquette by turning her clothes and other accoutrements into defiant expressions of autonomy and prestige. Although, as many scholars have pointed out, she did not evince a sustained interest in politics qua broad-reaching international or domestic policy, it is my belief that she identified fashion as a key weapon in her struggle for personal prestige, authority, and sometimes mere survival.[6] Her efforts in this vein became increasingly complex and sophisticated as she grew to adulthood and adapted to the ever-changing political climate around her. But it was quite early on, as an adolescent newcomer to France, that she first made a striking bid to seize control of her sartorial image. Initiating a lifelong series of bold stylistic experiments (which one aristocratic contemporary described as constituting "a veritable revolution in dress"), she challenged received wisdom about the kind and the extent of the power that a French royal consort ought to possess.[7]

Traditionally, such power was severely curtailed by a principle known as Salic Law, which excluded women from the line of royal succession.[8] Except in cases where a widowed queen acted as regent for a son still too young to rule on his own, the role of the French king's wife was restricted principally to her ability to bear royal children. But for the first seven years of her marriage to Louis Auguste, who became King Louis XVI in 1774, Marie Antoinette found this avenue closed to her. Because of a combination of debilitating psychological and sexual reticence, her young spouse refused to consummate their union, and this put Marie Antoinette—married off to cement a political union between Austria and France—in a profoundly uncomfortable position.[9] For as her mother, Empress Maria Theresa, never tired of reminding her, neither the Franco-Austrian alliance nor Marie Antoinette's own place at Versailles would be secure unless she gave the Bourbon dynasty an heir. Until that day, the many French courtiers who deplored the alliance (designed to reverse a centuries-old enmity between the two nations) would not hesitate to push for her replacement by a more fertile princess.

Isolated and unloved by these scheming factions, the Austrian newcomer was thus faced with two options: concede defeat and return to Vienna in disgrace, or find another means of establishing herself in France. With the high geopolitical stakes of her marriage placing the first alternative squarely out of the question, Marie Antoinette began to combat her enemies with style. Through carefully selected, unconventional outfits and accessories, she cultivated what she later called an "*appearance* of [political] credit," even as she faced continual failure on the procreative front.[10] From the male riding gear she sported on the royal hunt to the white furs and diamonds she favored for sleigh rides, and from the monumental hairstyles she flaunted in all of Paris's most fashionable haunts to the intricate disguises she donned for costume parties at Versailles, the startling fashions that Marie Antoinette unveiled announced her as more than just an inadequate spouse or the token of a foundering diplomatic effort. I will argue that these ensembles, too often dismissed as mere instances of the Queen's ill-advised frivolity, identified her as a woman who could dress, spend, and do exactly as she pleased.

To some extent, this strategy was not new. The Sun King, Louis XIV—to whom Marie Antoinette was distantly related and whose exploits she studied as a child—had furthered his absolutist pretensions in part by adopting such imposing, awe-inspiring costumes that viewers had little choice but to concede his supremacy.[11] He, too, had had a penchant for elaborate masquerade balls, oversized wigs, glittering gems, and hunting gear that connoted dominion over all creatures, great and small.[12] More recently, Mesdames de Pompadour and Du Barry, mistresses to Louis XIV's successor Louis XV, had made a show of their unrivaled influence on the crown by spending a king's ransom on gowns and jewels. For them as for the Sun King, dress functioned as a compelling and efficient vehicle for communicating political power.

Yet, because she was neither a king nor a king's mistress, Marie Antoinette's sartorial posturing represented a striking departure from established court custom. For a French consort to modify the conventions of royal appearance, or to seek attention or empowerment on her own terms, was virtually unheard of. But this is exactly what Marie Antoinette did, in ways that became even more daring after she acceded to the throne in 1774.[13] Her stature unchallenged by a competing royal mistress—for shy Louis XVI had none—the young queen promptly jettisoned the stagnant and dowdy royal style that had long functioned to evoke the timelessness of the Bourbon reign, and set out in heady new directions. Aided by a burgeoning class of gifted Parisian designers, the forebears to today's superstar couturiers, Marie Antoinette cultivated looks that were playful and coquettish, ephemeral and unpredictable, alluring and modern.

On the more whimsical side, one of her signature vogues was the *pouf,* a thickly powdered, teetering hairstyle that re-created elaborate scenes from current events (such as a naval victory against the British, or the birth of an exalted French duke) or from imaginary country idylls (complete with windmills, grazing beasts, laboring peasants, and babbling brooks). Less ostentatious but equally novel were the saucy, unstructured *chemise* dresses that the Queen came to favor as a reaction against the stiff hoops and whalebone stays of standard court wear. Adopted as the unofficial uniform of the Petit Trianon—the private country retreat Marie Antoinette received as a gift from her husband shortly after their accession—these free-flowing shifts facilitated distinctly nonroyal shenanigans such as picnics on the grass, games of blindman's buff, and frolics among pretty, perfumed flocks of sheep. Despite conservative courtiers' protestations that the dresses made their noble wearers indistinguishable from serving wenches, the Queen and her companions reveled in the freedom and comfort their new garb afforded them.

Among the nobility and the moneyed bourgeoisie, even those women who found such innovations shocking in the King's wife could not resist following her lead. "By one of those contradictions that are more common in France than anywhere else," wrote a contemporary observer, "even as the people were criticizing the Queen for her outfits, they continued frenetically to imitate her. Every woman wanted to have the same *déshabillé,* the same bonnet, that they had seen her wear."[14] Propelled to notoriety by the ingenuity of designers to whom the public came to refer as her "ministry of fashion," Marie Antoinette established herself as a force to be reckoned with—as a queen who commanded as much attention as the most dazzling king or mistress, and whose imposing stature had nothing to do with her maternal prospects.

Her celebrity, however, came at a price. Obsessively monitored by those around her, Marie Antoinette's unorthodox styles prompted a backlash among courtiers who strenuously opposed her rise, and who bristled at her defiance of time-honored royal customs. These aristocrats, in turn, reviled her as a reckless Austrian interloper who was blithely overstepping the bounds of her queenly station, eclipsing her husband as the center of her subjects' attention, and degrading his sacred authority in the process. They also charged her and her "ministry of fashion" with depleting France's coffers, which, because of a recent series of domestic and international crises, could ill afford to be tapped for endless bonnets and frocks.

Flowing from the nobles' palaces to the streets of Paris, often by means of vituperative underground pamphlets and caricatures, rumors of the Queen's sartorial exploits also prompted outrage among her lower-born subjects. Outside the privileged world of Versailles, Marie Antoinette's costly attire came to epitomize the vast economic inequalities that condemned so much of the French populace to abject misery. In addition, some of her critics resented her because they retained an expectation that the royal consort should respect the established limits of her position, should retain the air of docile conformity and anodyne polish that previous consorts (such as Louis XV's late wife, Maria Leczinska) had reassuringly conveyed.[15] Yet the new queen's provocative garb revealed that she had no intention of doing any such thing.

The resulting paradox of Marie Antoinette's career as a public figure was that despite her intuitive grasp of clothing's potential to express status and strength, she repeatedly misjudged the responses her attire would elicit from her subjects. That she was performing for a twofold audience—aristocrats and commoners—almost necessarily meant that she could not hope to please all of the people all of the time. But more often than not, her rebellion in dress generated or exacerbated grievances among both contingents, to the point where the nobility and the populace, worlds apart on so many political issues, reached an explosive consensus about their hatred of Marie Antoinette. Like Claudius, the illegitimately enthroned "king of shreds and patches" thought by Shakespeare's Hamlet to personify the whole of the rotten Danish state, this queen of *poufs* and feathers came to emblematize the worst aspects of royal privilege—and the best reasons for revolution.

. . .

IN THEIR SWEEPING REFORM OF FRENCH SOCIETY AND CULTURE, THE REVO-
lutionaries who toppled Louis XVI's régime succeeded in obliterating not
only a political system based on entrenched and iniquitous caste distinctions,
but also the emblems—palaces and prisons, coats of arms and crowns—that
gave these distinctions their material form.[16] Unfortunately for the purposes
of this study, the rebels' destructive frenzy reduced Marie Antoinette's own
magnificent clothing collection to, precisely, a pile of shreds and patches.
Before insurrectionary forces stormed Versailles in October 1789, the collection filled three entire rooms at the château: rooms that were open to the
public, and that granted visitors a firsthand glimpse of the Queen's countless accessories and gowns.[17] After the October uprising, the monarchs
were forced to relocate from Versailles to the Tuileries, their Parisian residence; a large number of Marie Antoinette's clothes, undamaged in the
invasion, were sent on to her there. Yet neither these outfits nor the new
ones she commissioned while in Paris survived the Revolution's subsequent
turmoil.

In June 1791, during the royal family's abortive attempt to flee the capital, a crowd of marauders reportedly broke into the Tuileries and looted the
runaway consort's armoires for articles that, during the revolutionary period, had remained billboards for her undiminished sense of monarchical
prestige—and had thus continued to draw the people's ire.[18] Fourteen months
later, on August 10, 1792, rioting hordes again laid siege to the Tuileries,
this time sending the King and Queen into an imprisonment that ended only
with their executions in 1793. With the exception of the diminutive, beribboned slipper she lost while fleeing the palace, and of swatches of ruined garments later preserved as relics by the monarchy's loyalists, almost nothing of
Marie Antoinette's wardrobe escaped the onslaught intact.[19]

The fragments that remain—scattered, stained, and harrowing to
behold—are woefully unequal to the task of re-creating the Queen's fashions
in all their grandiose glory. The history of Marie Antoinette's costuming
preferences can, however, still be gleaned from a variety of other eighteenth-
century materials: from formal portraits to satirical cartoons, from fashion
journals to pornographic pamphlets, and from her contemporaries' recollections to her clothing purveyors' and wardrobe manager's account books. In
addition, pieces of this history can be reconstructed from the research of
those biographers who, while not focusing primarily on Marie Antoinette's
love affair with fashion, pay close attention to the vagaries of her costumes.
Antonia Fraser's well-known recent biography has been particularly helpful
to me in this regard, for the splendid detail it offers about (and the concern

it demonstrates for) the Queen's style of dress. Like me, Fraser went through the none-too-self-evident process of obtaining permission to consult first-hand the few *gazettes des atours*—marvelous eighteenth-century "look books" containing fabric swatches and shorthand dress descriptions, on the basis of which Marie Antoinette selected her outfits each morning—that have been preserved in France's Archives Nationales.[20]

Admittedly, determining with utter certainty what Marie Antoinette wore and when is made almost impossible by the distortions and omissions that inhere in even the most "neutral" of historical records.[21] And when a subject generates as varied and severe a backlash as this controversial queen's outfits invariably did, the lines between biographical fact and cultural fiction can be especially hard to demarcate. (The same holds true for Marie Antoinette's actions in general; in charting the biographical elements most salient to her sartorial itinerary, I have therefore relied on the scrupulous research of generations of biographers, cited abundantly and gratefully throughout these pages.) Without purporting to resolve these difficulties with respect to Marie Antoinette's clothing, I have tried to address them by documenting my sources as painstakingly as possible, and by highlighting the places where an observer's overriding political agenda—be it anti-Austrian, antifeminist, pro-monarchist, or pro-revolutionary—calls the reliability of his or her claims most acutely into question.[22]

At the same time, I have made a conscious decision not to exclude from this study the distortions and fantasies that cropped up around the Queen's clothed persona, for these, too, tell us something valuable about how that persona was represented and perceived.[23] As Lynn Hunt has demonstrated in her work on revolutionary pornography, wildly exaggerated, often outright invented tales of Marie Antoinette's nymphomania, lesbianism, and other sexual "perversions" not only belied the deep-seated misogyny of republican politics, but were marshaled by the Queen's adversaries to build the legal case for her execution.[24] Such fabrications, Hunt has shown, can have real political weight and real historical significance. They have the power to change lives—even to end them.

In much the same way, I take the view that both the ostensibly neutral and the obviously exaggerated accounts of Marie Antoinette's costuming choices highlight these choices' capacity to provoke commentary and generate upheaval on a grand scale. As Michael Ondaatje has written in the voice of another of history's more elusive antiheroes, Billy the Kid, "blood a necklace on me all my life."[25] Reviled time and again for her crimes of fashion, Marie Antoinette might well have described herself in much the same way. Indeed, according to the biographer Carrolly Erickson, shortly after the guillotine sliced its own bloody version of a necklace into the Queen's throat, well-born women in Paris began tying "thin red ribbons around their necks as reminders of what they might soon suffer."[26] Even in death, the royal consort thus affirmed a powerful link between fashion and politics. But this was a link that, as the nation's most conspicuous and controversial fashion plate, she had spent a lifetime forging. Always imaginative, if sometimes imaginary, Marie Antoinette's wardrobe was the stuff of dreams, and the space of nightmares.

ONE

PANDORA'S BOX

April 21, 1770. Fifty-seven richly appointed carriages, laden with more than twice as many dignitaries and drawn by more than six times as many horses, had filled the Hofburg's majestic central courtyard since dawn.[1] But when the imperial family stepped out of the palace at nine o'clock, the crowds began to separate, making way for Maria Theresa, the stout fifty-two-year-old Empress of Austria and Queen of Hungary. Stately and imposing in her black widow's weeds, her daily uniform ever since her husband Francis Stephen's death five years earlier, the woman sometimes referred to as King Maria Theresa marched grandly through the courtyard.[2] Along with the usual cadre of courtiers and guardsmen, she was flanked by several of her ten living children, among them her eldest son and co-regent, the Holy Roman Emperor Joseph II, and her youngest daughter, fourteen-year-old Archduchess Marie Antoinette.

Stiff-backed imperial soldiers fired salvos from the ramparts; church bells pealed gaily throughout the city. Their voices raised above the din, court officials harangued the travelers and onlookers in German, French, Latin. *Bella gerant alii, tu Austria felix nube*. Although Marie Antoinette had lately been studying the classics with her private tutor from France, the Abbé de Vermond, she did not need to draw on his lessons to translate this particular line. It was the Hapsburg family motto, and her mother had repeated it to her often enough in recent months: "Let other nations wage war; you, happy Austria, achieve your ends through marriage."

The aphorism suited this morning's occasion, which celebrated one of

Maria Theresa's boldest diplomatic successes to date. This scheme involved marrying off Marie Antoinette to the Dauphin Louis Auguste, the fifteen-year-old grandson of France's King Louis XV, and the heir to the Bourbon throne. Arranged by the Austrian empress, the French king, and their respective advisers, the union was designed to cement a strategic alliance first begun by the Treaty of Paris in 1756. Before then, Austria and France had long been at loggerheads—bitter adversaries as recently as the War of the Austrian Succession (1740–1748), in which France had fought alongside Austria's hereditary enemy, Prussia. But seven years after that conflict, Frederick II of Prussia had done an about-face by signing a treaty with France's own long-standing foe, England. Alarming to both France and Austria, this development prompted the two countries to broker a mutually expedient defensive pact.³

The Franco-Austrians' inaugural joint military effort, the Seven Years' War (1756–1763), had proved disastrous, culminating in a resounding victory for Great Britain. Nevertheless, in its aftermath, Maria Theresa sought further to strengthen the ties between her nation and Louis XV's. True to her family's motto, the Empress decided to offer her youngest daughter as a bride for her Bourbon ally's conveniently unwed heir. Louis XV's most trusted and influential minister, the Duc de Choiseul, worked assiduously in support of the plan, and after years of delicate negotiations, the two countries agreed formally to the marriage. Now, on this spring morning, Marie Antoinette was to depart for France in triumph, a living emblem of her mother's foreign policy.

A trim strawberry blonde with wide blue eyes, rosy cheeks, and a gentle demeanor marred only by the prominent lower lip that identified her as a member of the Hapsburg clan, the bride-to-be fought back tears as she prepared to take leave of her family and her home, jostled by hundreds of Viennese well-wishers who showered her with bouquets and other mementoes.⁴ Though visibly moved, the young archduchess made a concerted effort to smile, and navigated the crowd with grace.⁵ Ever since her engagement the previous summer, she had been working intensively with the legendary French dancer and ballet theoretician Jean-Georges Noverre. At the court of Versailles, Noverre had reiterated in their rigorous sessions together, the ladies do not walk—they glide. Yes, their whalebone stays are painful and their shoe heels high, but they float as if their bodies are weightless. As if their feet never touch the ground.⁶

For the journey she was about to undertake, Marie Antoinette's ladies had dressed her in the sweeping folds of a *grand habit de cour*—the formal court dress of Versailles—cut from the most lustrous brocade that money could buy. With its lavishly beribboned, tight-fitting bodice, its voluminous hoopskirts draped over wide *paniers* ("baskets" fastened to the hips underneath the dress), and its long matching train hanging from stiff pleats behind her shoulders, the dress presented an impressive, if highly stylized, silhouette. Because Versailles stood as a beacon of style for virtually all the courts in Europe, the look was not unfamiliar to the Archduchess: she had sported modified versions of the *habit de cour* at official functions throughout her childhood.[7] However, like the late Emperor Francis Stephen, her brother Joseph II was opposed to excessively strict court etiquette, and upon his accession began a vigorous campaign to reduce the elaborateness of Viennese court costume.[8] Her assumption today of the *grand habit* thus represented a break with the relatively relaxed dress codes of her native milieu, and anticipated the world of unremitting formality that awaited her at Versailles.

ALTHOUGH HER COMPATRIOTS IN FRANCE WOULD LATER MAKE MUCH OF HER penchant for undignified, "Austrian" informality, Marie Antoinette's Viennese upbringing had afforded her some degree of training in matters of ornamentation and artifice: even as children, Hapsburgs were not exempt from ceremonial court appearances.[9] When she was just ten years old, she, Maximilian, and Ferdinand (two of her brothers who were closest to her in age) had danced in a ballet for the guests at the wedding of their brother the Archduke Joseph to Josepha of Bavaria. In Martin Mytens's lovely painting of the performance—which Marie Antoinette later had sent to her in France as a cherished memento from home—the Archduchess strikes an impressively graceful pose despite the stiffness and girth of her elaborate, hoop-skirted costume. (Plate 2.) Years before her tutelage under Noverre, she had appeared "exquisitely poised, her famous deportment already in evidence": a credit to her illustrious birth and her mother's high expectations.[10] Excelling in dance far more than in any other art form, the Empress's youngest daughter thus gravitated at an early age toward a skill that would be crucial to her assimilation in France.

Another of the Archduchess's fortuitous childhood pursuits was playing with dolls, a diversion that allowed her to practice manipulating and adorning the female form. Her interest in this pastime is captured in a 1762 portrait by her older sister, Archduchess Marie Christine, which today hangs in the Kunsthistorisches Museum in Vienna, and which depicts the imperial family gathered for an intimate breakfast on Saint Nicholas's Day. Most of the painting's elements suggest the invitingly relaxed domesticity that, unlike their relentlessly formal counterparts at Versailles, Maria Theresa and her clan cultivated when not participating in state occasions. Surrounded by various members of her family, all celebrating the holiday in an unstuffy, comfortable manner, seven-year-old Marie Antoinette plays excitedly with a large doll in a fancy yellow gown.

At first blush, there scarcely appears to be anything unusual about the future Dauphine's absorption in her doll, for Saint Nicholas's Day was then, as it is today, a gift-giving holiday that children ecstatically devote to their new toys. What *is* unusual about the image, and what suggests something singular about Marie Antoinette's relationship to this particular toy, is rather the outfit she is wearing. In marked contrast to her mother and her oldest sister, Marie Christine (whose outfit in the painting Antonia Fraser has aptly described as "more like that of a maid than [that of] an Archduchess"), the little princess is wearing an ornate *robe à la française,* a slightly less cumbersome variation on the ceremonial *grand habit,* identifiable by its tight, low-cut bodice and by the pleated train hanging from her tiny shoulders.[11] (At Versailles, the *robe à la française* was worn on all but the greatest state occasions.) Nothing in the surrounding scene explains or justifies the young Archduchess's hyperelegant costume—nothing, that is, except the presence of her doll, whose sumptuous attire she seems to be copying with her own.[12] Whether an actual historical fact or an imaginative embellishment on the part of the artist, this odd detail is a suggestive one, for it links Marie Antoinette's affinity for dolls—an affinity she would maintain throughout her girlhood—to what one observer described as her developing "ardor for new ensembles."[13]

Thus attuned to the joys of playing dress-up, Marie Antoinette was eminently well suited for one of the key activities in which her mother enlisted her a few years later to prepare her for Versailles—shopping for the bridal trousseau. This required the thirteen-year-old archduchess to spend countless hours with dressmakers and milliners summoned from Paris to provide her with a suitably luxurious wardrobe. To showcase their wares, the fashion purveyors often relied on jointed wooden or plaster *poupées de mode,* or "fashion dolls"—precursors to both the store mannequin and the runway model—outfitted in doll-sized versions of the latest Parisian styles.[14] Commonly known as Pandoras ("little Pandora" modeled morning and informal garb, while "big Pandora" was draped in ceremonial and evening wear), these dolls were crucial in disseminating the latest trends coming out of the city that was already recognized as the standard-bearer for international style.[15] According to the historian Daniel Roche, "in times of war, the *poupées* enjoyed diplomatic immunity, and were even given cavalry escorts to ensure their safe arrival."[16]

As the biographer Carrolly Erickson has noted, "scores of these dolls began arriving at the Hofburg as soon as [the Archduchess] turned thirteen, wearing miniature versions of the robes and gowns proposed for her"; and these included ball gowns, afternoon dresses, robes and petticoats in a score of delicate shades, the silks embroidered with floral designs or silk ribbon appliqué, the borders trimmed with serpentine garlands of silver and gold lace, . . . already over-decorated fabrics [trimmed] with fields of artificial flowers, feathers, tassels and silk ribbon bows, rosettes and ruffles, *passementerie* and beading and costly metallic fringe.[17]

Even for a future queen, the trousseau Marie Antoinette accumulated was a spectacular one. In being fitted for these sumptuous gowns, Pierre Saint-Amand has observed, the young archduchess herself became something of "a miniature mannequin, . . . carefully prepared for the enjoyment of the French court."[18] Indeed, much like a *poupée de mode,* she was to serve as a valued object of exchange between two nations, transcending diplomatic grudges and fostering mutual cooperation and goodwill. But her adoption of the dolls' lavish apparel had other implications as well. Marie Antoinette's transformation into a living, breathing fashion doll both allowed her to participate actively in the magic of sartorial transformations, and subjected her in the most literal sense possible to her future compatriots' exacting standards.

Indeed, her fittings with Parisian fashion purveyors were predicated on the notion that at the famously refined and discriminating court of Versailles, clothing was the currency of social acceptance and political survival. In fact, it was none other than the Duc de Choiseul, France's strongest advocate of the Hapsburg-Bourbon union, who had stipulated the Archduchess's wardrobe overhaul as a necessary precondition for the match. Louis XV himself had made it known that he could not possibly extend an offer of marriage on his grandson's behalf without first knowing that Marie Antoinette was attractive enough to be a credit to his court—and Choiseul had good reasons for wishing to oblige his master on this point. As Choiseul (like the rest of the monarch's subjects) was well aware, the King was a notorious womanizer, who had neglected his late consort, Maria Leczinska, in favor of a series of flashy mistresses.[19] Although the King's heir and Marie Antoinette's future husband, Louis Auguste, evinced nothing but frightened malaise around the opposite sex, Choiseul apparently hoped that providing the boy with a pretty, glamorous bride would, as Pierre Saint-Amand has put it, "stabilize the Bourbon monarchy and put an end to its reputation for adultery."[20] However, when Choiseul first asked his chief contacts in Vienna—Marie Antoinette's tutor, the Abbé de Vermond, and France's ambassador, the Marquis de Durfort—about the girl's physical appearance, both men complained of its many deficiencies. These, Maria Theresa and her emissaries were informed, would have to be remedied if the Austrians wished to secure their alliance with France.

The Empress took the directive seriously, sparing no expense to make her daughter a visibly worthy Bourbon bride. At a time when the wardrobe of an entire working-class French family had an average value of thirty livres, and when the collective wardrobe of a wealthy aristocratic couple was worth somewhere between two thousand and five thousand livres, Maria Theresa spent a staggering four hundred thousand livres on her youngest daughter's trousseau.[21] (According to Jean Sgard's useful if highly approximate metric, a livre in Marie Antoinette's day was probably worth between twenty and thirty U.S. dollars today.[22]) This amount far exceeded the sums the Empress had disbursed for all her other daughters' trousseaus combined. Just as important, every garment purchased was French-made. Only in clothes that boasted such a provenance could Marie Antoinette hope to pass muster with the French king and his courtiers.

Choiseul and his emissaries also suggested alterations to the Archduchess's physical person. During the marriage negotiations, they noted that the girl's teeth were lamentably crooked. Straightaway, a French dentist was summoned to undertake the necessary oral surgeries. Although the interventions were excruciating, performed without anesthesia and requiring three long months to complete, the Archduchess was rewarded with a smile that was "very beautiful and straight."[23]

Choiseul's contingent also decreed that something had to be done about the princess's hair. Marie Antoinette's unruly mess of reddish-blond curls was habitually worn pulled back off her forehead with a harsh woolen band that ripped at her scalp. The band, however, was beginning to cause unsightly bald patches along the Archduchess's hairline; what was more, because it created a towering "mountain of curls" atop the girl's head, the style accentuated what French officials viewed as an unacceptably high forehead.[24] To address these alarming problems, Choiseul's stylish sister, the Duchesse de Grammont, came to the rescue by dispatching Larsenneur, who had served as hairdresser to Louis XV's own queen, to Vienna to coif the Archduchess *à la française*.[25] Re-creating the coiffure made famous by Louis XV's beloved late mistress, Madame de Pompadour, Larsenneur tamed the Archduchess's locks into a low, powdered upsweep studded with decorative gems. The resulting look softened her prominent forehead, saved her from further balding, and brought her directly into line with the tonsorial conventions of Versailles. What was more, the change made a strong impression on the ladies of Vienna who, like their counterparts throughout Europe, looked to France's courtiers as paragons of style: before long, these women were "said to be abandoning their curls in favor of a style [called] *à la Dauphine.*"²⁶ Already at age thirteen, Marie Antoinette had become a closely observed and avidly copied trendsetter.

Louis XV's representatives also arranged for a French portraitist named Joseph Ducreux to travel to Vienna to do his part for the alliance. This painter was charged with documenting the effects of the Archduchess's extensive makeover; for Louis XV had declared that he would not definitively agree to the union until he saw what the bride-to-be actually looked like. Before Ducreux's arrival in January 1769, Maria Theresa had repeatedly stalled for time, putting off the Bourbon monarch's requests "as if no artist could really capture the beauty of her daughter."²⁷ After Marie Antoinette underwent her metamorphosis, the Empress grew more compliant and eagerly sent Louis XV Ducreux's first completed painting in April.

Unfortunately, the original canvas has been lost, but during the spring of 1769, Ducreux painted two more portraits in rapid succession, both of which were sent to Versailles and widely copied by French artists and engravers.²⁸ (Plate 3.) The replicas that survive depict a fetching young dauphine with an impeccably French hairstyle and outfit that apparently dispelled the King's doubts about her suitability once and for all—for he formally approved the match shortly after Ducreux's first portrait reached his court. The make-over had done the trick. Now, it would simply be up to Marie Antoinette to maintain the image in which her elders had so painstakingly refashioned her.

AS SHE STEPPED OUT OF THE HOFBURG TO BEGIN THE JOURNEY TO HER NEW homeland, the Archduchess's appearance did not, it seems, offer much obvious room for improvement. With her *pompadour* coif, her cosmetically enhanced smile, and her elaborate brocaded gown, she reportedly looked the very picture of the flawless French princess. And as she effortlessly maneuvered her outsized hoopskirts and train, she carried herself like one as well. Even her staunchest detractors at Versailles would later concede that Marie Antoinette knew how to glide with the best of them.²⁹

All of a sudden, her light floating movements gave way to actual, if momentary, flight, as her handsome brother Ferdinand swept her up into the capacious *berline* that Louis XV had sent to fetch her. Designed by the Parisian carriagemaker Francien with detailed input from the Duc de Choiseul, the *berline* looked for all the world like a giant jewel box.³⁰ Its front, side, and rear panels fashioned almost entirely of glass, and its ornate, garlanded trimwork wrought from white, rose, and yellow gold, drew whistles of admiration from the crowd. On its solid gold slab of a roof, "bouquets of flowers of gold in different colors waved gracefully in the slightest breeze."³¹ Magnificent golden harnesses tethered a team of eight white horses to the carriage; the tall feathers in their manes bobbed in time as they snorted and pawed at the ground.[32]

Inside the *berline*, plush crimson upholstery depicted the Four Seasons, painstakingly embroidered in golden thread by a master craftsman named Trumeau.[33] Of Spring, Marie Antoinette had already heard plenty of late. Over the previous week, she had been guest of honor at a seemingly unending series of state dinners and fêtes celebrating new beginnings, unspoiled youth, fruitful days to come. Yet amid all the merry-making, no one had thought to prepare the girl for the challenges her future held in store. She had simply been told that she had won the most glittering prize that anyone, even a Hapsburg archduchess, could possibly hope to obtain.[34]

Outside the *berline* stood the Archduchess's family, the palace where she had spent her girlhood, the friends and servants she had known her entire life. With very few exceptions, she would never see any of them again.[35] Through a wall of glass she stared out at the unsmiling Empress, who had recently consulted a psychic as to her daughter's prospects for success at Versailles, only to be told: "Every pair of shoulders has its cross to bear."[36] With a last, pleading look at her mother, the young woman began to cry.[37]

The trumpeters sounded their horns, and the Swiss Guards fired their guns in a deafening salute. Escorted by blue-and-gold-liveried outriders who would accompany it as far as the city gates, the Archduchess's carriage joined the vast, jostling cortège and rolled slowly out of the courtyard. In its wake, her childhood playmate Joseph Weber remembered, "the avenues and streets of Vienna resounded with expressions of sorrow."[38] Perhaps in an attempt to hide her emotion from the Princesse de Paar—a longtime friend of her mother's, and her only companion in the oversized *berline*—Marie Antoinette busied herself with the little pug dog, Mops, that lay curled up in her lap.[39] Still, spectators observing her passage noted with alarm that "her cheeks were bathed in tears."[40] According to Joseph Weber, her weeping became especially evident when the young girl poked her head outside the carriage window, craning her neck and staring back toward the Hofburg, until the Empress's black-clad figure at last disappeared from view.

But Maria Theresa remained with her in spirit. As a parting gift, Marie Antoinette had received from her mother a tiny gold watch, which was to remain one of her most prized possessions, even when her jewel collection expanded to include far more extravagant pieces. Just as important, when the cortège stopped at Freiburg days later, the Archduchess received a letter her mother had apparently penned as soon as her *berline* left the Hofburg. Entitled "Regulation to Read Every Month," the missive provided detailed, unstinting advice about how Marie Antoinette should conduct herself at Versailles. "You must not do anything unusual," the letter commanded. "On the contrary, you must absolutely lend yourself to what the court is accustomed to doing."[41]

Then, several lines later, the intimidating warning: "All eyes will be fixed on you."[42]

ONCE SHE BECAME DAUPHINE, ALL EYES WOULD INDEED BE FIXED ON Marie Antoinette as a figure at the very center of court ritual. In the spectacular ceremonies of Versailles, regulations governing when, how, and in whose company she dressed would serve as constant reminders that her body not only belonged to the crown but existed as visible proof of its splendor. Especially since the long reign (1643–1715) of Louis XIV, opulent personal adornment had functioned to underscore the Bourbons' absolute power. As subsequent historians have argued, even such seeming trivialities as "hair, embroidery, ribbons," precious metals, gemstones, and lace—those indispensable features of the French royal costume—were instantly recognizable to the Bourbons' subjects as "effects of force."[43] Wordlessly but eloquently, this ornamentation impressed upon all viewers their king's ability to channel limitless resources into his own, and his family's, supreme glorification. As the wife of the future French monarch, Marie Antoinette would have to embody this principle in every last detail of her appearance, and to present herself for the approval of countless tenacious stares.[44]

Yet even the most meticulously cultivated appearance could not guarantee that approval would be hers. Many French people blamed Austria for the failure of the Seven Years' War, in which France had been forced to cede her Canadian and Indian colonies to England.[45] In fact, a goodly number of courtiers at Versailles had since begun lobbying in earnest for a return to the kingdom's previous, uncompromising distrust of Maria Theresa and her compatriots. That the new policy had been the work of the Duc de Choiseul, whose vast political influence and controversial positions on philosophy and religion had earned him countless enemies at court, made these individuals even more determined to overturn the Austrian alliance.

Although loosely assembled under the catch-all name of "the French party," the anti-Austrian faction at court belonged to two otherwise distinct social cliques. The first of these was the cabal of aristocrats supporting the King's latest titular mistress, Madame Du Barry. Choiseul had benefited richly from the patronage of Du Barry's predecessor, Madame de Pompadour, and after she died, those who loathed him had cast about for a royal mistress who would further their own interests at his expense. Led by the conniving Duc d'Aiguillon and the Duc de La Vauguyon, tutor to the young Dauphin, this group attempted to trounce the great minister by installing Madame Du Barry—a bewitching former prostitute with a taste for luxury items and few political ideas of her own—in Louis XV's bed. On a personal level, there was no love lost between the new "favorite" (as the King's *maîtresses en titre* or *maîtresses déclarées* were commonly known) and Choiseul, whose sister, the Duchesse de Grammont, despised Du Barry for her lowly birth and promiscuous background.[46]

Yet Choiseul's foes recognized quite rightly that with the advent at court of another beautiful young woman, Madame Du Barry might not retain her monopoly on the notoriously fickle sovereign's good graces. (In fact, in the initial stages of his marriage negotiations with Maria Theresa, Louis XV had considered putting himself forward as the bridegroom, before concluding that his grandson represented the more sensible candidate.) Marie Antoinette thus posed a threat to Madame Du Barry herself, and to the group whose social advancement at court went hand in glove with the favorite's unrivaled standing there.[47]

The other important wing of the French party—more commonly known as the devout party, because of its members' staunch religious convictions—was headed up by Louis XV's three spinster daughters, Adélaïde, Victoire, and Sophie. Known collectively as "Mesdames" (the conventional name for royal female offspring) or "the Aunts" (because of their relationship to the heir to the throne), these pious, unattractive, and unhappy women despised Du Barry but, like her, had scores to settle with Choiseul.[48] These ranged from his friendship with the late Madame de Pompadour, whom they had bitterly envied, to his successful persecution of France's Jesuit priests, whom they had avidly supported.[49] These factors trumped even Mesdames' abiding hatred for the lowborn, simpering strumpet whose wiles held their father enthralled.[50]

For Mesdames as for the *barrystes,* then, Choiseul's stance on Austria presented yet another urgent reason to plot his demise. More to the point, the bride he had imported for the Dauphin became a target for all manner of strategic backstabbing and intrigue. Should she fail to produce an heir or perform in an exemplary manner, perhaps Marie Antoinette could be sent back home to Vienna. Should this occur, Choiseul's foreign policy (and his reputation) would be in tatters. This was the anti-Austrians' secret hope.[51]

The fourteen-year-old archduchess's future was also complicated by the fact that France was a terminally ailing kingdom. The nation's coffers were woefully underfunded and many of its people underfed. Its ruler—once referred to as "Louis the Well Beloved"—had in recent times lost his nickname along with his subjects' respect.[52] Badly damaged by the Seven Years' War, the King's reputation had also deteriorated because of his autocratic and bullying style of government, as well as the unpopular tax reforms he had imposed on his subjects by means of special sessions called *lits de justice*. In these sessions, the King personally overrode objections leveled against his proposals by the *parlements*, the judiciary bodies charged, in principle, with the task of registering royal edicts. "Le roi le veult" ("the King wishes it"): at a *lit de justice*, this was the only justification offered for riding roughshod over dissenting *parlementaires*.[53]

Reported among the flourishing Enlightenment circles of Paris, where progressive-minded intellectuals advanced new ideas about mankind's fundamental equality and heatedly debated the very legitimacy of monarchical rule, Louis XV's recourse to the *lit de justice* became a prime example of absolutism run amok. But the King seemed quite happy to conduct his political affairs in the spirit of Pompadour's infamous battle-cry, *"Après nous, le déluge"*[54] ("After us, the deluge"). As this dictum implied, the serious problems that had developed during Louis XV's rule gave him little cause for concern, for they would one day be someone else's to deal with.

And then there was the issue, already considered by Choiseul, of the King's extramarital shenanigans with Pompadour and Du Barry, who inspired loathing both within and beyond the court for the power they wielded, for the riches the King lavished upon them, for their complicity in his moral decline, and for the sheer, unjust arbitrariness of their exalted placement. For a long time and to a large extent, the French people succeeded in displacing onto these royal favorites many of their principal grievances against the monarch himself.

Louis XV, though, further alienated his subjects by indulging in sheer venal libertinism to boot. In addition to his official paramours, the ruler's conquests included countless young women culled from the so-called vile classes, many of whom he maintained in private brothels not far from Versailles. Established in an area called the Parc aux Cerfs (that is, the Deer Park, where Louis XIII had hunted more acceptable game), these brothels offered proof of the "Well-Hated"'s irreversible slide into immorality. It mattered little when Madame Du Barry, anxious to keep a closer watch on her lover, prevailed upon him to close the brothels down; as far as many of his subjects were concerned, the damage to the King's reputation had long since been done.

SO IT WAS THAT WHEN MARIE ANTOINETTE SET A TINY SILK SLIPPER ONTO THE stage of French public life in 1770, she was, without knowing it, facing a restless and bifurcated audience. On the one hand, a court fraught with rivalry and vendettas viewed her as a handy pawn in its high-stakes struggles for power. On the other hand, a nation on the verge of revolt expected her to breathe new life into its decaying monarchy. Although different in many respects, these groups shared one implicit conviction: that the way the Dauphine looked was crucial to her prescribed role. One of the prints produced in the period leading up to Marie Antoinette's marriage, a portrait of the bride dressed in a handsome *robe à la française,* expressed this view neatly in its caption:

> *With her beauty winning our hearts*
> *And virtue decorating her,*
> *Already France adores her;*
> *She will establish happiness here.*[55]

Maria Theresa could not have put it better herself. She had not spent 400,000 livres on her daughter's trousseau for nothing, understanding as she did that in France in general, and at Versailles in particular, one should never underestimate the power of the Bourbon strictures equating princely beauty with virtue, surface appearance with underlying essence.[56] Maintaining these equations would be one of Marie Antoinette's most important, and least negotiable, duties as Dauphine. Her success or failure in "establishing the happiness" of her subjects would depend at least in part on her continued willingness to dress for success.

DRIVING AWAY FROM VIENNA THROUGH HER MOTHER'S TERRITORIES, THE fourteen-year-old archduchess certainly looked to be on her best behavior. Arrayed in her lavish French finery, she gave herself over to innocent pursuits inside the glass *berline.* She stared out the windows at the passing scenery. She hid her tears, smiling and waving on cue for the droves of people who had lined the roads to cheer her on. She chatted brightly with the Princesse de Paar, upon whom the Dauphine would later bestow, as a reward for her companionship on this journey, a dress bodice embroidered with more than twelve hundred diamonds of different sizes.[57] And, hugging her little dog tightly for comfort, she reread her mother's letter. In keeping with the advice it set forth, the girl was not doing anything out of the ordinary . . . so far.

But unusual times breed unusual measures, and when, after two and a half weeks of traveling, she reached the border between France and Austria, she would confront the first of many singular circumstances marking her reign as French fashion's brightest star and its unhappiest victim. Meanwhile, back in Vienna, an anxious Maria Theresa was spending much more time than usual in prayer, imploring "the Almighty to avert a disaster that she alone had foreseen."[58] Time and again, this disaster would play itself out on the surface of her daughter's well-dressed body. As a political cartoon would charge years later, in sending Marie Antoinette to France, the Empress had blown the lid off Pandora's box.[59]

TWO

STRIPPED

Storm clouds hung heavy over the Black Forest on the afternoon of May 7, 1770, as Marie Antoinette's presentation carriage drew to a halt on the banks of the river Rhine, just across from the French city of Strasbourg. The evening before, at the Abbey of Schüttern, the royal traveler and her entourage had enjoyed their final night in Hapsburg territory, with local church and government officials addressing her in her native German and hailing her as a daughter of Austria. But now, the Archduchess was to leave her homeland once and for all.

With its front wheels parked on a bridge leading to a small island in the middle of the Rhine, and its rear wheels still on Hapsburg soil, the *berline* assumed, at the head of the fifty-seven-carriage cavalcade, a symbolically neutral locale between two kingdoms. Behind it lay Maria Theresa's empire, figured most proximately by the nearby town of Kehl. Across the river, France awaited her new Dauphine.

When Marie Antoinette alighted onto that bridge from her fairy-tale carriage, she was, in strict geopolitical terms, neither here nor there. In the course of arranging for her journey, French and Austrian diplomats had argued intensely as to where the handover (*remise*) of the bride to Louis XV's emissaries should occur. Representatives for each nation felt that to perform this important ceremony on the other's territory would be to grant that state, and that sovereign, undue precedence over the other. At last, deadlock was averted when one of the negotiators recalled the existence of an obscure islet, the Île des Épis, between Kehl and Strasbourg, and proposed it as a compromise venue. On this sandy and uninhabited piece of land, the diplomats ordered the construction of a *pavillon de remise,* built in haste from inexpensive wood but designed to resemble a miniature French château. The pavilion was divided into three parts. It contained a suite of rooms that opened out onto the right bank of the Rhine, built to house the Austrian contingent, and a matching suite facing the river's left bank, established for the delegation from Versailles. These two wings were separated in the center by a large *salle de remise,* "the great hall in which the Archduchess would be definitively metamorphosed into the heiress of the throne of France."[1]

The metamorphosis began as soon as Marie Antoinette entered the pavilion on the Austrian side, escorted by her "best man," Prince Starhemberg, Envoy Extraordinary from Maria Theresa's court. The building's interior proved cold and drafty on this overcast afternoon, and presented an unwelcoming aspect despite its would-be luxurious décor: a motley profusion of furnishings on loan from the leading families of Strasbourg and from Louis XV's own Garde-Meuble in Paris. Most notably, the latter source had supplied antique Gobelins tapestries to adorn the walls, but these hangings did little to insulate the space against the rising winds that whistled through the cracks of the pavilion's crude wooden planking. Standing at the center of her large assembled retinue, the Archduchess's slender frame was racked by uncontrollable shivers. Her cleavage-baring, snugly fitted formal *grand habit de cour*—beneath which she wore only a delicate *chemise* and a stiff assemblage of stays and *paniers* that gave the gown its exaggerated shape—offered little protection against the cold. Marie Antoinette, though, did not benefit long from even these comforts, for the first and principal task of the ladies who had accompanied her into the pavilion was to strip her naked.

From her heavy train to her voluminous skirts, from her ruffled lace sleeves to her ribbon-bedecked bodice, from the jewels in her hair to the buckles on her shoes, each of the articles painstakingly chosen to make the girl look French was removed, confiscated as a symbolic link to the House of Hapsburg. As one of her ladies-in-waiting at Versailles, Madame Campan, would later explain, Bourbon protocol required this ritual to ensure that the foreign bride-to-be "would not retain any trace of [her] court [of origin], not even her slip or her stockings."[2]

The fact that this particular foreigner wore only garments confected in France did not exempt her from the traditional undressing ritual.[3] Except for the little watch her mother had given her, which she somehow managed to hold on to as the ladies were confiscating her other possessions, "nothing was she to keep that might be endeared to her by memory, not a ring, not a cross, . . . [not] a buckle, a clasp or a favorite bracelet."[4] Parisian though these articles were, they apparently risked carrying with them unsuitable, Austrian associations. As such, they had to go, along with their owner's favorite nonsartorial accessory, her beloved, tawny-colored pug. Mops, Marie Antoinette's ladies informed her, would be sent back to Vienna instead of accompanying her hence; his dirty paws could simply not be trusted around a woman who, now more than ever, was going to have to look her best.

Whatever alarm this announcement may have caused Marie Antoinette went unnoticed as the women continued to dismantle her elaborate outfit, and to argue among themselves about which items each would take home as souvenirs of the journey. Some of these articles even found their way into the hands of the ladies' French counterparts at the pavilion, later sparking instances of surprised recognition on Marie Antoinette's part when they surfaced again, worn by members of her entourage at Versailles. Etiquette prevented her from protesting, much less from demanding the return of the purloined garments. She was supposed to bear the offense with the good grace befitting a future queen.

Like the women bickering over plum articles of her clothing, the men in the Austrian group were too preoccupied—with the logistics of the *remise* and of the long trip home—to pay much heed to the Archduchess's mounting dismay as her undressing proceeded apace. Clustered around Starhemberg, they greeted the spectacle of her nudity with casual interest, only occasionally interrupting their conversations to evaluate a newly exposed body part or swath of skin. (Her breasts may have elicited particular interest, as, during the marriage negotiations, Louis XV had inquired specifically as to their size and shape, only to receive Maria Theresa's assurances that the girl was young yet and would surely develop over time.[5]) All the while, a prisoner of the men's appraising glances and the women's officious ministrations, Marie Antoinette blinked back hot, angry tears. For the first time since she exchanged farewells with her mother on April 21, she began noticeably to buckle under the pressure of her new station.

No one had expected her to react in this manner. Trained from childhood to present to her subjects a façade of unimpeachable royal dignity, the ingénue had until this point acquitted herself admirably in the public eye. For the better part of a month now, she had endured an arduous eight-hour daily traveling schedule, during which she was on constant view through her carriage's glass panels. Dutifully she had smiled at the crowds despite her ever worsening cold.[6] In the evenings, she had sat, ramrod straight and still smiling, through interminable banquets and town celebrations held in her honor at each stop. She had listened to lengthy Latin declamations praising her youth and beauty. She had accepted bouquets from children dressed in quaint regional costumes. She had applauded appreciatively at countless musical performances, dance numbers, and fireworks displays.[7] She had never, apparently, forgotten that all eyes were upon her.

And yet, stripped naked in front of the entire Austrian delegation, the Archduchess finally began to lose her composure. This nudity business was not simply one obligation among the many that now comprised her royal mandate—it was something much harder to handle, especially for a girl exhausted by traveling, sick with a cold, and endowed, as many of her acquaintances would later note, with an acute sense of modesty uncommon in individuals of her rank.[8] "That day," one of the noblewomen present for the *remise* was to recall, not without a twinge of disapproval, "she cried a great deal."[9]

DESPITE HER TREMBLING AND HER TEARS, THE NAKED PRINCESS RETAINED plenty of the physical attractions about which Louis XV had inquired so insistently. The same observer who commented on her weeping also conceded that the petite, blue-eyed blonde had a beautiful complexion, which another contemporary described as "delicately nuanced with rose, [and] dazzling in its whiteness."[10] One of the ladies who turned out for the ceremony—a young Alsatian noblewoman called Henriette-Louise de Waldner, later to be known under her married name as the Baronne d'Oberkirch—similarly described Marie Antoinette's exposed skin as "literally blending lilies and roses."[11]

These compliments carried an underlying political message, for the rosy and lily-white color palette they invoked carried specific iconographical connotations. The rose, everybody knew, represented the House of Hapsburg, while the lily (fleur-de-lys) was the Bourbons' equally recognizable emblem. (It appeared, for example, in the delicately shuddering golden bouquets that festooned the roof of Marie Antoinette's traveling carriage.) Along with the metaphorics of springtime that had greeted the girl so often in Vienna—and that attached to her throughout her early years as consort—the twining of the Hapsburg rose and the Bourbon lily was a favorite image among the poets, orators, artists, and royal-wedding buffs of both countries. As one contemporary French quatrain announced:

The rose of the Danube and the lily of the Seine,
Mixing their colors, embellish both parts:
From a garland of these flowers, love forms a chain,
Happily joining the two nations' hearts.[12]

Considered from this perspective, it was significant that the Archduchess's luscious pink-and-white aspect appeared, to paraphrase Mademoiselle de Waldner, literally to blend the two nations' hopes for a harmonious Franco-Austrian union. To be sure, this literal blending was expected, eventually, to take the form of royal offspring: as Dauphine, Marie Antoinette was expected to ensure the dynastic continuity of the Bourbon line. But even before fulfilling this reproductive mission, the girl embodied what Maria Theresa, in a letter to the French king, called "the sweetest pledge that exists between our states and Houses."[13] Two days after the *remise,* a young priest called the Prince de Rohan sounded a similar note in his encomium at the Strasbourg Cathedral: "[Madame la Dauphine] combines the soul of Maria Theresa and the soul of the Bourbons."[14]

But Hapsburg and Bourbon were not to mix in altogether equal proportions. Certain commentators focused solely on "the dazzling whiteness of her complexion" and on the beautiful "white soul" it necessarily implied.[15] More accurately than the rhetoric of floral blending, these accounts identified the Dauphine's first political duty, which was to forsake the rose of the Hapsburgs for her new family's fleur-de-lys. In her whiteness, she was a blank slate. Cleansed of her Austrian markings, she was ready to be overwritten with exclusively French monarchical codes and interests.

To initiate this process, she had been required before her marriage formally to repudiate her fatherland and adopt her betrothed's national allegiance as her own—two actions that the patriarchal organization of the French royal family demanded of all its foreign brides. Like the rest of her Gallicizing makeover, Marie Antoinette's conformance to this exigency had begun while she was still at the Hapsburg court, when she took a French name to match her new appearance. By birth, she was Maria Antonia Josepha Johanna, and she had gone by "Antonia" until the Abbé de Vermond, the French tutor selected for her by Choiseul to prepare her for her life as Dauphine, began addressing her as "Madame Antoine," a moniker that had transmogrified into the similarly French "Marie Antoinette" shortly before she left home.[16]

On April 17, four days prior to her departure, she had officially renounced her hereditary succession rights as an archduchess of the empire. Two evenings later, dressed in a costly cloth-of-silver gown, she had married Louis-Auguste by proxy, with her brother Ferdinand standing in for the bridegroom.[17] Held by candlelight in Vienna's starkly majestic Church of the Augustine Friars—the same church where Marie Antoinette had been baptized as an infant—this service invested the bride with the legal title of Dauphine. The ceremony at the *pavillon de remise* was thus intended by its organizers to put the finishing touches on the Archduchess's newly minted Frenchness.

. . .

AS THE DRAFTS SEEPING THROUGH THE PAVILION'S SHODDILY JOINTED PANELS
gave way to heavy rain, Marie Antoinette's ladies-in-waiting hastened to complete their task. As a prelude to dressing the naked girl anew, they coated her
hairstyle with an extra layer of powder, then applied thick white makeup to her
face and fresh red circles of rouge to her cheeks: three requisite details among
the ladies of Louis XV's court, even those (like Marie Antoinette) whose naturally fair hair and rosy skin tone seemed to require no enhancement.[18]

After they had applied these touches, the women got to work on the girl's
clothing, slipping her first into a new, delicate batiste *chemise,* then cinching
new whalebone stays tightly around her waist. Next they secured *paniers*
over her hips and sheathed her legs in a pair of gold-embroidered stockings
woven from pale, shimmering silk. Finally, they maneuvered to help her put
on a weighty, gleaming ceremonial gown made from cloth-of-gold.[19] Like the
garment it replaced, this was a sweeping, formal *grand habit.* Its low-cut triangular stomacher was lavishly decorated with a "ladder" (*échelle*) of billowy satin bows, while additional flounces, ribbons, lace, gemstones, and silk
flowers decorated the rest of the dress.[20] A pair of high satin slippers, made
for her by a leading French shoemaker and trimmed with diamond buckles,
completed the look.[21] On the surface at least, the Dauphine's grand golden
gown had taken the place of all "that might be endeared to her by memory,"
and had transformed her definitively into a *Française.*[22]

Meanwhile, rainwater was gushing fast and furious through the pavilion's
flimsy ceilings and walls. Still a child despite her grown-up dress and high heels,
the Dauphine stopped crying long enough to laugh at the sight of her ladies'
rapidly decomposing, waterlogged hairdos.[23] Less offended by their charge's
laughter than fearful that her own artfully constructed coiffure would soon
suffer the same fate, the ladies nipped her merriment in the bud by reminding
her of what had to happen next. Now that she had given up her Austrian
clothes, they informed her, she must rid herself of her Austrian retinue as well.

At her companions' prompting, the Dauphine thus moved through the
antechamber to take her leave of everyone except Prince Starhemberg, who
was to accompany her into the central chamber for the signing of the formal
actes de remise. Her slender body once again shook with sobs as she said her
good-byes to the ladies and the gentlemen of her mother's court, many of
whom had waited on her since her infancy. Like Mops, now whimpering in
the crook of a servant's arm, these loyal longtime companions received particularly sentimental farewells from their mistress.

Such an outpouring of emotion constituted an unwelcome departure from
the regal solemnity of the proceedings, so Prince Starhemberg respectfully

but firmly cut short the girl's effusions, leading her into the great hall just outside the Austrians' door. There, three emissaries from Louis XV, the Comte de Noailles and Messieurs Gérard and Bouret, greeted her on a raised dais, positioned behind a long table draped in crimson velvet and designed to represent the Franco-Austrian border.

The rest of the Versailles delegation was waiting in state behind the closed door of a chamber just opposite the Austrians' quarters; they would be presented to the Dauphine only after the signing of the documents spread out on the table's surface. (The French courtiers' curiosity could, however, scarcely brook such a delay. One of the group's more enterprising women had deliberately caught the long train of her skirt in the doorway between the French antechamber and the central hall so that she and her compatriots would be able to sneak advance glimpses of their future queen.) Maneuvering carefully through the puddle-strewn *salle,* Starhemberg and Marie Antoinette stepped up to the dais and greeted the envoys of Louis XV.

The Comte de Noailles informed the Austrian pair that the King sent his regards, and that His Majesty greatly looked forward to meeting Marie Antoinette in Compiègne seven days hence. Like their sovereign, Noailles continued, the French people rejoiced at the prospect of a union between "two of the most ancient Houses in the universe," and expected her to bring unprecedented "felicity" to the nation.[24] Marie Antoinette accepted these compliments with a gracious nod, then allowed Noailles and Starhemberg to help her into the large thronelike armchair placed for her at the table's center. This was no mean feat, given the outsized unwieldiness of the girl's *paniers* and train. But, like the consummate courtiers they were, Noailles and Starhemberg tackled the job with aplomb. Once she was seated, the gentlemen followed suit and, reviewing the *actes de remise* arrayed before them, got down to the business of formalizing the exchange.

While they did so, Marie Antoinette seems to have been distracted by the sight of the Gobelins tapestries hanging on the wall behind the table. These, among the most precious ones borrowed from the French king's Garde-Meuble and displayed with no apparent thought for their subject matter, depicted the mythological union of Jason and Medea, as originally shown in some celebrated "cartoons by Raphael."[25] Her classical instruction with the Abbé de Vermond must have prepared Marie Antoinette to recognize the narrative, for upon first noticing the wall-hangings, she cried out to no one in particular: "Oh, look! What kind of omen is that?"[26] Ignoring her outburst, Starhemberg and his French counterparts continued their formalities; with the future of European geopolitics hanging in the balance, there was no time to acknowledge such girlish malaise.

. . .

ACCORDING TO AT LEAST TWO CONTEMPORARIES, HOWEVER, THE DAUPHINE'S somber-faced remarking of the tapestries seemed entirely understandable. The first of these contemporaries, a student at the University of Strasbourg named Johann Wolfgang von Goethe, had toured the pavilion just a few days before the *remise* and had been infuriated by the fact that some thoughtless French official had selected a wall-hanging showing "the most disastrous of all marriages" to greet the Austrian guest of honor.[27] In much the same vein, Mademoiselle de Waldner railed against the "stupid tapestries representing Medea and Jason, their massacres and domestic quarrels."[28] What kind of welcome, she later asked rhetorically, were such images supposed to provide to a fourteen-year-old dauphine?

Yet Waldner, who unlike Goethe was present for the *remise,* did notice that Marie Antoinette looked less upset than "struck" by the tapestries—a reaction that invites the question of what kind of "omen" the Archduchess actually took them to be.[29] For as her training with the Abbé de Vermond had surely taught her, Medea was, like Marie Antoinette, a princess brought by marriage into a foreign land—and a princess who used clothing to counter the challenges she faced there.

More precisely: Medea had left her home and family to marry Jason, who later, out of political expediency, decided to wed a different princess. Instead of accepting Jason's reasons for the new marriage, Medea created a gown and a diadem of irresistible beauty, lined them with poison, and sent them to her rival as wedding gifts. These accoutrements promptly melted the woman's flesh from her bones and destroyed her. After taking further revenge against Jason by killing the children she had borne him, Medea escaped in a chariot sent to her rescue by her ancestor Apollo, the god of the sun.

Marie Antoinette, not incidentally, boasted a quasi-divine, solar-oriented genealogy of her own. Through her late father, Francis Stephen, she was related by blood to her future husband's own ancestor, Louis XIV, who had cultivated his image as Sun King by appearing as Apollo in court masquerades. (Plate 4.) On the maternal, Hapsburg side, she traced her lineage to Augustus Caesar, who had claimed Apollo as his father. When contemplating Medea's machinations, the girl who had been greeted since birth as "the daughter of Caesars" might thus have identified something germane to her own predicament.[30] The tale might have suggested to her that even a lonely princess could, with the right outfit, resist the humiliations into which other people callously tried to force her.

The time was surely ripe for Marie Antoinette to engage in reflections along these lines, given that her encounter with the wall hangings followed right on the heels of her public divestment. How, indeed, could she stop herself from staring in amazement, when the scenario she deciphered in the tapestries so starkly opposed the one from which she had just emerged? In the latter vignette, a dress was removed, and a princess surrendered her power in meekness; in the former, a dress was donned, and the royal heroine asserted her absolute power. Though they stood as negative mirror images, both scenes reflected the same notion: that a woman's garb was a source of tremendous political potency, of transformational magic that was hers either to wield or to endure.

THE INK ON THE *ACTES DE REMISE* HAD BARELY HAD A CHANCE TO DRY BEfore the door to the adjacent chamber flew open, and French courtiers descended on the young bride by the dozen. Because protocol required that introductions be made according to rank, the exalted Comte de Noailles, whose wife Louis XV had appointed to serve as Marie Antoinette's *dame d'honneur* and titular guardian, presided over the process. Like his wife, Noailles, who came from one of France's greatest families, was a stickler for etiquette, and his presence ensured that the ceremony would come off as smoothly as a well-choreographed minuet.[31] Under his direction, the aristocrats lined up to meet her: the gentlemen looking debonair in the powdered wigs, plumed hats, and red-heeled shoes of their class, the ladies in their rich court dresses moving with the impeccable grace that Marie Antoinette's dance master, Noverre, had prepared her to expect. One after another, they bowed and curtseyed at their new mistress's feet, pledging themselves loyally to her service.

Yet according to at least one account, not all of the Dauphine's new compatriots were impressed by what they saw. The ladies, in particular, smirked at the sight of her "poorly chosen costume," as they wrongly assumed that she was wearing an "Austrian [rather than] a French dress."[32] (Unbeknownst to Marie Antoinette and her mother, it was common practice for French clothing merchants traveling in the Holy Roman Empire to try to palm off their outmoded or second-rate creations on unsuspecting German boors.[33] This phenomenon may have contributed to the French courtiers' skepticism about the foreign girl's ensemble.) What with her unimpressive outfit and her tear-streaked rouge, those who sympathized with the French party's anti-Austrian stance had found their first grounds for complaint with the new dauphine. Gleefully they filed the information away for later discussion with like-minded cronies at Versailles.

They also clucked their tongues quietly when Marie Antoinette, overwhelmed by the emotion of the moment—and perhaps also by the ladies' snide whisperings behind their fans—sought relief by flinging herself into the arms of the Comtesse de Noailles, to whom her mother had directed her to defer in all things.[34] (By "deference," Maria Theresa had not meant childish clinging; the Empress, who had never coddled her daughter, expected her to look to her new guardian for leadership, not love.) The prim, icy, middle-aged Comtesse "breathed etiquette," as Madame Campan once quipped, to the point where "she seemed as though she might suffocate at even the slightest disturbance in the consecrated order of things."[35] Even Louis XV, when presented with a thorny protocol question, never failed to inquire: "Has Madame de Noailles been consulted?"

As the Comtesse knew full well, etiquette held the bodies of French sovereigns to be so sacred that casual physical contact with them bordered on the unthinkable. An impromptu hug between a dauphine and a subject—even one as well-born and universally respected as Madame de Noailles—thus represented a gaffe of the highest order, and Marie Antoinette's new guardian recoiled to see it perpetrated on her watch. The rest of the French retinue now had another juicy piece of gossip to carry back to court.

Not yet aware of her faux pas, Marie Antoinette still clung to the Comtesse's waist and asked for guidance in adapting to her new position. In response, Madame de Noailles pursed her lips and briskly pulled the girl to her feet. Thereupon she curtseyed to her royal mistress and informed her in prickly tones that the show must go on. If Marie Antoinette really wanted to acquit herself well, she would take care to avoid, now and in the future, any further infractions of the rigid and unremitting propriety that etiquette demanded. This was what being a Bourbon wife called for—this and nothing less.

The Comtesse's harsh—and, of course, public—rebuke made clear that in Marie Antoinette's new life "there was no place for sentiment, which [was] not tabulated among the logarithms of courtly procedure."[36] She would find compassion in no quarter here. By the same token, her guardian's insistence that appearances be maintained at all costs likely heightened a dawning sense that her new life would be the stuff of surfaces, manipulation, theater. Hadn't her mother reminded her that in France, she would always be at the center of a large spectacle, and that she must never give her audience reason to fault her? The Dauphine released her hold on the grim-faced *dame d'honneur,* drew herself up with all the dignity she could muster, and said, in a clear, unwavering voice: "Forgive me, Madame, the tears that I have just shed for my family and my homeland. From this day forward, I shall never again forget that I am a Frenchwoman."[37]

Madame de Noailles received this speech with a curt nod to signal that the crisis had abated. Ceremonial presentations resumed as before, and as soon as they were completed, the Comte de Noailles led the Dauphine out of the pavilion. The rest of the court followed behind. As the last of the group exited the building, the roof over the *salle de remise* collapsed under the weight of the accumulated rainwater.

Outside the ruined pavilion, a clutch of indigent peasants from the surrounding region of Alsace huddled in the rain, hoping to see the Dauphine. As she stepped lightly into her *berline,* a liveried page carrying her golden train high above the mud, they cheered uproariously. Then they stayed behind to pillage the building from which she had come. Most of the tapestries and other furnishings that had adorned the place disappeared in the mêlée.[38]

FROM THE ÎLE DES ÉPIS, A STATELY PARADE OF FRENCH CARRIAGES, WITH Marie Antoinette's *berline* at its head, moved across the Rhine for the first of the marriage celebrations to be held on French soil. Through the now diminishing rain, Marie Antoinette rode to Alsace's capital city, Strasbourg, passing beneath lavishly garlanded gates and along roads lined with three companies of adolescent soldiers. The young men, dressed in the picturesque costumes of the Cent-Suisse guard, fired salvoes into the air as the procession moved past them and through the entrance to the Place Broglie, beneath the great triumphal arch erected in the Dauphine's honor.[39] At the top of the arch "were juxtaposed the arms of France and Austria joined by a blue and yellow ribbon bearing the optimistic inscription: *Perpetua imperiorum concordia*—'the perpetual concord between the two empires.' "[40] Across the city, the bells of Strasbourg Cathedral pealed out a jubilant welcome.

At length, the Dauphine's carriage stopped before the towering Archepiscopal Palace, where the head of one of France's foremost princely houses, the Cardinal Louis Constantin de Rohan, would play host to her for the night. This venerable churchman received Marie Antoinette on the palace steps, flanked by the city's chief magistrate, Monsieur d'Antigny. After the Cardinal's opening salutations in French, Antigny undertook to greet the Dauphine in her native tongue. Eager to compensate for any missteps committed during the handover ceremony, and to prove herself a Frenchwoman through and through, Marie Antoinette interrupted the well-meaning magistrate with a modified version of the speech she had just made to Madame de Noailles: "Please, my good sir, do not address me in German; from this moment on, I understand only French."[41] Pronounced with that hint of a German accent she would never manage to lose, the Dauphine's utterance delighted the crowds filling the town square. Like her "superb clothes sent from Paris," widely deemed "a thousand times more charming" than those she was thought to have worn before the *remise,* her gracious words confirmed the spectators' hopes that the Austrian princess would, indeed, adopt the nation's interests as her own.[42]

Accordingly, the people of Strasbourg took great pains to make their Dauphine's introduction to France a memorable one. After her interview with Rohan and Antigny, thirty-six young shepherds and shepherdesses, selected for their good looks and picture perfect in their sweet rustic costumes, offered her baskets overflowing with fresh flowers. Municipal representatives showered her with dozens more bouquets, and twenty-four maidens from Strasbourg's most eminent families, dressed up in colorful Alsatian garb, scattered still more blossoms beneath her feet. Particularly charmed by this last group, Marie Antoinette paused to ask each girl her name and to give a posy to each one as a memento.[43] The luckiest of them all received the gift of the fan the Archduchess was carrying with her that afternoon: an intricately carved, gem-encrusted ivory piece decorated with sprightly Rococo scenes.[44] Charmed by her generosity and grace, the people of Strasbourg heartily welcomed the foreign princess to their city.[45]

Their effusive, beautifully orchestrated reception could not have been further from the tense solemnity of the *remise.* Everywhere the Dauphine looked, she saw beautiful faces smiling up at her—no insignificant pleasure to a young woman who, one of her hairdressers would later remark, could not endure the company of unattractive people.[46] Little did she know that in this case, an ordinance had been passed in advance of her visit, "forbidding every person afflicted with any disgusting disorder to appear in her way."[47] According to Goethe, this decree had caused some disgruntlement among the population at large, but the end result was spectacular. The seamless show of beauty that greeted Marie Antoinette in Strasbourg revealed to her that the French national obsession with appearance was not without its benefits.

It was in this Alsatian city, too, that she first tasted the enjoyable side of French theatrics: hard-edged and daunting during the *remise,* uplifting and joyful in the festivities that followed. An eighty-foot-high screen, painted with life-sized porticoes and verdant formal gardens, had been hung across the Archepiscopal Palace's elegant façade, and transformed the whole of the Place Broglie into a glorious stage set in the round. When night fell, the rain clouds that had dogged Marie Antoinette's trip across the Rhine dispersed once and for all, and hundreds of lanterns were hung out to illuminate the city's streets and rooftops. Similarly lighted from its spire to its foundations, the pink sandstone of the Strasbourg cathedral, according to Mademoiselle de Waldner, "resembled a single flame, its ornate ornamentation shining like a constellation of stars."[48]

Fireworks depicting various mythological characters (though not, in all probability, Jason and Medea) cast more dazzling lights in the darkness, and their reflections danced across the surface of the river that ran alongside the Cardinal de Rohan's palace.[49] Ferrying back and forth across the shimmering waters, the city's boatmen further enhanced the scene by hanging "lampions like great red oranges [from] their masts, or [waving] colored torches" in their hands.[50] Some of them even gathered their boats together beneath the Dauphine's windows, their crafts laden with various kinds of shrubbery and forming an exquisite "floating garden" for her amusement.[51] Even the wine flowing in the fountains and the oxen being roasted in the streets could not compete with such marvelous visions. Mademoiselle de Waldner was surprised to notice that even the most impoverished revelers largely ignored the free foodstuffs, so awed were they by the splendor of their transformed surroundings.[52]

Although no stranger to extravagant parties, Marie Antoinette seems to have been similarly enthralled.[53] Miraculously ablaze in the middle of the night, the city appeared so magical as to resemble no other place on earth. "It looked," Waldner reminisced years afterward, "like the end of the world."[54] But for Marie Antoinette, the festival represented a new beginning: an introduction to a place where extravagant spectacle outstripped all other considerations.

THE FOLLOWING DAY, THE DAUPHINE AND HER ENTOURAGE ATTENDED SERvices at the Strasbourg Cathedral, where her host's nephew, the Prince Louis de Rohan, officiated on behalf of the Cardinal, who had already left for nearby Saverne to make arrangements for the evening's festivities there. Viewed with the hindsight of history, the encounter in the cathedral was a momentous one, for the younger Rohan, an inveterate roué with an unshakable sense of social entitlement, was fifteen years later to do irreparable harm to Marie Antoinette's reputation. Yet if any traces of Rohan's malevolence or loose morals were evident in his oration, his regal addressee appeared to pay them no mind. On the contrary: when he brought his remarks to a close, she treated the prince to a dazzling, appreciative smile.[55] In her effort to grasp the intricacies of the social hierarchy in which she was now enmeshed, she had rightly intuited that as one of France's leading noblemen, Rohan was someone, as Antonia Fraser has put it, "with whose claims—or pretensions— Marie Antoinette as Dauphine would have to learn to cope."[56]

As Dauphine, Marie Antoinette was in fact coping better and better with each passing day. After she and her 160-person entourage left Strasbourg, they embarked on the weeklong trip to meet Louis XV and his family in the forest of Compiègne. Over the course of her journey, the princess impressed her new subjects at each stop along the way. In all the towns she visited, residents welcomed her with great circumstance and pomp—more fireworks and flowers, more pretty faces and enthusiastic speeches. To express her gratitude, the Dauphine presented to her hosts an image of exemplary royal decorum. The mistakes of the *remise* were a thing of the past. With her French clothes and her French speech, she everywhere elicited euphoric shouts of "How pretty she is, our Dauphine!" and she responded to the compliments with winning modesty and grace.[57] "It did not take long," her old friend Joseph Weber asserted, "for everyone to be convinced that the beauty of her soul was equal to the beauty of her person."[58]

THE DAUPHINE'S TRIUMPH REACHED ITS APOGEE ON MAY 14, WHEN NONE other than the King himself deemed her "French graces" as exquisite as any he had seen.[59] Louis XV, Louis Auguste, and select members of the court had ridden out that afternoon to meet the young traveler in the forest of Compiègne, not far from the royal residence of that name. When her carriage pulled in to the sun-dappled clearing, the girl emerged on the arm of the ugly but urbane Duc de Choiseul, to whom the King had granted the privilege of joining her for the final stage of her journey.

Having first prettily acknowledged Choiseul as "the author of [her] happiness," Marie Antoinette glided through the phalanx of princes and dignitaries that stood in state, and swept a deep, impeccable curtsey at Louis XV's feet. When he bade her stand, she addressed him initially as "Majesty," then, more tenderly, as "Grandpapa." It was an instance of familiarity that no doubt displeased the Comtesse de Noailles, but the King seemed to find it endearing.[60] He kissed the girl lustily on both cheeks, looked her up and down for good measure, and with an approving smile stepped aside so that his grandson might do the same.

Louis Auguste, by contrast, seemed not so much excited as intimidated by the sight of his new bride. As the assembled courtiers noted—some with alarm, others with thinly disguised glee—he was visibly reluctant even to approach her. Etiquette required that he kiss her on the cheek; but unlike his grandfather, he did so as brusquely as possible, and then shuffled off to one side, leaving Louis XV to flirt with her.[61] Retaining her composure, Marie Antoinette gamely fielded the King's gallantries and greeted the rest of his entourage. But after the glowing reception she had received from virtually everyone else over the course of her journey, the younger Bourbon's standoffishness must have given her pause. Louis XV shared her befuddlement, remarking afterward that in his failure to respond to his bride's obvious charms, his grandson "was not a man like other men."[62]

Or, at the very least, the young bridegroom was not a man like his grandfather the King. In contrast to the dark-eyed, dashing Louis XV, who even at sixty retained his legendary smoldering good looks, the fifteen-year-old Louis Auguste was nearsighted, maladroit, and grossly overweight. As the Comte de Mercy-Argenteau, Maria Theresa's ambassador to Versailles, reported with distaste: "Nature seems to have denied everything to Monsieur le Dauphin." Everything, that is, except thick-lidded, watery blue eyes, a shambling gait, a nervous bark of a laugh, a hoggish appetite, and, in consequence of this last characteristic, a corpulent physique. The young man had, moreover, never wanted or expected to be King: only the premature deaths of his father and two older brothers had made him Dauphin, and he seemed curiously determined not to look or act in accordance with his role.[63] According to the court's crueler wags, as he waddled through the halls of Versailles he resembled nothing so much as "a peasant who had just left his plough."[64]

Nature had been equally unkind to the next members of the royal family presented to the Dauphine: Mesdames Adélaïde, Sophie, and Victoire. Like their nephew, these unmarried daughters of the King were physically unattractive and socially awkward—described by Horace Walpole, having met them at court, as "clumsy, plump old wenches [who never] knew what they wanted to say, and wriggl[ed] as though they wanted to make water."[65] Madame Campan—who served as reader to the trio before becoming a member of Marie Antoinette's retinue, and who later wrote one of the most detailed insider's accounts of life at late eighteenth-century Versailles—confirmed Walpole's opinion in her own humorously unflattering recollections of the three women. According to Campan, hefty Victoire had by the age of thirty-seven gained so much weight as to merit her father's teasing childhood nickname for her, Piggy (Coche). Although "remarkably lean," Campan remembered, the thirty-six-year-old Sophie was "horridly ugly" and known to the King as Grub (Graille).[66] Both Sophie and Victoire had painfully nervous temperaments. Forced during her early convent education to do penance in the burial vaults at Fontevrault Abbey, while a madman shrieked wildly from an adjacent cell, Victoire was susceptible to paralyzing nervous attacks. Sophie was terrified of crowds and storms, and had an unsettling tendency to dart around Versailles "like a frightened hare"—this was Campan's bemused simile—when something had rattled her.[67]

At thirty-eight the oldest of the bunch, Adélaïde was stronger-willed, though scarcely more attractive in body or demeanor. Her slovenly personal grooming and generally shabby, shopworn appearance earned her the paternal sobriquet Rag (Loque). At the same time, she adored beautiful clothes, and was almost poignantly vain about her physical charms, despite the fact that these had been limited at best even in her youth and had faded quite speedily thereafter.[68] According to the Marquis de Ségur, Madame Adélaïde was also "absurdly proud of her royal rank," opting not to marry a foreign prince in order to maintain her lofty standing as a Daughter of France.[69] Her sisters had followed her lead, as they did in the political vendettas Adélaïde directed against their father's foreign minister. Even before the new dauphine's arrival, the group had been gearing up for the latest of these vendettas, which aimed at precipitating both Choiseul's and his protégée's fall from grace.[70]

Over the years, Louis XV himself had done little to secure his daughters' cooperativeness or garner their support for his decisions. Although it was rumored that he had conducted an incestuous dalliance with Madame Adélaïde when she was young, the King opted to spend as little time as possible with her and her sisters. Their piety, in particular, seemed to him unspeakably dull; so he kept his ceremonial daily visits to their rooms to a bare minimum, and made no secret of the fact that he infinitely preferred the company of his prettier, more fun-loving mistresses.[71] Even on the trip to meet Marie Antoinette, he had ruffled the three princesses' feathers by inviting the Comtesse Du Barry to join in a banquet he hosted the night after the meeting in the forest of Compiègne. Du Barry had never before been accorded the privilege of dining with the royal family; Mesdames were incredulous that the King would grant her this honor on so solemn an occasion as his grandson's nuptials.[72]

It was at this dinner, held at La Muette, Louis XV's hunting lodge in the Bois de Boulogne, that the Dauphine got her first look at the Comtesse Du Barry. Conspicuous among the dinner guests for her extravagant clothing and jewelry, her lisping baby talk, and her scandalous habit of perching on the arm of the King's chair, the favorite caught Marie Antoinette's attention straightaway.[73] When she asked "what [were] that woman's functions at court," Madame de Noailles's quick-witted nephew, the Duc d'Ayen, proffered a euphemism: "To amuse the King." "Well, then I shall be her rival!" the younger woman replied, not catching the innuendo.[74] For Mesdames, however, the girl's rejoinder evoked a galling scenario—already anticipated, to their horror, by the fact that since meeting the Dauphine, their father could, Madame Campan observed, "speak of little else but her graces."[75] Such talk did not endear the newcomer to Madame Du Barry or her group of friends, either. With Choiseul's *Autrichienne* riding intolerably high, Mesdames and the *barrystes* had more reason than ever to seek her destruction.

MARIE ANTOINETTE ARRIVED AT VERSAILLES ON THE MORNING OF MAY 16. (Plate 5.) Constructed on a far more imposing scale than either the Hofburg or Schönbrunn, the eleven-hundred-room Hapsburg castle just outside

Vienna, this monumental château boasted a limestone façade over a quarter mile long. Its solemn, grandiose architecture bore the imprimatur of the great seventeenth-century architect Jules Hardouin-Mansart, enlisted by Louis XIV to make Versailles—originally a mere royal hunting lodge—the most magnificent palace in Europe. And so it was. From an unruly swath of marshland twelve miles east of Paris, Louis XIV had summoned forth waterways, parterres, and magnificent geometrical gardens that extended as far as the eye could see. Though several of the statues and fountains around the palace had fallen into disrepair during Louis XV's reign, and though, one contemporary visitor complained, poor sanitation caused "the park, the gardens, even the château [to] turn the stomach with dreadful odors . . . [of] urine and fecal matter," the overall effect was one of unmatched, unimaginable grandeur.[76] Even the stables that flanked the castle's series of imposing central courtyards were massive, capable of housing twenty-five hundred horses under their mansard roofs.

The palace itself was home to between two thousand and four thousand inhabitants, who vied for the supreme privilege of landing one of its 226 sumptuous apartments—or one of its five hundred less comfortable, but still prestigious rooms.[77] On a particularly crowded day, Versailles could accommodate up to ten thousand people: from the most august grandees to the lowliest domestic staffers, and from foreign dignitaries and their entourages to merchants hawking their wares in makeshift stalls. The castle was even open to tourists, provided that male visitors dress in the requisite hat and sword of the King's gentlemen. (A would-be visitor lacking his own could rent them for a small fee from the palace concierge.[78])

The Sun King had conceived of his incredible château above all as a place where his courtiers could remain constantly under his watchful eye—and he, in turn, under their awestruck gaze.[79] During his youth, Louis XIV had found the nobility dangerously resistant to the authority of the crown. In the last quarter of the seventeenth century, he brought them to heel by installing them at his newly expanded château as full-time worshippers in the cult of his own transcendent splendor.

Louis XIV codified daily life at Versailles in a way that both emphasized his divinely anointed status and forced the aristocracy into a role of worshipful subordination. Court etiquette construed virtually all gestures performed by the King and his family members as sacred rites, in which aristocrats served both as spectators and as officiants. On the surface, the duties assigned to the members of nobility might have appeared trivial enough: removing the sovereign's shoes at night or pouring out water for him to rinse his hands in the morning. But Louis XIV transmuted these functions into tokens of supreme prestige: "imaginary compensations"—as the cultural historian Jean-Marie Apostolidès has called them—for which court aristocrats competed fiercely among themselves, and which disguised their loss of real political power under the King's absolutist rule.[80] As the biographer and historian Olivier Bernier has explained of this system:

> Because the nobles [at Versailles] found themselves busy arguing abstruse points of precedence, the length of cloaks worn as a sign of mourning, or the exact placement of the cushions in the Royal Chapel, they had no time left to think of revolting against the government as their ancestors had so often done.[81]

Furthermore, as Bernier's reference to cloaks reveals, clothing externalized not only the King's own power but also each aristocrat's place in the delicately calibrated court hierarchy. When Louis XIV adopted a special coat with slashed sleeves to mourn the death of his father-in-law, for instance, he passed a law that prevented anyone but his courtiers from wearing the same ensemble.[82] Similarly, the monarch invented an outfit called the patent coat, which he distributed to only seventy of his favorite men. And "when they wore these blue coats with gold embroidery," recounts the fashion historian Mila Contini, the seventy chosen ones "could follow the King without needing any further permission"— a mark of unusual freedom and extreme privilege.[83] This set of distinctions was still alive and well in the eighteenth century, when a prominent nobleman, the Comte de Ségur, observed that "courtiers in France were even more the slaves of fashion than of the prince."[84] Indeed, for the denizens of Versailles, clothes and other seemingly superficial emblems remained concrete measures of their success . . . or failure. In this rarefied world, the surface was the substance. And the appearance of power, legible in everything from a slashed sleeve to a patent coat, was the real thing.[85]

WHEN MARIE ANTOINETTE FIRST ALIGHTED FROM HER CARRIAGE IN THE château's grandiose central courtyard, she had little time to ruminate on the peculiar culture of her new home. Because renovations were not yet finished on the grand set of first-floor apartments she was supposed to occupy, the Comtesse de Noailles hastily ushered her through the riot of ormolu, marble, ebony, ivory, glass, statuary, paintings, and tapestries that crowded the gargantuan palace, and into a temporary set of rooms on the ground floor.

Previously home to the Dauphin's late mother, Marie Josèphe, the suite consisted of "two antechambers, a large cabinet or library, two smaller sitting-rooms, an oratory, a bedroom and a bathroom."[86] Apart from some pretty boiseries on the walls and a pair of frothy paintings that hung over the bedroom doors—pictures of Venus, the goddess of love, cavorting with her son Cupid's paramour, Psyche—Marie Antoinette's new abode boasted few notable charms. Left almost untouched since Marie Josèphe's death from tuberculosis in 1767, the rooms were gloomy and dark; many of the sumptuous gilded furnishings were still draped with slipcovers or caked in dust. The ceiling, also heavily gilded but cracked and crumbling, threatened imminent collapse.

If this last architectural feature suggested a throwback to the *pavillon de remise,* the Dauphine's memories of the latter building may have resurfaced even more forcefully when her ladies began her *toilette.* Here, as at the *remise,* the princess had to stand half dressed and shivering while a large clutch of attendants briskly coated her hair with powder, her face with pasty white makeup, and her cheeks with large, precisely defined circles of rouge. Here, as at the *remise,* the women laced her into a stiff, fitted bodice and *paniers* and outfitted her in a richly brocaded *grand habit.*[87] Only the gown represented a notable departure from the exchange ceremony on the Rhine, insofar as the one provided for her today had been cut from luminous, white-hued cloth-of-silver: the traditionally prescribed material for a dauphine's wedding gown.

Already resplendent on its own, the silver gown was enhanced by masses of exquisite white diamonds, which she had received as wedding gifts from her mother, and which accentuated her official standing as the most important woman at court.[88] The ensemble would have been a masterpiece but for one tiny detail—a detail that may have made the girl's wedding *toilette* more upsetting even than the stripping at the border. For the dressmakers who had confected the wedding gown had misestimated her measurements, and cut the bodice far too small.

Try as they might, Marie Antoinette's helpers could not close the dress in back; there remained, as one of the wedding guests observed, "quite a broad stripe of lacing and shift quite visible, which had a bad effect between two broader stripes of diamonds."[89] This was a not insignificant glitch, for the bride was supposed to embody the splendor of the dynasty she was joining. Yet with thousands of people anxiously awaiting the Dauphine's appearance— scheduled to occur at one o'clock sharp—and with no other cloth-of-silver gown on hand as a substitute, there was little choice but for her to appear as she was. The palace clocks chimed one. On a cue from Madame de Noailles, the princess commenced her bridal march in the ill-fitting gown, her "lacing and shift" exposed for all to see. As she stepped out of her apartments, the façade Marie Antoinette had worked so hard to uphold began to crack. After just a few hours at Versailles, the perfect princess was already coming apart.

All the same, Marie Antoinette put on a brave face as she walked upstairs to join Louis XV and his family in the Cabinet du Conseil. Here for the first time, she met the Dauphin's two younger brothers, the Comtes de Provence and d'Artois, and his two sisters, Clothilde and Élisabeth, as well as several princes of the blood—who, apart from the King's immediate family, were the most important personages at court. Once these presentations were made, the group processed through the palace's vast, glittering Hall of Mirrors, where some six thousand splendidly attired aristocrats had gathered to watch them pass.

Reserved for important court occasions, the hall drew its name from the seventeen gigantic arched mirrors that lined its eastern wall. These captured the light both from the sun streaming through the windowed arcade on the opposite wall, and from the thousands of candles that flickered in the gallery's crystal chandeliers and golden torchères. (The artificial light would soon prove more a necessity than a decorating touch, as black thunderclouds had begun to clog the summer sky—"surely a bad omen," the aging Duc de Richelieu, who supported Madame Du Barry, hypothesized aloud.[90]) Crowded among the room's tall marble statues and heavy gold furniture, blossoming orange trees in thick silver pots filled the air with their fragrance. Overhead, gilt-framed frescoes depicted the heroic exploits of Louis XIV, who had presided over the hall's construction, and whose ubiquitous sunburst cipher had been stitched in gold onto the rich white damask drapery that lined the vaulted windows.

Typically, the room's bedazzling attractions were enough to impress upon both Frenchmen and foreigners the Bourbon monarch's unparalleled glory. But today, they were no match for the slender maiden gliding along its lustrous parquet floors. "From the first steps she took into the long gallery," Madame Campan wrote, "she drew six thousand pairs of eyes to her person."[91] Indeed, even with her stays and laces visible—and how unnerving it must have been for Marie Antoinette to see them reflected, a million times over, in the hall's countless mirrors—the bride cut a breathtaking figure as she made her way to the King's Chapel. While her magnificent diamonds refracted the sun- and torchlight in every direction, her natural dancer's movements and her glowing skin elicited murmurs of admiration throughout the massive gallery, as did the way in which she intuitively granted a nod or a smile to each person whose rank merited such favors.[92] With this admirable performance, Campan opined, the Dauphine "looked better than beautiful to every eye"—though this assessment no doubt overlooked whatever hostile or resentful murmurs the Dauphine's arrival may have prompted from members of the French party.[93]

When the bride, groom, and royal family reached the King's Chapel, the spectators poured in behind them for the religious ceremony. As viewed from the chapel's overcrowded pews and teeming second-story loges, the lithe and lissome Marie Antoinette, kneeling under the silver canopy stretched over the altar, offered a welcome contrast to that of poor Louis Auguste, who was manifestly uncomfortable in his opulent gold wedding suit (reportedly worth over 64,000 livres).[94] At least, this was the opinion of one of the wedding guests, the Duchess of Northumberland, who complained that the Dauphin was "not so well in his own Clothes" and "appear'd to have much more timidity than his little Wife. He trembled excessively during the service and blushed up to his Eyes when he gave the Ring."[95] Though the bride momentarily betrayed her own nervousness during the signing of the marriage register (she allowed a large inkblot to fall as she wrote one of her middle names, Jeanne), she made a quick recovery and ignored bystanders' murmurings about the dark future the blotch betokened.[96]

After another round of formal presentations, the party adjourned to the recently completed *salle de spectacles* for the royal family's public dinner, where Marie Antoinette continued to hold the assembly's rapt attention. The renovations to the *salle*—a lavishly gilded room lit by more than three thousand flickering candles—had been terrifically expensive and had taken the King's architect, Ange-Jacques Gabriel, over two years to complete.[97] But although the results were, as one spectator effused, "a hundred times more admirable than the Seven Wonders of the World," the thousands of guests perched in the room's gold-trimmed loges to watch the royals eat kept their eyes trained on the Dauphine.[98] Beneath the painting of Apollo that graced the hall's high, gilded ceiling, the daughter of the Caesars did her exalted lineage proud. In marked contrast to Louis Auguste, hunched greedily over his food, Marie Antoinette hardly ate a bite, sitting elegant and upright "like a statue of Beauty."[99]

Likewise, when the storm that had been gathering over Versailles finally broke, drenching the revelers and driving them indoors from the illuminated gardens, Marie Antoinette's poise did not falter, nor did her bandbox beauty suffer from the change. In the newspaper *Le Mercure galant,* one Mademoiselle Cosson de la Cressonnière published a quatrain echoing the adulation that the bride had elicited at her nuptials, and reprising the optimistic imagery that adorned the walls of her new apartments:

> *Bearing the wishes of her court,*
> *She comes, by noble marriage led;*
> *'Tis Psyche in the bloom of youth*
> *Conducted here to Cupid's bed.*[100]

Irritating as this widespread approval must have been for Marie Antoinette's foes, it was the matter of sending her off "to Cupid's bed" that may at last have brought them some consolation, if only by affording them a chance to watch the mask of graceful serenity slip from her face once and for all. The bride and bridegroom's conveyance to their wedding chamber for the *coucher,* the ceremony of getting into bed, essentially reprised the events that had left Marie Antoinette exposed and vulnerable on the banks of the Rhine. Every bit as demeaning as the rites that had attended the *remise,* the rituals surrounding the wedding night turned the goddess of love back into the frightened princess who, just two weeks earlier, had been dismayed by an altogether different mythological figure.

Marie Antoinette's preparations for her wedding night began, as had the *remise,* with a quasi-public undressing effected by a large retinue of women. In this case, not only her ladies-in-waiting but also all the highest-ranked princesses of the court participated in the undoing of the Dauphine's hairdo, the dismantling of her intricate wedding ensemble, and the donning of her virginal white peignoir.[101] Crammed *panier* to *panier* into the room reserved for the *toilette,* dozens of ladies unfamiliar to the bride fell into line to ready her for the *coucher.* As the most recently married princess of the blood, the young Duchesse de Chartres held the nocturnal *toilette*'s ultimate privilege, that of handing the embroidered nightdress to the Dauphine. But etiquette dictated that the garment pass through other privileged hands, as well, before arriving at the naked bride's body. To a princess at whose home court the ceremonies of the bedchamber were relatively uncomplicated, largely private affairs, this procedure may have come as something of a shock.[102]

But worse was yet to come. Having dressed their charge for bed, the Dauphine's ladies propelled her out into the wedding suite where, according to a royal custom that dated back to the Middle Ages, the bride and groom had to get into bed "before the whole world." This assembly included the Archbishop of Reims, Louis XV, the princes and princesses of the blood, foreign princes and dignitaries, the dukes, duchesses, peers, and peeresses of the realm, and the many other nobles whose titles afforded them Rights of Entry to the royal bedchambers. (These rights, needless to say, fell into the broad category of "imaginary compensations" by means of which the Sun King had managed to subordinate his nobles.) Though he was known to hate being the center of attention, the nightgown-clad Louis Auguste bore the ordeal without much fuss, facing his audience with an air of somnolent, bovine stolidity.[103]

Marie Antoinette, however, clutched desperately at the collar of her scanty peignoir and blushed to the roots of her hair.[104] According to one of her new attendants, the fifteen-year-old Mademoiselle de Mirecourt, the

Dauphine was "violently upset by all the public attention."[105] Scarcely waiting for the Archbishop to finish sprinkling holy water on their bed, the bride dove beneath the gold-embroidered coverlet in horror. A short moment of respite came when the curtains on the great four-poster bed drew closed around her and her husband. No sooner had this occurred, however, than the curtains flew open again, so that the courtiers, reassured that the royal marriage was indeed poised for consummation, could formally take their leave of the pair.

AS IT HAPPENED, THE NEWLYWEDS DID NOT CONSUMMATE THEIR UNION THAT night. The next morning, the servants who changed the couple's bed linens, finding no signs of blood to attest to the virginal Dauphine's deflowering, spread the news that no new royal offspring should be expected anytime soon. Following the lead of the Spanish ambassador, who bribed these servants to let him examine the sheets firsthand, diplomats from a host of foreign courts, including Austria, hastened to inform their sovereigns that the Bourbon-Hapsburg alliance had not yet been cemented in full.[106] Inadvertently or otherwise, Louis Auguste himself summed up the situation by noting in the journal he used to tally his successes and failures on the royal hunt: "May 17: Nothing."[107]

And yet, like another famous "nothing" from Louis Auguste's hunting diary—he would make the same pithy entry on July 14, 1789, when the people of Paris stormed the Bastille and set the Revolution on its world-changing course—this entry neglected to account for the fact that Marie Antoinette's traumatic bedtime appearance before the court established the tenor and the terms of her sojourn in France. Along with the *remise,* this incident may well have impressed upon her that her body was not hers to control; that the very garments she wore could be taken from her against her will. By the same token, if clothing could be turned against her to such mortifying effect (as it was when she found herself stripped of it in mixed company), then it also represented a possession worth reclaiming, a power worth exploiting. On the basis of Marie Antoinette's own subsequent reports that Louis Auguste had not so much as touched her hand, many biographers have speculated that on the couple's first night together, the young man fell asleep straightaway, ignoring his baffled new bride.[108] This scenario leaves room for the related possibility that while her husband dozed, the Dauphine was free to replay over and over in her mind the humiliations she had thus far endured in her new homeland—and maybe, just maybe, to dream a little dream of Medea.

THREE

CORSETED

The wedding celebration continued for nine more days and nights, with gambling in the Hall of Mirrors, dancing in the ballroom, and banqueting, opera, and ballet in Gabriel's *salle de spectacles*. On the festivities' final evening, Louis XV launched a fireworks display—postponed from the first night because of heavy rains—by flinging a flaming spear from an open window in the Hall of Mirrors.[1] The spectacle involved a volcanic eruption of fireworks over the palace gardens' Temple of the Sun, and culminated in the simultaneous detonation of twenty thousand rockets that crashed through the darkness like falling stars.[2] Afterward, 200,000 revelers in the castle's gardens spent the night dancing alongside the reflecting pool and fountain known as Apollo's Basin. Illuminated by scores of multicolored lanterns, the trellises, allées, archways, and obelisks that encircled the basin were reported as being "far more brilliant than when lit by the sun in all its splendor, [and outstripped] everything that one reads of Fairyland."[3]

As the festivities' guest of honor and its animating spirit, Marie Antoinette sparkled just as brilliantly as the Fairyland that had been created in her honor. To a certain extent, that sparkle was literal: on her wedding day, Louis XV had presented her with the coffer of jewels that tradition reserved for the Dauphine of France. Covered in richly embroidered crimson velvet, the coffer was nearly as tall and three times as wide as its new owner, whose hands shook with excitement as she unlocked it with a tiny golden key.[4] Inside, glittering on the robin's-egg-blue silk lining, she found a magnificent array of necklaces and earrings, fans and snuffboxes, bracelets and buttons—

all glittering with diamonds and other precious gemstones, and valued collectively at almost 2 million livres.[5] One of the collection's most stunning pieces was a necklace of priceless oversized pearls first worn in the seventeenth century by Louis XIV's mother, Anne of Austria, an ancestress Marie Antoinette happened to share with her bridegroom. Along with the set of splendid white diamonds she had brought with her from the Hofburg as part of her trousseau, these treasures became additional ornaments for the Dauphine's already resplendent court costumes. Even among a sea of courtiers "clad in brocades, silks, and other gorgeous robes, [and] flashing with jewels," the Austrian newcomer shone the brightest.[6]

A handful of the more critical wedding guests remarked that the girl's frame seemed far too slight to support such a hefty abundance of gems.[7] Nonetheless, in a palace where a trim torso was de rigueur, universally enforced through the adoption of whalebone stays, the girl's very delicateness redounded to her credit, as did her fair hair, wide blue eyes, and already much touted alabaster complexion.[8] Royal marriages always spawned tributes to the bride's physical charms, whether or not she actually deserved them, but in Marie Antoinette's case, the poets' encomia did not seem far off the mark. So "luminous and fragile" did she appear, according to her new lady-in-waiting, Mademoiselle de Mirecourt, that "we dreamed we were watching Spring incarnate."[9]

Her bearing provided viewers with additional grounds for approval, for, in Madame Campan's words, it was "simultaneously graceful and imposing."[10] By most accounts, her posture was indeed perfect, and she had a way of carrying her head that, her contemporaries agreed, marked her as a queen even in a room full of other great ladies.[11] Of course, Marie Antoinette had worked slavishly to win this acclaim: it had taken hours of training with Noverre before she could perform the "Versailles glide" without a misstep. Moving in such an airy, effortless fashion was no mean feat under the best of circumstances, much less among the profusion of obstacles littering the floors of the Bourbon court. Cleanliness did not feature heavily inside the palace, and those navigating its passageways had to steer clear of everything from the feces of palace pets to scraps of food dropped by careless servants to mud tracked in by peddlers and tourists. The long, cumbersome gowns of the formally attired court ladies also posed problems; the folds of a noblewoman's train—which, the courtier and noted writer Madame de Genlis complained, was always "of immoderate length"—tended to snag at the heels of nearby ladies' slippers.[12] Accidental contact caused severe mortification for everyone involved. But for Marie Antoinette, it was as if these pitfalls didn't exist: "she walked as if on wings."[13]

She danced more elegantly still. On May 19, the Dauphine and her husband were called upon to perform the first minuet at a dress ball held in the great, gilded *salle de spectacles*. Encircled by several thousand lookers-on, the heir to the throne shuffled through the dance in obvious discomfort, blushing and scowling in his usual unappealing way. His bride, by contrast, seemed only to become more graceful as the music played on, and in a world where the Bourbons' physical splendor was supposed to mirror their political supremacy, such easy elegance made a strong impression. During her début minuet, her movements were reportedly "so natural and so graceful that the immense hall was filled with nothing but murmurs of admiration."[14]

Insofar as they augured good things for the Franco-Austrian alliance, the Dauphine's public triumphs met with the approbation of both Louis XV and Maria Theresa, who had instructed her ambassador Mercy to send her regular dispatches about the girl's doings—dispatches that were to be kept secret from everyone at Versailles, including Marie Antoinette herself. "Our archduchess has surpassed all my hopes," Mercy informed the Empress shortly after the wedding. "The whole court and the general public are full of nothing but praise for her."[15] Louis XV in particular, he added, "remains very satisfied with Madame la Dauphine, and is always caressing and complimenting her in a very graceful and touching way."[16] Maria Theresa in turn wrote to her daughter to commend her for having "captured everyone's hearts," and reminded her that the King's heart was especially important quarry. She enjoined Marie Antoinette to "love him, obey him, try to anticipate his thoughts; you cannot do too much [on that front]."[17]

Marie Antoinette took this advice to heart, flirting prettily with Louis XV every chance she got, and calling him her "dear Grandpapa" in defiance of more formal rules of address.[18] To ingratiate herself further, she informed him that she "would be charmed to accompany him on the little voyages he had a habit of making" to his nearby residences at Choisy and Compiègne, Meudon and Fontainebleau—trips that usually featured regular hunting expeditions with the Dauphin, and in which the King readily included her.[19] (Marie Antoinette did not yet ride well enough to participate in these outings on horseback, so she followed the princes and their fellow hunters from the safety of an elegantly appointed calèche.) Although also something of a novice with a needle and thread, the Dauphine proudly announced her plan to embroider a vest for Louis XV and made winningly self-effacing little jokes about how long the project was taking her: "I hope that with the grace of God it will be finished in a few years."[20] When she extended this deadline to twenty years, her "dear Grandpapa" laughed and told her she should really try to complete the vest before he died. Even the girl's sewing mistakes drew indulgent smiles from the jaded old monarch.

. . .

MARIE ANTOINETTE WAS RIGHT TO HEED HER MOTHER'S COUNSEL IN CULTI-
vating Louis XV's affections, because for her as for the other members of his
court, all blessings flowed from him and him alone. As a result, competition
for the King's favor created an atmosphere of bitter acrimony and infighting
at the château.[21] A scandalized Mercy described the French court to his Empress as an "abode of treachery, hatred, and revenge . . . , [fueled] by intrigues and inspired by personal interest."[22] And while Marie Antoinette's
exalted position alone sufficed to earn the jealousy of those thousands of less
fortunate courtiers striving for advancement, her special rapport with Louis
XV made her particularly unpopular with the members of the French party,
for whom each of the Dauphine's little victories scored points not just for
her, but for Austria and Choiseul.[23]

Mesdames the Aunts remained at the forefront of this hostile group, but
their long years at Versailles had taught them the importance of dissimulation and tact. Jean de La Bruyère, the great moralist of seventeenth-century
Versailles, had written: "Do not ever hope for candor, frankness, fairness, . . .
benevolence or generosity from a person who has spent any time at court,"
and Louis XV's daughters had learned this lesson well.[24] They had little
trouble concealing their animosity from the girl—despite the fact that etiquette obliged Marie Antoinette to spend hours every day in their company,
from visits to their apartments each morning to obligatory card games at
night. In her presence, the older women behaved sweetly enough; but behind
her back, they railed against the girl they dubbed *l'Autrichienne*.[25]

In their effort to win their niece's trust, the Aunts benefited from the fact
that she had always taken orders from a strong older woman—Maria
Theresa, who, in the letter Marie Antoinette had retrieved at Freiburg, had
explicitly ordered her daughter to follow Mesdames' lead in adapting to life
at Versailles. With their veneer of piety and the august rank they enjoyed as
Children of France, the sisters seemed to the Empress the most trustworthy
mentors their new niece could hope to find. And this was precisely how they
presented themselves to the Dauphine. They even gave her a key to their
apartments, to encourage informal as well as formal visits. Such increased
intimacy would enable them to gather valuable information against Marie
Antoinette, information they could use to undermine her in the King's eyes.
By adopting them as her surrogate mothers, the unsuspecting princess would
make their job that much easier.[26]

The Aunts and their coterie of stodgy (if vindictive) friends were not the
only ones who blanched to see the Dauphine dazzle. On the opposite end of
the court's social spectrum, the wanton and beautiful Comtesse Du Barry,

herself a longtime victim of Mesdames' vicious prattle, shared the older women's antipathy to Marie Antoinette. The rambunctious, impudent, low-born royal mistress differed from Mesdames and their pious cronies in just about every way, except in the hatred that she, too, bore the Duc de Choiseul. Seconded by those in his cabal, the foreign minister incensed the Comtesse not only by crowing at having brought the girl to France, but by commenting pointedly on her obvious superiority to all the court's other noted beauties.[27]

With her striking combination of pale blond curls and sultry, violet-colored eyes, Du Barry was unaccustomed to competition from other women at court. ("You are the King's divinity," the legendarily lusty Duc de Richelieu was fond of reminding her.[28]) By the same token, she was aware that her lover bored easily. Like her predecessor Pompadour, Madame Du Barry had thus, in the words of one court memorialist, built her career on "dissipating his ennui by every means possible."[29] She organized licentious private parties for Louis XV and his friends, behaved with a saucy vulgarity that her lover found titillating, and shared with him the latest, illicitly published satirical verses and pornography (even when such publications took aim at her personally). The favorite's *choiseuliste* detractors maintained that she actually went so far as to place other young lovelies in the King's bed, so that she might control him even when he strayed from her side. His interest in Marie Antoinette, though, was something the Comtesse could not control, and so posed a notable threat to her position. Behind closed doors, palace gossips gave voice to Du Barry's worst fear: that before long, the old roué would look to his own granddaughter-in-law for a piquant change of pace.[30]

Adding insult to injury, the princess soon adopted the *choiseulistes'* habit of treating Madame Du Barry with open disdain. The favorite did not know it, but Marie Antoinette's coldness was the handiwork of the Aunts, who had ex-ultantly filled their nephew's wife in on Du Barry's scandalous past.[31] Born Jeanne Bécu, the favorite was the illegitimate daughter of a promiscuous seam-stress and a badly behaving monk. After a few years of education in a convent, she took a job as a shopgirl in a fashionable Parisian accessories store, but found a more lucrative sideline in a series of brothels, where she charged 24 livres for a night of love.[32] It was in this milieu—which Jeanne herself later flippantly described as her "Seminary of Debauch"—that the young prostitute became involved with an aristocratic but cash-strapped libertine named Du Barry.[33] When her new lover brought her into Louis XV's sights, he realized he stood to win the King's favor (and thereby resolve his own financial difficul-ties) by installing her as the newest *maîtresse en titre*. This was in 1768, four years after Madame de Pompadour's death, and although the King had been deeply afflicted by his trusted mistress's passing, his well-known sexual ap-petites made it highly unlikely that her post would remain vacant forever.

Acting fast, Du Barry arranged a marriage of convenience between the fifteen-year-old Jeanne and his brother, the Comte Du Barry, with Jeanne's own father officiating at the ceremony. The farce endowed Jeanne with an aristocratic title, and thus qualified her to receive the King's official attentions. Mesmerized by her beauty, which even the worldliest of noblemen concurred in finding "celestial," Louis XV eagerly installed her in Pompadour's place.[34] In April 1769, he arranged for her formal presentation at court—a ceremony usually reserved for the flower of the nobility—where the former shopgirl and prostitute shocked the world by mincing in among her betters with a hundred thousand livres' worth of jewelry on her person, and diamonds on the soles of her shoes.[35] But the King's courtiers weren't the only ones who recoiled to see a lowly tramp rise so high. Thanks in part to the efforts of the *choiseulistes,* who funded the publication of underground pamphlets about Du Barry's lubricious exploits (real and exaggerated), French commoners also became outraged at her ascendancy.[36] From the salons of Versailles to the streets of Paris, malcontents complained that Louis XV's new favorite would turn the very throne room into a Seminary of Debauch.

For the Aunts, passing such gossip on to Marie Antoinette had two related advantages. First, it would help them instill in the girl such a hearty aversion toward the Comtesse that Du Barry would face social humiliations beyond any she had previously known. Second, and more important, they seem to have hoped that the Dauphine's inevitable dislike of the favorite would get her into serious trouble with Louis XV.[37] Too naïve to detect this double game, Marie Antoinette played right into Mesdames' hands. Having received a fairly strict religious upbringing, she was obligingly horrified by the details of Madame Du Barry's salacious history and concluded that it would be indecent for her to acknowledge the favorite's existence.[38] In one letter to Maria Theresa, she justified her conduct by describing the King's lover as "the stupidest and most impertinent creature imaginable"—and this was not an opinion she felt compelled to confine to the printed page.[39] Whenever she encountered "the creature," the Dauphine's naturally haughty-looking lower lip—which the Cardinal de Rohan had already noticed at Strasbourg as being "scarlet as a cherry, but thick . . . , which one knows is the distinctive trace" of the Hapsburgs, curled into an unmistakable sneer.[40] She refused to address so much as a word in the favorite's direction, even when the King was looking on. Much to the Austrian ambassador's dismay (for Mercy realized that no good could come of snubbing the King's mistress), the Dauphine "made frequent jokes in public" at Du Barry's expense.[41] Laughing at these witticisms for reasons their young niece did not suspect, the Aunts encouraged her in the erroneous belief that hers was the course of righteousness.

Given her influence on the King, Du Barry's enmity could prove lethal to the already friendless Dauphine. The Aunts recognized, however, that it would take a more flagrant scandal to turn their father against the girl in earnest, for his propensity toward boredom and his sexual profligacy were not his only defining qualities. Another, his daughters knew as well as anyone, was a peculiar apathy that their enemy Choiseul once described as a "total inertia of the soul."[42] Louis XV excelled at making hot chocolate and prided himself on his knack for cutting the top off a boiled egg with one neat swipe of his spoon.[43] Apart from these talents, his sexual romps, and his passion for the hunt, very little interested him enough to rouse him from his indolence.

So the Aunts bided their time as, humiliated by the Archduchess's public slights, Du Barry retaliated by criticizing the girl sharply and frequently, and by sharing her views with "all those whose political ambitions had been thwarted, hurt, humiliated by Choiseul's ministry."[44] This group included not only the Duc d'Aiguillon, widely believed to be Du Barry's secret lover, but also the Duc de La Vauguyon, a singularly mean-spirited man whose chief claim to fame had been serving as Louis Auguste's boyhood tutor. Having worked actively to establish Du Barry as the King's favorite, the two *barryste* ringleaders did not appreciate seeing her power diluted—by Choiseul's protégée, no less—and they joined the favorite in running down the Dauphine whenever the King was within earshot.

Perhaps most notably, to neutralize the slew of compliments the Austrian princess had garnered for her elegance and beauty, the *barryste* crew referred to her as "that little redhead" (red hair being infinitely less desirable than Du Barry's own much admired blond), and pronounced with mock regret that the Dauphine "had no figure to speak of." Not surprisingly, the favorite's verdict was harshest of all: "I see nothing attractive in red hair, thick lips, sandy complexion, and eyes without eyelashes," she sulkily informed Louis XV. "Had she who is so beautiful not sprung from the House of Austria, such attractions would never have been the subject of admiration."[45] In a court where appearance was everything, these were fighting words, and like all gossip at Versailles, they quickly became fodder for widespread discussion. First making the rounds of the Oeil-de-Boeuf (the heavily trafficked antechamber outside the King's apartments, named for its "bull's-eye"-shaped window), the slurs quickly spread throughout the palace. But to the joy of both wings of the French party, it soon became apparent that caustic assessments of the girl's looks were not the only ammunition they had at their disposal.

. . .

IN HER FIRST FEW MONTHS AT VERSAILLES, THE DAUPHINE REMAINED LARGELY ignorant of these intrigues, as she was distracted by a different problem, one that had the whole of the court chattering about the state of her marriage. Aristocrats whispered about it in out-of-the-way salons and allées.[46] Servants mulled it over in the stables and the vegetable gardens. Visiting diplomats described it in their eagerly awaited dispatches to princes back home. Choiseul assessed the situation by declaring with characteristic bluntness: "unless [the Dauphin] changes, he will end by becoming the horror of the nation," a pronouncement by which Louis XV said he was "moved very deeply," though the sovereign also expressed hope that the worrisome circumstances would improve "when we least expect it."[47] Maria Theresa adopted a similarly optimistic stance when she chalked the issue up to her new son-in-law's "extreme youth and shyness."[48] Marie Antoinette, for her part, ventured no such opinions or theories, but simply reported the facts to her tutor, the Abbé de Vermond. Paraphrasing her remarks to the Empress's emissary, Starhemberg, Vermond recorded that "since the occasion of their meeting in the forest of Compiègne, Monsieur le Dauphin had not only not kissed her, but had not even touched her hand."[49] Louis Auguste, in short, had still made no effort to consummate his marriage.

According to a medical expert whom Maria Theresa consulted on the matter, this qualified as "strange behavior," even though the fifteen-year-old Dauphin was indeed, as the Empress had put it, still quite young, and even though the timidity she had accused him of was indisputably one of his most marked character traits.[50] Orphaned at the age of thirteen, both of his parents having died of tuberculosis, Louis Auguste had grown up under the more or less exclusive tutelage of the Duc de La Vauguyon, who had kept him isolated from other courtiers on the grounds that as a Bourbon prince, he was superior to them all. According to one critical contemporary, the greatest legacy of the boy's lonely upbringing was a "dread [of] conversation and [a] shyness so deeply rooted in [his] soul that it was impossible to cure" him.[51] In addition, La Vauguyon had instilled his pupil with a profound suspicion of Choiseul and the House of Austria—a sentiment that Louis Auguste's late father, Louis Ferdinand, one of the foreign minister's most implacable enemies, had fervently shared.[52] Between his antisocial character and his ingrained Austrophobia, it was thus perhaps not altogether startling that Louis Auguste should panic when confronted with the gregarious and attractive female emissary of the *choiseuliste* alliance.

Even so, in the context of a royal union, sex was a nonnegotiable duty, and all the more so in France at that particular time. Under the kingdom's previous two sovereigns, Louis XIV and Louis XV, the immediate heirs to the throne had met with untimely deaths, leading to worrisome generation gaps in the succession. Louis XV, great-grandson to the Sun King, had acceded to the throne at age five, after the deaths of his grandfather, father, and two older brothers, while Louis Auguste had lost two older brothers as well as his father before becoming Dauphin. Even with two younger brothers waiting in the wings—the Comte de Provence, aged fourteen, and the Comte d'Artois, aged thirteen, both slated to marry within the next few years—Louis Auguste had his work cut out for him. He and the Dauphine needed to start a family, without delay.

Yet delay Louis Auguste did, leaving both partisans and enemies of the Austrian alliance obsessively to monitor what Madame Campan called his undiminished "indifference and coldness"[53] toward his wife. Etiquette required that he dine with Marie Antoinette in public and join her and the rest of the royal family for daily gatherings in the Aunts' apartments. But when not at these command performances, the young man fled his bride with the terrified haste of a man swarmed by bees. He devoted his days to the hobbies that had filled his bachelorhood: hunting in the parks around the royal residences, and tinkering with locks and clocks in his private workshop, under the tutelage of a gruff professional smith named François Gamain.

Both pastimes excluded Marie Antoinette. Her inexperience as an equestrienne barred her from participating fully in her husband's beloved hunting jaunts; and she herself dismissed the idea of joining him in his smithy, on the grounds that she would be as incongruous there as "Venus at Vulcan's forge."[54] Here again, the princess found in classical literature an apt point of reference for her own life: Venus, the comely goddess of love, and Vulcan, the malformed blacksmith god, were among mythology's most improbable—and most unhappy—married couples. Stubbornly absorbed in his rough-and-tumble pursuits, Louis Auguste appeared all too willing to hold up his end of the analogy, leaving Marie Antoinette as pure and untouched as the painted images of Venus that gamboled across her bedroom walls.

Nor did the Dauphin's aloofness abate after dark. Instead of visiting his wife in her chambers, as princes with a dynastic mission were expected to do, Louis Auguste elected to spend most evenings in his own rooms, where he tried to deflect his attendants' inquiring stares with bizarre, infantile antics. For the ceremonial preparations he had to undergo before bed each evening, he developed a favorite prank involving the blue sash he wore over his coat as a mark of his adherence to the Order of the Holy Spirit. As his gentlemen attempted to remove his clothing, the Dauphin would grab the sash with both hands, wave it in the air like a lasso, and attempt to loop it through the earring of a nearby courtier or valet. If the sash reached its target, he would then proceed to rip the man's earlobe with a swift, gleeful tug.[55]

Such outbursts made it difficult, if not downright impossible, for the assembled crew to perform their prescribed functions—removing his coat and shoes, putting slippers on his feet, changing him into his nightgown, tucking his hair into a nightcap—with anything resembling gravity or ease. Like all other princely rituals, the *coucher* was supposed to affirm both the Bourbon family's dignity and the courtiers' own prestigious role in upholding it. By behaving in a manner that belied the nobility of his station and compromised his attendants' ability to serve him, Louis Auguste compounded the scandal emanating from his other "strange behavior."

MEANWHILE, THE YOUNG MAN'S RETICENCE IN THE BEDROOM WAS MAKING it downright impossible for Marie Antoinette to be, as the elderly *salonnière* Madame du Deffand put it, "a real dauphine."[56] But according to Maria Theresa, Louis Auguste's evasions did not relieve the Dauphine of her own marital obligations. Marie Antoinette, the Empress declared in her regular missives to France, could not content herself with charming Louis XV; she must also please her husband, and clinch the Franco-Austrian alliance by giving birth to a royal heir. "Everything depends on the wife," the Empress proclaimed, "on her being compliant, sweet, and amusing" toward her husband: a consort's "only business [must be] to please and obey" her man.[57] Having governed a vast empire while her own husband amused himself with horses and mistresses, Maria Theresa herself had not exactly lived by this advice. But for her daughter, she seemed to envision a more traditional path, directing the girl to combat the Dauphin's reserve with gentle but prodigious "caresses and cajoling."[58]

The young woman responded by declaring to her mother and anyone else who saw fit to inquire "that she was trying to win [Monsieur le Dauphin]'s confidence, and that she hoped to succeed in this."[59] She seems to have intuited that this reluctant future king suffered from a debilitating sense of his unsuitability for the role, especially when compared with the dashing Louis XV.[60] Compassionately, Marie Antoinette tried to bolster the boy's low self-esteem by announcing both in and outside of his company that she found him "more and more loveable each day."[61] With the King's permission, she began taking riding lessons on a donkey, so that she might one day be able to follow the royal hunt. She acted as peacemaker in the bitter fights Louis Auguste had a habit of getting into with his middle brother, the Comte de Provence, who mocked him cruelly for his clumsiness and lack of wit. And whenever she caught her husband emerging from his workshop, she extended her pretty white hands to him in an affectionate greeting, pretending not to notice how badly his own hands had been blackened by the forge.[62]

Where other courtiers looked upon him with barely disguised impatience or scorn, Marie Antoinette welcomed him with a smile.

Nonetheless, for the first few months of the marriage, the Dauphine's overtures had little discernible impact. Apart from hunting and smithing, the only topic Louis Auguste appeared willing to broach with his wife was their latest meal. As a rule, he consumed vast amounts of food each time he sat down to eat—downing at least "four cutlets, a chicken, a plateful of ham, half a dozen eggs in sauce, and a bottle and a half of champagne [in the mornings] before setting out to hunt."[63] Often these excesses drove him to serious bouts of indigestion, during which she cheerfully stayed by his side to tend to him.[64] Yet despite his frequent digestive troubles, the Dauphin returned ceaselessly to the same topic: the cooks were not feeding him enough. Trying to be as "sweet, compliant, and amusing" as her mother had commanded, his wife fielded these complaints with an empathetic air. Still, neither their tone nor their content was at all conducive to romantic intimacy.

Once the court embarked upon its annual summertime tour of the King's smaller châteaux in the region around Versailles, Marie Antoinette tried a different tack. One Sunday in July, while the court was at Choisy, she detained the Dauphin alone and confronted him directly about their sex life. "Since we must live in intimate friendship," she explained, "we must trust one another in speaking frankly about everything."[65] For all his shyness, her husband seemed grateful that she had raised the subject, and said that he shared her point of view. As Marie Antoinette later reported to Mercy, the Dauphin professed "that he was not ignorant of what was involved in the state of marriage, that from the beginning he had hatched a plan from which he had not wanted to deviate, and that once the court traveled from Choisy to [the royal residence at] Compiègne in August, he would live with her in the intimacy that their union required."[66] More specifically, Louis Auguste promised her that when he turned sixteen (his birthday would coincide with the visit to Compiègne), "all would be accomplished," and that he would visit her bedroom more frequently thereafter.[67] Like Versailles, Choisy was no place to keep a secret, and the château soon buzzed with news of a rapprochement. All signs seemed to point toward a happy resolution.

But the signs were misleading. For reasons Louis Auguste either did not know or did not care to explain, his sixteenth birthday came and went with no change whatsoever in the status quo. On a sporadic basis, the Dauphin might show up in Marie Antoinette's rooms—only to have his courage fail him. During these visits, Madame Campan recorded, the youth would simply crawl into bed without speaking to or touching his wife, and the next morning, he would try to sneak out while Marie Antoinette was still in slumber.[68] But more often, he left his wife to spend the night alone. By the summer's end, the scene that greeted the ladies who waited upon the Dauphine each morning was invariably the same as it had been back in May. Drawing back the curtains on the immense four-poster, they would find the girl all by herself, clinging pitifully to her little pug. Prince Starhemberg and Mercy had had Mops sent back to her from Vienna as a concession to the Dauphine's loneliness.[69]

FOR THE DAUPHINE WAS LONELY INDEED, ALTHOUGH SHE WAS ALMOST never alone. Whereas in Vienna, she had spent her days frolicking with her many brothers and sisters, she was now, like her husband, surrounded at all times by a large, official entourage.[70] Handpicked by the King, the group was presided over by Marie Antoinette's *dame d'honneur,* Madame de Noailles, and the Mistress of the Robes (*dame d'atours*), the Duchesse de Cossé-Brissac (whose husband had secured her the post through his close ties to none other than Madame Du Barry). Serving alongside these ladies were twelve noblewomen whose principal function was to accompany their mistress everywhere (*dames pour accompagner Madame la Dauphine,* known after her accession as *dames du palais de la Reine*). Like the *dames d'honneur* and *d'atours,* these women's positions were known as *charges d'honneur,* bestowed as a function of their families' exalted lineage and court connections. *Charges* at this level carried with them substantial pensions and, because they allowed for unequaled access to the future queen, unquantifiable, priceless prestige.

Serving beneath the *dames* were sixteen Women of the Bedchamber (*femmes de chambre*), recruited from the ranks of the local haute bourgeoisie. "The first four [of these women] performed their service by twos, for alternate fortnights, replaced in emergencies by their deputies among the twelve under-women."[71] (It was to this group that Madame Campan— whose father-in-law served as Marie Antoinette's personal librarian— proudly belonged.) The *femmes de chambre* in turn relied on the assistance of a cadre of *femmes rouges* or "red women," so called because of the distinctive red uniform they wore to perform their duties.[72]

Marie Antoinette also had a hundred officers and valets to manage her finances and run her household, two hundred servants to oversee the preparation and service of her meals, and a small cadre of priests to tend to her spiritual needs. Against her enemies' wishes, the tutor whom Choiseul had assigned to Marie Antoinette while still in Austria, the Abbé de Vermond, had been permitted to follow her to Versailles to continue her studies. "Six equerries, nine ushers, two doctors, four surgeons, a clock-maker, a tapestry-maker, eighteen lackeys, a fencing master, and two muleteers" rounded out the picture.[73] Like Marie Antoinette's ladies, these staffers shared a single objective: to serve the future Queen of France, upon whose benefaction their livelihood depended. Beset on all sides by their zealous ministrations, Marie Antoinette soon found she "could not make a gesture, take a step, utter a word without triggering a reaction in the attendants who never left her."[74]

Whereas she had grown up in a court marked by at least occasional lapses into bourgeois informality and comfort, Marie Antoinette was now treated with the unremitting solemnity accorded to all Bourbons under Louis XIV's system of etiquette. As Madame Campan observed, the protocol to which the princess was forced to adhere turned her into both an idol and a victim: an idol because her entourage had to worship her like a goddess, but a victim because their staunch service robbed her of whatever privacy she had enjoyed in Vienna.[75] Indeed, in the seventeenth century, the court moralist La Bruyère had expressed this paradox in much the same way when he asserted that at Versailles, "kings want for nothing except the pleasures of a private existence." This was certainly true for the young dauphine.[76]

Even at her bath time, Marie Antoinette found she could not escape her retinue, though she tried to preserve what Madame Campan described as her "excessive sense of modesty" and privacy by wearing a long cotton gown into the bathtub itself.[77] Such gestures, however, presented a flimsy defense against her courtiers' avid stares. Undergoing this awkward experience day after day—for unlike her French compatriots, the Dauphine evinced a "Germanic" devotion to regular baths—she was repeatedly confronted with the truth of her mother's maxim: "All eyes will be fixed on you."[78] Her body, she was learning, was most definitely not her own.

This drastic shift from her old way of living left the Dauphine tremendously nostalgic for Austria: "I swear to you," she wrote to her mother in July, "that I have not received one of your dear letters without having tears come to my eyes. . . . I ardently wish I could see my dear, my very dear, family for at least one more instant."[79] And in another missive, she confessed forlornly: "My heart is always with my family in Austria."[80] These proclamations may have stemmed more from homesickness than from outright filial affection—years later, Marie Antoinette would admit that she "feared [Maria Theresa] more than she loved her"—but still, the girl's sense of isolation seems to have been acute.[81] The Abbé de Vermond, who was just about the only familiar face Marie Antoinette encountered in her new household, detected "moments of sadness" beneath the sunny demeanor she tried to maintain in public.[82] "My heart," Vermond admitted to one Maria Theresa's closest advisers, "is absolutely wrung by all this."[83]

Initially, the Dauphine tried to make the best of the situation by cultivating friendships with the ladies who flanked her night and day. Though the majority of these women were far older than she, and not prone to spontaneous fits of hilarity, Marie Antoinette was thrilled to discover among some of her younger *dames* and their friends a spirit of merriment not unlike the one she had been given to indulging with her brothers and sisters back home. These newfound companions of hers, noted one contemporary,

> loved pleasure and hated restraint, laughed at everything, even the tattle about their own reputations, and recognized no law save the necessity of spending their lives in gaiety, behind a thin and sometimes deceptive screen of decorum, which concealed badly, or not at all, certain caprices which came near to creating scandal.[84]

Marie Antoinette's capers with this group ranged from chasing butterflies in the palace gardens to going for donkey rides in the forests around Versailles. Above all, though, her new chums encouraged her in making fun of the absurd characters who abounded at court. Among their favorite targets were the grotesquely dowdy, laughably self-important ladies of the older generation. Looking like creatures from another century (often their ceremonial court costume was just about that old), these women became known in the Dauphine's irreverent circle as "turned-up collars," "packages," and "centuries."[85] Failing to grasp these elders' importance as tireless purveyors of gossip and strict arbiters of politesse, Marie Antoinette dismissed them out of hand. "When one has passed the age of thirty, I don't know how one dares show oneself at [Versailles]," she sniffed.[86] Though the remark won her many unseen enemies among the palace's éminences grises, even within her own retinue, her young friends laughed and laughed.

In a similarly ill-advised manner, the Dauphine also enlisted her clique to join her in mocking Madame Du Barry, whose infantile lisp lent itself to parody and whose crude way of speaking and eating betrayed her lowly origins. Pompous despite her unimpressive background, the favorite had fifty footmen in her service and insisted upon being accompanied everywhere by "an exotic Bengali page [named] Zamor, who strutted along behind her in a pink velvet jacket and trousers, a white turban wound around his head, a small sword at his side."[87] Madame Du Barry's Blenheim spaniel, Dorine, boasted a similarly outrageous getup: a diamond-and-ruby-studded collar and leash, gifts from the King of Sweden.[88] Sometimes the Comtesse pushed her whims to insulting extremes, as for instance when she forced a visiting papal nuncio to bring her shoes to her while she luxuriated, half-dressed, in her bed.[89] Certainly, the money that Louis XV lavished upon her enabled her to dress like a queen—she had an income of 150,000 livres a year—and she spent it with abandon on dresses and jewels.[90] In fact, whenever she could she liked to combine these two indulgences, with jaw-dropping results: according to Olivier Bernier, "at a time when a well-to-do noble family could live luxuriously on 30,000 livres a year," Du Barry spent 450,000 livres on a single diamond-encrusted dress bodice.[91]

These pretensions provided Marie Antoinette and her companions with endless amusement. On one occasion, the Comtesse de Grammont, a *dame pour accompagner Madame la Dauphine* who was related to Choiseul by marriage, took the merriment so far as to step deliberately on Du Barry's train, tearing it "to atoms, [then] laughing most immoderately" with her friends.[92] More frequently, the Dauphine and her clique were content to titter none too subtly behind their fans whenever Du Barry, trailed by Zamor, entered their sights.

The young ladies' irreverent antics attracted the notice not just of the unhappy favorite, but of the King himself, whose intermediaries warned the Dauphine that his forbearance would not last forever. (Maria Theresa, briefed by Mercy, urged her daughter to make peace with the favorite, pleading with her at least to "say one word to her—about a dress or some bagatelle of that sort," possibly on the grounds that at least the two adversaries had a love of pretty clothes in common.[93]) But these admonitions fell on deaf ears. Marie Antoinette's escapades with her irrepressible *dames* remained just about the only bright spots on her otherwise dreary social horizon.

In the months that followed her wedding, the Dauphine also sought camaraderie among the children of her female attendants. Although Versailles was not traditionally a child-friendly place, its highest-ranked princess insisted on reviving her old girlhood games with the few youngsters who did cross her path. Two of them, the five-year-old and four-year-old sons of her *femmes de chambre* Madame Miséry and Madame Thierry, respectively, "never left Madame the Dauphine's apartments and caused a fair amount of disorder there"—to the chagrin of just about everyone but the Dauphine herself.[94] (Even the boys' mothers were horrified.)

Homesick for her two youngest brothers, Ferdinand and Max, Marie Antoinette amused herself by watching the little fellows "stain her dresses, tear down her wall-hangings, break her furniture, and throw her apartments into complete disorder," as Mercy wrote disapprovingly to the Empress.[95] For more sisterly diversion, she took up with Madame Miséry's twelve-year-old girl and with a lovely four-year-old daughter of still another of her women.[96] Together, the three girls would kneel on the floor of the royal apartments, playing dolls for hours on end, just as Marie Antoinette had done as a child back in Austria.

Despite the Dauphine's fondness for such interludes, they proved short-lived, thanks to the intervention of the Comtesse de Noailles, who did not miss a single opportunity to make the Austrian girl toe the Bourbon line and to remind her that she was, as Maria Theresa herself had put it, "a foreigner who, in every instance, [should] want absolutely to please the nation."[97] The Comtesse therefore railed against the girl's donkey-back jaunts because court protocol had no established precedent dictating how courtiers should behave "when a Dauphine of France falls off a donkey."[98] Marie Antoinette found the grievance a laughable one and baptized the older woman "Madame Etiquette" to register her contempt. But a mocking nickname from a poorly behaved Hapsburg princess was hardly enough to put Madame Etiquette off her mission.

Madame de Noailles objected in particular to Marie Antoinette's overfamiliar relationships with her staff members' offspring. Banishing the children from the Dauphine's quarters, the *dame d'honneur* announced, would reestablish the suitably dignified calm that had reigned there under the previous Dauphine, Louis Auguste's late mother, Marie Josèphe. (This princess had showed an exemplary docility with respect to court conventions, as Madame Etiquette liked to remind her unruly charge.[99]) To the Comtesse, the doll-playing was sufficiently horrifying to merit the attention of Louis XV himself. Far less stringent than his great-grandfather, Louis XIV, about matters of etiquette, the King's first instinct was to dismiss Madame de Noailles's complaint out of hand. Marie Antoinette was still so young; why not allow her to have some innocent fun? Besides, was it not far better for the Dauphine to busy herself with dolls than with politics?[100]

This rhetorical question betrayed the ever-growing influence of Madame Du Barry and her circle, who laced their criticisms of "the little redhead" with hints that she had come to court with the sole objective of establishing Austrian interests above France's own. Compared to threats of this nature, a bit of child's play did not at first present itself to Louis XV as cause for concern. However, as the Comtesse continued to barrage him with grievances about the Dauphine's "careless[ness] in matters of dignity and outward appearance," he conceded that his granddaughter-in-law must indeed find a way to rein in her "natural gaiety . . . when she is holding her court."[101]

THE SOVEREIGN'S COMMAND, WHICH MARIA THERESA FORCEFULLY REPRISED in her letters, did not allow Marie Antoinette much room for maneuver, as "holding her court" accounted for practically all of her time. Etiquette demanded that the Dauphine follow the same kinds of choreographed public rituals as those her husband was always trying to subvert. Beginning with her *lever,* ending with her *coucher,* and including just about everything in between—trips to mass, public meals, formal receptions, audiences, and visits—her day followed a strict, all-consuming schedule.[102] This regimen took literally the importance of "outward appearances," so that even the actions constituting her *toilette* served as a focal point for the court as a whole. "At eleven each morning," she wrote to her mother on July 12:

> I have my hair done. Then at noon, they call in the chamber . . . and I put on my rouge and wash my hands in front of everyone [*devant tout le monde;* also: "before the whole world"]. Then the gentlemen leave and the ladies stay, and I get dressed in front of them.[103]

Although describing one of the key features of her imprisonment in court routine, the language the Dauphine used here was deceptively neutral. Early on, Maria Theresa had warned her not to risk the expression of any personal feelings in her missives, lest unfriendly parties intercept the letters, and Marie Antoinette quickly came to share this aversion to prying eyes. (Arguably, her fears for her privacy were well founded: less than two months after her arrival, she caught the hateful Duc de La Vauguyon listening outside her bedroom door during one of Louis Auguste's rare visits there.[104]) The girl thus framed her updates in bald, uncomplaining terms that, as her mother had recommended, "all the world [again: *tout le monde*] might read," and which no one could turn against her.[105]

Yet, notwithstanding the bland way in which she described it, the ceremony of the Dauphine's *toilette* was extremely arduous, for it was supposed to overlay on her person all the established, outward signs of monarchical grandeur. This, indeed, was why she had had to be a blank slate upon arriving at court: there were layers upon layers of accoutrements that she, as a Bourbon princess, had to be primed to accommodate—beginning, in her *toilette,* with an intricate hairdo. To bring the Dauphine into conformity with court fashion, Monsieur Larsenneur, who had first waited on her in Vienna, had to tease her locks into shape by "frizzling" them with hot irons and curling papers.[106] He then piled them onto a scaffolded construction of wool and wire, and blew powder over the whole confection with a large instrument resembling fireplace bellows.[107] While Larsenneur did this, the women of Marie Antoinette's retinue were obliged to hold a mask over her face and a peignoir over her morning gown so that the heavy powder would not coat her skin or her clothes. The whole affair took at least an hour and represented a stunning departure from the years when an Austrian governess would simply scrape the girl's hair back with a cloth band and call it a day. At Versailles, the Dauphine was discovering, her appearance was a collaborative effort, subject to the ministrations of many hands, and to the opinions of many people; for her image was also the image of the Bourbon clan, whose magnificence underpinned and upheld the entire social order.

The application of rouge also put the Dauphine through her political paces, for it was also a highly public event, at which just about everyone with Rights of Entry to Marie Antoinette's chambers (granted as a matter of course to people of importance at Versailles) tended to put in an appearance. In keeping with the codes of the court, the Dauphine had to extend the appropriate greeting to each person who came into her chamber while her ladies were slathering makeup onto her cheeks. Depending on the rank of the person arriving, Antonia Fraser has noted, Marie Antoinette was expected either "to nod her head or to incline her body or—most graciously of all, when faced with a prince or princess of the blood—to make as if to rise without actually doing so."[108] Needless to say, Madame de Noailles grilled her charge relentlessly on the subject of the various courtiers' positions and of the type of salutation each was entitled to receive. Welcoming every spectator to her *toilette* with a different, intricately nuanced gesture thus required serious concentration on Marie Antoinette's part and left her vulnerable, when she slipped up, to the criticisms of her guardian and the court as a whole. This aspect of the ceremony, too, pointed up the highly politicized nature of Marie Antoinette's standing as a focus for "all eyes."

Logistics and politics became even more unwieldy when it came time to dress Marie Antoinette in her *robe à la française*. Custom held that the Dauphine could reach for nothing herself—which, for instance, meant that unless Madame de Noailles, who as *dame d'honneur* held the privilege of handing her a glass of water, was nearby, the princess had to go thirsty. A similar logic subtended her *toilette*, which Madame Campan described as a "masterpiece of etiquette" even by the extreme standards of Versailles:

> If the *dame d'honneur* and the *dame d'atours* were both present they performed the principal service together, aided by the *première femme [de chambre]* and two other women; but there were distinctions among their different roles. The *dame d'atours* handed [the Dauphine] her underskirt and presented her with her dress. The *dame d'honneur* poured out the water for [the Dauphine] to wash her hands and passed her the *chemise*. When a princess of the blood was present, she took over this last function from the *dame d'honneur,* who could not however hand her [the *chemise*] directly. Rather, the *dame d'honneur* had to pass [the *chemise*] back to the *première femme*, who in turn presented it to the princess of the blood.[109]

Like the carefully nuanced greetings that punctuated the application of the Dauphine's rouge, this elaborate sequence emphasized—to her and to all other participants—the deep ceremonial and political importance with which the stylized presentation of her body was invested.

The underlying political nuances of the *toilette* were thrown into especially strong relief whenever a noblewoman who had not been present for the beginning of the ritual entered the Dauphine's apartments once it was already under way. On these occasions, the new arrival had to be incorporated into the process according to her place in the court pecking order. If the latecomer ranked above the princess who was on the verge of handing Marie Antoinette an article of clothing, then the latter woman was obliged to return the garment to the *première femme de chambre,* so that the entire process might begin again. It was unthinkable that a lady of august standing could simply stand by while her social inferior usurped her right to perform the final honors in getting the Dauphine dressed. As Madame Campan averred, "All of the ladies scrupulously observed these usages, which they viewed as their [sacred] rights."[110] At the same time, none of these privileged women seemed the least bit concerned that while they performed their rightful duties, Marie Antoinette herself had to stand naked in their midst for extended periods of time—"her arms crossed over her chest and looking very chilly."[111]

On one especially cold morning, when the late entries of various countesses and duchesses caused even more than the usual number of stops and starts to her *toilette,* Marie Antoinette abruptly gave voice to her exasperation, exclaiming, "Oh this is odious! What an inconvenience!"[112] Uttered as they were in extended company, these words ruffled feathers among the Dauphine's proud, entitled entourage, and report of them spread quickly through the palace. The Comtesse de Noailles was horrified as ever—but in this case, she had a point. Given her continued failure to conceive a child, to gain her husband's friendship, or even to behave civilly toward the King's mistress, Marie Antoinette's position was precarious enough as it was. By disrupting her *toilette,* with its emphasis on making visible the sublimity of her station, she gave the French party further rationale for claiming that as Dauphine, she was an irredeemable failure.

AFTER HER INTERVIEW WITH THE DAUPHIN AT CHOISY IN JULY, DURING which he had pledged to live with her "in all the intimacy that their union required," Marie Antoinette had run straight to the Aunts, to whom this information came as unwelcome news.[113] Like the Comte de Mercy, in whom Marie Antoinette had also confided, they suspected that if Louis Auguste came to love her, the Dauphine would "be able to dominate him completely."[114] It went without saying that a baby would shore up her position—and, by extension, Choiseul's—considerably. And so, while Mercy, Maria Theresa, and the *choiseulistes* rejoiced at this prospect, Mesdames took it as an impetus to nip the Archduchess's triumph in the bud.

As usual, Madame Adélaïde took the lead. Despite her portliness and her often unkempt appearance, this daughter of the King remained, as a Bourbon family friend, the Comtesse de Boigne observed, "highly preoccupied with anything pertaining to her *toilette* . . . [and] had an extreme need for inventiveness and luxury" in her wardrobe.[115] Already it had been impressed upon the Dauphine that at the court of France, "a woman could not be seen wearing the same dress or jewels on several consecutive occasions."[116] Apparently, this discovery prompted her to seek sartorial guidance from an adviser she assumed to be more sympathetic than Madame Etiquette. Madame Adélaïde readily seized the opportunity to put her newest plan into effect.

The scheme drew its inspiration from Marie Antoinette's recent clashes with the Comtesse de Noailles and targeted specifically the domain of the young princess's *toilette,* which, along with the codified social interactions to which it subjected the Dauphine, had the added significance of imposing on her the identifying markers of her class. The huge circles of rouge and the high, powdered coiffure she evoked in her letter to Maria Theresa did not function so much to beautify the princess—whose blooming complexion and fair hair scarcely required such embellishments—as to symbolize her royal standing. Custom identified adornments such as heavy rouge as the province of high-born ladies, just as it conferred the wearing of red-heeled shoes (*talons rouges*) on male grandees.[117] In the case of both rouge and *talons rouges,* the exuberant hue served to set nobles apart from their more drably attired social inferiors and to call attention to their own enviable stature.[118] (One eighteenth-century Englishman visiting France took note, recalling: "The First time I saw the Ladies all rouged . . . they seem'd to me to look like a long Bed of high-colour'd full-blown Peonies in a garden."[119]) By suffering to have her cheeks reddened "before the whole world," Marie Antoinette thus repeated yet another crucial symbolic gesture: she publicly assumed the signs of aristocratic power.

The whalebone stays into which the Dauphine's attendants laced her at her *toilette* fell into the same important category. Like rouge, the stays emphasized her membership in the ruling caste as distinct from any other social group. A tightly corseted body evinced "the norms of stiffness and self-control" valued by aristocrats; in sharp contrast, the body of a lower-class individual, as the historian Daniel Roche has observed, tended either

to be "bent by hardship and toil, or [to] enjoy a freedom unrestricted by etiquette."[120] Well-born children of both sexes were therefore put into stays
early—often by age two—to "prevent deformities of the skeleton" and
"keep the waist under control."[121] When boys reached the age of six, they
traded their stays for breeches, but female aristocrats remained corseted all
their lives.

But if the whaleboned bodice was universal at Versailles, Marie Antoinette's position required her to wear it in a particularly inflexible form
known as the *grand corps*. In the costume symbolism of the court, this was a
mark of supreme distinction: France's greatest princesses alone had the right
to wear the *grand corps* on a regular basis.[122] Other noblewomen were allowed to don it only on the day of their presentation at court (the solemn
ceremony at which the scions of the aristocracy were formally "presented"
to the King and Queen), and, after that, at specially designated formal functions. The Marquise de La Tour du Pin, who served as a *dame du palais*
after Marie Antoinette's accession, described the rarefied *grand corps* as
follows:

> It was a specially made corset, without shoulder straps, laced up the back, but
> tight enough so that the lacings, four fingers wide on the bottom, allowed for a
> glimpse of a *chemise* of such fine batiste that it would be readily apparent to
> everyone if one's skin underneath was not sufficiently white. . . . The front of
> the corset was laced, as it were, with rows of diamonds.[123]

In Marie Antoinette's case, whiteness of skin was ostensibly not a concern; her "lilies and roses" complexion was said to show beautifully beneath the thin *chemise* that peeked through her lacings. Looking good in
the corset and feeling good in it were, however, two different matters entirely. The Marquise de La Tour du Pin recalled her own experience of the
grand corps as "extremely bothersome and fatiguing"; indeed, even more
than the regular corset, the stiff and tight-laced *grand corps* severely restricted its wearer's movements, especially around the arms.[124] Digesting
one's food and breathing were rendered equally challenging, and the
bodice caused frequent fainting among the court's prominent ladies, especially expectant mothers, for even pregnancy did not exempt one from the
corps. According to the corset's nonnoble critics, who saw it as a badge of
loathsome class vanity, other common side effects included heart palpita-
tions, asthma, vapors, "stinking breath, consumption, and a withering rot-
tenness."[125]

Though the Dauphine did not suffer from the worst of these symptoms,
she resented the basic discomforts that the *grand corps* imposed. The simple

corps she had grown accustomed to wearing while in Vienna was noticeably more flexible than the one she now had to endure each day at Versailles. Even her mother, who rarely acknowledged personal discomforts suffered for the sake of political glory, conceded that "those Paris-made corsets [were] far too stiff" to make for sensible wear, and offered to send Marie Antoinette some Austrian ones in their stead.[126] Given that she was quite thin enough to slip into her formal gowns without the *grand corps,* it did not take long before the Dauphine was questioning why she had to don it at all. "No one else, so far as she knew, wore such a garment [every day], so pray why should she do so?"[127] Particularly in the heat of her first French summer, Marie Antoinette approached the rigid bodice more as a torture device than as an indispensable emblem of her rank.[128]

As the Dauphine's trusted confidante, Madame Adélaïde had no trouble getting her to admit her aversion to the stays, and this became the basis for her new plan of attack. The court was of course already buzzing with stories of Marie Antoinette's etiquette infringements; by June, just a month after her wedding, these tales had even begun to circulate in Paris, where many of the court's denizens maintained splendid houses, and where the girl's enemies triumphantly spread the news of her failures.[129] If the Dauphine could be led to attract still more scandal to her name, through a continued eschewal of the *grand corps,* then perhaps she could be eliminated before Louis Auguste made good on his promise to bed her.

THE AUNTS WASTED NO TIME IN PUTTING THIS STRATEGY INTO EFFECT. Though as Children of France they, too, were required to wear the *grand corps,* they abruptly stopped doing so and urged the Dauphine to follow suit. Because they were aging spinsters, however, Mesdames had the option of keeping their corsetless state hidden during public appearances. They took to "enveloping themselves right up to their chin" in billowy black taffeta capes—especially, Madame Campan noticed, whenever the King was around.[130]

But neither Louis XV nor his courtiers paid Mesdames the same level of attention as they did Marie Antoinette, whose physical charms were expected to remain on constant display. In any event, not even the most loose-fitting taffeta cape could have protected the Dauphine from her guardian's eagle eyes. Present whenever the princess was getting dressed, Madame de Noailles could not help but notice—and fixate on—the girl's abandonment of the *grand corps.* By August 4, this irregularity was sufficiently public knowledge that the Comte de Mercy felt compelled to raise it with the Empress: "The *dame d'honneur* says that there is no way of convincing Madame la Dauphine to wear a corset."[131]

To a woman who viewed "even a pin misplaced on a court gown [as] a tragedy," this unprecedented rejection of the corset betokened nothing short of an apocalypse.[132] Madame Etiquette made it known that Marie Antoinette's "waist [was] growing misshapen, and her right shoulder out of kilter," a verdict that other courtiers rapidly disseminated far and wide.[133] "In the palace and beyond its walls, . . . the chief topic of conversation was the awful fact . . . that one of the future queen's shoulder blades was more protruding than the other."[134] Insofar as this news seemed to reveal the Bourbon princess's unwillingness to adapt to her role, it was received as important political gossip in other European courts. Fifteen years later, in fact, an English lord touring Marie Antoinette's apartments after she and her family had been sent to jail asked to examine a bodice of hers that revolutionary looters had left lying on the floor. (Plate 10.) He explained to his puzzled French companions that he had long ago heard tales of the young woman's misshapen right shoulder—attributable to her avoidance of the *grand corps*—and was curious to see whether her bodice was padded to disguise the deficiency.[135]

Another foreigner to weigh in on the affair of the *corps,* Maria Theresa's friend the Countess Windischgrätz, focused less on the alignment of Marie Antoinette's shoulders than on the general slovenliness that the missing undergarment occasioned. After her presentation at Compiègne in early August 1770, the Countess informed acquaintances in Paris, Brussels, and Vienna "that the Dauphine was *très mal mise* [very badly dressed] and that her figure was not good."[136] Whether she knew it or not, in eschewing the corset, the princess was playing with fire.

THE COMTE DE MERCY, FOR HIS PART, WAS ACUTELY AWARE OF THE DANGERS the girl's conduct posed for her future at Versailles and, by extension, for the Franco-Austrian alliance. After doing some discreet detective work, he established that Madame Adélaïde and her sisters had played a major role in the trouble. Identifying them as thoroughly "dangerous people," he notified Maria Theresa that her daughter would be far better off if she were to "behave exactly in the opposite manner to Mesdames her Aunts," who were deliberately setting the girl on the path to her own destruction.[137] This information prompted the Empress to reverse her initial view of the women as appropriate mentors for her daughter. Agreeing with Mercy about the Aunts' perfidy, she enjoined him to save the Dauphine from their clutches: "I am counting on your prudence in advising her so that she avoids any further missteps."[138]

To do so, however, Mercy needed to talk to Marie Antoinette in private, and that proved virtually impossible. As an ambassador to the court of France, he enjoyed Rights of Entry to the Dauphine's chambers for ceremonies like the *toilette*. Insofar, though, as these took place "before the whole world," they provided him with no chance to broach such a delicate subject as the Aunts' double-dealing. Complicating matters further, etiquette dictated that Marie Antoinette visit Mesdames' apartments several times a day, and because she had no other friends to call on, this was one Bourbon practice the Dauphine seemed all too eager to embrace. During the court's retreat at Compiègne, she spent most of her time with them. Whether on her long, donkey-led processions or on her recreational carriage jaunts in the forests around the château, the Dauphine was almost constantly flanked by the three older ladies.[139]

So it was not until August 24, 1770, three weeks after he had first written to Maria Theresa about the corset problem, that Mercy managed briefly to dodge the Aunts' blockade. With the court's stay at Compiègne drawing to a close—preparations were being made for a short trip to Chantilly on the twenty-eighth, before the return to Versailles on the thirty-first—Mercy took advantage of the hubbub to steal a few moments alone with the Dauphine. "I begged her," he informed the girl's mother afterward, "to watch herself very closely" in the future.[140]

By this point, however, the damage had largely been done. Both at Versailles and in Paris—for the French party was by no means above the *choiseulistes'* tactic of leaking damning gossip outside the bounds of the court—wags made clever quips about the Dauphine's rejection of "that belt, that precious ornament," and snickered openly about her conflicts with her guardian.[141] Even the Abbé de Vermond, who disliked Bourbon etiquette for the relatively low place it assigned him in the court hierarchy, recognized the enormity of his pupil's transgressions. The Dauphine's "refusal of the corset [and] the disfavor of the Comtesse de Noailles," he warned her in mid-September, had set "all of France complaining."[142]

To savvy Maria Theresa, that the French had gone from praising her daughter's comely, successfully Gallicized appearance to disparaging her as an unwashed, sloppy, and disrespectful foreigner could not but come as a threat to the Bourbon-Hapsburg alliance. After fielding reports from Mercy about the Dauphine's conduct, she wrote to Marie Antoinette chiding her for "tak[ing] poor care of yourself, apparently even when it comes to cleaning your teeth; this is a key point, as is your figure, which [people say] has worsened."[143] Closer to home, Madame Campan likewise discerned the political dangers that the Dauphine's physical neglect entailed; the *femme de chambre* noted in horror that the stalwarts of the French party had grown so emboldened as to entertain openly "the possibility of a divorce."[144]

Still, in order to justify such an extreme outcome as sending Marie Antoinette back to Vienna, her detractors would have to advance a somewhat subtle argument. Given the Dauphin's own history of etiquette violations, they could not exactly claim that he had shunned Marie Antoinette just because she had abandoned her *corps*. What they could and did do, though, was to keep the court and the public focused on the girl's untamed midsection—which, in light of each of Louis Auguste's widely publicized brush-offs, came to stand not just for diminished beauty and disrespected etiquette, but for chronic infertility as well. Maria Theresa herself adopted this line of reasoning when she wrote admonishingly to her daughter later that fall: "Reassure me about the corsets you are wearing, or else I will worry about it, for fear, as they say in German, of *auseinandergehen, schon die Taille wie eine Frau, ohne es zu sein*."[145] For fear, as they say in English, of letting yourself go and gaining a fuller, more womanly waistline, *without in fact being a wife*.

More than Vermond's solemn lectures, Mercy's furtive hints, or the Comtesse de Noailles's ceaseless nagging, the Empress's German aphorism appeared to hit home. A few months into her corset embargo, the Dauphine finally seemed to grasp that she had no business claiming unprecedented freedoms for herself when she was not yet "a real dauphine." Her relations with Louis Auguste grew steadily friendlier over the course of the autumn, as he began, despite his reticence, to "allow himself some little caresses, and one day even felt bold enough to give her a kiss."[146] Yet these little signs of the Dauphin's growing regard did little to quell the relentless gossip-mongering of his wife's detractors. "The possibility of a divorce"— or, more precisely, an annulment, which European princes sometimes secured to rid themselves of childless wives—still lingered menacingly on the horizon.

That fall, it became public knowledge that the Dauphin's younger brother Provence was going to marry Marie Joséphine, a Savoyard princess, in May of the following year. Ever vigilant about possible shifts in the court's delicate balance of power, the nobles of Versailles went into a frenzy of speculation. Would the new royal bride displace Du Barry, or the Dauphine, in the King's affections? Would an alliance with Savoy alter in any way the administration's stance on Austria? And, most worrisome of all from Marie

Antoinette's perspective: would Provence manage to sire a child ahead of the current heir to the throne?[147]

Provence—who resented the Dauphin and Dauphine for outranking him in the succession—bragged mercilessly about the sexual prowess that he, in contrast to his hapless brother, planned to display as a bridegroom. Louis Auguste was humiliated, and Marie Antoinette aghast.[148] Should the Comtesse de Provence bear a child before her, the Dauphine's own inadequacy as a consort would become more glaringly obvious than ever, and her superfluity at the court of France would be beyond question. To the extent that she allowed her waistline to grow progressively thicker "without in fact being a wife," she was only reminding both herself and the nation of this mortifying fact. And so, in the middle of October, the Dauphine capitulated. Summoning Mercy to meet with her alone, she confessed that she had been horribly "upset by some reports about her position and her person, and she cited the question of the corset."[149] From that moment on, Mercy reported, she "finally agreed to wear a corset quite regularly."[150]

ACCORDING TO MARIA THERESA'S AMBASSADOR, THE DAUPHINE'S CHANGE of heart led to a swift improvement in her political fortunes. On October 20, just a few weeks after she surrendered to the *grand corps,* he informed Maria Theresa that "recently the King has increased his tenderness, his attention, and all the marks of his caring friendship for Madame la Dauphine."[151] Four months later, Mercy reiterated: "His Majesty again takes a friendly tone with Madame la Dauphine and kisses her hands very often. When [she] ignores Mesdames' advice, the King is enchanted and displays a level of tenderness that he does not show toward any of his other children."[152] Unfortunately, Mercy lamented in the same dispatch, "nothing has yet come of Monsieur le Dauphin's supposed plans to live with Madame la Dauphine in the intimacy that their union requires."[153] Still, Marie Antoinette's reinstatement in Louis XV's good graces went some way toward fortifying her position and protecting her from the possibility of annulment or divorce.

The Dauphine's readoption of the corset had another, equally significant result. "Madame la Dauphine's figure," Mercy wrote in February 1771, "has been nicely restored by the usage of whalebone stays, and [she] now observes quite carefully all matters pertaining to grooming and dress."[154] This development had the immediate advantage of silencing the slew of negative publicity the French party had generated about Marie Antoinette's looks. No longer could Mesdames' or Du Barry's coteries justly impugn her appearance; her newfound scrupulousness, strict and unyielding as any *grand corps,* placed her beyond their reproach.

Still, disappointment among the French party did not mean unreserved happiness for Marie Antoinette, upon whom the corset affair appears to have had a sobering, if illuminating, impact. As Maria Theresa reminded her in the scandal's aftermath, the court culture of the Bourbons was founded on a strict equivalency between symbolic glory and political strength. And because the Aunts had knowingly encouraged her to upend this equation, she must no longer look to them for assistance in honoring it.

> Do not be negligent about your appearance. . . . I cannot caution you enough against letting yourself slip into the errors that the members of the French royal family have fallen into of late. They may be good and virtuous, but they have forgotten how to appear in public, how to set the tone [for the nation]. . . . I therefore beg you, both as your tender mother and as a friend, not to give in to any further shows of nonchalance about your appearance or court protocol. If you do not heed my advice, you will regret it, but it will be too late. On this point alone you must not follow your [French] family's example. It is up to you now to set the tone at Versailles.[155]

As was often the case, the Empress's advice was in equal parts intimidating and constructive. Her gloomy forecast—"you will regret it, but it will be too late"—put no balm on the wounds of a girl whose recent "shows of nonchalance" had already attracted so much scandal to her name. At the same time, however, by encouraging her daughter to step to the forefront of French court life, and to do so by means of a carefully cultivated appearance, Maria Theresa gestured toward a new strategy for survival. If Marie Antoinette could not defy the exigencies of "appearance and court protocol," perhaps she could turn them to her advantage. With Du Barry cornering the market on the King's erotic appetites, and the future Comtesse de Provence poised to unseat her as the mother of the next Bourbon heir, it behooved the Dauphine to find another way of shoring up her tenuous position at Versailles. And Versailles was a place where, as everything from the corset hullabaloo to the publicity and ceremony of her daily *toilette* had taught her, matters of costume were monitored as closely and taken as seriously as royal sex (whether recreational or dynastic).

This being the case, it seems not inappropriate to suggest that a heightened attention to the styling of her body presented itself to Marie Antoinette at this stage as a viable, alternative path to political security. It was her cross to bear that her husband's embargo on the marriage bed continued to disqualify her as "a real dauphine." But with a little more savvy about the way she looked and dressed, she could at least do her best to *resemble* a real dauphine—to appear, as one courtier later expressed it, "as if she had been born for the throne."[156] In a court where appearances were indeed everything, perhaps the appearance of majesty would suffice.

FOUR

RIDE LIKE A MAN

October 1770, Marie Antoinette's fifth month in France, was marked by two important steps in her progress as a Bourbon wife. The first was her resumption of the whalebone *corps;* the second was her graduation from riding donkeys to riding horses. This latter development, which would soon afford her a prime opportunity to assert herself through her clothing, coincided with the court's annual fall visit to the royal residence at Fontainebleau, where stag was in season and hunting the mainstay of the social agenda. On October 22 and 26, the Dauphine left the Aunts behind at the château and followed the hunt in her private calèche. During these outings, Mercy noted, Louis XV "devoted himself to showing her different things about the hunt . . . and singled her out for all kinds of special notice, in a much more avid way than he does when Mesdames are around."[1] Flattered by this renewal of the King's attentions, Marie Antoinette was emboldened to press for a boon that would enable her to attract them more frequently. It was time, she decided, to start following the chase on horseback.

Despite Mercy's admonitions about the Aunts, the Dauphine applied to Madame Adélaïde—who herself had been an impassioned rider in her youth—to advise her as to how to secure the King's permission on this score. From personal experience, Adélaïde knew that her father "might find [the request] unreasonable," for he had raised objections to her own equestrian ambitions when she was a girl.[2] The older woman did not, however, share this history with the Dauphine. Instead, on October 29, Madame Adélaïde flatly told her father that Marie Antoinette wished to begin riding, and was

likely gratified to find him—as Mercy was horrified to learn after the fact—
"a little vexed by the request."[3] For the Austrian ambassador, Madame
Adélaïde's maneuvering simply represented another of her flagrant efforts to
drive a wedge between the Dauphine and the King. But to Mercy's (and, in
all probability, Adélaïde's) surprise, Louis XV actually decided to grant
Marie Antoinette's wish. On October 30, three days before her fifteenth
birthday, he arranged for her to go riding in the forest with a stableboy leading her horse, and a group of donkeys nearby in case she needed to switch to
an easier mount.

While the Aunts, sulking at this unexpected turn of events, remained at
the castle, several aristocrats flocked to the forest to witness Marie Antoinette's début on horseback. When the lesson was over, these spectators reported back to their fellows at court about "the great joy that this new
exercise had brought" the princess—and the tidings traveled so quickly that
by that very evening, "all the world," as Mercy put it in a dispatch to Vienna, turned out to congratulate her on her triumph.[4] Louis XV himself was
so charmed by the Dauphine's infectious enthusiasm that on the very next
day, he signed an ordinance for 24,000 livres to furnish her stables with
hunting mounts. Not long afterward, she became a fixture on the royal
hunt, riding ably at her doting Grandpapa's side.

THE GIRL'S TRIUMPH COULD NOT HAVE COME AT A BETTER TIME. ALREADY
anxious about Provence's impending marriage, Marie Antoinette received
still greater cause to worry on December 24, 1770, when Louis XV abruptly
relieved her sponsor Choiseul of his position. Officially, the foreign minister
was dismissed because of a clash with the King over France's role in a military conflict between England and Spain in the Falkland Islands. Backed by
the *parlements,* those judiciary bodies whose aristocratic members had a
long history of resisting their monarch's policies, Choiseul had argued vociferously that France should enter the fray, to seek vengeance against the
British for the humiliations of the Seven Years' War. Never happy to let the
parlements dictate his decisions, and aware that the kingdom had scant resources to spare on another war, Louis XV had insisted on maintaining
France's neutrality. Soon afterward, Choiseul was exiled without warning to
his castle in Touraine.

But court politics had also contributed to the foreign minister's disgrace.
Over the course of the autumn, as the snubs Madame Du Barry received from
Marie Antoinette (and Choiseul's friends and family) became more pronounced, so, too, had the favorite's appetite for revenge. When the Falklands
affair erupted, she pounced, maintaining that the minister was inciting the

parlementaires to challenge the crown's authority and that a nationwide uprising would be the result. "Frightened by this dangerous possibility" (as Mercy explained to his sovereign), Louis XV acted fast, appointing the Duc d'Aiguillon, a fervent adversary of the *parlementaires*, to Choiseul's old position, and filling the rest of his cabinet with other *barrystes*.[5] Most notably, he selected as his chancellor the Abbé Maupeou, who was hell-bent on forcing the *parlements* into submission and on reinstituting unchecked absolutism.

Rumor had it that Maupeou, like Aiguillon, was a paramour of the favorite; at very least, they were both regulars at the dissipated parties she hosted in her apartments and her little private palace, Louveciennes. Viewed in this light, Louis XV's appointment of the Abbé and the Duc to such lofty positions confirmed fears that he had ceded his authority to a woman; as the author of the gossipy, clandestine newsletter the *Mémoires secrets*—which circulated in worldly Parisian circles from 1762 to 1789—put it, "in Du Barry . . . the female sex [was] governing [the King] far more than it had a right to."[6] At least one popular ditty emphasized the irony of the situation by opposing Joan of Arc, who had famously saved France from the English, to Du Barry, who had, anti-*barryste* sentiment held, prevented Choiseul from doing the same. "France," the anonymous poet warned,

> *It seems to be your destiny*
> *To be subjugated to Woman.*
> *Your salvation came from the Maiden;*
> *Your death will come from the Whore.*[7]

To skirt royal censorship laws, politically explosive texts like this one were generally written by hand or published anonymously or abroad. Disseminated surreptitiously at court and in Paris (among other cities), they were bankrolled not only by Du Barry's usual detractors, the *choiseulistes*, but by any number of other parties hostile to the King's corrupt new régime.[8] Across the board, the pamphlets attempted to discredit the monarchy by presenting its sexual decadence as a metaphor for its political weaknesses and corruption.[9] And Du Barry, whom one pamphleteer charged with reducing Louis XV and his ministers to "slaves crawling at the feet of a prostitute," figured in this literature as the ultimate villainess.[10] The day after Choiseul's dismissal, one French caricature showed Louis XV holding a basket full of body parts belonging to the *choiseuliste* parliamentary contingent. Casting these men's defeat in literal, bodily terms, the image depicted Maupeou gathering up his enemies' severed heads, while Du Barry, in her capacity as France's foremost castrating hussy, busied herself with the dead men's penises. When, in April 1771, Maupeou disbanded the refractory Paris

Parlement and replaced its members with puppet delegates of his own choosing, the cartoon's gruesome prediction appeared to have come true.

Yet far from recoiling at the negative publicity, the "Whore" at the center of the firestorm appeared perfectly content to remind her lover's subjects that it was her brazen sexual talents that had landed her at the top. Shortly before the December coup, the *Mémoires secrets* reported, she commissioned from the famed artisan Francien a carriage intended to outclass in "elegance and magnificence" the *berline* that he had made, at Choiseul's behest, for Marie Antoinette's marriage journey.[11] Emblazoned with the apt Du Barry motto, "Push forward!" (*Boutez en avant!*), the carriage's gold-painted panels displayed "baskets of roses, . . . two doves pecking amorously at each other's beaks, and a heart pierced through with an arrow."[12] The author of the *Mémoires secrets* added that the "voluptuous chariot"'s ornate golden trimwork, too, exhibited "attributes of the god of [love]": arrows, quivers, torches licked with flame.[13] "Finally," he concluded, "a garland of flowers in mother-of-pearl runs all around the panels, and frames them with glittering colors."[14] Although Louis XV reportedly found this creation in questionable taste (it was the Duc d'Aiguillon who had footed the bill), his mistress loved riding around in it. As the *Mémoires secrets* did not fail to point out, the carriage not only emblematized its owner's erotic potency but also cast a long shadow over "[the one] that had been sent to Madame la Dauphine in Vienna."[15] The fairy-tale princess, Du Barry's chariot seemed to be suggesting, was yesterday's news.

Marie Antoinette could certainly not compete with the favorite for pride of place in the hierarchized geography of the new Versailles. After her victory over Choiseul, Madame Du Barry set tongues wagging by relocating to sumptuous quarters linked by a staircase to the King's own apartments. But the favorite wanted more. And so, to decorate her new abode, she acquired for 24,000 livres—the exact sum that Louis XV had spent on Marie Antoinette's horses—a Van Dyck portrait of Charles I of England. According to the *Mémoires secrets,* whenever Louis XV showed signs of regretting his old adviser's dismissal, the Comtesse would point to the portrait and remind him that its subject had been executed by a gaggle of impudent parliamentarians.[16] "Has the Well-Beloved," she would then ask pointedly, "mislaid the rod of the great Louis XIV?"[17] This double reminder—of Charles I's defeat by his parliament and the Sun King's dominance over his—apparently boosted Louis XV's sense of purpose. It also bolstered the perception of Du Barry's unrivaled influence over him.

For the Dauphine, the favorite's ascendancy represented a monumental setback, for Choiseul's dismissal had eliminated any substantial counterweight to the French party at court. Empowered by the Comtesse Du Barry, this group's members could now proceed unhindered in their machinations against Austria—and its little archduchess, too. With the exception of Mercy and the Abbé de Vermond, whom the *barrystes* also tried to expel from court at this time, Marie Antoinette had no friends at Versailles. She would have to endure the onslaught, and shore up the alliance, virtually all on her own.

Needless to say, one surefire means of improving both her own prospects and those of the alliance would be to conceive a child. "It is beginning to aggravate me that you are not yet a [real] dauphine,"[18] Maria Theresa groused six weeks after Choiseul went into exile. Predictably, she reminded her daughter about "the future Comtesse de Provence," who "may well get ahead of you" in the race for a Bourbon heir.[19] "The position you are in makes me tremble," Maria Theresa declared. Only a baby could save the day.

All this advice was, of course, predicated on the assumption that it was somehow possible for Marie Antoinette to inveigle her husband into the marriage bed. But in truth, no amount of "caresses and cajoling," to use one of the Empress's favorite phrases, seemed liable to have this effect. For all that the Dauphin had begun to treat his bride with a marked increase in "preference, trust, and friendship," as Mercy confirmed, these overtures remained purely platonic.[20] Louis Auguste's conduct, the Austrian ambassador reported at the end of February, "remains inexplicable and vexing."[21]

Members of Du Barry's circle, for their part, seemed to delight in making sure the Dauphin would not change his mind. His former tutor La Vauguyon continued to hector him about the dastardliness of the Austrians and the disadvantages of a Hapsburg alliance, and even intimated (untruthfully) that Choiseul had had a hand in the untimely deaths of both of Louis Auguste's parents. La Vauguyon cast the deaths as part of a nefarious *choiseuliste* plot to weaken fatally the House of Bourbon and to cede French power to Austria.

The *barrystes* supplemented these conspiracy theories with attempts to place actual physical distance between the Dauphin and his bride. During one of the court's trips to Fontainebleau, for example, Marie Antoinette discovered that the men in charge of renovating the rooms designated for her and her husband had been bribed to keep the couple apart. Although the work was supposed to have been completed before his arrival, Louis Auguste's apartments, designed to adjoin his wife's, were in such disrepair that he had to move into a suite located at the exact opposite end of the castle.[22] According to Madame Campan, Marie Antoinette understood straightaway that her shy husband would never brave such a long, public promenade to visit her chambers; she complained to her "dear Grandpapa," who promptly intervened, and the rooms were ready in a week's time.[23] Yet even the couple's increased proximity at Fontainebleau did nothing to diminish the

Dauphin's sexual reserve. In exposing the *barrystes*' bribery, his wife may have won the battle, but in her childlessness, she was still losing the war.

IT WAS TIME, THEN, FOR MARIE ANTOINETTE TO TAKE A DIFFERENT TACK IN preserving her stature at court, and she appears to have hit upon this formula while riding. For in her loneliness, she had begun to ride on an almost daily basis, whether or not the King was hunting. When the weather was too cold and snowy to allow for excursions in the woods, she spent long afternoons galloping around the palace's indoor riding ring. Though preoccupied with the larger implications of the anti-*choiseuliste* coup, Mercy took the time to register his concern about "the many bad things that could befall such a young princess permitted to go about on horseback."[24] Informing the Dauphine that he was acting on Maria Theresa's authority, he devised three restrictions to keep these unnamed "bad things" at bay. First, he declared that the princess must "never ride to the hunt, no matter how fine the weather, and on no pretext whatsoever." Second, he urged her "to take her equestrian exercise moderately, at a trot, and only very rarely at a canter." Finally, he announced that she must "suspend totally all such exercise in the event that she had any cause to suspect" she might be pregnant.[25]

Though she bristled at all three directives, Marie Antoinette seems to have found the last one particularly easy to dismiss. "The whole world," including Mercy, knew full well that she was not—could not be—carrying a child, and she lost her patience when a woman in her retinue launched into an unsolicited lecture about the dangers that riding posed to an unborn child. Marie Antoinette interrupted the woman's officious little speech, snapping: "Mademoiselle, in God's name, leave me in peace, and know that I am in no way compromising any heir to the throne."[26]

Nor did she embrace Mercy's other proposed modifications to her riding regimen. To indulge "only very rarely [in] a canter" was not impossible so long as she confined her jaunts to the riding ring. But when wintertime melted into spring, the Dauphine, unable to hold back any longer, charged through the forests around Versailles at a full gallop, gleefully outpacing her bevy of breathless attendants. Sometimes, she rode just for the sake of riding. Sometimes, she followed the hunt; and though deer hunting was considered most appropriate for ladies, Marie Antoinette expanded her horizons to include the pursuit of boar and other game as well. Whatever the circumstances, the Dauphine's horseback outings appear to have infused her otherwise regimented, stressful, and desolate life at court with a much-needed sense of release, a joy from which even Mercy's fiercest objections could not dissuade her. "On her splendid Suffolk hunters," the biographer Carrolly

Erickson has written, "she could gallop to her heart's content, free of her mother, free of Madame de Noailles, free, for the moment, of the cares of her situation and of fretful thoughts about her future."[27]

Before long, this taste for freedom effected a striking change in the Dauphine's style of dress, a change that seemed less to ignore than directly to repudiate the mounting pressures she faced on the domestic front. Amid the ongoing chatter about her failure to conceive, and about the incompatibility of her dynastic duties and her new passion for horses, she devised a riding costume that quite clearly marked her distance from a Bourbon consort's conventional, maternal role. Given her recent experience with the *grand corps*—and given her mother's barbed references to the "future Comtesse de Provence's neat little waist," which, strangely, the Empress seemed to view as proof of the woman's sound reproductive health—Marie Antoinette did not eschew the corset that female riders were obliged to wear under their habits. (The royal riding habit was called the *justaucorps* ["just on the body"] for a reason; its smartly tailored silhouette, comprising a fitted jacket worn open over a matching waistcoat, cleaved closely to the body. On the female form, it made focal points of a prettily cinched-in waist and pushed-up breasts, which were the effects of a special riding *corps*.)

This time, Marie Antoinette's sartorial rebellion was more radical, and evoked a distinctly unfeminine form of political power. For her expeditions on horseback, she abandoned the long, flowing skirts of the sidesaddle rider for the slim breeches—and the straddled mount—of a man. And it was with this ensemble that Marie Antoinette first began to articulate a powerful new self-image, one that would—in the short term, at least—enable her to weather the intensifying political storms all around her.

IN PURELY STYLISTIC TERMS, THE DAUPHINE'S BREECHES WERE NOT ALTO-gether shocking, since the trim jacket and waistcoat that constituted the eighteenth-century female riding uniform had been directly modeled on the male version.[28] The jacket's masculine tailoring was based on that of the frock coat favored by sporting Englishmen, as were its back vent, tapered coat-tails, side pleats, narrow neck opening, turned-down collar, and long, cuffed sleeves.[29] The cutaway waistcoat worn underneath was made from matching or complementary fabric—velvet, wool, silk, or a worsted blend called cam-let. And beneath the waistcoat, riders of both sexes wore crisp, high-collared shirts; the female version disguised still another underlayer of corset and *chemise*. To emphasize the outfit's manly air, equestriennes often accessorized it with other masculine touches, such as a lace cravat and cuffs and a tricorn hat trimmed with feathers.[30]

Well-born Frenchwomen who engaged in vigorous outdoor activities such as riding and ice skating had for some time been in the habit of wearing knitted wool, silk, or velvet breeches beneath their petticoats. First introduced to the French court by Catherine de Médicis in the sixteenth century, the underbreech had both the practical benefit of keeping women warm while outside and the added advantage of preserving feminine modesty in the event of a tumble.[31] Though not known, as Marie Antoinette was, for her tendency to fall off her mount, the King's former mistress Madame de Pompadour had resembled the Dauphine in her love of the hunt. When Pompadour passed away in 1764, "hunting culottes" were duly noted in the inventory of her personal effects.[32]

Nevertheless, in 1771 masculine-style breeches—fitted tightly over the leg and gathered into a snug band around the waist—did not form part of the standard female riding outfit in France. And breeches worn without the supplementary cover of petticoats and skirts were far from common when Marie Antoinette adopted the look. As the art historian Patricia Crown has shown, John Collet—the European artist who produced the most extensive store of images depicting "sporting women" in the 1760s and 1770s—almost never portrayed a lady in breeches.[33] (The sole exception in Collet's vast catalog is a 1775 engraving that represents an actress in her dressing room, casting off her corset and donning trousers in its stead: a striking, if coincidental, conflation of Marie Antoinette's two early fashion rebellions.) According to Crown, the virtual nonexistence of breeches in Collet's artwork corresponded to the social reality of the day. Arbiters of feminine conduct disapproved of breeches because they "permitted women to assume the poses and gestures of men, to swagger, stride, swing the arms, and put hands on hips."[34] Even worse, breeches made it far too easy for their wearers to straddle a horse, whereas riding sidesaddle was—and remained until at least the early twentieth century—the norm for ladies in most European countries. Riding astride, it was believed, represented both an affront to common decency and a threat to a woman's reproductive health.

In the context of the French court, riding astride in breeches also violated standard guidelines for ladylike behavior insofar as it carried connotations of masculine royal authority. Since the Middle Ages, the ideal leader had been imagined as a chivalrous warrior-king, galloping boldly into battle to save his lady and his land. To preserve this ethos in times of peace, French monarchs adopted hunting as another means of showcasing their courage—a strategy that Louis XIV honed to perfection during his reign.[35] "Wishing to be great in everything," the eighteenth-century academician La Curne de Sainte-Palaye noted of the Sun King, "he surpassed in his hunting abilities all the Kings who preceded him."[36] And, as the historian Philip Mansel has hypothesized in his magisterial study on the politics of kingly uniform, Louis XIV's supreme talent as a hunter provided a strong basis for his absolutist pretensions: "Royal hunts symbolized royal mastery over . . . humans as well as animals," and so served as excellent shorthand for monarchical power in general.[37]

The Sun King further consolidated his reputation as a masterful sportsman by cultivating the trappings of equestrian prowess even when he was not riding to the hunt. Louis XIV mused in his memoirs that "the peoples over whom we reign generally base their judgments on what they see from the outside," and he seemed to conceive of a horseman's uniform as one of the "marks of superiority that distinguish [the King] from his subjects."[38] In numerous portraits and statues, he had himself depicted on horseback, dressed sometimes in contemporary riding costume or military uniform, and sometimes in the idealized garb of a conquering Roman emperor.[39] This posturing was not limited to artwork alone. Both in 1655 and again in 1673, when threatened with rebellion among his *parlementaires,* Louis XIV reacted by appearing among them dressed in hunting garb and boots. According to Voltaire, who served as court historiographer under Louis XV, it was this ensemble—and the "air of mastery" it imparted to its wearer—that enabled the Sun King to bring the seditious noblemen to heel.[40] Ubiquitous both during and after his lifetime, the image of Louis XIV as a lordly, indomitable rider became inextricably associated with the absolutist dictum "I am the State."[41] In fact, the associations between hunting costume and royal authority were so strong that when, in 1766, Louis XV went to the Paris Parlement to quell dissension among *his* unruly nobles, he, too, made his appearance in the *justaucorps,* breeches, and boots of a hunter.[42]

Louis XV was not the only eighteenth-century sovereign to take a page from the Sun King's sartorial playbook. Catherine the Great, too, reprised the great French monarch's equestrian pose when making her own daring bid for political power. In 1762, after the dramatic overthrow of her husband made her the Empress of Russia, the German-born princess appeared at her first military review astride a horse, with a male officer's uniform on her person and a feathered tricorn hat on her head. The Empress's aggressively masculine appearance served to remind her troops—and the rest of her subjects—that she was perfectly capable of doing a man's job.[43]

After her accession, engravings of Catherine the Great in her riding ensemble circulated widely, becoming, as in Louis XIV's case, a crucial component of her political iconography. One of these images, showing the Russian Empress "mounted astride a horse . . . dressed in a fur-trimmed, military jacket, [and] coiffed in a shallow hat topped with a tuft of large feathers," sold briskly in the Paris of Marie Antoinette's day.[44] With Louis XV's permission, it was peddled at a print seller's shop on the rue Saint-Jacques. The artist was thought to be a Frenchman, Robin de Montigny, whom Louis Auguste's two younger brothers later commissioned to paint portraits of their wives.[45]

Its possibly French origins notwithstanding, the popular picture of Empress Catherine riding astride functioned in Louis XV's kingdom less as an affirmation of female sovereignty than as an exception to the countervailing patriarchal rule. For France was governed by Salic Law, which, by banning widowed royal wives from succeeding their spouses on the throne, dictated that "three things were important at Versailles—the King, his mistresses, his court. A queen was nothing."[46] In rare cases, queen mothers with sons too young to assume the crown were allowed to rule, but only as regents. Held to derive "from Nature herself," Salic Law reserved the prerogatives and markers of supreme authority for the male sovereign alone.[47]

For this reason, Empress Catherine's cultivation of a kingly appearance was not, before Marie Antoinette's time, a strategy that would have seemed readily available to French royal women. It was well known that female regents such as Catherine de Médicis, who had introduced culottes to the women of the French court, and Anne of Austria, to whom Marie Antoinette owed both her Bourbon blood ties and her lustrous pearl necklace, had failed to win the French people's affections. Indeed, both widowed queens had presided over periods of intensely acrimonious civil strife, and the bias against women in power lasted into the eighteenth century. The hue and cry sparked by Du Barry's trouncing of Choiseul was a case in point: in 1771, anxiety about the country's "subjugation to Woman" continued to loom large in the French public imagination.

This anxiety extended to the realm of fashion. Carnival, the period of revelry that preceded Lent, saw an abundance of costume parties at which men quite frequently dressed top to toe in women's clothes. When women, by contrast, attempted to appear *en travesti,* they were not able, or encouraged, to go nearly so far. For them, the costume historian Nicole Pellegrin has noted, "the taboo against wearing breeches was so strong" that dressing as members of the opposite sex could go no further than donning a large, body-concealing cloak called a domino, and coiffing their hair in a more masculine style.[48] Outside the bounds of Carnival, female cross-dressing was even more unheard-of, and was construed as a strange erotic perversion.[49] So, at least, opined the Duc de Lauzun, whose catholic sexual proclivities and conquests earned him renown as one of France's greatest seducers in the last decades of the *ancien régime.*[50] When one of Lauzun's aristocratic mistresses paid him a visit "on horseback, wearing a dragoon's uniform and leather breeches," he found that he was "disgusted almost to the point of no return."[51]

And though he bedded the woman anyway, he claimed that he did so with considerable regret, identifying the encounter in his memoirs as one of the most shameful of his whole career.

IRONICALLY, IT TOOK THE WOMAN WHOSE SUBJECTS CALLED HER "KING Maria Theresa"— the woman whose own accession to the throne had met with fierce opposition because of her gender—to advise against Marie Antoinette's sporty, cross-dressing ways. Kept current by Mercy as to "Madame la Dauphine's cavalcades," the Empress decried her daughter's new hobby as yet another product of the Aunts' malevolent influence and warned the girl starkly of all the damage it could do:

> Riding spoils the complexion, and in the end your waistline will suffer from it and begin to show more noticeably. Furthermore, if you are riding like a man, dressed as a man [*si vous montez en homme*], as I suspect you are, I have to tell you that I find it dangerous as well as bad for bearing children—and that is what you have been called upon to do; that will be the measure of your success. If you were riding like a woman, dressed as a woman [*si vous montiez en femme*], then I would have less cause for concern. It is impossible to guard against accidents. Those that have befallen others, like the Queen of Portugal, who afterward were unable to have children, are anything but reassuring. . . . One day you will agree with me, but it will be too late.[52]

The maternal rhetoric was strong as always, but in this instance, the Dauphine, who was indeed riding astride and "dressed as a man," stuck to her guns. When Maria Theresa tried to make Marie Antoinette promise to stop riding altogether, the younger woman refused outright, remarking that Louis XV and his grandson would be unhappy to see her do so: "The King and Monsieur le Dauphin take pleasure in seeing me on horseback. . . . They have been enchanted to see me in the uniform of the hunt."[53] Though she was careful not to mention whether she wore this uniform with breeches or a skirt, Marie Antoinette for once forced her mother to back down. "Since you tell me that the King and the Dauphin approve of [your riding]," the Empress replied grudgingly, "then that is enough for me. It is up to them to command you; it is into their hands that I have placed my lovely Antoinette."[54]

For all her political acumen, Maria Theresa failed to grasp that the Dauphine's sudden and all-consuming love for the hunt may in fact have represented an effort to achieve an alternative "measure of success" at court—an effort to embrace and embody a standard that had nothing whatsoever to do with the procreative functions traditionally assigned to a Bourbon wife. As long as she was not "a real dauphine" in the reproductive sense, she had no hope of asserting her authority through the conventional, "womanly" channels of pregnancy and motherhood. Yet even for a French royal consort, Marie Antoinette was no ordinary woman, given her blood ties to such illustrious sovereigns as Louis XIV and the imperial Caesars. Neither her husband's late mother, Marie Josèphe of Saxony, nor Louis XV's late wife, Maria Leczinska of Poland, had boasted nearly so sublime a genealogy. Though they had fulfilled their husbands' and subjects' expectations by bearing children, these women were in no position to do what Marie Antoinette's rarefied lineage—to which she referred with increasing frequency in later years as "the great blood that flows through my veins"—entitled her to do.[55] And that was to command attention by dressing and riding "like a man" . . . just as her ancestor Louis XIV, sometimes directly copying her other ancestors the Caesars, had so effectively done before her.[56]

Given both her past and present life circumstances, it is unlikely that Marie Antoinette would have been inclined to ignore the model of the Sun King's artfully cultivated, astoundingly potent public image. In Vienna, she had not received much of a formal education before the Abbé de Vermond was sent to inculcate her with the basics of French language and culture. But in his tutorials with the Archduchess, Vermond managed to remedy her ignorance in large part by schooling her in French royal genealogy. According to Vermond, his pupil embraced the subject so enthusiastically that she was soon able to identify her two favorite French kings: "Henri IV, because he was so good, and Louis XIV, because he was so great."[57] And once she reached Versailles, she impressed her new compatriots with her command of Bourbon familial and political lore. Upon joining the Dauphine's retinue, for instance, Mademoiselle de Mirecourt found her new mistress "better versed than any other prince in everything having to do with the history of France and its leading families."[58]

Still, should she have needed reminders of Louis XIV's greatness, the Dauphine had only to look to her immediate surroundings at Versailles: to the gates and doors that bore his golden cipher, and to the ceiling frescoes, the statues, and the portraits that were everywhere on display. By design, these representations stood as ubiquitous proof of the Sun King's transcendent stature.[59] And if Marie Antoinette had arrived at the French court unprepared for other aspects of life there—the anti-Austrian party, the sexually reticent husband, the rigid system of etiquette—at the very least, the imagery of Louis XIV that surrounded her stood to confirm the opinions she had formed under Vermond's tutelage in Vienna.

In the summer of 1771, Marie Antoinette drew on this very imagery when she had her portrait painted at her mother's request. The Empress had specified that the painting should "depict you in your finery, not in a man's clothing, but in the place that has been assigned to you."⁶⁰ Ignoring these parameters, the young woman commissioned a portrait of herself in masculine-style riding garb. This canvas has been lost, but a few surviving portraits present her in similar attire: "just as she is," Maria Theresa later wrote of the lost portrait, "in her riding clothes, with a hat on her head."⁶¹ In the earliest of these paintings, a pastel that the Alsatian artist Josef Krantzinger executed later in 1771, the Dauphine is shown from the waist up, in an androgynous red *justaucorps* (the hunting uniform at the royal residence of Trianon), yellow kidskin riding gloves, and a three-cornered hat edged with gold braid.⁶² According to Marguerite Jallut, a former curator of the museum at Versailles, Marie Antoinette's excitement at posing in this special costume exceeded her enthusiasm for riding itself, and Krantzinger captured her joy so effectively that even Maria Theresa was mollified when she saw the painting, declaring it one of the most true-to-life images she had yet seen of her daughter.⁶³

The Empress might have looked less kindly on another equestrian portrait, which the Swiss-born court painter Louis-Auguste Brun painted from life (and from articles of clothing and footwear that Marie Antoinette gave him for this purpose) several years later.⁶⁴ Unlike the Krantzinger portrait, this painting depicts Marie Antoinette's full body as she rides to hounds, and so reveals her penchant for riding and dressing "like a man." Attired in a blue habit (the requisite uniform for hunting at Versailles) with masculine breeches, a fluttering lace cravat, high yellow boots, and a grandiosely feathered hat, Marie Antoinette sits confidently astride, and draws her mount up into a bold, rearing stance. (Plate 6.) In both the horse's position and the rider's masterful air, the Brun painting owes a marked debt to the great equestrian depictions of Louis XIV.⁶⁵ (Plate 7.)

IMITATION OF THE SUN KING'S SIGNATURE POSE WAS AN EXTREMELY BOLD move for a princess whose foothold at court remained far from secure, but Marie Antoinette may have drawn her courage from the unexpected dissolution, at around this time, of one of her biggest political obstacles: this was the threat that Provence's new bride, Marie Joséphine of Savoy, might pose to her position as the King's most cherished granddaughter. For when the court turned out to meet Marie Joséphine on May 12, 1771, it immediately became clear that she stood no chance of outshining the Dauphine. Although the Savoyard princess had been selected, like Marie Antoinette before her, for reasons of political alliance, Louis XV himself confided in Mercy that he found the new Comtesse de Provence disappointingly ugly; he objected in particular to her "villainous nose."⁶⁶ And that was just one of her defects.

"In the language of an officer of dragoons," another, more loquacious observer noted wryly,

> [Marie Joséphine] would have been described as a powerful, hairy animal. Her head was crowned with a thick forest of black hair, growing down low [over her] bushy eyebrows. . . . [Her] thick lips [were] surmounted with a pronounced moustache; and the whole was set off by a very dark complexion. So much for the face. Her Royal Highness's figure was broader than it was tall, [with an] ample bosom . . . and [a derrière] the likes of which the Paris brewers love to see gleaming on their horses' hindquarters. When Madame walked, this portion of her body quivered in a way which made the comparison still more obvious.[67]

Other courtiers extended this viewer's characterization to conclude that Provence's bride even had hair growing on her chest.[68]

So filthy, moreover, were Marie Joséphine's personal habits—even by the fairly lax hygienic standards of Versailles—that Louis XV charged his ambassador to Savoy with asking the princess's father, King Victor Amadeus III, to intervene. The French king asserted that at the very least, his grandson's wife ought occasionally to wash her neck, clean her teeth, and comb her hair. "Though it is embarrassing for me to discuss such things," the diplomat from Versailles confessed to Marie Joséphine's father, "these mere details are matters of vital importance to us in this country here [*ce pays-ci*]."[69] ("*Ce pays-ci,*" the colloquialism by which those attached to Versailles referred to the place, suggests the degree to which it represented a distinct cultural universe unto itself.) Marie Antoinette had by now had time to learn these lessons the hard way; for the Comtesse de Provence, less endowed with the basic, superficial prerequisites for success at the elegant French court, the failure to embrace her new homeland's grooming codes placed her at an even greater disadvantage.

Even more important in allaying the Dauphine's erstwhile fears that Marie Joséphine would surpass her was the fact that the latter girl almost immediately gave the lie to Provence's boasts about his supposed sexual vigor. When asked about her husband's claim that on their wedding night he had made her "happy four times," the Comtesse de Provence sighed to her *dame d'atours* that the young man had done no such thing.[70] It turned out that the bridegroom, partially lame from a hip deformity, and fatter by far than his brother Louis Auguste, was physically incapable of intercourse. The marriage would never bear fruit—and, as Marie Joséphine was wont to murmur, "it's not my fault."[71]

Perhaps not incidentally, the patent failure of the Provence union—and the widespread tittering over the bride's ungainliness—coincided with yet another show of the King's increased fondness for Marie Antoinette. Just after Marie Joséphine's arrival, Mercy recorded, Louis XV took to visiting the Dauphine each morning "by means of a hidden door which had remained closed until then," and to sharing his morning coffee with her, "looking happier and more content than usual."[72] It seemed that the Savoyard princess's presence only heightened the King's appreciation for his comelier granddaughter-in-law.

These developments might have allowed Marie Antoinette to breathe easier, had it not been for her ongoing—and worsening—feud with the Comtesse Du Barry. In the weeks that followed Provence's wedding, the royal favorite complained with increasing frequency about the Dauphine's treatment of her, until the King felt he had no choice but to take a stand. Summoning Mercy to his chambers, he urged the ambassador to talk sense to Marie Antoinette: "All [the Comtesse] wishes is that Madame la Dauphine should speak to her just once."[73] Maria Theresa, horrified that Louis XV should have been reduced to making such a request, took her daughter to task. Throughout the summer, the Empress and the King worked in concert with Mercy to broker a peace between the warring women. Where Maria Theresa had suggested "a dress or some bagatelle of that sort" as the Dauphine's opening gambit, Mercy encouraged the girl to make "some anodyne comments about the hunt—that would be enough to make the favorite happy."[74]

These recommendations, however, proved superfluous. Though "it was arranged that Marie Antoinette should speak to Madame Du Barry [on] Sunday evening, July 10, 1771," the Dauphine did not follow through with the plan.[75] No sooner did she enter the room where the favorite—and the rest of the court—eagerly awaited her overture, than she turned on her heel without speaking, ushered along by a gleeful Madame Adélaïde. The ensuing scandal prompted Maria Theresa and her ambassador to scold the girl all over again. But Marie Antoinette stood firm. "If you saw all that goes on here as I do," she informed her mother, "you would realize that this woman and her clique will not be content with just one word."[76] At this point, the Dauphine's pride was on the line: she was being asked to yield too much ground to the *barrystes,* and she seemed unable to stomach such a vast concession. Haughtily she countered the Empress's chiding: "You can be assured that I need guidance from no one in anything concerning proper, decent behavior."[77]

It was at precisely this time that the Dauphine, still regularly riding astride, "like a man," sat for that first equestrian portrait, now lost.[78] And while she was hardly the first Bourbon princess to be painted in riding garb—such portraiture had a long tradition in France and elsewhere—her attempt to stage herself both in paint and in life as a mighty, specifically manly horseman may well have assumed special significance at this point in her career. Viewed against the backdrop of Choiseul's dismissal, Provence's recently disclosed impotence, and Du Barry's mounting demands for recognition, Marie Antoinette's equestrian posturing can plausibly be construed both as an act of defiance and as an assertion of authority. For her appropriation of iconic kingly trappings coincided directly with her refusal to compromise with the hated *barrystes* and suggested a refutation of the label of worthlessness generally reserved for a childless consort. In this sense, Marie Antoinette indeed indicated that she "need[ed] guidance from no one," and so challenged common assumptions about how her success as Dauphine should be evaluated.

"Clearly you are not of our blood," Madame Adélaïde told her at this time, reluctantly praising the girl's new show of boldness and purpose.[79] But in fact, the so-called *Autrichienne*'s lordly horseback theatrics implied just the opposite. Louis XIV's breeches and boots had, as Voltaire had famously put it, forced the King's detractors to accede to "the authority of his rank, which until then had been little respected." Dressed in much the same way, the Sun King's female descendant now seemed to be endeavoring to do the same. Her conduct was all the more striking given that her husband, the one who actually stood to inherit Louis XIV's crown, consistently and adamantly refused to have himself depicted in such a heroic, mythologizing manner.[80] As it happens, in Brun's equestrian portrait of Marie Antoinette, Louis Auguste appears as a tiny figure in the background—also on horseback, but almost utterly eclipsed by his wife's commanding, kinglike pose.

THOUGH HER FLAGRANT DEFIANCE OF TRADITIONAL ROYAL GENDER ROLES would one day come back to haunt her—with accusations of lesbianism, monstrousness, and a brazen thirst for power leveled at her by the dozen—Marie Antoinette's first years of riding and dressing "like a man" seemed to serve her well. Her equestrian outings with Louis XV and Louis Auguste placed her on surer footing with both men. Not only did the King continue to honor her with informal visits each morning; the Dauphin himself began visiting her chambers with some regularity, and the uncomfortable strain between the young spouses started to turn into something more like friendly mutual regard. In late October 1772, the couple informed their grandfather that although Louis Auguste found intercourse painful (he may have had a deformity of the foreskin, which would only be diagnosed years later), they had attempted consummation several times. On July 22 of the following year, appearing before Louis XV with Marie Antoinette by his side, the Dauphin solemnly declared that he had at last made her "his wife."[81] Louis XV was delighted, and with visible emotion declared Marie Antoinette "his daughter."[82] Afterward, the trio celebrated by setting out together on a glorious stag hunt.

Just as her nemesis's star was rising, Madame Du Barry's had begun to wane. As Mercy was pleased to report to the Empress, "[His Majesty's] original affection for the favorite having diminished with time, and this woman having infinitely few resources of spirit and character, the King sees her only as a source of mediocre dissipation."[83] Sensing a decline in her fortunes, Du Barry was reduced to groveling for the Dauphine's favor. In a stunning display of desperation, she offered to buy Marie Antoinette a pair of diamond earrings, costing an outrageous 700,000 livres, from the Swiss jeweler Charles Boehmer. Declaring through an intermediary, the Comte de Noailles, that she already had more diamonds than she knew what to do with, Marie Antoinette refused the gift—and her refusal was an unmistakable show of power.[84] At last, she had established herself as someone with enough clout to rebuff Madame Du Barry.

By now, however, Marie Antoinette knew better than to assume that her husband's sporadic attentions alone would safeguard her future in France. Du Barry still had powerful friends at court, for instance, the formidable Rohan family, whose arrogant and debauched scion, Prince Louis de Rohan, was France's new ambassador to Vienna. It had already come to the Dauphine's attention that Rohan was spreading unflattering stories about her in her native city, but she became even more upset when she learned of his biting witticism about her mother's role in the Polish partition of 1772. (After the death of Poland's ruler, who had historically been a Bourbon ally, Austria, Russia, and Prussia had proceeded to divvy up the nation among themselves.) In a letter to the Duc d'Aiguillon, which the Duc read aloud to hoots of laughter in Madame Du Barry's boudoir, Rohan described Maria Theresa as "holding in one hand a handkerchief with which to wipe away the tears she was shedding over the woes of Poland, while in the other she wielded a sword with which to divide that unfortunate country."[85] News of this episode instilled in Marie Antoinette a lasting hatred of Rohan, but it also revealed that for all the progress she had made, the French party remained alive and well at Versailles.[86]

At the same time, her first official entry into Paris, which brought her face-to-face with the power of public opinion, revealed that she had other means to draw upon besides the support of her husband or her courtiers. On June 8, 1773, the capital's inhabitants turned out in record numbers to cheer their future sovereigns. After a procession through the city, whose narrow streets were so densely packed with well-wishers that the royal carriages were often stalled for forty-five minutes at a time, the young couple attended a solemn mass at Notre-Dame, then paid their respects at the Church of Sainte-Geneviève and listened to orations at the Sorbonne. At length, the Dauphin and Dauphine wound up at the Bourbons' Paris residence, the Tuileries, so named because it had been built on the site of an old tile factory. Once ensconced in this palace, they greeted the crowds from a high balcony. The masses of people in the castle gardens stretched as far as the eye could see, so astonishing Marie Antoinette that she asked the Governor of Paris, the Maréchal-Duc de Brissac, how many of them stood before her. Gallantly, Brissac informed her that there were 200,000 of them, and that they had all fallen in love with her.[87]

Though the level-headed Mercy estimated the turn-out at only "fifty thousand souls," the Duc's flattering remark about the Parisians' love for the Dauphine contained more than a small grain of truth.[88] During her appearance in the capital, Marie Antoinette had eclipsed her awkward husband just as wholly as she had on the occasion of their wedding.[89] Resplendent in diamonds and a sumptuous white *grand habit,* she commanded the spectators' rapt attention throughout her visit, as an ode published afterward in *Le Mercure de France* glowingly confirmed:

> Citizens, there she is! Ye gods, she is beautiful!
> What a noble, touching air! What sweet, appealing eyes!
> Her spirit, her gaiety, her graces—everything about her
> Is reflected in her dazzling features. . . .
> [Madame la Dauphine,] honor us often with your presence;
> Work toward the happiness of a people that adores you.
> Impatiently we ask in your absence:
> "When will we see her again?"[90]

That she could inspire such emotion in an entire people, simply by waving at them from a distance, moved Marie Antoinette deeply. "What really touched me," she mused to the Empress,

> was the love and enthusiasm of the poor people, who were ecstatic at the sight of us, even though they are burdened by taxation. . . . How fortunate we are that we can have such widespread popularity at so small cost. . . . That fact was impressed upon me, and I shall never forget it.[91]

To a public fed up with the excesses of the royal favorite and the abuses of the *barryste* cabinet, just "the sight of" Marie Antoinette, fresh-faced and elegant, seemed to give cause for rejoicing. It revived the expectations that her marriage to the Dauphin had first spawned three years before, expectations that she would reverse the Bourbons' shameful decline and lead France into a new golden age.[92] Inclined in this direction, public opinion—and a savvy manipulation of "her dazzling features"—could serve as a most effective weapon in the Dauphine's political arsenal.

For the moment at least, the "poor people" of that nation's capital appeared to have no interest in condemning Marie Antoinette's breeches. On the contrary, as long as these commoners wrung their hands over the rise of "the Whore" Du Barry, and longed for "the salvation [that had once] come from the Maiden" Joan of Arc, a cross-dressed equestrienne of seemingly limited sexual power was, if anything, bound to receive special exemption from their ire. For the horseman-ruler Louis XIV may have been France's greatest king, but Joan of Arc was one of its greatest soldiers, and she had saved the nation by riding astride into battle, dressed as a man. At the siege of Orléans in 1429, a contemporary chronicler reported:

> The people of the city had such great desire to see Joan the Maiden, that they could not have their fill of seeing her. It seemed a great marvel to all that she could keep her seat on horseback as elegantly as she did. And in truth, she comported herself as well in every regard as if she had known how to be a man-at-arms following the wars since her youth.[93]

Three and a half centuries later, the descendants of Joan's admirers "could not have their fill of seeing" the Dauphine, in or out of the saddle. On the heels of her Parisian début, it was still anybody's guess whether this new female cynosure would succeed in fulfilling the public's hopes, or whether, like Joan the Maid, she would be martyred on the pyre of their shifting affections. Though no one could as yet have anticipated the latter outcome, by 1791 it would seem inevitable enough, when an anonymous, antiroyalist writer presented Marie Antoinette's riding habits as sure evidence of treason:

> No doubt you wanted to take one of your ancestors, Louis XIV, as your model, and lay siege to Paris at the head of a huge army, dressed in boots and spurs and carrying a whip, as if you were coming to subjugate your slaves.[94]

But in 1773, this indictment was still a revolution away.

FIVE

THE *POUF* ASCENDANT

For Louis Auguste's coronation on June 11, 1775, sumptuous, tasseled wall hangings had transformed the Gothic Reims Cathedral "into a kind of Baroque opera house," more reminiscent of the seventeenth century than of the Middle Ages.[1] But the costumes of the men gathered at the altar seemed to stand outside time. Representing Charlemagne's original peers of the realm, twelve of the nation's most exalted princes, including the adolescent Comtes de Provence and d'Artois, wore polished coronets and "great cloaks of ermine over long, cloth-of-gold vests."[2] The captains of the Guard sported flat plumed hats and jackets shot through with gold, while other officers were outfitted in coats of crisp white satin, and the Guard of the Seals, Armand de Miromesnil, had donned a stylized golden toque. "It was most majestic," reported the Duc de Croÿ, who as a Knight of the Order of the Holy Spirit had a well-placed seat near the front. "All these ancient costumes were imposing, even more so because one sees them only on this day."[3]

At the center of the glittering group, Louis Auguste, now Louis XVI, knelt on a plush square of plum-colored velvet, looking in his long, cloth-of-silver coat "as though he had been transfigured by grace."[4] The aristocrats assembled in the cathedral's pews and temporarily constructed boxes looked on "in perfect silence" as the Archbishop of Reims, flanked by three other mitered church luminaries, led the twenty-year-old monarch through the sacred rites.[5] Louis XVI's shimmering coat and the scarlet camisole beneath it were laid open to reveal his pudgy, bare chest, which the Archbishop daubed with unguents from the same vial that Saint Rémy had used to anoint Clovis, the first king of France, almost thirteen hundred years before. He then presented Louis with the attributes of Charlemagne: an ivory-tipped baton called the Hand of Justice, and a gilded scepter that measured six feet long.

Praying aloud, the Archbishop exhorted France's young King to be virtuous and wise, and, in a somewhat stranger formulation, to carry out his duties with "the strength of a rhinoceros."[6] After this, Monsieur de Miromesnil summoned the twelve princes forward in a booming voice. Once they had encircled the King, the Archbishop lifted from the altar Charlemagne's heavy gold crown, "set with fat, precious uncut stones," and held it aloft with both hands.[7] The litany of blessings he uttered, asking God to bestow upon France's ruler "the crown of glory, the crown of justice, the crown of eternal life," served as the signal for the coronation proper. Now, in accordance with custom, the princes simultaneously extended their hands toward the diadem, and, together with the Archbishop, lowered it onto the kneeling Louis's head. According to Croÿ, "this superb moment created the greatest imaginable sensation in the cathedral."[8] But beneath the audience's jubilant cries, Louis XVI, already failing to display the rhinoceros-like force expected of a Bourbon king, was heard to gasp: "The crown is hurting me."[9]

Meanwhile, ensconced in a special grandstand that had been built especially for her, the nineteen-year-old Marie Antoinette wept happily at the scene. She had dressed for Louis XVI's coronation not in the timeless ceremonial garb of the male grandees, but, Croÿ noted, in the "contemporary, very gallant style" of which she had recently become enamored.[10] Covered in sapphires, other gemstones, and ornate but fanciful embroidery, her dress was the work of Rose Bertin, a rising star in the Parisian fashion industry and one of the greatest influences on the new queen's evolving taste; the gown was so heavy that Bertin had argued for sending it to Reims on a special stretcher.[11] Because Marie Antoinette was the first consort to attend a French coronation since Catherine de Médicis in 1547—the last three kings before Louis XVI having been unmarried when they received the crown—she had had no immediate precedent to follow in determining how to dress for the occasion.[12] The eminent modernity of her ensemble, though, suggested more devotion to of-the-moment sartorial caprices than to the ancient dignity of the French throne.

But it was Marie Antoinette's hairstyle, teased high above her forehead, heavily powdered, and topped with a cluster of nodding white feathers, that perhaps provided onlookers with the biggest surprise. So towering was the overall effect of this coiffure that her face appeared to be the midpoint between the top of her hair and the hem of her gown. The gallant Duc de Croÿ, for one, found his sovereign's headdress charmingly silly, and pretended to wonder how she and her ladies, who were similarly coiffed, had all managed to grow so much taller since he last saw them a year before.[13]

Other guests were less than amused. Afterward, some of them grumbled that Marie Antoinette's extravagant hairdo had blocked their view of the realm's new king.

Although the claim was spurious—the Queen's grandstand was positioned off to the side of the altar, where neither it nor its occupants could obstruct the shimmering figure of Louis XVI—there was no disputing the massive proportions of her new coiffure. Yet Marie Antoinette's slim neck showed no sign of bowing under the strain. By contrast, her husband appeared almost alarmingly unequal to the physical challenge that his new headgear imposed. "What is wrong with the King?" his wife asked anxiously, when she noticed the discomfort that his diadem seemed to be causing him. "Look how ill at ease he seems. Do you think the crown is too tight?"[14]

ON MAY 10, 1774, LOUIS XV HAD DIED AT AGE SIXTY-FOUR OF SMALLPOX, which he was thought to have contracted by sleeping with a milkmaid.[15] In the agony of his illness, he suddenly became concerned for the fate of his immortal soul and made his first confession in forty years. After receiving absolution for his sins, he could no longer keep Madame Du Barry, his longtime accomplice in fornication, by his side. With tears in his eyes, he expelled her from her palace apartments; she fled to Aiguillon's nearby Château de Rueil, where a small group of devotees rallied around her and hoped for the best. If Louis XV did not regain his health, the *barrystes* knew, their days at court were numbered.[16]

This faction's fears were justified. When at last the older king passed away, and the nineteen-year-old Louis Auguste acceded to the throne as Louis XVI, one of the young man's first decisions was to send both Du Barry and her longtime supporter, the Duc d'Aiguillon, into exile—an act that appeared to signal a decisive victory for Marie Antoinette.[17] Quite clearly, it meted out justice to those who had so consistently slandered her during the previous reign. (In Paris, crowds rejoicing at the change of régime burned Aiguillon's despicable colleague Maupeou in effigy, in part because they suspected him of having spread vicious rumors against their lovely new queen.) Better yet, the demise of the *barrystes* seemed to confirm Mercy's and Maria Theresa's forecasts about the great political influence Marie Antoinette might hope to exert as sovereign.

True to form, the Aunts hastily maneuvered to thwart this outcome. Shortly after Louis XV's death, they arranged a private meeting with their nephew, at which they urged him to assemble a cabinet that would not cede royal authority to the *parlements* and the *choiseulistes*. Reprising La Vauguyon's claims that Choiseul and his cadre wanted to destroy the French monarchy and hand over its power to the Austrian Hapsburgs, they convinced Louis XVI that he should select his ministers from among the French party. Apparently still under the sway of the anti-Austrian teachings of his youth, the new king complied, naming the Comte de Maurepas, Aiguillon's uncle and one of La Vauguyon's closest friends, as "his personal adviser and unofficial prime minister."[18] By the time Marie Antoinette learned of the nomination, it was a fait accompli. So, too, was that of the Comte de Vergennes, whom her husband invited to serve as his foreign minister, and who harbored no fondness for Austria.

To Marie Antoinette, these appointments came as devastating news. In her estimation, both Vergennes and Maurepas would labor "to maintain the King in the ideas . . . that the black-hearted La Vauguyon" had "invented against the House of Austria," and it galled to find her enemies still entrenched in a court over which, as Queen, she might have expected to preside unchallenged.[19] Despite the still-sporadic nature of their sexual interludes, she and her husband had grown relatively comfortable with, even fond of, each other. Like herself, Louis XVI had never had many people at Versailles whom he could trust, and he had seemed to appreciate the sweetness and compassion with which his wife generally tried to treat him. But the young king's affection for his wife did not, she now discovered, mean that he intended to involve her in affairs of state. It was a sad but true fact, as she explained some time later to her brother Joseph II, that her husband had no interest in her opinions on such matters as the composition of his cabinet:

> I have raised [the issue of the anti-Austrian ministers] more than once with the King, but . . . he does not often talk to me about great decisions. . . . When I reproach him for not having spoken to me on certain subjects, he looks somewhat embarrassed, and sometimes adds that he had not even thought to do so. So I can tell you that political affairs are those over which I have the least control. . . .[20]

Thus, although she was now Queen, Marie Antoinette's political prospects remained bleak, and were made bleaker still by the altered living arrangements at her husband's court. As King, Louis XVI was obliged to move from his old apartments into his grandfather's magnificent suite, a change to which the savvy Maurepas responded by taking over the rooms that Madame Du Barry had once occupied, and which were connected to the monarch's chambers by a hidden stair. This reallocation of palace real estate not only signaled the new minister's unrivaled clout, but increased the distance between Marie Antoinette's apartments and her husband's. A year after the old king's passing, she finally prevailed upon Louis XVI to construct a secret passageway linking their rooms. But until then, the shy and self-conscious young monarch was "condemned to make his sporadic marital visits by going through the Oeil-de-Boeuf antechamber" outside his bedroom—in full view of every gossipy courtier who idled there.[21]

Isolated both politically and spatially, Marie Antoinette once again turned to clothing to boost her precarious stature—although this time, she abandoned her masculine hunting uniform for a fancier kind of dress. Perhaps again borrowing from Louis XIV, who had presided over an era of dazzlingly extravagant court masques, she decided to start hosting two parties a week at Versailles—one of which was to be a Monday night masked ball.[22] For the first of these events, held on January 9, 1775, Marie Antoinette drew her inspiration from a recent snowfall, selecting "Norwegians and Lapps" as the theme.[23] Outfitted in sumptuous, faux-Scandinavian attire provided at the Queen's behest by the Surintendant des Menus Plaisirs (Steward of Small Pleasures), Papillon de La Ferté, and his staff, courtiers flocked to the party and lingered well past dawn. According to Mercy, who described the festivities to Maria Theresa, the Queen's "personal graces" stood out even among her exotically costumed guests—and held the whole crowd enthralled.[24] To behold Marie Antoinette looking radiant in her glittering winter-wonderland attire, one would never have guessed at her underlying political woes.

And that may have been exactly the point of the Queen's new fêtes. As Mercy noted, she was elated by the tremendous success of her first masked ball, and threw herself wholeheartedly into planning subsequent such affairs, with ever more inventive outfits and themes.[25] At her enthusiastic prompting, Tyroleans, Indians, and circus performers were just a few of the personae who danced through the castle's *petite salle de spectacles*—decorated in accordance with the revelers' attire—each Monday night.[26] Sometimes, Marie Antoinette prescribed an alluringly simple scheme for the colors and fabrics her guests were to wear: for example, "white taffeta with flowing tulle" for the ladies, and "blue velvet with white, [blue-embroidered] waistcoats" for the men.[27] On other occasions, she drew on her knowledge of French royal history to re-create the Renaissance courts of François I and Henri IV.[28] For these gatherings, partygoers were instructed to wear stylized sixteenth-century costume: trunk hose and jerkins for the gentlemen, gabled hoods and bell-shaped farthingale skirts for their damsels, and starched white ruffs for every neck.

Yet even when she required that her revelers display a certain degree of uniformity, Marie Antoinette took pains to set herself apart from the crowd. To emphasize her standing as the party's—and the court's—most important woman, she generally selected the plum costume for herself. Thus, at one of her Renaissance-themed extravaganzas, she turned heads not only by convincing Louis XVI to appear as Henri IV, but by herself masquerading as that king's legendarily powerful mistress, Gabrielle d'Estrées.[29] "The outfit," wrote the Marquis de Ségur,

> was truly resplendent. A black hat, trimmed with white plumes held in place by four large diamonds and a loop of precious stones valued at 2,000 livres. Her stomacher and her girdle were made of diamonds, her dress was white gauze studded with silver stars, trimmed with golden fringe, which was attached to the skirt by more diamonds. A fairylike vision, indeed, but a ruinous one, from the point of view of the treasury.[30]

For a queen whose conjugal visits with her husband were still—as her courtiers knew full well—few and far between, the decision to pose as a famed royal paramour may have struck some of her guests as incongruous. If Marie Antoinette really wanted to dress like a Renaissance heroine, then Catherine de Médicis would after all have been the more appropriate choice, given that Catherine's royal marriage, too, had been plagued by fertility problems. (Though she eventually succeeded in bearing heirs, Catherine had been woefully childless during her early years as Dauphine, and had also been threatened with the prospect of divorce and banishment from court.[31]) Yet however unsuitable it may have appeared given her sexual relations, or lack thereof, with the King, Marie Antoinette's Gabrielle d'Estrées ensemble indicated that she held his favor in another, important respect. Through its sheer, breathtaking extravagance, it implied that she enjoyed the spending power, as well as the conspicuous splendor, of a royal favorite.[32]

This was a radical notion to say the least. At Versailles, queens were traditionally expected to lead quiet, retiring lives, busying themselves with childbearing and prayer while pampered *maîtresses en titre* dipped freely into the kingly coffers. Certainly the women in Louis XV's life had conformed to this model. Whereas his consort, Maria Leczinska, had been a dowdy and unassuming woman whose greatest personal extravagance was "a quiet party of whist," the glamorous Mesdames de Pompadour and Du Barry had secured from their lover countless gifts of jewelry, clothing, and cash.[33] Similarly, Louis XIV's queen, Marie Thérèse, had "led a life of extreme piety, her chief pleasures being her religious faith and her collection of dwarves," while his favorites indulged in far showier delights.[34] In return for their favors, the King's mistresses even received private residences, which became venues for merriment unfettered by the regimented ceremonies of the court.

But Louis XVI, with his still crippling sexual reticence, had no mistress, made no effort to procure a mistress, and seemed perfectly happy to grant his wife a mistress's privileged financial position, if not her sexual functions. It was the Queen who now, with her priceless array of ostentatious costumes, eclipsed all the other noblewomen at Versailles; it was she who dominated the court and made it dazzle. And like a royal favorite's, her caprices seemed incapable of eliciting the King's disapproval, no matter how much money they cost. Indeed, Louis XVI raised eyebrows by refusing to restrict her party expenditures even after La Ferté, who was also in charge of planning the royal coronation for the following summer, complained that the weekly masquerades were cutting into the budget for that far more important state affair. Perhaps just as surprising, given his reputation for avoiding society, the young king actually deigned to attend his wife's parties. (He always left by eleven o'clock—his bedtime—but he graciously exempted the rest of the guests from the obligation to retire when he did.) And, at a party she hosted on January 23, he accorded her an even greater mark of royal favor, overcoming his fear of dancing enough to perform the opening minuet with her. Along with his financial largesse, his presence at Marie Antoinette's costume balls revealed that it was she, more than any other courtier, who enjoyed the monarch's invaluable esteem.

For the Queen, carte blanche in party planning thus served not only to distract her from her latest troubles, but also, in a roundabout way, to address them. With the appointment of the Maurepas cabinet, she had patently failed to exercise direct political influence of the sort once wielded by Pompadour and Du Barry. If, however, she entertained just as lavishly, and presented herself just as magnificently, as these mistresses past, then perhaps she might disguise—even improve—her disenfranchised state. As she confided some years later to Joseph II: "Without ostentation or lies, I allow the public to believe that I have more credit [with the King] than I do in reality, because, if people were not to believe me on this point, I would have less power still."[35]

And although predicated precisely on "ostentation," her posturing became an essential part of her campaign for increased popularity and prestige. Like her equestrian cross-dressing, her parties imbued her with an aura of influence that she otherwise sorely lacked. And indeed, her efforts seem to have paid off, for during the first few months of Louis XVI's reign, observers commented frequently on the Queen's apparent dominion over both him and his nobles.[36] At the top of the hierarchy, the royal family appeared, at least on the surface, to accept her as its center of gravity, with Provence, Artois, and their wives (Artois having married Marie Thérèse of Savoy, the sister of the Comtesse de Provence, in 1773) becoming fixtures at her weekly fêtes, and joining her and Louis XVI for intimate, royals-only dinners that she organized in defiance of court tradition. With the exception of the bitter old Aunts, who now sought less to manipulate their niece than to boycott her glittering dos, the rest of the courtiers followed suit in entering her indomitable orbit.³⁷ Her soirées won her new friends among the court's younger and jollier members, and even those who disliked her (including the secretly jealous Comtesses de Provence and d'Artois) "now sought at least outwardly to please her."³⁸ Maurepas and his ministers themselves got caught up in the excitement, and, as Mercy was gratified to notice, "redouble[d] the respect and the deference [they showed] Her Majesty, basing their conduct on the degree of influence and credit that the Queen enjoy[ed]."³⁹ It was not insignificant that in discussing this shift, both Mercy and Marie Antoinette ascribed it to her newly cultivated air of "credit." This term indicated quite clearly that in the absence of any direct political involvement, Louis XVI's consort had chosen to showcase her power of the purse.

At the same time, because they made such effective use of costume in flaunting her enviable prominence, the Queen's parties also established her as a leader in the realm of fashion—as a woman who, just as Maria Theresa had once enjoined her to do, alone "set the tone at Versailles."⁴⁰ For particularly among her new cadre of pleasure-seeking companions, Marie Antoinette's costume balls had sparked a new passion for whimsical dress. The handsome and debonair Comte d'Artois, who had become one of her closest male friends, so enjoyed her Renaissance masquerades that he started a movement to reinstitute sixteenth-century dress as everyday wear for the court. Though older and more conservative noblemen angrily vetoed the idea, demanding that "the usages of Louis XIV and Louis XV retain their dominance," the die was cast.⁴¹ Since the Sun King's era, these "usages" had imparted to the aristocrats an air of changeless permanency. But the new guard now had as its ringleader a queen who did not disguise her scorn for the outmoded "high-collars" and "centuries" of the older generation, and who had, moreover, wasted no time in shrugging off Madame Etiquette's unwelcome advice. (Madame de Noailles left Marie Antoinette's service not long after her accession.) For this group, the court's requisite costume had grown old and sorely needed a new look.

Egged on especially by Artois and his fast-living cousin the Duc de Chartres, Marie Antoinette set her sights on Paris, one of Europe's largest cities and its undisputed center of fashion.⁴² During the previous reign, aristocrats bored with the dowdy and stultifying atmosphere of Versailles had escaped as often as their court duties allowed to their residences in the smart, sophisticated capital.⁴³ The most significant of these aristocratic outposts was the Palais Royal, the urban stronghold of the Duc d'Orléans and his family. This mighty clan, known to be the richest in France, descended from

Louis XIV's younger brother, Philippe; Orléans and his son, the Duc de Chartres, were therefore princes of the blood, who stood just behind Louis XVI and his brothers in the line of succession. (In fact, when Louis XV was a child, it was his cousin Orléans who had served as regent, governing from the family seat in Paris.) However, the Orléanses had not approved of the late king's disbanding of the *parlements,* an act that they perceived as a dangerous move toward autocracy. The family members registered their discontent by shunning Versailles and establishing a kind of Parisian countercourt at the Palais Royal, where their relatively liberal politics earned them the loyalty of many of the city's lower-born inhabitants.[44]

The Orléanses' urban residence did, however, resemble Versailles in one important respect: it was open to the public. Anyone was free to wander through the gardens of the sprawling compound, which contained within its walls cafés, shops, gambling dens, bookseller-printer's shops, and prostitutes plying their wares. What was perhaps most important for Marie Antoinette, the complex encompassed the ultra-stylish Paris Opéra, where the aristocracy and the urban haute bourgeoisie gathered for see-and-be-seen performances and public masked balls. To attract the attention of these well-heeled crowds, luxury purveyors opened fancy boutiques all around the complex, especially on the nearby rue Saint-Honoré, which, then as now, was an epicenter of European fashion. It was at the Palais Royal that the Duc de Chartres's neglected young wife, who consoled herself with shopping while her husband dallied with other women, had established herself as one of the most modish women of her day. And it was on the rue Saint-Honoré that the Duchesse discovered a *marchande de modes* named Rose Bertin, who would soon launch the Queen's own quest for matchless chic. With Bertin's help, Marie Antoinette would cultivate an image of the very power that both her husband's ministerial appointments and her sexless marriage categorically denied her.

IN THE LAST THREE DECADES OF THE EIGHTEENTH CENTURY, *MARCHANDES de modes,* female fashion merchants, had begun to emerge as a major force in the French garment industry, in response to a paradigm shift in the Parisian clothing market. Driven by increases in textile production and changing attitudes toward consumption, the market during this period witnessed unprecedented levels of interest and variety "in garments and accessories, colors, and fabrics"—a development that Daniel Roche has described as an absolute "revolution in clothing."[45] "For the first time," writes another historian, Clare Haru Crowston, of this moment, "elements of personal taste, choice and superfluity entered the attire" of the middle and working classes.[46] In particular, women took to spending twice as much money as their husbands did on clothing and accessories.[47] Even their least expensive headdresses cost four times more than everyday men's hats.[48]

Capitalizing on women's burgeoning appetite for diversity and frivolity, the *marchandes de modes* offered their services not as seamstresses or tailors—these professions having received from the crown a legal monopoly on garment manufacture—but as stylists focusing on readily modifiable, everchanging trimmings and ornaments designed to alter and enhance already made dresses and skirts. Far more than the garments they adorned, it was the artful, decorative touches of the *marchande de modes* that established a woman's flair for dress.[49] Reflecting this idea, a 1769 technical treatise called *The Art of the Tailor* defined the labor of the *marchandes de modes* not as a "profession" properly speaking, but as a "talent" for "sewing and arranging according to the mode of the day the embellishments which they and the ladies constantly concoct."[50] It was a talent that, under the law, could only be practiced by members of the all-male mercers' guild and their wives.[51]

In October 1773, Rose Bertin, an unmarried twenty-four-year-old woman from Picardy, defied this law by setting up shop as a *marchande de modes* on the rue Saint-Honoré.[52] Exotically named the Grand Mogol, in reference to a putatively luxury-loving Asiatic grandee, her boutique boasted large windows filled with displays that were designed to divert foot traffic from the Palais Royal.[53] With their artistic arrangements of bonnets, shawls, fans, spangles, furbelows, silk flowers, gemstones, laces, and other accessories, the displays set up a bewitching siren's song.[54] Once lured inside, ushered through the door by a liveried footman, potential customers found themselves in a setting as luxurious as an aristocrat's salon: gilded moldings adorned the ceilings, full-length mirrors and fine oil paintings hung on the walls, and expensive furniture was scattered about among the piles of damasks, silks, brocades, and baubles that announced the place's true purpose.[55] This purpose, indeed, would have been hard to overlook, for, along with its piles of fabrics and ornaments, the Grand Mogol boasted indoor fashion displays of complete, one-of-a-kind ensembles, covered from neckline to hemline in luscious frippery.[56] On one occasion, the boutique housed an exhibition of 280 such dresses, each one trimmed by its celebrated proprietor, and collectively valued at 500,000 livres.[57]

The inspired genius behind all these delights, Bertin presided over her team of elegantly clothed shopgirls with an air of supreme authority, sometimes even issuing her recommendations from the comfort of her personal chaise longue. Though her portly build and vaguely porcine, ruddy-cheeked face squared ill with her boutique's refined, jewel-box décor, she impressed visitors as a "great personage in petticoats [who] never suffer[ed] contradiction"—so certain was she that whichever ornament she prescribed was just the one her client's outfit called for.[58]

In the early months of 1774, Bertin expanded her offerings to include a wildly innovative headdress called the *pouf*.[59] Developed in conjunction with a hairdresser named Monsieur Léonard, who had recently made a name for himself by devising flamboyant hairdos for prominent actresses and noblewomen, the *pouf* was built on scaffolding made from wire, cloth, gauze, horsehair, fake hair, and the wearer's own tresses, teased high off the forehead. After dousing the whole edifice heavily with powder, its architect installed amid the twists and curls an elaborate miniature still-life, intended either to express a feeling (*pouf au sentiment*) or to commemorate an event (*pouf à la circonstance*) of importance to the client. At a time when consumers were more anxious than ever to distinguish themselves through their accessories and adornments, these personalized mobile billboards effected a radical transformation in Frenchwomen's appearance.[60] As the costume historian Madeleine Delpierre has shown, "there were by 1780 a hundred and fifty different ways to trim a gown, and the variety of head-dresses was infinite."[61]

LIVING CONVENIENTLY CLOSE TO BERTIN'S STORE, AND HAVING UNTOLD riches to lavish on her wardrobe, the Duchesse de Chartres became one of the *pouf*'s early adopters. When she gave birth to a son, she celebrated by commissioning a headdress that featured "not only her African page and her parrot, but also a nursemaid seated in an armchair, clasping a newborn baby to her breast."[62] Not to be outdone, the wife of the disgraced Duc de Choiseul commissioned "a three-foot-high *pouf* that replicated a verdant garden, replete with flowers, grass, a bubbling stream, and a tiny windmill edged with jewels and powered by a clockwork mechanism that Louis XVI himself might have admired."[63] In a still more intricate variation on this theme, the Duchesse de Lauzun, who like the Duchesse de Chartres seemed to gravitate toward *la mode* as a compensation for her husband's notorious debaucheries, hired Bertin to decorate her locks with—as a bemused contemporary journalist reported—"a stormy sea, a hunter shooting at ducks, a mill where a female mill-worker was being seduced by a priest, and at the bottom, the mill-worker's husband walking along with his donkey."[64] Wild, witty, and containing "the whole, motley world . . . in their superstructure," *poufs* such as these were Bertin's calling card when, in the spring of 1774, the Duchesse de Chartres presented her to the Queen.[65]

Marie Antoinette's enchantment with the *pouf* seems to have been immediate and absolute—indeed, it is almost impossible to contemplate an accoutrement better suited to her campaign for increased public prestige.[66] Placing both Bertin and Léonard on her payroll, she adopted the fanciful headdress as her signature look and Paris as the right place to show it off. Despite vague expressions of disapproval from the Aunts, she began traveling to the city two to three times a week. This twelve-mile journey from Versailles transported the Queen into a different world: one where she was free to dance at the public Opéra balls, to browse through the open-air markets, to stroll along the swank promenades in the Palais Royal, the Champs Élysées, and the Bois de Boulogne. More even than her weekly costume parties, these venues provided Marie Antoinette with the wide audience that she craved and that her new hairdos deserved.

In the earliest days of her reign, this audience proved a gratifyingly adoring one. The once inconceivable sight of a queen mingling freely with her subjects provoked elated reactions from a populace that had long viewed its monarchs as unattainable and distant. Historically, the residents of the capital had construed any visit from their sovereigns as an exceedingly rare, divinely accorded grace.[67] Thus, when the Parisians spotted Marie Antoinette applauding fervently at the Opéra, or seated with some girlfriends in a public park, picnicking on strawberries and cream, they could scarcely contain their delight.[68] "In those first summer days," the Duc de Croÿ confirmed, "all Paris came out [to see her], and it was like one continual fête. Everyone looked happy and there was joyful shouting, and even the clapping of hands."[69] And of course, the hairstyles the Queen adopted for these trips quite literally heightened her visibility in the public eye.

Better still, because they were explicitly designed to convey topical messages, Marie Antoinette's *poufs* allowed her to play at politics and look fashionable at the same time. One of her first such successes was reportedly the *coiffure à l'Iphigénie,* a lyrical confection wound with black mourning ribbons, trimmed with a black veil, and topped with a crescent moon.[70] (Apparently introduced shortly after Louis XV's death, this headdress may have doubled as mourning garb at a time when the whole of the court was supposed to be wearing somber-toned clothing.) This *pouf* paid tribute to Gluck's opera *Iphigénie en Aulide,* which, just a few weeks before Louis XV passed away, had enjoyed a stellar début in Paris—thanks to the good offices of Marie Antoinette herself.

Gluck had been her childhood music tutor in Vienna, and she had rewarded him, now that she was a Bourbon princess, by supporting his efforts to break into the Parisian music scene. Yet his *Iphigénie* had not been guaranteed to succeed; this was partly because of the French public's reservations about "German" music, and partly because of active campaigning by

Madame Du Barry, who, in another effort to avenge herself on her rival, had decided to support the Italian composer Nicola Piccini at Gluck's expense.[71] Marie Antoinette had crushed the favorite's opposition by arriving at the opera's opening night with her husband, and along with more than half a dozen of France's highest-ranked princes, in tow, and by leading them and the rest of the audience in vigorous applause.

Onlookers had not missed the significance of this battle between the princess and the courtesan: the *Mémoires secrets* reported afterward that Marie Antoinette had emerged at the center of her very own cabal.[72] In this context, the *coiffure à l'Iphigénie* was not just another way to demonstrate her fondness for Gluck, but a pointed dig at the woman Marie Antoinette had publicly shamed at the Opéra. Like her masculine riding habits, the Queen's (towering, even phallic) *poufs* enabled her to suggest to her enemies, and to the rest of her subjects, that despite all the setbacks she had experienced as Louis XVI's wife, she remained very much in charge.

Another of the Queen's early, similarly self-promoting coiffures was the *pouf à l'inoculation,* which she is said to have unveiled after convincing her husband to submit to a smallpox inoculation.[73] The practice was common in Austria but, as evidenced by Louis XV's recent death from the disease, far less so in France. At first, the Queen had weathered a firestorm of criticism for wanting to impose this strange and foreign custom on her spouse; as the biographer Joan Haslip has observed, "numberless petitions were presented to Louis XVI begging him not to undergo such a dangerous procedure, and all those who were against the Austrian queen were loud in their denunciation."[74] When the King survived the inoculation and received a clean bill of health, Marie Antoinette thus had twofold reasons to be jubilant: her husband was safe, and her enemies had been routed. To celebrate, she apparently commissioned a gigantic *pouf* showcasing emblems of the inoculation: a serpent belonging to the Greeks' god of medicine, Aesculapius, twined around an olive tree that symbolized wisdom, a quality that of course belonged to medical science, but that also implicitly characterized medicine's staunch advocate the Queen. Behind the tree beamed a great golden sun: a nod to the new rulers' shared ancestor, Louis XIV, and a promise that the Sun King's glory had finally returned to the land—though whether in the person of Louis XVI or of his consort was left open to debate.[75]

However self-serving Marie Antoinette's agenda may have been in putting forth such an image, the notion of a revival of the French monarchy's *gloire,* after Louis XV's long and disappointing slide into debauchery, initially held tremendous appeal for the populace.[76] And the dizzy appreciation of the Queen's female subjects, at least, manifested itself in an outbreak of copycat *poufs* all across the city.[77] Many of these paid direct homage to the new rulers; one headdress, for instance, "showed a rising sun shining over a wheat-field, where Hope now grew"—an allusion to the reign's inauguration of a long-awaited golden age. Another *pouf* that became popular at this time was styled in the shape of a cornucopia, again symbolizing the prosperous future that awaited the realm under the stewardship of Louis XVI and his wife.[78] The Queen herself, in fact, lent credence to this hope by refusing the tithe French subjects traditionally paid to a royal consort on her accession. Known as the *droit de la ceinture de la Reine,* the right of the Queen's belt, this ancient levy was suspended when Marie Antoinette, making a self-effacing joke about her fondness for fashion, announced that belts were no longer in style anyway.[79]

Soon *poufs* vied with towering ostrich and peacock feathers—which sometimes measured up to three feet high, and were always terrifically expensive—as the hair accessory of choice.[80] Marie Antoinette, who favored both, continued to inspire imitators both within and beyond the capital. The result, according to a perceptive, worldly priest called the Abbé de Véri, was that "ridiculous feathers and coiffures have been propagated to the very remotest parts of the kingdom, and will perhaps soon conquer all of Europe."[81] In response to the feminine public's boundless fascination with the trendsetting consort, the production of French fashion plates and illustrated "fashion almanacs" underwent what Daniel Roche has called a "massive explosion."[82] Although these precursors to the modern fashion journal were expensive, and were mostly sold by subscription to noblewomen and rich bourgeoises, widespread pirating made the images accessible even to women of lesser means.[83] Not surprisingly, the "models" illustrated in engraving series like the *Galerie des modes* often resembled, or even directly represented, the Queen.[84] In one popular print, designed as a board game, the myriad hairstyles of the day were shown as stopping points along the way to the "winning" place, which was *la coiffure à la Reine:* a teetering, satin-wrapped *pouf,* studded with pearls and feathers, and perched atop Marie Antoinette's own, clearly recognizable visage.[85]

Meanwhile, Louis XVI's consort was reveling in her new role as a standard-bearer for Parisian panache; according to Madame Campan, the Queen treated fashion not as a frivolous sideline but as her "principal occupation" and began "introducing a new fashion almost every day."[86] The Comtesse de Boigne remarked that "to be the most *à la mode* woman alive seemed to [Marie Antoinette] the most desirable thing imaginable"—and although Boigne was far from alone in perceiving this dedication to stylishness as "unworthy of a great sovereign," Marie Antoinette may have begged to differ.[87] After all, as the monarch who had first established France's international preeminence in the realm of fashion, none other than Louis XIV had

1. *La Galerie des modes:* Fashion plate depicting Marie Antoinette (c. 1776)
(Bibliothèque Nationale de France, Paris)

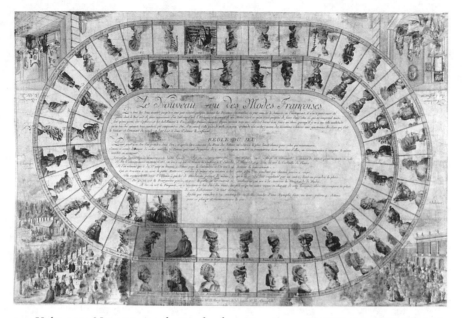

2.   Unknown, *Nouveau jeu des modes françoises* (c. 1778) (Bibliothèque Nationale de France, Paris)

strongly favored sartorial luxury in general and oversized, over-the-top wigs in particular.[88] At the peak of his obsession, the Sun King supposedly employed forty wig makers to maintain him in unrivaled tonsorial splendor, and declared hairstyles "an inexhaustible subject" of interest.[89]

For Marie Antoinette as for her astute Bourbon ancestor, clothing was serious business. To be sure, it provided a welcome distraction from the tedium of Versailles, and it allowed her to continue indulging her girlhood taste for playing dress-up. But in the context of the eminently adult political challenges that she faced as Queen, her involvement with fashion offered a compelling, added advantage. As Pierre Saint-Amand has written, it enabled her to present herself as "the court's supermodel, its ruling diva, the Queen of glamour."[90] Insofar as they attested to the King's generous financial backing—and to her own authority to "set the tone" for women everywhere— her mesmerizing ensembles could function as so many signs of her boundless royal "credit."

Instead of shunning the limelight and staying hidden away at Versailles like Louis XIV's and Louis XV's queens before her, Marie Antoinette thus actively sought publicity for her voguish coiffures. In a break with a long-standing royal tradition, which required those in a sovereign's service to cut ties to all other patrons, she allowed her purveyors to retain both their shops and their clients in the capital. In the first place, this breach of protocol enabled people like Bertin and Léonard to stay abreast of the latest trends; Marie Antoinette had warned them that she did not want them to fall behind the times by tending only to her. In the second place, Marie Antoinette's decision to share her stylists with a broader public gave nonnoble customers unprecedented insight into the Queen's personal tastes and habits. Bertin especially loved to brag about "my latest collaborations with Her Majesty," and agreed to sell eager clients copies of the pieces she had made for Louis XVI's bride.[91] The Queen approved of this practice, setting just one condition: that no sale occur less than two weeks after she had first unveiled the article in question. As long as her imitators did not threaten to unseat her as France's "most *à la mode* woman alive," Marie Antoinette seemed perfectly untroubled by their existence.[92] In fact, she proved an active and zealous manipulator of her own celebrity. According to Léonard's memoirs, she even urged him and Rose Bertin to "publish the philosophy of [their] art," as practiced on her royal person, in the pages of the women's newspaper *Le Journal des dames,* as a means of educating readers about her costume choices.[93] Gestures such as these, unprecedented for a French queen, allowed the consort to diffuse her impressive image far beyond the restricted world of Versailles. "As a fashionable woman," the art historian Mary Sheriff has noted, "Marie Antoinette represent[ed] herself not in terms of a position at court, but in terms of a position in a larger society."[94]

As the young woman would soon discover, the attempt to dissociate herself from her narrowly prescribed queenly role and establish herself as a famous figure in her own right would prove devastating both to her reputation and to her husband's régime. Yet for the moment, the larger society she sought out proved an avid market for her iconoclastic, exciting image. For the staunchest devotees of the fashions she launched, neither printed matter nor in-store gossip could compare with a direct sighting of Marie Antoinette. Léonard, who like Bertin acquired a huge following thanks to his association with the Queen, recalled the immense popularity of a style he created for one of his royal patroness's evenings at the Opéra: a "pyramidal head-dress . . . that included three white feathers placed at the left side and fastened in a rosette formed of curls of the hair with the assistance of a pink ribbon, and with a large ruby in the center."[95] The result, according to his memoirs, was a "*furore* at the Opéra! People in the pit, where at that time there were as yet no seats, crushed one another in their endeavors to see this masterpiece of cunning audacity: three arms were dislocated, two ribs broken, three feet crushed. . . . In short, my triumph was complete."[96]

However they gleaned their information, one thing was clear: French-women from all walks of life wanted to look like their queen. Madame Campan recollected that once her mistress began experimenting with wildly varied new modes of dress, "she was quite naturally imitated by all women. They wanted to have immediately the exact same ornamentation for their dresses as Her Majesty did; to wear the same feathers and garlands which her beauty (then at its peak) imbued with infinite charm."[97] So enthusiastic were Marie Antoinette's acolytes, in fact, that they did not hesitate to embrace styles more ridiculous than sublime. Thus, spotting in the Queen's *pouf à la jardinière* such implausible ingredients as an artichoke, a carrot, some radishes, and a head of cabbage, one lady of the court declared: "I shall never again wear anything but vegetables! It looks so simple, and is so much more natural even than flowers."[98]

Even the practical inconveniences imposed by the Queen's hallmark hairstyles did not discourage women from trying to emulate them. Like the powdered, "frizzled" coiffures of court tradition, the *poufs* were almost impossible to wash and so became breeding grounds for all manner of vermin. Special head-scratchers (*grattoirs*) "made from ivory, silver, gold, and even sometimes decorated with diamonds" were designed to provide relief, but a certain degree of itchiness and agony remained inevitable.[99] Sleeping, too, was uncomfortable at best, as it required a woman to wrap her coiffure in a huge conical "triple bandage which everything [went] under, false hair, pins, dye, grease, until at last the head, thrice its right size, and throbbing, [lay] on the pillow, done up like a parcel."[100] Thus coiffed, ladies were obliged to sleep quasi-upright, propped on a mountain of pillows.[101]

The headdresses also proved incommodious by day. One of Marie Antoinette's favorite *dames du palais* complained that the top-heaviness of the new hairstyle "quite spoilt the pleasure of dancing," and carriage travel, too, became deeply problematic:

> With their scaffolding of gauze, flowers, and feathers, coiffures reached such dizzying heights that women could no longer find carriages with roofs high enough to accommodate them, and quite often one would see a woman keeping her head down, or putting it out the window, while she rode. Other ladies opted instead to get down on their knees as an even surer means of protecting the ridiculous edifice with which they were encumbered.[102]

Even the Queen was not immune to such difficulties. In February 1776, the Duchesse de Chartres held a ball in her honor at the Palais Royal; for the occasion, Marie Antoinette had decided to sport "double-height" ostrich feathers in her hair. But in order to exit from her carriage without damaging her plumage, she had to have her ladies remove it first, and then replace it in her headdress after she disembarked.[103]

Similar challenges arose when ladies attempted to maneuver through

3. Unknown, *Servants Standing on a Ladder, Preparing a Pouf for Bed* (c. 1778) (The Picture Gallery at the New York Public Library)

doorways or into boxes at the theater, where, quite often, they were not the only ones who found their hairstyles problematic. According to one contemporary, "spectators at the theater complained that they could no longer see the stage, and even petitioned Monsieur Duvisme, the director of the Paris Opéra, to refuse orchestra seats to any woman whose [coiffure] was too high."[104] Duvisme granted the request and ruled that ladies wearing oversized *poufs* and feathers should be allowed only in the loges.[105]

To address these problems, a fashion merchant known as le Sieur Beaulard, a rival of Bertin's whom Marie Antoinette (to Bertin's tremendous chagrin) sometimes patronized, invented "a mechanical coiffure which could, when circumstances required it, be lowered a foot or two by touching a spring."[106] Although this device, slyly called the *coiffure à la grand-mère*, proved handy for young women who felt the need to modify their hairdo when confronted with a tongue-clucking grandmother, it never met with widespread success.[107] Proposals to make doorways higher, so that even excessively coiffed women could walk through them with ease, likewise failed to get off the ground.[108]

The inconveniences posed by the *poufs* soon appeared in anonymously disseminated caricatures produced both in France and abroad. These images depicted ladies with hairdos twice the size of their bodies, caught in a range of ludicrous positions: with their hair catching fire from chandeliers or getting snagged on streetlights, with hairdressers scaling high ladders to coif them, with hunters firing mistakenly at *poufs* shaped like gigantic birds in flight. Believing as she did in the sanctity of her mistress's station, Madame Campan was offended to discover that some of the women in these cartoons possessed "features which maliciously recalled those of the sovereign herself."[109]

UNFORTUNATELY FOR THE SOVEREIGN IN QUESTION, SUCH MALICE WAS NOT restricted to the underground lampoons. Despite the first *poufs'* optimistic wheat fields and horns of plenty, France in the mid-1770s was in dire economic straits. The disastrous Seven Years' War had left the kingdom teetering on the brink of bankruptcy, saddled with a deficit that totaled 22 million livres upon Louis XVI's accession and that was projected to grow by another 78 million livres forthwith.[110] Because the nobility and the clergy were exempt from taxation, the burden of making up the shortfall landed squarely on the shoulders of the Third Estate—the approximately 24 million to 28 million commoners who made up over 96 percent of the population at that time.[111] Crushed by inordinate taxes, much of the Third Estate lived in grinding poverty.

Because, moreover, the French economy was still largely agrarian, people's living conditions worsened drastically after a bad harvest. And the harsh, snowy winter of 1774–1775 led to one of the worst harvests in recent memory. That May, a scarcity of grain and misguided reforms by Louis XVI's Controller-General, Turgot, impelled starving people throughout the nation to stage riots known as the Flour Wars. Five thousand people charged the gates of Versailles, having been told that the royals were hoarding grain and bread. To quell the rioting both far and near, the historian Simon Schama has written, Turgot "call[ed] out twenty-five thousand troops and institute[d] summary tribunals and exemplary hangings."[112] The government's brutal response to the crisis left a bad taste in many commoners' mouths even after order was restored. At the Palais Royal, malcontents gathered to voice their fury over the episode, sometimes in earshot of Bertin's well-coiffed clientele.

Against this backdrop, Marie Antoinette's status as a style icon soon turned from enchanting to suspect, and her use of fashion to command her subjects' respect started to work against her. Already in the summer of 1774, as the novelty of her first urban appearances began to wear off, a chronicler of Parisian life observed that the people had begun viewing her in a harshly skeptical light and attributing to her all manner of unnamed and "mutually contradictory horrors."[113] The Flour Wars cast her frivolity into even sharper relief. "The Queen is constantly in Paris, at the Opéra, at the theater," groused the Comtesse de la Marck, who was married to one of Mercy's closest friends. "She runs into debt; she is adorned with plumes and furbelows, and makes fun of serious things."[114] Where Marie Antoinette's "plumes and furbelows" had once inspired admiration and awe, they now raised questions about her willingness or ability to consider more "serious things"; a 1776 fashion-plate caption described her beloved feathers as "symbols of levity" that revealed their wearer's correspondingly, and lamentably, unserious character.[115] According to Hector Fleischmann, an early-twentieth-century author who collected numerous scurrilous pamphlets written about Marie Antoinette during her lifetime, "the first attacks against the Queen [in the clandestine press] began with the trend for high hairdos that predominated in 1775."[116]

Popular distaste may have been exacerbated by the fact that flour was an ingredient of the powder used to coat her prodigious coiffures.[117] Indeed, although historians have established that Marie Antoinette never uttered the legendary remark "Let them eat cake" (*"Qu'ils mangent de la brioche"*), it is not implausible that the lasting association between her callousness and baked edibles in fact originated with her habit of parading her powdered, wedding-cake hairstyles before a bread-starved nation.[118] Equally impolitic was Rose Bertin's decision to celebrate the Flour Wars with a headdress called the *coiffure à la révolte*—a style of which no image survives, but whose very name bespoke a stunning co-optation of human suffering by high fashion.[119] Unveiled before an increasingly restive public and placed on conspicuous display at Louis XVI's coronation in June 1775, styles like these sent an inflammatory message. From the look of her, Bertin's overdressed royal patroness had no noticeable concern for her subjects' welfare.

Rather, as was implied in contemporary engravings that showed an ostentatiously plumed Marie Antoinette standing before a mirror, she appeared utterly absorbed in the spectacle of her own beauty. The charge of narcissism stood to damage her reputation to no end. For unlike the opulent ensembles traditionally worn by French sovereigns—by Louis XVI and his brothers at the coronation, for example—the Queen's fanciful modes now seemed designed less to enhance the monarchy's public grandeur than to accentuate her own, private charms. As Chantal Thomas has argued, Marie Antoinette's pursuit of stylishness represented "no longer the glamour of an entire caste being staged, but that of a woman."[120] In a land where royal glamour made sense only as a reflection and a consecration of state power, her extravagance risked seeming thoroughly self-indulgent and perilously unmoored from the kingdom's broader concerns.

PLATE I.   This sumptuous John Galliano creation weaves Marie Antoinette's dizzying rise and tragic fall into the very fabric of a dress. One of the gown's two embroidered hip panels depicts the notorious French queen frolicking at her country palace in a shepherdess costume; the other shows her walking to the guillotine in rags. These details rightly suggest that her fate was inextricably intertwined with her clothing choices.

PLATE 2.   Even as a small child, the Hapsburg Archduchess Maria Antonia was conscripted to perform in glittering celebrations at the imperial court of Vienna, such as the ballet staged in honor of her oldest brother Joseph II's wedding in 1765. The Empress Maria Theresa's youngest daughter moved with extraordinary grace—an attribute that would stand the girl in good stead at Versailles.

PLATE 3. The French King Louis XV refused to agree to a marriage between his grandson and Maria Antonia until the girl's looks had been brought into line with French standards. Louis XV dispatched the celebrated painter Joseph Ducreux to document the Archduchess's metamorphosis into a "*Française*." Although the 1769 portrait that clinched the deal has been lost, Ducreux executed this one later that year.

PLATE 4. Louis XIV, an ancestor whom Marie Antoinette shared with her husband, Louis Auguste, was known as "the Sun King." He was renowned for his love of costumes and for his savvy manipulation of his own image. Here he is dressed as Apollo for a performance of a ballet called *La Nuit* [Night].

PLATE 5. Marie Antoinette traveled from Vienna to France in a fairy-tale carriage, or *berline*, made from glass and gold. By the time it reached Versailles on May 16, 1770—the fourteen-year-old Dauphine's wedding day—the magnificent cavalcade surrounding the *berline* had swollen to gigantic proportions.

Garde françoise et Suisse

Les gardes

Les Chevaux Legers   Gens darmês de la garde

PLATES 6 AND 7.   At a time when
her failure to conceive an heir was
causing speculation, Marie Antoinette
scandalized many courtiers by dressing
in trousers and riding astride "like a
man." This form of rebellion may
have been inspired by her ancestor
Louis XIV (right), who had used
equestrian finery to enhance his own
authority. When Marie Antoinette
commissioned an equestrian portrait of
herself in the summer of 1771, she may
thus have been cultivating a form of
prestige that had nothing to do with
her maternal prospects. The canvas
above, painted almost a decade later,
depicts Marie Antoinette in the fitted
trousers and mannish riding habit she
first began wearing as a "barren,"
beleaguered dauphine.

PLATE 8. Upon acceding to the throne in 1774, Marie Antoinette became enamored of the teetering *pouf* hairstyle, first brought into fashion by an inventive Parisian *marchande de modes* named Rose Bertin. The *pouf* quickly became the young queen's signature look, spawning copycats among countless women both in France and abroad. This contemporary engraving depicts the startling juxtaposition of the modish, whimsical coiffure and the regal, timeless ermine-trimmed robe of a French sovereign.

PLATE 9. When France joined forces with the American revolutionaries, Marie Antoinette showed her support by wearing a *pouf à la Belle Poule*: an intricate hairdo displaying a French frigate that won a key victory against the British in June 1778.

PLATE 10. Just a few months after her arrival at Versailles, Marie Antoinette set tongues wagging by refusing to wear the intensely restrictive whalebone *corps* [corset]. Only under severe pressure from both her mother and the members of the French court did Marie Antoinette eventually agree to wear the corset. This apple-green bodice is one of the few garments of Marie Antoinette's to have survived the French Revolution.

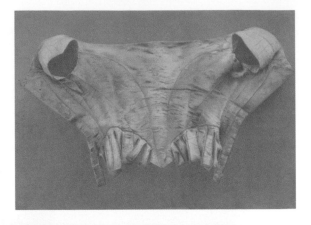

PLATE 11. In this 1775 painting by Jean-Baptiste Gautier-Dagoty, Marie Antoinette's imposing blue gown boasts the wide hoopskirts (*paniers*) and rigidly corseted bodice of the ceremonial *grand habit de cour*, and is topped with an unmistakably royal garment: a sweeping, ermine-lined robe embroidered with golden fleurs-de-lys. The lilies tucked into the dress's folds imbue it with a hint of unexpected freshness.

PLATE 12. Before the appearance of a bona fide French fashion journal in 1785, series of engraved fashion plates like the *Galerie des modes* were one of the chief means by which devotees of *la mode parisienne* gained information about the latest styles. This plate from 1778 depicts the flirty, ankle-baring *robe à la polonaise*, which was one of the many dresses that Marie Antoinette, her friends, and her imitators adopted as a reaction against the sweeping and uncomfortable *robe à la française* prescribed at court.

PLATE 13. The redingote was sometimes described as a "Germanic" sartorial aesthetic, which may have lent added credence to rumors about Marie Antoinette's penchant for lesbianism, "the German vice." This 1787 plate from the *Galerie des modes* represents a woman in a *redingote à l'Allemande* or "German riding-coat," whose oversized gold buttons and prominent cuffs and lapels also characterized the male fashions of the period.

PLATE 14. By the mid-1780s, Marie Antoinette's beloved man-tailored redingotes had become mainstays of every well-heeled Frenchwoman's wardrobe. In this miniature, the Queen is outfitted in a blue, gold-frogged redingote, a frothy white collar and cuffs, and a jaunty black hat adorned with black and white plumes.

PLATES 15 AND 16. One of the most widely emulated ensembles Marie Antoinette introduced at the Petit Trianon was a lightweight, informal *chemise* dress known as the *gaulle*. Made from airy, ruffled muslin (usually white) and structured by a wide sash at the waist and matching ribbon "bracelets" at the elbows, the *gaulle* eschewed the weighty silk fabrics and rigid architecture of the aristocratic *robe à la française*. Everyone, from the Queen's closest friends (like the Princesse de Lamballe, below) to her enemies (like Madame Dubarry, at left), fell in love with the style.

PLATE 17. Other staples of the Queen's Petit Trianon wardrobe included simple white muslin and linen bonnets and aprons; like the *gaulle*, these enjoyed a tremendous vogue in the 1780s. Also like the *gaulle*, these homespun bonnets and aprons were relatively inexpensive and easy to copy. The resultant democratization of French fashion—which one aristocratic observer dubbed "a revolution in linen"—eroded the class distinctions that had once been readily apparent in the way women dressed.

PLATE 18. During the *ancien régime*, ladies of style paid tribute to current events through their headgear, and this trend continued during the first few years of the French Revolution. This 1790 fashion plate presents two headdresses edged with the tricolor ribbon that was, by that time, an instantly recognizable sign of patriotic fervor. The bonnet at right is called the *Coiffure à la Nation*.

PLATE 19. This 1785 portrait by Adolf Ulrik von Wertmüller depicts Marie Antoinette and her two oldest children, Madame Royale and the Dauphin Louis Joseph, in the gardens of the Petit Trianon. Marie Antoinette turned thirty that year and announced her intention to begin dressing in a more conservative manner; the outfit she wears in this portrait (a tightly corseted dress of peachy-brown silk, edged with exquisite French lace) is consistent with that change.

PLATE 20. This contemporary engraving depicts Marie Antoinette in one of her favorite Trianon looks: a plain white bonnet and a gauzy, loosely draped gown that bears no traces of royal grandeur. Even the image's caption reveals how little she looks like a French queen: in describing her solely as "Marie Antoinette of Austria," the anonymous print-maker may be emphasizing her objectionable, "Austrian" informality and her preference for simple fabrics like muslin, imported from Hapsburg territories.

PLATE 21.   When Marie Antoinette and her family escaped the Tuileries in June 1791, her disguise consisted of an unassuming dark brown dress and a large black shawl and hat. However, in this engraving by the revolutionary artist Lesueur, the runaway sovereign is shown in her signature white gown and straw hat. During the scandal surrounding Vigée-Lebrun's *La Reine en gaulle* eight years earlier, an angry public had construed the rusticated ensemble as proof of Marie Antoinette's unqueenly conduct. By reintroducing this dress into his version of the Varennes episode, Lesueur again calls attention to this aspect of the Queen's bad reputation.

PLATE 22. In this 1789 lampoon, Marie Antoinette's head is superimposed onto the body of a harpy, whose claws are busy shredding a document labeled both "Declaration of the Rights of Man" and "Constitution of the French people." Several years earlier, the Queen had embraced a fashion known as *à la harpie* (a bold, triangular pattern that appeared on both headdresses and gowns).

PLATE 23. Published in August 1790, this fashion plate illustrates a "woman patriot in her new uniform," which is made up of of a simple, dark blue jacket faced with red, a matching dark blue skirt, a ruffled white collar and sleeves, and a black hat sprigged with bobbing feathers. Paradoxically, the outfit is strikingly reminiscent of the equestrian ensembles Marie Antoinette had made popular in the previous decade; indeed, female revolutionary costume repeatedly borrowed from the Queen's sartorial repertoire, even as the anti-royalist press virulently denounced her crimes of fashion.

PLATE 24. Upon learning of her husband's execution on January 21, 1793, Marie Antoinette immediately requested black mourning clothes for herself and her family. Painted sometime between 1793 and 1795, this work by the Marquise de Bréhan provides a richly detailed picture of the costume that the consort adopted to mourn Louis XVI's death. Particularly notable is her voluminous black widow's coif, the last headdress she ever ordered from Rose Bertin.

PLATE 25. Marie Antoinette's final fashion statement eloquently condensed her complex sartorial history into a single color with a host of different associations: white.

PLATE 26. Marie Antoinette went to the guillotine dressed in a plain but pristine white *chemise* and bonnet that she seemed, according to the girl who waited on her in prison, to have saved for precisely that occasion. At thirty-seven, the former queen was haggard, emaciated, and white-haired. The republican politician, artist, and propagandist Jacques Louis David hastily sketched her as a wretched crone.

Paradoxically, though, in her very quest to assert herself as a force to be reckoned with, the young queen failed either to consider or to grasp the scandal that her personal splendor represented to her people.[121] And since she had emancipated herself from Madame Etiquette and distanced herself from the Aunts (who dismissed her voguish plumes as "ornaments for horses"), she had no one in her immediate circle to challenge her behavior.[122] Certainly, the spendthrift Ducs d'Artois and de Chartres were disinclined to rein her in, given their own habits; and Chartres had ulterior motives, both political and personal, for encouraging the Queen's profligacy. Immensely jealous of his royal cousins' precedence, he dreamed of acceding to the throne in their place, and to that end cultivated the dissenters who flocked to the Palais Royal. Chartres also nursed a private grudge against Marie Antoinette because of the favor she showed Rose Bertin, who had once publicly and humiliatingly rebuffed his attempts to seduce her.[123] (To make matters worse, the always impudent Bertin had reportedly bragged to Marie Antoinette's *dame d'atours:* "If I wanted to, I could be the Duchesse de Chartres this very evening!"[124])

The women of the aristocracy, meanwhile, were too focused on keeping up with the Queen's ever-changing styles to question either their appropriateness or their cost. Whereas under previous monarchs, eminence of lineage, conformity to etiquette, and service to the crown had served as the nobility's chief arms of distinction, the nobles in Marie Antoinette's newly fashion-oriented court found that modishness represented a far surer path to royal favor.[125] Life at Versailles required several costume changes a day— "an outfit for the *lever* and an outfit for dinner, an outfit for receiving friends and an outfit for receiving clergymen, an outfit for promenading in Paris and an outfit for going to the country"—and a woman could easily fall from grace if the Queen found her badly dressed.[126] For this reason, the biographer Michelle Sapori has observed, "the ladies of the court lived in a state of constant anxiety about being dressed in just the right way, and at just the right moment."[127] Conversely, when Marie Antoinette approved of her noblewomen's appearance, there was no limit to the honors she would lavish upon them.

The Princesse de Lamballe, a sweet-faced young widow six years the Queen's senior, was a case in point. As daughter-in-law to the fabulously wealthy Duc de Penthièvre, the Princesse had plenty of money to spend on personal adornments and, like her sister-in-law the Duchesse de Chartres, was a devoted customer of Rose Bertin.[128] Her stylish, soulful appearance attracted the consort greatly, as did her foreign birth (she hailed from Turin) and her tragic marital history (the Prince de Lamballe, a notorious libertine in the circle of the Duc de Chartres, had died of syphilis in 1767). Although

Lamballe already held the rank of princess of the blood—her late husband's family descended from the last of Louis XIV's legitimated bastard sons—Marie Antoinette elevated her to an even more coveted position. In the fall of 1775, she made Lamballe Surintendante de la Maison de la Reine (Steward of the Queen's Household), a *charge* that had been long suppressed because it was thought to confer too much power on its holder, and that brought with it a princely annual income of 150,000 livres. That jealous nobles and cash-strapped commoners resented the promotion mattered little to Lamballe or the Queen.[129] What concerned them was that it allowed the Princesse constant proximity to her friend, and more money than ever to earmark for their voguish amusements.

Like Marie Antoinette, the Princesse de Lamballe had pearly white skin, blue eyes, and pale golden hair, and the two young women seemed to take pleasure in underscoring their resemblance through prettily coordinated ensembles. In the winter of 1776, after six weeks of heavy snowfalls, the friends caused a sensation by riding to the Bois de Boulogne in a horse-drawn sleigh, both of them glittering with white diamonds, adorned with powdered *poufs,* and snuggled under piles of fluffy white furs—all of which matched the white plumes bobbing in their horses' manes.[130] By her own admission, Madame Campan was in the minority in finding this vignette fetching and "spring-like."[131] To other onlookers, the pair's luxurious whiteness registered less as the color of springtime than as the color of money—and of ice-cold indifference to the people's suffering.[132] Louis XVI himself found the outing distasteful, declaring pointedly that he preferred to chop up some of his own old sledges as firewood for the poor.[133]

In fact, the King was the only member of Marie Antoinette's inner circle who seemed willing to challenge her immoderate ostentation, and whose rank placed him in a position to do so. While he had benignly supported her costume parties at Versailles, her Parisian fashion excesses began to alarm him as they assumed monumental, astronomically expensive new proportions. To get this point across, he presented her in January 1775 with a conservative queenly aigrette made from diamonds already in the crown's collection. According to Mercy, "His Majesty said he hoped that she would wear [the aigrette] in place of the new style of headdress, for which adornment she was too pretty to have a need."[134] The gesture's gallantry only thinly masked his disapproval of her showy *poufs* and feathers.

Finding, however, that his wife did not take the hint, Louis XVI resorted to humor. One morning not long after the Flour Wars, he visited Marie Antoinette in her apartments while she was trying on a new gown that Rose Bertin had brought in from Paris. (Although as a *marchande de modes,* Bertin was not supposed to sew dresses herself, she collaborated extensively with her clients in the design as well as the adornment of their gowns, whose fabrics were often woven, dyed, cut, and stitched to her precise specifications.[135]) When the Queen asked her husband how he liked the confection, which was made from taffeta of an odd pinkish-tan hue, he replied laconically: "It is the color of a flea [*puce*]."[136]

Once again, however, the King missed his mark. Instead of prompting Marie Antoinette to reject Bertin's latest creation, his comment sparked a frenetic new appetite for "puce" garments among the fashion-forward. "The next day," the Baronne d'Oberkirch remembered:

> every lady at court wore a puce-colored gown, old puce, young puce, *ventre de puce* [flea's belly], *dos de puce* [flea's back], etc. [And] as the new color did not soil easily, and was therefore less expensive than lighter tints, the fashion of puce gowns was adopted by the [Parisian] bourgeoisie.[137]

So great was the color's success that the Baron de Besenval, who became one of the Queen's preferred companions during this time, informed a young man new to court that all he needed to succeed was a jacket dyed puce—though for ladies, the Baron might well have prescribed the much coveted *pouf à la puce*.[138]

Louis XVI's failed campaign against his wife's follies left one last line of defense: Maria Theresa, to whom the Queen's "extravagances of fashion," faithfully related by Mercy, came as appalling news.[139] In March 1775, she asked her daughter what possessed her to wear her hair "rising [from] your forehead by as much as three feet, and made even higher by the addition of plumes and ribbons."[140] Marie Antoinette replied tersely, "It is true that I am concerned with my appearance," only to claim that she did not start, but was merely following, the trend toward pricey ostrich feathers.[141] But Maria Theresa was unconvinced, declaring nine days before the coronation at Reims that her overdressed daughter was "hurtling toward an abyss."[142] Sternly she reminded the young woman that "a queen only degrades herself . . . through unthrifty expenditure, especially in such difficult times," and that "simplicity of costume is better suited to her exalted rank."[143]

In 1777, Maria Theresa even charged her son and co-regent, Emperor Joseph II, who was traveling to Versailles on a diplomatic mission, with reinforcing her warnings. As an adamant critic of all that was frivolous—especially in the realm of clothing, which he had endeavored to make more informal and sensible at the Viennese court—he seemed an ideal candidate for talking some sense into his sister. When Marie Antoinette greeted him by asking how he liked the "quantity of flowers and feathers" in her hair, the Emperor struck a note of disapproval wholly of a piece with his mother's:

"If you wish me to speak frankly, Madame, I must say that I find it far too light to support a crown."[144] (Plate 8.)

LIKE THE KING'S VEILED CRITICISMS, HOWEVER, JOSEPH II'S BARB HAD NO apparent impact on the Queen, who persisted in her profligate ways even as the demand she herself had sparked for the creations of Bertin, Léonard, and their competitors drove their prices sky-high.[145] In the year 1776, Marie Antoinette spent 100,000 livres on accessories alone, although she had a fixed yearly allowance of only 120,000 livres to cover all her clothing expenses.[146] While the allowance may well have been inadequate even for a more frugal queen—it had been set in 1725 and never adjusted since—Marie Antoinette seemingly paid it no mind as she continued to stuff her wardrobe with novelty items.[147] And because Bertin refused to provide detailed accounts justifying her prices, the Queen's *dame d'atours* had no means of verifying the charges and no choice but to pay up, even if that meant applying to the King to provide "supplements" from his own privy purse. The overages increased every year, with the lion's share of the money invariably going straight to Rose Bertin.[148]

Admittedly, such overspending was not uncommon in the French royal family as a whole. Artois, for example, channeled huge sums into gambling, courtesans, and elegant clothing; in 1777 he ordered 365 pairs of shoes so that he might have a different pair for each day.[149] In that same year, he and Provence managed between them to rack up 31 million livres in debts—which they had to enjoin Louis XVI to settle for them. Even the pious old Aunts, who had an annual income of a million livres each, had no compunction about "using up 3 million livres in a six-week expedition to Vichy to drink the waters"; and Adélaïde, despite her pronounced disdain for Marie Antoinette's fashions, herself spent prodigiously on new clothes.[150] Only the King himself had a tendency toward thrift, except where his stables and his mealtimes were concerned. But like his relatives' more considerable excesses, Louis XVI's indulgences (like 2,190 livres for his year's supply of lemonade) were the custom of the country, construed—as the Abbé de Véri put it—as expressions of "royal decency and dignity" understood to reflect the glory of the monarchical institution as a whole.[151]

It was, in fact, a similar tradition that dictated at least some of the Queen's own budgetary madness, for one of her attendants' chief perquisites was the right to help themselves to those items for which she no longer had a need. As Antonia Fraser has pointed out, it was partly for this reason that those running the consort's household ordered eighteen new pairs of perfumed gloves and four new pairs of shoes each week, as well as "three yards of [brand-new] ribbon daily to tie the royal peignoir . . . and two brand-new yards of green taffeta daily to cover the basket in which the royal fan and gloves were carried."[152] After Marie Antoinette had finished with these "minor items," members of her staff either appropriated them for their own use or sold them to supplement their earnings.

The same fate befell the new dresses that were added to her wardrobe on a seasonal basis, from the thirty-six new gowns of varying formality that her *dame d'atours* ordered every winter and every summer, to the still larger array of light frocks and *déshabillés* that supplemented them.[153] In keeping with etiquette, a French queen changed clothes at least three times a day, selecting from her pattern book or *gazette des atours* each morning "a formal dress for mass, a *déshabillé* for hours of intimacy [in her chambers], and a gala dress for the evening."[154] Generally, if Marie Antoinette had worn a gown once, she did not wear it again; this practice had caused even her retiring predecessor Maria Leczinska to spend considerable sums on clothes.[155] Although Marie Antoinette disposed of all but her favorite outfits at the end of each season, the ones that remained in her possession still added up to a formidable collection, which filled three entire rooms at Versailles.[156]

However, neither these traditional expenses nor those of the other Bourbons sparked nearly as much public indignation as Marie Antoinette's more modish splurges, for the simple reason that these last, with their associations of private rapacity and unchecked narcissism, appeared better suited to a king's mistress than to a king's wife.[157] In particular, the Queen's infinitely diverse and costly hairstyles recalled the heyday of the celebrated trendsetter Madame de Pompadour twenty years earlier. "A hundred entrancing ways did she arrange her hair," one of that favorite's contemporaries recollected, "till the court nearly went mad attempting to imitate her inimitable coiffures."[158] Like Pompadour's excesses (upon which Du Barry, with her "voluptuous chariot," jewel-encrusted gowns, and diamond-soled shoes, had put her own notorious stamp), the Queen's grandiose adornments became emblems of the monarchy's dark side: the absolutist power that enabled a king capriciously to bankroll unbridled female acquisitiveness.[159] Picking up on this association, Marie Antoinette's brother-in-law Provence remarked with more than a hint of Schadenfreude that because of her gewgaws and gimcracks, she was "held in much the same estimation as were formerly the mistresses of Louis XV."[160]

Ironically, this very analogy suggested that the public perceived Marie Antoinette's political clout as much greater than it really was. "Truly," the *Mémoires secrets* proclaimed in June 1775, "the Queen's credit with the King increases each day, as she presides over pleasures and [weightier] matters."[161] Yet if Marie Antoinette herself had worked toward this "appearance of credit" to compensate for her actual disenfranchisement in other arenas, she had apparently not anticipated its downside—which was that the French soundly distrusted any woman they saw as trying to wrest control from their monarch. And so, faced with the seemingly empowered consort's excesses, they lashed out at her—just as they had reviled Louis XV's mistresses in the previous reign.[162]

As in the case of Louis XV's paramours, the public's growing mistrust for Marie Antoinette was fueled largely by anxieties about a feminine shadow government secretly ruling France. Where they had once deplored Du Barry's behind-the-scenes role in catapulting Aiguillon and Maupeou to power, observers now decried Marie Antoinette's elevation of Léonard—to whom she accorded the unprecedented privilege of weekly Sunday-morning sessions in her rooms at court—and Bertin, whose ascendancy was even more dramatic. Claiming that the new headdresses required the attention of an expert, the Queen demanded that Bertin participate in her daily *toilette*. This decree infuriated the ladies whose rank conferred upon them this same cherished right.[163] Refusing to stand by while a lowly *marchande* usurped their privileges, many of Marie Antoinette's noble attendants abandoned the *toilette* in protest and shook their heads to see a mere "fashion worker become the most important personage in the Queen's life."[164]

Though this defection turned much of the court against her, the Queen seemed to welcome the reduction in her entourage, which she used as a pretext to relocate her *toilette* to the pretty suite of small, private apartments that abutted her public chambers. By tradition, only the loftiest nobles gained admittance to this area: even Voltaire, the nation's greatest living philosopher and Louis XV's own court historiographer, had been denied such a boon.[165] But for Bertin, Marie Antoinette again breezily suspended the rules. Several times a week, the *marchande de modes* and her mistress disappeared behind closed doors for hours at a time. According to Madame Campan, this left the excluded aristocrats to stew angrily among themselves and to speculate about the "vexing ramifications" that "the admission of a milliner in the Queen's private rooms" would have for the world as they knew it.[166]

Beyond the court, as well, Bertin's career trajectory had begun to attract considerable public notice. In August 1776, the government allowed the *marchandes de modes* to separate legally from the mercers and form a largely female guild that included peddlers of feathers and flowers.[167] Along with emancipating all would-be *marchandes de modes* from the patriarchal strictures that had once governed their practice, this change represented a clear victory for Bertin, who had opted to break the law rather than allow her marital status to determine her career. It was, moreover, a measure of her enterprise's financial health and strength that she employed thirty shopgirls at the Grand Mogol and entered into trade contracts with dozens of male and female suppliers (tailors, seamstresses, fabric dyers, feather merchants, lacemakers, and so on).[168] With her success unmatched by any of her peers, Bertin was herself a great mogul [*grand mogol*] and put a woman's face on the French luxury trade.

This success also translated into booming business abroad. Well-dressed women from England to Russia so coveted the French consort's ensembles that Bertin had to produce a new, life-sized *poupée de mode*—much larger than other such dolls, and endowed with the Queen's own face, figure, and hair—as a mannequin for her latest clothing and coiffure designs. In the previous reign, another stylist had done something similar by making a fashion doll in the likeness of Madame de Pompadour, "with a complete wardrobe consisting of formal court dress, . . . a *robe de négligée* for morning wear, [and] all sorts of hairstyles with appropriate accessories as well as written explanations and directions on how to put together the latest look."[169] This *poupée* had sparked such a frenzy when it arrived in England that a satirist writing for the *London Spectator* complained about women's inability even to concentrate on church sermons, so preoccupied were they with this "completely dressed [Pandora] just come from Paris."[170]

That Bertin's invention had an obvious, recent precedent in the Pompadour effigy can only have lent further weight to the comparisons Provence and others were making between Louis XV's mistresses and Louis XVI's queen. Nevertheless, the Marie Antoinette mannequin was an ingenious marketing device, for in the courts and capitals where even unnamed, unidentified Parisian Pandoras were awaited with breathless anticipation, there seemed to be something particularly exciting about a doll dressed up to look like the Queen of France herself. According to Louis Sébastien Mercier, an editor of *Le Journal des dames* and one of the era's most assiduous chroniclers of Parisian mores, fashionable ladies throughout Europe welcomed the oversized, overdressed mannequin with practically as much adulation and excitement as if they were meeting the sovereign herself.[171] A celebrated contemporary poet, the Abbé Delille, captured the sense of wondrous power that radiated from the *marchande* and her royal Pandora when he wrote of the pair: "Thus the sovereign of female ornamentation transports our tastes into Northern terrain, [and her] despotic mannequin dominates the universe."[172]

Needless to say, such formulations as this one spoke to the monumental, international influence that Bertin and the Queen achieved in their stylish collaborations, and French clothing exports received a tremendous boost from the women's shared high profile.[173] Yet Bertin's prominence in particular sparked significant resentment along both gender and class lines. In an era when female fashion merchants were still a relatively new driving force in the Parisian garment trade, the idea that Bertin—and not, say, her chief male competitor, Beaulard—should "dominate the universe" marked her as infringing on men's economic territory.[174]

Similarly, Bertin's success sounded an offensive note to many in the caste-conscious world of the *ancien régime,* for she was shameless in trying to parlay her financial triumph into a dizzying social ascent. As the daughter of a provincial gendarme, Bertin had absolutely no claims to class superiority. Yet in reinventing herself as—to use the phrase on the sign she hung outside her shop window—"*Marchande de Modes* to the Queen," she seemed to feel that this title justified her in dismissing any customer whom she deemed unworthy of notice.[175] Once, for example, she refused to fill a would-be client's order because she did not wish to outfit "the wife of a mere prosecutor from Bordeaux!"[176] That a prosecutor's wife ranked well above a policeman's daughter was of little consequence to Bertin: in her view, her genius alone merited special treatment. Nor did she hide this attitude from the aristocracy. On more than one occasion, the *marchande* even dared to treat noblewomen with disrespect, prompting the Baronne d'Oberkirch, who made a pilgrimage from her native Alsace to shop at the Grand Mogol, to describe Bertin as "puffed up with self-importance, behaving as if princesses were her equals."[177]

Bertin's sometime collaborator, Léonard, was equally offensive in his class pretensions. To obscure his own unimpressive origins (he came from Gascon peasant stock), he dressed in noblemen's discarded clothing, purchased from valets who, like the Queen's attendants, received the garments as the spoils of their service.[178] In this manner, he even acquired a pair of red-heeled shoes—which, in principle, only aristocratic men were entitled to wear—and he crowed to his friends that he was routinely mistaken for a marquis. Léonard also bought an imposing six-in-hand so that he might travel between Paris and Versailles "in superb style, aping the gentleman."[179] Though many courtiers found his antics infuriating, Madame de Genlis observed that Marie Antoinette and her friends welcomed the coiffeur as adoringly "as if he were King."[180] Much like Bertin, he appears to have taken this mark of aristocratic favor to mean that other clients were beneath him; supposedly, he once shouted at the lackey of a rich banker's wife: "Tell your mistress that Léonard does not dirty his hands with the heads of the middle classes!"[181]

By assuming class prerogatives to which they had not been born, Bertin and Léonard threw fuel on the fires of resentment that had long smoldered in public discourse about the nature of royal government. "In the eyes of the public," Chantal Thomas has noted, the Queen's unfairly elevated minions became "the incarnation of arbitrary royal preferences—and of the gains to be made from them."[182] As a woman, Bertin inspired a particularly ferocious backlash. By the early 1780s, the public had derisively labeled her Marie Antoinette's "Minister of Fashion" and "Minister of Trinkets."[183] Also by this time, the underground press, once preoccupied with Du Barry's corrupt, effeminizing ministry, had turned its unforgiving spotlight on Marie Antoinette's coterie.[184] One illicit pamphlet, which first appeared in 1781 and was in its seventeenth printing by the end of the decade, avowed that the Queen "works with Bertin in the same way that her august spouse works with his ministers of state."[185] This text sarcastically deemed Bertin a better politician than France's greatest and best-known ministers to kings: "Happy had it been for France had Louis XVI discovered as much sagacity as Antoinette in his choice of ministers. Sully, Colbert, and Richelieu, for management and finesse, were scarce to be compared to la Bertin!"[186]

The idea that the *marchande de modes* could operate on the same level as legendary power brokers like Colbert and Richelieu had two disturbing implications. First, it implied that Marie Antoinette indeed presided over a shadow cabinet, where effeminacy and frivolity "perverted the seriousness of affairs of state."[187] Certainly this seemed apparent in the Queen's response to the naval clash that occurred in June 1778 between the British, who were attempting to quell a colonial uprising in America, and the French, who had elected to side with the rebels.[188] The French frigate *La Belle Poule* carried the day, but its victory represented the beginning of France's long and costly military engagement in the American Revolution, funding for which the already overburdened Third Estate would be forced to provide. And although Marie Antoinette preached personal sacrifice, piously declaring that the nation needed new warships more than she needed new diamond jewelry, she paid homage to the conflict with her flashiest *pouf* to date: an enormous, fully rigged replica of *La Belle Poule* sailing on a sea of hair.[189] This gross, and of course costly, trivialization of current events—reprised later by a similar *coiffure à l'Indépendance*—did nothing to endear Marie Antoinette and her stylists to an already wary nation. As the costume historian Mary Frasko has noted, "engravings of the Queen with a tall ship in her hair were widely distributed to illustrate [her] preposterous extravagance."[190] (Plate 9.)

The second alarming aspect of the Bertin "ministry" was the inversion of power it appeared to have wrought in the monarchy's upper echelons, allowing women to displace men, and arbitrarily selected underlings to usurp their sovereigns' God-given right to rule.[191] This double blow to Salic Law and class privilege rankled the more conservative partisans of the *ancien régime.* The Baron de Frénilly revealed as much when he recorded: "Never was a minister guilty of perverting the King's will more widely cursed than Bertin was, for providing ornaments to the Queen."[192]

Yet even as they censured the consort's deference to her "minister," her detractors held her responsible for subjugating the French people to the trifling "laws of fashion." Of course, her primary victims were the women eager to imitate her styles, the staggering costs of which drove many to squander family fortunes or accumulate vast debts.[193] An extreme example of the problem was the Queen's friend the Princesse de Guéménée, whose husband was forced to declare bankruptcy in 1783 with unpaid debts of 6 million livres, including a staggering pile of bills from the Grand Mogol.[194] Yet despite these occasional setbacks, Bertin happily enabled her customers' binges by selling on credit, sometimes at interest rates of 10 percent or higher; and those *marchandes de modes* competing for her business often did the same.[195] Whether one was a noblewoman shopping at the Grand Mogol, or a petite bourgeoise trying to re-create such expensive modes "with cheaper ribbons, kerchiefs, and other trinkets," irrational exuberance was the name of the game.[196] One pocket-sized fashion almanac, the *Recueil général des costumes et modes,* appended to its collection of engravings a little accounting ledger to help readers keep track of their clothing expenses.[197] But by and large, female consumers seemed to throw caution to the wind and, as Madame Campan lamented, "the general consensus was that the Queen would ruin all the women in France."[198]

The problem, however, struck many as more far-reaching still. In their blind desperation to be chic, ladies' moral values were seen to be deteriorating in tandem with their finances. According to Mercier, 1.5 million young women were depleting their dowries for the sake of "those trimmings, those ribbons, those gauzes, those bonnets, those feathers and hats" that Marie Antoinette had brought into fashion.[199] When informed that their spending would make it impossible for them to marry, the stylish demoiselles replied breezily that they "were just as happy [buying] *poufs* as [getting] a husband."[200] In Mercier's (doubtless exaggerated) account, the very institution of marriage— not to mention the traditional availability of women's dowries for reinvestment in land—threatened to disappear because of the Queen's bad example.

Some women, critics claimed, manifested their newfound financial and sexual insouciance in even more dangerous ways. One journalist wrote, toward the end of 1776:

The Queen, all unwittingly it is true, has done irreparable injury to the nation. In the passionate desire to copy her example, women's dress has become so enormously expensive, that husbands, generally, are unable to pay for what is required, so lovers have become the fashion. [In this way,] Her Majesty . . . is a danger to the morals of the people.[201]

Striking a similar note, Léonard's autobiography alleged that "little working girls" too poor to imitate Marie Antoinette's hairstyles on their own earnings were forced, against their better judgment, to accept the strings-attached "offers of generous lovers."[202] In these reports, the Queen emerged—"all unwittingly, it is true"—as a catalyst not just of indebtedness, but of promiscuity and prostitution. Fatally tempted by her extravagant coiffures, decent women could no longer maintain their principles.[203] Marie Antoinette's high Parisian profile and high Parisian hairdos appeared to be eroding the moral fabric of the kingdom.

SUCH CHARGES OF IMMORALITY AND SEXUAL LICENSE WERE SOON LEVELED at the Queen herself, whose success as a fashion plate had done nothing to change her failure in the marriage bed. In this respect, she was not unlike the demoiselles Mercier criticized for squandering their dowries on useless *poufs:* she was making a huge investment in her beauty but accruing no tangible—familial—benefits. By contrast, the newest Bourbon bride, the Comtesse d'Artois, won few accolades for her comeliness or charm—she had a haughty manner, crossed eyes, and a nose as "villainous" as that of her sister, the Comtesse de Provence.[204] Yet Artois's wife defeated the Queen in what remained, for the monarchy and its public, the far more important female competition. In August 1775, the Comtesse gave birth to a son, and almost exactly a year later, to a daughter as well. On the occasion of the little boy's birth, the women who worked in the Halles fish market in Paris followed tradition and trooped to Versailles to offer their rowdy congratulations. On that same visit, they took the opportunity to lambaste the Queen directly, and in unsettlingly vulgar terms, about her abiding infertile state.[205]

Contributing to Marie Antoinette's failure in this arena was the fact that sexual encounters with her husband remained sporadic and futile. Even as he had grown fonder of his wife, and thus perhaps shed some of his psychological biases against getting too close to an Austrian princess, Louis XVI nevertheless continued to find sex an uncomfortable proposition, and the doctors to whom he and Marie Antoinette turned for counsel ascribed his discomfort to the congenital defect of phimosis: an overly tight foreskin that made intercourse prohibitively painful. However, when these physicians raised the subject of a curative surgery, the young man blanched and demanded reassurance that "there was still hope without 'the operation.' "[206] Although both husband and wife tried to keep these discussions as private as possible, the court was soon abuzz with rumors that the King was physically incapable of intercourse. And because, following Marie Antoinette's lead, palace aristocrats were spending more time than ever in Paris, these allegations fast reached the capital, too.[207] A popular ditty mocking Louis XVI for his debility contrasted his "sticky *prépuce* [foreskin]" with the Queen's "inherent *puce*": one of the colors she had famously brought into fashion.[208] The song foretold dire things for the future of the Bourbon line, for it alleged that between the King's crippling impotence and the Queen's all-consuming fashion follies, the couple had no "inherent" propensity to parenthood.

But although Louis XVI's supposed physical defects were now publicized as a cause of the couple's reproductive woes, it was Marie Antoinette who remained a focal point for charges of gross sexual misconduct. Most notably, a spate of underground pamphlets speculated that if the stylish consort was not spending so much time and money to look beautiful for her husband, then she must be doing so for a lover.[209] The Duc de Chartres probably funded many of these publications through his rabble-rousing contacts at the Palais Royal; others were sponsored by Provence, who also had his eye on the succession, and who maintained his own Parisian outpost at the Palais du Luxembourg.[210] Meanwhile, the Aunts gleefully spread the damaging gossip at Bellevue, the residence they had received as a gift from their nephew; and at Versailles, Provence, his wife, the Comtesse d'Artois, and any number of other nobles with vendettas against the Queen engaged in like banter. Secret agents working for England and Prussia, too, disseminated sordid tales about Marie Antoinette both in France and abroad, as did underground publishers hoping that the French crown would pay them off to desist in their publications.[211] With the exception of this last group, whose motivations were largely financial, many of these parties had political reasons for casting aspersions on Marie Antoinette's moral character. For, like the anti-*barryste* pamphlets of the previous reign, these stories implied that Louis XVI's régime itself was disorderly and debased. And should this king's government falter in earnest, especially before he managed to produce an heir, then the likes of Chartres and Provence, England and Prussia, all stood to reap tremendous political gains.

Yet as high as the political stakes were, the tone of the intrigue was consistently low as the participants focused relentlessly on Marie Antoinette's alleged extramarital activities. As one of her best-looking and most frequent companions, the Comte d'Artois emerged as a prime suspect on the list of her possible lovers, and this notion spawned pornographic libels accusing

Artois and his sister-in-law of incest. One of these pamphlets, written in the voice of Maria Theresa, offered the Queen a scandalous bit of mock advice alluding to Artois's place in the succession: "My daughter, give birth to a successor; it does not matter who the father is—whether he sits on the throne, or right behind it."[212] This quip took aim at Louis XVI's masculinity and authority by targeting him as a hapless cuckold; but it also positioned Marie Antoinette as a brazen harlot who would not hesitate to contaminate the French royal line with a baby born of incest.

Those building a case against the consort's wifely virtue also found evidence in her clothing orders from the Grand Mogol. Because Bertin had a fondness for the romantic, the trimmings and fabrics she peddled bore such names as "stifled sighs," "Venus' sigh," "masked desire," "unfulfilled wishes," "the heart's agitation," "a sweet smile," "a sign of hope," "marked attention," "assured conquest," "indiscreet pleasures," "despair," and "regrets."[213] Such provocative nomenclature did little to dispel notions about the sexual immorality of fashion's devotees. When its terms were applied to the Queen, whose "unfulfilled wishes" in the marriage bed were a matter of public record, they marked her as an "assured conquest" for gentlemen other than her spouse.

Marie Antoinette's reputation also suffered when fabricated stories of her licentiousness achieved notoriety through new trends in clothing. One of the earliest pamphlets against her, written shortly after Louis XVI's accession, drew its inspiration from a real-life episode: a night when the Queen and some of her friends decided to stay up all night and watch the sun rise from the gardens behind their palace. Although the outing had, like so many of Marie Antoinette's rebellious adventures, been innocent enough, it had sparked furious court gossip that soon found its way into a clandestine, scurrilous pamphlet. This text, entitled "Le Lever de l'Aurore" ("The Sunrise"), retold the outing as a crazed sexual free-for-all, with Marie Antoinette and a slew of paramours copulating feverishly in the bushes.[214]

Virtually overnight, the story created a sensation in Versailles, Paris, and even abroad. (As France's new ambassador to Vienna, Louis de Rohan deepened the rift between himself and Marie Antoinette by gleefully circulating the text throughout her native city.[215]) Although an outraged Louis XVI moved to have all copies of the libel found and destroyed, and had its presumed author thrown in prison, the scene it described became part of public legend. Just three years later, the story resurfaced in the form of a fashionable and somewhat risqué new garment: a gauzy, sensuously billowing little cape called the *mantelet au Lever de l'Aurore*. In at least one contemporary fashion plate, the garment's wearer bore a marked resemblance to Marie Antoinette.[216]

Furthermore, because of the widespread emulation her fashions inspired, the clear social distinctions that had once been apparent in Frenchwomen's dress began to blur. The Comte de Camaran complained that "bourgeoises, artisans' wives, and chambermaids all try to approximate as closely as they can the outfits worn by women of quality; indeed, their eyes are always fixed on these outfits and they imitate them even in their most ridiculous details."[217] As a result, another aristocrat sneered, "it stopped being possible to tell a duchess from an actress."[218] In eighteenth-century France, "actress" was more or less synonymous with "prostitute," and women of both professions joined the Queen in frequenting the Palais Royal, where they all swooned over the same heady fashion displays. They also joined the Queen in patronizing Léonard, always a favorite with actresses and courtesans, and Bertin, whose client list included none other than the disgraced (if still moneyed) Madame Du Barry.[219] The resulting erosion of visible boundaries between sovereign and guttersnipe bred still more animosity against Marie Antoinette. As one underground writer noted with scorn, "The most elegant whore in Paris could not be more tarted up than the Queen."[220] Maria Theresa echoed this view when she scoffed that a portrait she had received of her daughter, dressed in full feathered regalia, surely depicted an actress and not a sovereign.[221]

The Queen was reportedly so infuriated by this remark that she responded by sporting even higher, flashier plumage than ever before. Court gossips were quick to publicize her gesture, and when the news reached the Empress, her relations with her daughter became noticeably chillier.[222] Yet Maria Theresa's criticism had been prescient, as the people located additional evidence for the putative kinship between Marie Antoinette and Paris's actress-prostitutes in the Queen's visits to the Paris Opéra balls. These events drew participants from a broad range of backgrounds—including courtesans—and were notorious hotbeds of romance and intrigue because people dissimulated their identities behind masks and cloaks (dominoes).[223] While under other circumstances the contact across class lines was limited, at the Opéra balls strangers were able to chat and flirt boldly with no concern for their respective social positions. Sometimes, illicit intercaste assignations ensued. This tantalizing possibility only existed, however, to the extent that revelers dressed homogeneously enough to keep their social rank a mystery.[224] "Kept women, duchesses, and bourgeoises," Mercier observed, "all of them hid beneath the same dominoes."[225] Apparently, female revelers took special pains to hide their hair, perhaps because their customized *poufs* were easily recognizable. Enterprising fashion merchants thus offered a "*pouf* covered with a transparent veil": a confection whose eponymous, see-through veil fostered the illusion of mystery, while still making visible the intricate headdress underneath.[226]

Although it required the temporary abandonment of her hallmark coiffures, the chance at anonymity was apparently what Marie Antoinette loved most about parties at the Opéra. "Wearing some coquettish domino," Stefan Zweig relates, "she could shake off the chill and exalted trappings of etiquette to descend into the warm turmoil of ordinary human life": thus, she adopted nonroyal stature as still another transgressive and exhilarating costume.[227] Most often, she would chat excitedly with a group of strangers until somebody recognized her. After being discovered (which happened every time, according to the Prince de Ligne, no matter how hard the Queen tried to remain incognito), she would gather her friends about her and take umbrage in a private loge, leaving the other revelers to murmur in astonishment at her daring.[228]

But although the Queen's Opéra capers were harmless enough, they were soon equated with those of the "kept women," actresses, and prostitutes also in attendance. One evening in 1778, when she was spotted flirting with the famous actor Dugazon, easily identifiable despite his fishwife's disguise, the public did not hesitate to imagine them as lovers.[229] On another night, a guest who recognized Marie Antoinette beneath her black domino allegedly excoriated her to her face "for failing in her duty as a good wife, who should remain at home with her husband and not go to balls without him."[230] It was true that Louis XVI rarely accompanied her on these excursions, a fact that only seemed to corroborate theories about her impure motives for making them.

Even her less risqué trips to the Opéra inspired censure along these lines. In the 1770s, Madame Campan remembered, a comely dancer named Marie Madeleine Guimard "always played the starring roles" at the Opéra, and Marie Antoinette rarely missed a performance.[231] Between this and the fact that Léonard served as the dancer's hairdresser, the pamphleteers seemed to feel justified in listing Guimard—who owed her fame as much to her string of wealthy lovers as to her artistic talent—among the Queen's dubious cronies.[232] Perhaps not incidentally, Guimard had during Louis XV's reign been a protégée of Madame Du Barry, at whose behest she had even received a small royal pension.[233] That the public now ascribed to Guimard a friendship with Marie Antoinette attests to the ever diminishing perceived distance between lofty sovereign and lowly trollop.[234]

One of the gossip sheets attested to this collapse in social categories when it identified the dancer as the nation's new "Minister for Muslins and Dresses": further proof that Marie Antoinette had the tastes of a whore.[235] Still another pamphlet asserted that Guimard colluded with Rose Bertin to "direct the amours of the Queen": "these Machiavellian females" were "deeply versed in the arts of Venus" and actively complicit in the Queen's "licentious dissipations."[236] In this account, Marie Antoinette did not simply dress like a prostitute—she *was* a prostitute, tricked up and pimped out by her lowborn, fashion-obsessed female lackeys.

Unleashed by her love affair with Parisian mode, aspersions of this kind would haunt the Queen until her death, gaining particular force and momentum after the Bastille fell in 1789. But already in these first years of her reign, her attempts to convey an "appearance of credit" backfired and told an infuriating, horrifying tale.[237] Rather than shower blessings on a starving land, Marie Antoinette had stolen flour from her people's mouths and led her imitators into a financial and moral abyss. Rather than uphold the King's sacred authority, she had relinquished it to a pack of parvenus and strumpets. Rather than purge Du Barry's "Seminary of Debauch," she had revived it in her own flamboyant style. And although this new seminary at first seemed confined to the nation's decadent capital, the people soon discovered that it had another headquarters: a little country palace called the Petit Trianon.

SIX

THE SIMPLE LIFE

In June 1774, a month after acceding to the throne, Louis XVI made his wife a gift of the Petit Trianon, a small but exquisite neoclassical château located just a quarter league from Versailles. Louis XV had first commissioned it in 1761 as a pleasure palace for Madame de Pompadour, but as she died before building was completed, he "inaugurated" it with Madame Du Barry in 1770. Sympathetic to his wife's distaste for the regimented life of the court, the new king appears to have recognized her need for a sanctuary all her own, and to have seen in the unoccupied villa a ready means of satisfying that desire.[1] "You are fond of flowers," he is said to have told her, "so I give you this whole bouquet."[2]

To Marie Antoinette, who indeed adored flowers, the building proved every bit as enchanting as Louis XVI's metaphor implied. A masterpiece of the late Ange-Jacques Gabriel, the same architect whom Louis XV had charged with completing the wondrous *salle de spectacles* for his grandson's wedding feast, the Petit Trianon had been designed with a delicate, light-hearted sensibility that seemed to emphasize its physical and spiritual distance from Versailles. Where that palace's architecture and décor functioned to overawe the people who walked through its doors, and to remind them of the sovereign's inconceivably superior glory, Trianon was intended to delight its visitors and put them at ease. Ceiling heights in the little castle were relatively low, the scale of the rooms comfortable and intimate. In place of heavy gilded moldings and thick slabs of marble, pale boiseries of garlanded wildflowers dominated the décor. Wall coverings and draperies were fashioned not from the heavy, regally colored satins and brocades that abounded at Versailles, but from light muslins and sweet, subtly patterned silks.[3]

Struck by the Petit Trianon's freshness and simplicity, the Queen promptly and enthusiastically set about transforming the place into a laboratory for a program of broad-based aesthetic and cultural experimentation. From the gardens to the interiors, and from the costumes she and her invited guests wore to the kinds of activities and behavior she encouraged there, Marie Antoinette designed virtually every aspect of life at her villa along the understated, informal lines suggested by its architecture. Taken together, her innovations established a domain where none of the usual courtly rules applied, and—in a different if no less dramatic way than her Parisian *poufs*—announced her ever-increasing confidence as she continued to forge her own, iconoclastic path as Queen. The Petit Trianon, too, would form part of her revolution in fashion, serving as both a backdrop and a showcase for a conspicuously emancipated, empowered consort.[4] Yet, like the glamorous styles she developed with Rose Bertin, the innovativeness of Marie Antoinette's country retreat would attract her subjects' fierce disapproval, even as it aimed to bolster her autonomy and enhance her prestige.

IT BEARS NOTING THAT IN RECONFIGURING THE PETIT TRIANON TO REFLECT her personal tastes and desires, Marie Antoinette, like many celebrated trendsetters, did not so much invent a brand-new stylistic vocabulary as draw on preexisting cultural currents and personalize them with her own, unmistakable flair. Chief among these currents was the tradition of the pastoral—the so-called cult of the simple life—which had long held an important place in French literary and courtly life.[5] Perhaps most notably, in the seventeenth century, aristocrats enamored of the long, bucolic novel *Astraea* had staged elaborate performances, disguised as the shepherds and shepherdesses that the book introduced as its protagonists.[6] A century later, the ideal of a natural existence, unspoiled by the corrupting elements of modern life, had very much returned to favor, thanks above all to the Swiss-born philosopher and novelist Jean-Jacques Rousseau. As is well known, Rousseau's writings linked the luxuries of "refined" civilization to underlying, deplorable socioeconomic iniquities, and thus assumed a deep and revolutionary political valence for critics of *ancien régime* social structures in the latter decades of the eighteenth century.[7] Yet these texts—some of which made their way into Marie Antoinette's library at the Petit Trianon—also spawned a somewhat more superficial, if no less passionate, vogue for all things unpretentious and rustic.[8] Certainly for Louis XVI's queen, with her pronounced aversion to the stifling protocol of Versailles, Rousseau's call to cast off the shackles of conventional luxury appears to have held considerable appeal.[9] In this context, the Petit Trianon provided her the perfect canvas on which to sketch out the contours of a freer and simpler—but still exhilaratingly stylish—life on the fringes of the royal court.

To begin her experiment in pastoral living, Marie Antoinette focused less on clothing per se than on the surroundings in which her unfettered new existence would unfold. After receiving the château from her husband, she went straight to work with Richard Mique, Gabriel's successor as the architect of the Petit Trianon, to deepen and expand the villa's alluringly unstudied ambience. To her bedroom, she added a lovely little salon whose boiseries featured lushly carved roses, traditional Hapsburg symbols, which happened to be her favorite flowers. For her new library, she ordered apple-green taffeta curtains and wooden paneling painted in the softest shade of white.[10] The private theater boasted airy ceiling frescoes representing Apollo (forebear of both Medea and the Caesars), robin's-egg-blue wall coverings, sculptures made of papier-mâché, and glass-stone ornamentation made to resemble precious gems.[11] Along with Marie Antoinette's collections of crystals, shells, Japanese lacquerware, and petrified wood, the villa's cabinets of curiosities were filled to bursting with flowers made of delicate china and enamel.[12] And throughout the place, light-colored textiles embroidered with cheerful bouquets—roses and jasmine, apple blossoms and lilies of the valley—brightened the furnishings and the walls and augmented the prevailing sense of relaxed, casual elegance.

To extend this cozy, countrified atmosphere to the grounds around the palace, Marie Antoinette elected to replace some of the existing, rigidly geometrical landscaping of André Le Nôtre—a holdover from Louis XIV's theatrically formal era—with the artistically untended atmosphere of a contemporary English garden. Brought into fashion by Rousseau's best-selling sentimental novel *Julie, or the New Heloise* (1761), the *jardin anglais* was meant to look as though it had been planted, as Rousseau himself had stipulated, "without order and without symmetry," for an effect that was "charming, but uncultivated and wild."[13] Adhering to this model, the English garden of the Petit Trianon therefore featured rolling meadows, a meandering river, random-looking plantings of trees and shrubbery, and, everywhere, casually strewn clusters of flowers.[14]

For outbuildings, Mique suggested a profusion of artificial ruins, but Marie Antoinette vetoed this detail as too obviously picturesque. Instead, she ordered the construction of a perfectly turned neoclassical belvedere, a mysterious grotto with a waterfall, and a small, columned rotunda called the Temple of Love, which sat on a tiny island overgrown with lilac bushes and rose trees. The result was a subtly romantic landscape—a fusion of pastoral charm and neoclassical restraint—opposed in every way to the imposing grandeur of Versailles.[15]

Its low-key ambience notwithstanding, the Queen's palace quickly emerged, like her court costume parties and her Parisian modes, as a symbol of her favorite-like ascendancy over Louis XVI, and not just because the place had originally been designed as a love nest for the former king and his paramour. As mistresses of their own private residences, Mesdames de Pompadour and Du Barry had attained an impressive, indeed enviable, degree of freedom when away from Versailles: they had hosted their own parties, seen their own friends, indulged in their own favorite hobbies and decorative whims, and, to a lesser or greater extent, abandoned the rituals of the court. In this way, the favorites' personal homes represented extensions as well as assertions of their unusual and unequaled power.

With the Petit Trianon, Marie Antoinette managed to achieve a similar degree of freedom and control, and she went to great lengths to underscore the notion that the realm of Trianon was ruled by her and her alone. For instance, it was her personal cipher—not her husband's—that she had affixed to the wrought-iron staircase in the central hall and embossed on the book bindings in the library. She also expressed her independence in the customized livery of scarlet and silver that she required the staff of the Petit Trianon to wear, to differentiate them from officers of the King's household, who wore uniforms of white, blue, and red, the traditional royal colors. Perhaps most strikingly, all regulations that governed Trianon were issued "By Order of the Queen"— an unprecedented feminization of the standard monarchical decree. Symbolically, this formula transformed even Louis XVI himself, who liked to stop by for the occasional hearty luncheon, into just another of the chatelaine's obedient subjects. His cheerful, uncomplaining subordination to his consort's wishes—an astonishing abandonment of the supreme mastery the King was thought to enjoy over all his people, including his wife—confirmed the impression that Marie Antoinette's "credit" knew no bounds.

Paradoxically, then, the Queen's very move toward a simplified lifestyle bolstered the appearance of her royal power, as members of the French public came very quickly to realize. For at court, noblemen's rank granted them varying degrees of royal access whether the monarchs wished to see them or not; at Trianon, admittance required a special invitation from the Queen herself. Similarly, whereas Versailles was open to all members of the public, the entrances to the Petit Trianon were locked and guarded to exclude unwanted visitors. And whereas at court, she was required to bear up constantly under the scrutiny of countless onlookers, now, in her new domain, Marie Antoinette took control of her image by withdrawing it from the public eye. The decision challenged both aristocrats and commoners in their expectation of finding the Queen, a living symbol of her husband's glorious reign, ever available for viewing; and it revealed the degree to which Marie Antoinette was willing to sally forth on her own, and to determine her own destiny, with no input from either the people or the King.

The funds that the Queen was able to channel into her new architectural project also enhanced her appearance of power, for as usual, her expenditures indicated her exalted place in the court pecking order—and, like her more extravagant Parisian fashions, the Petit Trianon's understated loveliness came at a terrific price. One year, she spent over 350,000 livres on landscaping improvements, which required, for example, relocating and replanting an entire forest from the royal nurseries at La Rochette.[16] And the party that she hosted in September 1777 to celebrate the completion of the Temple of Love cost a whopping 400,000 livres. Conceived as a *fête galante*—a relaxed outdoor idyll of the sort made famous in the paintings of Antoine Watteau—this event took place in a temporarily constructed village square containing fairgrounds, a marketplace with a variety of food stands, and a "tavern where the drinks were poured by the ladies of the court, while the Queen dispensed lemonade."[17] At dusk, twenty-three hundred colored lanterns bathed the gardens in rosy light, and the band of the Royal French Guard, outfitted in fanciful "Chinese" uniforms, provided the music for dancing.[18]

To those lucky enough to secure an invitation, this fête offered a titillating change of pace from the stuffier, more formal functions of the court. But those left behind at Versailles—those whom the hostess had overlooked without regard for the illustriousness of their name or the longevity of their service—groused bitterly about the costs. So, too, did the commoners, who were accustomed to flooding the parterres of Versailles whenever the court was having a party.[19] (Marie Antoinette apparently loathed this practice; when the public invaded the gardens of Versailles, she often dodged their curious stares by cloaking herself in a domino and wandering about incognito, as if she were at an Opéra ball.[20]) As when contemplating their Queen's sartorial follies, members of the aristocracy and the Third Estate found common ground in decrying her country soirées, which literally and figuratively declared her independence at their expense.

Marie Antoinette's subjects also recoiled at the drastic suspension of etiquette that she introduced at the Petit Trianon, thereby even more thoroughly repudiating the stultifying rigidity that held sway at her husband's court. "By Order of the Queen," guests at the estate were instructed not to stop talking and not to rise from their seats when their sovereign entered the room. "Conversations continued, ladies did not interrupt their embroidery or music making," Evelyne Lever has written. "The Queen took a seat among her guests, wherever she wished. . . . No one was to feel any constraint." [21] Nor was anyone to carry out the myriad other formalities that prevailed at Versailles. Not coincidentally, most of the attendants charged with overseeing rituals like the *toilette* and the *coucher* were unwelcome at Marie Antoinette's retreat, and in this, too, she signaled her unwillingness to abide by long-standing court tradition. In lieu of her *dame d'atours,* she kept Rose Bertin on hand to help her dress. In lieu of her *dames du palais,* she surrounded herself with friends like the Princesse de Lamballe and the heartbreakingly beautiful Comtesse Jules de Polignac, whom the Queen first adopted into her circle in the summer of 1776. [22] Although the favoritism she showed these companions represented a flagrant defiance of royal protocol, Marie Antoinette found their company infinitely preferable to that of the "centuries" and "high collars" whose rank entitled them to besiege her constantly at court, and whose stuffy formality she had never made a secret of despising. At the Petit Trianon, she told the Comtesse Jules, "I am me"—and for her, that transformation from a public consort into a private subject involved the unprecedented replacement of her retinue by friends of her own choosing. [23]

The men she invited to the Petit Trianon offered a similarly welcome change from the dullards of the old guard. Along with the perennially fun-loving Comte d'Artois, Marie Antoinette's preferred male guests included the Duc de Guines and the Duc de Coigny, both of them suave, well-mannered, and ambitious; the Baron de Besenval, who having reached his fifties was somewhat past his prime, but who remained a great raconteur of salty stories; the Comte d'Esterhazy, a handsome young man thought to be more trustworthy than Guines or Besenval, though he relied on Louis XVI to pay his gambling debts; the aging, debonair Prince de Ligne; and the legendary seducer the Duc de Lauzun, who had once bedded a cross-dressed equestrienne against his better judgment. [24] The most doted-upon of the crew was Count Axel von Fersen, an aristocratic Swedish officer the same age as Marie Antoinette whose virile manner and elegant, chiseled features first attracted her at an Opéra ball in 1775, and who in subsequent years became the great love of her life. [25]

Like Fersen, most of the Trianon regulars were foreigners—Lamballe came from the Piedmont, Esterhazy from Hungary, Besenval from Switzerland, and Ligne from Belgium—and so did not boast the genealogical or historical ties to the French monarchy that usually led to special royal favor. [26] By lavishing her attention on relative outsiders who did not, by the traditional standards of Versailles, deserve such privileged treatment, Marie Antoinette again provoked considerable jealousy among the courtiers excluded from her private domain. In this, too, she broke dramatically with court etiquette. But her chosen companions' very foreignness may have contributed to the appeal they held for her, for they, perhaps less than staunch French denizens of the court, were not prone to object when Marie Antoinette urged them to abandon the tiresome protocol of Versailles. (Besenval in particular was described as "full of new suggestions for the discomfiture of etiquette," though perhaps the fact that he was Rousseau's countryman contributed to this perception.[27]) During the day, they joined her in perching on the belvedere's moss-covered benches, boating in the lake beside the grotto, picnicking on the grass, and engaging in raucous outdoor games like *descampativos,* a version of blindman's buff.[28] At night, if they elected to stay inside, the friends held impromptu concerts (Marie Antoinette played the clavichord and sang, although she supposedly had little talent for either art), gambled recklessly, and traded wicked gossip about the people excluded from their clique. For evenings outdoors, they built great bonfires at the Temple of Love, transformed by the flames into "the brightest spot in the gardens, while the smoke twined wreaths among the branches overhead, and brightly colored figures moved through the shadows and the shafts of light."[29] Despite the mounting envy and disapproval of the courtiers she had abandoned at Versailles, these adventures allowed the Queen to liberate herself from the oppressive curbs and restraints of royal life.

She seized another opportunity along these lines beginning in the summer of 1780, when Mique put the final touches on Trianon's private theater. With this new resource at their disposal, the Queen and her crew took up dramatic productions with abandon, performing comedies and light operas by popular contemporary authors such as Rousseau, Sedaine, Marmontel, and Beaumarchais.[30] And whenever possible, Marie Antoinette insisted on playing the role of the saucy peasant or servant girl, like Colette in Rousseau's *The Village Soothsayer* and Rosine in Beaumarchais's *Barber of Seville.* According to Madame Campan, "the greatest happiness" her mistress derived from these productions "consisted in having the most elegant and faithfully observed costumes," though surviving drawings by the men in the Menus Plaisirs charged with designing the troupe's outfits show that Marie Antoinette's servant girls were sumptuously attired indeed: all flouncy, intricately embroidered skirts and high, bobbing feathers.[31] Yet notwithstanding the elegance of her stage clothes, her lowly character roles extended her fantasy of living a simple life and provided her with yet another escape from the demands of her rank. Resistant since his youth to these same demands, Louis XVI—who often constituted the players' sole audience—chuckled delightedly at his wife's daring masquerades.[32]

The King's subjects were considerably less amused by his consort's flirtation with lower-class existence. As Madame Campan noticed, those bluebloods whom Marie Antoinette kept away from the Petit Trianon were especially resentful, and they fixated on her nonroyal antics as proof that she had lost all respect for Bourbon dignity and tradition.[33] Originating in the Oeil-de-Boeuf, where courtiers gossiped peevishly among themselves while waiting for Louis XVI to enter or exit his apartments, tales of his wife's bad behavior traveled to Paris, often by way of those same courtiers, who through the usual avenues of gossip and clandestine literature incensed other members of the public over the Queen's blatant disrespect for the throne.

Public disapproval of Marie Antoinette's conduct intensified in the spring of 1779, when during a bout of the measles she decided to stay overnight at the Petit Trianon, and holed up there for several days. (Before this episode, she had made only day trips to the place, between command performances at Versailles.) This extended stay flew in the face of the long-standing custom by which the monarch remained constantly before the aristocracy's eyes, as a sublime object of their worshipful attention. For Marie Antoinette, having a palace to call her own—and to disappear to for days on end—meant shrugging off this most hateful of her royal burdens. Although La Bruyère, the great aphorist of Louis XIV's court, had famously remarked that Bourbon princes were entitled to everything but "the pleasures of a private life," these were the very pleasures to which the Queen tried to lay claim by making Trianon a true second home.

Besides excluding her official entourage and all other unwelcome visitors, Marie Antoinette took additional, aggressive measures in her pursuit of privacy. While lounging in the gardens of the Petit Trianon, she and her friends often congregated inside a blue taffeta tent equipped with Venetian blinds, which stymied voyeurs' attempts to gawk at them from afar.[34] During parties, they directed porters to expel unceremoniously any and all gate-crashers. The rule was strict enough that when Marie Antoinette found out in May 1782 that her enemy Louis de Rohan, by then a cardinal, had managed to sneak into one of her outdoor parties with his crimson cardinal's stockings insufficiently hidden under a dark cloak, she summarily fired the concierge who had allowed him onto the property.[35]

As a prince from one of France's most powerful families, Rohan was, like many other nobles barred from the Petit Trianon, having a hard time accepting banishment from his sovereign's presence.[36] But Marie Antoinette appeared utterly disinclined to gratify her adversaries' pretensions or to soothe their wounded pride. Every night, a special mechanism shuttered her villa's windows with mirrors that rose from the floors. Thus, even a would-be spy crafty enough to elude the guards, gates, and watchful guests would, upon attempting to peek indoors, see nothing but his own abashed reflection.[37]

. . .

HUMILIATED BY THEIR EXCLUSION AND OUTRAGED BY MARIE AN-
toinette's defiance, the shunned aristocrats revived the French party's old
moniker for the Queen, *l'Autrichienne*, and launched a new series of xenophobic attacks against her. Asserting that this Hapsburg princess had never
successfully adapted to the formal refinements of the French court—no one
had forgotten her long-ago war with the corset—they baptized Trianon "little Vienna" and "little Schönbrunn."[38] (One newcomer to Versailles heard
these terms used in such dead earnest that he actually referred to the Queen's
palace as "little Vienna" when writing to her secretary to request admittance.[39]) Despite her ritual divestment of all Austrian accoutrements when
she first arrived in France, her white blank slate of a body had failed to live
up to its promise as a site of inscription for Bourbon custom; as the historian
Thomas E. Kaiser has persuasively argued, Marie Antoinette "was suspected
of not having sufficiently exchanged national identities."[40] Starkly manifest
in her unconventional doings at Trianon, her aversion to protocol and her
desire for privacy were construed by her enemies less as extensions of a
proto-naturalist Rousseauean worldview than as damning signs of her unreformed "Austrian heart" and her vile "German" barbarism.[41]

When her brother Joseph II traveled to Versailles in the spring of 1777, he
did little to dispel the stereotypical image of Austrian crudeness that prevailed at Versailles at that time. Already, Kaiser has noted, Marie Antoinette's
subjects were predisposed against her brother because of his "erratic foreign
policy opposed to French interests."[42] And although he went a long way toward reversing this perception during his visit, the Emperor's success with
the French people had nothing to do with his attitude toward their aristocratic customs, to which he unapologetically declined to conform. He was a
serious reader of Enlightenment authors like Rousseau; and since his accession twelve years earlier, one of his pet projects had been to eradicate needless formality from Viennese court customs and dress.[43] His own clothing
was thus markedly sober and modest for a man of his standing; and when he
toured the French capital, the fishwives of the Halles market marveled aloud
at the difference between the bourgeois-looking Joseph II and the lavishly
overdressed Comte d'Artois. This incident won the Emperor points with the
common folk, but appalled certain members of the aristocracy.[44]

Joseph II caused perhaps an even greater stir when, attending his sister's
toilette at Versailles, he mocked her and her ladies for wearing too much
rouge and compared them aloud to the bloodstained Furies of classical
mythology.[45] The Queen, who had by now been living in *ce pays-ci* for seven
years, was horrified by her brother's flagrant criticism of this long-standing

local convention; she scarcely seemed to recognize the degree to which his resistance to court etiquette mirrored her own past and present rebellions. This point of commonality between the siblings may not, however, have been lost on Marie Antoinette's detractors, who alleged that in the event of her untimely death, she planned to leave "little Vienna" to Joseph II as a Hapsburg outpost right in Versailles's backyard.[46]

But despite the stir his Germanic oddities caused among some of his sister's compatriots, the Emperor had traveled to France to address two issues of considerable importance to that nation: Marie Antoinette's unrestrained spending and her husband's unaccountable sexual reticence.[47] By all accounts, the first part of his mission yielded no positive results. When Joseph II jested about the Queen's plumes being too flimsy to support a crown, she ignored him outright. And when he urged her more explicitly to stay her clothing expenditures, she replied that if she were to do so, "two hundred places of business would have to close their doors tomorrow."[48] (This was doubtless not far from the truth, given the copious sums the Queen funneled into the Parisian luxury market, and given the large network of suppliers and tradespeople who served the Grand Mogol alone.[49]) Like Maria Theresa, who since her reported outburst over her daughter's "actress"-like plumage was finding her ever more impervious to scolding, the Emperor could do nothing to curb Marie Antoinette's stylish follies. To these, the Queen remained staunchly committed, and neither her Austrian family nor her French subjects were going to sway her from her fashion-forward course.

Joseph II did, however, succeed in the second part of his mission, which involved treating the King to a frank lecture about the nature of the sex act and enjoining him to become "more than two-thirds of a husband" to the Queen. For although the Emperor's brusqueness bordered on menacing—he later admitted that he wished he could have just flogged his brother-in-law "until he ejaculated like an enraged donkey"—a rough harangue was, it seems, precisely what Louis XVI needed to hear.[50] Appearing finally to realize that neither psychological resistance nor physical discomfort could excuse him from his husbandly duties, the young man resolved to put his fears behind him once and for all. Not long after Joseph II left Versailles, the French king and his wife consummated their union "completely" for the first time in its seven-year history. After overcoming this hurdle, the couple began sleeping together on a somewhat more regular basis, and a year later, Marie Antoinette was pregnant. On December 19, 1778, after eight and a half years of thwarted dynastic expectations, she at last gave birth to a baby girl: Marie Thérèse Charlotte, to be known by the august title "Madame Royale" once she reached the age of five. The birth itself was traumatic because, like virtually all events in Marie Antoinette's life at Versailles, it had to take place in public, and the crush of spectators almost suffocated her. Nonetheless, she and her husband were ecstatic at the baby's advent, and they both gratefully attributed Marie Thérèse's arrival to the Emperor's blunt bedroom advice.[51]

YET NEITHER JOSEPH II'S GOOD OFFICES NOR HIS SISTER'S SUCCESS IN FI-nally bearing a child dispelled the animosity that "little Vienna" continued to inspire. Where Mercy, who as Austria's ambassador may have been particularly attuned to the xenophobic rumblings against the Queen, had expressed a hope that the blessed event would at last force the nation to "regard her as French," gossips dwelled instead on the possibility that the baby was illegitimate—fathered by Artois or one of the other dandies in the Trianon crowd.[52] Moreover, it seems unlikely that Marie Antoinette's decision to name her daughter after her Austrian mother bolstered the public's readiness to hail the new arrival as a Child of France.[53]

Indeed, when in March 1779 the royal family traveled to Notre-Dame in Paris for a formal celebration of Marie Thérèse's birth, their cavalcade was met not with the cheering masses that normally turned out for such occasions, but (as Mercy reported to the Empress) with crowds gathered alongside the roads in grim, stony silence. Only upon seeing the Queen and her husband wave toward Rose Bertin—who was watching the twenty-eight-carriage cortège from the balcony of the Great Mogul—did the bystanders become animated.[54] But their animation was anything but friendly. At a time when a nod or a smile from a monarch was a precious sign of royal beneficence, commoners and courtiers alike blanched to see a mere *marchande* receive such a boon—particularly the same *marchande* whom Marie Antoinette had just paid 500 livres to make a gold brocaded dress for the Virgin's shrine at Monflières, in thanksgiving for the birth.[55] Though ostensibly an occasion for sheer joy, the monarchs' procession thus revived long-standing animosities against the Queen and her "ministry of fashion" and cast a pall over the remainder of the day's festivities.[56]

The newborn's sex also elicited disgruntlement, since, being a girl, Marie Thérèse did nothing whatsoever to ensure her father's succession. Marie Antoinette herself tried to make the best of this far from optimal situation by declaring tearfully that a son would have belonged to the nation, whereas a daughter could be hers alone.[57] True to her word, after recovering from the delivery, the Queen began absconding more often than ever to Trianon, with only her baby, a nursemaid, and a handful of female friends in tow. This practice invited censure as well, for although Bourbon daughters could not inherit the crown, they were still expected to function as public figures at court.[58] (Even as infants, the Children of France provided courtiers with the opportunity to jockey for coveted positions in the royal service.) By taking Marie Thérèse away from Versailles on a regular basis, the Queen again disclosed—and seemed to be inculcating a French royal scion with—her offensive, "Austrian" disregard for local protocol.[59]

But the Queen's visits to Trianon posed even more serious problems for her public image. If, on the one hand, her cultivation of a private life implied a trivialization and degradation of her public duties, on the other, it pointed to the emergence of a hidden, separate sphere of influence where the usual rules did not apply.[60] On this second count, Bertin's rise to power had already generated tremendous anxiety, as it seemed to indicate that the King had ceded his authority to a pack of frivolous, scheming women. Marie Antoinette's establishment of the Petit Trianon as her explicitly private domain, populated only by intimates of her choosing, sent much the same message.

If, moreover, anxiety about the Bertin "ministry" had led Marie Antoinette's adversaries to condemn it in sexual terms, casting the Queen as a prostitute and the *marchande* as her procuress, alarm about the hidden doings at Trianon likewise fueled the public's mounting obsession with the consort's sex life. In particular, the mirrors that blocked the palace's windows at night inspired comment about what its mistress was endeavoring to hide. At a time when clandestine erotic literature featured mirror-lined, secret boudoirs as a key thematic device, this aspect of the Petit Trianon offered a titillating sign of debauchery.[61] At worst, such debauchery in the nation's queen—who, of course, remained a public figure despite her efforts to flee her ceremonial duties at court—implied a moral rot at the heart of the kingdom.[62]

Fanning the fires of this explosive idea, Marie Antoinette's detractors were not content merely to keep casting aspersions on her daughter's paternity and spinning yarns about her trysts with Artois and other gentlemen. (Ironically, the one person with whom she did in all probability become secretly involved, Axel von Fersen, mostly escaped mention in these libels, perhaps because his military duties and his service to the King of Sweden kept him abroad for years at a time.[63]) That she spent so much unchaperoned time in the company of known seducers like Artois and Lauzun seemed to point clearly toward adulterous dealings; and, unfortunately for Marie Antoinette, some of these men self-aggrandizingly hinted that her attachment to them was more than platonic.[64] More scandalously still, because so often she disappeared to Trianon accompanied only by her female friends, and because these women often spent the night there—whereas her husband never did—rumors began to circulate that Marie Antoinette was a lesbian.[65]

Conveniently for those disseminating such stories, a colloquial French term for lesbianism was "the German vice," and Marie Antoinette's adversaries, already up in arms about her "foreign" habits and friendships, made the most of this sexual stereotype.[66] As early as December 1775, the Queen had lamented to Maria Theresa that anonymous scandal-mongers "attribute to me a taste for both men and women."[67] A few years later, Artois himself—perhaps motivated less by anti-Austrian feeling than by a wish to defuse suspicions concerning his much gossiped-about friendship with the Queen—also hinted at her Sapphic tendencies, telling friends that he had caught her and the Comtesse Jules de Polignac in an impassioned embrace.[68]

As usual, tidbits like these traveled not just through court but to Paris, again thanks to the efforts of Chartres, Provence, and others with an ax to grind or an agenda to advance.[69] Tipped off by chatter of this sort, the *Mémoires secrets* reported pointedly on the "fêtes Her Majesty has at the Petit Trianon, that is to say at little Vienna, to which she admits only women—without any men."[70] The Comtesse Jules, the Princesse de Lamballe, and Rose Bertin, who were the most frequent female visitors to "little Vienna," figured in the scandal sheets as the Queen's lesbian lovers.[71]

These allegations implied that Marie Antoinette's licentiousness went beyond just garden-variety moral turpitude, as practiced by the late, lascivious Louis XV. Her supposed lesbianism—or "tribadism," perhaps the most prevalent eighteenth-century term for the "German vice"—may have seemed retroactively to account for her long history of childlessness, and to suggest an equation between the attention she lavished on her conspicuous female favorites and the sexual energies that she might have otherwise harnessed for more constructive (procreative) ends.[72] Like her frivolous but powerful fashion ministry, headed by her alleged lover Bertin, the Queen's "tribadism" also implied an even graver, twofold political sin: that of seizing the King's prerogatives and making him irrelevant. Whereas Louis XVI still did not have (and indeed would never have) a mistress, his "German" spouse arrogated to herself two of his best-known royal rights: the right to seek pleasure with other women, and the right to bestow the most dazzling favors upon them.[73]

Indeed, in 1775 Lamballe's lucrative appointment as Surintendante had marked her as enjoying the inordinate privileges of a favorite—not least because the *charge*'s 150,000-livre annual income matched precisely the sum Du Barry had received each year as Louis XV's mistress. The magnificent gifts and honors that Marie Antoinette showered on her other closest female friend, the Comtesse Jules de Polignac—whom in 1780 she made a hereditary duchess, and who competed openly with Lamballe for the consort's affections—also recalled the largesse of a king toward his lover. As the author of an underground pamphlet first published in 1781 observed, "The Queen's sublime passion [for Madame de Polignac] was equaled only by

Louis XV's imbecilic attachment to the Marquise de Pompadour. Like the Marquise, the Comtesse Jules cost the state immense sums."[74] Similarly, another pamphleteer writing at around the same time asked sarcastically: "So what if the Queen gives money to Madame Jules? And makes her husband [le Comte Jules de Polignac] a duke? Wasn't Du Barry made a countess? What's the difference?"[75] The difference, of course, was that Marie Antoinette was not a king. Her habit of pampering girlfriends pointed to a dramatic reversal of monarchical and marital roles, and so indicated that women were trampling sacred male authority beneath their dainty satin heels.[76]

From Marie Antoinette's point of view, however, the money and attention she lavished upon Lamballe and Polignac may simply have been the price of having friends—and of remaining in style.[77] Thanks in large part to Rousseau's novel *Julie,* the ideal of an extremely close, almost amorously tender bond between women was then very much in vogue. Like the *jardin anglais* also promoted in that book, the idea of an "inseparable" female friendship became an early Romantic touchstone: a triumph of nature (the spontaneous communion of kindred souls) over convention (the societal construct that was marriage). For the Queen, who even, it was reported, tried to breast-feed Marie Thérèse in deference to Rousseau's back-to-nature ideals, a handful of girlfriends thus served as welcome, perhaps even indispensable, additions to the décor.

That is not to say that Marie Antoinette did not enjoy her favorites' companionship for its own sake. After her long isolation as Dauphine and her often disappointing relationship with Louis XVI, there seems to be little doubt that she found real solace in the "highly charged feminine atmosphere" of the Petit Trianon, where, as the biographer Amanda Foreman has elegantly put it, "feelings ruled and kisses and embraces were part of the ordinary language of communication."[78] Yet as the Comtesse de Boigne firmly insisted, Marie Antoinette sought more than anything else "to be *à la mode,*" as much in her choice of friends and pastimes as in her choice of clothes.[79] (Boigne even suspected that her sovereign's affair with Fersen was motivated by the fact that foreign men were "particularly in style" among the ladies of Versailles; and the news that the Queen encouraged Fersen and his Swedish friends to wear their colorful national uniforms when visiting Trianon may have appeared to confirm this supposition.[80]) In any event, despite its roots in the vogue for Rousseauean sentimentality, Marie Antoinette's fondness for female company earned her no points with the underground press, which accused her of leading the whole of Versailles headlong into sexual depravity. "The court lost no time in going *à la mode,*" one pamphleteer later asserted. "Every woman became a lesbian and a slut."[81]

. . .

OF COURSE, MARIE ANTOINETTE'S TRIANON LIFESTYLE ALSO ALLOWED FOR
more direct—and, on the face of it, more innocent—indulgences of fashion.
For although her first years at the Petit Trianon coincided with her discovery
of *la mode parisienne,* she chose not to dress for the country in the over-
stated manner she had showcased in the capital; it was almost as if, in the
privacy of her bucolic retreat, she could relax her more conspicuous attempts to command attention and respect. With the exception of her
sumptuous theatrical costumes, she generally tried to match the cultivated
simplicity of the villa's design with a similarly unstudied and unfussy approach to dress. (Rousseau's writings, in fact, prescribed simplicity of apparel as an antidote to the overwrought, overpriced costumes of the French
capital.[82]) Far from her subjects' prying eyes, Marie Antoinette thus seems
to have asserted her power not so much by cultivating an ostentatious,
attention-grabbing persona as by wearing exactly what she pleased—and
these outfits were, yet again, distinctly at odds with the sartorial traditions of
Versailles. "I therefore kindly request," she directed her childhood friend
the Princess Louise von Hesse-Darmstadt before receiving her at Trianon,
"that you not come in formal attire, but rather in country wear."[83] With
Bertin on hand to cater to her caprices, and with the King still raising no
serious obstacles to her spending, Marie Antoinette zealously dreamed up
new outfits suited to her hideaway and predicated on the idea that she, as
Queen, could freely suspend the costuming dictates that she had trans-
gressed at her peril as Dauphine.

Perhaps surprisingly, given the *pouf*'s associations with the high-octane
glamour she embraced while in Paris, the looks she devised for the Petit Trianon did not call for the total abandonment of that headdress. As long as a
pouf included vegetables, fruits, and posies, it seemed entirely consistent
with Trianon's overarching pastoral aesthetic. There was, for instance, the
"*pouf* with a garland of roses, a white-striped gauze ribbon and a beautiful
white feather" that Bertin created for the young Marie Thérèse, and the *cor-
beille de fleurs* that involved wearing an actual basket or bucket of fresh
flowers on one's head.[84] Hairdos that directly mimicked the surrounding
landscape—"gleaming meadows, silvery brooks, a whole *jardin anglais,*"
"woodland groves, streams, sheep, shepherds, and shepherdesses"—also assumed pride of place at Trianon.[85] At a party Marie Antoinette hosted there
in 1782 for the Grand Duke and Grand Duchess of Russia, the Grand
Duchess's coiffure featured a jeweled bird whose wings could be made to
flap with the tug of a small filigreed chain, while French guests kept tiny bottles of water nestled within their curls and filled with sprays of fresh-cut

blossoms.[86] This style, the Baronne d'Oberkirch recalled fondly, "set spring on our heads, amidst a snow of powder."[87]

But the use of powder waned at Trianon, as did the use of makeup, which the blooming-cheeked, naturally gorgeous Madame de Polignac led the way in eschewing. A 1778 portrait by Antoine Vestier, *Marie Antoinette at the Petit Trianon,* represented Marie Antoinette's strawberry-blond hair and creamy complexion in all their fresh, natural splendor, untouched by the rouge and pomade of the arduous queenly *toilette.* Giddily casting off these time-honored emblems of aristocratic prestige, Marie Antoinette and her ladies sought other bonnet styles, less intricate than *poufs,* to complement their newly emancipated complexions and coiffures. By the late 1770s, they were thus all mad for the "milkmaid's bonnet" (*bonnet à la laitière*) and, of course, for the *bonnet à la Rousseau,* both of which were large, soft-crowned caps made from plain white cloth. As a rule, these bonnets' sole adornments consisted in a few jaunty fresh flowers, a plain satin ribbon, and a clutch of dainty ruffles around the face, designed to offset the natural beauty of the wearer's skin.[88]

Inspired by France's conquest of Grenada in the war against the British, the *bonnet à la Grenade* offered a slightly showier variation on this deliberately simple and naturalistic theme. The Grenada bonnet was a voluminous white lace or satin bonnet that attached to a circular straw band wound with ribbons and festooned with pomegranate flowers (*fleurs de grenadier*).[89] Over time, this minimally structured cap shape was transmuted into a variety of full-fledged hats, with the stiff crowns and wide, round brims hitherto characteristic of men's headgear. At Trianon, the hat of choice was usually made of straw. Garlands of real and artificial flowers, worn on the crown of a hat or directly on the hair, became another popular choice, which likewise emphasized the wearers' natural charms and eschewed the intensely artificial stylings of Versailles.[90]

This trend toward relatively modest materials and minimal ornamentation brought about a sea change in women's clothes as well as in their coiffures. Whereas in Paris and at Versailles, Marie Antoinette and her friends tended to pair their *poufs* and feathers with lavishly trimmed *robes à la française,* at the Petit Trianon they preferred styles less obviously contradictory to Rousseau's recipe for a simple life. For starters, the clique lost no time in eschewing the wildly glittery baubles that adorned their formal gowns. Surrounded outdoors by the untamed, natural beauty of the *jardin anglais,* and indoors by the charming floral woodwork that adorned the villa's walls, the Trianon ladies' "professed ambition was to resemble wildflowers."[91] To achieve this effect, they traded imposing gemstones for pretty lilac spangles; gigantic furbelows for silk flowers and gauze ribbons (fittingly known as *gaze reine* or "the Queen's gauze"); flashy gemstones for "rustic metal jewelry" and homespun, if often expensive, muslin kerchiefs or fichus.[92] Appropriately enough, the most elegant and prettily embroidered of these became known as fichus *à la Marie Antoinette*.[93]

Even during their appearances at court, the ladies' apparel changed in accordance with their newly rusticated tastes. In a Gautier-Dagoty portrait from 1775, for instance, Marie Antoinette wears a beautiful blue *grand habit de cour* whose cut adheres to traditional court standards, but whose primary garnishes are lifelike sprigs of lilies (the Bourbon *lys*) tucked into pert, gauzy bows. (Plate 11.) And the trend toward simpler ornamentation went further in other ensembles. According to Mademoiselle de Mirecourt, the muslin fichu, which covered up the whole of the chest and the neck, grew so popular at court that the ladies stopped wearing their fine diamond necklaces "more than five or six times a year," even though the deep décolleté of their *robes à la française* was designed to display glittering jewelry to maximum effect.[94]

The underlying form of the noblewomen's gowns simultaneously metamorphosed to reflect what Mademoiselle de Mirecourt, perhaps nostalgic for the days of showier court dress, grumpily termed "this peasant look that the Queen [has] imposed on everyone."[95] For the female courtiers' official costume, Marie Antoinette prevailed upon her husband to allow for substantial modifications in the *grand habit,* whose ten- to twelve-foot circumference she pronounced "obsolete and unbearable."[96] At her request, Louis XVI permitted the ladies of Versailles to adopt smaller *paniers* and a shorter train for most palace functions, thereby lending his official sanction to the campaign Marie Antoinette had long ago begun against the court's stringent and uncomfortable sartorial dictates.[97]

At the Petit Trianon, the Queen grew even bolder in her iconoclasm and began to introduce even more radical silhouettes, which likewise flew in the face of the customs of courtly attire. Beginning in 1775, for instance, she and her friends became partial to the *robe à la polonaise*. According to a caption in the *Galerie des modes,* which showcased the look in its illustrations, the *polonaise* was "in keeping with the principles of Rousseau," insofar as these included a critique of artificial, aristocratic dress.[98] And indeed, the *polonaise* did represent a significant move away from such costumes by eliminating the restrictive *paniers* and train of the *grand habit* and the *robe à la française* and replacing them with a pert little bustle made from layers of glued cotton. The cut of the overdress was loose, "like a waisted coat," and its overskirt was looped up around the hips into three jaunty swags.[99] (These three swags were what gave the dress its name, after the three-way partitioning of Poland by Austria, Russia, and Prussia that had inspired Rohan to make jokes about the

Empress's rapacity.) Like the overskirt, the circular, flounced petticoat worn underneath the *polonaise* boasted a much higher hemline than that of the gowns worn at court. Instead of "grandly sweeping the floor," it exposed the wearer's feet and ankles, a feature that allowed for unfettered romps through Trianon's rolling fields.[100] To underline this advantage, contemporary fashion plates often showed *polonaise*-clad lasses in the great outdoors, accessorizing their gowns with parasols and walking sticks. (Plate 12.)

Another garment well suited to the ladies' rustic existence, and starkly divergent from the structured dresses required at court, was the *lévite*, a loose-fitting gown inspired by the togalike costumes of classical French theater.[101] Eliminating not only the court costume's *paniers* and train but its whalebone bodice as well, the *lévite* accentuated the waist with a simple, loosely knotted scarf worn as a belt, a feature that the Queen found especially attractive while she was pregnant with Marie Thérèse. She may also have discovered that the relaxed, oversized shawl collar with which the *lévite* replaced the plumped-up décolletage of the *robe à la française* facilitated her efforts to breast-feed once the child was born.[102] But the informality of the *lévite*, which by 1782 accounted for over a third of the dresses in her wardrobe, seems to have appealed to her aesthetically as well.[103] Where the *grand habit* and the *robe à la française* featured skintight, elbow-length sleeves edged with triple layers of lace, the *lévite* boasted the relatively loose-fitting, wrist-length sleeves of the Queen's beloved riding habits.[104]

Actual equestrian gear also entered into rotation at the Petit Trianon, whose habitués shared a passion for horse-racing, an English craze that first took France's fashionable circles by storm in 1776. Among the Queen's intimates, the Comte d'Artois and the Duc de Lauzun were particularly enamored of the sport; they abandoned the fancy, fitted jackets of the male courtier for the informal, open frock coats (*fracs*) and vests (*gilets*) favored by Englishmen and jockeys. Palace conservatives declared the style indecent to the point of naughtiness (any man thus attired was said to be *en polisson*—"dressed like a rascal"), and Louis XVI himself, in an uncharacteristic sartorial crackdown, forbade his courtiers to wear it at Versailles. Though the King's decision drew groans from the fashionable set, it seemed entirely sensible to Mercy, who was shocked that gentlemen should dare to appear before their queen *en polisson*.[105]

Marie Antoinette, for her part, adored the rascally aesthetic, no doubt because of, not despite, the challenge it posed to the costuming standards of the court. Indeed, not only did she encourage her male friends to sport it in her presence, in defiance of the King's distaste; she soon introduced its turned lapels, cuffed sleeves, and buttoned plackets into her own wardrobe, making masculine-tailored *gilets, fracs,* and redingotes (this word, which began life as a bastardization of the English "riding coat," has passed back into that language with a French accent) all the rage in ladies' fashion. As adapted for female wear, these jackets boasted little ornamentation besides large, stylized buttons, contrasting-color lapels and cuffs, and subtle embroidery in the fabric, like the tiny cream-colored sunbursts that adorned a turquoise redingote she wore in 1782.[106] (Plate 13.) As a rule, the woman's redingote called for spartan, mannish accessories: riding boots, a stiff-brimmed, feathered black "jockey's cap," and a man's club-shaped ponytail called a *catogan.* Like the order she placed in November 1781 for thirty-one new riding outfits, these ensembles revealed that Marie Antoinette had by no means lost her taste for the androgynous costume that had long accompanied her penchant for riding "like a man."[107] Against the backdrop of the Petit Trianon, which was explicitly coded as her private fiefdom, such experimental garb as the redingotes and, indeed, the *polonaises* and *lévites,* flaunted her newfound, unchallenged freedom from court practice and even from kingly approval. Already, as Dauphine, she had insisted that she needed "guidance from no one in anything concerning proper, decent behavior," and she had made her point by dressing in masculine attire.[108] Now that she was the sublimely independent queen of Trianon, this belief manifested itself more clearly than ever, again making itself apparent in the very cut of her clothes.

It was evident, as well, in the fabrics and colors toward which Marie Antoinette gravitated as she worked up a wardrobe for her country retreat; and in this respect, too, she flagrantly abandoned the sartorial conventions that aristocrats had hitherto embraced both at court and in the capital. For despite their many differences, Versailles and Paris shared a culture of ostentation and one-upmanship that required the aristocracy to don weighty brocades, lush velvets, and lustrous satins—all in bright, vivid jewel tones and regal, large-scale patterns that loudly broadcast their supreme wealth and privilege.[109] Indeed, as Chantal Thomas has observed, the "glaring colors" of aristocrats' clothing had historically functioned, like heavy rouge, as a means for the nobility to assert itself as a class, and especially as a class distinct from the bourgeoisie, whose own economic fortunes had been on a dramatic upswing since Louis XIV's era but whose somewhat more practically minded members "preferred grey or beige to hot pink and orange."[110] However, the creamy white walls and light-colored upholsteries of the Petit Trianon were anything but showy—and as Marie Antoinette sought the most suitable costumes for her villa, she came to replace the brighter shades of her caste with more "bourgeois" greys, beiges, and subtle pastels.[111] In addition, she abandoned bolder, grand-scale patterns for only the most delicate "broken" stripes, tiny dots, diminutive bouquets, and tiny sunbursts. (Her *gazette des atours* for 1782 reveals how much she loved this last pattern, which graced one of the pastel-blue redingotes and several of the *lévites* she purchased that year.[112]) These changes in color and pattern were far from insignificant, for they again revealed Marie Antoinette's readiness to shrug off the trappings and suits of traditional royal elegance and to play the game of fashion by her own, unconventional rules.

She rewrote the rules as well by expanding the repertoire of fabrics used in her clothing to include more than just the rich silks and satins that customarily made up court dress. Although she retained those fabrics in their newly patterned and colored iterations, Marie Antoinette also began wearing plainer and less formal textiles, such as the printed cottons known as *toiles de Joüy,* whose miniature landscapes in some cases directly recalled the picturesque gardens around her château. She and her followers also placed gauze, muslin, and linen at the forefront of fashionable dress, and while sometimes these materials were also dyed in quiet colors, at other times they were simply, elegantly white.[113] By the summer of 1780, one of her favorite ensembles for Trianon was a white muslin shift known as the *gaulle,* which Bertin had copied from "Creoles" and colonialists' wives unable to wear silk in the Caribbean heat.[114] This garment was slipped on over a flexible cloth bodice instead of whalebone stays, and was free of any other structuring elements except a ruffled drawstring neck, puffy sleeves held up by ribbon "bracelets," and a wide ribbon sash at the waist. Wearers accessorized it sometimes with a saucy white apron, sometimes with a white fichu, and almost always with a soft white bonnet or wide-brimmed straw hat, perched atop hair that was loose and unpowdered.[115]

As costume historians have observed, the popularity of the loosely draped, flowing white *gaulle* attested in part to a Continent-wide revival of neoclassical taste, prompted by the recent discovery of the ruins at Herculaneum and Pompeii, and reprised by Marie Antoinette in many of the neoclassical decorative elements she introduced into her homes. (This was an aesthetic later labeled "Louis XVI style," though, as Stefan Zweig and others have pointed out, "Marie Antoinette style" might have been a fairer designation.)[116] And in part, the airy lawn gown was viewed as an English trend, though Georgiana, Duchess of Devonshire, seems only to have made it a sought-after ensemble in Britain after receiving a *gaulle* as a present from Marie Antoinette, with whom she enjoyed a friendship.[117] But above all, the look and feel of this dress corresponded perfectly to the pared-down look and feel of the Queen's Trianon, where neoclassical purity and pastoral simplicity were everywhere merged, and everywhere trumped the overdone elegance of Versailles. Controversial though this style would prove to be, women of fashion soon followed suit: by 1782, "the boulevards of Paris were flooded with plain white dresses."[118]

INSOFAR AS IT EXPRESSED A WHOLESALE REJECTION OF ARISTOCRATIC AND royal traditions, the Queen's move toward stylized simplicity did nothing to defuse the anger that her otherwise very different, hyperdecorated Parisian fashions had also provoked in her subjects. On October 22, 1781, she finally did her duty by the kingdom and provided the nation with a dauphin, a sickly child named Louis Joseph—Louis for his father (and countless other royal predecessors), and Joseph for his Austrian godfather, Joseph II. Nonetheless, the public's growing distaste for the Queen's inappropriate behavior seemed once again markedly to overshadow their response to this long-awaited dynastic event.[119] Viewed through the lens of her other doings at Trianon, the clothes Marie Antoinette wore there attracted the indignant attention of courtiers and commoners, who alike seem to have construed them as additional signs of her "Austrian" deviancy, her defiance of French mores, her thoughtless extravagance, and her theft of the King's sacrosanct power.

It was telling, in this context, that the Queen's new masculine hairstyle, the *catogan,* elicited the disapproval of Louis XVI himself, though with his characteristic gentleness and indirection, he expressed his displeasure by means of a joke. In May 1783, he showed up in his wife's apartments with his hair whipped up into a womanly chignon. When Marie Antoinette laughingly asked him why he had done such a frightful thing, he replied that although the hairdo was indeed "villainous,"

> it is a fashion that I would like to start, since I have as yet launched no trends of my own. . . . [Besides,] men need a hairstyle that distinguishes them from women. You have already taken from us the plume [and] the hat. . . . Until recently, we still had the *catogan,* but you have appropriated that as well, and I find *that* extremely villainous on women.[120]

According to the *Mémoires secrets,* which was just one of the gossip sheets to report on this incident, Marie Antoinette accepted the King's prank as the reproach it was, and "immediately gave orders to have her *catogan* undone."[121] Yet this token show of docility did not dispel her reputation as a queen who did not know her place, and who had not only cross-dressed but had, scandously, forced her emasculated husband to do the same.

The Queen's daring ensembles were criticized not just for the disrespect they manifested toward her spouse, but for the refractory attitudes that they—like her overpriced *poufs*—seemingly inspired in other ladies of fashion. In 1787, an unknown author writing under the pen name Mademoiselle Javotte addressed a satirical open letter to the "handsome messieurs" of France, on the subject of women's mannish headgear. "You messieurs think that you are our masters, but really we are leading you around by the nose," Javotte taunted:

> Yet you persist in wearing hats, which you know we have been wearing constantly for several years now. Shouldn't our adoption of this style have forced you to renounce it? Your mental faculties are so limited that we will spell it out for you: Messieurs, we hereby declare that the hat is ours. "But what will we wear?" you may ask. Well, you dear little men, we will leave you our bonnets, which we no longer wear. A light, transparent bonnet, tilted just so above the face, enhances the skin's whiteness, . . . [and worn with] just a soupçon of rouge will make you look oh so charming.[122]

Reminiscent of the King's pointedly bizarre chignon, this sarcastic style tip expressed the degree to which contemporary women's fashion was thought to have compromised male dignity. Like Samson shorn of his hair, Frenchmen stripped of their hats were, in Javotte's account, reduced to powerless weaklings—condescended to as "little" and "limited," feminized in rouge, and, perhaps most humiliatingly of all, outmoded in last year's bonnets.

According to critics, the informal apparel of the Petit Trianon imbued its wearers not just with a general disregard for men, but with the same sense of sexual emancipation ostensibly enjoyed by the rebel queen herself. Fashion-plate captions made frequent, provocative allusions to the sexual escapades in which their models were wont to indulge, one example being a redingote-clad "prudent Amazon advancing cautiously toward a secret grove where her lover is to meet her, taking care not to be seen."[123] Whereas, under Louis XV's reign, Marie Antoinette's self-aggrandizing masculine garb had placed her in opposition to the wanton seductress Madame Du Barry, the Queen's cross-dressed aesthetic now seemed more redolent of sexual depravity than of selfless heroism. (Indeed, at around this time one Parisian dressmaker is said to have invented a *polonaise à la Jeanne d'Arc,* the bodice of which completely exposed the wearer's bosom, and which thus transformed Joan of Arc herself from a virile military champion into an immodest female libertine.[124]) Likewise insisting on the new fashions' suitability for erotic misdeeds, certain observers remarked that the loose cut of gowns like the *lévite* and the *gaulle* allowed for easier access to women's breasts and genitals, and thus enabled hasty dressing after covert rendezvous.[125]

So sexually corrupting were these garments thought to be, in fact, that when the Count of Aranda, Spain's ambassador to Versailles, commissioned a trousseau for his young new bride, he stipulated that the collection must not contain a single *lévite* or *chemise*.[126] Perhaps Aranda was alarmed because one of the most popular *lévites* of the day was the *lévite à la Prussienne* (Prussian *lévite*), which in both its name and its detailing—frogged and tasseled military trim and man-tailored, brass-buttoned "cavalier's" sleeves—announced an unsettling potential for the "German vice," as well as a cultural connection to France's reigning *Autrichienne*.[127] Indeed, during the revolutionary period, when pornographic literature attacking Marie Antoinette became even more prevalent thanks to the suspension of royal censorship laws, one popular image depicted her straddling a chair and allowing her girlfriend Polignac to fondle her breasts beneath her conveniently loose *lévite*. Between her suspiciously unstructured outfit and her masculine way of sitting on the chair—reminiscent of her penchant for "riding like a man"—the Queen appeared in this print as a flagrantly perverted transgressor of heterosexual norms. Indeed, as the historian Elizabeth Colwill has remarked, whether "astride a man, woman, or beast, a woman on top spelled disorder, [and] no woman spelled disorder more flamboyantly than Marie Antoinette."[128]

Although it was English designs that had originally inspired Marie Antoinette's vests and riding coats, the way these garments masculinized female wearers also may have implied a penchant for "Germanic" sexual inversion. One of them, accordingly, was known as the redingote *à l'Allemande*—the German riding coat—and was described in a fashion plate as an ideal outfit for "a young woman ready to straddle a horse" (Plate 14), while another, the *frac à la bavaroise*—or Bavarian frock coat—was modeled by a "masculine-dressed" lady doing just that.[129] Though far less explicit than the print that showed Marie Antoinette locked in a lascivious embrace with la Polignac, this image gestured toward the gender-bending habits of the Austrian-born queen.

In addition to upending accepted rules for female eroticism, the designs that flowed from the Petit Trianon were thought to destabilize larger-scale geopolitical boundaries. One inveterate trend-watcher, the Baron de Frénilly, declared of the new look: "An auxiliary army of jackets . . . round hats, and frock coats [has] charged like so many Huns into the heart of [our] kingdom."[130] With this metaphor of military invasion, the Baron accentuated growing concerns about vulnerability in the body politic—concerns sparked not just by France's expensive ongoing involvement in the American Revolution and by the nation's ever dwindling domestic resources, but also, increasingly, by the frock-coated, tribade queen's apparent treasonous desire to "Germanize" her husband's government. Certainly her *polonaises,* whose tripartite overskirts directly evoked Austria's complicity in the 1772 partition

4. Anonymous, *Marie Antoinette Embracing the Duchesse Jules de Polignac* (late eighteenth-century French caricature) (Bibliothèque Nationale de France, Paris)

of Poland, did more to enhance than to dispel suspicions of this kind, leading hostile commentators like the academician Jean-Louis Soulavie to reprise the French party's long-standing rhetoric about Marie Antoinette as an agent of Austria.[131]

A similar perspective informed reactions to the patronage the Queen extended to the Chevalier d'Éon, a high-ranking member of the French military and diplomatic corps whose confusing gender status had made him famous throughout Europe.[132] Under Louis XV, Éon had served as a dragoon in the Seven Years' War, then as a spy disguised as a woman in the court of Catherine the Great, and next as France's minister plenipotentiary in London, where a fascinated public concluded that Éon had in fact been born a woman and had abandoned his "natural" state in order to undertake a man's career. The speculation turned to aggressive betting and merciless publicity, which by 1778 led Louis XVI to demand Éon's return home. As plans were being made for his arrival, Marie Antoinette singled him out for her attentions by enjoining Rose Bertin to make the Chevalier a costly "trousseau" of women's clothing, and by sending him an elegant fan which she urged him to wear in place of his gentleman's sword.[133] In the fall, while working on her new project, Bertin and Éon raised eyebrows in Paris by dining together twice in her home—with the Chevalier dressed one night as a man and the other night as a woman.[134] Given the *marchande*'s reputation as the Queen's lesbian lover, Parisians may not have found her choice of a dinner companion altogether surprising, but they did declare it "in very bad taste."[135]

Similar complaints arose when Éon was presented to the sovereigns in November of that year. Versailles was packed to the rafters that day with spectators who were curious to see how the notorious character would dress for the occasion . . . and who were gratified, if appalled, by his hybrid appearance.[136] On his chest, the Chevalier wore the Cross of Saint Louis, which he had earned, as only men were permitted to do, in service to the

5. Unknown,
The Chevalier d'Éon
(late eighteenth century)
(Bibliothèque Nationale
de France, Paris)

throne. According to Léonard's memoirs, Éon stomped forcefully through the palace like the dragoon he had once been, speaking in "the most masculine of voices" and sporting a "thick beard which, if it did not betray virility, [at least] simulated it wonderfully well by some freak of nature."[137]

These characteristics contrasted grotesquely with his lace sleeves, long train, and "blue satin skirt like the Holy Virgin Mary's"—which Bertin had designed in homage to Marie Antoinette, who of course shared the Virgin's name.[138] But to Madame Campan, at least, there was nothing at all virginal about this crudely androgynous creature. Although the Queen had charged Madame Campan's parents with giving Éon a crash course in ladylike deportment before his court appearance, the perennially proper *femme de chambre* deemed the Chevalier "the worst company one could imagine."[139]

The Queen, though, found Éon utterly delightful. Having herself refused to conform to certain of the strictly imposed, gendered requirements of her station, she responded warmly to this individual who, swaggering like a man yet dressed as a woman, flouted the royal authorities' attempts definitively to establish his sex. Before the whole of the court, she effusively praised his "new uniform" and with mock solemnity declared him "the female-knight [*chevalière*] commander" of "my regiment of white skirts,"[140] thereby helping him to retain the gender ambiguity he seemed determined to put forth. Indeed, a denatured she-male emblematized perfectly the gender reversal implied in Marie Antoinette's bon mot: with her putative army of women, whose "white skirts" declared their allegiance to the radical Trianon style, she herself was seen as effectively taking over her husband's realm. A year later, rumors circulated that she was pushing Louis XVI to name Éon his Minister of Foreign Affairs. Although the rumors were patently false—Éon had retreated quietly to his country estate to avoid the "jokes and prying" that his indeterminate sexual identity inspired—their proliferation fed fears that the Queen's monstrous "German" tastes were now shaping monarchical policy at the highest level.[141]

MARIE ANTOINETTE'S LATEST SARTORIAL CAPRICES ALSO GENERATED BAD press because the fabrics she had made fashionable at Trianon were by and large foreign imports, whereas the silks traditionally worn by the aristocracy were domestically produced, and in fact French silk manufacturers relied heavily on the court for business. Disregarding this custom, too, in her pursuit of freedom and fashion, the Queen obtained many of her muslins and linens from Britain, where, a diplomat named the Marquis de Bombelles reported, Rose Bertin was revered as a national savior for her zealous patronage of Scottish manufacturing plants.[142] At home, by contrast, the *marchande* and her mistress were reviled for "leveling a fatal blow" to the silk industry, which accounted for thousands of jobs in manufacturing in cities like Lyon.[143] According to Soulavie, harsh as always about the dreaded *Autrichienne,* no less than three quarters of the silk workers in Lyon lost their jobs in the 1780s, as "our fine silk stuffs fell out of fashion" due to the Queen's unpatriotic patronage of foreign textile plants.[144]

To counter the damaging new mode, French silk makers reportedly disseminated a cautionary tale about the dangers of wearing muslin: "a case . . . where a young lady wearing a flounced muslin dress had come too close to the fire, and was burnt to death."[145] This alarming anecdote had as little success in stemming the tide of fashion as had had the satirical prints of the 1770s, in which women's *poufs* tangled worrisomely with street lamps and chandeliers. And so the Queen, who had launched the muslin craze, was blamed in at least one contemporary pamphlet for "reducing the silk workers of Lyon and other cities to beggary, and leaving their enterprises in shambles."[146]

To the Anglophobic French, a preference for British-made over domestic goods was offensive enough, especially while France was still at war with England in the American colonies. After the war ended in 1783, though, a new trade treaty with England flooded the French market with British textiles, and the Queen could no longer be singled out as their sole consumer.[147] As "Anglomania" became a staple of French fashion—even the nation's leading fashion journal was entitled *Le Magasin des modes nouvelles françaises et anglaises*—the public excoriated Marie Antoinette instead for importing muslins and linens from Hapsburg-controlled Belgium. Because Joseph II had recently undertaken a vigorous campaign to revitalize the Flemish textile industry, Marie Antoinette was accused of "revolutioniz[ing] French clothing and fashion" out of a treacherous "attachment to the commercial interests of her House."[148] Again tarring their sovereign with a xenophobic brush, observers fulminated that "the *Autrichienne* [was] conspiring to ruin our manufacturers of beautiful silks."[149]

This notion gained added currency when the producers of Lyon banded together and petitioned the throne about "the need to protect their business and to prohibit the new styles which proliferated in France to the detriment of her commercial prosperity."[150] Unluckily for Marie Antoinette, they first took their complaint to the Aunts, who were doubtless all too pleased to confirm the workers in the view that Marie Antoinette considered her subjects' plight with—as Soulavie put it—"the haughtiness of a sovereign whose heart is foreign to the French."[151] After the meeting with Mesdames, tellers of tales grew even more adamant that the Queen's covert agenda was to channel "hundreds of millions in profits" to Hapsburg Flanders.[152]

In this context, it was either supremely ironic or peculiarly fitting that one of the greatest boosts the silk makers experienced during this time occurred with the death of Maria Theresa in November 1780. To honor the Queen's late mother, dead at sixty-three after a protracted illness, the members of the French court had to order masses of sumptuous velvet and satin clothes in the somber colors of mourning. Although her relationship with Maria Theresa had been strained for some time, Marie Antoinette was crushed by the news of her death. To mourn her mother in appropriately regal, respectful style (Maria Theresa herself having worn nothing but "widow's black" from the time of her husband's death in 1765 until her own), Marie Antoinette spent almost 66,000 livres on silk stuffs in late 1780 and early 1781.[153] This represented a dramatic 50 percent increase over her expenditures on silk during her first year on the throne.[154]

Yet even the rise in silk orders sparked by the Empress's death did not absolve her daughter of the charge that she was laying waste to one of France's proudest industries. Although mourning fabrics, which ran a predictable spectrum of blacks, violets, blues, grays, and whites, were easy enough to produce, the unusual color palette required for the Queen's Trianon costumes called for significant changes in the silk makers' business practice. For years they had been able to churn out a fairly consistent array of regally toned materials, with colors and patterns changing five or six times a year at most.[155] But Marie Antoinette—as one lampoonist scoffed, echoing Madame Campan's somewhat more neutral comment about her mistress's boundless appetite for sartorial novelty—"wanted to appear every hour, as it were, in a brand-new guise."[156] And this led to a dizzily accelerating cycle of production and obsolescence in the silk industry.

The manufacturers' schedule turned chaotic as they worked overtime to accommodate Marie Antoinette's capricious requests for brand-new, of-the-moment colors, such as the flame-toned *incendie de l'Opéra,* designed to commemorate the fire that ravaged the Paris Opéra in June 1781, and the dull brown *caca dauphin* inspired by the newborn Louis Joseph's soiled swaddling clothes four months later.[157] Due to the lightning speed at which tastes changed, silk makers often found that by the time they had finished producing a particular line of fabrics, the shade or pattern they had created had gone out of style.[158] A pale-gold silk that at the height of its popularity commanded 86 livres per *aune* (a unit of measurement equivalent to about 1.2 meters) sold for less than half that sum after it fell out of favor.[159]

Equally challenging for the silk manufacturers was the fact that they could no longer begin work on a product line until they had received word about what newly invented colors and patterns Her Majesty desired to see made.[160] In one famous instance, Bertin sent the producers at Gobelins a lock of Marie Antoinette's hair and ordered them to weave a silk of the same burnished-blond hue, to be known as *cheveux de la Reine*.[161] While awaiting such directives, Mercier reported, the silk workshops "languished in inaction," leaving the owners to wring their hands over the lost income and wasted time.[162]

Nor were the silk makers the only economic casualties of the Queen's new wardrobe. Much like her costly headdresses, Marie Antoinette's countrified ensembles were deemed by her detractors to be financially ruinous to the countless Frenchwomen who aspired to her style. These critics pointed out that although the fabrics used to achieve the Trianon look were less expensive than silk, they were also less durable and so had to be replaced more often.[163] They also objected that the sheer modishness of such materials made them pricier than their workmanship—which was a hallmark of painstakingly crafted French silks and satins—deserved. Gauze, for instance, cost between 9 and 10 livres per *aune,* whereas satin had an average price of 12 to 14 livres, but used many more silk threads per *aune* and was thus more labor-intensive to produce.[164] Like the Queen's English garden, whose unfussy effect came at a tremendous price, her fondness for flimsy cloth encouraged women to spend great sums on what struck the uninitiated as an essentially inelegant style.

The style presented social as well as economic problems, for it obfuscated long-standing sartorially coded differences in class. Just as the Queen's *poufs* were said to make prostitutes and petites bourgeoises look like duchesses, so the pared-down frocks of the Petit Trianon were thought to make noblewomen look like peasant girls.[165] The Baron de Frénilly dubbed this phenomenon a "revolution in linen"—and the Goncourt brothers, two of Marie Antoinette's most clothes-oriented biographers, called it "the revolution of simplicity"—precisely to underscore its radical consequences for the social order as a whole.[166] By tradition, a lady of the court was made immediately recognizable by the *paniers,* corset, and weighty silk materials that structured her gown. By doing away with these things, the fashionable *gaulle* and its related accoutrements (the linen or muslin fichu and apron; the straw hat) stripped female aristocrats of their prime identifying markers.

Conversely, Mademoiselle de Mirecourt complained, the resulting disappearance of visible social distinctions "enabled women of low birth to try to compete with, [or even] be mistaken for, ladies of quality."[167] Exemplary in this regard was Madame Du Barry, whose "low birth" remained a matter of public knowledge despite her illicitly acquired noble title, and who, tellingly, proclaimed her wish to wear "only dresses of white muslin, winter and summer, no matter what the weather was like."[168] Although there was no hope of her ever securing an invitation to the Petit Trianon, Du Barry became so enamored of the place's costuming aesthetic that she hired Marie Antoinette's own favorite portraitist, Élisabeth Vigée-Lebrun, to paint her in a muslin *gaulle* and straw hat. (Plate 15.) Bearing a distinct resemblance to portraits painted at around this same time of Trianon regulars like the Princesse de Lamballe (Plate 16), this portrait of Du Barry reveals that Marie Antoinette's country-girl look had indeed traveled a long way from its privileged point of origin.

But imitation was by no means restricted to former royal favorites. In contemporary fashion plates, the frilly aprons and "milkmaid" bonnets of the Petit Trianon were depicted on such humble characters as "the provincial kitchen-maid who is beginning to take on the airs of an elegant Parisienne"—a mini-narrative that hinted at the garments' democratizing reach.[169] Similarly, engravings series like the *Galerie des modes* depicted bourgeoises whose attire (particularly their headdresses) looked virtually indistinguishable from that of women whom the captions identified as "ladies of the court."[170] Although sumptuary laws—those regulations that, in placing certain restrictions on sartorial luxury and excess, had historically served to prevent superficial confusion between the classes—had been suspended early in Louis XV's reign, both convention and expense had to a large extent succeeded in upholding such distinctions ever since.[171] But with the advent of a more rustic style, infinitely easier to copy than a lavish *robe à la française,* women's costume no longer transmitted reliable messages about background and class. (Plate 17.) Like Marie Antoinette's playful adoption of menial roles on the stage at the Petit Trianon, this trend suggested an unsettling possibility for confusion between high and low, princess and peasant.

In a society that was still organized along strictly demarcated class lines, such a development was bound to provoke a backlash. One of the aristocracy's great doyennes, the Maréchale de Luxembourg, so hated seeing her granddaughter the Duchesse de Lauzun dressed "like a servant" that she sent her a pointed gag gift: a lace-trimmed apron made of crude packaging material.[172] But commoners, too, were alarmed by the decline of clearly established social boundaries, especially when Marie Antoinette, a foreigner who by all accounts understood and respected so little of their culture, was doing so much to destroy them. In 1783, the Queen lent direct, substantial credence to these charges when she allowed Vigée-Lebrun to include in that year's public exhibition at Paris's Salon du Louvre a portrait of her entitled *La Reine en gaulle* ("The Queen Dressed in a *Gaulle*").[173]

In this painting, Marie Antoinette's figure was utterly devoid of the accoutrements conventionally found in royal portraiture.[174] Gone were the *grand habit de cour,* the regal ermine cape with fleur-de-lys embroidery, the priceless jewelry, the heavily powdered hairdo, and the outsized circles of rouge. (Even in the Gautier-Dagoty portrait of 1775, for which she accessorized her outfit with naturalistic sprigs of lilies, Marie Antoinette had retained these other, more traditional features of queenly dress.) Instead, Vigée-Lebrun's sovereign wore only a broad-brimmed straw hat and, as the title of the painting announced, a muslin *gaulle* fastened with a wide sash of pastel-blue gauze. Apart from the roses she held, and which recalled her Hapsburg birth, absolutely nothing in the portrait hinted at her august identity—and this was apparently just what the Queen wanted. Like her onetime nemesis Madame Du Barry, Marie Antoinette was so taken with her new, simplified style of dress that she was eager to have its flattering effects commemorated on canvas . . . royal representational expectations be damned.[175]

The understated charms of this unqueenly ensemble were, however, largely wasted on the crowds at the Paris Salon, who fulminated that the consort had finally gone too far.[176] With this latest affront to the dignity and sanctity of the throne, she had proven definitively what her other fashion follies already implied: Marie Antoinette deserved neither her special standing nor her subjects' respect. The exhibition was open to the public, and the news that it displayed a portrait of the Queen "dressed up like a serving-maid," "wearing a chamber-maid's dust-cloth," brought the hecklers and critics out in force.[177] Even the progressive-minded Honoré Gabriel de Mirabeau, an aristocrat who a few years later would galvanize members of the bourgeoisie in their sweeping attack on the political foundations of the *ancien régime,* sniped that "Louis XIV would be rather surprised if he could see the wife of his great-grand-successor in the gown and apron of a country wench."[178] Indeed, Marie Antoinette had traveled a great distance from her early years aping the Sun King's grandeur. In the Vigée-Lebrun portrait, her rejection of courtly luxe represented a stark departure from her forebear's commanding *gloire.*[179] And in making that departure, Mademoiselle de Mirecourt reflected, the Queen violated "the fundamental law of this kingdom, [which is] that the public cannot suffer to see its princes lower themselves to the level of mere mortals."[180]

As in their lamentations over Marie Antoinette's louche romps at Trianon, the public's anxieties over her depiction by Vigée-Lebrun were tinged with sexual malaise. To the uninitiated, the dress in the portrait resembled nothing so much as a *chemise*—an article that a woman either wore under her other clothes or donned as casual wear when lounging in the intimate space of her private boudoir. As Vigée-Lebrun herself later

6.   Élisabeth Vigée-Lebrun, *La Reine en gaulle* (1783) (© Board of Trustees, National Gallery of Art, Washington)

recalled, the similarity between the *gaulle* and the *chemise* led many viewers to conclude that she "had painted the Queen in her underwear."[181] (As a matter of fact, the term *gaulle* eventually gave way to *chemise à la Reine*, a designation that, in addition to highlighting the garment's resemblance to a woman's slip, forever linked it to its most infamous wearer.) Thus *La Reine en gaulle* registered not only as undignified but as indecent, and it conflated Marie Antoinette's social self-abasement with her alleged sexual immorality.[182]

Furthermore, the Queen's wantonness was again seen as bearing an unmistakably Germanic stamp. One irate Salon-goer pronounced that the Vigée-Lebrun portrait ought to have been titled *France Dressed as Austria, Reduced to Covering Herself with Straw*.[183] As the art historian Mary Sheriff has suggested, this quip revealed that the painting "was read as indicating the Queen's desire to escape being French, to bring what was alien into the heart of the French realm"—what was alien being the putatively Belgian, symbolically Austrian fabric of her *gaulle*.[184] And needless to say, as signifiers of her Hapsburg heritage, the roses she held in the portrait only further highlighted her supposed foreign loyalties.

So virulent was the outcry over *La Reine en gaulle* that Vigée-Lebrun had to remove it from the Salon and replace it with another, hastily executed canvas called *La Reine à la rose*. This painting represented Marie Antoinette in a blue-gray silk *robe à la française* and rich pearl jewelry, attributes that better attested to both her majesty and her Frenchness.[185] A rebel with unconventional, informal tastes, twenty-eight-year-old Vigée-Lebrun herself preferred the Queen in more "natural" attire and had strongly supported her abandonment of more sumptuous sartorial trappings.[186] (Interestingly enough, the painter's iconoclastic aesthetic program led certain members of the public to perceive her as a disgrace to her sex and to qualify her as a hermaphrodite of sorts, not unlike Marie Antoinette's other gender-bending protégé, the Chevalier d'Éon.[187]) But in the royal portraits she executed after *La Reine en gaulle,* the painter dutifully returned to more traditional depictions of the consort, overwriting the hated *chemise* with piles of ermine, gemstones, and lush *lyonnais* silks, satins, and velvets.[188]

Yet Marie Antoinette herself was apparently too fond of her simple ensembles to abandon them—even after the Salon fiasco, and even after the passage of a protectionist law forbidding the importation of foreign muslins.[189] Again flouting her husband's authority and her subjects' distaste, she held fast to her *gaulles* and straw hats, sporting them not only at her country palace but even at Versailles, where she now refused to don formal costume except on the most solemn occasions.[190] For most court soirées, she cast off the masks and dominoes in which she had previously hidden from importunate gawkers at Versailles, and shocked these people with her unapologetically peasantlike attire. (Plate 18.) She even went so far as to nickname her daughter "Muslin" (Mousseline) and to dress the girl in simple country-girl outfits that coordinated fetchingly with her own. Fanned by these acts of defiance, indignation over the Queen's undignified, anti-French frocks lingered long after *La Reine en gaulle* had disappeared from view.

SEVEN

GALLED

Two years after the outcry over Vigée-Lebrun's *La Reine en gaulle*, the controversial gown featured in the portrait resurfaced to play a small but pivotal role in another, even more widely publicized and far-reaching scandal. Remembered today as the Diamond Necklace Affair, this scandal erupted at the very moment when the French public was gaining new information both about the woeful state of the national economy and about the shocking extent of the Queen's clothing expenditures. Now known and decried among a broader public than ever before, Marie Antoinette's iconoclastic indulgences of style again figured forth a host of damning connotations—from sexual depravity to financial rapacity to treasonous, anti-French political loyalties—that damaged her already tarnished reputation beyond repair and drastically compromised the stature of the monarchy as a whole.[1] Incredibly, this whole process was set in motion, at least in part, by a sartorial smoking gun: one of the Queen's trademark white *gaulles*. And although the legal case addressing the Diamond Necklace Affair was closed by the summer of 1786, the case against Marie Antoinette's clothing, and the manifold scandals it was thought to comprise, remained wide open.

AS IT WAS LATER RECONSTRUCTED BY WITNESSES, LAWYERS, AND JUDGES IN the courtroom drama that turned the Diamond Necklace Affair into national news, the tale of the *gaulle*'s revealing reappearance went something like this:

The Cardinal de Rohan moved swiftly through the hedges in the moonlight-dappled Grove of Venus. Despite the August heat, he had donned a long black cloak to cover his watered-silk scarlet vestments and stockings. Only his lace cuffs and collar flashed brightly against the dark sky. These exquisite pieces, like the shallot-sized gemstone that sparkled in his pastoral ring, were renowned for "filling the most fashionable beauties with envy."[2] But Rohan had chosen his accessories well—for at last, France's most stylish and most powerful beauty had turned her beneficent gaze upon him. After nine years of snubbing him, shaming him, and barring him from her presence—a fate that scarcely befitted a prince of his exalted stature—Marie Antoinette had agreed to talk with the Cardinal alone, in the gardens behind Versailles.

It was Rohan's lover, the ambitious and resourceful Comtesse de La Motte-Valois, who had brokered this watershed encounter. Earlier that year—1784—she had taken it upon herself to recommend him to the Queen, who needed someone trustworthy to perform services that she wished to keep hidden from Louis XVI. In view of the many stories he had heard (and spread) about Marie Antoinette's dubious dealings, Rohan saw no reason to question La Motte's claim and zealously declared that he stood ready to serve. Tonight, he would be given a chance to prove it.[3] Even the great sorcerer Cagliostro—who had communed with the deities of ancient Egypt and read clearly into the future—had assured him that he would prevail.[4]

All at once, a white form, blurry and shifting, glided toward Rohan from the far corner of the grove. Behind it, he caught a glimpse of the Comtesse de La Motte and her companion, Réteaux de Villette, standing guard to protect his and the Queen's privacy. The shape moved closer, and even in the darkness, even to his fifty-year-old eyes, its contours became as clear as day. Gradually he made out a frilly muslin shift tied with a ribbon sash, pale blond hair streaming out from beneath a straw hat, and a fair, dainty hand reaching out to give him . . . a rose: the Queen's signature flower. "You know what this means," the apparition whispered, already backing away. Deliriously the Cardinal lunged for the blossom. Clutching it to his chest, he fell to the ground to kiss the hem of her *gaulle*. Then came La Motte's urgent whisper: "The Comte and Comtesse d'Artois are coming!" Before Rohan could raise himself up off the grass, the white sylph had disappeared.

Brief though it was, the rendezvous gave Rohan exactly what he had been looking for: proof that the Queen was willing to overlook the past and extend to him her special, enviable favor.[5] Back at the Palais-Cardinal in Paris, he had the rose enshrined in a gold-embossed, red leather box. In the months that followed, La Motte acted as the intermediary between him and the consort, furnishing him with additional information about the task Her Majesty wanted him to perform. The jewelers Boehmer and Bassenge, La Motte explained, had designed an extravagant, twenty-eight-hundred-carat diamond necklace called the Slave's Collar, which they had originally hoped Louis XV would buy for Madame Du Barry, but which Marie Antoinette was now desperate to call her own.[6] However, La Motte continued, the necklace was priced at 1.6 million livres, and because the King had reached his wits' end over her spendthrift ways, Marie Antoinette had been forced repeatedly to refuse Boehmer's offers to sell it to her. If Rohan would be willing to purchase it on her behalf, under a veil of total secrecy, the Queen would gladly repay him—and be forever in his debt.

With naïve eagerness, the Cardinal assented. In February 1785, after a protracted series of written negotiations with Boehmer, he gave the necklace to the Comtesse to convey to her royal friend. He had had no further contact with Marie Antoinette, but La Motte trained him to identify subtle signs of the Queen's appreciation: a furtive smile or a tilt of her head in his direction when she passed him without speaking. Although Rohan avidly kept watch for each of these little gestures, he grew anxious for the day when his patroness would wear the necklace in public and acknowledge him more openly still.

But that day never came. Instead, on August 15, 1785, as he was preparing to perform Assumption services in the King's Chapel at Versailles, the Cardinal was abruptly summoned into Louis XVI's study. There, the King, the Queen, and the Minister of the Royal Household, the Baron de Breteuil—who shared Marie Antoinette's longtime hatred for Rohan—confronted him about his role in a recently uncovered crime. Twelve days earlier, Boehmer had informed Madame Campan that Rohan had purchased the "Slave's Collar" in Marie Antoinette's name.[7] The Queen, though, had never entrusted him with any such mission. As Marie Antoinette now angrily informed the Cardinal, she had never wanted the necklace, which she found gaudy and distasteful. She had never heard of a Comtesse de La Motte, and she had certainly never singled Rohan out for her special favor.

Thunderstruck, the Cardinal produced a letter signed by "Marie Antoinette of France" to prove that he had been acting on her orders. Louis XVI and his wife immediately pronounced the letter a fake—as the botched signature, which according to royal protocol ought to have included the Queen's Christian names alone, made clear. Brusquely they ordered him to withdraw into the Hall of Mirrors, where, before of a crowd of astounded courtiers, the Baron de Breteuil bellowed to an ensign: "Arrest the Cardinal!" Before the royal guards closed around him, the astonished prince managed to instruct an underling to burn all incriminating papers at the

Palais-Cardinal. Rohan acted none too soon, for moments later he was carted off to the Bastille.

THE NEWS OF THE GREAT ROHAN'S ARREST SENT SHOCKWAVES THROUGH the court, the capital, and the nation, but it was to be another nine months until the matter went to trial in the Paris Parlement, the kingdom's highest court of justice. Beginning in the spring of 1786, the *parlementaires* sought to unlock the mystery of the Diamond Necklace Affair by deposing a slew of intriguing witnesses and defendants: the Comtesse de La Motte, a penniless provincial aristocrat who, it turned out, had masterminded the scheme so that she could break up the necklace and sell its 647 diamonds abroad; the magician Cagliostro, whose self-proclaimed mystical gifts had already earned him both renown as a seer and infamy as a quack; Réteaux de Villette, an amateur forger who had penned the missives that Rohan assumed to be from the Queen; and Nicole Le Guay, a reportedly promiscuous blond milliner from the Palais Royal who bore more than a passing resemblance to Marie Antoinette, and whom La Motte had hired to impersonate the consort on that pivotal evening in the Grove of Venus. As the historian Sarah Maza has shown, after the "feverish anticipation" with which the public had awaited the trial's commencement, all these individuals became celebrities overnight, their juicy testimony circulated in trial briefs, newspapers, and pamphlets that reached an audience of "at least 100,000 readers": a vast, unprecedented number by eighteenth-century French standards.[8]

Yet the readers who voraciously consumed published reports on the Diamond Necklace Affair—more commonly known at the time as the *affaire du Cardinal*—were not attracted solely by its deliciously shady cast of secondary characters. Along with fascinating figures like the Comtesse de La Motte (who, despite her alleged descent from France's Valois kings, had worked as a lowly dressmaker's assistant) and Cagliostro (who insisted that he was three hundred years old, though he looked only thirty), the drama was riveting for its two starring, impossibly privileged antagonists, Marie Antoinette and the Cardinal de Rohan.[9]

Far more than the ultimately banal matter of the jewel heist, Sarah Maza has argued, it was the adversarial relationship between this rarefied pair that captured the public's attention. Because the affair pointed to corruption and conflict in the loftiest echelons of French society, contemporaries followed it with bated breath to see how the *parlementaires* would handle the two enemies' opposing claims. According to Maza, what the French people wanted to know above all was this:

Should the Cardinal be charged with "criminal presumption" and "lèse-majesté" for believing that the Queen would stoop to dealing with the likes of Madame de La Motte and assigning [him] a nocturnal rendezvous? Or should he be acquitted, on the implicit grounds that such behavior on the part of Marie Antoinette was not at all implausible?[10]

To Louis XVI and his wife, these questions urgently required just one, absolutely unequivocal response. By presuming that the Queen had invited him to a covert assignation and allowed him to kiss her gown, the Cardinal had "violated with unheard-of insolence . . . the respect due to the Royal Majesty," and thus deserved severe punishment.[11] But to many of Marie Antoinette's subjects, and certainly to her myriad enemies, her own record of compromising the Royal Majesty pointed toward a different conclusion. Here was a queen who (as several of the lawyers pointed out) often ventured out at night without a chaperone. Who fraternized with lowlifes. Who defied and cuckolded her husband at every opportunity. Whose fashions were publicized by references to trysts in secret groves and other sexualized transgressions. Whose favorite-like excesses made it wholly believable that she might have craved a "Slave's Collar" intended for the tawdry Du Barry. Who dared to dress "like a serving maid," in foreign fabrics, *en gaulle.*

This last attribute received frequent mention as the *parlementaires* pieced together the origins of the scam, and it led the public to construe Marie Antoinette—and not the Cardinal—as the real villain in the affair. For although the witnesses' testimony revealed that the Queen had had no involvement whatsoever in the conspiracy to steal the necklace, the judges and lawyers returned time and again to Le Guay's impersonation of her in the Grove of Venus. And this was a scene that inevitably recalled the uproar over *La Reine en gaulle,* which had already laid the groundwork for connecting the Queen's bad behavior to her immodest, inappropriate taste in clothes.[12]

Indeed, the Comtesse de La Motte seemed to have had the Vigée-Lebrun portrait in mind when she devised Nicole Le Guay's Marie Antoinette costume. This became evident when authorities confiscated La Motte's personal effects while searching for the stolen diamonds and found in her jewel case an exquisite tortoiseshell *bonbonnière* that, the police report noted,

> [was] encircled by a band of enormous diamonds evenly matched and perfect in color; the lid, on which a rising sun was painted, would fly up at the touch of a certain secret spring to reveal a portrait of the Queen in the very costume

[a white muslin dress] and posture [holding a rose] assumed by Mademoiselle [Le Guay] in the Grove of Venus scene.[13]

La Motte herself confirmed the implications of this find when she admitted to the court that her little box bearing the "portrait of the Queen wearing her simple white dress, as was the fashion at the time, and holding a rose in her hand" mirrored "precisely the attitude and the costume that Mademoiselle [Le Guay] adopted in the grove at Versailles."[14] Along the same lines, Le Guay testified that for the meeting with Rohan, the Comtesse "dressed me in a ruffled white linen dress; it was, as far as I can remember, a *gaulle,* the kind of garment more often described as a *chemise*"—that was to say, a *chemise à la Reine.*[15]

It had been a stroke of genius on La Motte's part to intuit that Rohan would read the *gaulle* as proof not just of its wearer's identity, but also, implicitly, of the Queen's willingness to engage in nonroyal behavior. But for Marie Antoinette, the results were disastrous. Having already provoked public outrage when depicted on the Queen's person at the Salon of 1783, the plain white gown now figured, to a bigger-than-ever reading public, as a clear sign of her multifaceted wickedness. Perhaps recalling the "Austrian" connotations of the gown's muslin, some of Marie Antoinette's detractors now accused her of conveying state secrets to Joseph II (who had taken over as the sole ruler of Austria after Maria Theresa's death) and of diverting French monies to him in order to strengthen Hapsburg rule.[16] Equally harmful to the Queen's reputation was the insinuation that the lower-class appearance the *gaulle* imparted to its wearer had necessarily led the Cardinal to assume Marie Antoinette's complicity in an act of lèse majesté.

In this context, Rohan's "presumption" in the rendezvous with the impostor-Queen registered as an honest (if ill-advised) mistake, and his case became a cause célèbre for a staggeringly diverse array of interest groups: from *parlementaires* eager to establish their autonomy from the crown to courtiers with personal grudges against Marie Antoinette, and from princes and churchmen eager to protect one of their own to political progressives who decried the Cardinal's imprisonment as an egregious case of royal despotism.[17]

Women's fashion followed suit with a trend that the Queen, for once, decidedly ignored: the *Cardinal sur la paille,* "Cardinal on the straw," a headdress that one contemporary described in his journal as being "in the shape of a cardinal's hat, with cardinal-red ribbons and a straw brim—symbolic of the heap of straw on the floor of the Bastille cells."[18] It was true that the Baron de Breteuil had, as Rohan's lawyer, the Abbé de Georgel, asserted before the court, "assigned His Eminence one of those hellish dungeons, those tombs for the living," thereby playing into the Bastille's existing reputation as a dreaded symbol of monarchical law and order.[19] But in deference to Rohan's princely standing, the prison warden had placed the Cardinal instead in his own private apartments, where the doors were never locked and where the prisoner feasted on oysters and champagne with the countless friends and supporters who were allowed to visit him there.[20] The luxuriousness of Rohan's circumstances notwithstanding, the well-heeled women of Paris and Versailles romanticized his plight and proudly wore their "Cardinal" bonnets in support.[21]

On May 31, 1786, the *parlementaires* resolved to acquit Rohan of all charges. The margin of votes (twenty-six to twenty-three) was perhaps narrower than some of his supporters would have liked; nonetheless, the ruling represented a crushing defeat for Marie Antoinette, whom the judges directly censured in one brutal clause: "With Her Most Christian Majesty's reputation for frivolity and indiscretion, with her succession of male and female 'favorites' of dubious repute, we find it entirely plausible that the Cardinal de Rohan did so presume."[22] With these lines, the *parlementaires* lent official credence to the charges that the gossip sheets had long leveled against the Queen and confirmed her rebellious exploits (at Trianon and elsewhere) as the real cause of the scandal. The French public overwhelmingly agreed with this assessment, as even Marie Antoinette's own good friend, the Baron de Besenval, could not help but attest. Reporting on the moment when the verdict was handed down, he observed:

> The Palais de Justice was full to overflowing and the joy was universal when it was known that the Cardinal was declared innocent. The judges were applauded and received such a welcome that they could hardly pass through the crowd, so great was the hatred for the opposite side, so deeply unfavorably disposed were the people against the Queen.[23]

An infuriated Louis XVI tried to lessen the affront to his wife's honor by banishing Rohan from court and forcing him to resign as Grand Almoner of France, but these gestures only prolonged the popular hue and cry over the crown's "despotic" ways. Meanwhile, the King's actions appear to have brought little solace to Marie Antoinette herself. When news of the Parlement's verdict first reached her at Versailles, she burst into tears and, according to Madame Campan, she never fully recovered from the blow.[24] Little did she know how much darker her days were soon to become. As the Comte de Beugnot, a lawyer who had enjoyed what he tried to downplay as a "youthful dalliance" with Madame de La Motte, wrote years later: "The

Revolution was already present in the minds of those who could contemplate such an insult to the King in the person of his wife."²⁵ But to Marie Antoinette's infinite misfortune, one of the most glaring "insults to the King" had been traced to her own, unseemly wardrobe. A central feature of her perceived involvement in the Diamond Necklace Affair, her revolution in fashion had, on a larger scale than ever before, turned public opinion squarely against her.

THE FACT THAT HER *GAULLES* CAME TO SIGNIFY HER COMPLICITY IN THE Cardinal's offense against the throne may have come as something of a surprise to Marie Antoinette, for, a full year before the trial's devastating conclusion, she had begun to dress more conservatively—indeed, rather more like a conventional queen. Early in 1785, she had announced to Rose Bertin that, as she would be turning thirty that November, she intended to "reform her accessories and adornments, which were better suited to a younger woman, and [to] stop wearing both feathers and flowers."²⁶ Duly Marie Antoinette renounced her whimsical coiffures in favor of what Antonia Fraser has described as "more matronly" headdresses made from gauze, satin, and velvet, and trimmed with fur or regal jeweled aigrettes.²⁷ The Queen modified the rest of her wardrobe as well, leading the contemporary chronicler François Métra to observe at the end of February "that Her Majesty's approach to dress has altered, that she no longer wants *chemises,* or redingotes, or *polonaises,* or *lévites*" (all of which had once predominated at Trianon) and that she "has taken up again the more serious" *robes à la française.*²⁸ According to the Baronne d'Oberkirch, Marie Antoinette required the ladies of Versailles to do the same and "to abdicate, like herself, plumes, flowers, and even the color pink" if they were thirty or older.²⁹

Admittedly, these changes may have been motivated more by vanity than by her subjects' disapproval. Though the Duke of Dorset, Britain's ambassador to Versailles, found it silly that the Queen should consider herself "an old woman" at thirty, she seemed acutely aware of the changes that age had wrought in her appearance.³⁰ In particular, she worried about losing her complexion, which her airy pastel gowns and flower-basket bonnets had offset so beautifully in earlier years. Indeed, Madame Campan maintained that the Queen first began to change her style of dress when she noticed that a new, rose-studded collar from the Grand Mogol made her skin look washed out and dull. The Marquise de La Tour du Pin corroborated this report by noting that Marie Antoinette "showed jealousy toward those young ladies whose seventeen-year-olds' complexions shone more dazzlingly than hers in the harsh light of day."³¹ While the Marquise was serving as one of the consort's youngest *dames du palais,* a well-meaning older duchess informed her that under no circumstances should she stand by a window when Her Majesty was present, lest the sunlight show off her skin to enviable effect. The fresh-faced La Tour du Pin discovered how sound this advice was only after she inadvertently disregarded it one afternoon and was promptly rebuked by the Queen for the inordinate showiness of her ensemble.[32]

Marie Antoinette had also apparently grown insecure about her hair, much of which had fallen out during her pregnancy with the Dauphin in 1781. Unfortunately, the higher coiffures Marie Antoinette had once preferred required extensive "frizzling" and teasing, which had only produced additional embarrassing bald patches. So dramatic was the Queen's hair loss that the ever-resourceful Léonard had felt compelled to disguise it with a cropped cut known as the *coiffure à l'enfant,* which other ladies of fashion hastened to emulate.[33] Léonard's relatively low-maintenance new style presented a more practical alternative to the towering coiffures of her youth and protected her against further unseemly balding.

In all likelihood, Marie Antoinette's return to the whalebone-bodiced *robe à la française* was also driven by vanity, for her proportions had ballooned in recent years: her bust now measured forty-four inches, and only the tightest of lacings could squeeze her waist down to a more acceptable silhouette.[34] These changes were, however, due as much to serial pregnancy as to aging: on March 27, 1785, the Queen gave birth to a second son, Louis Charles. Despite a new spate of rumors about the child's dubious paternity (Charles, after all, was the first name of the Comte d'Artois), his parents were delighted, as a second son placed the succession on a very strong footing.[35] Elated, Marie Antoinette dubbed the boy, who was much more beautiful than either of his older siblings, her *chou d'amour,* or sweetheart, and devoted herself more enthusiastically than ever to motherhood. Madame Royale, as little Marie Thérèse was then known, was growing into a sulky, ill-tempered girl, but Marie Antoinette doted on her nonetheless, as she did on the two little boys.[36]

Joined by the Duchesse de Polignac, whom the Queen had named Governess of the Children of France, and sometimes by Fersen, who made several extended trips to France during this period, Marie Antoinette and her little ones absconded frequently to Trianon to play at "normal" domestic life. Louis XVI, whose undiminished shyness and hatred of ceremony drove him to flee the court as frequently as his role would allow, joined them there almost every day for lunch and gave no sign of suspecting anything improper between his wife and the dashing Swedish count.

To increase the already considerable attractions—and faux rustic simplicity—of her hideaway, the Queen oversaw the construction of her now-famous Hameau (Hamlet), a picturesque, half-timbered country village that was erected between 1783 and 1787. Nestled in a pretty spot not far from the Petit Trianon, the Hameau was a place where she and her little family could gambol among the perfumed flocks of sheep and cows, feed the birds in the dovecote and the henhouse, eat freshly picked strawberries and cherries, and drink fresh milk from Sèvres porcelain cups reportedly molded on the Queen's own breasts.[37] Marie Antoinette's postnatal stoutness— further increased when she gave birth to an ailing, malformed daughter, Sophie Hélène Béatrice, on July 9, 1786—was apparently a small price to pay for such domestic bliss. Although Madame Sophie was to die only eleven months later from a tubercular ailment, Marie Antoinette would describe her surviving offspring to the Duchesse de Polignac as "my sole resource" against the vicissitudes of public life.[38]

The Queen's deepening passion for motherhood resulted in another notable sartorial shift besides the return of the corset. Although she reassumed the tightly trussed silhouettes of the *robe à la française,* she dressed her children in a thoroughly relaxed, modern fashion. Except for swaddling clothes in infancy, and one-piece gowns worn over a diminutive whalebone *corps* between the ages of three and four, the clothing of the children of the aristocracy had long resembled that of their parents in almost every particular. This, however, was a convention against which the Petit Trianon's patron saint, Rousseau, had argued forcefully, on the grounds that such restrictive attire could have deleterious effects on a child's health and development.[39] Apparently eager to extend the naturalness and freedom of her country haven to all aspects of her offspring's life, Marie Antoinette outfitted Madame Royale in the simple, unstructured muslin *gaulles* that she and her adult friends had made famous, and the young princes in sporty, unconfining sailor suits.

These were the costumes worn by Marie Antoinette's two oldest children in a portrait that the Swedish artist Adolf Ulrik von Wertmüller painted of them and their mother—posing in front of the Petit Trianon's Temple of Love—for Gustavus III, King of Sweden. (Plate 19.) And when the painting was shown at the Paris Salon of 1785, the public again railed against the inappropriate clothing styles it placed on display, even though the Queen herself had been represented wearing altogether traditional *paniers,* a cinched corset, lace sleeves, pearl bracelets, and a low headdress that Rose Bertin had confected from a slate-blue satin that highlighted the blue of the consort's eyes.[40] For the Wertmüller portrait, Marie Antoinette had even abandoned her signature Hapsburg roses, though Madame Royale held a clutch of them, as if reprising, in miniature, her mother's pose in *La Reine en gaulle*. In this way, the royal children's unconventional outfits may have reflected badly on their mother, despite her visible effort to rein in her own previous excesses of fashion.

Yet despite the unremarkable ensemble captured by Wertmüller's painting, the Queen nevertheless continued to develop at least a few experimental new styles for her own—rather than her children's—enjoyment. One of her sources of inspiration during this period came from her infant son's wet-nurse, a salty peasant known as Madame Poitrine ["Mrs. Chest"], who often hummed an old-time ditty, "Marlborough Goes Off to War," to lull the child to sleep.[41] As was reported widely in the scandal sheets of the day, Marie Antoinette became so infatuated with the tune that she not only baptized the little turret at the Hameau "Marlborough Tower," but launched a fad for the *chapeau à la Marlborough,* which was an extremely wide, flat straw hat worn low over the forehead and tilted up at the back by a gigantic bow underneath the brim.[42] (A close cousin to this hat was the *chapeau à la Devonshire,* named for Marie Antoinette's elegant English friend Georgiana, Duchess of Devonshire.[43]) According to one unnamed trend watcher, after it was adopted by the Queen, "the Marlborough mode spread like an epidemic throughout all of France."[44] And although the *Mémoires secrets* dismissed the prized cha-peaux as "grotesque hats in which [the ladies] are pleased to bury their charms," the ladies in question ignored this, and Rose Bertin busily whipped up Marlboroughs and Devonshires for clients both at home and abroad.[45]

Beginning in 1784, Marie Antoinette and her fellow fashion devotees also drew inspiration from reports that circulated about the discovery in Peru of a mythical beast called the harpy, described as "a two-horned monster with bat's wings, and a human face and hair, which was said to devour daily one ox, or four pigs."[46] To pay homage to the fascinating creature, French *marchandes de modes* devised a ribbon printed with blocky, abstracted tri-angles that may have been meant to evoke horns, wings, or fangs. The stark geometrical pattern reportedly captivated the Queen and almost overnight, stylish Parisian promenades were awash with hats and dresses adorned *à la harpie.*[47] Unfortunately, the harpy's reputation for gluttony supplied ready ammunition for those taking aim at Marie Antoinette's spendthrift tenden-cies; one 1784 pamphlet, apparently published by her duplicitous brother-in-law Provence, contained a caricature of a harpy whose flowing and unpowdered blond hair identified the monster with the Queen herself.[48] And this identification was visible not only in her hair, but, according to another unidentified lampoonist, in her adoption of this latest trend in dress:

> *Everything now is* à la harpie:
> *Ribbons, gowns, and bonnets;*
> *Ladies, you are getting smarter:*
> *You have given up your other trinkets*
> *For ones that show your true character.*[49]

And the fact was that as far as her putative true character was concerned, the Queen remained very much a slave to fashion, at least in terms of the money she was prepared to spend on her wardrobe. For in 1785, even as she was swearing off flowers and feathers in the name of a dignified old age, she spent a whopping 258,000 livres—more than twice her 120,000-livre yearly allowance—on new "fashions and jewels."⁵⁰ Of all the purveyors listed in the account books, Rose Bertin, as usual, was owed the largest amount, 91,947 livres. When she was asked how she could charge so much money for mere bits of gauze, satin, and straw, the *marchande* haughtily compared herself to a great painter the value of whose work, by definition, far exceeded that of the canvas and oils with which it was made.⁵¹

This remark provided little help to the Comtesse d'Ossun, Marie Antoinette's conscientious *dame d'atours,* who was responsible for disbursing payments to her mistress's many suppliers. And although the Comtesse had applied to the King for extra funds every year since she first assumed her *charge* in 1781, she found it quite difficult to explain the gigantic 1785 shortfall of 138,000 livres. When petitioning the King's Household for the necessary supplement, Madame d'Ossun acknowledged that it was a "veritably excessive sum" and apologized profusely—without invoking Bertin's explanatory quip about the high price of haute couture.⁵²

THE TIMING OF THESE FINANCIAL REVELATIONS COULD NOT HAVE BEEN worse, for the Comtesse d'Ossun filed her petition for the 1785 supplement on July 16, 1786, just sixteen days after Rohan's acquittal in the Diamond Necklace Affair.⁵³ In the realm of *la mode,* women expressed their disapproval of Marie Antoinette's presumed role in the debacle, to which the judges had alluded in such harsh terms, by wearing hats *au collier de la Reine.* (The crowns of these hats were studded liberally with real or fake gemstones meant to recreate the infamous "Slave's Collar."⁵⁴) That the missing necklace, whose constituent diamonds the Comtesse de La Motte, now imprisoned in the Salpêtrière Prison, had successfully smuggled abroad before her arrest, was now dubbed "the Queen's" (*collier de la Reine*) perpetuated the view that the consort had been responsible for the whole tawdry affair. News of her record-breaking wardrobe supplement now only strengthened this perception, according to which the spendthrift queen would have stopped at nothing to acquire a new accessory—even one costing an unthinkable 1.6 million livres.

Concerns about Marie Antoinette's spending had moreover assumed new urgency because of the financial crisis besetting the kingdom as a whole. In 1781, Louis XVI's widely admired Controller-General, the Swiss banker Jacques Necker, had published a report on the state of the nation's treasury, outlining not a huge deficit, as was commonly feared, but a modest revenue surplus of 10 million livres.[55] Necker had endeared himself to the French people for making public, for the first time ever, the royal accounting books. As the King's Minister of the Army, the Comte de Ségur, recalled of this dramatic move:

> Hitherto the nation, a stranger to its own affairs, had remained most completely ignorant as to the receipt and expenditure of the public revenue, the debts of the state, the extent of its wants and the resources it possessed.... [Necker's] appeal to public opinion was thus an appeal to liberty; and as soon as the nation had satisfied their curiosity, respecting these important objects, which had always been kept concealed from their view, they began to discuss and to judge, to bestow praise and to censure [on those who governed].[56]

In truth, Marie Antoinette's clothing expenditures accounted for a negligible portion of the overall budget outlined in Necker's report, but her ostentatious image belied the economic reality. While she was reviled, Necker emerged as a hero for his "democratic" willingness to furnish the people with information by which their sovereigns might be judged—and found wanting.

Yet the Controller-General's publication had not told the whole truth about the economic straits in which France actually found herself. His reporting of a small surplus was likely intended to boost investor confidence and public credit at a moment when he hoped to raise funds, at attractive interest rates, for France's involvement in the war in America.[57] Necker's emphasis on the surplus downplayed the alarming fact that since Louis XVI's accession, the treasury had racked up debts of 530 million livres, on which interest payments alone now consumed half of the annual national budget. When, in 1783, Necker was replaced in his duties by Charles Alexandre de Calonne, the new minister deemed his predecessor's much-touted publication "an absurd fraud, a pretense that all was well when, in fact, all was very much ill."[58]

All was very much ill indeed, but like Necker before him, Calonne discovered that he had little choice but to try to mitigate actual and potential creditors' skittishness about the health of the French economy. To that end, Calonne devised a policy that counterintuitively encouraged additional, and even more conspicuous, state expenditures, in the form of public works, trade subsidies, and even the creation of a new East India Company. The minister thus oversaw a period of intense investment, which the government could afford only by borrowing more and more money, at higher and higher rates. By 1786, Calonne had borrowed 650 million livres with the paradoxical goal of enriching France through spending.[59]

On a personal level, too, Calonne's profligacy was legendary (in a notable contrast to Necker, whom the people also admired for his modest, bourgeois lifestyle). Calonne's private art collection featured works by Rembrandt, Titian, Watteau, and Fragonard; the interiors of his coaches were lined with expensive furs; and the feasts he hosted at his two châteaux and his house in the capital assumed such epic proportions that he had to retain three servants and a kitchen boy just to look after the roasted meats. In 1784, the historian Simon Schama relates, the Controller-General commissioned Vigée-Lebrun to paint him dressed in opulent lace cuffs and a taffeta coat from "the sharpest and most expensive clothiers in Paris."[60] Rumors circulated afterward that he was the portraitist's lover and that he had once presented her with a box of candies in which each treat was wrapped in a 300-livre bill.[61] Vigée-Lebrun herself denied the allegation, which historians have been unable definitively to confirm or dismiss.[62] However, Calonne's choice of Marie Antoinette's official portraitist as his own, along with his taste for grandiosity and his close friendship with the family of the Duchesse de Polignac, linked him in the public imagination with the spoiled, self-indulgent queen.[63] Quick as always to seize upon the gossip of the day, fashion merchants began peddling a Trianon-worthy straw hat, the *chapeau à la Calonne,* whose overwhelming profusion of trimmings included a wide band of Marie Antoinette's beloved triangular *harpie* pattern.[64] Like the mythical creature that gave the *harpie* its name, both the Queen and her supposed protégé appeared to be endowed with ravenous financial appetites.

Truth be told, the association was an unfair one: Marie Antoinette disliked Calonne intensely because of the ties he maintained to the Rohan clan.[65] (Indeed, to her great disillusionment, many members of the Duchesse de Polignac's coterie had done the same, thereby casting a pall over the pretty favorite's friendship with the consort.) Worse still, from the Queen's perspective, the urbane Controller-General was a longtime friend of the Duc d'Aiguillon. Since his appointment, Calonne had taken special pains to ensure that Aiguillon's former lover Du Barry, now involved with Paris's governor, the Duc de Brissac, continued to live in high style. Calonne even increased the modest pension Du Barry had received upon her exile, to an incredible 1.2 million livres.[66] Understanding, however, that it also behooved him to curry favor with Louis XVI's beloved wife, the Controller-General did not hesitate to advance her large sums whenever presented with updates about her financial distress. "Whenever I asked for 50,000 livres, they gave me 100,000," Marie Antoinette later explained, to emphasize how little she had known of the economic difficulties that existed while Calonne controlled the purse strings.[67]

All this changed in the wake of the Diamond Necklace Affair and the

Comtesse d'Ossun's petition for extra wardrobe monies. In the summer of 1786, the Controller-General completed an extensive review of the nation's finances; and on August 26, he informed Louis XVI that, contrary to Necker's earlier assertions, the treasury was running a current deficit of over 100 million livres, with 250 million livres of additional debt in arrears.[68] Calonne further announced that no more creditors could be induced to cover the shortfall, even at higher interest rates; that trade had slackened too much to feed the beast; that "public confidence in government was at its lowest ebb in memory"; and that only a massive overhaul of the taxation system and the royal budget could begin to reverse the damage.[69]

At the heart of Calonne's solution lay the premise that the nobility should no longer receive inordinate tax exemptions and that taxes ought to be made "equal and proportionate for all."[70] Under normal circumstances, this was a proposal that the King would have charged the Paris Parlement with ratifying, but after that body's ruling in the Rohan trial, he no longer trusted its members to support his policies. Besides, taxation had long stood as a point of conflict between the parliamentary aristocracy and the King; as noblemen, the *parlementaires* had everything to lose by endorsing Calonne's suggested reforms. To circumvent the Parlement, Louis XVI and his Controller-General therefore resolved to convene an Assembly of Notables—144 aristocrats selected, in theory, for their ability to advise their sovereign on the fiscal morass, but in reality chosen because they were expected to support the King in whatever measures he saw fit to undertake.

Louis XVI had, however, misjudged his Notables. Like the *parlementaires,* these men saw no reason to forfeit their tax exemption, especially insofar as its purpose seemed to be to pay off the extravagances of the royal family. In protest, fashionable noblemen sported waistcoats embroidered with the faces of all the Notables—and with the figure of the King, whose right hand was deliberately positioned to appear to be dipping into the wearers' pockets.[71] When the Assembly of Notables convened in late February 1787, its members refused to ratify Calonne's reforms; instead they demanded, and secured, his dismissal. Calonne retaliated by publishing his findings on the grim state of the French economy, so that before long the word *deficit* figured prominently in the public's mounting complaints against the throne.

Many blamed the bad news on Calonne himself and on his presumed protectress, Marie Antoinette. Print sellers in Paris marketed an image called *Pandora's Box* showing the Controller-General carrying an open box, which holds a large figurine labeled "Antoinette" and outfitted in a white muslin scarf and bonnet. To the courtiers who have gathered around to inspect the doll—one of whom sarcastically dubs it "this beautiful present that the court

7. Anonymous, *Pandora's Box* (c. 1787) (Bibliothèque Nationale de France, Paris)

of Vienna sent to us"—Calonne explains, "Here is the only German jewel upon which one can place a price." A sly euphemism for the female genitals, "jewel" evoked Marie Antoinette's supposed collaboration with a prostitute in the Diamond Necklace Affair, while "German" played on her Austrian allegiances, additionally figured by her muslin (thus possibly Hapsburg-manufactured) fichu. But above all, it was Marie Antoinette's background in fashion that the cartoonist had singled out for attack. For the "Antoinette" doll recalled precisely the large traveling mannequin or "Pandora" by means of which, it had once been said, she and Bertin had "dominat[ed] the universe."[72] The message was clear: Marie Antoinette's clothing excesses, recklessly indulged by the dandyish Calonne, were the uncontrollable evils that, once released from Pandora's box, could never be contained again. Small wonder, then, that when crowds at the Palais Royal burned Calonne in effigy, they festooned his dummy with pamphlets that roundly condemned the Queen.[73]

Calonne's successor, Étienne Charles de Loménie de Brienne, came from the opposition party in the Notables. But because he had served as the Abbé de Vermond's longtime protector, and because it was Marie Antoinette herself who pushed for his nomination to the post, he was fated to inspire just as much loathing as Calonne had done. News of Brienne's appointment to the long defunct position of Prime Minister was greeted with furious cries of "It is the Queen who governs!"[74] Partly because of this reaction and partly because, like his predecessor, Brienne had to advocate tax changes unfavorable to the aristocracy, his policies, too, met with fierce political resistance. This time, the problems came from the *parlementaires,* to whom the affair had been entrusted after the deadlock among the Notables, and who, as Louis XVI had correctly surmised, had no intention of supporting the necessary reforms.

On August 6, the King called a *lit de justice* to register edicts supporting the imposition of a stamp tax and a land tax, measures the Paris Parlement opposed so strenuously that he sent its members into exile. They were allowed to return to Paris only when violent protests against Louis XVI's actions threatened to engulf the city in chaos. On November 19, the monarch again presented his ideas for economic reform and threw the Parlement into an uproar when he called for the issuance of 420 million livres in new loans. Adding his voice to the outcry was the Duc d'Orléans, erstwhile Duc de Chartres, to whom the Orléans title had passed upon his father's death in 1785. Amid the clamoring *parlementaires,* Orléans stepped forward and declared, "This register is illegal." Flabbergasted by this unthinkable affront to his authority, the Duc's royal cousin blushed and stammered for a long, uncomfortable moment. Finally, he succeeded in blurting out an infamous rejoinder: "Yes, it is legal, legal because I say so."[75]

Afterward, with Marie Antoinette's encouragement, the King exiled Orléans for his insubordinate behavior. But like Louis XVI's eminently quotable, autocratic outburst, his dismissal of the Duc proved a political boon to the latter man by casting him as a martyr to absolutist whim. Now more than ever, Orléans could credibly position himself as a friend of the common man and an enemy of royal despotism. Fearsome demonstrations attended his exile, and the legitimacy of the Bourbon rule was again—as during previous unpopular moves by Louis XVI and his predecessor—called furiously into question.

In both aristocratic and Third Estate circles, news of the deficit and confusion about what course the government would take next sparked a panicked indignation directed in no small part at the Queen. And so, while her husband sank into a deep depression over his failures with the Notables and the *parlementaires,* Marie Antoinette had to shoulder terrifyingly overt displays of public anger.[76] In February 1787, she found on the door to her loge at the theater an anonymous note that warned: "Tremble, tyrants, your reign must end!"[77] Audiences at the theater and the Opéra seemed to share this sentiment, greeting her with frosty silence or sharp hisses and applauding vociferously whenever an actor declaimed against a royal despot.[78] Her subjects' behavior so mortified her that she more than once gave way to crying jags in private, begging her intimates to explain why the people hated her so. Eventually she agreed to avoid public performances altogether.

Her other favorite Parisian haunt, the Palais Royal, had become just as inhospitable, especially after Orléans's newsmaking exile. With that prince's tacit protection, booksellers hawked the incendiary memoirs of the Comtesse de La Motte, who, after staging an amazing escape from her cell in the Salpêtrière, had wound up relocating in London. There, enemies of the Queen, including the recently dismissed Calonne, enlisted La Motte as their ally. Thought by Marie Antoinette herself to have been commissioned by Choiseul (who blamed her for his fall from grace), the Comtesse's memoirs insisted that the Queen had been guilty in the Diamond Necklace Affair and accused her of lesbianism and adultery, thereby reopening the wounds that the public had nursed over the course of Rohan's trial.[79] The lieutenant of police advised Marie Antoinette that it was no longer safe for her to appear in Paris, with the Palais Royal, that hotbed of scurrilous writings against her, posing the most obvious threat to her safety.

Somewhat oddly, rumor held that La Motte's text had been smuggled into the country by none other than Rose Bertin and that Marie Antoinette had punished the turncoat *marchande* by imprisoning her in the Bastille.[80] No doubt this was an outcome that many of Bertin's detractors would have enjoyed witnessing, and perhaps it served as the basis for the fantasy. But as it happened, the culprit was a *marchande de modes* unconnected to either Bertin or the Queen. The woman's name was Henriette Sando, and she owned a shop called The Court's Taste that, despite its name, Marie Antoinette apparently never frequented; in March 1788, Sando was arrested for smuggling La Motte's licentious text into France.[81] However, when combined with renewed discussions of *gaulles* and diamonds, and with the more recent disclosure of Ossun's exorbitant wardrobe request, the claims that Bertin had acted as the smuggler kept the public focused on the sordid capriciousness that always seemed to characterize the Queen's involvement with fashion.

Even more harmful to Marie Antoinette's reputation were the bankruptcy rumors swirling around her favorite *marchande* in early 1787. Just a month before the Assembly of Notables first gathered, the savvy Bertin had decided to stage a fake bankruptcy in order to force her clients to pay her for all that they had purchased on credit. And although it was common knowledge that Mademoiselle Bertin ran her business on credit, she astounded the public by announcing that her uncollected debts totaled somewhere between 2 and 3 million livres. "It is true that hers is hardly a plebeian bankruptcy," the Baronne d'Oberkirch noted wryly. "Two million? This is the bankruptcy of a *grande dame!*"[82]

For the Baronne, who had long bemoaned Bertin's tendency to act above her station, the bankruptcy was of a piece with the *marchande*'s other pretentious antics. Yet just as appalling as this latest proof of Bertin's arrogance was the suggestion that Marie Antoinette had again behaved with breathtaking financial irresponsibility. It was believed that the lion's share of Bertin's outstanding accounts were in the Queen's name; or at least, this was the assumption underlying the rumor to which the Parisian bookseller S. P.

Hardy alluded on January 31, when he recorded that upon declaring bankruptcy, Bertin "instantly received an ordinance for 400,000 livres drawn on the royal treasury"—a sum that, as was now all too well known, the royal treasury could ill afford to spare.[83] Once again, the news made its way onto stylish women's heads in the form of a novelty headdress. Hung with a dour black veil, this one was called the *caisse d'escompte* or "savings account": its crown [*fond*] had been sliced off in a sarcastic emulation of the national treasury's "bottomless" [*sans fond*] coffers.[84]

Like Bertin's alleged imprisonment in the Bastille, though, the story about the 400,000-livre note was pure fiction. When the *marchande* came to Versailles to collect her debts on January 28, the Queen refused to see her, presumably because she guessed that Bertin was trying to embarrass her into settling her accounts. Nevertheless, it did not take Bertin long to convince Marie Antoinette that malicious souls had started the bankruptcy rumors in order to discredit them both. Relieved not to face betrayal from this quarter—especially at a time when another of her favorites, the Duchesse de Polignac, seemed to be drifting ever further into the enemy camp—the Queen forgave her star *marchande*. And Bertin, for her part, wisely never mentioned her bankruptcy again.

Even so, Bertin's much-vaunted "collaborations with Her Majesty" diminished considerably after this incident, which along with the other events of 1786 and 1787 seemed at last to show Marie Antoinette how little—politically and financially—she could afford any further extravagance. In 1787, she reduced her total household expenses by a staggering 900,000 livres. As for her wardrobe budget during this year, the Queen requested a mere 97,187-livre supplement—40,000 livres less than she had required in 1785.[85] Furthermore, much of her money now went to the overhauling of existing dresses and skirts rather than to the purchase of brand-new, of-the-moment creations. On March 19, while the Assembly of Notables fought with Calonne over the nation's economic future, the Queen directed a relatively obscure *marchande des modes* called Madame Éloffe to repair one of her old dresses, described in Éloffe's records as "a green satin dress garnished with pearls and red beads."[86]

According to the Comte de Reiset, who published and extensively annotated Éloffe's account books in the late nineteenth century, this was in all likelihood the first time that Marie Antoinette ever had a dress mended rather than simply throwing it away.[87] This unusual decision soon became a bona fide trend, with Marie Antoinette regularly enlisting Éloffe to perform minor repairs and to provide inexpensive new trimmings for her luxurious old gowns. Exemplary entries from Éloffe's 1787 ledgers show her charging the Queen for "3 *aunes* of *blonde Alençon* [a delicate lace woven from silk], to be used to edge the sleeves of a black-striped, blue satin redingote" (28 livres); "3 *aunes* of faux silver fringe for the hem of a festooned skirt" (102 livres); and "2 *aunes* of black lace to put on the brim of a rose-colored gauze hat" (36 livres).[88]

Such unimpressive orders probably held minimal appeal for Rose Bertin, whose twelve-year bonanza of total creative and financial liberty had finally come to an end. Marie Antoinette still entrusted the great *marchande* with her most significant orders, for example the red velvet and blue satin gowns and headdresses she wore in portraits by Vigée-Lebrun in 1787 and 1788. More and more, though, Bertin was obliged to turn her attention to other wealthy customers as the Queen cut back on frivolities. Thanks to the generosity of Calonne and Brissac, Madame Du Barry still figured on Bertin's elite client list and commissioned from Bertin such lavish costumes as a dazzling 2,000-livre frock embroidered with seed pearls, blue gemstones, and golden sheaves of wheat.[89] The Comtesse was still spending and dressing as luxuriously as she had during the reign of Louis XV, while Marie Antoinette, who remained the only love interest in the reigning king's life, renounced her mistresslike glamour for good.

But however great a turning point 1787 may have represented in the Queen's spending on clothes, the change seems to have been lost on the public at large. In August of that year, at the Paris Salon, a picture frame hung empty to herald the forthcoming appearance of Vigée-Lebrun's latest portrait of Marie Antoinette. This was a tactical maneuver on the part of the Salon officials, who after the scandals of 1783 and 1785 had decided that at least some degree of popular outcry could be avoided if the painter simply waited until after the opening to display her work.[90] Yet this effort at circumspection only served to provide Salon-goers with a different means to lash out at the King's wife. Before Vigée-Lebrun placed her canvas in the frame, a jokester affixed to the empty space a label reading "Voici le portrait de Madame Déficit"—"Here is the portrait of Madame Deficit."[91] The nickname took, and it hovered like a restive phantom over subsequent discussions of the nation's moribund economy.

FOR THE NEXT TWO YEARS, THE QUEEN PURSUED HER COURSE OF DIMINISHED personal expenditure and restrained sartorial display. No more did she sport headdresses *à la Marlborough* and *à la harpie;* no more did she indulge in the less whimsical, yet equally pricey, trimmings she had embraced after turning thirty. Observers now noticed in her a "total love of simplicity," which meant not the coquettish *gaulles* and fanciful bonnets of yore, but understated, generally unremarkable satin and taffeta dresses draped over narrow *paniers.*[92] In lieu of the pretty, custom-colored and -patterned pastels she had once brought into fashion, she gravitated toward somber shades enlivened only by the occasional bright stripe. For headgear she elected "the very simplest of hats," and diamonds she avoided assiduously.[93] They appeared only at the court's most formal occasions, such as New Year's Day, Easter, Pentecost, and Christmas, when etiquette required that she appear in full, formal dress, showcasing the crown's magnificence.

The economies Marie Antoinette introduced into her wardrobe were part of an effort to reduce expenses in almost all aspects of her household, a program that resulted in a dramatic savings of 1,200,600 livres in 1788 alone.[94] But her cost-cutting measures won her no acclaim. At court, aristocrats who lost their *charges* for budgetary reasons blamed Marie Antoinette for their diminished income and prestige, even as they disparaged her as "Madame Déficit." These disgruntled gentlemen and ladies joined the already swollen ranks of nobles who had been hoping for her downfall—little suspecting, as Madame Campan would note after the Revolution, that the Queen's demise might also entail their own.[95]

For Marie Antoinette, the unreservedly bitter complaints of Trianon habitués like the Baron de Besenval and the Duc de Coigny were especially painful. If she had hitherto been blind to her so-called friends' greed and self-interest, these qualities became much more apparent as she began scaling back on her former largesse.[96] Relations cooled still further between her and the Duchesse de Polignac, whose family and friends had always been unabashedly forward in seeking extravagant royal favors. Increasingly ill at ease in this self-serving company, the Queen began spending more time with the serious but trustworthy Comtesse d'Ossun and with Louis XVI's shy, deeply religious younger sister, Madame Élisabeth. Although less fun-loving, exciting, and attractive than her usual crowd, at least neither of these women appeared to begrudge Marie Antoinette her newfound frugality. Yet the Queen's asceticism took its toll on the culture of stylishness over which she had once presided. Even friends who remained loyal to her, like the Prince de Ligne, expressed shock and dismay at how "badly dressed" Frenchwomen of fashion had grown, thanks to the drastic "change for the worse in manners and customs" that the Queen's change in lifestyle had occasioned.[97]

Beyond the confines of Versailles, too, Marie Antoinette's pared-down clothes seem to have inspired distaste, on the by now familiar grounds that these outfits did not adequately reflect her royal standing. The bookseller Hardy noted in his diary that when the King and his family made a ceremonial public appearance at the Invalides in Paris on June 23, 1788, "the rumor spread that [Her Majesty's] exceedingly modest ensemble made for a striking contrast with that of Madame Royale, the Comtesse de Provence, and

Madame Élisabeth, who were by her side, and who were wearing costumes of the greatest formality."⁹⁸

It is hard not to believe that the harsh reaction to her simplified attire came as a complete surprise to Marie Antoinette, given the tremendous public animosity that the Diamond Necklace Affair had brought to the fore. Still, it may have stung her to find that at the very moment when she was forced to abandon her stylish endeavors, French modes continued to flourish without her, nurtured in no small part by the appearance in 1785 of the nation's first major fashion journal, *Le Cabinet des modes,* the name of which changed a year later to *Le Magasin des modes nouvelles françaises et anglaises,* and then again in 1790 to *Le Journal de la mode et du goût.* Unlike the fashion almanacs and engravings from which well-heeled women had previously obtained their style tips, *Le Cabinet des modes* and its later incarnations offered extensive commentary on the latest trends and zealous, knowing advice about how to emulate them.⁹⁹ Illustrated with three color plates per issue, these periodicals appeared on a more or less biweekly basis; subscriptions, at 21 livres a year, were costly but less expensive (and therefore more accessible) than the deluxe engraved almanacs of years past.¹⁰⁰

It is unknown whether Marie Antoinette subscribed to these journals, but she retained a palpable presence in their voguish pages. While the nomenclature of bonnets and gowns changed as rapidly as ever, reflecting the popularity of a newly discovered actress or color, their basic shapes and styles often traced their origins straight to the Queen. In the first issue of *Le Magasin des modes nouvelles,* for instance, the editor declared that the originally shocking "man's redingote" had, in recent years, become a staple of every elegant female wardrobe.¹⁰¹ At around the same time, a popular fashion plate purported to reproduce exactly a simple redingote of pale-gray taffeta that Marie Antoinette had been seen wearing on a recent stroll outdoors.¹⁰² This same image also reproduced the androgynous *catogan* ponytail and billowing white fichu that the royal consort had originally brought into style, and that now appeared as indispensable additions to the popular redingote ensemble.

Flower-trimmed straw hats that recalled the Petit Trianon, and silk dominoes that evoked Marie Antoinette's famous Opéra outings, also dominated the fashion press during this period, as did the *pouf,* which, according to an April 1787 issue of *Le Magasin des modes,* was still unsurpassed in the domain of ultra-fashionable headgear.¹⁰³ Other repeats of the Queen's modish innovations included delicately patterned taffetas "printed with tiny motifs [of] stylized flowers, dots, and dashes," which remained all the rage at this time, and "gowns of white gauze or muslin" such as the once-scandalous *chemise à la Reine,* which, in part thanks to Marie Antoinette's gift of the *gaulle* to her fashionable friend Georgiana of Devonshire, were prized in keeping with a general frenzy for things English.[104] When promoting these "Franco-English *robes en chemise*," the editor of *Le Magasin des modes nouvelles* recommended that they be paired, as they had been at the Petit Trianon, with loose, unpowdered hair, muslin or gauze fichus, and bouffant white bonnets, sometimes aptly identified as *bonnets à la paysanne de cour* ("peasant girl of the court").[105] In these respects, although the consort's budgetary restrictions and her self-imposed exile from Paris diminished her prominence as a trendsetter, the fashion periodicals carried on her legacy of experimental modern style.[106] Indeed, as the aristocratic chronicler Félix de Montjoie remarked, "even as the people were criticizing the Queen for her outfits, they continued frenetically to imitate her."[107]

Yet if Marie Antoinette felt any sadness as the scepter of fashion fell from her hands and into those of an increasingly unfriendly public, by 1788 she had a new avocation that was consuming much more of her time.[108] Whereas she had once approximated real political "credit" principally through her costumes and expenditures, she was now, for the first time, actively helping to shape the policies of her husband's government. Since the death of Louis XVI's favorite minister, Vergennes, in 1787, the King had become increasingly overwhelmed by tensions and conflicts among his remaining ministers and had turned to his wife as the only person he could genuinely trust.[109] This reversal of his longtime effort to exclude Marie Antoinette from substantive political discussions brought the couple closer together, even as courtiers angrily decried her ascendancy. According to the historian Timothy Tackett, Louis XVI came to rely so heavily on his wife's advice that "even when she was not [present for a meeting of his council], he would sometimes leave the room in the midst of discussions to consult with her—much to the consternation and bewilderment of his royal ministers."[110] Although she complained to Madame Campan that her newfound responsibility weighed heavily on her shoulders, this did not stop the Queen from influencing Louis XVI in some of his most important political decisions, from the appointment of Brienne to the exile of Orléans.[111]

In August 1788, she went even further, encouraging her husband to take what would prove to be one of the most fateful steps of his rule. As her protégé Brienne grew more and more unpopular and the deadlock between royal and parliamentary factions persisted, Marie Antoinette informed the King that the only solution lay in recalling an earlier Controller-General, Jacques Necker, whom the public still held in high esteem despite recent revelations about his overstatement of the nation's resources in 1781.

Louis XVI himself had always loathed Necker, thinking him unbearably conceited. (Years before, the Swiss banker had avowed in print that "if men are made in the image of God, then the Controller-General, next to the King, must be the man who most closely approximates that image."[112]) Though such insolence in a commoner sat little better with Marie Antoinette than it did with her husband, she was nevertheless convinced that Necker was the only one whom the French public would trust to find a way out of the present crisis. On August 25, after much grumbling, the King acceded to her suggestions. Brienne was persuaded to tender his resignation, and Marie Antoinette acted quickly to secure Necker as his successor. That same day, she wrote to Necker herself, imploring him to return to Versailles and resume his former duties. Afterward she sent a note to the Comte de Mercy, who continued to serve Austria under Joseph II, relating what had happened. "If [Necker] can get to work tomorrow," she concluded,

> so much the better. There is urgent work to accomplish. I tremble at the thought—forgive me this weakness—because it is I who am responsible for his return. My fate is to cause bad luck, and if infernal machinations cause him to fail, . . . then people will hate me all the more.[113]

At first, Marie Antoinette's premonitions seemed unfounded. Without acknowledging the Queen's role in Necker's return, the people of Paris were ecstatic at the news, parading his bust and that of the Duc d'Orléans through the streets around the Palais Royal and burning Brienne in effigy.[114] As a man of "enlightened," democratic convictions, Necker had indeed managed to retain the Third Estate's trust and support. A recent disastrous harvest had compounded commoners' fears about France's failing economy and had infused their debates about the legitimacy of the present régime with mounting urgency. In the cafés and bookshops of the Palais Royal, people imbued with the philosophy of the age—the egalitarian precepts of Voltaire, Diderot, and Rousseau, whose works Marie Antoinette had favored at Trianon without grasping their seditious political implications—excitedly discussed the idea of a constitution that would curb the iniquities of the present order.[115] That the ideals of liberty and equality had triumphed in the American Revolution, whose architects owed a heavy philosophical debt to the thinkers of the French Enlightenment, made it seem all the more likely that they could carry the day in France as well. That Necker, moreover, seemed to share these ideals only increased the surge of optimism that attended his return.

When Necker encouraged Louis XVI to address the government's problems by convoking the Estates General, a special advisory assembly that had not been summoned since 1614, the public was therefore primed to believe that the result would be the equitable political reforms for which it had long been hoping.[116] As one *cahier de doléances,* or formal grievance, drawn up in advance of the meeting announced: "The universal cry which goes up from the Nation announces that the moment has finally come to determine its Constitution, . . . [and] that no general law whatsoever [will] be introduced except in the Estates General, by mutual cooperation between the King's authority and the consent of the Nation."[117] Such sweeping changes as these went far beyond what the King—who appears to have viewed the convocation as only an inevitable, if risky, step toward solving the realm's fiscal woes—had envisioned.[118] Still, the discontented and the democratically minded rejoiced that the Estates General included representatives from the Third Estate, not just from the clergy and the nobility, in whom virtually all privilege had hitherto been concentrated. This—and the fact that Necker prevailed upon Louis XVI to double the number of representatives usually granted to the Third Estate—suggested that at last the people might be given a voice in the shaping of the nation.[119]

A staunch royalist by conviction as well as by birth, Marie Antoinette neither grasped nor sympathized with such egalitarian notions. To her, divine right and absolute rule were as much a part of the natural order as the grassy knolls around the Petit Trianon and the orange trees that shaded her bedroom windows at Versailles.[120] Apparently, she hoped that the bourgeoisie's and the clergy's natural reverence for the monarchy would lead their representatives in the Estates General to counteract the nobility's refractory measures and push for a solution acceptable to the King.[121] Yet in the Diamond Necklace Affair, her subjects' loathing for her had proven far stronger than whatever respect they harbored for her husband as a ruler or the crown as an institution. So the meeting of the Estates General, scheduled to take place in May 1789, did not promise to be a sure public relations victory for the Queen, her role in Necker's recall notwithstanding. With between eleven hundred and twelve hundred deputies from the three Estates, and countless excited spectators from throughout France, descending on Versailles for the historic meeting, the convocation would place her before hordes of the very people whom she had been staying away from Paris to avoid.

Perhaps to preempt fresh criticisms from this dauntingly large new audience, Marie Antoinette planned her outfits for the event with tremendous care, abandoning her more personal whims of style for the time-honored conventions of queenly pomp. For the formal procession and the religious services on May 4, 1789, she settled on a lustrous cloth-of-silver gown, which, viewed beside Louis XVI's resplendent cloth-of-gold jacket, would cast her as "the moon to the King's sun."[122] (If ever there was a time to cede the Sun King's glamour to her unassuming spouse, this would be it.) In addition, both she and Louis XVI would emphasize the Bourbon *gloire* by wearing the most precious white diamonds in the crown's collection. Along with a diamond-encrusted sword, diamond buttons on his jacket, and diamond buckles on his shoes, her husband would wear the so-called Pitt or Regent Diamond (later known as the Hope Diamond) affixed to his hat, while Marie Antoinette would place in her tresses the legendarily flawless Sancy Diamond.[123] "And on her person," Antonia Fraser has written, the Queen decided to wear "a series of other diamonds called the De Guise and Mirror of Portugal, with vast drops of single gems. . . . [She would] not, however, wear a necklace," lest hostile onlookers be inspired to reference the *affaire du Cardinal.*[124]

For the opening of the Estates General on May 5, Marie Antoinette chose another irreproachably dignified ensemble, one that would likewise present her as an avatar of an entire, august class rather than a lone, untamed consort concerned solely with her own beauty and pleasure. Abandoning the ministrations of Madame Éloffe, she commissioned Rose Bertin to supply her with "what was to be the last of [her] grand gala dresses, . . . a dress of purple satin over a white skirt embroidered with diamonds and paillettes."[125] Again eschewing any kind of necklace, she decided to accessorize this glorious confection with only a clutch of white ostrich feathers and a single band of diamonds in her hair.[126] Unlike the modest gown she had worn to the Invalides in June of the previous year, her garb for the Estates General would remind everyone present that, for all the ink that had been spilled in calumnies against her, she remained every inch their transcendent Queen, divine Bourbon dazzle incarnate.

But this was most definitely not how the people greeted her on May 4. On that day, as a prelude to the opening of the Estates General, Louis XVI and his consort headed a long, glittering procession through the town of Versailles, beginning at the Cathedral of Our Lady and ending at the Church of St. Louis. Just ahead of the royal couple, the Comte de Provence, the Comte d'Artois, and Artois's two young sons bore aloft a regal purple canopy over the Holy Sacrament. Behind this cortège came the three orders in the costumes that the Master of Ceremonies had, following the rules that had been laid out for the last such gathering in 1614, required them to wear: the clergy in sumptuous red, violet, and gold ecclesiastical robes; the aristocracy in rich, gold-embroidered black jackets, black silk knee-breeches, white silk stockings, and the plumed hats of Henri IV's court; and the 610 members of the Third Estate in plain black suits, white cambric cravats, and untrimmed black tricorn hats.

Putting a dramatic end to days of heavy rains, the sun broke through the clouds and glinted brightly on the aristocrats' ensembles. Marie Antoinette and her husband, in particular, shimmered from head to toe as their diamonds refracted the light in a thousand rainbows. The dark-suited deputies of the Third Estate, by contrast, appeared to blot out the sunshine as well as the light of the candles they carried in their hands. Many of them were galled by what the historian Claude Manceron has dubbed the "aggressive opulence of the nobles' costumes" and by the galling plainness of their own outfits— which, though dictated by ceremonial tradition, seemed designed expressly to highlight their inferior status.[127] As one Third Estate representative, Rabaut Saint-Étienne, recollected, his fellow deputies "looked as if they were in mourning" in their grimly humble garb.[128] But if the death of the old order was at hand, many of these plainly dressed individuals were perhaps less inclined to mourn than to rejoice. "What is the Third Estate?" one of their colleagues, the Abbé Sieyès, had asked several months earlier in a pamphlet that rapidly became a touchstone for their class. "Everything. What has it been up until now, in the political order? Nothing. What is it asking for? To become something."[129] Despite the mortification visited upon them by the day's dress code, this was the common-born deputies' mission in attending the Estates General; this was their righteous task.

According to contemporary accounts, the people who had flocked to Versailles from around the kingdom shared these deputies' outrage over the glaring sartorial differences between the Third Estate and the nobility. As Rabaut Saint-Étienne later recalled, many of the spectators who witnessed the procession had never before seen the court or any of its members. Familiar only with "the spectacle of miserable poverty that afflicted their own cities and villages," he wrote, these individuals were, like their representatives, deeply shocked by the unapologetic "evidence of expense and voluptuousness" among the aristocrats and the royals. Consequently, Saint-Étienne explained, "the people recognized the men in the [cambric] cravats as its fathers and its defenders, and the others as its enemies."[130] This explanation may have bordered on self-serving, given Saint-Étienne's own role in the proceedings, but it evinced an awareness of the gross, class-based discrepancies in clothing that subsequent commentators have characterized as "sartorial apartheid" and "sartorial humiliation."[131]

Needless to say, these striking differences in costume in no way redounded to the benefit of the Queen, whose luminescent court costume contrasted markedly with the commoners' homespun garb. To make matters worse, her husband's cousin the Duc d'Orléans had chosen a bourgeois outfit rather than the aristocratic accoutrements to which his birth entitled him; solidifying his image as the people's prince, he had elected not just to march with the Third Estate but to dress every bit as unassumingly as they. Orléans had also recently made a great show of selling off 8 million livres' worth of art from his family's collection, and, as the Marquise de La Tour du Pin recalled, of earmarking the proceeds "for the easement of the people's misery after the hard winter."[132] His credibility shored up by these astute maneuvers, the Duc won acclaim for a class masquerade of the very sort that the public deplored so virulently whenever Marie Antoinette cast off the trappings of her rank.

This discrepancy in the public's reaction toward the two royal celebrities may have had something to do with all the outrageous stories, widely disseminated in the Diamond Necklace Affair, about Marie Antoinette's extravagant tastes in clothing and jewels, and about her perverse hijinks at the Petit Trianon. Indeed, unbeknownst to the Queen, some of the spectators lining the streets of Versailles that day were already planning to pay an uninvited visit to her little country palace, to glimpse her decadent headquarters for themselves. According to Madame Campan, these malcontents would shortly descend in droves on the villa, angrily demanding to see its "richly furnished rooms . . . decorated with diamonds . . . sapphires and rubies," and reacting with intensified ire when they found that their expectations of luxury were misplaced.[133] But at the moment, they stood before a consort decked out in precisely such sumptuous gemstones; and in their resentment, not one person in the audience proffered the traditional cry of "Long live the Queen!" as she passed. Instead, the crowds shouted pointedly: "Long live the Duc d'Orléans!" Seeming to grasp that the compliment to her husband's cousin was intended as an insult to herself, Marie Antoinette turned deathly pale and looked as though she might faint.[134]

With the help of the nearby Princesse de Lamballe, the Queen managed to regain her composure, but at the Church of St. Louis she would suffer yet another brutal blow. For although the rich décor inside the church announced a supreme respect for the crown—regal violet satins and velvets, all embroidered with gold-threaded fleurs-de-lys, draped the ceiling, the altar, and the special armchairs in which the royal family took their seats—the priest presiding over the day's services was far from sharing it.[135] Henri de La Fare, the thirty-seven-year-old Bishop of Nancy, was a First Estate deputy who, like many of the Church's younger and poorer representatives, sympathized with the disenfranchised Third Estate. Once he reached the pulpit at St. Louis, he launched into an unexpectedly polemical sermon in which, according to a bourgeois representative named Duquesnoy,

> the Bishop compared the opulence of the court with the destitution of the countryside. He asked how it could be that under a wise and thrifty King, expenditure should so increase. . . . And there, he painted a very faithful picture of the life of the Queen, even to the point of saying that, weary of riches and grandeur, it had become necessary for her to seek pleasure in a childish imitation of nature—an obvious allusion to the Petit Trianon.[136]

During this part of the sermon, all eyes except those of Louis XVI, who had nodded off in his armchair a good half hour beforehand, were riveted on the Queen.[137] Sunlight streamed through the stained-glass windows in the transept and the nave; in the colored rays, Marie Antoinette's diamonds and cloth-of-silver gown shone with irrepressible sparkle. Whereas the outfit had perhaps been calculated to overwrite her image as the *gaulle*-clad mistress of the Petit Trianon, in fact, it merely showcased the "riches and grandeur" that, according to La Fare, she continued to enjoy at the people's expense.[138] Washed out by her glittering ensemble, the Queen's face had grown as cold and ashen as the moon.

Even Marie Antoinette's foes among the aristocracy were unprepared for the Bishop's vitriol; when the sermon came to an end, they sat silently, registering varying combinations of stern disapproval and outright disbelief. The Third Estate deputies, however, hailed the sermon with wild applause. This reaction, which the church setting, the presence of the King and Queen, and the presentation of the Holy Sacrament all strictly forbade, announced the commoners' fierce refusal to kowtow to their betters any longer. It also, of course, revealed their thorough dislike of their sovereign's consort. Stricken, the target of La Fare's harangue responded to the clapping and whistling with a barely perceptible pursing of her Hapsburg lip.[139] Taking note of Marie Antoinette's pallid, unhappy mien, the liberal aristocrat Mirabeau, who like the Duc d'Orléans had marched with the Third Estate, whispered to a neighbor: "Behold the victim."[140]

And so she was: of a revolution that had planted itself firmly at her doorstep, and against which no costume in the world would protect her. Whether she dressed like a princess or a peasant girl, "Madame Déficit" had been singled out as the people's most heinous foe. As such, she was indeed doomed to bring bad luck—to the *ancien régime,* to her family, and, most of all, to herself.

EIGHT

REVOLUTIONARY REDRESS

The interplay of clothing and politics only became more combustible after the opening procession of the Estates General.[1] The following day, May 5, 1789, at the formal convocation of the three orders, the deputies of the Third Estate expressed their rejection of the class hierarchies their costumes were supposed to establish by daring to place their hats back on their heads at the end of a speech delivered by Louis XVI. Because custom dictated that only the King and his noblemen had the right to don their hats at that point in the ceremony—the commoners were supposed to remain bareheaded and kneeling in the sovereign's presence—the gesture sent shockwaves through the vast hall where the deputies had assembled. For a few tense moments, indignation among deputies from the First and Second Estates threatened to derail the proceedings altogether. But Louis XVI, in an uncharacteristic show of self-possession, swiftly doffed his hat once again, thereby obliging everyone present to follow suit.[2]

Despite her husband's success in momentarily defusing tensions among the three orders, Marie Antoinette, seated in a great gilded throne at his side, seems to have been appalled by the Third Estate's behavior. As during La Fare's stinging sermon the day before, she struggled visibly to maintain an air of dignity and calm, but those observing her closely detected the turmoil beneath the façade. The Marquise de La Tour du Pin noted that her royal mistress seemed unusually "irritated and sad" as she fanned herself in "almost compulsive movements" with an enormous, jeweled fan. Her Majesty, the Marquise continued, further gave herself away by casting "frequent glances to the side of the room where the Third Estate was seated . . . and where she already had so many adversaries."³ Gouverneur Morris, an American lawyer and a newcomer to Versailles, suspected that the Queen deeply resented her husband's conciliatory hat-doffing maneuver. In Morris's account, Marie Antoinette "look[ed] with contempt on the scene . . . and seem[ed] to say, 'for the present, I submit, but I shall have my turn.' "⁴

Nevertheless, it was the Third Estate's turn to flex its newfound political muscle. And, inadvertently or otherwise, the deputies of this order did so by borrowing a tactic from the despised consort herself, who of course had, on more than one occasion, used attention-grabbing costumes and coiffures to assert her prominence in a government that sought to deny her any substantial role. In much the same way, the representatives of the Third Estate—whom the other orders would hasten to marginalize in the business of fiscal and governmental reform—now signaled through this use of their headgear that they were a force to be reckoned with. In their view, the fact that they represented at least 96 percent of France's population imbued them with a political weight and significance that the *ancien régime* could not rightfully ignore. Symbolically, then, their brief, hat-based mutiny expressed the refusal of millions of people to remain disenfranchised any longer. Indeed, at least one commentator has described the episode as heralding "the beginning of the French Revolution"—the beginning, that is, of the commoners' determined effort to achieve liberty, equality, and justice.⁵

Over the course of the summer, this effort gained dizzying momentum, fueled throughout the land by chronic famine and poverty, and, within the Estates General, by the aristocracy's reluctance to grant their social inferiors equal voting powers on key matters such as tax reform. On June 17, 1789, the members of the Third Estate retaliated by declaring themselves France's only legitimate legislative body, which they baptized the Assemblée Nationale to emphasize its allegiance to "the Nation" as a whole, with its massive, nonaristocratic majority. The founders of the Assemblée declared that it would be illegal for the other orders to raise taxes without their consent. Inviting the other two orders to join them in this new, nationally representative sovereign body, they announced that they would draft a constitution to establish the political rights and freedoms of the many, not the few.

Not surprisingly, these pronouncements did not sit well with the *ancien régime*'s more conservative stalwarts, who on June 20 arranged to have the rebel deputies locked out of the great hall at Versailles where the Estates General usually met. In response, the representatives of the Third Estate retreated to a nearby tennis court, where they swore an oath "never to be separated, and to continue assembling . . . until the Constitution was established and placed on solid ground."⁶ The "Tennis Court Oath" was a resounding shot across the monarchy's bow: a declaration that the people would not be cowed, no matter what measures the First and Second Estates took to thwart them.[7]

Louis XVI, for his part, was horrendously ill-prepared for a development of this magnitude. In part, he seems to have found it inconceivable that his subjects should arrogate to themselves a legislative power that God had invested in him alone.[8] And in part, he was distracted by personal difficulties, namely the death of his son, the seven-year-old Dauphin Louis Joseph, on June 4. Marie Antoinette, who had witnessed the heart-rending spectacle of the sickly boy's decline over several long weeks, was likewise stricken with grief and retreated with her husband to their château at Marly for a few days to mourn their untimely loss. But the political circumstances were changing too rapidly to allow the royal couple much time for grieving. Marie Antoinette forced herself back into the fray at the behest of her two brothers-in-law, who persuaded her to join them in urging the King to take a hard line against the Third Estate.

In truth, she did not require much persuading. Like Louis XVI's brothers, the Queen maintained that the Estates General had to be disbanded quickly, before its refractory members dared to carry their rebellion even further.[9] Additionally, after years of bad experiences with backbiting aristocrats, Marie Antoinette was convinced that her enemies within the court were covertly orchestrating these grave affronts to her husband's prerogatives. Above all, she suspected the Duc d'Orléans of exploiting the political situation to his own ends and of seeking support from the people to establish him as King in Louis XVI's place.[10] Both outraged and terrified by the prospect of a conspiracy against her family, she passionately supported Artois and Provence as they tried to impress upon their brother the importance of nipping the Revolution in the bud.

But the King was indecisive under the best of circumstances—sarcastic Provence had once said that trying to get Louis XVI to make up his mind was like "vainly trying to hold together a set of well-oiled billiard balls"—and when his family members pushed him to take drastic action, he reacted with reluctance and alarm.[11] Instead of heeding their arguments against the Revolution, Louis XVI temporarily acceded to Necker's countervailing assertions that he would do better to compromise with the rebels than to combat them. On June 24 and 25, a majority of the clergy and forty-seven liberal noblemen echoed this view when they announced that they, too, were throwing in their lots with the Assemblée. Now the King was compelled to acknowledge the validity of the new legislature; he urged the holdouts among the First and Second Estates to join it as well. But shortly afterward, he changed his mind again, calling for a strong military presence to maintain public order in Versailles and Paris and, his wife and brothers hoped, eventually to dissolve the Assemblée by force.[12] On July 1, having been informed that several companies in the regiment of French guards intended to side with their countrymen in the event of an uprising, the King summoned thirty thousand soldiers, many of them foreigners and mercenaries, to Versailles and to the capital. Ten days afterward, Necker, who disagreed forcefully with Louis XVI's about-face, was sent away from court in the middle of the night.

In Paris, where a majority of the public strongly favored the Assemblée Nationale—which on July 9 renamed itself the Assemblée Nationale Constituante—both Necker's dismissal and the King's call for military reinforcements were seen as grave threats to the salutary advances of the Third Estate.[13] And under these circumstances, clothes and accessories became clear signs of political intent. Those who supported the Third Estate's rise to power signaled their position by wearing large ribbon *cocardes*—cockades— tucked into their hats or pinned to their clothing.[14] According to revolutionary legend, the first such cockade was actually a leaf, which on July 12 the journalist Camille Desmoulins snatched from a tree in the Palais Royal while inciting his fellow citizens to take up arms against the crown; in his harangue, he described his new adornment as being "the color of hope." Cockades modeled on Desmoulins's were, however, quickly abandoned because green also happened to be one of the livery colors of the widely unpopular Comte d'Artois.[15] Instead, blue and red soon became the cockade colors of choice. These were the colors of the capital, worn in memory of one its earliest antiroyalist heroes, a draper named Étienne Marcel, who in 1358 led his fellow Parisians, all cloaked in red and blue hoods, in a revolt against the future King Charles V.[16] To what extent eighteenth-century revolutionaries were aware of this historic clash between the people and the crown remains unclear. Nevertheless, the so-called *cocarde à la Nation* or *cocarde nationale* was zealously adopted as a badge of its wearers' willingness—indeed, their desire—to contest absolutist oppression.[17]

The blue and red cockade also stood as a challenge to the monarchy in that it replaced the traditional royal *cocarde,* which was solid white to mimic the Bourbon fleur-de-lys.[18] (Red, by contrast, was conveniently enough the heraldic color of the Parisians' beloved Duc d'Orléans.) Like the deputies who donned their hats on May 5, the revolutionaries sporting the *cocarde nationale* took their cue, consciously or otherwise, from none other than Marie Antoinette. For it was through color—the color of the special scarlet and white livery she devised for her household staffers at Trianon—that the Queen had once sought to distinguish her dominion from Versailles. By similarly refusing the crown's signature white and replacing it with colors of their own choosing, the people made visible their sense of emancipation from the old order. As an emblem of this sentiment, various historians have since observed, a *cocarde* sported on a citizen's outfit "allowed others to decipher immediately the [wearer's] attachment to the revolutionary cause" and as such became one of that cause's most potent "symbolic forms of political practice."[19] It announced from the Revolution's very outset the key role that clothing and adornment would play in the politics of the era.

Partisans of the national cockade promptly reviled as "enemies of the Revolution" those who failed to affix it to their costume—or who, worse still, dared to wear rosettes in colors other than red and blue. When soldiers from foreign and mercenary regiments began filling the capital's streets in early July, for example, Parisians looked with suspicion upon the black cockades that perched in many of the newcomers' hats. For black was recognized as the color of the aristocracy and, to make matters worse, was one of the two colors of the House of Hapsburg (yellow being the other).[20] Black also happened to be the predominant color worn at court that summer, as the royal family and the nobility mourned the passing of the young Dauphin. As an aristocratic Austrian in mourning, Marie Antoinette was triply associated with this dark shade.[21] To a public that distrusted and despised her (some even whispered that she had poisoned the Dauphin herself, lest he grow up to favor his subjects' bid for freedom), the black cockades of the crown's new soldiers were therefore deeply suspect and had to go.[22]

According to the Romantic historian Thomas Carlyle, the troops' black cockades turned them into targets for harassment and violence on the streets of Paris. In his typically overblown but highly suggestive account of the turbulence that rocked the capital in the Revolution's early months, Carlyle writes:

> Truly, it is time for the black cockades to vanish. . . . On the bridges, on the Quais, at the patriotic cafés [of the Palais Royal], . . . ever as any black cockade may emerge, rises the many-voiced growl and bark: *À bas!* Down! All black cockades are ruthlessly plucked off: one individual picks his up again, kisses it, attempts to reaffix it, but a hundred canes start in the air, and he desists.[23]

More often than not, militant Parisians forcibly replaced the black cockade with the "politically correct" version in red and blue. Sometimes, though, the people's sartorially inspired rage pushed them even further. In one instance, Carlyle maintains, an angry crowd came dangerously close to hanging a man from a lamppost after he refused to cast off his black cockade. Having been unceremoniously seized as a menace to "the Nation," this fellow escaped death only because a group of patrolling soldiers happened to pass by before the mob had finished with him.[24]

It was not long before the people brought their enforcement of revolutionary fashion to bear on the royal family itself. This occurrence followed fast on the heels of 1789's best-known popular uprising. On July 14, hordes of Parisians intent on arming themselves against a possible crackdown by the King and his mercenaries stormed the Bastille prison to seize the munitions stockpiled within. At five o'clock in the afternoon, after trading fire with the prison guards for almost four hours, the assailants carried the day, invading the Bastille and liberating the paltry seven prisoners who were confined there. They then commandeered as much gunpowder as they could carry. After brutally dragging the prison's governor, Bernard-René de Launay, through the streets of Paris, they murdered him with a motley assortment of daggers, pistols, and bayonets, and decapitated his corpse on the steps of the Hôtel de Ville.

With Louis XVI's own troops refusing to quash the rebellion, the people's victory was complete. For centuries, the Bastille had loomed in the eastern end of Paris as a living symbol of absolutist oppression: a "palace of vengeance," as Voltaire dubbed it in a celebrated poem, where iniquitous royal vendettas relegated innocent people like the Cardinal de Rohan.[25] (That the seven prisoners freed by the insurgents included four counterfeiters, one madman, an aristocrat found guilty of incest "and other atrocious crimes," and a fellow who had attempted to murder Madame de Pompadour by anonymously sending her a box of explosives went unmentioned in subsequent, idealizing legends about the Bastille's unjustly shackled "victims of despotism."[26]) Now, the once impenetrable fortress had been sprung open, and its exultant destroyers controlled the city.

Early that same evening, Louis XVI, who had been hunting all day around Versailles and had as yet not heard of the uprising—whence his famous journal entry for July 14, "Nothing"—ordered the withdrawal of his troops from the capital. This was a move for which the members of the Assemblée had been forcefully lobbying for days. Almost a week before, Mirabeau had stated clearly that the capital's inhabitants would tolerate only militias whose membership was drawn from the Third Estate and was committed to safeguarding the nascent Revolution.[27] Thus, although on the evening of July 14 he acceded to these demands, the King's decision came several hours too late; the storming of the Bastille demonstrated clearly that the time for any sort of coup against the Assemblée had come and gone. The people of Paris, aided and abetted by Louis XVI's own turncoat soldiers, would never stand for it.

Adding insult to injury, the people of Paris demanded that Louis XVI appear in their midst to acknowledge their triumph. Seconded by the Comte d'Artois, Marie Antoinette again recommended a drastic alternative—

escaping as a family to Metz, near the border between France and the Hapsburg Netherlands, and working to quash the Revolution from there—but the King could not decide whether or not to take this advice. Eventually, he agreed that Artois and the Duchesse de Polignac, both of whom the public reviled in no small part because of their ties to the Queen, should flee the country for safety's sake. Artois and Polignac assented and in separate carriages promptly escaped abroad. Marie Antoinette herself had pushed strongly for this outcome, but the loss of her dear friends pained her deeply. Too heartbroken to see the Polignac family's convoy off in person, she sent her favorite a sorrowful note of farewell, along with a purse brimming with gold.

As for Louis XVI, he concluded that it was his duty to remain in France and to face the insurgent populace head-on. On July 17, he traveled to Paris for a public appearance at the Hôtel de Ville, presumably hoping to regain the affection of the subjects to whom he still optimistically referred to as "my good people." Many of the good people who awaited him there, however, were hungry, unemployed, and not wholly trustful as to where his sympathies really lay. When the King shuffled up to the dais, he appeared to the British ambassador, Lord Dorset, "more a captive than a King, being led along like a tamed bear" in the custody of the revolutionary officials who surrounded him.[28] And indeed, at least some of the spectators in the crowd seemed not only aware of Louis XVI's visible diminution in stature but gleeful about it, greeting him not with the customary shouts of "Long live the King!" but with a defiant new motto: "Long live the Nation!"

As if to drive the point home, the capital's newly elected mayor—Jean Sylvain Bailly, a bourgeois astronomer who had presided over the Third Estate's Tennis Court Oath—presented Louis XVI with a *cocarde nationale*.[29] Baffled but compliant, the King fumbled to pin the blue and red ribbons to his hat, on top of the royal white rosette already there. As he did so, the people burst into electrified cheers, hailing him as the "Restorer of French Liberty" and recognizing the move as an unheard-of concession to their will. Indeed, as the historian Dorinda Outram has pointed out, the *ancien régime* "was an order which relied on the continual proclamation of difference. In this order, the King—its political and ritual center—was as close to God as other men were far from the King. He was of a nature incommensurate with theirs . . . , and [was] therefore the fount of difference."[30] By accepting the *same* blue and red badge as those worn by thousands of lowborn Parisians, Louis XVI visibly ceded his God-given difference and so dismantled the very underpinnings of his power.

This effect of the gesture was not lost on Marie Antoinette's old adviser the Comte de Mercy, who was among those present at the Hôtel de Ville, and who afterward reported grimly that "the [French] people now play the part of the King."[31] Nor was it lost on Bailly, who later marveled at his own daring in orchestrating the scene, admitting that he had entertained some doubts as to "how the King would react, and whether there was not something inappropriate in giving [the cockade] to him."[32] Yet the gesture's inappropriateness was precisely the point, insofar as it simultaneously undermined Louis XVI's sacred stature and lent his tacit approval to the events of July 14.

By the same token, the King's symbolic concession did not, in his subjects' eyes, necessarily exclude him from the political regeneration that was expected to follow. To one of the Revolution's leaders, the aristocratic but progressive-minded young Marquis de La Fayette, who had distinguished himself as a hero in Louis XVI's service (and as a friend of George Washington's) while fighting for the American colonists years before, the accidental combination of blue, red, and white in the sovereign's hat suggested a harmonious "fusion between the royalty and the people."[33] This idea of "fusion" was important: for the moment, some leading members of the Assemblée envisioned a constitutional monarchy similar to England's, where commoners and aristocrats would share with the King in the business of government.[34] Such an outcome—La Fayette later claimed to have impressed upon his revolutionary colleagues—was best expressed visually in a blue, white, and red cockade. Whether or not it was (as the Marquis insisted) his own invention, the *cocarde tricolore* forthwith became the ubiquitous symbol of the revolutionary Nation.[35] Its colors were also adopted for the newly formed, bourgeois National Guard, of which La Fayette was named commanding general.

Interestingly, blue, white, and red had also long been the colors of the French king's livery; but since the revolutionaries had infused it with a radical new political meaning, the color combination became highly unpalatable to the devotees of absolute monarchy. The Comtesse de Boigne recalled in her memoirs that her whole family despised the National Guardsmen's tricolor uniform as a sign of despicable antiroyalist insubordination.[36] Certainly Marie Antoinette seems to have espoused this point of view.[37] Far less optimistic than La Fayette about a royal-populist "fusion," she reportedly saw Louis XVI's acceptance of the Parisians' cockade as a shameful defeat for the throne. When he left for the Hôtel de Ville on the morning of July 17, she watched him depart with tears streaming down her face, worried that Parisian rabble-rousers would hold him prisoner in the capital, or worse.[38] But when he reappeared in the castle's Marble Courtyard late that night with his makeshift tricolor rosette still tucked in his hatband, the Queen "instinctively recoiled" at the sight of him.[39] According to Mercier (who could not have been present for the scene, and whose political sensibilities may have inspired him to exaggerate it at Marie Antoinette's expense), she took one, withering look at her husband's new adornment and snapped: "I thought I had married a King of France, not a commoner."[40]

Whether Mercier exaggerated or invented her chagrin at this moment, Marie Antoinette did find her patience tried in the weeks that followed, when the Duc d'Orléans's son Chartres and his confidante, Madame de Genlis, both of whom shared Orléans's revolutionary leanings, showed up at Versailles sporting an oversized *cocarde tricolore* and tricolor dress ribbons, respectively.[41] Nor did it escape the Queen's notice when the wife of her old enemy, the Duc de La Vauguyon, commissioned Madame Éloffe to whip up "8 *cocardes,* in blue, rose-colored, and white ribbons," right after the Bastille toppled. (Stylish pink was a popular substitute for red in the "revolutionary" palette at court.[42]) But perhaps the greatest insult of all came when Marie Antoinette's aging royal aunts, Mesdames Adélaïde and Victoire, jumped on the tricolor bandwagon, hiring Madame Éloffe to furnish them with great supplies of rose-and-blue ribbons *à la Nation;* to trim their formal court gown bodices with patriotic-colored satin *échelles;* and to outfit them with dozens of ready-made tricolor rosettes.[43]

It bears noting that in all these cases, the aristocratic purchasers of "revolutionary" paraphernalia were sworn enemies of Marie Antoinette. (The Aunts had turned their private residence at Bellevue into "a center of opposition" where they and their cronies "continued to fulminate against *l'Autrichienne,*" and the Duc d'Orléans's Palais Royal likewise continued to serve as a safe haven for talk of this kind.[44]) Sometimes motivated by particular grudges, sometimes not, pro-revolutionary sentiment indeed existed, at this point, among certain strong factions of the nobility. And at court as in Paris, those individuals wishing to align themselves with the new order spelled out their intentions on their costumes in red, white, and blue—even if, as the royalist *Journal de la cour et de la ville* noted with distaste, this meant wearing "expensive *cocardes nationales* as large as cabbages."[45]

As summer turned to fall and the official two-and-a-half-month mourning period for the Dauphin came to an end, the Queen was compelled to abandon her sad black gowns and reenter the fraught new world of revolutionary fashion. However, given her apparent aversion to the *tricolore* and its attendant political significance, it is not surprising to discover that, according to Madame Éloffe's records at least, she did not hasten to adopt the styles inspired by current events.[46] Unlike many of her well-heeled contemporaries, Marie Antoinette placed no orders for tricolor cockades, not even the relatively expensive, elegant ones that Rose Bertin—less out of revolutionary enthusiasm than out of a need to keep her inventory up-to-date—had begun offering at the Grand Mogol.[47] And neither Bertin nor Madame Éloffe was commissioned to trim Marie Antoinette's gowns with red ribbon in the new shade called *sang de Foulon* ("Foulon's blood"), which a relatively unknown *marchande de modes* opportunistically launched after Parisian marauders murdered a seventy-year-old nobleman by that name, a low-ranking minister in Louis XVI's cabinet, on July 17.[48] Nor did Marie Antoinette rush to acquire necklaces and earrings set with stones from the Bastille's demolished walls. (By contrast, Madame de Genlis jubilantly sported a locket of this variety, set with diamonds that spelled out the word *"Liberté,"* "and tied at the top with a national cockade."[49]) Despite her erstwhile penchant for current-events headgear, the Queen likewise eschewed the *bonnet à la Bastille* (which was topped by crenellated white satin "towers" and edged with a wide black lace "balustrade" in imitation of the prison's pre-siege architecture) and the *coiffure à la Nation* (trimmed with festive bunches of tricolor ribbon).[50] (Plate 20.) The shoe buckles engraved with the people's July 17 victory chant, "Long live the Nation," also failed to earn the Queen's approval, though admittedly they were designed less for women than for men.[51]

Repudiating these pro-revolutionary emblems, Marie Antoinette took pains instead to dress in a way that, as Carrolly Erickson has noted, "made no concessions to the changing times."[52] In the wake of such radical developments as the Assemblée's so-called August decrees, which ordered the wholesale abolition of the feudal system in France and led to many an aristocrat's financial ruin, she pointedly reintroduced her most magnificent jewels, including diamonds, into her daily costume.[53] Although she had stopped wearing such gems for stylistic reasons at the Petit Trianon, and for political reasons after the Diamond Necklace Affair, she may now have found in them a handy means of opposing the Revolution's advances without saying a word. Thus, as Madame de la Tour du Pin remembered, when a delegation from the city of Paris, led by Bailly and La Fayette, called on the royal family on August 25 at Versailles, Marie Antoinette chose to receive them in "an everyday gown, but elaborately decorated and absolutely covered in diamonds."[54] To the revolutionaries whom she greeted with undisguised disdain, the Queen's "defiantly glittering" appearance was likely meant as a strong signal that whatever their impertinences of action and of dress, an irreducible gap still stood between them and her royal self.[55]

NEVERTHELESS, IT WAS PRECISELY THIS GAP THAT MANY OF THE QUEEN'S own most highly publicized clothing experiments had, in earlier years, gone a long way toward diminishing. In fact, if Louis XVI had been in a teasing mood on the night of July 17, when his wife supposedly chastised him for looking like "a commoner," he might well have replied with an allusion to the rusticated style she herself had introduced at the Petit Trianon and flaunted, by way of Vigée-Lebrun's scandalous portrait, at the Paris Salon. With the Revolution's advent, strict social differences were rapidly losing ground in France. But this was a process that the Queen's own "revolution in dress," as Félix de Montjoie termed it, had initiated long before 1789, by eliding the class distinctions that had once been clearly legible in women's costume. It was no small irony that at the very moment when the Queen was attempting to reestablish herself as incommensurable with her subjects, these latter turned to her own repertoire of once controversial, simplified ensembles to make the opposite claim: that all women were created equal.[56]

In September 1789, for instance, the fashion journal *Le Magasin des modes nouvelles* presented two new headdresses that referred directly to the drastic societal changes the Revolution had effected. The first of the head-dresses was called the *bonnet aux trois ordres réunis ou confondus* ("bonnet of the three united, or commingled, orders"); according to an explanatory caption, it was meant to show that "we no longer accept class distinctions in France: all of us are now mere citizens."[57] To convey this notion, the helmet-shaped white gauze bonnet featured not just a tricolor cockade, but an elaborate embroidered pattern depicting a golden sword (the aristocracy) and a blue spade (the Third Estate), which together formed a large cross (the clergy): a blending of class attributes that, the caption explained, evoked "the reunion or rather the commingling of the Three Estates."[58] The second bonnet, a simple, "old-style" muslin cap "trimmed with a *cocarde à la Nation*" and matching artificial roses, also celebrated the Revolution's advances.[59] The text that accompanied this unnamed confection described it as a tribute to "the conquest of liberty," which the deputies of the Third Estate courageously achieved despite the other orders' "long-standing attempts to humiliate [them]."[60]

With their progressive political overtones, nothing about these bonnets would necessarily have pointed to Marie Antoinette's legacy had it not been for their underlying fabric, form, and color, all of which recalled the white milkmaids' bonnets and Grenada hats of the Petit Trianon.[61] By qualifying the second of the two hats shown as "old-style," the fashion editor blithely conceded its pre-revolutionary origins, even as he deemed it a tribute to the new régime. Perhaps more significantly, the illustration presenting the *bonnet aux trois ordres* paired the headdress with an unfussy white linen skirt and dark blue, *lévite*-like overdress. These garments, in their utilitarian plainness, were meant to underscore the bonnet's populist message: "all of

8. *Le Magasin des modes nouvelles françaises et anglaises:* Fashion plate depicting the *bonnet aux trois ordres* (1789) (Bibliothèque Nationale de France, Paris)

us are now mere citizens." But they were also well-known mainstays of the Queen's Trianon wardrobe. Like the color-obsessed Parisian mobs and the hat-wearing deputies of the Third Estate, *Le Magasin des modes nouvelles* thus based its rejection of "class distinctions in France" on a sartorial rebellion famously initiated by Marie Antoinette herself.[62]

Needless to say, those advocating a broad-based "conquest of liberty" recognized that their rebellion sprang from fundamentally different motives than Marie Antoinette's. If the King's consort had cultivated a "mere citizen's" way of life and dress at her country villa, she had done so not to free the French people from dire social and economic oppression, but to emancipate herself from the superficial inconveniences of court etiquette. This much had been a matter of public record ever since her detractors first began to shine a spotlight on her violations of protocol at Trianon. And the rumors about the obscene sexual practices (her alleged lesbianism) and extravagant décor (her supposed penchant for gem-studded furnishings) that characterized the villa only solidified her reputation for self-indulgence. Through their association with this milieu, Marie Antoinette's linen skirts, long-sleeved *lévite* wrap dresses, and milkmaids' hats thus evoked her fundamental egotism and caprice. By modifying these garments with tricolor symbols, revolutionary fashion simultaneously exposed their origins in royal selfishness and reclaimed them for "the conquest of liberty." This appropriation showed up the hypocrisy behind the Queen's peasant-girl posturing, even as it reallocated her style ideas to a larger, and ostensibly more deserving, demographic.

In an interesting coincidence, it was on a day dedicated to the equitable redistribution of property that another of Marie Antoinette's signature outfits, the infamous white *gaulle,* was reinvented as an apt ensemble for women of a revolutionary bent. On September 7, 1789, in response to continuing anxiety about the state of the French economy, a delegation of eleven women from Paris—some of them artists' wives and daughters, some of them artists in their own right—made a dramatic appearance in the Assemblée at Versailles. Declaring that they cared more about the nation's financial health than about their own finery, the ladies approached the table where the Assemblée's president was seated and one by one laid before him heavy cases stuffed with jewels.[63]

Organized by a sculptor's wife named Adélaïde Moitte, who drew her inspiration from a famous episode in Plutarch's *Lives,* this outpouring caused a sensation in the Assemblée. The deputies burst into wild applause and according to at least one account promptly "took the silver buckles out of their shoes and laid them on the President's table" alongside the women's treasures.[64] Excited impromptu speeches followed, in praise of the ladies' selflessness, which, significantly, was apparent not only in their generous offer of jewelry but also in the floaty white dresses, simple ruffled bonnets, and modest muslin fichus they had all worn for the occasion. In all likelihood selected to emphasize their gesture's origins in classical antiquity, these unfussy outfits paid homage to Madame Moitte's injunction that "we abandon, for a moment, our foolish amusements and precious adornments" out of respect for "a Nation afflicted by so many painful blows, and sapped by poverty and fatigue."[65] Accordingly, as a journalist for the newspaper *Le Moniteur* reported, the women's gowns boasted "no ornamentation, no showiness," being "adorned only with that beautiful simplicity that is the mark of virtue"—though some of the women *had* accessorized their understated ensembles with tricolor sashes and cockades.[66]

Here again, the Revolution dispossessed Marie Antoinette of one of her most famous fashion statements, which for years had figured in the public imagination as a mark not of virtue but of vice. During the scandal of *La Reine en gaulle,* the understated muslin dress had been taken as proof of her hatred for the French people, many of whom lost their livelihood as a result of her love of foreign imports, and proof, too, of her disrespect for Louis XVI, whose stature was seen to suffer from his wife's undignified transgressions. During the Diamond Necklace Affair, it had retained these associations, while also being marshaled as proof of the Queen's involvement in the century's most monumental jewel theft.

Yet the same garment assumed another meaning altogether when it was sported by women who wished not to bankrupt France but to enrich it; who sought not to enlarge their private jewel collections but to place them in the service of an eminently worthy, public cause; whose pared-down attire aimed not to humiliate the King but to honor the Nation. Understood in this way, the women's attire indeed functioned as a "mark of virtue"—of a lofty, revolutionary goodness that definitively trumped the Queen's "old-style" wickedness. Indeed, it was as paragons of this change that the white-clad female patriots were hailed as they left the Assemblée and marched through cheering crowds from Versailles all the way home to Paris. The next day, the newspapers duly compared the jewel donors with "the most illustrious heroines of ancient Rome"—with the very women from whom, Madame Moitte preached in a contemporaneous pamphlet, the ladies of the Revolution could best learn "not to enrich themselves at their countrymen's expense, but, on the contrary, to ease the sufferings of the indigent."[67]

Hereafter, the art historian Laura Auricchio has noted, the ladies' "picturesque [appearance in the Assemblée became] a standard part of the Revolution's visual record, as it was disseminated through prints" by such artists as Pierre-Étienne Lesueur.[68] Fashion quickly followed suit: white dresses of a relaxed, neoclassical cut—some of them billowy and ruche-sleeved, like a *gaulle*, others more sleekly draped and long-sleeved, like a *lévite*—became a mainstay of patriotic female costume. The painter and revolutionary propagandist Jacques-Louis David, whose wife had figured among the jewel donors, immortalized this apparel in his classicizing female portraits of the period, and the contemporary fashion press cast it in the same pro-revolutionary light. As the newly renamed *Journal de la mode et du goût* explained: "Freedom has restored the taste for classical purity in France."[69] Still, the term *restored* belied one important fact: the plain white dress and its pastoral-cum-neoclassical variants had been a staple of French elegance long before *freedom* became a household word. And it was, to a great extent, the Queen who had made it so.[70]

Perhaps for this very reason, what soon emerged as the revolutionary woman's outfit par excellence—itemized by the costume historian Aileen Ribeiro as "the simple white dress, the muslin scarf knotted carelessly round [the] neck, and the plain white . . . bonnet"—was especially prized when its Bourbon-white links to the *ancien régime* were overwritten with mitigating touches of red and blue.[71] A few months after the female patriots' highly publicized trip to the Assemblée, *Le Journal de la mode et du goût* promoted a long-sleeved white muslin gown called the *chemise à la Constitution*, "embroidered with tiny red, white, and blue bouquets" and worn with a muslin fichu and a wide red sash.[72] (Once condemned as ruinous to the domestic silk industry, muslin could now be worn as a sign of patriotic ardor, along with even cheaper stuffs like cotton and wool, since the nobility's costumes at the Estates General had marked "sumptuous silks and velvets as enemies

9. Pierre-Étienne Lesueur, *The Citizenesses of Paris Donating Their Jewels to the Convention Nationale* (1789) (© Photothèque des Musées de la Ville de Paris)

of the Revolution."[73]) And now, when stylish ladies wanted to introduce some glamour into their simplified, patriotic wardrobes, they simply reverted to the *poufs* of the Queen's heyday—but with a key, contemporary twist: they wound their high, ornately styled hairdos with tricolor ribbon, and called them *poufs à la tricolore*.[74]

The blue, white, and red color scheme also assumed pride of place in the costume that women less interested in following beauty trends than in advancing a radical political agenda devised to make their proclivities known; and this costume, too, quite clearly harked back to one of the Queen's better-known fashion statements. In October 1789, the female revolutionary activist Théroigne de Méricourt—who entered the debate over the formation of the bourgeois National Guard by arguing that women, too, ought to be allowed to fight for their country—famously approximated the male Guardsmen's tricolor uniforms by donning a blue redingote with a white foulard at her neck and a red cap on her head.[75] To the Revolution's largely sexist, male chieftains, Méricourt's claim was far from welcome; women, they would later argue forcefully, were much better off staying home and furnishing the Nation's army with hardy patriotic sons.[76] Nonetheless, Méricourt's act of assuming quasi-masculine clothing to assert a female bid for power strongly recalled the horseman's posture Marie Antoinette had affected while Dauphine. It was striking that in both cases, the adoption of a gender-bending costume offered an alternative to a more conventional view by which women's influence resided in procreative and maternal capabilities alone.

Though not overtly insisting on this dimension of Méricourt's shocking clothes, the fashion press did claim them for revolutionary fashion, just as it had claimed the Queen's redingotes in earlier years. In August 1790, *Le Journal de la mode et du goût* presented its readers with an illustration of "a woman patriot in her new uniform": a blue cloth riding habit with a white and red collar and a feather-trimmed, black felt hat.[77] (Plate 21.) If one overlooked the *cocarde aux couleurs de la Nation* in the model's hatband, it would have been easy to mistake the ensemble for one of Marie Antoinette's own. With or without emphasis on its controversial feminist connotations, this outfit, too, entered the lexicon of pro-revolutionary women's dress.

YET EVEN AS THOSE SYMPATHETIC TO THE REVOLUTION'S AIMS APPROPRIATED the Queen's signature garments for their own, countervailing purposes, they did not cease to identify her as France's most dangerous scourge. To some extent, this claim found its justification in her aversion to the people's political agenda, which she exhibited in the defiantly glittering face she presented to advocates of the new order. Not surprisingly, then, when the Assemblée decreed the freedom of the press in August 1789 and the number of libels written about the Queen grew exponentially, pamphleteers turned with increased venom on her relationship to clothing.[78] With the liberalization of the publishing market, Elizabeth Colwill has pointed out, such scurrilous writings became cheaper and easier to diffuse and increasingly "came within the reach of Parisian artisanal classes as well as elites."[79] When revolutionary lampoonists posited the Queen's "love of fashion as [a telltale] sign of her vicious nature," as Chantal Thomas has justly observed, their claims thus reached a wider audience and assumed greater potential for political mobilization.[80]

One particularly important strain of invective against her during this period was political pornography, which, as during the *ancien régime,* operated on the premise that "sexual degeneration went hand in hand with political corruption."[81] Already before 1789, the defamatory rumors and pamphlets about Marie Antoinette's private life had of course served to discredit her as a political figure and to position her as a force for degradation at the heart of the Bourbon government. During the Revolution, this line of thought became all the more expedient, as it appeared both to justify the dismantling of a régime that the Queen had presumably harmed beyond repair and to necessitate the replacement of that régime's leaders by people of sounder moral fiber.[82] (It was far from incidental, in this context, that one of the Revolution's most influential leaders, the bourgeois lawyer Maximilien Robespierre, was nicknamed "the Incorruptible.") An emphasis on Marie Antoinette's inappropriate, erotically tinged clothing functioned within the pornographic genre as one effective means of reiterating her sexual depravity—or "uterine furors," in one pamphlet's colorful parlance—which in turn implied the degradation of the monarchy as a whole.[83]

For this reason, pornographers presented Marie Antoinette's *gaulles* as implicit proof of her wickedness, despite the morally upstanding connotations these ensembles now enjoyed when worn by just about anyone else. In a 1789 erotic pamphlet called "The French Messalina," for example, it was the Queen's appearance "in nothing but a long *gaulle* made of white muslin, and wrapped round her waist with a pink ribbon" that signaled her lascivious intentions to a stranger she was about to seduce.[84] The gown, her new lover was delighted to find, provided virtually unobstructed access to "her white, silky skin, divine breasts, and pretty pink nipples" and so made it all too easy for Marie Antoinette to prostitute herself to random passersby.[85]

In much the same vein, a pamphlet called "The Royal Dildo," also from 1789, described "Juno, Queen of the gods" (Marie Antoinette) cavorting obscenely with her female attendant Hebe (probably the Princesse de Lamballe or the Duchesse de Polignac), who proclaimed that wearing "only a *chemise*" greatly facilitated "fucking in the antechambers" of her mistress's palace.[86] Like "The French Messalina," "The Royal Dildo" reprised the urban legend that the Queen preferred relatively loose, unstructured gowns because she could put them back on hastily after tawdry flings with her favorites, or because they allowed her lovers easy access to her sexual "antechambers."[87] In both these pamphlets, flowing white *gaulles* or *chemises à la Reine* quite literally exposed Marie Antoinette's underlying sexual decadence and affirmed her status as "Queen of Vice."[88]

These dresses were not, though, the only articles of clothing that served as weapons against the royal consort; nor was political pornography the lampoonists' only medium. Satirical cartoons, as well, established Marie Antoinette's dastardly qualities through reference to a whole gamut of articles known to form part of her wardrobe. One such reference involved the towering, famously expensive ostrich feathers she had made voguish after her accession and, more recently, had worn to the opening of the Estates General. These plumes figured in a print called *La Poule d'Autru/yche*, which grafted Marie Antoinette's head, complete with a posh *catogan* hairdo and an elaborately bedecked bonnet, onto the body of a female ostrich. The grotesque figure was a visual pun based on the one-letter difference between "ostrich" (*autruche*) and "Austria" (*Autryche*), with the word *poule* (hen) establishing the Queen as a female of the species.

Read on this level alone, the cartoon condemned Marie Antoinette as Austria's creature—as an agent in a presumed conspiracy, much under discussion by the fall of 1789, between the Hapsburgs and the hard-line French royalists to suppress the Revolution and restore absolutism in France.[89] A close look at the *Poule*'s face underscored this intimation, as it revealed a tiny copy of the Nation's (as yet uncompleted) constitution clenched between her teeth. At the same time, the ostrich feathers in Marie Antoinette's hair invited another, equally damning interpretation, for combined with the word *poule* they evoked one of her most infamous headdresses, the *coiffure à la Belle Poule*. This hairstyle had sparked indignation largely because of the sanctimonious pronouncement the Queen had made shortly before she first unveiled it.[90] In 1776, Marie Antoinette had declared that she would rather see her husband spend his money on a warship for France than on more diamonds for herself . . . yet, not long afterward, she had appeared in public with an exceedingly intricate, quite obviously expensive replica of a warship, the *Belle Poule*, perched on her head. Ten years later, her ostensible guilt in the Diamond Necklace Affair compounded the appearance of hypocrisy and greed.

Now, in 1789, with the female artists' jewelry donations standing as a shining example of selfless patriotism, Marie Antoinette's well-established love of adornments appeared more hateful than ever and marked her values as utterly irreconcilable with those of the new régime. The caption of *La Poule d'Autru/yche* affirmed as much by ascribing to her the following statement:

> *I digest gold and silver with ease,*
> *But the Constitution is something I cannot swallow.*

In this representation, the lavishly plumed consort was no longer a human being but a monster.[91] And this monster's Austrian loyalties and gross extravagance would surely destroy the Revolution—if the Revolution did not take care to destroy her first.

This supposition formed the basis of another lampoon that likewise invoked the Queen's sartorial tastes. First appearing in the summer of 1789 and published by a prominent revolutionary engraver named Villeneuve, this print depicted a stern-faced Marie Antoinette trampling fiercely on a document.[92] (Plate 22.) In one version of the image, the document was identified as being the celebrated Declaration of the Rights of Man, the preamble to the Constitution that declared that all men were born equal and enjoyed

10. Anonymous, *La Poule d'Autru/yche* (c. 1789) (Bibliothèque Nationale de France, Paris)

certain inalienable rights (such as freedom of speech and of conscience, equality under taxation, and equality before the law). This cartoon depicted the Queen in a harsh, grotesque manner: a human face attached to a scaly body equipped with giant wings, cruel talons, and a long, forked tail. These, as a caption confirmed, were the characteristics of a harpy, the voracious beast of legend to which Marie Antoinette, just a few years earlier, had paid homage through her trendsetting costumes *à la harpie*.

Indeed, her affinity for a vogue named after a monster of boundless appetite had raised eyebrows about her unbridled spending habits as early as the mid-1780s and had already spawned at least one cartoon likening her to that rapacious beast. In the revolutionary era, the Queen's record as a spend-thrift fueled mounting anxiety about her presumed desire to enslave her subjects and thwart their Revolution. Whether by earmarking national resources for her own frivolity, or by conspiring to suppress the Constitution and the Declaration of the Rights of Man, she would, the revolutionary lampoonists maintained, tear the people's dreams to tatters with her brutal harpy's claws. Her erstwhile harpy ensembles, then, provided the basis for an analogy that corroborated assertions about the threat she posed to freedom, equality, and social progress. As one pamphleteer warned, in the "horrible conspiracy" brewing among those nobles and foreigners who surely wished to thwart the French revolutionaries' great advances, "there could not be a more fitting leader than this inhuman woman."[93] Supporting this view, the satirical press abounded with images and texts that labeled Marie Antoinette "the female harpy," an epithet inspired by her modish dress.[94]

CONDITIONED BY CHARGES SUCH AS THESE, THE FRENCH PEOPLE WERE BY the fall of 1789 primed to believe the worst about their queen and to seek added proof of her nefariousness in her relationship to fashion. In September, an incendiary pamphlet dubbing her "Austria's deputy" cautioned Parisians that to see proof of her treasonous nature they need look no further than her hair and costume: the former being reddish like that of Judas who betrayed Jesus Christ and the latter characterized by a "passion for disguise" that marked her as untrustworthy to the core.[95] On October 2, a stark confirmation of that untrustworthiness surfaced in widespread allegations that the night before, at a banquet held in honor of the Flanders Regiment at Versailles, Marie Antoinette and her friends had appeared among the soldiers and exhorted them to turn their weapons against the Nation. More precisely, it was claimed, the cadre of ladies had led the revelers in ritually trampling on the tricolor cockade, an act that the Queen—true to her image as a Constitution-shredding monster—had performed with particular gusto.[96] Those *tricolores* that escaped physical desecration were worn back-to-front, so that only their solid white backing was visible. And to supplement these makeshift royalist badges, the women handed out additional white Bourbon *cocardes* and black, aristocratic or Austrian ones as well.[97] All the while, frenzied cries of "Down with the Nation!" reverberated throughout the palace, and the whole affair concluded in an orgy of unspeakable lewdness.

Like so many of the rumors that targeted Marie Antoinette, this one sensationally exaggerated her actual doings. On October 1, the royal *gardes du corps* had indeed hosted a banquet for the officers of the Flanders Regiment, who were newly arrived at Versailles. And the banquet had indeed culminated in an effusive show of royalist sympathy (including hearty cries of "Long live the King!") when Louis XVI and his family made an unexpected appearance among the guests. "Dressed in white and pale blue, with matching feathers in her hair," Antonia Fraser has written, Marie Antoinette had captured the soldiers' hearts as she graciously made the rounds of the banqueting tables with the new Dauphin, Louis Charles, and Madame Royale by her side.[98]

Perhaps the Queen's white dress provided some inspiration to the rumormongers' tale about the mass distribution of white cockades that she supposedly initiated. But according to Madame Campan, the Marquise de La Tour du Pin, and the Marquise de La Rochejaquelein, all of whom were present at the banquet, no such distribution took place.[99] Only "Madame de Maillé," the Marquise de La Tour du Pin recalled, who was "a foolish young woman of nineteen, [had] detached from her hat a single knot of [white] ribbon" to assert her Bourbon loyalties.[100] According to La Tour du Pin's account, none of the officers followed suit. And although some of the revelers indeed appeared at the banquet wearing the black cockades of the aristocracy—according to the chronicler Antoine-Joseph Gorsas, one officer made a disparaging comment about "the cockade of colors" and declared that "the black one is the finer one"—it seems that no *cocardes nationales* were stomped underfoot.[101]

Unexceptional as the real events of the evening were, gossips and journalists hastily transformed them into "imaginary crimes of *lèse-nation* [which soon] reverberated through all the street corners of Paris to summon the citizens to vengeance," and which centered on the all-too-believable image of Marie Antoinette desecrating the Revolution's most sacred accessory.[102] A gaggle of courtiers reportedly led by the Queen's longtime nemesis, the Duc d'Aiguillon, disguised themselves as women of the people—a rabble-rousing practice traditionally adopted by male rioters during the *ancien régime*—and traveled to taverns throughout the city to fan the flames of indignation that the Flanders banquet rumors had ignited.[103]

Invoking the widespread scarcity of bread and the contrasting extravagance of the royal consort, the disguised noblemen incited their compatriots "to take up arms [against the throne, and] . . . vociferously to curse Marie Antoinette."[104] Large numbers of the people they encountered welcomed these harangues, and by October 5 the real women of Paris were echoing the imposters' outraged cries.

On the afternoon of the fifth, between five thousand and six thousand of these women flocked to the Hôtel de Ville and, after protesting the (genuine) dearth of reasonably priced bread in the capital, decided to take their complaints directly to the King and Queen. The women seized all the armaments they could get their hands on, while the soldiers of the National Guard, whom the stories of the Flanders Regiment's banquet had likewise incensed, actively did nothing to stop them. Then, with Théroigne de Méricourt (dressed in a man's hat and bright red redingote) galloping in their midst, and with large groups of male revolutionaries, cross-dressed or otherwise, bringing up the rear, they marched on Versailles.[105] After they left Paris, they were followed by approximately fifteen thousand sympathetic National Guardsmen, who threatened General de La Fayette with murder if he failed to join them. By the time the demonstrators congregated in front of the palace at dawn, their ranks had swollen to gigantic proportions.

Because La Fayette sent a courier ahead to Versailles to warn the court and the Assemblée of the insurgents' impending arrival, the soldiers of the royal guard were able to gather at the palace gates and brace themselves for trouble. And trouble they eventually got when the people—whose temper had been aggravated by their six-hour march and then by a long period of inaction as they awaited news of a response from the King and the Assemblée Nationale to their demands for bread—engaged them in combat and, easily overpowering the guards' relatively paltry numbers, streamed into the castle in droves.[106] Together the Parisians trampled through the gilded, lavishly decorated rooms in search of the King and Queen, whom they disrespectfully apostrophized as "the Baker and the Baker's Wife," and whom they vowed to bring back to Paris to guarantee increased supplies of food. Virulently, the invaders lambasted the royal *gardes du corps* for failing to wear the national cockade and threatened to slit their throats if they did not cast off their royalist rosettes.[107] Those royal guards who tried to stay their passage through the château were assaulted with pikes and muskets, daggers and broomsticks. Two royal soldiers were murdered and their heads promptly decapitated and set victoriously on pikes.

But the mob's most belligerent intentions were reserved for Marie Antoinette. In fact it was chiefly against her, Madame Campan recalled afterward, that the whole invasion appeared to be directed. Stampeding through the palace en masse toward her bedroom (several witnesses later claimed to have seen the Duc d'Orléans himself, dressed in a suspiciously unassuming gray coat, leading the way), they rehearsed an unending litany of menaces against the Queen.[108] Most of these involved calls for her head, but some of them were gorier still. The women from the fish market at the Halles, for instance, declared volubly that they planned to eviscerate Marie Antoinette, empty her entrails into their aprons, and, from the resulting mess, fashion brand-new red *cocardes*.[109] Outside the palace, too, seething crowds took up this threat, shrieking beneath the windows of the royal apartments: "We have come for Queen's skin, so that we can make ribbons for our rosettes!"[110] It hardly needs pointing out that this stated desire to transmute Marie Antoinette's body—her bloody entrails or her legendary white skin—into tricolor cockades revealed a specifically sartorial dimension to the people's fury.

Meanwhile the woman they had come to punish stood terrified in her bedroom, where two attendants rushed in to inform her that she did not even have time to dress if she hoped to elude the marauding horde. Nevertheless pausing long enough to slip on a yellow redingote and a black hat over her half-fastened petticoat, Marie Antoinette fled her bedroom through a secret door, which gave onto the hidden passageway joining her rooms with the King's.[111] She left the tall, paneled main doors to her apartments locked behind her, and by the time the mob arrived and kicked them in, she was already deep in the bowels of the passageway, safely en route to Louis XVI's chambers.

Her would-be assailants, however, had whipped themselves up into too much of a frenzy to realize straightaway that the target of their hatred was gone. In the belief that Marie Antoinette lay sleeping under her richly embroidered coverlet, the people rained down blows upon the bed and slashed the mattress, bedclothes, and pillows to ribbons. As soon as they realized their mistake, they sought another target for their fury and promptly found it in the gilt-edged mirrors lining the walls of the chamber. These, Léonard recorded later, they "smashed with blows of their muskets, doubtless to punish the unoffending crystal for having reflected the features of the woman whom they had been prevented from assassinating."[112] If the bed had been destroyed as a stand-in for the Queen herself, the mirrors were shattered as accomplices to her infamous, fashion-fueled narcissism.

Later that same day, the people would find another way to castigate her for this trait, but not before accepting a temporary truce brokered by General de La Fayette and some of his less bellicose guardsmen. Appalled by the destruction the crowds had wrought, these soldiers worked quickly to prevent any further acts of violence against the royal *gardes du corps*. The General then assured the insurgents that the *gardes* were not traitors to the Nation: he even ceremoniously pinned a tricolor cockade on one royal bodyguard's hat.[113]

But the people wanted more. Crammed into the Marble Courtyard in front of the palace, they shouted for Louis XVI and his wife to step outside the King's apartments and onto the balcony to face them; then they watched with a mixture of skepticism and elation as the royals pledged to return to Paris with them and to provide them with bread. Some of the marauders may have bristled to see Marie Antoinette dressed in yellow and black, the colors of the Austrian Hapsburgs; a few voices in the crowd continued to threaten her with bodily harm. But as the royal governess, Madame de Tourzel, who was waiting in the wings with Madame Royale and the Dauphin, remembered, the Queen's "air of grandeur and heroic courage in the presence of danger . . . had such an effect on the mob that they at once abandoned their sinister designs and [were] struck with admiration."[114] The low, dignified curtsey Marie Antoinette swept to acknowledge her subjects appeared to have an especially placating effect. "Her courage and noble air," one young royal page noted, "disarmed the bloodthirsty tigers."[115]

Any truce between the tigers and the Queen would, however, be of short duration. Early in the afternoon, Louis XVI, his wife, his children, his sister Madame Élisabeth, and Madame de Tourzel piled into a carriage that joined a great, disorderly cavalcade bound for the capital. In theory, the Parisians had every reason to rejoice. After all, they were transporting both the royal family and huge supplies of grain from the château's storerooms back to the city. But the victors were also half-drunk from fatigue, alcohol, and carnage.[116] And as the twelve-mile journey, conducted at a snail's pace because of the sheer size of the procession, wore on (it took something like eight hours this time around), the rioters' original animosities again bubbled to the surface. Undeterred by the presence of La Fayette and the other soldiers who flanked the royal family's carriage, they swarmed around its wheels and hung onto its doors. They repeated "Long live the Nation!" until their throats grew raw from screaming. They brandished their pikes, upon which they had impaled stolen loaves of bread, and reiterated imprecations against "the Baker and the Baker's Wife." They ripped the branches off trees as they passed, wrapped them with tricolor ribbons, and shook them furiously at the carriage.[117] They sang lewd songs about Marie Antoinette's supposed promiscuity and taunted her with vigorous, obscene gestures while doing so.

Yet it was only when the cortège arrived in the town of Sèvres that the rioters hit upon the punishment most befitting the Queen's unique history of offensive conduct. While the cavalcade stopped to regroup, a handful of its more thuggish denizens reportedly slipped away and went in search of a coiffeur. Finding a few, a page from the royal household recorded, they "placed a knife to [the hairdressers'] throats and constrained them to frizzle and powder" the hair on the severed heads of the two murdered royal guards.[118] The ruffians then set the heads, intricately coiffed and abundantly powdered, back on their pikes and returned to the royal carriage. As the procession resumed, the pike bearers waved their gruesome trophies right beside Marie Antoinette's window, to make sure that she could see to what good use her beloved hair powder had been put.[119]

If this account (reported by one of the King's ministers as well as by his young page) is to be believed, then it seems clear that the pranksters were taking the opportunity to chastise the royal consort for having sported her powdered *poufs* while her subjects clamored for bread. This was an insult the people had been forced to swallow thirteen years earlier during the Flour Wars, and in all the years that followed, as the Queen persisted in her selfish, frivolous ways. But today, as the procession pulled slowly out of Sèvres, and Marie Antoinette was confronted with the coiffed, bloody heads, the people at last had their revenge. Not only had they laid claim to the Baker's Wife and to her obscenely plentiful stores of grain; they had also forced her to consider something that she herself had unwittingly impressed upon them throughout her tenure on the throne: in certain cases, extravagance of style can be nothing short of a crime.

Along with its obvious symbolic satisfactions, this encounter between the revolutionaries and the Queen benefited the former in one other important way. For when one of the pike-wielding hooligans lunged too close to Marie Antoinette's place by the carriage window, she is said to have shrieked: "Somebody get that sans-culotte away from me!"[120] This remark was an unequivocal insult: as Richard Wrigley has shown, before the Revolution, "to be deemed *sans-culotte* was equivalent to lacking an essential sign of proper dress"—the knee breeches or *culottes* of the nobility and the bourgeoisie— "and therefore to be consigned to society's lower ranks."[121] But according to one aristocratic chronicler, the Queen's use of the term in this context inspired revolutionaries to adopt the coarse, full-length trousers or *pantalons* of young workingmen as a gesture of class defiance and as proof of their anti-aristocratic "pure patriotism."[122] To be sure, in a climate where "pure patriotism" increasingly meant hatred for the King's wife, her alleged disapproval of the shabbily dressed masses invested the *pantalon* with a newfound power to evince opposition, outrage, and a lust for vengeance.[123] Again in spite of herself, Marie Antoinette had, it seems, provided her foes with a sartorial road map to rebellion.

THE QUEEN AND HER FAMILY ARRIVED AT THEIR SEMI-ABANDONED PARIS residence, the Tuileries, at ten o'clock on the night of the sixth. With the 670-odd attendants who had accompanied them from Versailles for the purpose of reestablishing the court in Paris, they struggled to find suitable lodgings among the numerous state pensioners who traditionally inhabited the château. The royal family had not resided at the Tuileries since 1722, when a very young Louis XV had moved from there to Versailles; of the current generation of Bourbons, Marie Antoinette was the only one to have made regular use of the place, occasionally retiring to a small suite of rooms, renovated at her behest, to refresh her *toilette* before or after evenings at the Opéra. Now, as pensioners were shuffled around and odd bits of furniture reallocated to different parts of the palace, the royals settled into their haphazard new quarters for a sorely needed night's sleep.

Sleep, though, was something the people of Paris had no intention of affording their sovereigns. Although La Fayette had surrounded the Tuileries with members of the National Guard (the soldiers of the *garde du corps* having been dismissed on account of their monarchist loyalties), the Queen and her family were awakened just a few hours after their arrival by the sound of crowds streaming into the gardens and courtyards, demanding to see them. In Madame de Tourzel's estimation, some of these people had shown up "for the pleasure of enjoying the fruits of their victory, [and] the majority merely out of curiosity."[124] But they all seemed eager to convey tidings of the Revolution's indomitable might. The market women, in particular, aggressively requisitioned other bystanders' tricolor cockades for themselves.[125] Then, despite what Tourzel noted as the visible reluctance of Marie Antoinette in particular, the mob forced all the members of the royal family to affix such *cocardes* to their own clothing.[126]

Like Louis XVI's acceptance of the blue and red *cocarde* two months prior, the incident had significant symbolic implications, allowing the people to assert power over the sovereigns who were now essentially their prisoners. Yet the Queen was determined, as she wrote to Mercy on October 7, to "win back the more sane and honest of the bourgeoisie and the people—despite all the malicious things that they keep doing to me."[127] Quite obviously, by forcibly relocating the King and his court to Paris, the commoners had marshaled a show of strength that even the fall of the Bastille had not foretold. Newly sensitized to the upstarts' capabilities, Marie Antoinette seems for the first time to have grasped the necessity of at least appearing to respect their goals—and their favorite symbols. With this in view, on her very first day at the Tuileries she enlisted Madame Éloffe to make 150 *cocardes tricolores,* "to be distributed to the market women of Paris on behalf of their Queen."[128] By reaching out to the very people who had just the day before threatened to make cockades of her entrails, she not only displayed a queenly capacity for forgiveness—a standard feature of sublime royal dignity—but also dispelled the rumors of her supposed disdain for the *tricolore.*

The market women were impressed, especially because the cockades she gave them, which Madame Éloffe had priced at 1 livre each, were considerably pricier and more luxurious than anything they could buy on a street corner or assemble at home.[129] Recognizing in the Queen an unexpected new source of munificence, the women gathered outside her apartments at the Tuileries the very next day, and after successfully clamoring for her to appear among them, demanded that she give them "the ribbons and the flowers from her own hat."[130] Marie Antoinette promptly dismantled her headdress and handed out its trimmings to the women, who gratified her by cheering her kindness and generosity for more than half an hour. Perhaps for the first time, the Queen's detractors found her willing to share the wealth that she had once reserved exclusively for her own adornment.

After festooning their dirty aprons and shopworn bonnets with bits and pieces of her costly apparel, the women of the Halles pushed their advantage further, still focusing on clothing as the area in which Marie Antoinette ought first and foremost to provide assistance. From Madame de Tourzel, who, summoned by their shouts, reappeared outside the palace after the Queen had returned to her rooms, they extracted a promise that the consort would redeem the articles of clothing that their poverty had forced them to put into hock.[131] Unfortunately for the Queen, though, the market women hurried to their local pawnshop at once, well before she had a chance to send her instructions to its proprietor.

When the women reached the pawnshop, they were enraged to discover that money had not yet arrived to redeem their belongings, and in a fury they laid waste to the store's windows, doors, and contents. Then they returned to the Tuileries, "crying out that the *Autrichienne* had tricked and made a mockery of them" and threatening to do the same damage there that they had done at the pawnshop.[132] Bailly hastened to the scene to prevent a full-scale riot, but weeks later, the women's anger was still simmering. It turned out that repurchasing all their pawned possessions would cost the crown 3 million livres—an impossible sum given the grim state of the nation's finances. As a compromise, Louis XVI issued a declaration stating that the people had misinterpreted his wife's generous pledge and that all she would be able to redeem on the women's behalf was "their body linens and their winter clothes."[133] This in itself was not an insignificant boon, but it failed to dispel the women's impression that the Queen, yet again, had betrayed them. Forgotten were her conciliatory gestures, and remembered, once more, were her manifold, unforgivable crimes against the people— crimes that scurrilous pamphlets continued to broadcast throughout Paris.

Yet even in the face of the public's animosity, the Queen seemed determined to deflect it with an image of peaceable compliance. At the Tuileries, where hostile

Parisians assembled to gawk at her every day, and where pro-revolutionary National Guard members monitored her every move, she found herself just as intensely scrutinized as she had ever been at Versailles.[134] The Parisians' appetite for revenge remained robust, as did the famine and poverty that had fueled their outbursts in the first place. And although the Assemblée, which had moved its quarters to the capital to follow Louis XVI's displaced court, was struggling to contend with social unrest and economic suffering both in the city and around the nation, popular violence continued to erupt in frightening, unpredictable ways. In this volatile situation, placating the subjects by whom she was surrounded presented itself as the safest course Marie Antoinette could follow.

That is not to say it was an easy one. As the Queen confessed in letters to her aristocratic friends—more and more of whom were emigrating to safer havens abroad—the stresses of life at the Tuileries tested her courage and her patience daily.[135] But if she was going, as she put it, to "win back . . . the bourgeoisie and the people," she would have to do so by convincing them of her good intentions and by manifesting those intentions not just in her behavior, which now involved unstinting kindness toward the Revolution's adherents, but in her style of dress as well. As was evident in the ferocious outcry over her reported aversion to the *cocarde nationale,* in the steady stream of libels taking aim at her fashion choices, and in her dealings with the women women from the Halles, the people were monitoring her clothing with an acutely critical eye and were prepared to lash out at the slightest provocation.

Thus, on October 7, 1789, when she announced to a large crowd that she and the King wished to coexist peacefully with the Parisians and that "all hatred must end," Marie Antoinette reportedly adopted a tricolor costume: a blue-and-white-striped gown and a white bonnet and fichu, both of which were edged with red ribbon.[136] On that same day, she also directed Madame Éloffe to provide her with dozens of *aunes* of rose, white, and blue ribbon for cockades for her own personal use.[137] Quietly but powerfully, her externalized change of heart toward the Revolution's emblems corroborated her message of friendship and peace. As she admitted years afterward to Mercy, "it behooved me to appear in good faith to adopt the people's cause as my own . . . for the best way to subvert those new ideas [was] to seem to share them."[138] During the early days of her reign, her costume choices had appeared to invest her with a degree of political authority that she actually lacked. Now, inversely, her manner of dress conveyed a false allegiance to the revolutionary public's "new ideas."

In the months that followed, Marie Antoinette continued to use clothing to express her superficial faith in the people's "new ideas." She purchased more cockades. She paid Madame Éloffe thousands of livres to overhaul old blue, white, and rose-colored dresses—brought to Paris from her wardrobe at

Versailles—and to trim them with extra, tricolor trappings.[139] Even when she received word of her brother Joseph II's death from a lung ailment at the end of February 1790, she took pains to incorporate these motifs into her mourning. In March she placed an order for twelve *aunes* of "narrow ribbon *à la Nation* as a concession to the ideas of the day."[140] Enthusiastically proclaiming the Revolution's egalitarian impact on fashion, the March 25 issue of *Le Journal de la mode et du goût* criticized royal mourning as an elitist practice (since traditionally, all of a monarch's subjects wore mourning to show respect after his or her passing) and called for its abolition.[141] By adding tricolor ribbons to her mourning costume, the Queen mitigated the political incorrectness of her ensemble and fell into step with revolutionary style.

Furthermore, though she had arrived at the Tuileries clutching a casket full of her most valuable diamonds, she abandoned the aggressively jeweled stance she had assumed during the Revolution's first summer. And despite the occasional orders she continued to place with Rose Bertin for formal gowns—the timeless ceremonies of Versailles having resumed at the Tuileries not long after the court's relocation there—mostly she spent her clothing allowance on ribbons, dress repairs, and simple caps and kerchiefs.[142] For her daily promenades in the Tuileries gardens, she seems to have favored the unfussy white bonnets and fichus that the populace had by now made its own, and that, along with tricolor accessories and clothes, the fashion journals of the day continued to promote as laudably "patriotic" markers.[143]

Indeed, ending her marked leave of absence from the world of fashion, Marie Antoinette might have stepped directly out of these periodicals' pages when, on July 14, 1790, she appeared before the 400,000 people who had crowded into the capital's Champ de Mars to celebrate the first anniversary of the Bastille's fall. For this event, called the Fête de la Fédération, she had selected a simple white dress not unlike those that all the female attendees had been required to wear (along with a tricolor sash) for the occasion. And she chose to accessorize her gown not with a staggering array of crown jewels, but with a headpiece of graceful tricolor feathers and fluttery matching ribbons.[144] After many long years of alienating her people through her dress, she now appeared instead as their friend and supporter, with her revolutionary sympathies plainly evident from her ensemble.

These sympathies were also on display in the outfit she had chosen for the five-year-old Dauphin, Louis Charles. For in contrast to the King himself—who remained partial to the fancy breeches, glittering jacket, and plumed hat of court culture—the little boy wore the tricolor uniform of the National Guard.[145] At the sight of this patriotically attired prince, the crowds went wild and extended some of their pleasure to the woman whose outfit coordinated so prettily with her son's. For the first time in many years, Marie Antoinette was welcomed with zealous cries of "Long live the Queen!"—cries that reached a fever pitch when the clouds overhead gave way to heavy rains, and, to the audience's ecstatic approval, she gently draped the Dauphin's uniform with her own diaphanous shawl. At last, it seemed, the people were encountering the kind of queen they had hoped for all along: a tender-hearted mother of France whose clothing spoke of generosity, not selfishness, of patriotic virtues, not foreign loyalties and aristocratic vice.[146]

Despite the foul weather, the Fête de la Fédération was held to be a resounding success, in no small part because of the reconciliation it seemed to have effected between the capital and the crown. Yet from Madame de Tourzel's point of view, the experience was bittersweet at best, for the populace would never receive the royal consort so benevolently again. Years later, Tourzel wistfully recalled the festival, during which she had stood by the royal family's side in the rain-soaked Champ de Mars, as her mistress's "last auspicious day."[147] For Marie Antoinette, history was about to follow an entirely different course, during which auspicious days would indeed be in short supply. Never again, after this day, would the revolutionaries fête her as their loyal queen of fashion.

NINE

TRUE COLORS

If the people were momentarily swayed by the sight of their Queen's tricolor garb at the Fête de la Fédération, the fact remained that her acceptance of the Revolution's sartorial codes in no way corresponded to an underlying conversion to its politics.[1] In January 1790, she explained in a secret letter to Mercy that although as a rule she considered herself too well-born to stoop to deception, "my current position is so unique that for everyone's sake, I have to change my frank and independent character and . . . [learn] how to dissimulate."[2] Her successful performance at the Fête de la Fédération was therefore just that, a performance: "One has to participate," she confessed to Mercy in advance of the festival, "but oh, how I dread it."[3]

Indeed, even as she sought to appease her subjects' wrath and diminish their hatred, she never warmed to the notion that they ought to have a hand in governing her husband's kingdom. Over the course of the Revolution's second year, she watched in horror as it took ever bolder swipes against the ancient pillars of the absolutist régime: in June 1790, the deputies of the Assemblée abolished all hereditary aristocratic titles and chivalric orders; in July, they drafted a "Civil Constitution of the Clergy," which, in an unprecedented repositioning of the Church's hierarchy, deemed all clergymen servants of the state; and in December, they pushed the King to accept this Civil Constitution, very much against his will. In the face of these radical changes, Marie Antoinette came to despise the Revolution more than ever.[4]

Louis XVI deplored the Assemblée's actions as well, and like his wife he dreaded the moment when the deputies would finish work on France's new constitution, which was bound to decree marked diminutions of his power.[5] However, in his perennial indecisiveness, he seemed unable or unwilling to consider taking any forceful steps to counteract the revolutionaries' maneuvers. Marie Antoinette, by contrast, drew daily more convinced that she and the King could not remain passive if they hoped to save their family, their position, and their kingdom from ruin.[6] Her behind-the-scenes preparedness to act with courage made a strong impression on the liberal aristocrat Mirabeau, who said of her on June 20, 1790: "There is only one man siding with the King now—his wife." Then, perhaps referring to her past as an intrepid, cross-dressed equestrienne, he added: "Soon the time will come when we will have to see what a woman can do in the saddle."[7]

In a satirical ditty published in a royalist newspaper at around the same time, Marie Antoinette was similarly praised for her "masculine" force of character, as contrasted with the sneaky feminine costume that the Duc d'Aiguillon had been said to adopt when provoking the October 1789 march on Versailles:

> We have been transported to a miraculous time:
> While d'Aiguil-- dresses up as a woman,
> Antoinette becomes a courageous man.[8]

As Mirabeau's quip may have done, this observation cast the Queen precisely as she had once attempted to cast herself by means of her masculine riding gear: as a lordly figure who would not cede her royal stature without a fight.

Needless to say, this was not a posture that endeared Marie Antoinette to those revolutionaries who remained skeptical about her commitment to their cause. One pornographically inclined lampoonist warned of the underlying wickedness of the Queen's equestrian exploits, imagining a sexual encounter between her and Artois in which she was "mounted on a superb palfrey and habited like an Amazon."[9] Here, her history of cross-dressing and her supposed penchant for her brother-in-law combined to yield a portrait of a perverse, denatured woman who was quite literally sleeping with the enemy. (Artois had never been a favorite of the French people, but since his clandestine departure from France in July 1789 and his involvement in an overtly counterrevolutionary émigré community abroad, their dislike of him had developed into implacable hatred.)

Whereas many of the Revolution's supporters still wanted to believe in the King as the "Restorer of French Liberty," a worthy leader for a new constitutional monarchy, they had no such hopes for his consort. Between her family ties to the Austrian Emperor and the long-standing gossip about her special friendship with Artois—two men who posed potential threats to the budding revolutionary state—there seemed every cause to fear that the inappropriately virile and power-hungry Marie Antoinette would, as one pamphlet noted, "take one of [her] ancestors, Louis XIV, as [her] model, lay siege to Paris at the head of a huge army, dressed in boots and spurs and carrying a whip, as if [she] were coming to subjugate [her] slaves."[10] And even if one dismissed the possibility that she was a dangerous foreign agent, the persistence of famine on the domestic front made her an easy target for accusations that she, France's most famous squanderer of flour, actively "wanted to reduce us [the people] to the harsh condition of beasts of burden, while reserving all the best grain for [her] superb hunting mounts."[11] Much like her powder-intensive hairstyles, Marie Antoinette's equestrian past was reframed by her detractors as proof of her spendthrift, selfish, and generally sinister character.

Though the fantasies the Queen harbored were likely nowhere near as extreme as the pamphleteers imagined, by the summer of 1790 she was, in fact, discreetly putting out feelers to see what might be done to reverse the Revolution's aggressive forward march. She began meeting and corresponding secretly with a variety of loyalists to the crown, including Mirabeau, who remained one of the leading lights of the Assemblée but who, following the gory events of October 1789, had begun in private to rethink his once vigorous opposition to royal power. In her dealings with the renegade nobleman, Marie Antoinette gained ample practice in "learning to dissimulate." Disguising her thorough aversion to the man—whose terrifically ugly, pockmarked face and oversized, leonine head had little appeal for the beauty-loving Queen—she seems to have brought him easily under her spell. Mirabeau's fervent pledges of assistance seemed to offer some hope that, as he reportedly promised her, "the monarchy [would be] saved."[12]

Considerably more disheartening, if allowing for greater honesty, was the correspondence she undertook during this time with her brother Leopold II—who had succeeded Joseph II on the throne, but to whom Marie Antoinette had never been close—and with other leaders throughout Europe. Her goal in approaching them was to see what they might do to help, in her words, pull France "back from the abyss" into which the people seemed hell-bent on flinging it. For philosophical and political reasons of their own, however, these rulers displayed woefully little interest in rescuing France from chaos; they simply urged her and Louis XVI to stay calm and hope for the best, advice that Marie Antoinette found extremely difficult to follow. As she remarked in a fit of desperation to the Spanish ambassador, who reported to her husband's cousin on the throne of Spain: "It is easy enough to recommend prudence and temporizing when one is far away from all of this—but not when one has a knife at one's throat."[13]

These words were more accurate than perhaps any of the Queen's royal correspondents cared to consider. As time passed, they also proved more literal than figurative, insofar as the revolutionaries' knives seemed to hover increasingly close to Marie Antoinette's physical person. Not long after the Fête de la Fédération, National Guardsmen apprehended an armed man who had infiltrated the gardens of the court's country retreat at Saint-Cloud with the express purpose of assassinating the Queen. Once this individual was caught, secret police hired by Louis XVI promptly uncovered another plot to kill his wife, this time by poison.[14]

Almost as frightening, from the royal family's perspective, was a proposal that gained considerable momentum during the fall, both among the general public and in the revolutionary government. Strengthened in no small part by the outpouring of political pornography that "documented" the gaulle-clad consort's sexual misdeeds, this proposal called for trying her as an adulteress, securing a divorce for her husband, and leaving him free to marry a woman more palatable to the revolutionary public, such as the Duc d'Orléans's eligible daughter. As for the adulterous Autrichienne, her punishment would be either permanent confinement in a convent or execution. Even La Fayette, for all his talk about a happy union between the people and their princes, did not mince words when informing the Queen that the public might well seek to get rid of her in this way.[15]

In light of these mounting dangers, it became painfully clear to Marie Antoinette and even, at last, to her husband that they could no longer avoid taking drastic action.[16] Toward the end of 1790, they concluded that they had little choice but to escape the Tuileries with their family and flee to a location controlled by a strong monarchist sympathizer, either outside France (the Queen's preference) or within it (the alternative Louis XVI favored, out of a desire not to disappoint his "good people"). Mirabeau, among others, had already proposed a solution of this kind over the summer; now more than ever, it seemed the only way out.[17]

Just what would happen afterward—whether Leopold II or other foreign rulers would offer to help them, and how or to what extent they would succeed in restoring the monarchy's powers—remained to be determined.[18] But at least the royals would be free of the Tuileries and of the constant menaces that confronted them in the revolutionary nerve center that was Paris. Marie Antoinette's old paramour Axel von Fersen, who had settled in the capital earlier that year and had been unstinting in his offers of assistance, stepped forward to help orchestrate the escape. Louis XVI, as always, seemed willfully blind to any romantic ties binding the Swedish nobleman to his wife and raised no objections as Fersen set about planning their flight.

While Fersen and a handful of other trusted confidants busied themselves with the necessary arrangements, the Queen herself was operating under the almost constant surveillance of the National Guard and, less officially, of her assigned palace domestics, most of whom she distrusted as revolutionary spies. Under these conditions, her policy of strategic dissimulation remained paramount, for the smallest false step could betray her to the Assemblée and dash her plans for good. Besides, there was no denying by this point that the Revolution had a vocabulary all its own, a language of political fervor and egalitarian virtue that included accessories such as the *tricolore*. So why not, she asked rhetorically, "speak to [the people] in the only language they understand?"[19] As she bided her time and awaited her flight to freedom, Marie Antoinette therefore continued to speak this language through her clothing. At least if Madame Éloffe's account books are any indication, during this period she adhered to a conciliatory, mostly blue-and-white dress code.[20]

In this respect, Marie Antoinette paradoxically began advancing the very same agenda that her enemies had long insisted on reading into her "counterrevolutionary" appearance.[21] In the pamphlets that had flooded the capital since the summer of 1789, the Queen's detractors had cautioned that her outfits most definitely did not speak the language of democratic conviction and populist virtue; that her Austrian connections, metaphorically figured in her ostrich feathers, represented a real danger to France's budding constitutional government; that her masculine ensembles bespoke her treasonous will to power; and that even her simple white dresses, bonnets, and kerchiefs did not so much celebrate the upright new régime as recall her attachment to the decadent old one. By late spring 1791, as she and her helpers put the finishing touches on the escape plans, these paranoid charges had taken on an indisputable element of truth. The cunningly bedecked Marie Antoinette was *not* to be trusted. She *did* harbor something akin to the unpatriotic intentions that her enemies deciphered in her clothing. As one contemporary pamphlet observed, "the public saw in [her] nothing but a theater actress" whose superficial displays of patriotic probity masked a deep-seated aversion to the revolutionary cause.[22] To be sure, her extravagant, inappropriate costumes had long since identified her with the corrupt population of Parisian actresses—a fact that made her protestations of good will seem unreliable in the extreme.[23]

Yet as the Queen had confessed to Mercy, the desperate straits in which she found herself necessitated her recourse to dissimulation and disguise. However ambivalent she said she felt about telling lies, they were stepping-stones to a future that would restore her "frank and independent character" once and for all. In this regard, it is telling that in the months leading up to June 1791 and her planned flight, Marie Antoinette stopped asking Madame Éloffe to provide her with tricolor cockades, ribbons *à la Nation,* and dresses strategically rehabbed in red, white, and blue. In the wardrobe she assembled for her journey, she instead began gravitating toward the unrepentant green of Artois, the lavish violet of royalty, the black of Austria and of royal mourning, and the white of the Bourbon fleur-de-lys.[24] Gradually increasing her clothing orders from both Madame Éloffe and Rose Bertin, she put together a trousseau fit for a queen—a queen, that is, who had every intention of reclaiming her crown.

Madame Campan, whose help Marie Antoinette enlisted in completing her apparel purchases, begged her mistress to remember that "a Queen of France will be able to get the dresses she requires, wherever she may find herself" and warned that acquiring so much clothing in advance "could be useless, even dangerous."[25] Certainly, by stepping up the time and money she spent with Rose Bertin, Louis XVI's consort was exposing herself at worst to the possibility that someone would catch on to her scheme, and at best to a new spate of negative publicity. And in fact, both of these risks materialized. Although she did not denounce the royals' escape until after it occurred, one of the women working in the royal wardrobe grew suspicious as to Marie Antoinette's motives for suddenly ordering such a large number of new gowns. A die-hard revolutionary with a lover in the National Guard and no affection whatsoever for the Queen, this woman began cautioning her compatriots that the royals were preparing to flee.[26] Marie Antoinette, in turn, grew so apprehensive of the wardrobe woman's spying that she arranged to defer the escape from Paris until one day after the woman had left her service.[27]

Revolutionary journalists, likewise, sat up and took notice of Bertin's renewed regular presence at her patroness's side. Unlike the wardrobe woman, the pamphleteers did not make the connection between the dress orders and the escape plot; but they did reintroduce the *marchande de modes,* alongside old standards like Artois, Polignac, and Lamballe, as a key player in Marie Antoinette's coterie of detested favorites. According to one tale, probably apocryphal, a maidservant working for the Princesse de Lamballe was once attacked outside the Tuileries because she was mistaken "for someone belonging to the Queen's milliner Madame Bertin, who, [her aggressors] said, was feasting upon the public misery."[28] If this incident did occur, perhaps it drew its rationale from pamphlets such as the one that, reprising the same litany of complaints unleashed against the fashion merchant a decade earlier, indignantly asserted: "Nothing equals the impertinence of this *demoiselle* since she has been admitted to the intimacy of the Queen, to whom she dictates the laws of fashion—of which she is, she says, the most fervent priestess."[29] Renewing old grudges against the frivolous and arbitrarily empowered "ministry of fashion" over which Marie Antoinette presided, this passage again presented her devotion to clothing as compelling grounds for the public's mistrust. In January 1791, the revolutionary journalist Camille Desmoulins—he who had donned the first, leafy green cockade in July 1789—took up this line of argument by describing Marie Antoinette in his newspaper as "that Fury who has detached all the snakes from her hair and turned them loose on the French Nation."[30] In this formulation, the Queen's intricately styled hairdo harbored poisonous elements that would lay her subjects low.

Yet this latest round of journalistic attacks did nothing to deter the Queen as she selected clothes for her impending journey. In the months leading up to the escape, Madame Campan recalled, Marie Antoinette paid an inordinate amount of attention to the way she would dress once away from Paris—as if her royalist-hued ensembles stood as so many promises of the prerogatives she thought she was on the verge of recapturing.[31] By abjuring the colors of revolutionary militancy and reverting to those affiliated with the *ancien régime,* and by convening her erstwhile "ministry of fashion" to outfit her for her imminent triumph, Marie Antoinette indicated that henceforth the only political agenda displayed in her dress would be her own. She had just one last misleading costume to wear before she and her family would be free at last.

ON THE NIGHT OF JUNE 20, 1791, AFTER GOING THROUGH THE MOTIONS OF the formal royal *couchers* that still concluded each day at the Tuileries, Louis XVI, Marie Antoinette, their children, Madame de Tourzel, and Madame Élisabeth sneaked out of the palace under cover of darkness, slipping past the patrolling National Guardsmen at carefully timed intervals. Axel von Fersen, dressed as a coachman, picked them up in an inconspicuous carriage. Like Fersen, the escapees had donned new costumes and social identities to make their escape. Madame de Tourzel was disguised as a Russian aristocrat's widow, the Baronne de Korff (the real Baronne had loaned the royals her passport for their journey); the Children of France as the Baronne's two young daughters; Marie Antoinette as the children's governess; Madame Élisabeth as the children's maid; Louis XVI as a valet; and their three loyal bodyguards as manservants.[32] When presented with his unusual outfit for the evening, a little frock made from brown-striped calico, the six-year-old Dauphin is said to have speculated happily, "So we are going to play a comedy," thereby recalling his mother's amateur theatrics at the Petit Trianon.[33] Indeed, the unassuming dark brown tunic and voluminous black shawl and bonnet she sported that night revealed that, as during the performances at her country villa, she had deliberately elected not to play the role of the Queen.[34] Whereas once, her interest in assuming a commoner's identity had represented an amusing diversion from the burdens of royal life, it was now quite simply a matter of survival.

The royals' plan was to travel to the fortified city of Montmédy, which stood close to the border between France and Hapsburg Flanders, the very territory whose muslin exports to the Queen had caused such an outcry in the early 1780s. Once in Montmédy, they were to receive military protection and backing from the Marquis de Bouillé, an aristocratic general who controlled a sizable number of troops in the area.

Six miles outside of Paris, they switched carriages and drivers: Fersen was to make haste to Flanders ahead of them, while his royal charges rode in relative luxury in a capacious, custom-made green-and-yellow *berline* packed with the huge piles of luggage they insisted on bringing into exile.[35] One of the many precious items Marie Antoinette brought on the journey was a small jade manicure set painted with a miniature of herself on horseback—a token that perhaps served to steady her resolve and to remind her, in Mirabeau's words, of just "what a woman [could] do in the saddle" as she led the charge from Paris.[36] Had her detractors known about its inclusion in her travel gear, they almost surely would have seen it as confirmation of their worst fears about this menacing royal huntress.

But the scheme unraveled well before the travelers reached their destination. From the outset, the *berline*'s eastward progress was hindered by substantial travel delays; these in turn caused problems in connecting with the cavalry detachments that were slated to meet it en route.[37] The Queen's hairdresser Léonard was at least partly responsible for the ultimate catastrophe. Marie Antoinette had chosen him to participate in their flight so that she might "still appear as queen of fashion when she and Louis received the acclamations of their loyal troops at Montmédy or when she visited her [Hapsburg family members] at Brussels."[38] Unfortunately for his patroness, Léonard's skills as a hairdresser did not translate into aptitude as a diplomatic envoy and military scout. He and the young Duc de Choiseul-Stainville (the loyal but inexperienced nephew of Marie Antoinette's old supporter at court, Choiseul) awaited the *berline* for several hours at a designated meeting spot. When it failed to appear, Léonard rode ahead to Varennes, a town forty miles outside of Montmédy. There, swaggeringly self-important as ever, he persuaded a waiting company of loyalist soldiers to disband on the grounds that the royal family had been detained in the Tuileries and would not require their assistance that night.[39] At the same time,

he also unwisely handed off Marie Antoinette's casket of priceless diamonds—
which he had been directed to deliver to Montmédy himself—to a soldier, who
was found murdered and empty-handed the next day.[40]

Meanwhile, early in the morning of June 21, the news of the Bourbons'
disappearance spread like wildfire through the French capital, disseminated
by the palace staffers and National Guardsmen whose surveillance they had
eluded. The tidings stirred indignation in the populace (which was already
on a hair trigger) and fostered rumors of an imminent counterrevolutionary
coup to be led against Paris by the Queen and the Austrian Emperor. Fearing
a city-wide descent into chaos, the deputies of the Assemblée held an emer-
gency meeting and directed La Fayette to dispatch mounted couriers to the
surrounding countryside with warrants for the royal family's arrest. The
couriers sped through the provinces while the heavily laden *berline* crept
along toward the border.

At the end of its first long day on the road, the *berline* was also pursued,
and fatally overtaken, by a young postmaster named Drouet, who had happened to see the royals pass through the town of Sainte-Menehould and had
recognized Louis XVI's face (the valet disguise notwithstanding) from a
50-livre note.[41] As the royals journeyed on to Varennes, their last stop on the
way to Montmédy, Drouet sped on horseback behind them. Failing to find
the expected change of horses when they first arrived in town, the royals met
with still another unanticipated delay. In the meantime, Drouet reached
Varennes, sounded the tocsin, and gathered a group of local National
Guardsmen and other revolutionary militants who lost no time in throwing
up a barricade that would prevent any nearby royalist troops from entering
the town to assist the fugitives. Drouet and his men then prepared an am-
bush along the town's main street, and the *berline* soon drove straight into
it.[42] Before the passengers knew what was happening, they were surrounded:
by Drouet and his helpers, by swarms of irate townspeople, and by teeming
arrivals from other towns in the area—all of them scandalized by the King's
and Queen's ignominious flight.

To protect the royals from this volatile mob, a local official and grocer
named Monsieur Sauce squired them into his house, where he detained them
while awaiting further instructions from Paris, Drouet having informed him
that anyone allowing the escapees to move on "would be guilty of high treason."[43] The wait was agonizing for the royals, besieged as they were by cat-
calls and hissing from the townspeople who surrounded the house, and
anxiously wondering if their loyalist soldiers in the area might still be able to
come to their aid.[44] Just after dawn, they were forced to abandon this hope
when two of La Fayette's men appeared in Sauce's house and served Louis
XVI with an arrest warrant. Incredulous that his people were daring to seize

control of his sacred person, the monarch cried: "There is no longer a King of France!" Marie Antoinette, characteristically, displayed more defiance, snatching the piece of paper out of her husband's hands and hurling it to the floor. She would not, she announced, allow her children to be defiled by such a preposterous document.[45]

But the Queen's protestations were in vain. She and her family were hemmed in by hordes of seething revolutionary sympathizers who were determined to carry out the Assemblée's arrest orders, and Louis XVI, in particular, was unwilling to let the paltry crew of loyalists who finally had managed to enter Varennes use force against them. And so, for the second time since October 6, 1789, the royal family became prisoners of the French people. On the morning of June 22, they piled into their glossy green *berline*, bound for the city they had so desperately wanted to flee. In a slow-moving cortège flanked by National Guardsmen as well as by "people armed with scythes and muskets, pikes, pitchforks and sabers," they drove along roads lined with commoners who had turned out to heckle and curse them.[46] In one village, the rabble went so far as to tear at the dresses of Marie Antoinette and her sister-in-law, reducing both women to tears.[47] Once again, the Queen's outfit—as humble and unassuming as it had been designed to look—served as a focal point for her subjects' rage.

After four days' travel in the sweltering summer heat, neither Marie Antoinette's clothes nor her family's were in especially presentable condition as their cortège at last came to a stop in front of the Tuileries on June 25, flanked by an escort that had grown to include between fifteen thousand and thirty thousand people.[48] When the royals piled out of the *berline*, the angry crowds who had gathered there were astonished to see their faces and traveling disguises caked with grime. But before they could retire to their rooms— Marie Antoinette was clamoring to take a bath and Louis XVI, to consume a roast chicken—they had to run one last popular gauntlet.[49] According to one of the King's pages, "the crowd was immense. La Fayette [had been] going around the gardens, urging the people to stay calm, but inviting them to keep their hats on their heads at the sight of the monarch[s], in order to signal their indignation."[50] In this reprise of the show of defiance that the Third Estate's members had staged two years earlier, the General's orders were, Madame de Tourzel observed, "so strictly obeyed that several hatless scullions covered their heads with foul and dirty napkins."[51]

Madame Campan, for her part, was less shocked by the people's latest demonstration of hostility than by what she saw when her royal mistress removed her own hat after the journey. Over the past few days, the thirty-five-year-old Queen's hair had "turned as white as that of a seventy-year-old woman."[52] Straightaway, Marie Antoinette sent a lock of it to the Princesse de Lamballe, whom she had dispatched to England on secret business just as she and Louis XVI fled the Tuileries, and who was anxiously awaiting news of the escape. For Marie Antoinette, the lock of hair was all the news the Princesse would require; she had it set in a ring inscribed with the pithy but telling phrase "whitened by misfortune."[53] In the friends' early years together, whiteness—white skin, white-powdered hair, white diamonds, white furs incandescent against a snowy landscape—had meant the unrestricted pursuit of enjoyment, luxury, and beauty. In this very different day and age, it bore witness to the trials the Queen had undergone in her attempted flight.

Those trials only intensified after her return to the capital. Because their clandestine departure had registered as an outright betrayal of the revolutionary cause, the royals lost whatever residual political credibility they had enjoyed before leaving, and the very idea of a constitutional monarchy, still supported by more moderate revolutionaries, underwent a dramatic fall from favor. "Now that this 'patriotic' King has fled," ranted the political journalist Jacques-Pierre Brissot, "he has been unmasked . . . [and] has destroyed his crown with his own hands."[54] Indeed, the day before the sovereigns' reappearance in the capital, members of the leftist political Club des Cordeliers, led by the charismatic Georges Danton, gathered six thousand signatures on a petition demanding the establishment of a republic and the concomitant elimination of all royal privileges.[55] Shortly afterward, thirty thousand more people signed another such petition. As Marie-Jeanne Roland, the wife of the politician Jean-Marie Roland, observed at this time, "the word 'republic' is now being uttered almost everywhere."[56]

Rendering the situation of the monarchy even more precarious, the Queen's old ally Mirabeau had died in April, depriving her and her family of their most potent, if covert, revolutionary ally. And in early September, the Assemblée presented Louis XVI with a completed constitution that downgraded him to a "representative of the Nation" and thereby reduced the crown's pretensions to being divinely ordained.[57] On September 14, fighting back bitter tears, and wholly under duress, the King swore to uphold the Constitution, while the onlooking deputies of the Assemblée again pointedly failed to remove their hats in his presence.[58] Four days later, a hot-air balloon trimmed with tricolor ribbons flew over the Champs Élysées to commemorate the landmark oath.[59] But although the balloon's fluttering decorations suggested that the long-awaited fusion of the people and the crown had finally come to pass, the latter's future remained uncertain at best. Just after Louis XVI pledged his support for the Constitution, Marie Antoinette remarked bitterly: "These people do not want sovereigns. [With] their perfidious tactics, they are demolishing the monarchy stone by stone."[60]

The so-called flight to Varennes certainly gave the people abundant new reasons to distrust their sovereigns, and, as usual, they directed a large portion of their anger at the Queen.[61] Perhaps the most damning evidence that the court of public opinion held against her was the fact that she and her family had been caught on the road to the Hapsburg border. This discovery not only confirmed the *Autrichienne*'s significant involvement in the escape, but retroactively corroborated anxieties that had fermented since the days of *La Reine en gaulle* about an "Austrian conspiracy" to ruin France. Echoing Desmoulins's depiction of the Queen as a Fury with dangerous snakes slithering out of her hair, one pamphleteer lambasted her as a "Fury [seeking] the destruction of [the] twenty-three million people" in her husband's realm.[62] Another unknown writer emphasized that this plan grew out of her nefarious Hapsburg upbringing. Eliding any mention of the impeccably Gallic appearance that the Dauphine had presented to her subjects when first arriving in their midst, this writer imagined Marie Antoinette referring to her adopted homeland as "France, the sole object of my resentment; France, which I have hated since the day I was born."[63] Visually, this claim may have found corroboration in the pro-revolutionary artist Lesueur's popular engraving of the Varennes arrest, which showed the Queen (and her daughter, "Muslin") dressed in the instantly recognizable flowing white dress and rusticated straw hat of "little Vienna."[64] (Plate 23.)

An abiding mistrust of her Austrian connections was not, however, the only aspect of the Varennes flight that intensified the people's anger with the Queen. For many observers, the episode also highlighted the strong underlying link between Marie Antoinette's treasonous agenda and her obsession with fashion. Had she not, after all, adopted an artful disguise to elude potential captors, just as she had been wont to do during the scandalous Opéra visits of her youth? Had she not encouraged the King to don a costume, too, and to demean himself by masquerading as a mere valet? (Jérôme Pétion, one of the three deputies who had accompanied them on the final leg of their trip from Varennes to Paris, emphasized afterward that the sovereign's clothes "could not have been more shabby."[65]) Had Marie Antoinette not, as the wardrobe woman's denunciation specified, ordered an inordinate quantity of new clothes in the months leading up to June 20?[66] Had she not called upon the haughty, frivolous Bertin in preparing for her escape and upon her equally loathsome hairdresser in trying to carry it off?[67]

Of course, the Queen's easy adoption of bogus personas, her degradation of the kingly office, her boundless vanity, and her close association with fashion's artificers had long struck her critics as proof of her malevolence and moral bankruptcy. But for the partisans of the new régime, these qualities, all abundantly evident in the flight to Varennes, represented severe political dangers—especially when placed in the service of what was assumed to be a plan of counterrevolutionary military action. In this light it is not entirely surprising that when the news of the royals' escape was made public, masses of Parisians flocked to the Tuileries gardens, some of whom reportedly charged into the palace and made straight for Marie Antoinette's wardrobe. Whatever garments they could lay their hands on, the interlopers were said to have seized, tried on, and then carried home to resell or wear themselves.[68] Like the mirrors in her apartments at Versailles, the consort's clothes—signs of her vanity and self-indulgence—again attracted the people's marauding ire.

Exploiting this relationship between the public's outrage and the Queen's sartorial obsessions, the numerous satirical prints that came out after the botched escape took pains to highlight the starring role that fashion had played in the episode. In one caricature that depicted the royal family's detention at Sauce's house, Marie Antoinette stood before a mirror, adjusting a scarf at her neck, too enraptured with her own image to notice that La Fayette's emissaries had just arrived to arrest her and the King. This representation identified narcissism as her besetting sin: her profound self-absorption prevented her from recognizing the perils that faced her family, just as it had ostensibly (during the Flour Wars, for example) inured her to her subjects' suffering.

In another contemporary image that also placed the Queen before a mirror,

11.   Anonymous, *The Gourmand: Scene at Varennes on June 21, 1791* (1791) (Bibliothèque Nationale de France, Paris)

her principal offense was not so much vanity as a willful assault on her husband's masculinity and authority. In this print, she was seated at a *toilette* table while Louis XVI, dressed in a distinctly feminine smock, diligently brushed out her hair. Ever since her flirtation with the *pouf* in the mid-1770s, the public had worried that Marie Antoinette's unchecked expenditures, showy self-presentation, and cultivation of a "ministry of fashion" added up to a degrading feminine appropriation of Louis XVI's kingly powers. With the flight to Varennes, in which she had presumably forced her husband to participate, she had again overstepped her bounds. She had reduced the King to a lowly minion who—like her "other" coiffeur, Léonard—existed solely to serve her egotistical whims. Yet this, the cartoon suggested, had deleterious effects on the monarchy as a whole. If Louis XVI himself had admitted at Varennes that his authority was no more, he had no one but his wife to blame for the loss. As the caption to the image, which was entitled *Tit for Tat*, suggested, he had made a bad trade in trying to substitute "Montmédy for Paris" and "coiffure for crown." The failure of the enterprise had effectively cost Louis XVI his crown and had left him with nothing better to do than to tend to the hairstyle of his reckless, domineering wife.[69]

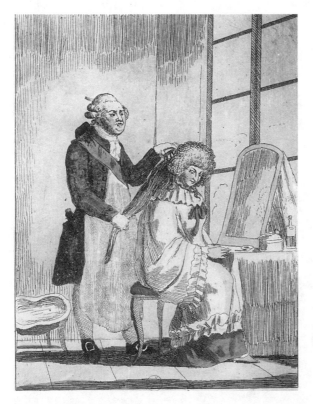

12. Anonymous, *Troc pour troc, coiffure pour couronne* (1791) (Bibliothèque Nationale de France, Paris)

Still another caricature attacked Marie Antoinette's involvement in the flight to Varennes by grafting her head—complete with snake-infested, Fury-like locks—onto the body of a leopard, above a satirical caption about the false identity she had assumed for her voyage.[70] While the coiffure, of course, reprised Desmoulins's terrifying warnings about the Queen's monstrous appetite for destruction, the introduction of the leopard's body added two further caveats. First, by offering a visual pun (*léopard*) on Léonard's name, it reminded viewers that the royal consort had drafted one of her notorious "ministers of fashion" to connive with her against the French people. Having for over a decade despised the shady characters in her effeminate "shadow cabinet," the public could now, the cartoon revealed, feel wholly vindicated in its antipathy. Thanks to the revelations of the Montmédy fiasco, despicable hangers-on like Léonard (who, not coincidentally, disappeared abroad after learning of the royal family's arrest) could legitimately be construed as threats to the Nation.[71]

Secondly, by endowing the Queen with a leopard's body, the image harshly refuted the peace-making gestures she had offered the public in the Revolution's earlier phase. Despite her reassuring adoption of tricolor costumes and cockades, her stealthy decampment to the Hapsburg border revealed that the leopard had by no means changed her spots. For all her protean self-styling techniques, she remained the same, perfidious foreigner she had always been. If, in the future, she wished to adorn herself with tricolor ribbons, then she would be doing so in vain; the people would not be fooled again.[72] "Go ahead and wrap yourself in your royal purple mantle,"

13. Anonymous,
*Her Excellency Madame
la Baronne de Korff*
(c. 1791) (Bibliothèque
Nationale de France, Paris)

the revolutionary journalist Louis Prudhomme angrily directed her in his newspaper, Les Révolutions de Paris. "We don't expect you to display any civic virtues; you weren't born with any!"[73]

By opposing Marie Antoinette's "royal purple mantle" to the people's "civic virtues," this statement forged a connection between her newly commissioned wardrobe of violet (and white, and green) dresses and her unreformed, counterrevolutionary beliefs. And the politically incorrect colors of her new costumes may well have been viewed in this manner, even beyond the realm of leopard cartoons and newspaper harangues. Shortly after the royal family's return from Varennes, a group of fist-shaking market women hastened to the Tuileries and tore to shreds the green sash that one of the Queen's female attendants—Madame Campan's sister—happened to be wearing. By way of an explanation, the women declared that green was the color of Artois, "whom they would never forgive" for his own counterrevolutionary machinations, and that the lady sporting that loathsome hue was obviously "the slave of the Autrichienne."[74] In this context, it is hard to imagine that the Queen's replacement of revolutionary with royalist colors of clothing did anything but worsen her already catastrophic public image.

Nonetheless, the irredeemable failure of the Montmédy effort seems to have left Marie Antoinette with little appetite for further sartorial deceptions. After Varennes, twelve of her first twenty orders with Madame Éloffe were for garments in either Artois green, royal purple, or both, and one of the first court dresses she commissioned from Rose Bertin was also royal purple.[75] Politically, however, she resumed her program of dissimulation, this time working with the moderate revolutionary deputy Antoine Barnave (who, along with Pétion, had ridden with her in the berline as she and her family reentered Paris in June), to convince him that she and Louis XVI were devoted to the cause of constitutional monarchy, and that she could get her brother Leopold II to lend it his diplomatic support. Just as she had with Mirabeau, Marie Antoinette was engaging Barnave in a double game. In a letter written in code to Mercy, she dismissed the Constitution as a "tissue of impracticable absurdities."[76] Far from garnering her brother's support for the new régime, she wanted him and the other European monarchs to form an armed congress that would intimidate the fledgling revolutionary government and, as Antonia Fraser has put it, "essentially . . . threaten the French into better behavior toward their King."[77] Unshakable in her royalist convictions, the Queen seemed to view this as a perfectly reasonable course to pursue. "Far from asking the impossible," she wrote on August 7, "I simply demand the reestablishment of the [old] régime."[78]

Yet even as she manipulated Barnave to this end, Marie Antoinette no longer took any pains to wear her false political sentiments on her sleeve.

From the "duck-green" taffeta cloak she ordered on July 13 to the "green Florence *chemise* shot through with violet" that she purchased on September 16, and from the green redingote she bought on September 24 to the violet satin gown she commissioned on November 18, the Queen emphatically reintroduced the regal colors of the *ancien régime*. What was more, she spent princely sums to do so: in the last two quarters of 1791, her debt to Rose Bertin rose 30 percent over the already inflated sum she had funneled into her Montmédy purchases in the first two quarters.[79]

Nor, apparently, did these changes in the Queen's attire go unnoticed by her subjects. In the summer of 1791, at least one pamphleteer complained about her "aversion to our national costume"—meaning the tricolor uniform of the National Guard—and marshaled this aversion as proof that "all [France's] calamities past, present, and to come, have always been and will always be her doing."[80] Equally critical of the consort's newfound, royalist-tinged elegance was La Fayette, who scoffed that despite her tenuous political position, she was "more concerned about looking beautiful in the face of danger than about staving it off."[81] By contrast, Barnave, young and starstruck, found the Queen's resplendent appearance more captivating than objectionable. "You can move the French people with ribbons, with a charming smile," he flattered her, insisting that she could still win back her subjects' affections by simply looking lovely.[82] (Barnave's own admiration for the elegant consort was such that when he went to the guillotine in November 1793, he carried a treasured swatch from one of her dresses in his coat pocket.[83]) Yet what Barnave, Lafayette, and the anonymous pamphleteer all failed to see in Marie Antoinette's manner of dress was the expression of a cherished goal, which she confided in more explicit terms to Fersen alone: "to become, once again, so powerful as to prove to all these beggars that I was never their fool."[84]

But defiant as it was, the change in Marie Antoinette's clothing repertoire also evinced some pathos, for since the return to the Tuileries, the monarchy was losing support not only within France but without, and not only among the people but among the nobility. The Comte de Provence, who had made a separate, successful escape on the night of June 20, had reunited with his brother Artois and a large group of other aristocratic émigrés at Coblentz, a city just south of Cologne that was ruled by the French princes' maternal uncle. From the safety of their foreign outpost, which they styled as France's only legitimate court, this rabidly counterrevolutionary group rejected the Assemblée's political pretensions, threatened violence against the Nation, and railed against Louis XVI's weakness in accepting the Constitution. Prompted by the former controller-general Calonne, who still blamed Marie Antoinette for his dismissal from his post, this faction entertained the idea of establishing the ever ambitious Provence as regent "on the grounds that the King was held under duress," and of formally establishing the French monarchy abroad.[85]

Heartbroken by what she saw as a familial as well as a political betrayal, Marie Antoinette wrote to Provence, begging him not to follow this route.[86] Still, the émigrés continued to posture aggressively against the Revolution and its officially pro-Constitution king—gestures that placed great additional pressure on the royal family's already strained relations with their subjects. Thus, if the Queen insisted on regal colors in her costume, perhaps it was to remind her foreign audience as well as her domestic one that, for all the humiliations they had been forced to endure, she and her husband still occupied the French throne.

It was a lonely stance to take, and a lonely time Marie Antoinette had of it trying to assert herself as a sovereign when so few people were stepping forward to acknowledge her as such. The Constitution had stripped the Queen and King of their divine aura; under the new régime, they were "no longer to be called 'Majesty' . . . and no one was to show [them] any of the traditional marks of honor, such as remaining standing in [their] presence or uncovering their heads."[87] By and large, those courtiers who had not yet emigrated had little interest in participating in the ceremonies of a drastically desacralized court, particularly when the National Guardsmen surrounding the Tuileries had received strict orders to bar anyone not wearing a national *cocarde*.[88] Given the increasingly punishing antiaristocratic timbre of the revolutionary movement, this emblem had grown much less palatable to nobles who had once worn it for fashion's sake; according to an Englishwoman traveling in Paris at the time, aristocrats who did adopt the cockade for fear of the masses' reprisals preferred to hide it "under a tuft of ribbons."[89] After Varennes, though, this was an effort that fewer and fewer nobles seemed willing to make for the privilege of attending their sovereigns. "They are punishing us for our misfortunes," Marie Antoinette complained indignantly, scandalized that people had stopped attending even her husband's *coucher*.[90] Although as doyenne of the Petit Trianon she had blithely dodged her courtiers' ministrations, she now craved their help in shoring up the very prerogatives she had once made a game of renouncing.

Apart from the Princesse de Lamballe, who returned from exile loyally sporting three black, pro-Austrian, and pro-aristocratic feathers in her "bewitching English beaver hat," and bringing her animal-loving friend the gift of a fluffy dog named Thisbée, the Queen had few sources of immediate comfort and support.[91] From abroad, Fersen was still plotting actively to rescue his royal friends, but except for one clandestine visit to the Tuileries in late February 1792—his last face-to-face encounter with Marie Antoinette—circumstances kept him from her side. Almost as painfully, Madame Élisabeth, with whom the Queen usually enjoyed amicable relations, had grown bullheadedly conservative, supporting without question her émigré brothers' imprudent saber-rattling across the border. With Marie Antoinette holding a very different opinion of the princes' activities, the two women's friendship cooled. As for Louis XVI, he deplored the current political changes as strongly as his wife did, but he fell prey to a depression that, combined with his indecisiveness, made him a less than zealous participant in her feverish plotting.[92] No longer permitted to ride out to hunt, he whiled away the hours indoors, reading works of history and tallying the number of outings he had made "away from *chez moi*" in all the years of his reign. The result of his calculations, 2,636, offered a small boost to his morale, but provided no solace to the Queen.[93] Writing to Fersen on October 31, 1791, she described her domestic situation as "sheer hell."[94]

At the same time, perhaps unbeknownst to her, Marie Antoinette did receive a show of allegiance from at least one unexpected source: *Le Journal de la mode et du goût*. Whereas this fashion journal's editor, Jean-Antoine Le Brun, had initially waxed enthusiastic over the Revolution's political and sartorial accomplishments, in recent months he had grown increasingly disenchanted.[95] In the realm of fashion, in particular, Le Brun disliked the capital's turn toward radicalism, as the equation of simplicity with patriotism had wrought havoc in the French luxury industry. As during Marie Antoinette's Trianon years, the trend toward plain, inexpensive fabrics had come as a terrible blow to French silk manufacturers, causing rampant unemployment and poverty in that important sector of the economy.[96] It had also, Le Brun remarked in his journal, alienated "women of quality" who, now that the Assemblée had abolished aristocratic titles and privileges, would have liked at least to distinguish themselves through the kind of sumptuous, exorbitantly priced apparel that had once been the hallmark of their class. Yet such ladies—still the principal subscribers to *Le Journal de la mode et du goût*—found their efforts thwarted by the vogue toward "economical dresses" and the dearth of more elegant styles.[97]

Exacerbating this scarcity was the declining number of *marchandes de modes* in Paris. The fashion business in the capital had suffered terribly from the mass emigration of wealthy aristocrats, many of whom left town without settling their debts.[98] French fashion workers maintained in a 1791 petition to the Assemblée that "embroiderers were going bankrupt, fashion shops closing their doors, dressmakers sacking three quarters of their workers."[99] Indeed, apart from the occasional, handily reversible "antipatriotic cockade" (with royalist white on one side and a *tricolore* rosette on the other) or royalist "rallying outfit" (dyed green to show sympathy for Artois and the émigrés, or black to mourn the death of the old order), few stylistic innovations appealed to those aristocrats who remained in Paris. As a result, the dwindling population of Parisian *marchandes* was largely displaced by "provincial *fagotières* ['bad dressers']" whose outmoded, second-rate bonnets and trimmings, shipped into the capital from unglamorous locations around the country, were "maliciously called [styles] *à la Constitution*" to accentuate their origins in the political crisis.[100]

The few Parisian fashion purveyors whose businesses survived were reduced to catering to a far less spendthrift and fashion-forward customer base.[101] Even the great Rose Bertin, whose enterprise stayed afloat largely because of her undiminished popularity with rich foreign buyers, found her domestic sales increasingly dependent on inexpensive, unaffected products like the *cocarde tricolore*.[102] "Since liberty came," sniped the royalist *Journal de la cour et de la ville,* observing the diminution in sartorial splendor, "the only Parisian commerce is in *cocardes*."[103] Aghast at these developments, Le Brun ceased lauding the Revolution's impact on modern fashion. As a man whose job was to track and to stir up excitement over the ever-changing, effervescent creations of France's leading designers, he could not but lament what he described as the drastic demise of Parisian style.[104]

Where he had once promoted modes that the staunchly royalist Marie Antoinette could not abide, Le Brun now began to favor ones that directly mirrored her own contrarian sensibilities. In the spring of 1791, for instance, just as she was assembling her queenly trousseau for Montmédy, the fashion editor featured such garments as a green satin gown worn with a black, pro-aristocratic or pro-Austrian cockade (March 15), and a "violet-striped gauze skirt fastened with a pistachio-green ribbon," paired with a black felt hat (May 15). Beneath the pistachio-green ribbons and pair of black cockades that adorned this hat, moreover, was a short, curly hairdo identified as a *coiffure à la Reine*.[105] Two weeks later (June 1), the journal featured a simple but pretty *pouf à la Reine,* made from white linen and trimmed with royal violets.

These allusions represented Le Brun's first explicit tributes to the beleaguered queen. In subsequent issues, the editor broached similarly risky political territory by showing a "little white gauze *pouf à la contre-Révolution*," whose dominant adornment was a wreath woven from black and yellow ribbons: the colors of Austria and, indeed, of "counterrevolution."[106] As a pendant to this ensemble, the journal displayed a matching male *costume à la contre-Révolution,* comprising a black jacket, yellow waistcoat, and green cashmere *culottes*. Although it is nearly impossible to establish to what extent they were actually worn in royalist circles at the time, historians like the Goncourt brothers have maintained that such ensembles did find favor among the capital's shrinking population of loyalist nobles.[107]

Whether or not Le Brun's readership actually followed his fashion directives, after Varennes his coverage of royalist-inflected modes increased markedly. Upon the monarchs' return to Paris, he commended to his readers two white-and-green-striped dresses, one wrapped with a muslin fichu edged in Austrian yellow, and in his two July issues he showcased several "*cocardes* striped with violet and pistachio green," which directly reprised Marie Antoinette's favorite color combination at the time.[108] For the rest of the year, he offered endless variations on the same theme—a violet taffeta hat worn with a green taffeta gown; a white gauze bonnet embroidered with green leaves and trimmed with knots of violet ribbon—as well as white satin Bourbon cockades, *chemises* and *coiffures à la Coblentz,* and an old-fashioned hairstyle labeled the *coiffure à la Louis XIV.*[109] Needless to say, these colors and designations evinced strong royalist sympathies, to the point where, in January 1792, Le Brun felt compelled to acknowledge that the clothes in *Le Journal de la mode et du goût* bore "symbolic colors." (In wintertime, this meant more black and gold—the colors of Austria—and less purple and green, which were better suited to spring.) On one level, of course, this admission simply reiterated the well-known politicization of colors in the revolutionary milieu: this was an era in which virtually all colors seemed vested with political meaning. But on another level, it was telling that the particular "symbolic colors" Le Brun featured were the very ones the Queen was using to flout the public's avid attachment to the *bleu, blanc et rouge.*

None of this, however, was of any help to Marie Antoinette. In the year that followed Varennes, she had to chart an ever more perilous course among warring factions: moderate and militant revolutionaries; an untrusting populace and untrustworthy émigrés; the foreign monarchs whom she and her husband continued to beg for support, and Louis XVI himself, whose powers she still hoped to restore to their full, prerevolutionary glory. Navigating these groups' and individuals' often irreconcilable interests consumed all of Marie Antoinette's time but yielded few results. And the experience exacted a psychological toll that no prideful, optimistically royalist-toned ensemble—such as the sumptuous white-and-lilac dress she wore to the third annual Fête de la Fédération, in July—could hope to reverse.[110] According to a story recounted both in Léonard's memoirs and in Émile Langlade's classic biography of Rose Bertin, some time after her return to the Tuileries the Queen confessed to her favorite *marchande de modes* that she had had a most unnerving dream. In this dream:

> You were bringing me ribbons of all colors, my dear Rose, and I chose several. But as soon as I had taken them in my hands, they turned black, and I threw them back into your boxes in horror. I took up others: green, white, and lilac, and no sooner did I hold them than they became covered with the color of death. I was weaker in that dream than I am ordinarily; I began to weep, and you wept also.[111]

Although it goes unmentioned in both Léonard's and Langlade's commentaries on this exchange, the colors of the ribbons Marie Antoinette remembered from her nightmare were, of course, the very ones she had taken to wearing since the flight to Varennes. Since then, her existence had grown more precarious by the day: she and her family were now even afraid to eat the food prepared in the Tuileries kitchen, given the strong possibility that it might be poisoned. In this context, there seemed little reason to keep believing that the symbolic strength of heraldic *ancien régime* colors, even when marshaled by Rose Bertin's king-making genius, could save her from disaster. Indeed, the Queen is said to have believed that the nightmare was an omen warning of the most horrific scenario she could imagine: "that the cannibals of the 5th and 6th of October are going to force their way into my apartments again," insatiably thirsting for her blood.[112]

DURING THE SUMMER OF 1792, THE QUEEN'S NIGHTMARE BECAME A REALity. In March, her brother Leopold II had died after agreeing to join a coalition of European monarchs to combat the French revolutionary upstarts. Then, upon ascending to the Austrian throne, his son and successor, the hawkish young Francis II, allowed the aristocratic French émigrés to assemble troops on Hapsburg territory. These provocations in turn justified the bellicose stance of revolutionary leaders who, hoping to inspire neighboring peoples to rise up and join the fight against royal despotism, were already eager for an armed confrontation; and on April 20, France declared war on Austria.[113]

No sooner were they mobilized, though, than the French troops met with a slew of crushing defeats that exacerbated both the people's anxiety about the Nation's future and their animosity toward the *Autrichienne* (who, unbeknownst to her subjects, had actually leaked some of the revolutionary army's plans of attack to Fersen and Mercy). One consequence of this was a renewal of the old proposals that Marie Antoinette be imprisoned in a convent or—as one of the Third Estate's original ringleaders, the Abbé Sieyès, proposed—sent back to Austria like the foreign enemy she was.[114]

As usual, the public's desire for vengeance targeted the Queen's clothing choices as well. According to Madame Élisabeth, revolutionary officials tried to prevent Marie Antoinette from publicly wearing mourning for the late Leopold II.[115] She defied this order to the extent that she commissioned Madame Éloffe to provide her with an extensive wardrobe of black clothes: in a grim coincidence, the Queen placed one such order on March 21, the same day that the guillotine was adopted as France's new means of capital punishment.[116] It is unknown whether, or to what degree, she dared to sport her somber weeds in public. But when one of her guards was seen in the gardens of the Tuileries wearing the black crepe armband of royal mourning, he was—a horrified Madame Élisabeth recorded—violently "insulted and mistreated" by a revolutionary mob.[117]

On June 19, Louis XVI aggravated public opinion still further by vetoing a proposal for the establishment of a camp of twenty thousand National Guardsmen just outside Paris.[118] (The Constitution, as it was then written, invested the King with the power to veto legislative decrees coming out of the Assemblée.) Because the prevailing view was that such reinforcements would protect against an Austrian onslaught—not to mention prevent the royals from staging a counterrevolutionary coup—the veto provoked a savage backlash. In the halls of the Assemblée, Louis XVI's decision gave the more radical deputies added ammunition for their attacks on both the Constitution and the crown. In the streets of Paris, it had a still more violent effect. On June 20, several thousand people stormed the Tuileries, shouting "Down with Monsieur and Madame Veto!" while Marie Antoinette, her children, and the Princesse de Lamballe hid from the mob in the palace's Council Room, agonizing over what might befall Louis XVI and Madame Élisabeth—who were trapped in a different part of the palace—as well as themselves.

By the time they spilled into the Council Room, where Marie Antoinette and her companions stood barricaded behind a heavy table and guarded by a handful of devoted courtiers, the marauders had already encountered Louis XVI and his sister. Ignoring Madame Élisabeth, the mob had virulently harangued the King about his abuse of the royal veto, and then foisted on his head a "liberty bonnet": the drooping wool cap, usually colored red and historically associated with emancipated slaves and prisoners, which during this period became a widespread sign of revolutionary militancy.[119] But for the Queen, who did not yet know whether her husband was alive or dead, the insurgents held even greater horrors in store as they charged into the Council Room and surrounded her and her family. Several of the invaders brandished pikes speared with bloody animals' organs, and one of them taunted her with a female doll dangling from a miniature gallows: a gruesome variation on the celebrated *poupée de mode* that had once disseminated her style preferences, and her likeness, throughout Europe.[120] In the face of these threats, the Queen allegedly retained enough presence of mind to refuse the liberty bonnet that her aggressors likewise attempted to force onto her head, along with a clutch of tricolor ribbons they claimed to have received from her old adversary Orléans.[121]

In fact, it was significant that instead of treating her and her husband with brute violence, the crowd tried to assert its dominance and express its outrage by subjecting them to the latest element of the revolutionary dress code. (Even before reaching the monarchs, the sartorially attuned rioters had attempted to expel all so-called *noirs*—courtiers whose royalist proclivities were visible "in [their] black coats, mostly decorated with the Cross of Saint Louis"—from the palace by force.[122]) It is also telling that Marie Antoinette, in contrast to her husband, thwarted the insurgents by rejecting their political accessory of choice.[123] If, as one orator at the Club des Jacobins declared that summer, the moment had come when "true republicans [were to be] recognizable by their coiffures" (that is to say, their liberty bonnets), the moment had also come for the Queen explicitly and publicly to abandon any further semblance of sympathy for her foes.[124] Though Marie Antoinette and her people paradoxically shared a view of symbolic clothes and coiffures as matters of life and death, the haughty consort emphatically challenged the Revolution's politics by refusing the emblems that proclaimed its glory.

The Queen's courageous rejection of the liberty bonnet, however, represented only a momentary triumph over her aggressors. Over the course of the summer, as the war dragged on and the nation's economic problems grew even more severe, the Revolution entered a new phase of violent radicalism. In lieu of the drably but neatly attired bourgeois deputies who had established the Assemblée three years earlier, working-class and lower-class sans-culottes—identifiable by their shabby workman's pants, short jackets, filthy shirts, wooden clogs, and crude red bonnets—became the new harbingers of revolutionary change. Their anthem was "*Ça ira!*" ("It Will Go On"), which, set to the music of a ditty Marie Antoinette had often played on her clavichord at Trianon, incited the people to hang aristocrats from the lampposts.[125] Their heroes, moreover, were not moderates like Barnave and La Fayette, but more radical politicians like Danton of the Club des Cordeliers, and Robespierre, president of the increasingly militant Club des Jacobins.[126]

This roilingly discontented demographic was also targeted by rabble-rousing journalists like Jacques-René Hébert and Jean-Paul Marat. For over a year, the latter man had been inveighing violently against the sovereigns in his newspaper, *L'Ami du peuple*. Hébert's paper, *Le Père Duchesne*, which was written in a raunchy argot meant to duplicate the speech of the common man, now took a similar tack. This publication had long since targeted Marie Antoinette as an execrable foe, challenging her in December 1790 to "get rid of those f—ing chiffons, gauzes, and other foreign merchandise," and so highlighting her status as a dangerous foreign agent who wore her allegiances on her sleeve. Shortly after Louis XVI's ill-fated vetoes, Hébert turned his attention to the King, but only to disparage him as "Madame Veto's valet"—a reprise of the Varennes caricature in which the monarch humiliatingly waited on the Queen at her *toilette*. The couple were nonetheless well matched in their hatefulness, Hébert maintained, and declared on behalf of the French people that "we will not rest until the last royal head is cut off!"[127]

Fearing for Marie Antoinette's safety, members of her entourage begged her to begin wearing a special undergarment, which Madame de Tourzel recalled as being "made from twelve folds of [glued] taffeta [and] 'impenetrable by bullet or dagger.'"[128] Though she tried the garment on for size, and even instructed Madame de Tourzel to try stabbing through it with a knife, the Queen ultimately rejected it, explaining that "if the upstarts assassinate me, it will be a blessing, as they will be delivering me from the most painful existence imaginable."[129] Indeed, with the rise of the sans-culottes and their ferocious political rhetoric, exemplified by the likes of Marat and Hébert, Marie Antoinette's "deliverance" by violent means appeared none too improbable, whether or not she was protected by a few extra layers of taffeta. In early August, the Queen reflected in private that, to confront the dangers head-on,

> I could act, and mount a horse if need be; but if I acted, it would put weapons into the hands of the King's enemies; a general outcry would be raised in France against the Austrian woman, against female domination. . . . A queen who is not regent must, in such circumstances, remain inactive and prepare to die.[130]

Although this declaration of passivity squared ill with the indomitable image she had cultivated for so long, beginning with the heroic equestrian gear she had favored as Dauphine, it revealed her understanding that her posturing had made her the crown's worst liability. It also betrayed her awareness of the gravity of the situation she and her husband now faced. By the time she uttered these words, Paris had become a powder keg, with a fuse that was growing shorter each day and contents poised for a shattering explosion.[131]

The blast occurred on August 10, when Marie Antoinette's fears of a palace invasion came true once again. However, this time it was not twenty thousand people, but, as the municipal officer Roederer put it, "all of Paris," abetted by reinforcements from throughout the land, that marched on the château. The immediate provocation was a manifesto in which France's allied foreign enemies threatened the Parisians with harsh retribution should any harm come to the royal family. Intended to cow the French public, the document, which Fersen had assured the Queen would only bolster the position of her and her family, had precisely the opposite effect, driving antimonarchist sentiment in the capital to a fever pitch. Before dawn on August 10, the tocsin began to sound from bell towers throughout the capital, calling the people to arms and warning of an imminent, city-wide revolt. A sleepless Marie Antoinette and Madame Élisabeth stood at a palace window to watch the sun rise, ominously bloodred, over the rooftops of Paris. Keeping vigil with them and the King in the Council Room, a gaggle of mournful, black-clad courtiers chanted the name of each church as its distinctive chime joined in the general alarm.

Though confronted with what Evelyne Lever has described as "the monarchy's death knell tolling in the depth of the night," the Queen apparently still hoped at this point that she and her family might hold their ground at the Tuileries, defended by a few hundred loyal *noirs* and by those Swiss Guards and National Guardsmen who were charged with protecting the château.[132] Unfortunately for the royals, though, many of the latter soldiers harbored strong revolutionary leanings and had for the past day been working assiduously to prevent would-be monarchist champions among the *noirs* from entering the palace, on the grounds "that it was not the moment to pay court to the King and that no one entered except in the coat of the National Guard and to give reinforcement to that Guard."[133] Here again, clothing, and more specifically the uniform for which Marie Antoinette herself was thought to harbor an aversion, defined the terms of the battle between the people and their sovereigns—a battle that, in this instance, the royals had scant hope of winning.

The situation's gravity became even more apparent when, at his wife's suggestion, Louis XVI stepped outside to review his troops. Although he took this step to demonstrate his own resolve to stay the course and to bolster royalist sentiment among his soldiers, the King met with jeering hollers from members of the hostile crowd that had already begun to assemble in the palace gardens. He was even heckled by some of his own guards, whom the Queen was forced to dismiss as victims of "bad will and cowardice."[134] This humiliating encounter indicated to the King and his family that, in the unavoidable event of a siege, they would have to rely chiefly on their small cadre of loyal Swiss Guards. It was only when they grasped this horrifying fact that they acceded to Roederer's repeated pleas that they seek refuge in the Assemblée, which was quartered nearby in the palace's former riding

14. Marie Antoinette's shoe, lost on August 10, 1792 (Bibliothèque Nationale de France, Paris)

ring or Manège. Leaving with nothing but the clothes on their backs, they fled the château under a torrent of abuse from the gathering hordes: "Down with the tyrants! Death! Death!"[135] They made their escape so quickly, in fact, that the Queen lost a shoe—a delicate high-heeled slipper with ruched ribbon trim—in flight.[136] Behind them, Marie Antoinette and her family, accompanied by the Princesse de Lamballe, Madame de Tourzel, and Madame de Tourzel's daughter Pauline, left a relatively meager crew of monarchist defenders. In the confusion surrounding his departure, Louis XVI forgot to order these men to refrain from firing on the mob when it made its move.

And move the indomitable crowds did, not long after the royals appeared among the Assemblée's flabbergasted deputies—who happened already to be in session. While the legislators began debating what course to take next, and whether the monarchy as an institution could even survive such a massive vote of no confidence, the assailants who swarmed past and around the Manège seemed to give them their answer. Armed with every conceivable kind of weapon, including cannon which they pulled straight up to the palace doors, the rioters prepared to attack the Tuileries. Though hopelessly outnumbered, the Swiss Guards and other loyalist combatants refused to capitulate, and the two sides traded heavy fire. Ensconced in a cramped journalists' loge inside the Manège, the royal family could hear the sounds of the deadly clash—including the cries of the massacred Swiss, whose corpses began piling up both outside and within the château. The King, realizing that his troops planned to defend his palace to the death, sent word that they should cease fire. When the Swiss Guards received his message and laid down their arms, the mob massacred them by the dozens, heatedly cursing "Monsieur and Madame Veto" for having allowed them to fight in the first place. Trampling over the corpses, and more convinced than ever that the monarchs sought their ruin, the people took control of the Tuileries.

The royal family spent the next three days confined in their tiny loge, whose ceiling was so low that the adults in the group were unable to stand upright, while the members of the Assemblée continued to debate ways of handling the crisis, eventually voting to suspend the King's powers until further notice.[137] Outside, insurgents seeking revenge for their fellows' "murder" by the Swiss Guards vociferously demanded that the sovereigns be deposed, tried, and executed. The immense congregation of rioters around the Assemblée prevented the royals from going any farther than the Feuillants Convent, which was adjacent to the Manège. It was to this convent that Marie Antoinette and her companions retired on their first two nights away from the Tuileries, just long enough to nap briefly and change their clothing. (Having brought nothing with them in their flight, they all had to wear borrowed clothes—even borrowed body linens—provided by various sympathetic donors.[138]) But at the Feuillants, too, the raging horde dogged its princes, "even trying to break down the grating at the end of the corridor which led to the cells" in which they were quartered.[139] Hearing the crowds shout invective against his wife, Louis XVI asked balefully: "What did she ever do to them?"[140] At that moment, with her mismatched clothes, disheveled coiffure, and missing shoe, she can scarcely have resembled the glittering fashion icon her subjects had come to know and loathe.

Indeed, it cannot have been the image of this poorly dressed, dirt-streaked, fallen sovereign that in the first few days after August 10 led scores of female commoners to Marie Antoinette's old rooms at the Tuileries, to pillage her abandoned *garde-meubles*. During the uprising itself, those who abhorred the Queen had, like their predecessors in the 1789 march on Versailles, symbolically shattered her beauty and punished her narcissism by breaking every last mirror in her apartments.[141] After the dust settled, though, the members of the populace seemed eager not so much to destroy the deposed consort's glamorous trappings as to lay claim to them: a young Dutchman living in Paris at the time recalled that "everyone sought to decorate his or her person with some fragment of the devastation" in the royal wardrobe.[142] Another contemporary, who paid a visit to the Tuileries on

August 12, was struck by what he saw when he reached Marie Antoinette's apartments: a mass of shabby, cackling women tumbling over piles of cadavers to root through her lavish assortment of dresses and hats. "How many curiosity-seekers had assembled there!" this witness reported. "How many bonnets, elegant hats, rose-colored skirts, and white petticoats flew out of the bedroom doors!"[143]

As privileged signs of the Queen's despicable personality and politics, these confections provoked the women to acts of jubilant thievery that left the room's other contents untouched. (These contents included a pianoforte, a bust of the Dauphin, a clutch of priceless tapestries, and two small decorative paintings by Vigée-Lebrun: one depicting a dog, the other a vase of flowers.[144]) By targeting this specific aspect of Marie Antoinette's privileged past, one might say that the women aimed, as Pierre Saint-Amand has noted of the revolutionaries in general, brutally to cleave the consort "from the world of ostentation, ornamentation, and finery" she had so infuriatingly personified.[145] Even if the rose-colored skirts and comely bonnets they pilfered had little place in their modest, workaday wardrobes, the looters effectively established their dominion over the Queen by stripping her of the very trappings she had deployed to assert her own potency and stature. Watching them do so, one municipal official hypothesized that in so avidly appropriating the tokens of their queen's erstwhile prestige, the women were modeling themselves on "the rooster, who after a struggle climbs up on the booty he has won from his foe to crow about his victory and establish his dominion."[146]

The people's victory was complete the following summer, when what remained of Marie Antoinette's wardrobe was sold in a state auction to a motley crew of specialists: secondhand clothing and fabric dealers with an eye for quality and a nose for a bargain.[147] Yet this final blow to the Queen's priceless clothing collection merely extended the work that the female pillagers had begun in August 1792.[148] Though some of the items wound up in royalist hands, where they were preserved as precious relics of a vanished reign, most of the wardrobe's voguish contents were reallocated to a host of improbable wearers and scattered to the four winds.[149] A case in point: the last *pouf* that Marie Antoinette ever commissioned—that daring, violet-and-green creation she ordered from Bertin on August 7—was irretrievably lost in the fray.[150]

So, too, was the unreformed monarchist vision that Marie Antoinette had expressed with this *pouf*. Throughout the capital, the unkempt garb of the sans-culottes became more ubiquitous and significant in its stark opposition to the Queen's annihilated glamour.[151] According to a visiting Englishwoman, Helen Maria Williams, "every man who had the boldness to appear [in

Paris] in a clean shirt" was branded an aristocratic fop, while another commentator was shocked to note that the men who flocked to the republican clubs after August 10 wore "such filthy, neglected costumes that they could have been mistaken for beggars," whatever their actual social and economic standing.[152]

Even the moneyed and princely Orléans, who renamed himself Philippe-Égalité in homage to the radicalism of the day, made a point of dressing down. As Marie Grosholz, who would later achieve renown as the waxworks doyenne Madame Tussaud, noted, Orléans strategically abandoned the costly frippery he and his cousin Artois had once adored in favor of "a short jacket, pants [*pantalon*], and a round hat, with a kerchief worn sailor-style loose around the neck . . . [his] hair cut short without powder . . . and shoes tied without strings."[153] As a scion of the House of Bourbon, the self-styled Philippe-Égalité faced mounting skepticism from dyed-in-the-wool republicans, but his change in costume mirrored the widespread disappearance of class distinctions from Parisian apparel.[154] And although to some extent it had begun years earlier, with the frolicsome casualness of the Petit Trianon, and with the confusion between duchesses and actresses brokered by the Queen's star designers in Paris, this democratization of French clothing now truly marked the end of an era—an era when, abandoning her more informal dress habits, Marie Antoinette had flouted her subjects' festering hatred and wrapped herself in the colors of royal power.

TEN

BLACK

In addition to chasing the sovereigns from their domicile, August 10 saw the rise of a popular municipal government, the Commune de Paris, whose rabidly antiroyalist leadership clamored to take charge of the Bourbons' fate. Three days after the uprising, exhausted and overwhelmed by the ongoing mayhem in the capital, the Assemblée yielded to the Commune's demands that the royals be placed "under the safeguard of the Nation." To the members of the Commune, this meant imprisoning the royal family in the Temple, a thick-walled, turreted palace and fortress that in the Middle Ages had been the headquarters of the Knights Templar. In more recent years, the Comte d'Artois had used the Temple as his city residence, and Marie Antoinette had grown familiar with the place during her erstwhile jaunts to Paris. But she had never liked the Temple's gloomy architecture, which, as Stefan Zweig has put it, "reminded onlookers of the horrors of the Middle Ages [and] the Inquisition; of witches' sabbaths and torture chambers."[1] According to Madame de Tourzel, who on August 19 was, along with her daughter and the Princesse de Lamballe, separated from the royal family and incarcerated in the Prison de La Force:

> The Queen shuddered when she heard the Temple proposed, and said to me under her breath: "They will put us in the Tower—you'll see—and turn it into a veritable prison for us. I have always had an absolute horror of that tower, which I asked Monsieur le Comte a thousand times to tear down."[2]

Yet again, Marie Antoinette's dark forebodings came to pass. At dusk on August 13, she and her family were transported through Paris to the Temple past crowds of people who hurled insults at them, and who, predictably by now, refused to doff their hats.[3] Upon reaching their destination, the royals were initially placed in the most hospitable part of the compound, the graceful seventeenth-century palace that Artois had called home, only to be redirected at eleven o'clock to the smaller of the two turreted structures that together constituted the Tower. It was there, in the so-called Little Tower, that they were to reside until the Great Tower was made ready for occupancy (renovations ended that fall). That they were to be captives was obvious from the start. At dinner that evening, Evelyne Lever recounts, "the presence of the slovenly-looking municipal guards, smoking their pipes ostentatiously [while the princes ate], reminded them that the grand old days were over."[4]

The same reminder was implicit in the bedding they were allotted: bug-infested sheets, which, according to François Hüe, one of the few royal servants who had been permitted to wait on the sovereigns in their confinement, were "flung at us as if it were a favor."[5] This sentiment was implicit as well in the "indecent engravings" with which the guards had decorated the prisoners' rooms. (These Louis XVI swiftly tried to efface before they attracted the notice of his thirteen-year-old daughter, Madame Royale.) From these insulting decorative touches to the conspicuous lack of insulating fabrics on the Tower's walls and windows, everything about the setting conspired to impress upon the Bourbons just how far they had fallen. As a municipal officer gloatingly remarked to Hüe, the Temple was a far cry from the gilt-paneled luxury of the Tuileries and Versailles. But, the officer went on to point out, as "assassins of the people," the newcomers deserved no better.[6] Little did they know that outside the Temple, this very accusation was being leveled at them with mounting frequency, as republican politicians and self-proclaimed patriots continued to reframe the siege of August 10 as the night when the monarchy tried to slaughter its own people.

In the weeks that followed, the prisoners gradually adjusted to life in captivity, which—their new identity as "assassins of the people" notwithstanding—the Commune tried to make reasonably comfortable. Furnishings that had survived the sacking of the Tuileries were transported to the Tower to redecorate the King's and Queen's four-room suites; the bounty included green damask-upholstered chairs from Marie Antoinette's old apartments, and blue taffeta curtains for the windows.[7] Hundreds of volumes from Louis XVI's personal library were also provided, as were a clavichord and needleworking supplies for the ladies, and an assortment of toys for the children.[8] Even Thisbée, the little dog Marie Antoinette had received as a gift from the

Princesse de Lamballe, was allowed to join her owner.[9] And though the baked goods and fruits served at mealtimes were first cut open by a guard— in case they contained messages from royalist conspirators plotting the Bourbons' escape—the Commune allotted bountiful foodstuffs to its captives.[10] Marie Antoinette, too disconsolate by now to do much more than pick listlessly at her food, lost her womanly voluptuousness and grew downright skeletal.[11] (Even here, her clothing told a story, as a seamstress named Roussel billed the Commune for "taking apart a corset [belonging to the Queen], and taking it in on all sides."[12]) Louis XVI, however, retained his Rabelaisian appetite, downing more than two hundred bottles of champagne during their first month in the Temple alone.[13]

Of necessity, the royals were also allowed to shed the odd bits of clothing their friends had loaned them for their sojourn in the Feuillants Convent, and to order new wardrobes of their own. (Apparently they had been told that none of their personal effects had survived the pillaging of the Tuileries, though, as the government's auctioning off of these effects the following year indicated, this was far from true.[14]) Paid for with funds that the revolutionary state now deemed the people's rather than the monarchs', the prisoners' choices were far from extravagant, costing a mere fraction of their habitual clothing purchases. Nevertheless, their orders betrayed some elements of personal taste and of their lasting attachment to a bygone era.[15] Louis XVI, for instance, commissioned two suits of pale chestnut-colored silk, several Bourbon-white piqué waistcoats, a courtly black hat, and ten pairs of black silk breeches. Even in prison, he had no intention of dressing like a sans-culotte. Perhaps in a wistful concession to the fashion crazes he had once chided his wife for indulging, he also procured "a riding-coat colored *cheveux de la Reine*"—the shimmering, pale-gold shade that the Lyon silk manufacturers had dyed to match a lock of the royal consort's hair, years before it was "whitened by misfortune."[16]

As for Marie Antoinette herself, any nostalgia she might have harbored for her modish past manifested itself less in her costume selections, which were modest enough, than in her choice of purveyors. Though she ordered a handful of necessary garments from Madame Éloffe and other, lesser-known suppliers, she elected, as always, to spend her largest sums with Rose Bertin. Now that the Queen was a prisoner, "largest sums" was of course a relative matter. The amount she was given to cover her expenses with Bertin was a meager 602 livres—thirteen livres less than what she had paid the *marchande* just to put new trimming on an old "violet-on-violet-striped" gown the summer before—but it was still about four times what she spent with Madame Éloffe during this period.[17] From Bertin, Marie Antoinette received two white bonnets, nine gauze and organdy fichus of varying sizes, "one very fine, embroidered muslin skirt," one white linen capelet, one black taffeta capelet, and three lengths of white ribbon.[18] She also acquired several shifts, made from linen and muslin; a brown, floral-printed dress of *toile de Joüy;* a puce taffeta gown (this color, one of her early innovations, had recently come back into vogue); a pair of black ribbons to wear around her throat; a jaunty black "jockey" hat; and, continuing the equestrian motif, a "taffeta *chemise*-dress with a redingote collar in the color of 'Paris mud.' "[19]

These paltry selections, of course, could by no means approximate Marie Antoinette's extravagant wardrobe of yore—the dozens of formal gowns and countless lighter shifts commissioned for each season—and her style of dress became drastically simplified as a result. Each morning, she donned a plain white *chemise,* performing her *toilette,* once a task that high-born duchesses had vied with high-flying Rose Bertin to undertake, with the unpracticed assistance of Madame Élisabeth and Madame Royale alone.[20] For afternoon and evening wear, the princesses helped her change again, into one of her three principal dresses, the "Parisian mud," the brown toile, and the puce taffeta, all of whose colors had the utilitarian advantage of not showing dirt easily, and so reflected, perhaps, a concession to her less-than-immaculate living conditions in the Tower.[21]

Her accessories, too, were anything but glamorous. Her jewelry collection was now confined to her wedding ring, one other small, jeweled ring, a necklace with lockets containing pieces of her children's hair, and the little gold watch that she still treasured as a memento of her late mother. Similarly, she had to give up the imposing headdresses that had once perched atop her powdered mane, like the violet-and-green *pouf* she had ordered from Bertin just three days before the Tuileries fell. Instead, remarked Claude Antoine Moelle, one of the members of the Commune assigned to monitor goings-on at the Temple, "simple linen bonnets became [Marie Antoinette's] habitual headgear"; these she sent out to Rose Bertin for the occasional retrimming and repair.[22] And while Bertin was reduced to such menial functions on the Queen's behalf, Léonard, her onetime male counterpart in the "ministry of fashion," was displaced altogether. (He had returned to France several months after the Varennes debacle, but retained a prudently low profile.[23]) Whereas the great coiffeur had once earned thousands of livres a year to comb her locks into a series of alluring and varied new looks, his job now fell to Cléry, a valet who had previously been in the Dauphin's service.[24] Because Cléry had little experience with fashionable female hairstyles, his ministrations were limited to brushing out the Queen's hair as simply as possible, then applying a tiny dash of powder.[25]

Like her bold royalist color schemes and regal ensembles, Marie Antoinette's fabled frocks, jewels, coiffures, and "ministers of fashion" thus fell by the wayside as she adapted to a humbler, more constrained mode of existence.[26] Given their usual political associations, however, her white and black ribbons may have been subtle signs of Bourbon, aristocratic, and Hapsburg ardor. Similarly, the redingote-collared gown and jockey hat she continued to wear may have evoked the kingly authority and unrestricted freedom she had once conveyed by riding and dressing like a man. As for her simple white shifts, linen bonnets, minimal jewelry, and unassuming hairstyles, perhaps these served as bittersweet reminders of the Petit Trianon, where she had temporarily laid her crown aside, never dreaming she would one day lose it for good.

In fact, in a strange way, life in the Temple gave Marie Antoinette and her family an opportunity to pursue much the same kind of simplified, bourgeois routine they had willingly cultivated at her Petit Trianon. With all other stresses and distractions out of the way, from beautiful favorites like Fersen and Madame de Polignac to tension-inducing conflicts over the monarchy's future, Marie Antoinette's affection and respect for her kindly, devoted husband seems to have deepened considerably during this time.[27] Together, they spent many more uninterrupted hours with their children than their *ancien régime* schedule had ever allowed, and devoted themselves actively to the youngsters' upbringing. While the Queen read and sewed with Madame Royale, the King spent hours each day tutoring the Dauphin and watching him play with his little collection of toys. Before the Revolution, intimate family activities such as these had been restricted to stays at Trianon. Also reminiscent of this lost country idyll were the other pastimes that filled their days in the Tower. These included card games, embroidery, and music—though Marie Antoinette's offerings on the clavichord were consistently mournful.[28] The group was also allowed to take daily strolls in the Temple's dreary garden, under an allée of chestnut trees that alone had survived the construction of new walls: reinforcements against any possible security breach.[29]

The addition of these walls left little room for doubt about the true nature of the royals' confinement, whatever the modest pleasures it afforded them *en famille*. Adding insult to injury, the stringently republican Hébert was appointed the princes' chief jailer, and under his stewardship they were subjected to frequent indignities. The valet Cléry recalled that when his masters went on their daily walks in the garden, "the guards stationed at the base of the Tower took pains to put their hats on," in open—and, again, sartorially inflected—shows of disrespect. Cléry also bristled to see the sentinels mock the captives with "songs that were always revolutionary, and often obscene, in nature."[30] To torment the royals still further, the soldiers scribbled insults, obscenities, and frightful images of death and execution on the

Tower's interior walls. On one occasion, the King retired to his bedroom to find that someone had scrawled on the door: "The guillotine is permanent, and awaits the tyrant Louis XVI."[31]

Even such banal pastimes as reading books and doing needlework provoked the Temple staffers' aggression. According to Cléry, one night Marie Antoinette happened to be reading aloud to her children from a book of French history, narrating the episode "when the Connétable de Bourbon took up arms against France": not an obscure story, but one that prompted a guard to denounce the Queen to the Commune on the grounds that "by this example, [she] wanted to inspire her son to wreak vengeance upon the Nation."[32]

Not surprisingly, given its long history as a source of popular complaint, Marie Antoinette's clothing likewise became an object of mistrust, as for instance when a journalist charged that she and a clutch of coconspirators outside the Temple had "already exchanged letters smuggled in the folds of a bodice."[33] Taking this charge seriously, the Temple guards regularly checked the Queen's body linens for counterrevolutionary writings in invisible ink.[34] They also scrutinized, and sometimes confiscated, the pieces of needlework that she and her sister-in-law busied themselves with making, on the grounds that these might well contain ciphered royalist communiqués.[35] Whereas the textiles associated with the Queen had once symbolically revealed her anti-French or counterrevolutionary political stance, they now came under suspicion as literal vehicles of the same deplorable agenda.

Despite the sentinels' vigilance, invisible ink, cipher, and secret code did find their way into the family's prison, as Marie Antoinette tried to keep tabs on current events.[36] Fervently hoping that her nephew Francis II was hastening to her rescue, she was particularly keen to know how the European allies were faring against the Revolution's armed forces. But in order to keep the royal family in the dark about the allies' maneuvers, officials had banned newspapers from the Temple; and, apart from one early letter the prisoners were allowed to read from the Aunts (who had fled to Rome in February 1791), correspondence was strictly forbidden.[37] As a result, the Queen had to seek her updates through more furtive means, such as the scraps of paper scribbled with code that a few trusty underlings surreptitiously carried into the Tower. (Whether they did so via bodices and linens remains unknown.) She and her sister-in-law Madame Élisabeth also devised a system of subtle hand gestures through which they encouraged the Temple's more sympathetic staffers to provide them with the latest news.[38] Between these precious tidbits and shouts from town criers strolling outside their prison windows, the Queen and her family were able to keep at least somewhat abreast of developments occurring outside the fortress walls.

The world outside had in fact changed dramatically, and not at all in the Bourbons' favor. Though war still raged between the revolutionaries and the allies, with some crucial early victories going to the latter, Marie Antoinette's nephew the Austrian Emperor did not seem overly concerned about the fate of an aunt he had never met.[39] The August 10 rebellion had, moreover, thoroughly discredited moderate and constitutional monarchist politicians, and had shown the Assemblée to be woefully ineffectual in managing the Parisians' discontent.[40] In the wake of the uprising, the Assemblée had therefore disbanded to allow for the election of a new Convention Nationale, which was charged with rewriting the articles of the Constitution that had organized the monarchy, and in which a formidable minority of radicals like Robespierre and Danton militated vehemently for a republic.[41] The die was cast, and the monarchy's days were numbered. As the pro-revolutionary *Chronique de Paris* noted with a touch of black humor: "The only living creature in France who still cried 'Long live the King!' [that autumn] was a parakeet."[42]

Aristocrats repelled by this new political direction and outraged by the monarchs' imprisonment now expressed their resistance as Marie Antoinette herself had done before her incarceration, by incorporating coded royalist colors and emblems into their dress. Jean Augeard, the former Secretary of the Queen's Command, loyally donned a jeweled necklace decorated with fleurs-de-lys, crosses, and forget-me-nots, and engraved with the royalist parakeet's motto, "Long live the King!"[43] In the same spirit, Madame Campan noted, female royalists began wearing "enormous bouquets of lilies in their bosoms, and upon their heads, and sometimes even bunches of white ribbon."[44]

Perhaps not incidentally, such adornments were on prominent display in a portrait that Marie Antoinette had commissioned from François Dumont sometime before she went to jail: a portrait of which two noblewomen formerly in her service may have received miniature copies, and which by 1793 was circulating among royalists in lithographic form.[45] In this image, Marie Antoinette wore a drooping cap resembling the liberty bonnet and a neoclassically draped Greco-Roman tunic connoting "republican" virtue. At first blush, this costume appeared startlingly incongruous on the Queen, because it was the same garb favored by the militant republican artist and politician Jacques-Louis David in his paintings of idealized female citizens. (Furthermore, by 1793, this ensemble was the standard uniform for the Nation's new allegorical incarnation, the Marianne: yet another example of the uncanny overlap between Marie Antoinette's fashion choices and those of her republican enemies.) In Dumont's depiction, though, the Queen dramatically undercut her outfit's ostensibly pro-revolutionary meaning by holding to her breast an oversized clutch of lilies. With this arresting juxtaposition, the portrait implied that despite the Revolution's manifold triumphs, figured so clearly in the Queen's improbable toga and bonnet, it was the Bourbon *lys* that stayed closest to her heart.

Nor were white flowers and ribbons the only accessories to be invested with such bold, oppositional significance. First promoted in Le Brun's *poufs* and *costumes à la contre-Révolution* in the summer of 1791, yellow and black fabrics and ribbons also figured prominently in disenfranchised aristocrats' ensembles after the monarchy fell. For despite the anti-Austrian sentiment that had flourished at court during the *ancien régime,* those nobles who had remained in France now, even more avidly than in 1791, hailed the Hapsburgs as their saviors from the rabble's untrammeled menace. Le Brun's *Journal de la mode et du goût* alluded to this vogue in the fall of 1792, when presenting a new variation on the black and yellow *pouf à la contre-Révolution.* Either conflating Austria with Germany or referring to the Prussians' involvement in the allied war effort, Le Brun designated the colors' counterrevolutionary symbolism by specifying: "It is not merely to be fashionable that women of distinction have taken to combining yellow and black; for this they have a secret motive which is understood perfectly well in Germany."[46]

15. François Dumont, *Marie Antoinette, Archduchess of Austria, Queen of France* (c. 1792) (Réunion des Musées Nationaux/Art Resource, New York)

Yet if the "secret motive" of the ladies who dressed in this way was to emancipate the imprisoned sovereigns and restore the monarchy's (and their own) former "distinction," they had little hope of realizing these goals in a milieu increasingly dominated by ferocious antiroyalism. That ferocity was not without a strong sartorial component; as one man who claimed to have taken part in both the storming of the Bastille and the August 10 attack on the Tuileries declared to the Assemblée six days after the latter uprising: "Let us no longer cap liberty with a crown! She is much fairer in her woollen bonnet!"[47] This view quickly gained currency in Paris, where revolutionary sentiment remained the strongest. As Carrolly Erickson has noted, in the wake of the royals' expulsion from the Tuileries: "priests, gentlemen, anyone who did not dress like a sans-culotte was liable to be set upon, beaten and forced to put on a red cap. If the victim had the impudence to resist, he was stripped naked and cudgeled with a thick hawthorn branch."[48] According to Madame Campan, Parisians regularly shouted down Bourbon accessories as "dangerous insignia"—not only in the streets, but in the theaters—and "sentinels in every corner of the city stopped all who wore [them]."[49]

The militancy with which revolutionary hard-liners monitored and attacked royalist accoutrements even extended to the royal prisoners themselves—which made sense, given Marie Antoinette's long history of politically subversive attire. Indeed, Cléry recorded that after the republic was declared, municipal officers commanded the consort to unstitch by hand the monogrammed crowns that bedecked some fine new linens she had recently managed to acquire.[50] This order was as fitting as it was pointed, for once upon a time, beautiful fabrics had functioned to signify Marie Antoinette's prominence: from the opulent, custom-dyed silks she and Bertin had brought into vogue, to the airy muslins and linens worn "by Order of the Queen" at the Petit Trianon. Now, through the calculated cruelty of her jailers, sumptuous textiles were reinvented as reminders of her shattering political fall. As Chantal Thomas has remarked of this episode, in being forced "to unpick the last vestiges of her splendor herself, . . . the Queen literally 'came undone.' "[51]

YET AS FAR AS MANY OF MARIE ANTOINETTE'S SUBJECTS WERE CONCERNED, even the enforced loss of her erstwhile elegance did not sufficiently punish her sins. With almost two decades' worth of grievances stored up against her, the people had still more afflictions and acts of vengeance in store for their wicked queen—especially as the Austro-Prussian allies' troops drew closer to the capital. Beginning on September 2, enraged mobs broke into prisons throughout Paris to kill the aristocrats and royalist priests who had been incarcerated after August 10, incited by rumors that these captives themselves planned to slaughter "all good republicans" as soon as the Germans arrived in town.[52] Unsurprisingly, some of the rioters made straight for the Temple and the *Autrichienne,* but, upon arriving there, did not force their way inside; according to Madame Royale, the people's hands were stayed by the sight of a large tricolor sash that a resourceful official named Daujon had thought to drape across the Temple gates, correctly anticipating that no self-respecting patriot would dare to desecrate the *bleu, blanc et rouge.*[53] "At the sight of the honored symbol," one municipal officer asserted, "the murderous frenzy in the hearts of these men, drunk with blood and wine, seemed to yield to a feeling of respect for the national badge."[54]

In this curious turn of events, Marie Antoinette thus owed her safety to the very emblem she had come to despise, the symbol of the same forces that had laid her low. However, the unfurling of the *tricolore* outside her jail did not—could not—protect her completely from the people's wrath. Among the other prisons the marauders flocked to was the Prison de La Force, where the Princesse de Lamballe and the Tourzel women had been confined since late August. Lamballe was of particular interest to the mob, since she was the only "favorite" of the Queen's who was still in Paris (the Duchesse de Polignac had remained in exile since July 1789). Arriving at La Force early in the morning on September 3, the mob made a beeline for Lamballe's cell, where, falling upon her like a pack of wild animals, they bludgeoned and stabbed her to death, and then sliced off her head with a butcher's knife.

That the slaying was intended, or at least subsequently reframed, as an attack on the Queen herself is borne out by the story of what happened next. Though some subsequent commentators have qualified this tale as an (admittedly "persistent and revelatory") exaggeration, several self-proclaimed eyewitnesses insisted that the Princesse was, indeed, singled out for a grisly honor that none of the uprising's other victims received.[55] Like the heads of the two royal guards slain in the 1789 march on Versailles, Lamballe's head was, one of these observers related, taken from La Force to a wig maker's shop to "be curled, made up with vermilion, [and] a tricolor ribbon placed in her hair, [so that it would] be beautiful for her friend, [Marie Antoinette]."[56] Or, as another chronicler asserted, omitting the ribbon detail but expanding upon the attackers' motives for "beautifying" their trophy:

> They requisitioned a wig-maker so the princess might not show herself thus neglected before the Queen. He had to wash, untangle, plait, and powder the stained blond hair. . . . "At least, now, Antoinette will be able to recognize her!" exclaimed the people present.[57]

Whether or not they are true, these narratives are revealing indeed, insofar as they implicitly linked Lamballe's posthumous degradations to her best friend's reputation for extravagantly styled and powdered hair. Long associated both physically (the identical white skin and white hair) and sartorially (the matching sleigh-riding outfits, Bertin-made *poufs*, and white *gaulles*) with Marie Antoinette, the Princesse functioned in these tales as a double or a stand-in for the consort herself.[58] In particular, the plaiting and powdering of Lamballe's "stained blond hair" evoked the blond *Autrichienne* who had notoriously doused her locks with flour while her starving subjects clamored for bread.

Nor was powdered blond hair the only physical attribute that, in linking Lamballe to the Queen, received emphatic attention in chronicles of the former favorite's murder. For according to another contemporary account, "a black man . . . and a cut-throat repeatedly sponged the bodily remains to make sure the people noticed the exquisite whiteness of la Lamballe," and "exquisite whiteness" was likewise a trait belonging to the Queen.[59] Might not such a complexion, which still another alleged witness to Lamballe's murder suggestively described as being "pale as her linen," have recalled the vignettes in which the two friends had so often starred together?[60] Vignettes in which they made a display of their fine-tuned stylishness "in a sleigh, on the snow; in white dress[es] and powdered wig[s], adorned with pearls and ivory jewelry; at the Trianon, surrounded by sheep, barely distinguishable from the background of white marble"—and from the background of white muslin and linen *gaulles?*[61] Perhaps, then, it was in retaliation for these scenes of appalling aristocratic coldheartedness that the insurgents vowed to make the white-haired, white-skinned, well-dressed princesses suffer— Lamballe through her brutal death and ritual coiffing, and the Queen through a forced encounter with her friend's savagely styled head.

To ensure that this encounter took place, the contingent from La Force impaled the Princesse's head on a pike and carried it and the decapitated body through the streets of Paris to the Temple. There, Marie Antoinette's daughter later recollected, municipals granted the hooligans permission to "make the tour of our prison with Madame de Lamballe's head, on the condition that they left the corpse at the door."[62] When informed what the howling deputation had brought for her to see, "my mother was seized with horror," Madame Royale noted in her memoirs: "it was the only moment when her firmness left her" during the whole of the family's stay in the Tower.[63] But even after the Queen fainted dead away, Lamballe's "waxen white" face continued, Antonia Fraser relates, to "bob . . . up and down outside the windows of the dining room of the Tower, [with] the famous blond curls . . . floating as prettily as they had done in life, [making] the head . . . instantly recognizable."[64]

Marie Antoinette only came to after the thugs had left the premises, taking the Princesse's head and corpse with them. (She could not have known it, but upon stripping Lamballe's corpse of its clothing, the hooligans had discovered the ring that contained a lock of the Queen's hair "whitened by misfortune"; this they handed over to the Commune as further evidence of the two women's suspect relationship.) For the rest of the night, as the sounds of continuing riots swirled around the Temple and as the gutters outside ran red with the blood of other murdered prisoners, she gave herself over to uncontrollable sobs.[65] Just when it seemed her circumstances could not grow any more torturous, the revolutionary mob had confronted her with a newly shocking instance of brutality, becoming, in one royalist commentator's lyrical parlance, a "one hundred-headed monster that rose up against the throne to cut down its lilies and wither its roses."[66]

This last metaphor, whose terms recalled the effusive praise Marie Antoinette's complexion had garnered while she was Dauphine, was perhaps even better chosen than its author may have realized. Heralded twenty-two years earlier as a symbol of blissful Franco-Austrian cooperation, the consort's lily-and-rose palette was reinvented in September 1792 as a terrifying display of popular vengeance, visible not only in Lamballe's pallid, bleeding remains, but also in the "scrap of her *chemise,* drenched with blood," which one of the brigands reportedly "held hung from a lance" in the menacing procession through Paris.[67] As in the dream about Bertin's colorful wares turning black when she touched them, the Queen's fashionable past—her peaches and cream countenance, her snow-white coiffures and *chemises*—had literally returned to haunt her, wearing the gore-streaked mask of death.

The so-called September massacres continued for three days and claimed about thirteen hundred victims, some of them children as young as eight.[68] Yet just because the royals had emerged from the debacle unscathed did not mean their future safety was assured. Over the course of the autumn, French forces continued to do battle with the armies of Prussia and Austria, and as long as these nations remained hostile to the revolutionary state, the people's animosity to their German-born Queen would continue to smolder— expressed, in at least one pamphlet from the period, with yet another bloody variation on the lily-and-rose motif. This pamphlet, titled "The Life of Marie Antoinette," described Lamballe as cavorting lewdly with Madame de Tourzel in the Prison de La Force, and enjoining Tourzel to secure a dildo on her genitals with the help of a wide red ribbon. "The bright scarlet ribbon," the text's unnamed author averred, "contrasted beautifully with [Lamballe's] white skin."[69] In this single image, a whole host of associations—

depraved sexuality and the "German vice," the sashes usually worn with white muslin *gaulles,* and a strikingly pale complexion—coalesced to form a subtle portrait not just of Lamballe, but of her royal mistress.[70] For it was the latter who, under the sign of "bright scarlet" blood, remained the chief villainess of "The Life of Marie Antoinette": "The blood spilled from 1789 to September 1792 was her doing, with her mad passion to have the French destroy themselves."[71] Once again, the "mad passion" Marie Antoinette was thought to harbor against the French was yoked to another of her most notorious penchants: an inordinate devotion to physical beauty and personal adornment.

DESPITE THIS LATEST OUTPOURING OF VITRIOL AGAINST THE QUEEN, IT would be wrong to say that she was, by the fall of 1792, the only resident of the Temple whom the people had come to view as a redoubtable foe. On September 21, the newly elected deputies of the Convention Nationale met in the Tuileries palace, which they had claimed as their meeting hall, and declared the abolition of the monarchy and the founding of the First French Republic.[72] As one *conventionnel,* Henri Grégoire, declared on that day: "We must destroy the very word *king,* which remains a talisman whose magical powers are capable of stunning the multitudes [into submission]."[73] In this context, Louis XVI himself, already fatally discredited by the flight to Varennes, now stood as anathema to the republican *conventionnels,* who by early November were hotly debating the notion of trying him for crimes against the Nation.

Under the *ancien régime,* a proposal of this kind would have been unthinkable, for, as the historian David P. Jordan explains, "the legal maxim that 'the King can do no wrong' had always protected the monarchy" against formal recriminations from his subjects.[74] As Jordan further points out, even the 1791 Constitution had upheld this aspect of royal ideology, by declaring the King " 'sacred and inviolable,' and hence immune from prosecution."[75] The declaration of a republic, however, called for a radical rethinking of the monarch's position.[76] As Louis-Antoine Saint-Just, Robespierre's incongruously pretty, unnervingly coldhearted young acolyte, announced to his fellow *conventionnels* on November 13: "Louis is an enemy [who] must reign or die . . . : *no man can reign innocently.*"[77]

Now remembered as one of the Revolution's most infamous lines, Saint-Just's formulation electrified the legislature. And just one week later, the aspersions he cast on the King's innocence seemed borne out when, on a tip from François Gamain, the locksmith who had assisted Louis XVI in his workshop for some twenty years, an iron strongbox was extracted from the wreckage of the Tuileries. This box, which the now pro-revolutionary Gamain said he had made at his master's behest, contained secret letters exchanged with Mirabeau, the émigrés, and the leaders of the foreign coalition, and so laid bare the counterrevolutionary agenda that many had suspected the French royals of nurturing all along.[78]

The *conventionnels* sifted through the damning materials for several weeks, releasing them for widespread publication so that the populace could learn the full extent of the King's betrayal.[79] On December 3, Robespierre reiterated Saint-Just's demand that Louis XVI be punished in the harshest way possible. "Regretfully I speak this fatal truth," Robespierre intoned in his nasal, dispassionate lawyer's voice: "Louis must die because the Nation must live. . . . I ask that the Convention declare him, from this moment on, a traitor to the French nation, a criminal toward humanity."[80] Marie Antoinette, he added, ought to stand trial separately for her own despicable doings.[81]

For the moment tabling the issue of the consort's guilt or innocence, the deputies voted to bring to trial the man they now addressed by the pointedly nonroyal name Louis Capet—Capet being the surname of one of the French sovereigns' earliest forebears—or by the equally alarming designation "*cidevant* [erstwhile] king."[82] On December 11, the King was brought before the bar of the Convention to face his accusers for the first time. For the occasion, he donned his lustrous *cheveux de la Reine* riding coat, but if in choosing this garment he hoped to arrogate to himself some of his wife's and his royal predecessors' self-assured equestrian swagger, he did not entirely succeed.[83] Because traditionally the King was not addressed unless he spoke first, Louis was deeply unnerved by "all the questions they put to me" during his trial; these unsolicited queries, he admitted afterward to his valet, often left him too flustered to respond.[84] And though in his maladroit way, he did manage to insist that "my conscience in no way reproaches me," the 707 *conventionnels* were not impressed.[85] On January 15, they unanimously found the defendant guilty of "conspiring against liberty and public safety."[86] By a narrower margin, and with the King's own cousin Philippe-Égalité casting a deciding vote against him, they found in favor of the death penalty. On the afternoon of January 20, 1793, Marie Antoinette and her family heard town criers outside the Temple announcing that Louis Capet would be guillotined on the Place de la Révolution—the rebels' new designation for the square that had once borne the name of his grandfather Louis XV—the very next day.

MARIE ANTOINETTE HAD THOUGHT SHE WOULD BE PERMITTED TO SEE HER husband one last time before he died. Although he had had separate rooms in the Great Tower since October, where he was held in isolation for the duration of his trial (even on Christmas and New Year's Day), he was allowed to gather with her and the rest of the family for two hours on the evening of January 20. When the emotional interview came to a close, he assured his loved ones that he would meet with them again the following morning. Like Madame Élisabeth, the Queen had cried inconsolably throughout the King's visit, but at this heartening promise, she nodded her assent and urged him to come at seven o'clock, rather than eight as he had suggested, to prolong their final hours together.[87]

When morning came, though, Louis failed to appear as promised, having concluded with the priest who heard his last confession that further goodbyes would only add to his family's pain. In an agony of incertitude (for the guards would tell them nothing), Marie Antoinette and her children and sister-in-law listened to the neighborhood carillons confirming the passage of time. The bells tolled seven, then eight, then nine . . . but still there was no sign of Louis XVI. Finally, just after nine o'clock, they heard drumrolls and, as Marie Antoinette later put it, "the movements of men and horses" outside their windows.[88] From this unusual commotion, the captives deduced that the man they had called husband, brother, father, and King was leaving for the scaffold. Aghast, they waited for another excruciating hour until, at just past ten-twenty, more drumrolls and cannon fire, punctuated by cries of joy echoing throughout the streets of Paris, let them know Louis XVI was dead.[89]

According to a municipal officer called Goret and a Temple kitchen staffer named Turgy, both of whom published their memoirs during the Bourbon Restoration of the following century, Marie Antoinette reacted to the news by tearfully hailing the seven-year-old Dauphin as Louis XVII.[90] The words that accompanied the gesture—"The King is dead, long live the King"—were an ancient monarchical formula, but since the monarchy had been abolished four months earlier, they flew directly in the face of the now prevailing republican doctrine. Indeed, describing the sweeping political implications of the Convention's recourse to regicide, Simon Schama has observed:

> The theoretical immortality by which, when a king died, royalty lived—*le roi est mort, vive le roi*—was now reversed. It was the Citizen who had become the heroic immortal; it was the death of the King that was made to kill kingship.[91]

But, as Marie Antoinette had reminded Fersen under less challenging circumstances, she had never been the revolutionaries' fool; and she was not about to embrace their notions now.[92] In the name of equality, the Revolution's devotees had cast her and her family out of their home and into prison;

in the name of justice, they had mutilated her best friend and guillotined her husband. The *conventionnels,* in particular, had cloaked their actions in the language of moral rectitude—"no man can reign innocently"—yet their own hands were drenched in blood. And so, instead of refusing her son his royal birthright, she insisted upon it. Just as important, instead of remembering her spouse as an enemy of "liberty and public safety," she determined to honor his memory as an august King of France. Jailed and heartbroken though she was, she would not allow her adversaries to "kill kingship" entirely. She would keep the flame alive. (Plate 24.)

Characteristically, this attitude manifested itself in a new program of sartorial defiance. The *ci-devant* queen's mother, Maria Theresa, had famously paid tribute to her late husband by wearing widow's weeds from the day of his death till her own passing fifteen years later. Now a widow herself, Marie Antoinette, who had informed a childhood friend just a month before her imprisonment that she was growing daily "prouder and prouder to have been born a German," did not hesitate to steer the same course.[93] Despite the "near-catatonic state" into which her daughter remembered her falling after the King's execution, Marie Antoinette lost no time in requesting proper clothes for mourning.[94] On the afternoon of January 21, just hours after her husband's death, Goret came into her apartments, where, he recalled, the Queen "interrupt[ed] her sobbing to pronounce these words: 'We are aware of the tragedy that has befallen us; . . . our own tragedy is certain, and we wish to go into mourning.' "[95] Even when faced with unspeakable loss, Marie Antoinette tackled her difficulties as she always had—by choosing costumes that emphasized her resilience of spirit.[96]

Moved by the dignity that the newly widowed prisoner managed to display in her sorrow, Goret promised to see to it that she and her family obtained the outfits they required. Marie Antoinette, in turn, stipulated that these ensembles should be "as simple as possible," and then provided him with the name and the address of the dressmaker she wanted to make them.[97] Initially, revolutionary officials protested against the idea, on the grounds that the *Autrichienne*'s chosen seamstress, one Mademoiselle Pion, might be a monarchist or foreign secret agent.[98] (Perhaps the fact that her surname meant "Pawn" seemed further to support this possibility—and indeed, Pion did manage to report to Madame de Tourzel, now safely ensconced in a provincial castle, about the health and well-being of the surviving Bourbons.[99]) But Goret prevailed on the royal widow's behalf. Mademoiselle Pion was admitted to the Temple for two days' worth of fittings, so that less than a week after Louis XVI's death, each of the prisoners was in possession of serviceable black clothes for mourning. Marie Antoinette's new uniform consisted of a melancholy gown of plain black taffeta.[100]

What Goret's memoirs do not mention—but what an order form signed by Pierre-Joseph Tison of the Temple commissary on January 26 confirms— is that the Queen also managed to procure a small collection of mourning accessories from none other than Rose Bertin.[101] An itemized bill, also dated January 26 and signed by Bertin, specifies that the *marchande* furnished her former patroness with two widow's bonnets (trailing headdresses trimmed with ribbons and a long veil), three fichus, two pairs of kidskin gloves, one pair of silk gloves, and a fan—all of them black.[102] Three weeks later, Marie Antoinette received another package from her erstwhile "minister of fashion," this one containing a selection of black stockings and socks. This was the last shipment she would ever receive from the Grand Mogol, for Bertin fled France sometime in the last two weeks of February.[103] It was, however, significant that the Queen again turned to Bertin to help her make this last, deadly serious fashion statement—even if it meant equipping herself with the very black ribbons that had once haunted her dreams as portents of disaster.

As her jailers would only much later come to realize, allowing the woman they now disparaged as "Widow Capet" to mourn her husband's passing in this way constituted a grave tactical error, insofar as her clothes preserved through their symbolism a monarchy that the Revolution had already gone to great lengths to suppress once and for all. As the historian Abby Zanger has noted, during the *ancien régime* "the death of a monarch pose[d] a crisis for dynastic continuity," and one of the crown's ways of handling the crisis was to institute a nationwide period of mourning (set during Louis XV's childhood at six months) that allowed the people to process the old ruler's death, even as his successor adapted to the job of governing.[104] This ritual was so ingrained in prerevolutionary French culture that it held sway even when very few subjects were sorry to see the old monarch go, as had been the case with Louis XV. According to the childhood recollections of Jacques de Norvins, an aristocrat who was five years old when that king died:

> Mourning could be seen everywhere from the blazing chapel of Versailles and the funereal luxury of the princely residences to the lowliest shops in the suburbs. Everyone took pains to make his [or her] clothing look melancholy. All of France went into mourning.[105]

Needless to say, this ritual assumed different levels of magnificence depending on the social class of the person practicing it. At Versailles, "making [one's] clothing look melancholy" was elevated to an art form, as the new rulers and their courtiers were required to order new, somber-toned ensembles of the most extreme splendor. In addition, the biographer André Castelot has observed, the aristocrats' very carriages, "furniture, and beds had to be covered with dark drapery. Even the officers and livery servants had to dress in black, [with] mourning requir[ing] 1,365 new suits for the stable [hands] alone."[106] As the six-month period progressed, the mourning costume underwent a series of modifications: noblewomen, for instance, were allowed at specified points to resume wearing their jewelry and to substitute "little mourning" colors, such as gray, for the "great mourning" of violet and black.[107] Like all aspects of life at the château, these carefully regimented minutiae formed part of a broader symbolic program to highlight the Bourbons' *gloire*. But unlike other court ceremonies, this one included thousands upon thousands of commoners in its scope, uniting "all of France" in a tribute to the late king's immortal might.

Louis XVI's execution, though, necessarily demanded an altogether different response; it followed that if he had had to "die because the Nation must live," he deserved no homage whatsoever once deceased. Besides, royal mourning had been falling from popular favor at least since 1790, when the then pro-revolutionary Le Brun had dismissed it as inconsistent with the hard-won social equality that the Revolution had brought about.[108] In a surprising exception to this view, Mirabeau's death in April 1791 had been followed by a period of national mourning; this tribute to him as "the father of his people" had demonstrated the same concern for political continuity that had animated the practice under the *ancien régime*.[109]

But the discovery in November 1792 of the royals' secret correspondence with Mirabeau had posthumously destroyed the latter man's reputation (his corpse was even disinterred from its place of honor in the Panthéon, tomb to the Revolution's heroes), and now, in the age of legalized republicanism and regicide, the pomp and circumstance of mourning seemed less appropriate than ever.[110] Savage glee presented itself as the far more suitable reaction, as evidenced by the frenzied singing, dancing, and cries of "Vive la République!" that erupted among the masses of people who witnessed Louis Capet's beheading on the Place de la Révolution. To some of the revelers, the executioner even sold scraps of the victim's blood-drenched clothes and hair as souvenirs.[111] Buried naked in the Madeleine cemetery—not in the Saint-Denis Cathedral, where French kings had historically been laid to rest—Louis XVI was, even in death, treated as thoroughly deserving of his ignominious end.[112]

A similar attitude also informed the popular prints that revolutionary engravers like Villeneuve produced to commemorate the execution. In Villeneuve's iconic image, Louis's severed head dangled above a triumphant line from the radicals' new rallying song—and France's present-day national anthem—"La Marseillaise": "Let impure blood saturate our fields."[113] From this perspective, the shedding of Capet's blood, "impure" because of his abhorrent royal lineage and his established criminal conduct, was a cause not for mourning, but for celebration.

Royalists in France and abroad held quite the opposite view, of course. In England, the execution of an anointed monarch was decried as an abomination, and the British agreed to join forces with the other European allies in their war against the men they called "those murderers in Paris."[114] Within a month of the King's execution, Spain and Holland, likewise horrified by the republicans' bloody excesses, followed suit, and several months later the Pope declared Louis XVI a martyr of the true Catholic faith.[115]

Meanwhile, in France, black ribbons and armbands multiplied among the increasingly small and endangered population of monarchists in Paris—and among like-minded individuals in the provinces, where a formidable counterrevolutionary groundswell was under way.[116] To the liberal chronicler Mercier, these black accoutrements identified their wearers as "caterpillars gnawing at the tree of liberty," and thus invited harsh retribution from committed republicans.[117] Indeed, it seems likely that, for sheer self-preservation's sake, monarchists wore their mourning badges chiefly among friends and behind closed doors.[118] But it is telling that, however privately, these partisans of the throne adopted the same kinds of accessories that Marie Antoinette had had brought to her in the Temple. Even in her incarceration and bereavement, she remained at the forefront of an intensely politicized clothing trend.[119]

The trend was also a dangerous one, and not just because of the bouts of street violence it was capable of unleashing. Legally as well, the politics of personal appearance assumed higher and riskier stakes as the leaders of the new republic took stock of the regicide they had just committed and worked to solidify their new, kingless state. One of the great challenges they faced as they did so was to stamp out lingering monarchist sentiment wherever they could find it, on the grounds that the very "word *king* remain[ed] a talisman" capable of engendering royalist sedition. In this effort, they carefully scrutinized people's material talismans, such as accessories and outfits, for signs of either allegiance or betrayal.[120] As one group of zealous, *tricolore*-wearing patriots declared before the Convention in March 1793, their "uniformity of costume" corresponded to an underlying "uniformity of hearts."[121] Clothes presenting exceptions to this uniformity, perceived as the sole guarantor of stability in the new régime, necessitated strict government intervention.[122]

It was in this spirit that after the King's death, the republicans banned silk—once the pride of the French luxury industry—for its noble associations and decreed that in the future all cockades should be made from "patriotic" (because less expensive) wool.[123] In addition, all *cocardes* other than the tricolor were banned; citizens were encouraged to denounce people wearing "deviant cockades"; and the legal punishment for those who persisted in wearing such rosettes was death.[124] In July 1793, Marie Antoinette's former favorite shade of defiance, green, was added to the list of antipatriotic markers because a young woman named Charlotte Corday, who had stabbed to death the revolutionary journalist Marat in his bathtub, had been apprehended with a green ribbon in her hat. Following Corday's summary execution, Simon Schama has pointed out, her memorable headgear made green "the color of counter-revolution—prohibited, to the ruin of drapers and haberdashers, from any public dress."[125] Even grubby sans-culotte garb no longer protected its wearers from suspicion, as conspiracy theorists hypothesized that counterrevolutionaries might well be adopting it to bamboozle unsuspecting patriots into overlooking their concealed monarchist views.[126]

Surprisingly, however, the sartorial vigilance that came into effect as the republican government struggled to get its bearings did not immediately affect Marie Antoinette and her widow's weeds. Like the purloined letter that, several decades later, Edgar Allan Poe's eponymous short story would describe as being hidden in plain sight of those hunting for it, the Queen's symbolically charged black wardrobe seems to have attracted little attention during the early months of her bereavement.[127] Apart from their preliminary doubts about allowing Mademoiselle Pion into the Tower for fittings, Marie Antoinette's captors apparently interfered with her mourning efforts only to the extent that they denied her request for black wall coverings to hang in her apartments.[128] Presumably, they rejected this one petition on class grounds, for under the *ancien régime,* only the most elevated princes and courtiers had enjoyed the right to drape their homes while mourning the late king, and it would hardly have been fitting for a prisoner of the republic to be granted such an obviously aristocratic privilege.[129] But the revolutionaries seemed content to impose this single limit on the royal widow's pretensions.

Some degree of pity toward the former queen may also have contributed to the revolutionaries' leniency about her choice of costume, for her health had declined noticeably since her husband's death. Besides growing even thinner and more haggard, she had also begun hemorrhaging large amounts of blood, a symptom that, Antonia Fraser has hypothesized, attested to the beginnings of menopause, the presence of uterine fibroids, or perhaps "the first signs of cancer of the womb."[130] (The scabrous 1791 pamphlet that had spoken of the Queen's "uterine furors"—meaning her insatiable sexual appetites—could hardly have anticipated this grim scenario.[131]) Whatever the underlying malady, it took a dramatic toll on Marie Antoinette's appearance, as is clear from a portrait by the Polish artist Alexandre Kucharski, who had succeeded Vigée-Lebrun as the Queen's favorite painter after the latter's emigration, and who through obscure means managed to sneak into the Queen's prison to see her, painting her afterward from memory.[132] To look at Kucharski's painting is to see a woman who has aged far beyond her thirty-seven years, a woman whose morbid black headdress, haunted gaze, and hollowed-out features bespeak a condition even more harrowing than death.[133] Divested of her crown, her palaces, her friends, her liberty, and now her husband, she appears in Kucharski's portrait as a figure of complete and irrevocable ruin. To deprive her of her clothes on top of all this—especially of clothes as pitifully bleak and simple as the ones she had selected—may thus have struck her jailers as superfluous.[134] The woman was almost dead as it was: let her keep her shroud.

Alternatively, it may be that the republicans allowed Marie Antoinette to make so brazen a show of her royalist sensibilities for the simple reason that they were uncertain what to do with her now that the King was dead. Because their act of regicide was unprecedented in French history, there was no established protocol for them to follow in handling his widowed queen. In fact, in the first month after Louis's execution, it seemed eminently likely that instead of remaining a prisoner, or standing trial like her husband before her, the Widow Capet would simply be packed off to her relatives in Austria.[135] In February, Moelle assured her that his colleagues in the Commune had dismissed the idea of executing her as a "gratuitous horror"; and Madame Royale likewise remembered that "the guards thought we were going to be sent away."[136] There could be little doubt as to nature of the views Marie Antoinette would be free to advance, in her clothing or otherwise, once she was reunited with the counterrevolutionary Hapsburgs. With black as Austria's national color, and with widow's weeds as the late Maria Theresa's signature outfit, her mourning ensemble would be entirely in keeping with the politics of her new homeland. In this light, to rein in the *ci-devant* queen's self-presentation in the Temple would surely have seemed at least to the more sensible of her captors as a waste of political energies better directed elsewhere.

Over the course of the spring, however, Marie Antoinette's chance at freedom disappeared as the new government faced a barrage of daunting new threats. In March, the European allies scored key victories on France's northern and southern borders alike. At around the same time, in the Vendée region of the country, sedition among conservative Catholics who bitterly opposed the Revolution's dismantling of sacred *ancien régime* institutions was fast gaining ground, spawning bloody civil conflict in the process.[137] With war now threatening their supremacy both at home and abroad, and

16.   Alexandre Kucharski, *Marie Antoinette in Widow's Dress in Prison* (1793)
(Réunion des Musées Nationaux/Art Resource, New York)

having instituted a Revolutionary Tribunal in Paris to try people for suspected unpatriotic behavior, republicans now took a harder line on their
black-clad royal hostage. On March 27, Robespierre informed his fellow
conventionnels that it was "time for patriots to rekindle their vigorous and
immortal hatred for those who are called *sovereigns*"—meaning Marie
Antoinette—and Hébert took the opportunity to show his patriotic leanings
by instituting random searches of the royals' apartments in the Temple.[138]
Unfortunately for the Queen, one of these searches turned up a small scrap
of fabric embroidered with a crucifix, a crown, and Jesus's arrow-pierced Sacred Heart: the rallying symbol for the Catholic rebels in the Vendée.[139] The
discovery of this emblem among her possessions justified the republicans in
viewing her as an agent of counterrevolution, and in preparing to treat her as
such.[140]

Another item that Hébert's men confiscated from Marie Antoinette while
rooting through her personal effects was a small wax medallion of the
mythological antiheroine Medea. Apparently, she had received it from a
Temple officer named Augustin-German Jobert, who later explained to the
Revolutionary Tribunal that the bauble was "just one of about four thousand like it that I have at home"—most of them "allegories of the Revolution," and therefore harmlessly shared with the prisoners.[141] Yet Jobert
could not explain why, of all the cameos in his collection, the Queen had
chosen to hold on to that particular one.[142]

Unlike the Vendéens' Sacred Heart, the image of Medea had no established political or religious valence during this period, and therefore raised
puzzling questions about what it could possibly mean to its owner. For their
part, Jobert's questioners in the Tribunal wondered aloud whether the
mythological figure did not constitute "some sort of allusion" to the Queen
herself.[143] They did not expand upon this notion, but since the revolutionary press had already cast her as a harpy, a Fury, a Messalina, and other
deadly figures of legend, perhaps Jobert's interrogators were giving him the
benefit of the doubt and speculating that he had meant to insult the Queen
with the gift of a medallion featuring one of mythology's most notorious female villains.[144]

The few letters Marie Antoinette drafted while in the Temple make no
mention of the cameo and therefore offer no clues as to why she kept it.
Given her memorable encounter with the Medea tapestries at her girlhood
remise, though, it seems not at all implausible that the medallion held a particular kind of totemic appeal for her. In 1770, Medea had kept watch from
a Gobelins tapestry as the foreign princess was divested of her clothing and
formally severed from her homeland and her past. Twenty-three years later,
in the Temple, this same mythological figure resurfaced in a new medium as

Marie Antoinette was again faced with absolute, soul-shattering dispossession. But this time around, following in the mythical queen's footsteps, the real-life queen refused to cede control to those who would wrest it from her; for, like the poison gown Medea made for her enemies, Marie Antoinette's mourning costume suggested a prideful resistance to her antagonists' schemes. Whether by an astonishing coincidence, then, or by the Queen's conscious design, Medea's appearance in the Tower indeed presented an apposite "sort of allusion." It evoked the sartorial daring that Marie Antoinette had always reverted to when the going got tough, and that continued to prevail in the form of her royalist black dress.

AT THE SAME TIME, THE MEDEA CAMEO MAY HAVE INSPIRED THE REVOLU-tionaries to take an even closer and harsher look at their widowed captive and at her methods for shoring up her power. "By what magic," one republican author demanded to know, "has this infernal Antoinette taken control of our countrymen's hearts? Has she held in her possession the secrets of cruel Medea? Yes, without a doubt!"[145] If, by Medea's secrets, this writer meant extraordinary manipulations of clothing (as opposed to, say, a flair for infanticide), then the charge was more than a tad disingenuous. After all, for the past many years Marie Antoinette's fashion sense had done quite the opposite of winning over her "countrymen's hearts." This accusation may, however, have been aiming at something similar to the *conventionnel* Grégoire's comment about the potential of the "very word *king*" to uphold or revive the monarchy. For even when it alienated her subjects, Marie Antoinette's clothing had time and again conveyed insubordination, autonomy, and strength—qualities again on display in her mourning garb.[146] Given the tremendous opposition that they faced from royalist groups both within and outside France, the republicans could not afford to tolerate such intransigence in their captive queen. On June 2, Hébert invoked another of the best-known elements of the Medea myth—the part where she chops her and her straying husband's children to pieces—when he proposed that, in punishment for her obvious and abiding treasonous intentions, "the *Autrichienne* be hacked to bits, like pieces of pâté."[147]

LESS THAN A MONTH AFTER HÉBERT THREW DOWN THIS GAUNTLET, THE REV-olutionaries hit upon what was perhaps an even crueler strategy for handling the Widow Capet, whose passionate attachment to her children had not been lost on her captors.[148] Acting on rumors of a royalist plot to kidnap Marie Antoinette's son and install him as the new King of France, the *conventionnels* decreed on July 1 that "Louis Charles, son of Capet, [was] to be taken from his mother and placed in a separate apartment, the best-guarded one in the Temple."[149] (Directly beneath the princesses' rooms, this was the same apartment to which Louis XVI had been confined during his trial.) Two days later, six officers appeared in Marie Antoinette's apartments to carry out the Convention's orders. According to Madame Royale, who witnessed the heart-wrenching scene, Marie Antoinette opposed the soldiers so violently that it took them over an hour to tear the eight-year-old Louis Charles, sobbing and shrieking, from her arms.[150] Marie Antoinette's *chou d'amour* would, she was appalled to learn, be placed in the care of a fanatically republican, alcoholic cobbler named Simon, whom the Commune had charged with "deroyalizing" the little prince.[151] The Widow Capet had dared to treat her son like a king; under Simon's rough tutelage, he would be molded into a patriot.

Although the cobbler's mission, which he carried out with sadistic zeal, was to include plying Louis Charles with alcohol, beating him whenever he cried for his mother, teaching him to sing republican battle hymns like "La Marseillaise," and making him curse the monarchy loudly enough for his bereft family to hear from their apartments, all this was preceded by one simple but revealing act. As Madame Royale recalled: "The first thing that Simon did was to take away [my brother's] black suit," even though Marie Antoinette had "said before he left that she hoped he would not give up his mourning."[152] This account is telling for two reasons. First, it confirms the significance that Marie Antoinette attached to her family's mourning outfits: for her to remind her child how to dress at the very moment he was being taken from her indeed suggests that to her, wearing black for Louis XVI was a matter of utmost importance. Second, the fact that Simon hastened to override the Queen's directives on this score indicates that her enemies were finally on to her—that they recognized both how much the mourning gear meant to her and how brazenly it flouted their own, antiroyalist worldview. According to Madame Royale, the cobbler wasted no time in clapping a liberty bonnet on Louis Charles's head and dressing him in the dingy rags of a sans-culotte.[153]

Destroying his visible ties to the monarchy, this act claimed the boy for the Revolution and so turned Marie Antoinette's own strategy of sartorial defiance against her. If anyone possessed the "secrets of cruel Medea" now, it was the republicans, not the Queen: they had struck at her through her costume choices and her child, and the blow was devastating. For the rest of July, Marie Antoinette was almost prostrate with grief at losing her youngest child: her *chou d'amour* and her king. According to Madame Royale, her mother's "only pleasure, only expectation, only occupation" was to stare fixedly through a crack she had found in the wall of the Tower parapets, straining for occasional glimpses of Louis Charles in his horrifying red bonnet.[154]

But at two in the morning on August 2, the Widow Capet's jailers deprived her of even this last, meager source of comfort when they appeared in her rooms and declared that she was to be relocated to the Conciergerie prison, there to await trial by the Revolutionary Tribunal. With the allied forces drawing ever closer to Paris, the Convention had made its decision: the *Autrichienne* was a prime suspect in the counterrevolutionary conspiracy, and she had to be dealt with accordingly.[155] As if to prevent her from devising any further sartorial schemes as she prepared to leave the Temple, the guards who came for her allowed her no privacy as she changed from her nightclothes into her mourning gown.[156]

By now in tatters, this was the only dress she would be allowed to take with her to her new living quarters. Her request to bring with her some needlework—a pair of stockings she had been sewing for Louis Charles—was flatly refused.[157] As for the small bundle of other personal effects she assembled for her trip, the guards commandeered it for inspection by the Tribunal.[158] (Upon opening the packet, officials would confiscate several of the Queen's most precious possessions: locks of hair from her husband and her children, a miniature portrait of the Princesse de Lamballe, and a pocket mirror she had relied upon in the Tower to perform her meager *toilette*.[159]) Rosalie Lamorlière, the young serving woman who was assigned to wait on Marie Antoinette in the Conciergerie, would later recall her astonishment at seeing the legendarily modish consort arrive with only the shabby clothes on her back.[160]

It is worth noting that not all the republic's high-born, high-profile bêtes noires were so ruthlessly shorn of their elegant apparel. In March 1793, Philippe-Égalité had been arrested as a counterrevolutionary suspect, despite his strategically chosen nom de guerre and his vociferously proclaimed patriotism. Yet during his incarceration—first in a prison in Marseilles, later in the Conciergerie—Philippe-Égalité was allowed to maintain an extensive wardrobe full of all the luxurious trappings he had eschewed while trying to pass as a revolutionary comrade-in-arms.[161] It was as if, now that his militant charade had fallen apart, the *ci-devant* duke had no reason not to resume dressing like the scion of privilege he really was.

Things could not have been more different for Marie Antoinette. As Pierre Saint-Amand has shown, beginning with her arrival in the Tower, the revolutionaries had subjected her to a "slow process of subtraction" or "denarcissization" conceived precisely to punish her for her stylish, self-absorbed past.[162] And once the government officially identified her as a suspected royalist agitator, the process accelerated markedly. Upon reaching the Conciergerie, she was placed in a dank, squalid, and sparsely furnished cell whose floors were so filthy that her shoes—badly worn, high-heeled slippers made from "plum-black" satin—came to look to Rosalie Lamorlière as though the Queen had been "walking on the rue Saint-Honoré."[163] Because of the sympathetic, even admiring tone of Lamorlière's reminiscences, published during the Bourbon Restoration, the irony of this remark is likely unintentional.[164] For the rue Saint-Honoré had, of course, been the site of the Grand Mogol and thus of some of Marie Antoinette's most memorable adventures in fashion. In the dreary and sinister Conciergerie, though, this world was forever lost to Marie Antoinette—except for the grime on her shoes.[165] Requesting new slippers was, however, out of the question. According to a young woman who later claimed to have seen the royal prisoner at this time, "the [republicans'] fear that even a shoe might betray an important secret prevented them from allowing any replacement of this kind."[166]

Nor could Marie Antoinette expect to receive replacements for the other pieces of her mourning costume, which, after over six months of daily wear, was becoming as bedraggled as her shoes. When her widow's coif—the last headdress she ever received from Bertin's shop—threatened to fall to pieces, she asked Rosalie Lamorlière to help her transform it into two smaller, less intricately constructed bonnets.[167] The tenderhearted serving woman's assistance was essential in this effort because the revolutionaries had also taken away Marie Antoinette's sewing scissors, so that she had to tear pieces of thread off with her teeth whenever she tried to mend anything herself.[168] Various other female employees of the prison pitched in by making occasional repairs to the Queen's ragged mourning dress.[169] Yet the garment continued to deteriorate as its sweeping hemline dragged daily along the grime- and rust-streaked prison floors.[170] It was subjected to additional wear and tear because, according to Fersen, "the Queen always slept fully dressed in black: she expected to be killed or guillotined at any moment, and she wanted to go to the scaffold dressed in mourning."[171] (Though Fersen remained abroad, he continued to keep anxious tabs on his beloved and to lobby the allied leaders—as indifferent as ever to the widowed queen's fate—to hasten to her aid.[172]) The thick humidity and boiling heat of the Parisian summer must have made the gown—designed for the frigid months following Louis XVI's January execution—terrifically uncomfortable to sleep in.[173] Still, Marie Antoinette clung to it night and day, apparently determined that it remain with her till her death.

She was less successful in trying to preserve other treasured relics from her royal and familial past. The first of these, which she had somehow managed to sneak into the Conciergerie, was the little gold timepiece her mother had given her just before her departure for France twenty-three years earlier. This she hung on the wall soon after her arrival in her new cell, as if to infuse her dilapidated surroundings (peeling wallpaper, a shabby mattress, and crude straw chairs) with at least one pretty, personal touch.[174] Five days later, though, the watch attracted her jailers' notice. When they confiscated it, the usually stoic princess broke down and cried as if her heart would break.[175]

She was thwarted as well when she asked to be given the needlework she had begun in the Temple; once again, she expressed her eagerness to finish making a pair of stockings for her son. Although Madame Élisabeth and Madame Royale packed up the materials and sent them to the Conciergerie, the officers refused to give them to the Queen, on the grounds that she might hurt herself with the needles.[176] Desperate for something to do in her barren cell, and perhaps anxious to provide her son with clothing of a nonrepublican provenance, Marie Antoinette resorted to picking threads out of the faded, torn tapestry that hung on the wall over her bed. Using a pair of toothpicks, she "knitted" these threads into a pair of garters which she begged the prison concierge to send to the Temple.[177] The gift never reached Louis Charles, who died under mysterious circumstances in prison, possibly sometime in late 1793 or early 1794.[178] It was only in December 1795 that Madame Royale, Marie Antoinette's sole surviving child, received the garters—a striking testament to the piteous conditions of her mother's last confinement.[179]

But even as the republicans worked systematically to dismantle her once-elegant image, Marie Antoinette refused to assist them in this endeavor. Just a few days after she was placed in the Conciergerie, she succeeded in filching a scrap of paper in order to write the following note to Madame Royale, who had had to stay behind in the Temple with Madame Élisabeth:

> I want to let you know, my dear child, that I am all right; I am calm, and I would be altogether so if I knew that my poor daughter were not worried. I embrace you and your aunt with my whole heart. Please send me some lace stockings, a cotton redingote, and an underskirt.[180]

Like Marie Antoinette's parting directives to Louis Charles about his mourning wear, this letter placed an explicit emphasis on the question of dress and announced her refusal to embrace the utter abjection prescribed by her jailers. Straightaway Madame Élisabeth fulfilled her sister-in-law's request, entrusting a sympathetically disposed municipal officer named Michonis to bring a package of clothes to the Queen's room in the Conciergerie. This package contained an array of "beautiful batiste *chemises* and pocket kerchiefs; linen fichus; black silk stockings; a white *déshabillé* dress to wear in the mornings; a few night-caps; and several different-sized lengths of ribbon."[181] Marie Antoinette was apparently overcome by emotion as she sorted through her lovely new possessions and reacted in much the same way when Rosalie brought her a cardboard box in which to store them.[182] For the Queen's cell had no armoire, and without the box, her new finery would have been exposed to the dirt and moisture of the prison floors. According to the maid, Marie Antoinette received this box "as if it had been the most beautiful piece of furniture in the world."[183]

Rosalie also won her mistress's gratitude by offering her a cheap little red-painted mirror that she had bought from a trinket dealer by the Seine, for the Queen's formal requests for a mirror had been repeatedly denied.[184] Lamorlière was pleased to see "Her Majesty [treat the mirror] as an object of great importance" and happily performed other services for her, too: especially keeping the fastidious princess's body linens as clean as possible.[185] Thanks to these acts of kindness, and to the assistance of another prison employee, Madame Harel, who helped coif her hair every day with a white ribbon and a touch of powder, Marie Antoinette was able to preserve some semblance of decency in her appearance.[186] Certain chroniclers have speculated that this may have been particularly important to her given the vast numbers of people who visited her cell at all hours of the day and night—some of them revolutionary officials, some of them mere curiosity-seekers who had bribed the guards for a glimpse of the fallen queen.[187] At the Temple, she had lived in utter seclusion, but at the Conciergerie, once again finding "all eyes fixed upon" her, Marie Antoinette seems determinedly to have upheld a dignified façade, despite her captors' best efforts to humiliate her.

These efforts intensified considerably after September 4, when prison officials uncovered a royalist plot to help Marie Antoinette escape from the Conciergerie. (The botched attempt became known as the Carnation Affair, after the flower that the Queen's would-be rescuer, the Chevalier de Rougeville, used to smuggle a note into her cell.[188]) Although the discovery of the plan occurred shortly after the republicans had already decided to hasten to bring the Widow Capet to trial, it led them to crack down even more severely on her for the remainder of time in jail—and again to punish her, above all, in the domain of her physical appearance.[189] In addition to moving her to still smaller and more wretched quarters, her captors placed her under the twenty-four-hour surveillance of a gendarme who, in an uncanny throwback to her *remise* ceremony and wedding night, insisted on remaining present even when she undressed. Like Marie Antoinette's serving women at Versailles, Rosalie Lamorlière was struck by her mistress's "excessive modesty"; for this reason, she tried to block the guard's view with her own body whenever the Queen had to change her clothes.[190] Rosalie's obvious sympathy for the captive attracted her supervisors' suspicion. When she tried to style her mistress's locks (Madame Harel having been dismissed on the heels of the Carnation Affair), she was told that only the prison's concierge himself, Monsieur Bault, would be allowed to perform this function. Marie Antoinette flatly declined Bault's services and was reduced, perhaps for the first time in her life, to dressing her hair on her own.[191]

But the republicans carried their severity even further. During her transfer from the Tower, the Queen had managed to hold on to two rings set with gemstones—one of them was her wedding ring—and according to Larmorlière, she seemed to find comfort in these tiny traces of her glittering past, shifting them constantly from finger to finger with a dreamy look in her eye.[192] After the Carnation Affair, prison officials took these rings away from her without warning. In addition, they decided to stop providing her with sufficient clean body linens to stanch the blood from her continued uterine hemorrhaging. At best, Rosalie Lamorlière noted, "the clerk from the Revolutionary Tribunal doled out the linens one by one, and very far apart."[193] More often, the Queen had to rely on little strips of cloth torn from her maid's own humble *chemises,* which Rosalie thoughtfully left hidden beneath the mattress whenever she made up her mistress's bed.[194]

In this way, Marie Antoinette and her adversaries engaged in a fierce tug-of-war to control her sartorial body: a struggle she had been waging in some form or other since her first day on French soil. But the conflict entered its deadly, final act when Marie Antoinette was summoned before the Revolutionary Tribunal at eight o'clock in the morning on October 15. Seated calmly on a bench at the front of the crowded courtroom, she had to listen—and sometimes to respond—as the court's president, Armand Herman, and its prosecuting attorney, Antoine-Quentin Fouquier-Tinville, rehearsed a long litany of her supposed counterrevolutionary crimes. As historians have since pointed out, hard evidence against the Queen was scant, and the witnesses' testimonies relied shamelessly on inference and hearsay.[195] Against the backdrop of the ongoing battle over her appearance, though, it is interesting to note the number of clothing- and accessories-related anecdotes that were marshaled to show how she had "conspired against France." The prosecution and its witnesses brought up the Sacred Heart fabric and the Medea medallion; the costumes she had chosen for the flight to Varennes; the white cockades she was thought to have distributed at the "orgy" of October 1789; her nomination of "perverse" ministers and her manipulation of the King himself; her suspicious, financially ruinous involvement with the "infamous and execrable Calonne" and the Comtesse de La Motte; her direct responsibility for the famines that had plagued her subjects; the vast costliness of the Petit Trianon; the enormous sums she had supposedly channeled to Joseph II in Austria.[196] (This last charge, of course, had first been leveled against Marie Antoinette in connection with her imported-muslin *gaulles,* but at the trial, these garments received no explicit mention.) Somewhat oddly, given the pitiful state of the defendant's slippers, Herman even decried her prerevolutionary habit of ordering more shoes than she actually wore. He also averred that before the June 20, 1792, siege of the Tuileries, she had had a special dress made to disguise the pistols with which she had planned to open fire on the populace: an allegation that played explicitly on fantasies about the extreme danger the Queen's clothing posed to her subjects.[197]

In an attempt to defuse these incendiary charges, Marie Antoinette insisted that she had always loved her late husband's kingdom and that she had never wished for anything but France's happiness. Yet combined with even more dramatic charges concerning her monstrous nature—such as Hébert's claim that she had molested Louis Charles in the Temple in order to ruin the boy's health and improve her own chances at becoming an all-powerful, female regent—the prosecution's stories fueled its characterization of her as "the scourge and the blood-sucker of the French people."[198] Fouquier-Tinville placed the finishing touches on this portrayal by repeatedly referring to the Widow Capet's supposed cadre of "counterrevolutionaries and co-conspirators" as "that shadowy council," "that black council," or "that council that met in the shadowy black of the night."[199]

This emphatic rhetoric of blackness not only reinforced the idea of the defendant's participation in the dark crime of incest but also framed the outfit that the Queen had worn to the courtroom—her mourning dress—as an externalized mark of her criminality. In the eighteenth century, the French had a proverb that held that a person "is not so much a devil as he [or she] is black," meaning that said individual's underlying character is less horrific than his or her appearance might suggest.[200] But in depicting Marie Antoinette's activities "in the blackest of terms," the revolutionary prosecution implied that on the contrary, her dark costume perfectly externalized her devilish soul.[201] As Lynn Hunt has argued in her examination of Fouquier-Tinville's and Herman's reliance on the pamphlet pornographers' scurrilous tales, "the revelation of the Queen's true motives and feelings came [above all] from the ability of the people or their representatives to 'read' her body."[202] Particularly in the context of her other dastardly sins, Marie Antoinette's gown may have likewise offered itself to the people's condemnatory deciphering. Indeed, at least one of the militant neighborhood groups lobbying for her execution railed against the "new levels of blackness [to which] this impious, barbarous woman had sunk with her transgressions."[203]

Nonetheless, in drawing attention to the Queen's black attire, the republicans may have underestimated the degree to which it actually stood to elicit sympathy among the spectators at the trial.[204] One of the courtroom guards, Louis Larivière, asserted that "her long black dress rendered her extraordinary pallor all the more striking."[205] In this description, the black of Marie Antoinette's royalist mourning threw into relief the pallor for which she had once been famed, but to which her long confinement indoors and her chronic blood loss apparently lent a sickly new cast.[206] As stark manifestations of the many tragedies she had endured since the monarchy's fall, both the Queen's dirty, threadbare widow's weeds and her paper-white skin had the potential to establish her less as an insatiable "bloodsucker and scourge" than as a horrendously mistreated, manifestly bereaved individual whose sufferings were already well in excess of her alleged crimes.[207]

Indeed, it was in the latter light that Marie Antoinette managed to present herself at least once during the proceedings—when she responded to Hébert's incest accusation with undisguised heartbreak and shock. ("I call upon all mothers present," she is said to have cried, "to say whether such a thing is possible!"[208]) According to her lawyer, Claude-François Chauveau-Lagarde, this pathos-ridden outburst "excited in the courtroom a movement of admiration that momentarily suspended further debate"; and in the biographer Maxime de La Rochetière's version, even hardened revolutionary women were moved to tears and to fainting by the defendant's noble, long-suffering air.[209] Reportedly, when Robespierre "heard what a sensation the sublime manner in which the Queen had met the charge had made, and the effect it had on the audience, he, being then at dinner, broke his plate with rage."[210]

But Robespierre broke his plate in vain, because there was little doubt as to how the jurors—who, like the witnesses, had been handpicked in advance for their "patriotic" fervor—would ultimately find.[211] Still, the audience's unexpected show of sympathy for the Queen appears finally to have alerted her enemies to the tactical dangers of allowing her to dress like a tragic royalist martyr. At four in the morning on October 16, the Revolutionary Tribunal formally convicted Marie Antoinette as "a declared enemy of the French nation . . . the accomplice or rather the instigator of the majority of the crimes of which the *ci-devant* tyrant [Louis Capet] was found guilty."[212] Like her late husband, she was to be guillotined on the Place de la Révolution; but unlike him, she would not be allowed to say good-bye to her remaining family members, and her execution was set for that very same day.

Not long after this verdict was handed down, republican officials compounded its harshness by informing their victim that she must under no circumstances wear her mourning gown to the scaffold. According to Rosalie Lamorlière, the revolutionaries insisted that this was because the monarchist overtones of the costume "might incite the people to insult" Marie Antoinette when they turned out to watch her execution. Yet "to all of us in the prison," Lamorlière recalled, it seemed obvious that the officials "in fact were afraid of the interest that she might inspire as the King's widow."[213] In all the revolutionaries' systematic attempts to erase any remaining signs of royal privilege from the surface of the Queen's body, her black gown alone had escaped their clutches. Now, notwithstanding her wish to die in mourning, this dress was verboten. As she prepared to face the guillotine, Marie Antoinette had to find something else to wear.

ELEVEN

WHITE

October 16, 1793. Her trial had lasted twenty hours, but upon returning to her cell after the ordeal, Marie Antoinette did not fall asleep. At half past four in the morning, she requested a candle, some ink, and some paper (all of which had been denied her throughout her stay in the Conciergerie) and drafted a letter to Madame Élisabeth. In this missive, she declared her love for her family, asked "God's pardon for all the mistakes I have made," preached Christian forgiveness for her enemies, and expressed hope that she would be able to die with courage.[1] After completing the letter, Rosalie La-morlière tells us, the Queen stretched out on her lumpy little bed and turned her face to the wall, weeping without sound. At this point, she was still fully clothed in her widow's weeds.[2]

Hours passed, day broke, and Rosalie, who had withdrawn respectfully after trying to feed Marie Antoinette a few sips of broth, returned to help her dress. The gendarme who had been stationed inside the cell refused to leave even when the Queen, who had been hemorrhaging very badly and needed to change her blood-soaked body linens, implored him to do so for decency's sake.[3] Blushing furiously, she crouched down next to her bed, removed her soiled linens, and tucked them into a small hole in the wall.[4] Rosalie, who stood before the Queen so as to obstruct the guard's view, was struck to find that her mistress seemed to have kept a special white *chemise* at the ready, just for this occasion. "I realized," the serving woman recalled afterward, "that it was her intention to appear in public as decently dressed as her impoverished circumstances allowed, just as she had done for her trial."⁵ Even as she faced execution, Marie Antoinette's will to control her image, to manage it through her clothing, had not left her. All across Paris, crowds were spilling out into the streets to witness her procession from the Conciergerie to the scaffold. More crowds were gathering at the Place de la Révolution to see her die, and thirty thousand soldiers had been called out to keep the peace. On her last day in France as on her first, all eyes would be upon her. And although she had been forbidden to dress as a widow, she had something else up her sleeve.

And so, shedding the ragged black dress in which she had faced her accusers, Marie Antoinette slipped into her plum-black shoes, a fresh white underskirt, and her pristine white *chemise*.⁶ To complete the ensemble, she put on the white *déshabillé* dress Madame Élisabeth had sent her from the Temple and wrapped the prettiest of her muslin fichus around her neck. She even removed the dangling black ribbons from her makeshift widow's coif: the result was a pared down, ruffled linen bonnet as colorless as her hair. Paler than ever from her severe recent blood loss, the Queen became a figure of pure, radiant white.⁷ (Plate 25.)

Though imposed by her enemies' restrictions and her own meager resources in the Conciergerie, Marie Antoinette's white outfit just may have been the most brilliant fashion statement of her entire career.⁸ Both royalists and revolutionaries who witnessed her journey to the scaffold remarked upon her spotless ensemble.⁹ (Unlike Louis XVI, who had been conveyed to the guillotine in a closed carriage, the Widow Capet was forced to travel in an open cart, just like any other criminal.) To the republican *conventionnel* and artist David, who executed a quick, brutal sketch of her as she was driven past his window, her outfit was pathetic and contributed to his overall depiction of a hideous, haggard crone, justly deprived of all her *cidevant* splendor. (Plate 26.) But among other spectators, expressions of outright derision were apparently few and far between. By most accounts, as the spectral white figure was escorted through the double hedgerow of navy-blue-coated soldiers who lined her path, the crowds reacted with stunned, leaden silence.¹⁰ Past them rode a woman not covered in jewels, not crowned with feathers; a woman neither outlandishly dressed up nor offensively dressed down; a woman so bereaved that her very mourning gown had been taken away; a woman whose modest pile of remaining clothes was to be shipped off to the female prisoners of the Salpêtrière after her death.¹¹ As David's cruel drawing made clear, Marie Antoinette's famously stylish, unfailingly contentious wardrobe had vanished forever.¹² Even before she reached the guillotine, this aspect of her history, her body, her being, had been erased—leaving her only white.

But the erasure perhaps revealed even more than it concealed, condensing as it did the whole of her perilously fashionable past. White the color of the fleur-de-lys and of a young bride's complexion. White the color of a corset's whalebone stays. White the color of costume parties and sleigh rides in the snow. White the color of a powdered head, coiffed by Bertin and Léonard— or by the mob. White the color of a muslin *gaulle,* imported or otherwise: pretty at Trianon, perverse in Paris. White the color of Boehmer's diamond necklace and of "Austrian" ostrich feathers. White the color of the monarchist cockade that launched the march on Versailles. White the color of the Princesse de Lamballe's skin and hair, mirror images of Marie Antoinette's own, and fatally sullied for her sake. White the color of true-blue loyalist emblems. White the simultaneous coexistence of all colors: revolutionary blue and red, royalist violet and green. White the color of the locks that she saw the executioner slip into his pocket as he sheared her head to prepare her for her fate.[13] White the color of martyrdom, of holy heaven, of eternal life. White the color of a ghost too beautiful, or at least too willful, to die. White the color of the pages on which her story has been—and will be—written. Again and again and again.

FASHION VICTIM

I have seen everything, known everything, forgotten everything.
—Marie Antoinette, on the bloody events of October 1789

Louis XIV, who knew what he was talking about, once dubbed fashion "the mirror of history."[1] But so often nowadays, those of us who care about fashion track its never-ending variations through a glass, darkly. For a week, a month, a year, we recall the discreet charms of the trench coat or the ballerina flat, the sailor pant or the Kelly bag, only to lose sight of them as soon as other, "newer" looks start crowding them from view. Pantsuits and pencil skirts hang neglected in our closets' darkest corners until a designer's ingenious reinterpretation or a glossy magazine spread prompts us to reach for them once again. Season after season, we edit our clothing history in order to rewrite it anew. Selective memory is the handmaiden of fashion.[2]

In late December 2005, this fact impressed itself upon me in a curious way when I took a break from working on this book to do some Christmas shopping at Barneys New York. The department store's seasonal motto, emblazoned on each of the four giant plateglass windows that flank its Madison Avenue entrance, was "Have a Royal Christmas": a call to retail indulgence underscored by four elaborate and enticing window displays. Already, as I approached one of the displays for a better look, the hordes of window shoppers it had attracted put me in mind of Rose Bertin, the Grand Mogol, and the mad acquisitive frenzy that her innovative, glassed-in tableaux famously unleashed in the rue Saint-Honoré. Yet even in my quasi-delusional state—for I had reached the point in my research where my protagonists haunted me night and day—I had no reason to believe that once I made my way through the crowds to view the display at closer range, I would find myself face-to-face with Marie Antoinette.

But so I did. Or rather, I found myself staring at one black-and-white, close-up image of her face, cropped from an eighteenth-century portrait, reproduced ad infinitum, and arranged into wallpaper covering the display's backdrop and floor. On the side walls, the same Warholian technique had been applied to the cover of a box of cake mix—Duncan Hines Classic Yellow—to underscore the inevitable "Let Them Eat Cake!" spray-painted near the glass and behind the display's central figure. And that central figure was a female mannequin with a powder-gray *pouf* so enormous that it had been made to look as though it were breaking through the ceiling overhead. The rest of the outfit consisted in a frilled white linen blouse, a fitted dove-gray jacket, and, draped over twelve-foot-wide *paniers*, a billowing skirt of transparent black gauze. Beneath the skirt, movie-marquee bulbs flashed in wild, syncopated rhythms, as if a thousand unseen paparazzi were lurking somewhere in the shadows, snapping picture after picture of the big star in the giant dress. As for the star's identity, a note pinned to a freestanding, flower-studded wig near her right foot told me what I—and, doubtless, my dozens of companions in gawking—already knew: "Marie Antoinette would like to thank Olivier Theyskens of Rochas for the beautiful frock."

Initially failing to notice the small wooden guillotine that hung, swathed in tattered white netting, from the ceiling, next to a crazy chandelier festooned with metal whisks and wooden spoons, I stood at the window transfixed, hopelessly enthralled. Worthy heirs to the ingenious Rose Bertin, the creators of both the display (Simon Doonan) and the outfit (Olivier Theyskens) had all at once made me desperate to have a royal Christmas, to deck myself out like a movie-star queen. I wanted the dove-gray jacket. I wanted the frilly white blouse. I even wanted the Duncan Hines cake mix, not to mention the kitchen-appliance chandelier. Like an adult Alice in Wonderland with a (Kelly) bag full of credit cards, I had tumbled headfirst into fashion's funhouse mirror. I had remembered Marie Antoinette—only to forget her.

I had forgotten Marie Antoinette in the sense that during her lifetime, her clothing assumed a tremendous political significance that has all but disappeared from our present-day variations on her stylish myth, and which was certainly absent from the shallow, consumerist cravings that beset me until I thought harder about what the Barneys window had actually put on display. When I first began working on this book, I envisioned locating the French queen in a longer genealogy of prominent women who were recognized and evaluated more for how they dressed than for what they "did." The nineteenth-century French empresses Joséphine and Eugénie sprang readily to mind; so did the twentieth century's two most celebrated style icons, Jacqueline Kennedy Onassis and Diana, Princess of Wales. And without a doubt, there are striking parallels between these women's lives and Marie Antoinette's. For all of them, of course, were thrust by marriage into the harsh glare of an unrelenting media spotlight, where fashion entered power-fully into the equation as they negotiated their difficult, often conflicting du-ties as wives and mothers, public figures and private citizens.[3]

As I delved deeper into my subject, though, I became acutely aware that for Marie Antoinette, this negotiation occurred differently than it did for her successors on fashion's throne. Why? Because she alone lived and died in a milieu where, as the historian and biographer Horace de Viel-Castel has ob-served, "the crime of *lèse-costume* was expiated on the scaffold."[4] What was more, this was a circumstance that Marie Antoinette herself colluded in bringing about. Unlike an Eugénie or a Jackie, but quite like her ancestor the Sun King, Marie Antoinette helped invent fashion as a high-stakes political game—one that she played in dead earnest, and with deadly results. A winner-take-all affair, her program of singular sartorial defiance implicated not just her autonomy and her prestige, but her crown and, eventually, her life. Her clothing expressed the battles she waged at a time of the most ex-treme societal unrest, and at the highest echelons of both royal and revolu-tionary government. A mirror of history indeed, and it engulfed Marie Antoinette completely within its frame, like the reflecting pond that captured mythology's luckless, self-loving Narcissus. The politics of costume held her—far more than any of history's subsequent fashion queens—quite firmly by the throat.

This, then, is what I momentarily lost sight of while mesmerized by the Doonan/Theyskens tableau, and what the presence of the tiny guillotine near the mannequin's head, along with a more thoughtful look at her outfit's telling colors, soon prompted me to recall. Yet I am tempted to suggest that it was precisely in forgetting Marie Antoinette that I began to remember her again. After all, from start to finish, a dynamic interplay between remem-brance and oblivion informed her own adventures in fashion. Upon first reaching the border between her mother's and her future husband's domains, she was stripped of her "Austrian" clothes, themselves expressly commis-sioned as reminders of her Frenchness, in order to obfuscate her true na-tional origins. She recalled her great forebear Louis XIV by dressing and riding like a man, but disavowed her queenly stature by adopting styles ac-cessible to women outside her own, rarefied sphere. At the Paris Opéra and the Petit Trianon, she gleefully checked her august identity at the door, only to reclaim it with a vengeance once her revolutionary foes demanded a more systematic and lasting suspension of royal authority. Even the white gown she wore for her execution simultaneously overwrote and underscored her status as the fallen monarchy's martyr. Time and again, as she dressed for revolution, Marie Antoinette blurred the lines between remembering and forgetting.[5]

In this respect, we might say that she herself established the parameters for the legend that would attach to her name in death—and by which fashion, perhaps more faithfully than any other medium, remembers her still. For if contemporary culture has by and large acknowledged her voguish frivolities only to ignore their underlying political import, some of today's leading clothing designers have, appropriately enough, painted a more nuanced picture. Upon closer examination, for instance, I realized that in creating his Marie Antoinette frock for the Barneys display, Olivier Theyskens combined the manifold delights of her *pouf*'d Parisian style with the sad and somber palette of her prison wardrobe: the gray that masked the dirt, the black that mourned her loss, the white that took her to the scaffold. Like the Galliano dress discussed in the introduction to this book, the Theyskens ensemble thus presented a fashion queen hovering impossibly between defiance and suffering, sublimity and defeat. And Theyskens's is not the only recent confection to evoke the complexity of this unique sartorial narrative. Just last week, a fashion writer for *The New York Times Magazine* observed that the Paris couture's latest collections paid resounding homage to Marie Antoinette, and not merely in "the clouds of tulle and lace and feathers" through which the likes of Chanel and Givenchy masterfully reprised Rose Bertin's lavish, hyperdecorated aesthetic.[6] No. As a pendant to these luscious offerings, John Galliano again brought to light the darker facets of the doomed consort's life of style. In so doing, the designer conjured up a world in which even Marie Antoinette's martyrdom looked amazing—and in which, conversely, glamour was inseparable from gore. "Judging from the faux blood-splattered hems and the wild, haunted look in all of the models' eyes," the *Times Magazine* noted admiringly, "the Revolution was in full swing, and the poor Queen had already lost her head."[7]

· NOTES ·

Introduction

1. See Edmund Burke, *Reflections on the Revolution in France,* ed. Conor Cruise
O'Brien (Baltimore: Penguin, 1969 [1790]), 169–170; and Stefan Zweig, *Marie Antoinette: The Portrait of an Average Woman* (New York: Harmony Books, 1984
[1933]). For Zweig, it was paradoxically Marie Antoinette's very "ordinariness"—
manifest in what he presents as her laughably banal love of fashion—that made her a
prerevolutionary icon. "Instead of becoming a great figure for all time," Zweig writes,
"she became the embodiment of her own epoch. Even though she squandered her energies upon trifles, her existence had its peculiar significance, in that it was a fitting expression of and an appropriate close to the eighteenth century" (93). Between Burke
and Zweig, other biographers have likewise elevated Marie Antoinette to the position
of rococo or *ancien régime* icon; in the nineteenth century, for instance, she received
this treatment from the royalists Edmond and Jules de Goncourt, in their effusive, if at
times unself-consciously misogynistic, paean, *Histoire de Marie Antoinette,* preface by
Robert Kopp (Paris: Bourin, 1990 [1858]).

2. References to Marie Antoinette in today's fashion press are too extensive to document here; my favorite example is Marc Jacobs's wry comment about John Galliano's
provocatively insensitive 2000 "Homeless" Collection: "It all sounds very 'let-them-eat
cake' to me," Jacobs told *Women's Wear Daily,* adding darkly: "You know, they cut
off [Marie-Antoinette's] head over that." Popular films include the 1938 Norma
Shearer vehicle, *Marie Antoinette;* Charles Shyer's 2001 production, *The Affair of the
Necklace;* and the upcoming Sofia Coppola film *Marie Antoinette* (2006), based on
Antonia Fraser's splendid biography. Madonna has appropriated Marie Antoinette's
image on at least two well-known occasions: first, in her performance of "Vogue" for
the 1990 MTV Music Awards (where she and her dancers dressed in the costumes and
headdresses of Marie Antoinette and her court), and second, in the promotional materials for her 2004 "Reinvention" tour (in which the pop star wore a corseted eighteenth-
century-style gown by Christian Lacroix, a powdered wig, and a pearl earring said to
have belonged to Marie Antoinette herself). The ad campaign I mention is for the Swiss
watch manufacturer Brequet, which claims to have been "asked in 1783 to make a

watch as a gift for the Queen [Marie Antoinette], probably by a secret admirer," and offers twenty-first-century consumers the opportunity to buy replicas of the vanished timepiece. This advertisement appeared in winter 2005–2006 issues of *The International Herald Tribune* and *Le Figaro*.

3. Dena Goodman (ed.), *Marie Antoinette: Writings on the Body of the Queen* (New York and London: Routledge, 2003), 1.

4. Pierre Saint-Amand, "Terrorizing Marie Antoinette," in Goodman (ed.), 253–272, 271 n. 20. See also Mary Sheriff, "The Portrait of the Queen," in Goodman (ed.), 45–71; and Pierre Saint-Amand, "Adorning Marie Antoinette," in *Eighteenth-Century Life*, vol. 15, no. 3 (November 1991): 19–34—an early, and equally insightful, version of the "Terrorizing" essay.

5. See Chantal Thomas, *The Wicked Queen: The Origins of the Myth of Marie Antoinette*, trans. Julie Rose (New York: Zone Books, 1999), Chapter 2, "Queen of Fashion," 81–104. It is from this source that I have respectfully drawn the title of the current work.

6. Two of the many authors to insist on Marie Antoinette's supposed lack of interest in or aptitude for politics are Stefan Zweig, whose book I cited above, and Munro Price, *The Road from Versailles: Louis XVI, Marie Antoinette, and the Fall of the French Monarchy* (New York: St. Martin's Press, 2002). Price notes that the Queen's "interventions in politics were fitful and short-lived, and thus, though often conducted with great sound and fury, signified nothing. Unlike her mother, Marie Antoinette did not have the stuff of a statesman, because she simply lacked the patience and application to see a policy through from beginning to end. Further, as defining proof that she was no intellectual, she saw politics as a matter of personalities rather than issues" (8–9). Similarly, Zweig asserts that Marie Antoinette "never dreamed of playing such a part as her mother played, of becoming a second Elizabeth of England, a second Catherine of Russia. She lacked energy for so lofty a role, was too slothful, too narrow of outlook. . . . Her wishes were well-nigh exclusively personal" (72). In my view, the latter formulation is interesting above all for its reference to Elizabeth I and Catherine the Great, both of whom used clothing to reflect and enhance their authority. (Catherine's strategic adoption of male equestrian garb is discussed briefly in Chapter 4 of this book; Elizabeth's astute manipulation of apparel is discussed in Carole Levin, *"The Heart and Stomach of a King": Elizabeth I and the Politics of Sex and Power* [Philadelphia: University of Pennsylvania Press, 1994], 33–34, 125; Susan Frye, *Elizabeth I* [New York: Oxford University Press, 1993], 3–4; and Christopher Haigh, *Elizabeth I* [New York: Longman, 1998], 10, 90.) Contrary to Zweig, I believe that Marie Antoinette's loaded costume choices—which, though "personal," had far-reaching political implications and effects—establish some degree of commonality between her and these two other female sovereigns. By the same token, I do not tend to read her sartorial experiments as proof of an aggressive desire to shape French governmental policy as such—a desire attributed to her by some writers, including Paul and Pierrette Girault de Coursac and Simone Bertière. See Paul and Pierrette Girault de Coursac, *Le Secret de la Reine* (Paris: F. X. de Guibert, 1996); and Simone Bertière, *Les Reines de France au temps des Bourbons: Marie Antoinette, l'insoumise* (Paris: Fallois, 2002).

7. Félix Christophe Louis de Montjoie, *Histoire de Marie Antoinette Josèphe Jeanne de Lorraine, Archiduchesse d'Autriche, Reine de France* (Paris: H. L. Perronneau, 1797), 101. Although Montjoie's royalist proclivities are quite apparent in his text, the historian François Macé de Lépinay has insisted on his reliability as a witness. See François Macé de Lépinay, "La Conciergerie," in Jean-Marc Léri and Jean Tulard (eds.), *La Famille royale à Paris: De l'histoire à la légende (Musée Carnavalet 16 octobre 1993–9 janvier 1994)*, 73. Certainly, the publication date of Montjoie's memoirs precludes the facile supposition that they were written at a time when it was

fashionable, even politically expedient, to idealize Marie Antoinette and exaggerate the misdeeds of her revolutionary foes. That time would only come with the Bourbon Restoration of 1815, and as I point out in note 22 below, there are limits even to the proroyalist "idealizations" of Marie Antoinette, especially where her clothing is concerned.

8. First established in Frankish times, and codified during the Middle Ages, Salic Law is discussed in more detail in Chapter 4. For more on the original law, see Katherine Fischer Drew (trans. and ed.), *The Laws of the Salian Franks* (Philadelphia: University of Pennsylvania Press, 1991); and Karl August Eckhardt, *Lex Salica* (Hanover, N.H.: Hahn, 1969). The implications that Salic Law held for female consorts in the early modern period are most extensively treated in Katherine Crawford, *Perilous Performances: Gender and Regency in Early Modern France* (Cambridge, Mass.: Harvard University Press, 2004). The implications of this principle for Marie Antoinette in particular are discussed in Thomas, 162; and Sheriff, "The Portrait of the Queen," in Goodman (ed.), 46–47. Sheriff suggestively refers to this law as "Salic/Phallic Law" because of its codification of female subservience and disenfranchisement.

9. Louis Auguste's reasons for avoiding sex for so long continue to divide biographers and historians, and are discussed at greater length in subsequent chapters.

10. *Correspondance de Marie Antoinette*, 2 vols. (Clermont-Ferrand: Paléo, 2004), I, 205. Here and for all French-language sources cited, translations are, unless otherwise noted, my own.

11. Examined in detail later in this book, the complex, politicized nature of clothing and appearance at the court of Versailles has given rise to many important studies, which include Jean Apostolidès, *Le Roi-machine: Spectacle et politique au temps de Louis XIV* (Paris: Minuit, 1981); Louis Marin, *Le Portrait du roi* (Paris: Minuit, 1981); Norbert Elias, *La Société de cour*, trans. Pierre Kamnitzer and Jean Etoré (Paris: Flammarion, 1985); Peter Burke, *The Fabrication of Louis XIV* (New Haven and London: Yale University Press, 1992); and Philip Mansel, *Dressed to Rule: Royal and Court Costume from Louis XIV to Elizabeth II* (New Haven and London: Yale University Press, 2005).

12. See Mansel, 57.

13. As Chantal Thomas has remarked: "Marie Antoinette . . . was the first Queen of France to break with the tradition of self-effacement to which the wives of Louis XIV or Louis XV had submitted before her. She was the first to lend Versailles her style, to impose her imprint on it, and to promulgate the dictates of fashion. Under Louis XIV or Louis XV, this initiatory role belonged to the King or his favorite" (22). I discuss this point at greater length in Chapter 5.

14. Montjoie, 101.

15. The contrast between Marie Antoinette's and Maria Leczinska's self-presentation, as depicted in various royal portraits, is the principal subject of the excellent Sheriff essay to which I have already referred. See, again, Sheriff, "The Portrait of the Queen," in Goodman (ed.), 45–71.

16. Although it became official republican policy after August 10, 1792, the revolutionaries' impulse toward destruction manifested itself in a less programmatic form as early as 1789, with the (gradual) leveling of the Bastille and the (spontaneous) attack on the Queen's bedroom at Versailles. For more on revolutionary vandalism, see Erika Naginsky, "The Object of Contempt," in Caroline Weber and Howard G. Lay (eds.), *Fragments of Revolution, Yale French Studies*, no. 101 (special issue, 2002): 32–53; and Laura Auricchio, "Portraits of Impropriety: Adélaïde Labille-Guiard and the Careers of Women Artists in Late Eighteenth-Century Paris" (Ph.D. diss., Columbia University, 2000), Chapter 4, "Representing Revolution." On the broader project of symbolically purging France of its monarchical past, see Peter Brooks, "The Opening

of the Depths," in Sandy Petrey (ed.), *The French Revolution: Two Hundred Years of Rethinking* (Lubbock: Texas Tech University Press, 1989), 113–122; Marie-Hélène Huet, *Mourning Glory: The Will of the French Revolution* (Philadelphia: University of Pennsylvania Press, 1997); and Caroline Weber, *Terror and Its Discontents: Suspect Words in Revolutionary France* (Minneapolis: University of Minnesota Press, 2003).

17. Even this enormous collection was incomplete, since the consort usually discarded all but her favorite outfits at the end of each season. Castoffs went to her female attendants, who incorporated them into their own wardrobes, cut them up and employed the fabric for other purposes, or sold them off to used-clothing merchants. On the Queen's dress display at Versailles, see Mansel, 172 n. 97.

18. This account appears in Gustave-Armand-Henry, Comte de Reiset, *Modes et usages au temps de Marie Antoinette: Livre-journal de Madame Éloffe,* 2 vols. (Paris: Firmin-Didot, 1885), II, 245—a work that is above all useful for its reproduction of Marie Antoinette's dress orders from the fashion merchant Madame Éloffe, but that also supplies countless other details pertaining to the Queen's sartorial history. On the historical reliability and value of this work, see Maurice Tourneux, *Marie Antoinette devant l'histoire: essai bibliographique* (Paris: Henri Leclerc, 1901), v–vi. As Tourneux points out, Reiset's study is especially useful because, unlike Marie Antoinette's chief fashion purveyor, Rose Bertin, Madame Éloffe did not destroy her records of the orders the consort had placed with her. (Bertin did this as a self-protective measure during the Reign of Terror, when the revolutionaries sought her accounting books as further evidence of the former queen's objectionable, spendthrift ways.)

19. On the destruction of Marie Antoinette's dresses, both by pillaging revolutionaries and by relic-seeking royalists, see, especially, J. G. Millingen, *Recollections of Republican France from 1790 to 1801* (London: 1848), 120; Émile Langlade, *La Marchande de modes de Marie Antoinette: Rose Bertin* (Paris: Albin Michel, 1911), 226, 255; and Michelle Sapori, *Rose Bertin: Ministre des modes de Marie Antoinette* (Paris: Éditions de l'Institut français de la mode, 2003), 160. On the revolutionary government's appropriation and resale of those clothes of hers that the looters left behind, see Pierre Joseph Alexis Roussel d'Épinal, *Le Château des Tuileries* (Paris: Lerouge, 1802). Although small, perhaps the best collection of vestimentary relics from Marie Antoinette is conserved at the Musée Carnavalet in Paris. This collection includes the shoe Marie Antoinette lost on August 10, 1792, during the storming of the Tuileries.

20. See Antonia Fraser, *Marie Antoinette: The Journey* (New York: Doubleday/Nan A. Talese, 2001), xx. On the same page, Fraser cites a wonderful line from Marie Antoinette's clothes-obsessed nineteenth-century biographers, the brothers Goncourt: "A time from which one does not have a dress sample is a time dead to us, an irrecoverable time."

21. The question of historical "objectivity" and its limits is, of course, deeply complicated and lies beyond the scope of the current project. In my own thinking about this question, however, I have learned much from two thought-provoking essays in a volume coedited by Jonathan Arac and Barbara Johnson, *Consequences of Theory: Selected Papers from the English Institute 1987–88* (Baltimore and London: The Johns Hopkins University Press, 1991). Those essays are Anthony Appiah, "Tolerable Falsehoods: Agency and the Interests of Theory" (63–90), and Lynn Hunt, "History as Gesture, or the Scandal of History" (91–107). Hunt's reading of Friedrich Nietzsche's critique of "objectivity" as "disinterested contemplation" strikes me as particularly fruitful.

22. Conversely, many of the memoirs cited in this work—Madame Campan's foremost among them—were published during the Bourbon Restoration (1815–1830). Because the historical focus of this book does not extend to the Restoration, I do not discuss that period's politics here. However, it is important to note that whether or not

they were writing during the Restoration, royalist authors like Campan, Montjoie, the Comtesse de Boigne, the Marquise de La Tour du Pin, and others seem never to present Marie Antoinette's fashion choices in a particularly flattering light. To the contrary: even as they lament the Queen's demise (and, more to the point, lament the Revolution that occasioned it), these writers tend to complain about her inappropriate and extravagant taste in clothes. These authors, in other words, stand to make no obvious gains from lying about what Marie Antoinette wore; their complaints about her fashions do not serve their larger project of praising her and her martyred family. For this reason, I tend to find these writers' accounts more reliable—when it comes to documenting the Queen's fashion choices—than, for instance, political pamphlets that were published, during her lifetime, by people (aristocratic or bourgeois) with an undisguised interest in discrediting her. One of the most useful overviews I have come across of the relative reliability, and the varying shortcomings, of the different memoirs written by those who knew Marie Antoinette is Emmanuel Bourassin's introduction to the memoirs of the Comte d'Hézècques, a page in the service of Louis XVI. See Félix, Comte d'Hézècques, *Page à la cour de Louis XVI: Mémoires du Comte d'Hézècques,* ed. Emmanuel Bourassin (Paris: Tallandier, 1987 [1804]), ii–xxvi.

23. A similar approach informs Antoine de Baecque's insightful study, *Glory and Terror: Seven Deaths Under the French Revolution,* trans. Charlotte Mandell (New York and London: Routledge, 2001). Like Marie Antoinette's clothes, the Revolution's corpses are no longer available for direct examination, but nevertheless, de Baecque notes, assume a powerful afterlife in print culture.

24. See Lynn Hunt, *The Family Romance of the French Revolution* (Berkeley: University of California Press, 1992), Chapter 3, "The Bad Mother," 89–123; as well as "The Many Bodies of Marie Antoinette," in Goodman (ed.): 117–138, and a chapter bearing the same title in Lynn Hunt (ed.), *Eroticism and the Body Politic* (Baltimore: The Johns Hopkins University Press, 1991): 108–130.

25. Michael Ondaatje, *The Collected Works of Billy the Kid* (New York: W.W. Norton, 1974), 6.

26. Carrolly Erickson, *To the Scaffold: The Life of Marie Antoinette* (New York: William Morrow, 1991), 333.

CHAPTER ONE: PANDORA'S BOX

1. Annunziata Asquith, *Marie Antoinette* (London: Weidenfeld & Nicolson, 1974), 27. Antonia Fraser uses the same figures as Asquith—57 coaches, 376 horses, and 152 dignitaries—but notes that the last of these categories was "swollen to twice that number by doctors, hairdressers and servants including cooks, bakers, blacksmiths and even a dressmaker for running repairs." See Fraser, 41.

2. Although the nickname was not always applied lovingly, it may have originated with Maria Theresa's own statement, uttered two months after her contentious accession to her father's throne, and reminiscent of a famous declaration by Elizabeth I of England: "I am but a poor queen, but I have the heart of a king!" Cited in Victor Lucien Tapié, *L'Europe de Marie Thérèse: du baroque aux lumières* (Paris: 1973), 58–59.

3. As Fraser notes of the new alliance, "if either country was attacked, the other would come to its aid with an army specified to be 24,000 strong" (10).

4. Joseph Weber, *Mémoires de Joseph Weber concernant Marie Antoinette, archiduchesse d'Autriche et reine de France et de Navarre,* ed. MM. Berville and Barrière, 3 vols. (Paris: Baudouin Frères, 1822), I, 16–17.

5. Asquith, 26; Dorothy Moulton Mayer, *Marie Antoinette: The Tragic Queen* (New York: Coward-McCann, 1968), 15.

6. See Henriette-Lucie Séraphin Dillon, Marquise de la Tour du Pin de Gouvernet, *Mémoires: Journal d'une femme de cinquante ans (1778–1815),* ed. Christian de Liedekerke Beaufort (Paris: Mercure de France, 1989 [1907]), 91. The Marquise de La

Tour du Pin's memoirs were first published fifty-four years after their author's death. The editor of the edition cited here suggests that locating the date of the memoirs' composition is difficult, but that they were likely written after 1815 and before the end of the Restoration. See La Tour du Pin, 553 n. 3.

7. On the "absolute reign of French dress" in Austria, Prussia, and Russia in particular, see Michael and Arianne Batterberry, *Mirror Mirror: A Social History of Fashion* (New York: Holt, Rinehart & Winston, 1977), 173–175. As the Batterberrys point out, in Spain, Italy, and the American colonies, the French *habit* was subject to extensive, locally determined modifications. For the simplifications that the *habit* underwent in England at this time, see Aileen Ribeiro, *Dress in Eighteenth-Century Europe: 1715–1789* (New Haven and London: Yale University Press, 2002), 184.

8. Mansel, 26. This campaign would only, however, reach its pinnacle years after Marie Antoinette's departure, when, in 1783, Joseph II tried to ban corsets and hoops altogether. On this point, see Ribeiro, *Dress in Eighteenth-Century Europe,* 184. For more on the general cultural differences between the Austrian and French courts at this time, see Jeroen Duindam, *Vienna and Versailles: The Courts of Europe's Dynastic Rivals 1550–1780* (Cambridge, Eng.: Cambridge University Press, 2003).

9. As Antonia Fraser points out, Marie Antoinette was not even four years old when she was conscripted to sing "a French vaudeville song" at her father's name-day celebration. Public performance was thus a part of her life from a very young age. See Fraser, 19.

10. Ibid, 24.

11. Ibid, 15.

12. As Fraser observes of this portrait, Marie Antoinette "looks much like a doll herself" (16). For more on the distinctions between the *grand habit* and the *robe à la française,* see Ribeiro, *Dress in Eighteenth-Century Europe,* 188–190.

13. Montjoie, 25.

14. More frequently, the dolls were sent to foreign courts unaccompanied by their creators, but with luminaries as exalted as Maria Theresa and the Duc de Choiseul demanding their presence, the purveyors themselves traveled to Vienna to peddle their offerings, along with their dolls. See Erickson, 37.

15. Batterberry, 170. The American colonies were another story entirely; the Batterberrys write that "upon arrival in New England, the Pandoras ran into the Puritan ethic. When the Bay Colony suffered an earthquake, women took it as a sign of 'awful Providence' and generally laid aside the 'hoop petticoats' " they had adapted from the *poupées* (171).

16. Daniel Roche, *The Culture of Clothing: Dress and Fashion in the Ancien Régime,* trans. Jean Birrell (Cambridge, Eng., and New York: Cambridge University Press, 1944), 475. Roche is here alluding in particular to a famous incident in 1712, when a *poupée de mode* received an "inviolable passport" to travel between France and England, despite the fact that the two countries were at war and had imposed strict embargoes on enemy imports. For a discussion of this episode, see Joan Dejean, *The Essence of Style: How the French Invented High Fashion, Fast Food, Chic Cafés, Style, Sophistication, and Glamour!* (New York: Free Press, 2005), 67. For an account of how, similarly, "during the Napoleonic blockade, the combatants arranged for the passage of Big and Little Pandora to London, Rome, and Vienna," see Batterberry, 171. For more on the eighteenth-century fashion doll in general, see André Blum, 77–78; Mansel, 8–10, 165; Madeleine Delpierre, *Dress in France in the Eighteenth Century,* trans. Caroline Beamish (New Haven and London: Yale University Press, 1997), 177; Mila Contini, *Fashion from Ancient Egypt to the Present Day,* with a foreword by Count Emilio Pucci (New York: Crescent Books, 1965), 156–157; and Rose-Marie Fayolle and Renée Davray-Piekolek (eds.), *La Mode en France 1715–1815: de Louis XV à Napoléon Iᵉʳ* (Paris: Bibliothèque des Arts, 1990), 146. Whereas Dejean claims the *poupée de mode* as a seventeenth-century French innovation (Dejean, 63), other scholars have traced its origins to Renaissance Italy: see

Mansel, 165; and Sergio Bertelli, Franco Cardini, and Elvira Garbeo Zorzi, *Italian Renaissance Courts* (New York: Sidgwick and Jackson, 1986), 176. More detail on the eighteenth-century fashion press is provided in Chapters 5 and 7, below.

17. Erickson, 38–39.

18. Pierre Saint-Amand, "Terrorizing Marie Antoinette," in Goodman (ed.), 261.

19. On the political consequences of Louis XV's reputation for debauchery, see, especially, Robert Darnton's groundbreaking research, cited in Chapters 4 and 5, below.

20. Pierre Saint-Amand, "Terrorizing Marie Antoinette," in Goodman (ed.), 261.

21. These comparative clothing statistics are given in Roche, *The Culture of Clothing*, 96–97. The figure of 400,000 livres—spent on the young Maria Antonia's bridal trousseau—appears in Erickson, 38; Fraser, 43; and Mayer, 13–14, among other sources.

22. This metric, first proposed by Jean Sgard at a colloquium in the 1980s, appears in Annemarie Kleinert, "La Mode, miroir de la Révolution française," in Catherine Join-Dieterle and Madeleine Delpierre (eds.), *Modes et Révolutions: Musée de la mode et du costume (8 février–7 mai 1989)* (Paris: Éditions Paris-Musées, 1989), 78; the currency values provided in that article have been adjusted to yield a rough, weighted-average equivalent in 2006 U.S. dollars. But as Aileen Ribeiro, among many others, has noted, it is tremendously difficult to establish monetary values for the early modern period. In her excellent study on eighteenth-century European costume, Ribeiro provides a sense of relative values by referring to the incomes of people in different social classes: the average skilled laborer in France earned roughly 500 livres a year, whereas an exalted nobleman might have an annual income well above 10,000 livres. See Ribeiro, *Dress in Eighteenth-Century Europe*, 293.

23. Jean Chalon, *Chère Marie Antoinette* (Paris: Perrin, 1988), 21; also cited in Pierre Saint-Amand, "Adorning Marie Antoinette," 21.

24. Erickson, 39. The phrase "mountain of curls," coined by an unnamed contemporary, is cited in Marguerite Jallut, *Marie Antoinette et ses peintres* (Paris: A. Noyer, 1955), 10.

25. Madame Campan, *Mémoires de Madame Campan: Première femme de chambre de Marie Antoinette,* ed. Jean Chalon (Paris: Mercure de France, 1988 [1822]), 49, 537. As Emmanuel Bourassin has noted in his preface to the memoirs of the Comte d'Hézècques, Madame Campan's account was discredited for political reasons during the Restoration; for she had (somewhat surprisingly) enjoyed Napoleon's favor during the régime that preceded the Bourbons' return to power in 1815. Yet Bourassin, like Chalon in his own critical introduction, makes a convincing case for the relative reliability and even clearsightedness of the *femme de chambre*'s memoirs, which, as Bourassin notes, "remain a unique and irreplaceable account of both the private and the public life of the last queen of Versailles." See Hézècques, xvi–xvii.

26. Fraser, 37.

27. Sheriff, "Portrait of the Queen," in Goodman (ed.), 53.

28. For more on these three Ducreux paintings, their copies, and their dissemination, see Jallut, 10–13.

29. Testimonies about the elegance of Marie Antoinette's carriage abound, and so are too numerous to list exhaustively here. Three of the better-known contemporary accounts, however, are Campan, 52; Alexandre, Comte de Tilly, *Mémoires du Comte Alexandre de Tilly, pour servir à l'histoire des moeurs de la fin du XVIIIᵉ siècle,* ed. Christian Melchior-Bonnet (Paris: *Mercure de France*, 1986 [1804–1806]), 72; and Élisabeth Vigée-Lebrun, *The Memoirs* of *Élisabeth Vigée-Lebrun,* trans. Siân Evans (Bloomington: Indiana University Press, 1989): "Of all the women in France, she had the most majestic gait, carrying her head so high that it was possible to recognize the sovereign in the middle of a crowded court" (32).

30. Evelyne Lever, *Marie Antoinette: The Last Queen of France,* trans. Catherine Temerson (New York: Farrar, Straus & Giroux, 2000), 17.

31. Asquith, 26.

32. Helen Augusta, Lady Younghusband, *Marie Antoinette: Her Early Youth 1770–1774* (London: Macmillan & Co., 1912), 542.

33. André Castelot, *Marie Antoinette* (Paris: Perrin, 1962), 24; Mayer, 13. NB: Because Castelot published several different books entitled *Marie Antoinette,* I distinguish them in these endnotes by providing the publication date each time I cite any of them.

34. Joan Haslip, *Marie Antoinette* (New York: Weidenfeld & Nicolson, 1987), 16.

35. According to Joseph Weber, Marie Antoinette herself made this observation aloud at the moment when her carriage crossed the border between her mother's territories and Louis XV's; see Joseph Weber, 18. In point of fact, while at Versailles she received visits from two of her brothers and one of her sisters. But after her departure in 1770 she never saw her mother, or her native land, again.

36. The psychic was the famous Abbé Gassner (1727–1779). His prediction is cited in, among other works, Philippe Amiguet (ed.), *Lettres de Louis XV à son petit-fils Ferdinand de Parme* (Paris: B. Grasset, 1938), 92; and Maurice Boutry, *Autour de Marie Antoinette* (Paris: Émile-Paul, 1908), 138.

37. Rudolf Khevenhüller-Metsch and Hans Schlitter (eds.), *Aus der Zeit Maria Theresias: Tagebuch des Fürsten Johann Joseph Khevenhüller-Metsch,* 8 vols. (Vienna: Hozhausen, 1972 [1907–1925]), VII, 18.

38. Joseph Weber, 17.

39. Mops is commonly given as the name of this dog of Marie Antoinette's (see, for instance, Younghusband, 276). And although I read in one source that "mops" was in fact the generic term for pugs at the time, an extensive search through the dictionaries and encyclopedias of eighteenth-century France does not confirm this claim. See http:// humanities.uchicago.edu/orgs/ARTFL.

40. Joseph Weber, 5.

41. Maria Theresa to Marie Antoinette, 21 April 1770, in Marie-Thérèse, Marie Antoinette, and Comte de Mercy-Argenteau, *Correspondance secrète,* ed. Alfred von Arneth and Mathieu Auguste Geoffroy, 3 vols. (Paris: Firmin–Didot Frères, 1875), I, 2. In subsequent endnotes, references to this collection are designated "Arneth and Geoffroy." Because this has, until recently, been the most extensive and widely available of the editions of Marie Antoinette's, Mercy's, and Maria Theresa's three-way correspondence, it is the edition to which I refer wherever possible throughout these notes. Yet as Simone Bertière has pointed out, Arneth and Geoffroy excluded from their volume certain letters pertaining to Marie Antoinette's and her husband's sexual problem (706–707). I cite other editions only when they contain letters that do not appear in Arneth and Geoffroy. Unfortunately, Evelyne Lever's wonderfully comprehensive new edition of Marie Antoinette's correspondence (Paris: Tallandier, 2006) came out after I had already completed work on this manuscript; otherwise, I would have used that as my reference of choice.

42. Arneth and Geoffroy, I, 32.

43. Sheriff, "The Portrait of the Queen," in Goodman (ed.), 49. For more on the link between "elegance" and "force" at the court of Louis XIV, see above all Louis Marin, whom Sheriff herself cites in this connection and whose works are referenced throughout the endnotes to the present work.

44. Sheriff's above-cited essay remains the best meditation I have encountered on the notion that the French consort was supposed to reflect her husband's glory in her very person.

45. Madame de Pompadour herself famously reproached the Prince de Ligne, a

Belgian-born officer who fought for the Austrians and later became attached to the French court, because she and her compatriots had been reduced to "selling off our plate to pay for your war." See Charles-Joseph Lamoral, Prince de Ligne, *Mémoires du Prince de Ligne,* preface by Chantal Thomas (Paris: Mercure de France, 2004 [1809]), 95.

46. The Duchesse de Grammont—not to be confused with her sister-in-law the Comtesse de Grammont, who became a member of Marie Antoinette's retinue—was reportedly also hostile to Du Barry because she, the Duchesse, had herself aimed to become Louis XV's favorite. See Olivier Bernier, *The Eighteenth-Century Woman* (New York: Doubleday, 1981), 86.

47. Étienne-Léon Baron de Lamothe-Langon, *Memoirs of Madame Du Barri* (New York: Stokes & Co., 1930), 55; Madame la Comtesse d'Armaillé, *Marie-Thérèse et Marie Antoinette* (Paris: Didier & Cie., 1870), 126.

48. Louis XV had another unmarried daughter, Louise, a nun in the Convent of the Carmelites at Saint-Denis. Despite her removal from court life, her sisters back home managed on occasion to involve Madame Louise in their machinations against Marie Antoinette. See Edmond and Jules de Goncourt, *Histoire de Marie Antoinette,* 53–55.

49. For a good summary of Choiseul's conflicts with other powerful factions at court, see John Hardman, *Louis XVI* (New Haven: Yale University Press, 1993).

50. As one member of the devout party put it, "God allows this evil [Du Barry] in order to cure a greater evil, . . . [which] is the existence of Monsieur Choiseul." Cited in Bernier, *The Eighteenth-Century Woman,* 89.

51. Erickson, 69; Fraser, 82.

52. One of the King's contemporaries, the Marquis d'Argenson, went so far as to remark that by this time, Louis had earned a new nickname: "Louis the Well-Hated." See the Marquis d'Argenson, *Journal et mémoires du marquis d'Argenson,* ed. E.J.B. Ratherty, 9 vols. (Paris: J. Renouard, 1839), V, 371.

53. Simon Schama, *Citizens: A Chronicle of the French Revolution* (New York: Vintage Books/Random House, 1989), 80. For more detail on the acrimonious relationship between Louis XV and the *parlements,* see also Schama, 103–109.

54. Though this line is frequently misattributed to Louis XV himself, he echoed it in his own famous pronouncement: "Things as they are will stay that way during my lifetime. Afterwards. . . ." Cited in C. A. Sainte-Beuve, *Portraits of the Eighteenth Century, Historic and Literary,* trans. Katherine P. Wormeley, 2 vols. (New York: Ungar, 1964), I, 452; translation modified.

55. Bibliothèque Nationale de France, Département des Estampes: *Portraits de Marie Antoinette, Reine de France,* tome I, vol. 1181, D 205801.

56. Arneth and Geoffroy, I, 84.

57. Younghusband, 17.

58. Zweig, 11; translation modified.

59. This cartoon is reproduced and discussed in Chapter 7, below.

Chapter Two: Stripped

1. Zweig, 11. In fact, Marie Antoinette was by no means the first royal French consort to be handed over in this fashion. In the seventeenth century, Louis XIV's wife was likewise "exchanged" on an island in the Bidaossa River, between France and Spain.

2. Campan, 52.

3. Younghusband, 13.

4. Zweig, 13. That Marie Antoinette managed to hold on to her watch is borne out by the fact that she still had it with her when she was imprisoned during the Revolution. It may be worth noting that André Castelot disputes Campan's and other

biographers' claims that the Dauphine lost everything during the *remise*. Without citing his sources, he intriguingly stipulates that she "was able to keep her little girl's jewelry: necklaces, aigrettes, 'pretensions,' 'dog's earrings,' and a 'diamond beak' for her hair." See Castelot, *Marie Antoinette* (1962), 33.

5. Amiguet (ed.), 136.

6. Ian Dunlop, *Marie Antoinette: A Portrait* (London: Sinclair Stevenson, 1993), 51.

7. Ibid, 47.

8. In this respect, my reading of the *remise* differs from that of Antonia Fraser, who suggests that Marie Antoinette found nothing unusually humiliating about the experience. (See Fraser, 60–61.) This interpretation does not consider the experience in the broader context of European costume history and tradition, in which, as Jean Cuisenier has observed, "the practice of ritualized undressing" consistently functions to express "a sense of condemnation and the imposition of an indignity." From witches in the Middle Ages to women accused of fraternizing with the Nazis at the end of World War II, and, throughout French history, from prisoners being led to the scaffold to officers being stripped of their military honors, punishment involves a preliminary "ritual public denuding" that carries with it "unequivocally" shameful connotations. See Gérard Klopp (ed.), *Mille ans de costume français,* preface by Jean Cuisenier (Thionville: Klopp, 1991), 18. I should also note here that although Marie Antoinette's ritual disrobement is described in virtually every biographical and scholarly account I have read of the *remise,* the biographer Evelyne Lever dismisses it as the product of "some historians' lewd imagination." She does not, however, offer any compelling evidence to support this view. See Lever, *Marie Antoinette: The Last Queen of France,* 18.

9. Henriette-Louise de Waldner de Freudenstein, Baronne d'Oberkirch, *Mémoires de la Baronne d'Oberkirch sur la cour de Louis XVI et la société française avant 1789,* ed. Suzanne Burkard (Paris: Mercure de France, 1970 [1853]), 58. According to Burkard, Oberkirch first wrote her memoirs in 1789, but they were not published until the 1850s: 1852 in English, 1853 in French. It bears noting that the hardcover and the paperback copies of this edition have markedly different pagination; the page references in these notes refer to the paperback.

10. Étienne-Léon, Baron de Lamothe-Langon, *Souvenirs sur Marie-Antoinette et la Cour de Versailles,* ed. L. Mame, 4 vols. (Paris: Bourgogne et Martinet, 1836), II, 87. Scholars as diverse as Élisabeth de Feydeau, John Hardman, and Munro Price have attributed this work to the Comtesse d'Adhémar, a woman in Marie Antoinette's entourage. However, the late Trianon curator Pierre de Nolhac persuasively argues against such an attribution and describes the text instead as a compilation of memoirs produced around the time of the Restoration. See Nolhac, *Autour de la Reine* (Paris: Tallendier, 1929), 51–52. On this point, see also Tourneux, 37.

11. Oberkirch, 57.

12. Cited in Fraser, 51; my revised translation.

13. Cited in Pierre de Nolhac, *La Dauphine Marie Antoinette* (Paris: 1896), 46–47.

14. Delorme, 40.

15. Vigée-Lebrun, 32; Tilly, 72; Lamothe-Langon, *Memoirs of Madame Du Barri,* I, 57; Ligne, 85; Oberkirch, 57. Secondary sources compiling various contemporary accounts of Marie Antoinette's white complexion include Mayer, 19; Fraser, 24, 65; and Christian Melchior-Bonnet in his introduction to the *Mémoires du Comte Alexandre de Tilly,* 20–21.

16. Lever, *Marie Antoinette: The Last Queen of France,* 17.

17. Maurice Boutry, *Le Mariage de Marie Antoinette* (Paris: n.p., 1904), 62.

18. Lamothe-Langon, *Souvenirs sur Marie-Antoinette,* II, 87.

19. Lever, *Marie Antoinette: The Last Queen of France,* 18.

20. Akiko Fukai (ed.), *Fashion from the Eighteenth to the Twentieth Century* (Cologne: Taschen, 2004), 8.

21. Zweig, 13.

22. See also Pierre Saint-Amand, "Adorning Marie Antoinette," 21.

23. Lever, *Marie Antoinette: The Last Queen of France,* 18.

24. Boutry, 165.

25. Johann Wolfgang von Goethe, *Mémoires,* trans. Baronne de Carlowitz, 2 vols. (Paris: Charpentier & Fasquelle, 1855), I, 207.

26. Oberkirch, 58; Younghusband, 14. It bears noting that although the Abbé de Vermond did not find Marie Antoinette an exceptionally gifted or motivated student, she seems to have acquired a more than passing competency in the domain of Greek and Latin mythology. Throughout her life, she peppered her speech with classical allusions—comparing herself and Louis XVI to Venus and Vulcan, a friend's lovely young daughter to a combination of Venus and Diana, and the like. These references, while not exceptional in a person of her background, would seem to disprove Evelyne Lever's sweeping assertion that she "had little knowledge of mythology." See Lever, *Marie Antoinette: The Last Queen of France,* 18. For the classical allusions here mentioned, see *Correspondance de Marie Antoinette,* I, 68–69; and Gabriel de Broglie, *Madame de Genlis* (Paris: Perrin, 1985), 148.

27. Goethe, I, 207–209.

28. Oberkirch, 58.

29. Ibid.

30. Campan, 52; Arthur, Baron Imbert de Saint-Amand, *Marie Antoinette and the Downfall of Royalty,* trans. Elizabeth Gilbert Martin (New York: Charles Scribner's Sons, 1895 [1891]), 213.

31. Zweig, 14.

32. Lamothe-Langon, *Souvenirs sur Marie Antoinette,* II, 87.

33. Delpierre, *Dress in France in the Eighteenth Century,* 60.

34. Arneth and Geoffroy, I, 32.

35. Campan, 53.

36. Zweig, 14.

37. Lamothe-Langon, *Souvenirs sur Marie Antoinette,* II, 88.

38. Armaillé, 91.

39. Oberkirch, 56.

40. Dunlop, 50.

41. Oberkirch, 56.

42. Ibid, 58.

43. Ibid, 57.

44. Unlike the majority of Marie Antoinette's personal items, this fan survived the Revolution. It is on permanent display at the Musée Carnavalet in Paris.

45. Lever, *Marie Antoinette: The Last Queen of France,* 18–19.

46. Jean-François Léonard [Authier, or Autié], *The Souvenirs of Léonard, Hairdresser to Queen Marie Antoinette,* trans. A. Teixeira de Mattos, 2 vols. (London: n.p., 1897), I, 74. According to one early-twentieth-century author, Émile Langlade, Léonard's heirs disputed the authenticity of this text when it was first published in 1838. Unfortunately, Langlade does not provide archival evidence to support this claim, and I have not succeeded in uncovering any such material myself. Furthermore, Langlade concedes that the extraordinary level of detailed "insider" knowledge evinced in the *Souvenirs* suggests a deep, contemporary familiarity with Marie Antoinette and her inner circle, and that at very least the book can be seen as a composite of "all kinds of narratives and memoirs from that time." (See Langlade, 16–17, 89.) It is no doubt for this reason that Langlade himself quotes extensively from the *Souvenirs,* as does Desmond Hosford, who, likewise without archival evidence, calls the text apocryphal, even as he concedes that it "contain[s] a degree of truth supported by other sources." (See Desmond Hosford, "The Queen's Hair: Marie Antoinette, Politics, and DNA," in

Eighteenth-Century Studies, vol. 38, no. 1 [autumn 2004]: 183–200, 187.) Tellingly, moreover, many recent, painstakingly researched biographies (e.g., by Antonia Fraser and Michelle Sapori) cite the *Souvenirs* with no reference at all to its possibly apocryphal status; and, as Emmanuel Bourassin has pointed out, the great Marie Antoinette biographer André Castelot himself lends the text credence (see Hézècques, xxvi). Because this status has not been definitively established, because it so clearly draws on other, important eighteenth-century sources, and because it is so widely referenced in the existing scholarship on Marie Antoinette, I have elected to retain the *Souvenirs* as a source in this work.

47. Cited in Dunlop, 51.

48. Oberkirch, 57.

49. Ibid, 56.

50. Zweig, 15.

51. Dunlop, 50.

52. Oberkirch, 56–57.

53. Mayer, 19; Dunlop, 51.

54. Oberkirch, 58.

55. Frantz Funck-Brentano, *L'Affaire du Collier* (Paris: Hachette, 1903), 11–13.

56. Fraser, 63.

57. Joseph Weber, 20.

58. Ibid.

59. Campan, 54.

60. Haslip, *Marie Antoinette,* 12, 26.

61. Boutry, 170.

62. Arneth and Geoffroy, I, 12. Although Fraser attributes this expression to Maria Theresa (see Fraser, 85), Mercy himself reports it as coming from the lips of Louis XV.

63. Mayer, 22.

64. Marquis de Ségur, *Marie Antoinette* (New York: E. P. Dutton & Co., 1929), 81. Before leaving for France, Marie Antoinette received a portrait of the Dauphin helping to plow a field. But this image—a crowd scene, no less—disguised his less fortunate physical traits and thus bore none of the cruelty of the anonymous courtier's jest. See *Monsieur le Dauphin labourant sous la conduite de son précepteur le Duc de La Vauguyon,* in the Bibliothèque Nationale de France, Département des Estampes; reproduced in André Castelot, *Marie Antoinette* (Paris: Hachette, 1967), 14.

65. Horace Walpole, *Letters of Horace Walpole,* ed. P. Cunninghan, 9 vols. (London, 1891), IV, 414.

66. Campan, 24.

67. Ibid; Fraser, 65.

68. Campan, 29.

69. Dunlop, 18.

70. Bertière, 33.

71. Campan, 24.

72. Lever, *Marie Antoinette: The Last Queen of France,* 22.

73. Campan, 28.

74. Younghusband, 29.

75. Campan, 55.

76. Cited in Auguste Cabanès, *Moeurs intimes du passé,* 11 vols. (Geneva: Farnot, 1976), I, 254.

77. Lever, *Marie Antoinette: The Last Queen of France,* 29.

78. François Bluche, *La Vie quotidienne au temps de Louis XVI* (Paris: Hachette, 1980), 87.

79. Four indispensable studies on this subject are Jean Apostolidès, *Le Roi-machine: Spectacle et politique au temps de Louis XIV* (Paris: Minuit, 1981); Louis Marin, *Le Portrait du roi* (Paris: Minuit, 1981); Norbert Elias, *La Société de cour,* trans. Pierre Kamnitzer and Jean Etoré (Paris: Flammarion, 1985); and Peter Burke, *The Fabrication of Louis XIV* (New Haven and London: Yale University Press, 1992). It is nonetheless important to note, as Elias does, that Louis XIV did not so much invent French court etiquette as consolidate and systematize it (76–77). A more colorful, less analytical account of etiquette under Louis XIV appears in W. H. Lewis, *The Splendid Century* (New York: Sloane, 1953), 54–66.

80. Apostolidès, 46. Or, as Apostolidès says later in the same work: "Those men who had been political actors became spectators of a political performance, devoted to the glory of the King [alone]" (63). For additional, detailed analyses of this complex and important system, see all the four authors cited in note 79, above. See also Voltaire's history of Louis XIV's reign, cited in Chapter 4, below.

81. Olivier Bernier (ed.), *Secrets of Marie Antoinette* (New York: Fromm, 1986), 9–10.

82. Contini, 166.

83. Ibid.

84. Comte de Ségur, *Memoirs and Recollections of Count Ségur* (Boston: Wells & Lilly, 1825), 63.

85. The well-known observation of the seventeenth-century aristocratic French aphorist La Rochefoucauld—"It may be said that the world is made up of appearances"—is especially apposite here, and its political effects have been discussed by a variety of latter-day authors, many of whom I have cited in note 79, above, and of whom I will cite just two more here. The first is Tom Conley, who notes in his foreword to the English translation of Louis Marin that "in the arts of representation are found the real origins and organs of social control." See Thomas Conley, "The King's Effects," in Louis Marin, *The Portrait of the King,* trans. Martha M. Houle (Minneapolis: University of Minnesota Press, 1988), vi. In a related vein, the Batterberrys remark that by so carefully regulating the splendid "clothes of the French courtiers, Louis trapped [his] nobility in an intricate net of financially depleting trivia." See Batterberry, 148.

86. Younghusband, 37.

87. Fraser, 69.

88. Campan, 57.

89. Elizabeth Seymour Percy, Duchess of Northumberland, *The Diaries of a Duchess* (London: Hodder & Stoughton, 1926), n.p.; also cited in Dunlop, 75, and Mayer, 25.

90. Lamothe-Langon, *Souvenirs sur Marie-Antoinette,* 88–89.

91. Campan, 54.

92. Besides Madame Campan, the two eyewitnesses who dwell the most emphatically on the Dauphine's beauty are the Duchess of Northumberland and the Duc de Croÿ. See Northumberland, cited above; and Emmanuel, Duc de Croÿ, *Journal inédit du Duc de Croÿ (1718–1784),* ed. Paul Cottin and Vicomte de Grouchy, 4 vols. (Paris: Flammarion, 1907), II, 396–397. The Duchess of Northumberland's diaries evince no particular political biases that would lead her to exaggerate the bride's attractions, and while Croÿ was an avid monarchist, certain parts of his journal are critical of Marie Antoinette, which in turn suggests that his description of her at the wedding is not inordinately or unjustly flattering.

93. Campan, 54–55; Bertière, 35. Seeing the Dauphine not long after her wedding, Edmund Burke similarly described her as a "delightful vision . . . glittering like the morning star, full of life and splendor." See Burke, 169.

94. The cost of Louis XVI's wedding coat is given in Mansel, 31.

95. John Lough (ed.), *France on the Eve of Revolution: British Travellers' Observations, 1763–1788* (London: Croom Helm, 1987), 263.

96. Zweig, 18.

97. According to the Duc de Croÿ, who pronounced the new *salle de spectacles* "the most beautiful room that had ever been seen in Europe," the renovations cost about 800,000 livres. See Croÿ, II, 398.

98. Madame du Deffand, *Lettres de la Marquise du Deffand à Horace Walpole (1766–1780)*, ed. Mrs. Paget Toynbee, 3 vols. (London: Methuen, 1912), II, 113.

99. Horace Walpole, *Correspondence*, ed. W. S. Lewis (New Haven and London: Yale University Press, 1965), XXXII, 254.

100. Cited in Castelot (1962), 39.

101. Stéphanie Félicité, Comtesse de Genlis, *De l'esprit des étiquettes* (Paris: Mercure de France, 1996), 40.

102. Duindam, 215.

103. Lever, *Marie Antoinette: The Last Queen of France*, 24.

104. Castelot (1962), 56; Kunstler, 27.

105. Mademoiselle de Mirecourt, *L'Autrichienne: Mémoires inédits de Mademoiselle de Mirecourt sur la reine Marie Antoinette* (Paris: Albin Michel, 1966), 28.

106. Zweig, 23–24.

107. Cited in Lever, *Marie Antoinette: The Last Queen of France*, 25.

108. Castelot (1962), 58; Haslip, *Marie Antoinette*, 19; Lever, *Marie Antoinette: The Last Queen of France*, 25. This speculation is further supported by the reported exchange between Louis XV and his grandson during the nuptial feast. Noting how much the Dauphin was eating, the King warned him not to overstuff himself on his wedding night, to which the younger man replied: "But why not? I always sleep better when I have eaten well." Cited in Philippe Delorme, *Marie Antoinette: Épouse de Louis XVI, mère de Louis XVII* (Paris: Pygmalion/Gérard Watelet, 1999), 54—Delorme does not provide reference information for his quotations—and elsewhere.

CHAPTER 3: CORSETED

1. Christopher Hibbert et al., *Versailles* (New York: Newsweek Book Division, 1972), 103.

2. Dunlop, 80. See also Younghusband, who cites Madame du Deffand as saying: "The illuminations, as well as the spectacle of the ball, were of the greatest and most superb magnificence" (55).

3. Louis Petit de Bachaumont, *Mémoires secrets pour servir à l'histoire de la république des lettres en France* (London: Gregg International, 1970), V, 113. In these notes, I have respected the widespread bibliographical convention of identifying Bachaumont as the author of the *Mémoires secrets,* even though, as Jack Censer has recently pointed out, Bachaumont died in 1771, whereas the *Mémoires* continued to appear until 1789. See Jack R. Censer, "Remembering the *Mémoires secrets,*" in *Eighteenth-Century Studies,* vol. 35, no. 1 (winter 2002): 291–295.

4. Kunstler, *La Vie privée de Marie Antoinette,* 27.

5. Goncourt, *Histoire de Marie Antoinette,* 17–18 n. 3.

6. Zweig, 33. See also Croÿ, II, 111.

7. Dunlop, 75.

8. According to Carrolly Erickson, the aging Cardinal de Rohan (not to be confused with Prince Louis de Rohan, who would later become Cardinal) was, upon welcoming the Dauphine onto French soil at Strasbourg, especially impressed with her "unblemished porcelain skin." Cited in Erickson, 45.

9. Mirecourt, 26.

10. Campan, 54.

11. See Tilly, 72; Vigée-Lebrun, 32; Goncourt, *Histoire de Marie Antoinette,* 75; and Reiset, I, 109.

12. Genlis, *De l'esprit des étiquettes,* 26. On the difficulty of walking in female court dress, see also La Tour du Pin, 91.

13. Zweig, 34.

14. Kunstler, *La Vie privée de Marie Antoinette,* 29.

15. Arneth and Geoffroy, I, 10, 14.

16. Ibid, 14.

17. Ibid, 6.

18. Ibid, 88.

19. Ibid, 12.

20. Ibid, 19; Kunstler, *La Vie privée de Marie-Antoinette,* 45.

21. Lever, *Marie Antoinette: The Last Queen of France,* 30.

22. Arneth and Geoffroy, I, 154.

23. Erickson, 57.

24. Jean de La Bruyère, *Les Caractères ou les moeurs de ce siècle,* ed. Robert Garapon, no. 62: "De la Cour" (Paris: Garnier, 1962 [1688]), 241.

25. Thomas, 67.

26. Haslip, *Marie Antoinette,* 26, 29.

27. Erickson, 64–65.

28. Cited in Mayer, 24.

29. Bachaumont, VI, 123.

30. Campan, 55–56.

31. Lever, *Marie Antoinette: The Last Queen of France,* 33–34.

32. Bernier, *The Eighteenth-Century Woman,* 82.

33. Mayer, 31.

34. The Comte d'Espinchal cited in Bernier, *The Eighteenth-Century Woman,* 82.

35. Edmond and Jules de Goncourt, *Les Maîtresses de Louis XV et autres portraits de femmes,* ed. Robert Kopp (Paris: Robert Laffont, 2003), 460; Erickson, 63.

36. For more on this subject, see Robert Darnton's indispensable *The Literary Underground of the Old Régime* (Cambridge, Mass.: Harvard University Press, 1982), 139–146. Pamphlet literature against Du Barry and Marie Antoinette is discussed in greater detail in Chapters 4 and 5, below.

37. Erickson, 67–68; Lever, *Marie Antoinette: The Last Queen of France,* 34.

38. Lever, *Marie Antoinette: The Last Queen of France,* 34.

39. Arneth and Geoffroy, I, 17.

40. Cited in Erickson, 45.

41. Arneth and Geoffroy, I, 31.

42. Étienne-François de Stainville, Duc de Choiseul, *Mémoires,* ed. Jean-Pierre Guicciardi and Philippe Bonnet (Paris: Mercure de France, 1982 [1790]), 191.

43. Campan, 25.

44. Goncourt, *Les Maîtresses de Louis XV,* 436.

45. Cited in Lillian C. Smythe (ed.), *The Guardian of Marie Antoinette: Letters from the Comte de Mercy-Argenteau, Austrian Ambassador to the Court of Versailles, to Marie Thérèse, Empress of Austria (1770–1780),* 2 vols. (New York: Dodd, Mead, 1902), I, 15.

46. See, for instance, the comments of Madame du Deffand in du Deffand, II, 237; and those of the Comtesse de la Marck, sister-in-law to Madame de Noailles, cited in Kunstler, *La Vie privée de Marie Antoinette,* 34.

47. Younghusband, 175; Amiguet (ed.), 161.

48. Georges Girard (ed.), *Correspondance entre Marie-Thérèse et Marie Antoinette* (Paris: Grasset, 1931), 53.

49. Cited in Dunlop, 86.

50. This was the assessment of a medical expert named Van Swieten whom Maria Theresa decided to consult about the Dauphin's "frigidity"; see Fraser, 91.

51. Pierre Griffet, *Mémoires pour servir à l'histoire de Louis Dauphin,* cited in Dunlop, 63.

52. Campan, 38; Haslip, *Marie Antoinette,* 11; Price, 11–12.

53. Campan, 61.

54. *Correspondance de Marie Antoinette,* I, 69.

55. Ligne, 99.

56. Deffand, II, 237.

57. Arneth and Geoffroy, I, 6.

58. Ibid, 157; Girard (ed.), 42.

59. Cited in Dunlop, 86.

60. Lever, *Marie Antoinette: The Last Queen of France,* 90.

61. Cited in Dunlop, 88.

62. Lever, *Marie Antoinette: The Last Queen of France,* 91.

63. Hibbert, 102. See also Charles Kunstler, *La Vie quotidienne sous Louis XVI* (Paris: Hachette, 1950), 171; and Alex Karmel, *Guillotine in the Wings: A New Look at the French Revolution and Its Relevance to America Today* (New York: McGraw-Hill, 1972), 52–53. After relating the young man's incredible capacity for gluttony, Karmel adds: "He ate with such voracity that the naturalist Buffon said the sight reminded him of a monkey in the zoo" (53).

64. Arneth and Geoffroy, I, 25.

65. Ibid, 26.

66. Ibid, 25–26.

67. Ibid, 26.

68. Campan, 61; Kunstler, *La Vie privée de Marie Antoinette,* 28.

69. Kunstler, *La Vie privée de Marie Antoinette,* 28; Mayer, 24.

70. For a complete list of the individuals constituting the Dauphine's household at this time, see Lamothe-Langon, *Souvenirs sur Marie Antoinette,* I, 75–79.

71. Younghusband, 266.

72. Hézècques, 200.

73. Erickson, 59.

74. Ibid, 100.

75. Campan, 90.

76. La Bruyère, *Caractères,* "Du souverain et de la république," 145.

77. Campan, 96. See also Élisabeth Feydeau, *Jean-Louis Fargeon, Marie Antoinette's Perfumer,* trans. Jane Lizzop (Paris: Perrin, 2004), 86–87.

78. This habit was in distinct contrast to the behavior of Bourbon princes themselves: Louis XIV had only bathed twice a year.

79. Maxime de la Rochetière and the Marquis de Beaucourt (eds.), *Lettres de Marie Antoinette,* 2 vols. (Paris: n.p., 1895–1896), I, 8.

80. Cited in Erickson, 79.

81. Arneth and Geoffroy, I, 404.

82. Cited in Younghusband, 176.

83. Cited in Ibid, 178.

84. Léonard, I, 74.

85. André Castelot, *Marie Antoinette d'après des documents inédits* (Paris: Perrin, 1989), 30. See also Delorme, 100.

86. Cited in John E. N. Hearsey, *Marie Antoinette* (New York: E. P. Dutton & Co., 1973), 36.

87. The citation comes from Erickson, 64. For more information on Zamor and his dizzying array of "specially made suits," see Bernier, *The Eighteenth-Century Woman,* 87–88.

88. Erickson, 82.

89. Goncourt, *Les Maîtresses de Louis XV,* 508.

90. Ibid, 509.

91. Bernier, *The Eighteenth-Century Woman,* 86.

92. Lamothe-Langon, *Memoirs of Madame Du Barri,* 58.

93. Arneth and Geoffroy, I, 217–218; also cited in Delorme, 82.

94. Arneth and Geoffroy, I, 36.

95. Ibid, 176.

96. Ibid, 36.

97. Ibid, 3.

98. Cited in Fraser, 77.

99. Pierre de Nolhac, *The Trianon of Marie Antoinette,* trans. F. Mabel Robinson (London: T. F. Unwin, 1925), 151.

100. Léonard, I, 75–76.

101. Arneth and Geoffroy, I, 14–15, 142.

102. See Elias, 144–145.

103. Arneth and Geoffroy, I, 19.

104. Ibid, 17.

105. Ibid, 4.

106. Sainte-Beuve, I, 254.

107. Fraser, 77.

108. Ibid, 75.

109. Campan, 89–90.

110. Ibid, 90.

111. Ibid.

112. Ibid.

113. Arneth and Geoffroy, I, 77–78.

114. Ibid, 27.

115. Adèle d'Osmond, Comtesse de Boigne, *Mémoires de la Comtesse de Boigne, née d'Osmond: récits d'une tante. 1. Du règne de Louis XVI à 1820,* ed. Jean-Claude Berchet (Paris: Mercure de France, 1999 [1907]), 64. According to Berchet, the Comtesse de Boigne began to write her memoirs around 1837, but they were not first published until seventy years after her death (vi).

116. Lever, *Marie Antoinette: The Last Queen of France,* 29.

117. See Edmond and Jules de Goncourt, *La Femme au XVIIIᵉ siècle* (Paris: Flammarion, 1982), 257.

118. For more on the significance of rouge at the court of Versailles, see Thomas, 87–88.

119. Sir Harry Beaumont, *Crito: A Dialogue on Beauty* (1752), cited in Richard Corson, *Fashions in Makeup from Ancient to Modern Times* (London: Peter Owen, 2003 [1972]), 218.

120. Roche, *The Culture of Clothing,* 123.

121. Sixteenth- and seventeenth-century sources cited in Valerie Steele, *The Corset: A Cultural History* (New Haven and London: Yale University Press, 2001), 12.

122. Genlis, 34.

123. La Tour du Pin, 86.

124. Ibid, 87.

125. John Bulwer, *The Artificial Changeling,* cited in Steele, 14.

126. Arneth and Geoffroy, I, 85.

127. Younghusband, 262.

128. Erickson, 73–74.

129. Bachaumont, V, 121–123.

130. Campan, 23.

131. Arneth and Geoffroy, I, 33.
132. Hibbert, 103.
133. Arneth and Geoffroy, I, 33.
134. Younghusband, 262.
135. Roussel d'Épinal, 360–361. Roussel d'Épinal's text, which purports to be a firsthand account, is the most richly detailed description I have found of the condition of the Tuileries after the royals' enforced departure in August 1792. Among other scholars, the historians and curators organizing the 1993 museum exhibition "La Famille royale à Paris," have used it as a valuable and reliable historical source. See especially the various essays in Léri and Tulard [eds.], cited throughout this work, and the scrupulous bibliographical and archival research of Maurice Tourneux that supports this view; see Tourneux, 58–59. For these reasons, I am strongly disinclined to write Roussel's account off as apocryphal or even—given its publication date in 1802— as a piece of mere royalist propaganda.
136. Cited in Younghusband, 283. See also Arneth and Geoffroy, I, 83–84.
137. Arneth and Geoffroy, I, 65.
138. Ibid, 27.
139. Ibid, 49–50.
140. Ibid, 50.
141. Bachaumont, V, 121–123.
142. Arneth and Geoffroy, I, 55–56.
143. Ibid, 85.
144. Campan, 61.
145. Arneth and Geoffroy, I, 83.
146. Kunstler, *La Vie privée de Marie Antoinette*, 33.
147. Arneth and Geoffroy, I, 129.
148. Fraser, 96–97.
149. Arneth and Geoffroy, I, 67.
150. Ibid, 65.
151. Ibid.
152. Ibid, 135.
153. Ibid, 137.
154. Ibid.
155. Ibid, 83–84.
156. Yolande-Gabrielle, Duchesse Jules de Polignac, cited in Goncourt, *Histoire de Marie Antoinette*, 75, as well as in Reiset, I, 109. Marie Antoinette's strikingly regal appearance is also discussed in Vigée-Lebrun, 32; and Tilly, 72.

CHAPTER FOUR: RIDE LIKE A MAN

1. Arneth and Geoffroy, I, 90.
2. Ibid, 91.
3. Ibid.
4. Ibid.
5. Ibid, 127.
6. Bachaumont, VI, 241. On the public perception of Maupeou, in particular, as a dangerous and denatured "species of she-man," rendered effeminate by his many hours in Du Barry's "delicious boudoirs," see Sarah Maza, "The Diamond Necklace Affair Revisited (1786–1786): The Case of the Missing Queen," in Goodman (ed.), 73–97, 78.
7. Bachaumont, V, 257.
8. Jeremy Popkin, "Pamphlet Journalism at the End of the Old Régime," in *Eighteenth-Century Studies* 22 (spring 1982): 351–367. See also Jeremy Popkin and Jack R. Censer (eds.), *Press and Politics in Pre-Revolutionary France* (Berkeley and London: University of California Press, 1987).

9. The publication and circulation of clandestine, politically combustible literature written under the *ancien régime* is a complex, fascinating subject that this book does not purport to address in depth. Pathbreaking works on this topic include Robert Darnton, *The Literary Underground of the Old Régime, The Corpus of Clandestine Literature in France 1769–1789* (New York: W.W. Norton, 1995), and *The Forbidden Best-sellers of Pre-revolutionary France* (New York: W. W. Norton, 1995); Sarah Maza, *Private Lives and Public Affairs: The Causes Célèbres of Pre-revolutionary France* (Berkeley: University of California Press, 1993); and the essays in Popkin and Censer (eds.), cited above.

10. Anonymous, "Les Fastes de Louis XV, de ses ministres, généraux, et autres notables personages de son règne" ("Villefranche: Chez la Veuve Liberté," 1782), xlix.

11. Bachaumont, V, 172.

12. Ibid.

13. Ibid, 173.

14. Léonard, I, 49.

15. Bachaumont, V, 172. See also Goncourt, *Les Maîtresses de Louis XV,* 480.

16. Bachaumont, VI, 13.

17. Léonard I, 49.

18. Arneth and Geoffroy, I, 129.

19. Ibid.

20. Ibid, 136.

21. Ibid.

22. Campan, 61–62.

23. Campan, 62.

24. Arneth and Geoffroy, I, 93.

25. Ibid.

26. Campan, 62.

27. Erickson, 81.

28. Ribeiro, *Dress in Eighteenth-Century Europe,* 45.

29. C. Willett and Phillis Cunnington, *Handbook of English Costume in the Eighteenth Century* (Philadelphia: Dufour, 1957), 305.

30. Ribeiro, *Dress in Eighteenth-Century Europe,* 45, 214.

31. See Leonie Frieda, *Catherine de Medici: Renaissance Queen of France* (New York: Fourth Estate/HarperCollins, 2003), 311–312. However, given Frieda's contention that Catherine de Médicis was also "credited with having brought the side-saddle to France" (50), the bloomers this queen introduced to the French court should not be thought of as enabling or encouraging women to ride astride, as Marie Antoinette did two centuries later.

32. Ribeiro, *Dress in Eighteenth-Century Europe,* 150.

33. Patricia Crown, "Sporting with Clothes: John Collet's Prints in the 1770s," in *Eighteenth-Century Life,* vol. 26, no. 1 (winter 2002): 119–136, p. 126.

34. Crown, 121.

35. Philippe Salvadori, *La Chasse sous l'ancien régime* (Paris: Fayard, 1996), 194–224.

36. Cited in Salvadori, 194.

37. Mansel, 57.

38. *Mémoires de Louis XIV* (Paris: Communication & Tradition, 1995), II, 15; also cited in Elias, 116.

39. An excellent example is the depiction of Louis XIV as a Roman emperor in Charles Perrault's *Festiva ad capita annulumque decursio a rege Ludovico XIV* (1670), which is now in the British Library in London. A longer list of Louis XIV's equestrian representations is provided in note 65, below.

40. François-Marie Arouet Voltaire, *Siècle de Louis XIV,* 2 vols. (Paris: Garnier-Flammarion, 1966), I, 310.

41. See Marin, *Le Portrait du roi*, 19–20; and Roger Chartier, *The Cultural Origins of the French Revolution*, trans. Lydia G. Cochrane (Durham, N.C., and London: Duke University Press, 1991), 133. Whereas Marin focuses principally on the ideological aims of portraiture displayed at the King's court, for the benefit of his nobles, Chartier discusses the formative impact that popularly disseminated images had on the populace as a whole.

42. Mansel, 57.

43. Fournier-Sarlovèze, *Louis-Auguste Brun, peintre de Marie Antoinette* (Paris: Goupil, 1911), 49–50.

44. Ibid, 49.

45. Ibid, 50.

46. John Garbor Palache, *Marie Antoinette, the Player Queen* (New York: Longmans, Green & Co., 1929), 13–14.

47. Bignon, *De l'excellence des roys et du royaume de France* (1610), cited by Sheriff in "The Portrait of the Queen," in Goodman (ed.), 47. See also Guy Coquille, *Institution du droit des François* (1588), which Sheriff cites as well in her excellent overview of the history of Salic Law in France. Additional sources on Salic Law are provided in note 8 to the Introduction.

48. Nicole Pellegrin, *Vêtements de la liberté: abécédaire de pratiques vestimentaires en France de 1780 à 1800* (Aix-en-Provence: Alinéa, 1989), 125. On this subject, see also Crown, 126–127.

49. On female cross-dressing for the purposes of "erotic stimulation," see Rudolf M. Dekker and Lotte C. van de Pol, *The Tradition of Female Transvestism in Early Modern Europe* (New York: St. Martin's Press, 1989), 7–8; as well as Crown, 128–129.

50. Lever, *Marie Antoinette: The Last Queen of France*, 80.

51. Armand-Louis de Gontaut-Biron, Duc de Lauzun, *Mémoires du Duc de Lauzun*, ed. Georges d'Heylli (Paris: Édouard Rouveyre, 1880), 188.

52. Arneth and Geoffroy, I, 104.

53. Cited in Delorme, 65.

54. Arneth and Geoffroy, I, 104.

55. *Correspondance de Marie Antoinette*, II. For a useful discussion of how special and rarefied Marie Antoinette's origins and stature were thought to be, even for a future French queen, see Bertière, 20.

56. Following the theoretical paradigm established by Marjorie Garber in her brilliant work on cross-dressing, one might say that Marie Antoinette dressed like a male ruler in order to *seem* to have (phallic, masculine) powers that she lacked. Such a reading is wholly supported by Marie Antoinette's own later confession to her brother Joseph II that she sought to cultivate "an *appearance* of [political] credit" at court, even though she had none in reality. (This letter is discussed at length in Chapter Five, below.) This "fetishistic" gesture—covering over an originary lack by means of an artificial phallus—becomes even more interesting when one notes that for Freud, the conventional female response to "penis envy" is to have a baby. As I have emphasized throughout this chapter, virtually the only avenue to power available to a French consort was child-bearing. In this sense, Garber's psychoanalytic understanding of cross-dressing is almost uncannily appropriate for Marie Antoinette's situation at Versailles: lacking the standard, compensatory recourse to motherhood, the young dauphine addressed her political vulnerability by endeavoring to *appear* what she was *not*: a powerful man. See Marjorie Garber, *Vested Interests: Cross-Dressing and Cultural Anxiety* (New York: Routledge, 1992), especially Chapter 5, "Fetish Envy," 118–127. I particularly appreciate Garber's reading of a performance in which Madonna, imitating Michael Jackson (the so-called *King* of Pop, I might add), grabbed her crotch: "Squeezing the crotch of her pants became for her, onstage, the moment of the claim to *empowered*

tranvestism, to seem rather than merely to have or to be—*not* (the distinction is important) just a claim to empowered womanhood" (127). In another, more theoretically oriented study, it would be possible, and fascinating, to explore many more of Marie Antoinette's costumes from the point of view of "empowered transvestism": I am thinking in particular of the strikingly phallic hairstyles—*poufs*—which I discuss in more sociocultural terms in Chapter 5.

57. Cited in Asquith, 23. Lafont d'Aussonne corroborates this episode by insisting on Marie Antoinette's "overwhelming respect for the memory of Louis XIV"; see N., Abbé Lafont d'Aussonne, *Memoires secrets et universels des malheurs et de la mort de la reine de France* (Paris: A. Philippe, 1836), 473.

58. Mirecourt, 35.

59. Marin, 7–22.

60. Arneth and Geoffroy, I, 104–105.

61. Ibid, 167. Besides the two equestrian portraits discussed here, I should mention the one painted much later (in 1788) by the Swedish artist Adolf Ulrik von Wertmüller. This work shows a notably stouter and older Marie Antoinette, from the waist up, dressed in a striped gray riding habit; it is now in the collection of the Musée de Versailles et de Trianon.

62. Antonia Fraser suggests that the Krantzinger portrait is the one for which Marie Antoinette first sat during this time (Fraser, 86). However, the art historian Fournier-Sarlovèze and the Versailles museum curator Marguerite Jallut have demonstrated that a first version of the portrait in question was begun by Michel Van Loo, who died before it was finished; then Jean-Étienne Liotard was commissioned for the job. The correspondence of Maria Theresa, her ambassador, and her daughter corroborates Fournier-Sarlovèze's and Jallut's claim, which Mary Sheriff echoes by likewise asserting that the first equestrian portrait Marie Antoinette sat for in France is now lost. See Fournier-Sarlovèze, 52–54; Jallut, 15; and Sheriff in Goodman (ed.), "The Portrait of the Queen," 54.

63. Jallut, 15.

64. For more on this painting, see Jallut, 41; and Fournier-Sarlovèze, 52–54.

65. These portraits are too numerous to catalog here, but some of those that adorned the walls of Versailles—and with which Marie Antoinette would thus have likely been familiar—are: Pierre Mignard, *Louis XIV at Maastricht* (1673) and *Louis XIV Crowned by Victory* (1692); Adam Frans van der Meulen, *Defeat of the Spanish Army Near Bruges Canal, August 31, 1667;* and René Antoine Houasse, *Louis XIV on Horseback* (1679–1690). Also in the collection at Versailles, other representations of the Sun King on horseback include Bernini's famous equestrian statue in the palace gardens; Antoine Coysevox's *Victory of Louis XIV over the Enemies of France,* a stucco relief in the Salon de la Guerre; and the several panels devoted to Louis XIV's military victories in the Gobelins tapestry series, *History of the King* (1665–1680), from the studio of Jean-Baptiste Mozin.

66. Arneth and Geoffroy, I, 166.

67. Léonard, I, 105–106. Simone Bertière cites Marie Antoinette herself as writing jubilantly to her sister about the Comtesse de Provence's "moustache" (144). Unfortunately, however, the letter Bertière quotes is most likely apocryphal, as it appears in Paul Vogt, Comte d'Hunolstein (ed.), *Correspondance inédite de Marie Antoinette* (Paris: E. Dentu, 1864), 28. This is a collection of letters that Maurice Tourneux has convincingly, on the basis of a whole series of mid-nineteenth-century articles by other experts (including Alfred von Arneth), dismissed as a hoax. See Tourneux, 2–4.

68. Delorme, 80.

69. Amiguet (ed.), 178; also cited in Fraser, 96.

70. Delorme, 80.

71. Paul Christoph (ed.), *Maria Theresia und Marie Antoinette: ihr geheimer briefwechsel* (Vienna: Cesam, 1952), 52.

72. Arneth and Geoffroy, I, 165.

73. Hearsey, 26.

74. Cited in Delorme, 85.

75. Hearsey, 27.

76. Arneth and Geoffroy, I, 221.

77. Ibid.

78. Fournier-Sarlovèze, 53.

79. Arneth and Geoffroy, I, 89.

80. Annie Jourdan, *Monuments de la Révolution 1770–1804: Une histoire de représentation* (Paris: Champion, 1997), 51–52. Jourdan does not mention this in her book, but Louis XVI did have himself painted in a heroic equestrian pose many years later, in a portrait by Jean-Baptiste Carteaux (1791), which remains in the collection of the Musée de Versailles et de Trianon. It seems to me significant, though, that Louis XVI only allowed himself to be painted in this way once the Revolution was well under way—and more specifically, in 1791, when he was under pressure to accept a new constitution that curbed his absolutist powers. Like Louis XIV and Louis XV—and Marie Antoinette—before him, Louis XVI resorted to the iconography of equestrian heroism only when his authority was dramatically threatened.

81. Delorme, 91.

82. Fraser, 106.

83. Arneth and Geoffroy, I, 462.

84. Ibid, II, 95.

85. Arthur Baron Imbert de Saint-Amand, *Marie Antoinette and the Fall of the Old Régime,* trans. Thomas Sergeant Perry (New York: Scribners, 1891), 64. Rohan's much quoted observation recalled a similar witticism by Maria Theresa's longtime foe, Frederick II of Prussia, who after colluding with her in Poland's partitioning remarked: "She cried and cried, but she took and took."

86. Haslip, *Marie Antoinette,* 40; Fraser, 143.

87. Lever, *Marie Antoinette: The Last Queen of France,* 44–45.

88. Arneth and Geoffroy, I, 466.

89. Fraser, 105–106. Indeed, according to her admiring biographer Lafont d'Aussonne, she regularly outshone her husband at Versailles as well. See Lafont d'Aussonne: "The whole of [Marie Antoinette's] appearance . . . made such a lively impression on the multitude that people went to Versailles in the sole aim of seeing the Queen—as, under Louis XIV, they had gone there solely to contemplate the King" (149). Needless to say, this formulation is particularly interesting in the context of Marie Antoinette's equestrian posturing *à la Louis XIV,* for it again suggests the degree to which she arrogated to herself her husband's—and her ancestor's—kingly aura.

90. *Le Mercure de France* (July 1773): 184–185.

91. Arneth and Geoffroy, I, 459.

92. On the public perception of Marie Antoinette as the avatar of a golden age, see Campan, 83. The importance that the public, at least judging by the effusive ode cited here, seems to have attached to the princess's "dazzling features" at this time confirms the notion, implicit in her makeover back in Vienna, that how she looked was fundamental to her success. As discussed in Chapter 1, this ideological privileging of female beauty may have been related not only to the French cult of royal appearances in general, but also to Choiseul's supposed expectation that a pretty royal bride would prevent Louis XV's successor from lapsing into gross debauchery. On this point see, again, Pierre Saint-Amand, "Terrorizing Marie Antoinette," in Goodman (ed.), 261.

93. Cited in Régine Pernod and Marie-Véronique Clin, *Joan of Arc: Her Story,* ed.

Bonnie Wheeler and trans. Jeremy du Quesnay Adams (New York: St. Martin's Griffin, 1998), 42.

94. Anonymous, "Louis XVI et Antoinette, traités comme ils le méritent" (Paris: Imprimerie des Amis de la Constitution, 1791), 5–6.

CHAPTER FIVE: THE *POUF* ASCENDANT

1. Lever, *Marie Antoinette: The Last Queen of France*, 74. See also Croÿ, III, 171, where the Duc complains that the cathedral "looked too theatrical, like a *salle de spectacles,* enclosed in the most superb vessel of a Gothic church."

2. Croÿ, III, 181–182.

3. Ibid, 182.

4. Lever, *Marie Antoinette: The Last Queen of France*, 74.

5. Croÿ, III, 178.

6. Castelot (1962), 127.

7. Croÿ, III, 184.

8. Ibid, 185.

9. Campan, 105; Bertière, 199.

10. Croÿ, III, 174. See also Bertière, 198, and Evelyne Lever, *Marie Antoinette: la derniere reine* (Paris: Fayard, 1991), 158. I should specify here that despite its title, this book by Lever is altogether different from her later and longer Marie Antoinette biography, *Marie Antoinette: The Last Queen of France,* which I also cite in these notes.

11. Joseph-Alphonse, Abbé de Véri, *Journal de l'Abbé de Véri,* ed. Baron Jehan de Witte, 2 vols. (Paris: Jules Tallandier, 1928), I, 303; Fraser, 134; and Lafont d'Aussonne, 52.

12. In fact, as Joan Haslip points out, this long gap between Catherine de Médicis's accession and Marie Antoinette's also meant that "there was no law of precedence to prevent [the latter Queen] from being crowned" right alongside her husband. But Maurepas and Turgot, two puissant members of Louis XVI's cabinet, had succeeded in quashing this possibility, thus reducing Marie Antoinette to a mere spectator at her husband's coronation. She was crowned separately, in a small private ceremony, with no other women in attendance. See Haslip, *Marie Antoinette,* 76–77.

13. Croÿ, III, 174.

14. Lamothe-Langon, *Souvenirs sur Marie-Antoinette,* II, 268.

15. Hearsey, 35.

16. Lever, *Marie Antoinette: The Last Queen of France*, 51.

17. As Antonia Fraser notes, the perception was that Marie Antoinette was solely responsible for Aiguillon's dismissal, whereas Louis XVI, too, found the Duc "personally odious" and welcomed the chance to ban him from court. See Fraser, 125.

18. Hardman, *Louis XVI,* 20. Formally speaking, the position of "prime minister" had not existed in France since 1726; but before his exile, Choiseul had unofficially held this title while serving as foreign minister.

19. *Correspondance de Marie Antoinette,* I, 205.

20. Ibid, 204–205.

21. Fraser, 126.

22. On Louis XIV's fondness for costume balls and court masques, see especially Apostolidès, 22, 52.

23. Arneth and Geoffroy, II, 280.

24. Ibid, 295.

25. Ibid.

26. Ibid, 295–296; du Deffand, III, 60.

27. Mayer, 72.

28. Lamothe-Langon, *Souvenirs sur Marie Antoinette,* 570; Ségur, *Mémoires,* I, 41; du Deffand, III, 60 n. 2.

29. Evelyne Lever, *Louis XVI* (Paris: Fayard, 1985), 148.

30. Ségur, *Marie Antoinette,* 87.

31. See Frieda, 57–60.

32. Indeed, according to Evelyne Lever, it was the couple's appearance as Henri IV and Gabrielle d'Estrées that led the public to begin comparing Louis XVI to his grandfather and Marie Antoinette to a royal mistress. Lever, *Louis XVI,* 148.

33. Ségur, *Marie Antoinette,* 88.

34. Mary Frasko, *Daring Do's: A History of Extraordinary Hair* (Paris and New York: Flammarion, 1994), 61.

35. *Correspondance de Marie Antoinette,* I, 205. Marjorie Garber's concept of "empowered transvestism," discussed in Chapter 4, note 56, is of considerable relevance here as well.

36. Arneth and Geoffroy, II, 281; Croÿ, III, 124.

37. Arneth and Geoffroy, II, 355.

38. Campan, 71.

39. Arneth and Geoffroy, II, 281.

40. Ibid, I, 84.

41. du Deffand, III, 60 n. 2. According to the Baron Lamothe-Langon, the fabric merchants of Lyon also protested against the idea of a Renaissance revival in daily court costume, fearing the change would hurt their business. See Lamothe-Langon, *Souvenirs sur Marie Antoinette,* I, 570.

42. Munro Price sets the French capital's population at 700,000 people and declares it second in size only to London, whereas Evelyne Lever cites a figure of 600,000 and deems eighteenth-century Paris the largest city in Europe. See Price, 148; and Lever, *Marie Antoinette: The Last Queen of France,* 43.

43. Louis Sébastien Mercier, "De la cour," in Jean-Claude Bonnet (ed.), *Tableau de Paris,* 2 vols. (Paris: Mercure de France, 1994), II, 953–954. As the Duc de Lévis famously noted, whereas Versailles was once "the theater of magnificence of Louis XIV," under his successors it became "a mere provincial town whither one went reluctantly, and whence one fled as soon as possible." Cited in Pierre de Nolhac, *The Trianon of Marie Antoinette,* trans. F. Mabel Robinson (New York: Brentano, 1909), 168.

44. To some extent, this had also been the case during the Regency, the period of Louis XV's childhood when his older cousin, the Duc d'Orléans, ruled on his behalf. Once Louis XV acceded to the throne, court life again centered at Versailles, but the courtiers, having tasted the pleasures of Parisian life, were loath to give them up altogether, and Marie Antoinette's frequent urban expeditions justified palace aristocrats in following suit.

45. Clare Haru Crowston, "The Queen and Her 'Minister of Fashion': Gender, Credit and Politics in Pre-revolutionary France," in *Gender and History,* vol. 14, no. 1 (April 2002): 92–116, 96; Daniel Roche, *Histoire des choses banales, naissance de la consommation, XVIIe–XVIIIe siècles* (Paris: Fayard, 1997), and *The Culture of Clothing,* 159–162.

46. Crowston, "The Queen and Her 'Minister of Fashion,'" 96.

47. Roche, *Histoire des choses banales,* 232.

48. Françoise Tétart-Vittu, "1780–1804 ou Vingt ans de 'Révolution des têtes françaises,'" in Join-Dieterle and Delpierre (eds.), 47.

49. See "Mode: marchands, marchandes de," in Denis Diderot and Jean Le Rond d'Alembert (eds.), *Encyclopédie, ou dictionnaire raisonné des sciences, des arts et des métiers par une société de gens de lettres* (Lausanne/Berne: Chez les Sociétés Typographiques, 1779), XXII, 18–19.

50. Cited in Daniel Roche, *The Culture of Clothing,* 309; as well as in Crowston, "The Queen and Her 'Minister of Fashion,'" 97. For other, more detailed technical de-

scriptions of the work of the *marchandes de modes,* see Sapori, 28, and Diderot and d'Alembert, cited above.

51. In the eighteenth century, four out of five fashion merchants were women. See Michelle Sapori, *Rose Bertin: Ministre des modes de Marie Antoinette* (Paris: Regard/Institut Français de la Mode, 2003), 292 n. 105. On the legal status of the *marchandes,* before and after they were granted legal separation from the mercers' guild, see Roche, *The Culture of Clothing,* 308.

52. Despite previous uncertainty about her birthdate, often given as 1744, Émile Langlade has convincingly shown that Rose Bertin was born on July 2, 1747. Her legal name was Marie-Jeanne Bertin.

53. According to Michelle Sapori, the boutique's Asian-inspired name may have been modeled on that of a prestigious silk merchant's store, the Grand Turk. See Sapori, 40. It may also be the case, however, that Bertin named her shop in honor of a fashionable London theater troupe, called the "Great Mogul's Company of Comedians." For more on this troupe, see Kathryn Shevelow, *Charlotte: Being a True Account of an Actress's Flamboyant Adventures in Eighteenth-Century London's Wild and Wicked Theatrical World* (New York: Henry Holt, 2005), 14.

54. As Joan Dejean has pointed out, shop windows themselves were a late seventeenth-century innovation that dramatically transformed the experience of shopping and, along with the displays they harbored, "quickly made Paris the fashion capital of the Western world." See Dejean, 12.

55. Oberkirch, 196; Sapori, 37–38.

56. Gisèle d'Assailly, *Les Quinze révolutions de la mode* (Paris: Hachette, 1968), 126–127.

57. Bernier, *The Eighteenth-Century Woman,* 126.

58. Cited in Langlade, 170–171.

59. This headdress came immediately on the heels of Bertin's first *succès de scandale,* the *quès aco,* which drew its name from a satirical pamphlet by Beaumarchais (the title was a Provençal expression meaning, roughly, "What's up?") and featured a trio of high, curling feathers gathered in the shape of a question mark at the back of the wearer's head. In April 1774, the *Mémoires secrets* declared that the newly invented *pouf* was thought "infinitely superior to the *quès aco.*" See Bachaumont, VII, 165.

60. Campan, 88; Mercier, "Marchandes de modes," I, 1481–1483.

61. Madeleine Delpierre, "Rose Bertin, les marchandes de modes et la Révolution," in Join-Dieterle and Delpierre (eds.), 23–24. According to the Marquis de Valfons, there were 250 ways to trim a dress by this time. See Quicherat, 599.

62. Nolhac, *Autour de la Reine,* 10. See also Bachaumont, VII, 165.

63. Olivier Bernier, *Pleasure and Privilege: Life in France, Naples, and America 1770–1790* (New York: Doubleday, 1981), 74.

64. Nolhac, *Autour de la Reine,* 10.

65. Zweig, 96–97.

66. In a recent academic article, the scholar Desmond Hosford has argued that Marie Antoinette's hairdos—like the *poufs* discussed here—were a "site of her attempt to assert personal agency" over and against the strictures that governed her life as Queen. Hosford's thesis thus resembles mine, although his discussion also focuses on how Marie Antoinette's hair, disinterred during the Restoration and later examined for DNA, functioned posthumously "to play a performative dynastic role." See Desmond Hosford, "The Queen's Hair: Marie Antoinette, Politics, and DNA," in *Eighteenth-Century Studies,* vol. 38, no. 1 (autumn 2004): 183–200.

67. Mercier, "La Galerie de Versailles," II, 949. On Mercier's activities as a fashion editor, see Roche, *The Culture of Clothing,* 482.

68. Haslip, *Marie Antoinette,* 57.

69. Croÿ, III, 118.

70. The assertion that Bertin made this headdress and that Marie Antoinette wore it appears in Castelot (1962), 116. This is one of the most richly documented biographies of the Queen, but unfortunately, because several of the identification codes for Castelot's archival sources have been changed since the book's publication, I have been unable to track down the evidence for the claim that Marie Antoinette, with Bertin's help, indeed introduced the *pouf à l'Iphigénie*. Langlade, however, makes the same claim; see Langlade, 38–39, and Métra's *Correspondance secrète* maintains that this coiffure became one of the most sought-after styles in the late spring and early summer of 1774. One detailed description of it appears in André Blum, *Histoire du costume: les modes au XVIIᵉ et au XVIIIᵉ siècle,* introduction by Maurice Leloir (Paris: Hachette, 1928), 79.

71. The intricacies of this quarrel are nicely summarized in Fraser, 112–113.

72. Lever, *Marie Antoinette: The Last Queen of France,* 50.

73. Both Émile Langlade and Evelyne Lever assert that Marie Antoinette was the first to wear this *pouf.* See Langlade, 47, and Lever, *Marie Antoinette: The Last Queen of France,* 70.

74. Haslip, *Marie Antoinette,* 59.

75. A. Varron, *Paris Fashion Artists of the Eighteenth Century,* a special issue of *Ciba Review,* no. 25 (Basel, September 1939): 878–912, 896.

76. Pierre-Victor, Baron de Besenval, *Mémoires sur la Cour de France.* Ed. Ghislain de Diesbach (Paris: Mercure de France, 1987 [1805]), 223. See also Haslip, *Marie Antoinette,* 56; and Fraser, 121.

77. Maxime de la Rochetière cites a poem from this period that captures well early public sentiments toward the *pouf:* "Behold the coiffure of our Queen, whose perfect taste is therein seen, 'twere well her style to imitate, herself in acts both small and great." See La Rochetière, 117.

78. Nolhac, *Autour de la Reine,* 10. According to Émile Langlade, it was Bertin who launched the cornucopia *pouf* trend. See Langlade, 40.

79. Montjoie, 81; Haslip, *Marie Antoinette,* 54.

80. According to Bernier, the more expensive feathers could cost about 240 livres— twice the amount one would pay even if one "wanted to go all out" on a hat from Rose Bertin. See Bernier, *The Eighteenth-Century Woman,* 119.

81. Véri, I, 241.

82. Roche, *The Culture of Clothing,* 477–478.

83. For information on the different kinds of publications that covered fashion during Marie Antoinette's time, see especially André Blum, 23–28; Roche, *The Culture of Clothing;* Annemarie Kleinert, *Die frühen Modejournale in Frankreich: Studien zur Literatur der Mode von den Anfängen bis 1848* (Berlin: Eric Schmidt Verlag, 1980); Kleinert, *Le "Journal des dames et des modes" ou la conquête de l'Europe féminine;* and Caroline Rimbault, "La presse féminine de langue française au 18ᵉ siècle" (Paris: Thèse doct., 1981), 50–78, 250–288. In her study of seventeenth-century "glam" (13), Dejean airily asserts that as early as the 1680s, a French "woman could turn to [the newspaper] *Le Mercure galant* for print coverage, to the [fashion] plates for visual— and *voilà!* She had a fashion magazine!" (69). However, both Annemarie Kleinert (*Le "Journal des dames et des modes,"* 13 n. 8) and Daniel Roche (*The Culture of Clothing,* 479–480) persuasively refute the notion that the early, separate media conflated by Dejean could or did function like the illustrated "fashion press periodicals" that emerged during the latter third of the eighteenth century. Indeed, because the development from fashion plates and almanacs to full-fledged journals occurred later in Marie Antoinette's reign, this important aspect of the French fashion press receives additional treatment in Chapter 7, below.

84. See, for instance, *Galerie des modes et des costumes français, dessinés d'après nature,* 16 vols. (Paris: Chez les Sieurs Esnauts & Rapilly, 1778–1787), II, 1, and VII,

30–31. See also Langlade, 103. For more on the *Galerie des modes,* which was published between 1778 and 1787, usually in portfolios of six engravings at a time, see Stella Blum (ed.), *Eighteenth-Century French Fashions* (New York: Dover Publications, 1982), v.

85. *Nouveau jeu des modes françoises,* coiffure no. 62, in the Bibliothèque Nationale de France, Département des Estampes, Collection: De Vinck no 346, Qb_1778; cote: 80C 103422.

86. Campan, 89.

87. Boigne, 43.

88. Mercier, "On porte ses cheveux," II, 1089–1090; J. Quicherat, *Histoire du costume en France depuis les temps les plus reculés jusqu'à la fin du XVIIIe siècle* (Paris: Hachette, 1875), 513–514; Richard Corson, *Fabulous Hair: The First Five Thousand Years* (London: Peter Owen, 1980 [1965]), 215, 227. Although she surprisingly devotes only one short paragraph to Louis XIV's legendary wigs, Dejean provides a catalog of other fashion items he favored, both as a client and as a formative early patron of the French luxury trades. See Dejean, 1–20, 83–104, 161–176.

89. Corson, *Fabulous Hair,* 215; d'Assailly, 110.

90. Pierre Saint-Amand, "Terrorizing Marie Antoinette," in Goodman (ed.), 262.

91. Oberkirch, 197.

92. Langlade, 183.

93. Léonard, I, 161. The publication history of *Le Journal des dames,* which beginning in 1774 was explicitly "dedicated to the Queen," is treated extensively in Nina Rattner Gelbart, *Feminine and Opposition Journalism in Old Régime France: Le Journal des dames* (Berkeley: University of California Press, 1987); "The *Journal des dames* and Its Female Editors: Politics, Censorship, and Feminism in the Old Régime Press," in Censer and Popkin (eds.), 24–74; and Suzanna van Dijk, *Traces de femmes: Présence féminine dans le journalisme du XVIIIe siècle* (Amsterdam and Maarssen: Holland University Press, 1988), 134–187.

94. Sheriff, "The Portrait of the Queen," in Goodman (ed.), 59.

95. Léonard, I, 89.

96. Ibid, 91.

97. Campan, 89–90. See also Lamothe-Langon, *Souvenirs sur Marie Antoinette,* II, 113–114; and Montjoie, 101.

98. Paul Lesniewicz, *The World of Bonsai* (London: Blanford, 1990), 31; cited in Frasko, 63.

99. Quicherat, 596.

100. Cited in Erickson, 99.

101. Frasko, 55.

102. La Tour du Pin, 90; and Campan, 89. One famous contemporary caricature showing *pouf*'d ladies cramped in a carriage appears in Mary Darly, *Darly's Comic Prints of Characters* (London, 1776), plate 10.

103. Bachaumont, IX, 42–43.

104. See Mary Darly, "The Optic Curls, or the Obliging Head-dress" (1777), reproduced in Frasko, 64. See also Quicherat, 596.

105. Corson, *Fabulous Hair,* 351.

106. Ibid.

107. Goncourt, *La Femme au XVIIIe siècle,* 286.

108. La Rochetière, 116.

109. Campan, 89.

110. Fraser, 134.

111. Saul K. Padover, *The Life and Death of Louis XVI* (New York and London: D. Appleton-Century, 1939), 154.

112. Schama, 84.

113. Abbé Baudeau, "Chronique secrète de Paris sous Louis XVI," in Jules-

Antoine Taschereau (ed.), *Revue retrospective ou bibliothèque historique* (Paris: H. Fournier, 1833–1838). Also cited in Langlade, 51.

114. Cited in Ségur, 93.

115. N. Dupin, "La Dame de Cour, 1776," from Le Père (ed.), *Costumes françois représentans les différens États du Royaume, avec les Habillemens;* reproduced in Ribeiro, *Dress in Eighteenth-Century Europe,* 182.

116. Hector Fleischmann, *Les Pamphlets libertins contre Marie Antoinette, d'après des documents nouveaux et les pamphlets tirés de l'Enfer de la Bibliothèque nationale* (Paris: Publications Modernes, 1911), 59.

117. See Frasko, 72; and Akiko Fukai, "Le vêtement rococo et néoclassique," in Fayolle and Davray-Piekolek (eds.), 109–117 n. 7. For more on the ingredients contained in eighteenth-century French hair pomade, see "Paté de cheveux" and "Perruque," in Diderot and d'Alembert (eds.), *Encyclopédie* (1780), XXIV, 449, 397–420.

118. As Antonia Fraser rightly emphasizes, "Let them eat cake" was a "royal chestnut," with a long and varied history of attributions going back at least as far as Louis XIV's queen, Marie Thérèse, in the seventeenth century. Fraser, 135. Indeed, a journalist for the *Financial Times* recently reminded his readers that "the haughty phrase '*qu'ils mangent de la brioche*' [was] quoted by Rousseau in his *Confessions* when Marie Antoinette was just ten years old." See Peter Aspden, "Gilt Verdict," *Financial Times* (November 26, 2005).

119. Haslip, *Marie Antoinette,* 66; Zweig, 99.

120. Thomas, 83.

121. On this point, see, again, Mary Sheriff, "The Portrait of the Queen," in Goodman (ed.), 59. Speaking of Marie Antoinette's attempt to present herself as "a fashionable woman" and not a consort tied to Versailles, Sheriff notes: "What Marie Antoinette failed to realize . . . was that a queen could not do as she pleased. She was the first subject of the King of France, the model of all others subjected to his power."

122. Jean-Louis Soulavie (l'aîné), *Mémoires historiques et politiques du règne de Louis XVI,* 6 vols. (Paris: Treuttel & Würtz, 1802–1803), II, 75. The virulent anti-Austrianism of Soulavie's memoirs raises obvious questions about his "objectivity" on the subject of Marie Antoinette, but illuminates, precisely, the ways in which xenophobia, misogyny, and political and cultural hostilities informed what her enemies said about her. (For a helpful commentary on Soulavie's anti-Austrian stance, see Hardman, *Louis XVI,* 87–88.)

123. G. Lenôtre [Théodore Gosselin], *Versailles au temps des rois* (Paris: Bernard Grasset, 1934), 230–231.

124. Cited in d'Assailly, 132.

125. Sapori, 87.

126. Ibid.

127. Ibid.

128. Delpierre, "Rose Bertin," 22. Joan Haslip goes so far as to declare that "Madame de Lamballe was chiefly responsible for the Queen's extravagant fashions." See Haslip, *Marie Antoinette,* 87.

129. Marie Antoinette's first *dame d'atours,* the Duchesse de Cossé-Brissac, resigned to protest Lamballe's promotion. Behind only the *dame d'honneur*—after Madame de Noailles's dismissal, this was the Princesse de Chimay—the *dame d'atours* had held the highest rank in the Queen's retinue until Marie Antoinette instated her friend as Surintendante. The Duchesse de Cossé-Brissac was succeeded by the Duchesse de Mailly, who held the post until 1781, when it devolved to the Comtesse d'Ossun.

130. La Rochetière, 140.

131. Campan, 117.

132. Haslip, *Marie Antoinette,* 84.

133. Ibid, 86.

134. Arneth and Geoffroy, II, 453. This anecdote is also reported in Métra, *Correspondance secrète,* 18 vols. (London: John Adamson, 1787–90).

135. According to the *Encyclopédie,* the *marchandes de modes* did traditionally confect "a few particular articles of clothing: the little cape, the *pelisse,* and the court mantilla." See "Modes, marchands & marchandes de," in Diderot and d'Alembert (eds.), *Encyclopédie* (1779) XXII, 18–19. Rose Bertin, however, overstepped these boundaries by helping to create all manner of dresses—from frothy *déshabillés* to elaborate *robes à la française*—for her royal patroness.

136. Augustin Challamel, *The History of Fashion in France, or, the Dress of Women from the Gallo-Roman Period to the Present Time,* trans. Mrs. Cahsel Hoey and John Lillie (London: Sampson Low, Marston, Searle, & Rivington, 1882), 167.

137. Oberkirch, 69; also cited in Challamel, 167–168. See also Mayer, 73.

138. Besenval, 174; also cited in Goncourt, *La Femme au XVIIIe siècle,* 286–287. The *pouf à la puce* appears in the already cited *Nouveau jeu des modes françoises,* coiffure no. 10.

139. Arneth and Geoffroy, II, 293. Indeed, as Madame Campan observed, "only a husband or a mother" was in a position to challenge the Queen's sartorial follies. See Campan, 139.

140. Arneth and Geoffroy, II, 306.

141. Ibid, 307.

142. Ibid, 342.

143. Ibid; also cited in Zweig, 99; Arneth and Geoffroy, II, 306.

144. Mathurin de Lescure (ed.), *Correspondance secrète inédite sur Louis XVI, Marie Antoinette, la cour et la ville de 1777 à 1792* (Paris: Henri Plon, 1866), 61.

145. According to Pierre Mariel, Bertin's prices in 1779 were triple what they had been in 1774. See Pierre Mariel, "Mademoiselle Bertin, fournisseur de la reine" (8 février 1941), 2.

146. Nolhac, *Autour de la reine,* 16.

147. Pierre de Nolhac, "La Garde-robe de Marie Antoinette," in *Le Correspondant* (September 25, 1925): 840–859, 849. On the basis of extensive research, Nolhac, the late curator of the Petit Trianon at Versailles, has proposed that 160,000 livres would have been adequate to cover clothing expenses "normally" expected of a French queen.

148. See Sapori, 78–86.

149. Véri, II, 429 n. 39.

150. Ibid, 431 n. 22; Fraser, 150. Indeed, Madame Éloffe's account books reveal that Adélaïde spent even more than Marie Antoinette on fashions in the period from 1787 to 1792. During this time, in fact, Adélaïde spent more than any of Éloffe's other customers: a total of 76,427 livres in six years. (Over the same period, Marie Antoinette's expenditures ranked second to Adélaïde's and totaled 72,546 livres.) See Reiset, II, 511.

151. Véri, II, 106, 431 n. 22.

152. Fraser, 150. The figure about the gloves is provided in Feydeau, 83.

153. Feydeau, 91.

154. Haslip, *Marie Antoinette,* 87.

155. On Maria Leczinska's lavish—but noncontroversial—clothing expenditures, see Jean-Paul Leclerq, "Sur la garde-robe de Marie Leczinska et de Marie Antoinette," *L'Oeil: Magazine international d'art* (janvier-février 1996): 30–39.

156. Again, see Mansel, 172 n. 97.

157. See Michèle Bimbenet-Privat, "L'Art et le commerce au service de la reine: une mosaïque d'archives," in Yves Carlier et al. (eds.), *Les Atours de la Reine: Centre historique des Archives nationales (26 février–14 mai 2001)* (Paris: RMN, 2001): 5–13, 11; as well as Pierre Saint-Amand, "Adorning Marie Antoinette," 33 n. 7.

158. Cited in Corson, *Fabulous Hair,* 329. It bears noting that Pompadour was not the first royal mistress to set trends in hairdressing at the court of Versailles. As Dejean points out, it was Louis XIV's young paramour the Duchesse de Fontanges who launched the eponymous *fontange* coiffure—"the favorite look of the seventeenth century's final decades" (30). (Like Marie Antoinette's *pouf,* the *fontange* was a towering style that received additional height from fabric and padding.) French royal favorites, then, had a history as taste-makers in hair; in this respect, Marie Antoinette was most definitely stepping outside her own, queenly role.

159. Confirming that Marie Antoinette's fashion excesses led to comparisons between her and Madame Du Barry, Chantal Thomas has noted that Louis XV's last favorite was rumored to have purchased a dress made of solid gold while her lover lay dying, and was attacked in the underground press for "being constantly engaged in dressing up," as the pamphleteer Théveneau de Morande put it. See Thomas, 97–98. Also attesting to the perceived similarity between the two women is the fact that some biographers have conflated their shopping habits. Antonia Fraser, for instance, states that "during the previous reign," Du Barry had spent 100,000 livres on "silks and laces" from Rose Bertin (see Fraser, 149). However, surviving ledgers from Bertin's business prove that the royal favorite only began patronizing the *marchande de modes* in 1778, four years after being exiled from court. See Bibliothèque Nationale de France, Ms. 8157, 8158, and Bibliothèque de Versailles, Ms. 402 (254F).

160. Cited in Ségur, *Marie Antoinette,* 93. To be sure, Provence's jealousy of his sister-in-law's precedence over him may have motivated this remark. Marie Antoinette herself was aware of the rivalry, and, interestingly, was supposed to have said to one of her ladies: "The Comte de Provence accuses me of taking away his credit." See Lamothe-Langon, *Souvenirs sur Marie Antoinette,* II, 18.

161. Bachaumont, VIII, 82.

162. Arneth and Geoffroy, II. In this connection, the Abbé de Véri recorded on March 1, 1775, an interesting story which he admitted to be a fabrication, but which he claimed had been circulating widely in Parisian society, and which captured "the general attitude of the public" toward Marie Antoinette. The story was that "the Queen, seeing a lady dressed less elegantly than the others, teased her about her parsimony, and that this lady replied with impatience: 'Madame, it is not enough for us to buy our own dresses—we are forced to pay for yours as well.'" See Véri, I, 243. The "general attitude of the public" was thus, of course, that the Queen was bleeding the nation dry for her own fashionable amusement.

163. In much the same way, Olivier Bernier has noted, Marie Antoinette infuriated her *dame d'atours* by insisting on ordering her clothes herself from Rose Bertin: traditionally, placing such orders was the privilege of the *dame d'atours* alone. See Bernier, *The Eighteenth-Century Woman,* 122.

164. Véri, I, 303–304; see also Feydeau, 88–89.

165. Mercier, "Marchandes de modes," I, 1481; Zweig, 95. Conversely, André Castelot has pointed out that Bertin could dress Marie Antoinette only in these smaller chambers, since she did not, as a commoner, have Rights of Entry to the Queen's official bedchamber. See Castelot, *Marie Antoinette* (1989), 37.

166. Campan, 88.

167. Similarly, in September 1777, six hundred female hairstylists were admitted to the previously all-male guild of Master Barbers and Wigmakers, on the grounds that "the coiffure of the [female] sex has become so important that we must absolutely multiply the artists who build its gallant edifices" (Bachaumont, X, 213).

168. Sapori, 60–68.

169. André Blum, 23.

170. Cited in Batterberry, 170.

171. Mariel, 2; Mercier, "Marchandes de modes," I, 1482, and "Le Bal de l'Opéra," II, 608; Sapori, 91, 107–108.

172. Abbé Jacques Delille, *De l'imagination* (Paris: Guiget & Michaud, 1806); also cited in Sapori, 53.

173. Oberkirch, 94. In this connection, see also Delpierre, "Rose Bertin," 25, for a citation from an unidentified economist who, in 1775, wondered at how "the immense and costly coiffures that have come into fashion increase considerably our commercial production."

174. Sapori, 51–52. For a more general discussion of how the female fashion merchants came to "invade this male preserve," see Dejean, 42.

175. Oberkirch, 197; Sapori, 41. For more on how Bertin overstepped the bounds of her class, see Sapori, 75–76, and below.

176. Cited in Langlade, 183.

177. Oberkirch, 196. Similar complaints against Bertin appear in Lamothe-Langon, *Souvenirs sur Marie Antoinette,* II, 14–15.

178. For more information on the secondhand-clothing market through which parvenus like Léonard acquired their outfits, see Laurence Fontaine, "The Circulation of Luxury Goods in Eighteenth-Century Paris: Social Redistribution and an Alternative Currency," in Maxine Berg and Elizabeth Eger (eds.), *Luxury in the Eighteenth Century: Debates, Desires, and Delectable Goods* (London: Palgrave Macmillan, 2003), 89–102, 94–97.

179. Zweig, 99; Delorme, 111.

180. Stéphanie Félicité, Comtesse de Genlis, *Mémoires inédits de la Comtesse de Genlis,* 10 vols. (Paris: L'Advocat, 1825), I, 225.

181. Léonard, I, 228.

182. Thomas, 94.

183. Sapori, 135; Métra, VI, 146; Anonymous, "Essai historique sur la vie de Marie Antoinette d'Autriche, reine de France" (Paris: Chez la Montensior, 1789), 66. As Simon Schama notes, this text was "first published in 1781, again in 1783, and then with annual revisions to keep up with events right through to her execution in 1793. Five hundred and thirty-four copies were burned by the public hangman at the Bastille in 1783, but it was still a favorite item of the clandestine book smugglers and widely distributed in Paris." See Schama, 224. Indeed, as Vivian Gruder has noted, copies of the "Essai" were " 'liberated' from the Bastille" after the uprising of July 14, 1789, and so were able to reenter circulation. See Vivian Gruder, "The Question of Marie Antoinette: The Queen and Public Opinion Before the Revolution," in *French History,* vol. 16, no. 3 (September 2002): 269–298, 282. Additional detail on this text's complicated publication history is provided in Tourneux, 44–45.

184. Whereas most scholarship on Marie Antoinette's treatment in the clandestine press focuses on the revolutionary period, Vivian Gruder has done pathbreaking work on the pamphlets that proliferated as early as the mid-1770s, and Jacques Revel on texts that emerged in 1779. See Gruder, 269–298; and Revel, "Marie Antoinette and Her Fictions: The Staging of Hatred," in Bernadette Fort (ed.), *Fictions of the French Revolution* (Evanston, Ill.: Northwestern University Press, 1991), 111–129. The archival evidence presented in these articles serves to modify the commonly held view, advanced by Sarah Maza among others, that "open attacks on the Queen were very rare before the mid-1780s." See Maza, *Private Lives and Public Affairs,* 176.

185. Anonymous, "Essai historique," 66.

186. Ibid.

187. Thomas, 95.

188. For one contemporary account of this battle, see Véri, II, 129–130. The French government had recognized American sovereignty in March 1778 and broken off diplomatic relations with England the following month.

189. Marie Antoinette's famous line about preferring ships to diamonds appears in in Campan, 236. Contemporary depictions of the *Belle Poule* headdress appear in the

Recueil general des costumes et modes contenant les différens habillemens et les coëf-fures les plus élégantes (Paris: Chez Desnos, 1780), 14; and in the Bibliothèque Nationale de France, Département des Estampes, Coll: Qb_1778, cotes 46.B.2139 and 67.A.16387.

190. See Frasko, 68. Indeed, from my own extensive review of the fashion caricatures in the massive collection of the Département des Estampes, at the Bibliothèque Nationale de France, I have concluded that the *Belle Poule* coiffure appears more often in contemporary images than does almost any other headdress made famous by the Queen.

191. Crowston, 109.

192. Auguste-François, Baron de Frénilly, *Mémoires 1768–1828: Souvenirs d'un ultra-royaliste,* ed. Frédéric d'Agay (Paris: Perrin, 1987 [1905]), 60.

193. Mercier, "Marchandes de modes," I, 1481–1482; Campan, 88–89.

194. Bernier, *The Eighteenth-Century Woman,* 126.

195. Crowston, "The Queen and Her 'Minister of Fashion,' " 100–104.

196. Crowston, "The Queen and Her 'Minister of Fashion,' " 97.

197. *Recueil général des costumes,* 24–48.

198. Campan, 89.

199. Mercier, "Marchandes de modes," I, 1482.

200. Ibid, 1483.

201. Cited in Ségur, *Marie Antoinette,* 87–88.

202. Léonard, I, 133.

203. See also Léonard, I, 133: "At that time, no principles in France were defense against the attractions of a new mode [launched by the Queen]." (In this instance, the mode under discussion is a headdress called the *coiffure à la comète,* which reportedly became all the rage after Marie Antoinette wore it to the theater in Paris.)

204. Fraser, 108; Lever, *Marie Antoinette: The Last Queen of France,* 108.

205. Campan, 106.

206. Cited in Delorme, 125; and in Fraser, 156. Along the same lines, Frederick II of Prussia himself received an update in April 1777, stating that "the lack of physical interest that up to now His Most Christian Majesty feels, either for his wife, or for women in general, is undoubtedly the effect of an internal defect, very easy to correct in the doctors' opinion; but the prince has refused treatment, either out of fear of the painful consequences of the operation, or because his temperament does not accept it"; cited without bibliographical information in Antoine de Baecque, *The Body Politic: Corporeal Metaphor in France, 1770–1800,* trans. Charlotte Mandell (Palo Alto, Calif.: Stanford University Press, 1997), 42. Whether or not Louis XVI ever did (or even needed to) undergo surgery for phimosis remains open to debate: some scholars, among them Antonia Fraser and Simone Bertière, maintain that his sexual problems were largely psychological, whereas others, like John Hardman and Alex Karmel, claim that these problems indeed stemmed from a condition that surgery eventually cured. A useful, abbreviated overview of the surgery-versus-psychology debate appears in Price, 12–13. A far less commonly advanced hypothesis is the highly dubious contention of Paul and Pierrette Girault de Coursac that "Marie Antoinette, whose education had made her frigid, barred the door of her bedroom to the young prince," thereby making conjugal relations impossible. See Girault de Coursac, 15.

207. As Mercier pointed out, the Queen did not simply make courtiers' Parisian jaunts fashionable; she made them convenient, by arranging to have street lamps installed all along the roads from the gates of Versailles to the city entrance at Vincennes. See Mercier, "La Galerie de Versailles," II, 950.

208. Cited and discussed in de Baecque, *The Body Politic,* 49.

209. Véri, I, 152.

210. See de Baecque, *The Body Politic,* 47–48.

211. See Gruder, 275–275, on the oft-overlooked financial motivations underlying many of the prerevolutionary pamphlets against the Queen.

212. Cited in Delorme, 125.

213. Challamel, 169–170; Castelot, *Marie Antoinette* (1989), 37. Admittedly, Bertin was not alone in her penchant for suggestive product names; it was shared by her chief rival, a male fashion merchant called Beaulard. But Marie Antoinette's patronage of Beaulard was quite limited—largely, it seems, to placate Bertin, who often refused her services to his customers. On the rivalry between Beaulard and Bertin, see Varron, 899–900. It should also be noted that provocatively named accessories had formed part of French court costume for some time. Under Madame de Pompadour, for instance, *robes à la française* boasted "a pleated lace border artfully called *tâtez-y* [touch here]" and a ribbon "in the middle of the neckline [called] a *parfait contentement* [perfect happiness]." See Contini, 192. And under Louis XIV, female hairdos bore names like "heartbreaker." See Dejean, 30.

214. No copies of this pamphlet's two-thousand-copy print run survive, but it is mentioned widely in contemporary and historical writings about the Queen. For more on the publication, dissemination, and eventual confiscation of this text, see Lafont d'Aussonne, 123–125.

215. Fraser, 152–153.

216. Paul Cornu (ed.), *Galerie des modes et costumes français: 1778–1787*, 4 vols. (Paris: Émile Lévy, 1912), II, plate 93. This reprint does not contain all the images that appeared in the original *Galerie des modes et costumes français*, cited in note 84, above. Because, however, the reprint is more widely available, wherever possible I will refer to it instead of the original, designating the former as Cornu (ed.) and the latter as *Galerie des modes*.

217. Comte de Caraman, *Mémoires* (Paris: Revue de France, 1935), 637.

218. Montjoie, 101. On this subject see also Sapori, 89–90, as well as my discussion of sumptuary laws in Chapter 6.

219. Langlade, 94–102. For more information on the conflation of actresses and prostitutes in the eighteenth-century French cultural imagination, see Léonard Berlanstein, *Daughters of Eve: A Cultural History of French Theater Women from the Old Régime to the Fin-de-Siècle* (Cambridge, Mass.: Harvard University Press, 2001); Jean Duvignaud, *L'Acteur: Esquisse d'une sociologie du comédien* (Paris: Gallimard, 1965), 40; and Béatrice Didier, *Diderot, dramaturge du vivant* (Paris: Presses Universitaires de France, 2001), 16.

220. Anonymous, "Essai historique," 67.

221. Cited in Soulavie, II, 76.

222. Bachaumont, VIII, 149. As Simone Bertière points out, even Marie Antoinette's half-hearted attempt to appease her mother by sending her fashion-plates depicting the latest styles—presumably proof that she, Marie Antoinette, was doing nothing wrong in dressing in such a manner—only met with the Empress's disapproval: "I must admit, I find these French styles extraordinary; I should never have been able to believe that things like this were worn, especially not at court." See Bertière, 242.

223. According to the Baron de Frénilly, only the women at the Opéra balls wore masks; see Frénilly, 41. Other accounts, however, suggest that male guests wore disguises as well; see Philippe de Courcillon, Marquis de Dangeau, *Journal du Marquis de Dangeau, publié en son entier pour la première fois*, ed. MM. Soulié, Dussieux, de Chennevières, Mantz, and de Montaiglon, 19 vols. (Paris: Firmin-Didot, 1854–1860), XVI, 291–292.

224. Richard Semmens, *The bals publics at the Paris Opéra in the Eighteenth Century* (Hillsdale, N.J.: Pendragon Press, 2004), 97–98.

225. Mercier, "Bal de l'Opéra," I, 607; Frénilly, 41.

226. Bernier, *The Eighteenth-Century Woman,* 195. One such *pouf* appears in *Galerie des modes,* II, plate 122.

227. Zweig, 101–102.

228. Ligne, 125; Frénilly, 41; and Campan, 140.

229. Hector Fleischmann, *Les Pamphlets libertins contre Marie Antoinette,* 59–61, and *Les Maîtresses de Marie Antoinette* (Paris: Editions du Bibliophile, n.d.), 51.

230. La Rochetière, 141.

231. Campan, 137.

232. Guimard's highly placed lovers included Jean-Baptiste de La Borde, the Prince of Soubise, and the Bishop of Orléans. In 1789, she married the choreographer Jean-Etienne Despréaux. See C. W. Beaumont, *Three French Dancers of the Eighteenth Century: Camargo, Sallé, Guimard* (London: n.p., 1934).

233. Bachaumont, VI, 237.

234. Similarly, as Elizabeth Colwill has noted, Marie Antoinette's " 'dazzling' patronage of public women such as Mademoiselle Arnould of the Opéra and Mademoiselle de Raucourt of the Comédie Française reciprocally confirmed their (bad) reputations." See Elizabeth Colwill, "Pass as a Woman, Act Like a Man: Marie Antoinette as Tribade in the Pornography of the French Revolution," in Goodman (ed.), 139–169, 149.

235. Anonymous, "Essai historique," 66. During the revolutionary period, another vituperative pamphlet related that "Bertin and Guimard, in presiding over [the Queen's] august *toilette,* have saved prostitutes the trouble of having to hide among honest women," because now all women dressed alike. See Louise de Keralio, "Les Crimes des reines de France" (Paris: Chez Prudhomme, 1791). This text was printed under the name of Keralio's publisher, Louis Prudhomme. On the publication history of "Les Crimes des reines de France," see Hunt, *The Family Romance of the French Revolution,* 109, 110 n. 50.

236. Anonymous, "Memoirs of Marie Antoinette, ci-devant Queen of France" (Paris: n.d. [translated and reprinted in the U.S., 1794]), 22–23.

237. This same observation appears in Frénilly, 60.

CHAPTER SIX: THE SIMPLE LIFE

1. According to Mercy, Marie Antoinette had been hinting heavily for some time about her wish for such a palace.

2. Dunlop, 191.

3. Asquith, 80.

4. Pierre Saint-Amand and Rachel Laurent likewise consider the Petit Trianon as an extension of Marie Antoinette's interest in clothing, though they view it as a symptom of her narcissism and not as an instance of stylistic self-assertion. Saint-Amand notes that "Trianon was like an extension of the Queen's body," where "everything was constructed to reflect [her] image back to her"; while Laurent describes Marie Antoinette as "contaminating architecture with the art of the *toilette* [and] conceiving of the décor as a [personal] adornment." See Pierre Saint-Amand, "Adorning Marie Antoinette," 23–24; Rachel Laurent, "Marie Antoinette: le caprice et le style," in *Art-Presse* (1988): 113.

5. This expression comes from Harry Levin, *The Myth of the Golden Age in the Renaissance* (Bloomington: Indiana University Press, 1969), 59.

6. The subject of Renaissance and seventeenth-century pastoral traditions is too large to treat in a work on Marie Antoinette's clothing. Scholars who have examined these traditions in more detail include Levin, cited above; and Jean-Pierre van Elslande, *L'Imaginaire pastoral du XVIIᵉ siècle: 1600–1650* (Paris: Presses Universitaires de France, 1999).

7. Although I have written extensively on Rousseau elsewhere, I cannot possibly hope to do justice to the complexity of his thought in these necessarily condensed paragraphs. Readers interested in Rousseau's critique of luxury and societal refinement

should look in particular at his *Politics and the Arts: Letter to M. d'Alembert on Theater,* 17–25; his *Discourse on the Sciences and the Arts;* his *Discourse on the Origins of Inequality;* and his *Discourse on Political Economy.* These discourses are reprinted in the second and third volumes of Roger Masters and Christopher Kelly (ed. and trans.), *The Collected Writings of Jean-Jacques Rousseau,* 4 vols. (Hanover, N.H.: University Press of New England for Dartmouth College, 1990–1992).

8. As both Madame Campan and the Prince de Ligne pointed out in their memoirs, Marie Antoinette proudly identified herself as someone who hated reading and literature (see Campan, 128; and Ligne, 265), and it is unknown to what degree she was actually familiar with the work of Rousseau apart from in its bastardized, "fashionable" form as a call to (idealized, romanticized) bucolic simplicity. For an excellent overview of the Rousseauean cult of nature, see Schama, 150–51 and 155–162; and Norman Hampson, *A Cultural History of the Enlightenment* (New York: Pantheon, 1968). Rousseau's rejection of civilization is also discussed in Peter Gay, *The Enlightenment: An Interpretation—The Rise of Modern Paganism* (New York: Knopf, 1966).

9. In 1782, Marie Antoinette even went so far as to make the pilgrimage to Ermenonville, Rousseau's celebrated retreat and burial place—a pilgrimage that, according to the *Mémoires secrets,* was commonly undertaken by people of fashion. See Schama, 156–157.

10. André Castelot, *Marie Antoinette* (Paris: Perrin, 1989), 73.

11. As Élisabeth de Feydeau has noted, the public condemned this theater as "an entire room decorated with precious stones," not knowing that all the trimmings were inexpensive fakes. See Feydeau, 109.

12. Lever, *Marie Antoinette: The Last Queen of France,* 133. For more on the Queen's collection of curiosities, see *Marie Antoinette, Archiduchesse, Dauphine et Reine: Exposition au château de Versailles 16 mai–2 novembre 1955* (Paris: Editions des Musées Nationaux, 1955); and Monika Kopplin (ed.), *Les Laques du Japon: Collections de Marie Antoinette* (Paris: Réunion des Musées Nationaux, 2002).

13. Jean-Jacques Rousseau, *La Nouvelle Héloïse: Julie, or the New Heloise,* trans. Judith H. McDowell (University Park: Pennsylvania State University Press, 1968), 304–305. On the "immediate and overwhelming" success of this novel, see McDowell's introduction, 2.

14. Dunlop, 198. As John Garbor Palache has shown, the Queen was not alone in establishing a "fashionable, informal English garden as described by Rousseau." Many other princely estates boasted the same voguish feature. See John Garbor Palache, *Marie Antoinette, the Player Queen* (New York and London: Longmans, Green & Co., 1929), 73.

15. The Prince de Ligne once remarked that the Petit Trianon, although accessible from Versailles by means of either a long walk or a short ride, felt as though it were one hundred leagues from court—a quite substantial distance by eighteenth-century standards. See Ligne, 98; also cited in Bertière, 326.

16. Asquith, 84.

17. Hearsey, 51.

18. Delorme, 138.

19. Campan, 155.

20. Nicolas de Maistre, *Nicholas de Maistre: Marie Antoinette Archiduchesse d'Autriche, Reine de France,* ed. Paul Del Perugia (Mayenne: Yves Floc'h, 1993 [1793]), 74–75; Nolhac, *The Trianon of Marie Antoinette,* 140.

21. Lever, *Marie Antoinette: The Last Queen of France,* 135.

22. Campan, 122.

23. Bertière, 326.

24. Palache, 78.

25. Because Fersen burned much of his correspondence before he died, it has been impossible for historians to ascertain the precise nature and extent of his involvement with the Queen. Virtually all of her biographers take it for granted that the two were in some kind of a relationship, though the debates rage on—with very little hope of resolution—as to whether or not the relationship involved sex. Two classic books that focus on this issue are: Stanley Loomis, *The Fatal Friendship* (New York: Doubleday, 1972); and Evelyn Farr, *Marie Antoinette and Count Fersen* (London and Chester Springs, Pa.: Peter Owen, 1995). A short but excellent overview of Marie Antoinette's and Fersen's relationship—including all the historical difficulties in establishing when, or even if, the relationship became sexual—can be found in Fraser, 203–204.

26. The sole exception to this charge was the Princesse de Lamballe who, although foreign-born, had become a princess of the blood by marriage and had in fact maintained this status after her husband's death by refusing to remarry and by devoting herself to her rich and respected father-in-law, the Duc de Penthièvre.

27. Palache, 78.

28. Castelot, *Marie Antoinette* (1967), 106.

29. Palache, 75.

30. For more on the Queen's private theatricals, see Nolhac, *The Trianon of Marie Antoinette*, 189–199. As Nolhac points out in the same book, the Trianon library's collections were weighted heavily toward works of drama. This was perhaps not an accident, as Marie Antoinette's librarian, Monsieur Campan, was sometimes invited to participate in her troupe's performances.

31. Campan, 69; on the costumes designed for Marie Antoinette's theatricals, see especially André Blum, 136.

32. Campan, 191; Castelot, *Marie Antoinette* (1967), 103–104; Nolhac, *The Trianon of Marie Antoinette*, 191–192.

33. Campan, 225.

34. Dunlop, 208.

35. Campan, 201.

36. Imbert de Saint-Amand, *Marie Antoinette and the Downfall of Royalty*, 67.

37. Castelot, *Marie Antoinette* (1989), 73.

38. Campan, 102.

39. Ibid.

40. Thomas E. Kaiser, "Ambiguous Identities: Marie Antoinette and the House of Lorraine from the Affair of the Minuet to Lambesc's College," in Goodman (ed.), 171–198, 173.

41. Campan, 104.

42. Kaiser, "Ambiguous Identities," in Goodman (ed.), 177.

43. Castelot, *Marie Antoinette* (1989), 31; Ribeiro, *Dress in Eighteenth-Century Europe*, 228.

44. Campan, 152; Quicherat, 604–605. Years later, Félix de Montjoie would look back on Joseph II's visit to France as the thin end of the wedge, blaming the Emperor for a degradation of royal etiquette and stature more generally attributed to Marie Antoinette. Montjoie wrote that Joseph II "forgot his rank and his dignity, and took care to eradicate from his person all that could have drawn the respect of the masses. Thus, by an almost inconceivable fatality, those very [rulers] who should have shown themselves to the people as nothing short of gods, took it upon themselves to prove that they were no greater than the lowliest of men." See Montjoie, 131.

45. Campan, 152; Feydeau, 77.

46. Fraser, 220.

47. Joseph II had also made the trip to seek Louis XVI's support for his plan to oppose Frederick II of Prussia in a brewing conflict over the future of Bavaria, but that matter falls outside the scope of this book.

48. Cited in Langlade, 86.

49. On this point, see Delpierre, "Rose Bertin," 25.

50. Bernier, 217–218.

51. Campan, 170–171; Price, 12–13. See also Derek Beales, *Joseph II: In the Shadow of Maria Theresa* (Cambridge, Eng.: Cambridge University Press, 1987), 375 n. 66.

52. Campan, 168. According to Mercy and others, Provence was one of the prime culprits in diffusing this particular rumor. See de Baecque, *The Body Politic,* 47.

53. As Antonia Fraser has pointed out, Maria Theresa required that all firstborn granddaughters be given her name, which "meant that there would in the end be a grand total of six princesses in various countries named Maria Theresa." Fraser, 163.

54. Bachaumont, XIII, 299; Sapori, 1.

55. Bachaumont, XIII, 299; Langlade, 106.

56. Antoine de Baecque has shown that "pamphlets and songs" produced in the wake of these official ceremonies "did not hesitate to turn the official images upside down," transforming the Queen's ostensible triumph into further grounds for complaint among her subjects. For further discussion of these libels, see de Baecque, *The Body Politic,* 49.

57. Campan, 173–174.

58. Palache, 75.

59. de Baecque, *The Body Politic,* 48.

60. Revel, 123.

61. As Pierre Saint-Amand writes in "Terrorizing Marie Antoinette": "The Trianon conveys a sort of libertinage of appearances . . . for example, in its use of . . . mobile mirrors, in the way it constantly transforms space" (262). Mirror-lined boudoirs feature in such classics of eighteenth-century erotic literature as Vivant Denon, *Point de lendemain* (1777), Choderlos de Laclos, *Les Liaisons dangereuses* (1782), and the Marquis de Sade, *La Philosophie dans le boudoir* (c.1793–1794).

62. This notion has become a commonplace in scholarship on Marie Antoinette, thanks above all to the groundbreaking work of Chantal Thomas, Lynn Hunt, and Robert Darnton. Other scholars to analyze the insistently sexualized rhetoric about the Queen include Dena Goodman, Jacques Revel, Elizabeth Colwill, Mary Sheriff, Sarah Maza, and Pierre Saint-Amand. I refer with greater specificity to the work of each of these authors elsewhere in the notes.

63. For a discussion of Fersen's absence from the scandal sheets at this time (by the Revolution, he would appear in them alongside the Queen's other closest male and female companions), see Hearsey, 66.

64. For instance, after Marie Antoinette was seen wearing a feather that the Duc de Lauzun gave her, it was rumored that the two of them were having an affair, and the cocky Lauzun did nothing to dispel the rumor. A greater betrayal occurred when the Queen met with the Baron de Besenval privately to seek his assistance on a conflict between two other gentlemen at court—only to find out that Besenval afterward cast their meeting as a romantic assignation. (He even wrote about it in his memoirs.) On these incidents, see Campan, 144 (Lauzun) and 159–160 (Besenval).

65. Mary Sheriff explains that the Petit Trianon invited accusations of this sort because, although it once bore witness to Louis XV's virile debaucheries, it was "feminized by Marie Antoinette and her female friends. Male sexuality was banished and replaced by an intimacy among women." See Sheriff, "The Portrait of the Queen," 62. Sources documenting these charges of lesbianism are provided in note 71, below.

66. Fleischmann, *Les Pamphlets libertins,* 104; Schama, 225.

67. Arneth and Geoffroy, II, 404.

68. Ligne, 127.

69. Chartres's grudge against the royals had grown even worse after Louis XVI

banished him from court because of his bad behavior in a naval battle. See Fraser, 165–166.

70. Cited in Fleischmann, *Les Pamphlets libertins,* 241–242.

71. Contemporary sources addressing the Queen's supposed lesbianism include Campan, 144–145; Soulvaie, X, 49; Emile Raunié, *Chansonnier historique du XVIIIe siècle* (Paris, 1884), X, 229–237, 287–295; Baudeau, III, 281; and Anonymous, "Portefeuille d'un talon rouge" (Paris: Imprimerie du Comte de Paradès, 178 . . . [*sic*]), reprinted in Fleischmann, *Les Maîtresses de Marie Antoinette,* 201–233. (This list does not include the myriad publications that appeared after the outbreak of the Revolution, when allegations of Marie Antoinette's sexual involvement with women proliferated even more abundantly.) Secondary sources commenting on this phenomenon include: Madelyn Gutwirth, *Twilight of the Goddesses: Women and Representation in the French Revolutionary Era* (New Brunswick, N.J.: Rutgers University Press, 1992), 145–149; Fleischmann, *Les Maîtresses de Marie Antoinette* and *Les Pamphlets libertins contre Marie Antoinette;* Delorme, 136–137; Gruder, 280 n. 37; Thomas, 119–124; Colwill, "Pass as a Woman, Act Like a Man," in Goodman (ed.), 139–170; and the numerous works of Lynn Hunt, cited throughout these notes.

72. In this context, it is perhaps significant that the Abbé Baudeau, cited above, was one of the authors to accuse her of a lesbian relationship with Rose Bertin, for Baudeau was a Physiocrat, concerned with the efficacious marshaling of the kingdom's resources. Considered in terms of procreative payoff, the Queen's "tribadism" would thus perhaps have appeared as wasteful as the flour on her *poufs.*

73. As Elizabeth Colwill has said in more general terms, in the eighteenth century "female same-sex [intercourse] signaled the double transgression of abandoning man and assuming his sexual prerogatives." See Colwill, "Pass as a Woman, Act Like a Man," in Goodman (ed.), 148. In this context, abandoning the King and *his* sexual prerogatives represented a transgression of a particularly heinous order. Or, as Chantal Thomas has put it, "behind the fantasy of a lesbian plot lay the fear that men were losing their grip on the political reins" (121).

74. Anonymous, "Essai historique," 64.

75. See Anonymous, "Portefeuille d'un talon rouge," 206–207. In *Les Pamphlets libertins contre Marie Antoinette,* Fleischmann concludes on the basis of contemporary police records that the police seized and destroyed this text in May 1783, and maintains that it was written sometime between 1780 and 1783. Vivian Gruder suggests that it might have been published in 1781, while Chantal Thomas assigns it a date of 1780; see Fleischmann, *Les Maîtresses de Marie Antoinette,* 308; Gruder, 275; and Thomas, 159 n. 12.

76. Anonymous "Essai historique," 64.

77. Fleischmann underscores the mercenary aspect of the Comtesse Jules de Polignac's relationship with Marie Antoinette in his memorable chapter title on the subject, "Friendship on 50,000 Livres a Year." See Fleischmann, *Les Maîtresses de Marie Antoinette,* 180.

78. Amanda Foreman, *Georgiana, Duchess of Devonshire* (New York: Random House, 1999), 40. Not incidentally, Foreman provides this apt description of eighteenth-century female sentimentality when discussing Marie Antoinette's English friend Georgiana, who, like the French queen, was a supremely fashionable woman in a less than satisfactory marriage. Also like Marie Antoinette, Georgiana had intense female friendships that drew accusations of lesbianism.

79. Boigne, 43.

80. Ibid, 44; Ernest Daudet (ed.), *Dans le palais des rois: récits d'histoire d'après des documents inédits* (Paris: Hachette, 1914), 162. Similarly, Carrolly Erickson writes that "the Swedish uniform of the King's dragoons, with its blue cloak, white tunic, tight chamois breeches, and dashing shako with its blue and yellow plumes, had been spcially designed by King Gustavus III to show off the male figure to the greatest ad-

vantage. When worn by Count Fersen . . . it attracted the attention of every woman in the room, beginning with the Queen" (113).

81. Anonymous, "Les Fureurs utérines de Marie Antoinette" (n.p., [1791]), 6. Although written during the revolutionary period—when, as mentioned above, and as discussed in more detail in Chapter 8, pornographic texts against the Queen proliferated and circulated in larger numbers—the lines cited here refer *back* to Marie Antoinette's prerevolutionary antics at the Petit Trianon.

82. On this point, see especially Rousseau, *Politics and the Arts: Letter to M. d'Alembert on Theater*, 17–25. As Edward Hundert points out, simplicity of dress played a role in Rousseau's own professional notoriety, as the French public "paid considerably less attention to his economic views [which condemned spending on luxury items] than to his rejection of fashionable dress when he adopted the rustic 'Corsican' costume which came to serve as his public emblem." See Edward Hundert, "Mandeville, Rousseau, and the Political Economy of Fantasy," in Berg and Eger (eds.), 28–40, 34.

83. *Correspondance de Marie Antoinette*, I, 164.

84. Lenôtre, 228; *Nouveau jeu des modes françoises*, coiffure no. 52.

85. Métra, I, 158; also cited in Fleischmann, *Les Pamphlets libertins*, 45 n. 2; Mercier, "Parures," I, 398. See also Soulavie on the Queen's "superb coiffures representing English gardens, mountains, parterres, and forests" (II, 75).

86. Popular mythology has since reassigned the singing-bird *pouf* to Marie Antoinette herself; in the 1938 film *Marie Antoinette,* our heroine is shown wearing it at the first of her Versailles costume parties. Interestingly, moreover, this scene follows directly on the heels of a scene in which Marie Antoinette is openly humiliated by the *barrystes,* who send her an empty cradle to mock her barrenness; the abrupt cut between the empty cradle and the extravagant coiffure seems to support the argument I am advancing here, that the Queen turned to fashion as a bold alternative to motherhood.

87. Nolhac, *The Trianon of Marie Antoinette,* 162.

88. *Recueil général des costumes,* 7.

89. Cornu, II, plate 116.

90. Feydeau, 111–112.

91. Ibid, 112.

92. Cornu, II, plate 240; Goncourt, *La Femme au XVIIIᵉ siècle,* 288.

93. A. Étienne Guillaumot, *Costumes du XVIIIᵉ siècle* (Paris: Roquette, 1874), 3, plate 6.

94. Mirecourt, 131.

95. Ibid.

96. Kraatz, "Marie Antoinette: la passion des étoffes," 78.

97. Ibid.

98. *Galerie des modes,* VII, 27.

99. Delpierre, *Dress in France in the Eighteenth Century,* 18. For another good description of the *polonaise*—as well as of the *lévite* and the redingote, described at length below—see T. Anderson Black and Madge Garlan, *A History of Fashion* (New York: William Morrow, 1980), 154–155.

100. Fraser, 177; *Galerie des modes,* VII, 1.

101. Cornu, II, plate 83. According to Cornu, the *lévite* was inspired by the costumes worn by the Jewish priests in a 1780 performance of Jean Racine's play *Athalie,* at the Théâtre Français. (The name *lévite* was meant to evoke a "Semitic" exoticism.) Interestingly enough, this same play was performed during Marie Antoinette's wedding celebrations, and she had found it deathly boring; see Bertière, 41. It was thus the costuming of the more recent production that captured the Queen's, and her followers', attention.

102. Whether Marie Antoinette actually breast-fed her children has remained open to debate, but this advantage of the *lévite* is underlined in Delpierre, *Dress in France in the Eighteenth Century,* 19; and Quicherat, 601.

103. See the Archives Nationales de France, AEI 6 n°2: *Garde-robe des Atours de la Reine, Gazette pour l'année 1782* [referred to hereafter as "the 1782 *gazette des atours*"]. This ledger, which is one of the best surviving sources of information on Marie Antoinette's wardrobe, contains swatches of fabric and short descriptions of dresses purchased for the Queen to wear in 1782. As mentioned earlier, Marie Antoinette referred to this ledger, maintained by her *dame d'atours,* to select her outfits each day. Of the ninety-seven entries in the 1782 *gazette* (for which seventy-eight swatches survive), twenty-one entries designate *lévites* and fourteen *robes turques,* close cousins to the *lévite.*

104. Cornu, II, plate 83.

105. Campan, 188; Fournier-Sarlovèze, 43. Similarly, the Marquis de Bombelles recorded how, as late as 1789, aristocrats in the Parisian salon of the Comtesse de Brionne, who encouraged her guests to trade vicious stories about the Queen, were still complaining about this trend in dress. See Bombelles, II, 276–277.

106. The 1782 *gazette des atours* lists seven redingotes in the Queen's wardrobe, of which five are blue—sky blue; pale robin's-egg blue; and a blue the color of faded denim. The other two are purplish-toned: one mauve, one eggplant. It is likely that her orders for such ensembles only increased after the French and British signed a peace treaty in 1783, for after that, "English" redingotes became more desirable and prevalent than ever.

107. See Jallut, 41.

108. Arneth and Geoffroy, I, 221.

109. Chantal Thomas has identified the prerevolutionary aristocracy's fondness for "glaring color" as a political or politicized bias: "Censure by good taste, by the bourgeoisie, who preferred grey or beige to hot pink and orange, did not exist at that time: aristocratic pride went hand in hand with . . . a conspicuous presence" (88). In this sense, Marie Antoinette's gravitation toward paler hues—which included gray and beige as well as a broad range of pastels—can be understood as yet another move away from the codified ostentation of her class.

110. Thomas, 88. Though she does not discuss the implications of Marie Antoinette's shift in color preferences, Thomas herself poetically describes the Petit Trianon as "a tiny oasis of sweetness and light, . . . a refuge in white linen and pastel greys." See Thomas, 62. I should note, however, that Marie Antoinette was not the first French trendsetter to flirt with lowlier fabrics: as Joan Dejean points out, the late seventeenth century saw a boom in "hot fabrics" other than silks, such as "an inexpensive, grey serge cloth known as *grisette,* [which in 1677] was the talk of the town." Although she does not cite specific examples of *grisette*—until then associated with lowly shopgirls—being worn at the French court, Dejean implies as much when she notes that it was "as if denim had been used to fashion a ball gown for a fête at Versailles." See Dejean, 52. Still, as the costume historians Michael and Ariane Batterberry observe, "courtiers clung stubbornly to silk clothing" throughout the reigns of Louis XIV and Louis XV. See Batterberry, 130.

111. Even the Queen's riding gloves—though still luxuriously embalmed "between two beds of fresh flowers for eight days before wearing"—were now made from pale, unobtrusive-colored skins that contributed to their functional, understated air. See Feydeau, 82.

112. Again, the 1782 *gazette des atours* provides the most insight into what patterns and colors the Queen preferred at this time. For detailed studies of this *gazette*— and of the sea change in fashion that it documents—see Nolhac, "La Garde-robe de Marie Antoinette"; Kraatz, "Marie Antoinette: la passion des étoffes"; Jean-Paul LeClercq, "Sur la garde-robe de Marie Leczinska et de Marie Antoinette," in *L'Oeil: Magazine international d'art,* no. 478 (January–February 1996): 30–39; and two articles in Yves Carlier, Stéphane Castelluccio, Anne Kraatz, and Françoise Tétart-Vittu (eds.), *Les Atours de la Reine* (Paris: Centre Historique des Archives Nationales, 2001): Anne Kraatz, "La 'Gazette des atours' de Marie Antoinette" (25–38) and

Françoise Tétart-Vittu, "La Garde robe de Marie Antoinette et le regard des historiens" (39–44).

113. See, for instance, Kraatz, "Marie Antoinette: la passion des étoffes," 76–77.
As Kraatz rightly points out, the emergence of white as a popular color was in no small
part due to the discovery of ruins at Herculaneum and Pompeii, which led to a general
interest in "classical" styles. Kraatz attributes the appetite for muted, melancholy
shades to the massive popularity of Goethe's brooding novel *The Sorrows of Young
Werther* (1774).

114. On the West Indian origins of the *gaulle*, see Ribeiro, *Dress in Eighteenth-
Century Europe,* 227–228; Stella Blum, 29; and Batterberry, 29.

115. Along with the cites provided above, costume histories describing the *gaulle*
or *chemise à la Reine* include R. Turner Wilcox, *The Mode in Costume* (New York:
Scribner's, 1958), 201–214; and Blanche Payne, *A History of Costume* (New York:
Harper & Row, 1965), 437–440.

116. On the Marie Antoinette style, see Pierre Saint-Amand, "Terrorizing Marie
Antoinette," in Goodman (ed.), 262. Neoclassicism, however, has a long and convo-
luted history, not treated in detail here. For more on the rise of classical taste in the
eighteenth century, see, among others, Hampson, 248; and Gay, 50–51.

117. Foreman, 171. Georgiana, for instance, wrote in 1784: "I went to a concert in
one of the muslin *chemises* with fine lace that the Queen of France gave me." See Georgiana, Duchess of Devonshire, *Extracts from the Correspondence of Georgiana,
Duchess of Devonshire,* ed. Earl of Bessborough (London, 1955), 91; and Ribeiro,
Dress in Eighteenth-Century Europe, 228.

118. Quicherat, 602.

119. See Montjoie, 134: "The public's indifference, especially in Paris, was very obvious to [the Queen], and it must be admitted that this indifference was outright scandalous. She had given France a dauphin on October 22, and at the beginning of the
following January, the Hôtel de Ville in Paris had still not organized any celebrations.
[Marie Antoinette sarcastically] asked if she was going to have to wait until her newborn could attend and dance at a party himself, before any such event was thrown to
celebrate his arrival."

120. Bachaumont, XXII, 332–333.

121. Ibid.

122. Cornu, IV, plate 269.

123. Stella Blum, 42.

124. Quicherat, 600. Similarly, one 1778 fashion engraving describes the startling
detail on a breast-baring gown as an *ajustement à la Jeanne d'Arc.* See *Galerie des
Modes,* I, 9ᵉ suite, n.p. Significantly, during the revolutionary period, one antiroyalist
pornographer printed a cartoon that showed Marie Antoinette herself in a breast-
baring *lévite,* fondling the genitals of the Marquis de La Fayette. In this image, the presumed lasciviousness of women partial to the *lévite à la Jeanne d'Arc* is clearly evident,
and Marie Antoinette herself emerges as a prime example of this phenomenon. Kindly
brought to my attention by my colleague, Serge Gavronsky, this cartoon is reprinted in
Gilles Néret, *Erotica Universalis* (Cologne: Taschen, 1994), 346.

125. Keralio, 447.

126. Marc Marie, Marquis de Bombelles, *Journal (1744–1822),* ed. Georges,
Comte Clam Martinic, 3 vols. (Geneva: Droz, 1982), I, 327.

127. Cornu, II, plate 117.

128. Colwill, 149.

129. Cornu, IV, plate 250; *Galerie des modes,* XXI, 15. It seems that *bavaroise*
was also a term for the frogging on coats such as these, more generally referred to by
the similarly Germanic name, *brandenbourgs.*

130. Frénilly, 55.

131. Soulavie, VI, 75.

132. More specifically, Louis XVI, embarrassed by the notoriety that his grandfather's agent was acquiring abroad, recalled the Chevalier to France in August 1778; he found Éon, exhausted by the obsessive scrutiny of the English public, eager enough to comply with his command. Éon was, however, less enthusiastic about the royal stipulation that, upon returning to France, he accept the legal status, and retain the clothing of, a woman. (On his death, Éon was found to have been a man.) For more details of this fascinating story, see the two following monographs: Gary Kates, *Monsieur d'Éon Is a Woman: A Tale of Political Intrigue and Sexual Masquerade* (New York: Basic Books, 1995); and André Franck, *D'Éon: Chevalier et chevalière* (Paris: Amiot-Dumont, 1953). Marjorie Garber offers an astute theoretical discussion of Éon—whose name, she points out, inspired Havelock Ellis to label transvestism "eonism"—in her work on cross-dressing. See Garber, 259–266.

133. Langlade, 88.

134. According to his *Souvenirs,* Léonard dropped by to see Bertin on each of these evenings and did not initially recognize in the "tall, stout and ugly lady" the "captain of dragoons" he had met the first time around. See Léonard, I, 204.

135. Bachaumont, X, 216–217.

136. Ibid, 289.

137. Léonard, I, 205. Éon's swagger may have been deliberate, if we consider the letter he wrote from Versailles at around this time: "I cannot express my repugnance, my grief, my pain, my troubled state, my vexation, and my shame, at having to appear thus publicly at court in the dress and position of a female, . . . stripped of a man's estate and of my [very] uniform." Cited in Garber, 263. As Garber points out, what is so interesting about Éon is the fact that he insisted on the undecidability of his gender, whereas that was precisely what "the French could not tolerate, what they had to erase, or at least, put under erasure" (263).

138. Kates, 26; Campan, 163.

139. Campan, 163.

140. Cited in Kates, 29–30.

141. Du Deffand, III, 512; Soulavie, V, 116–117.

142. Bombelles, II, 12.

143. Ibid. Elsewhere in his memoirs, Bombelles explains that the court traditionally upheld some strict protectionist regulations on the silkmakers' behalf, such as the requirement that military officers not wear their uniforms to court, except on the first day of their arrival there, or on the day of their departure for active duty. This ban forced aristocratic officers to spend money on civilian, silk-based court dress. See Bombelles, I, 246. For more on the silk manufacturers' long-standing dependence on the court, see also Mansel, 9, 71.

144. Soulavie, VI, 41.

145. Varron, 910.

146. Keralio, 446–448. See also Mathurin de Lescure (ed.), *Correspondance secrète inédite sur Louis XV, Marie Antoinette, la cour et la ville 1772–1792* (Paris: Plon), II, 228.

147. Mirecourt, 131.

148. Soulavie, 41–42.

149. Henri Martin, *Histoire de France, depuis les temps les plus reculés jusqu'en 1787* (Paris: Furne, 1865), XVI, 514.

150. Soulavie, VI, 42. For more on the silkmakers' petitioning of the royal family, see Pierre Arizzoli-Clémentel (ed.), *Soieries de Lyon: Commandes royales du XVIIIe siècle (1730–1800)* (Lyon: Sézanne, 1989), 96.

151. Soulavie, 42.

152. Ibid, 43.

153. Fraser, 25.

154. These figures are provided in Nolhac, "La Garde-robe de Marie Antoinette," 849. More extensive detail on the mourning worn for Maria Theresa, by Marie Antoinette and the rest of the French court, is available in the Archives Nationales de France, K1017(1), bobine no. 539.

155. Soulavie, 41.

156. Keralio, 51.

157. On these custom colors see, among other references, Paule Adamy (ed.), *Recueil de lettres secrètes: année 1783* (Lausanne: Droz, 1997), 100 n. 116.

158. For more on this phenomenon, see Nolhac, *Autour de la reine*, 264–265.

159. François Boucher, *20,000 Years of Fashion: The History of Costume and Personal Adornment* (New York: Harry N. Abrams, 1987 [1965]), 320. See also Varron, 909.

160. Sapori, 64.

161. Goncourt, *La Femme au XVIIIe siècle*, 287.

162. Mercier, "Marchandes de modes," I, 1482.

163. See Fleischmann, *Les Pamphlets libertins*, 50–52.

164. Kraatz, "Marie Antoinette: la passion des étoffes," 78.

165. Frénilly, 55.

166. Ibid.; Goncourt, *La Femme au XVIIIe siècle*, 288.

167. Mirecourt, 132.

168. Cited in Bernier, *The Eighteenth-Century Woman*, 92.

169. See the 1779 plate reproduced in Stella Blum, 5.

170. As Daniel Roche observes of this time period, the fashionable luxuries that "had once been confined to the narrow circle of the high aristocracy or the very rich bourgeoisie had become a general phenomenon, [leading to] the social scrambling of conditions and ranks. Valets and masters, maidservants and mistresses were confused in the urban theater" that was Paris. See *The Culture of Clothing*, 111.

171. Mercier, "Lois somptuaires," II, 496–497. These laws had been suspended in 1724.

172. Goncourt, *La Femme au XVIIIe siècle*, 289 n. 1.

173. For more on the relationship between Marie Antoinette and Vigée-Lebrun, see Gita May, *Elisabeth Vigée Le Brun: The Odyssey of an Artist in an Age of Revolution* (New Haven and London: Yale University Press, 2005), Chapter 4, "Marie Antoinette's Portraitist."

174. Marie Antoinette's controversial self-presentation in this portrait receives detailed treatment in Sheriff, "The Portrait of the Queen," in Goodman (ed.).

175. Jallut, 37.

176. The "general public" that frequented the Salon was nevertheless largely an elite, educated bourgeois audience. For more on the eighteenth-century Salons, see Thomas Crow, *Painters and Public Life in Eighteenth-Century France* (New Haven and London: Yale University Press, 1985).

177. The first of these quotes is cited in Nolhac, *The Trianon of Marie Antoinette*, 169; the second appears in Mirecourt, 133.

178. Cited in Nolhac, *The Trianon of Marie Antoinette*, 170.

179. Although he was remembered principally for his magnificence—and for his minister Colbert's forceful and effective support of the French silk industry—Louis XIV had, at certain moments in his reign, passed edicts calling for greater simplicity in fabrics and clothes. See Quicherat, 517.

180. Mirecourt, 133. It is telling, moreover, that a portrait of Marie Antoinette's sister-in-law the Comtesse de Provence, dressed in much the same outfit, hung right beside *La Reine en gaulle* at the Salon, but contemporary accounts emphasize that only the Queen's portrait provoked public outrage (see Jallut, 37). In this sense, Mirecourt's suggestion should be modified: it was not that the people could not bear to see "its

princes" depicted like commoners. The problem, rather, was that the people could not forgive *Marie Antoinette* this latest transgression of royal sartorial standards. The Comtesse de Provence, who, whatever her faults, had no established track record of offending her subjects through dress, seems to have been relatively immune to anger of this kind.

181. Vigée-Lebrun, 33.

182. For contemporary observations about the indecency of the *gaulle/chemise*, see Friedrich-Melchior Grimm et al., *Correspondance littéraire, philosophique et critique*, ed. Maurice Tourneux (Paris: Garnier Frères, 1877–1882), XIII, 441–442; and Bachaumont, XXII, 116–117.

183. Cited in Henri Bouchot, "Marie Antoinette et ses peintres," in *Les Lettres et les arts*, no. 1 (January 1, 1887): 46.

184. Sheriff, "The Portrait of the Queen," in Goodman (ed.), 61; in the same essay, Sheriff notes that "the silk makers at Lyon . . . charged her with ruining a national industry for the profit of her brother Joseph, the Hapsburg ruler," then adds: "How they thought her brother would benefit from the change is not clear" (61). The benefit, as I have shown, was economic, and derived from the Hapsburgs' interests in the linen and muslin manufacturers of the Low Countries.

185. Ariane James-Sarazin, "Le Miroir de la reine: Marie Antoinette et ses portraitistes," in Carlier et al. (eds.): 13–24, 22.

186. May, 138.

187. Mary Sheriff, "Woman? Hermaphrodite? History Painter? On the Self-imaging of Elisabeth Vigée-Lebrun," in *The Eighteenth Century*, vol. 35, no. 1 (spring 1994): 3–27.

188. See, for instance, Vigée-Lebrun's 1785 and 1786 portraits of Marie Antoinette and her 1787 *Portrait of Marie Antoinette with Her Children*.

189. Sapori, 64.

190. Langlade, 116.

CHAPTER SEVEN: GALLED

1. As Simon Schama aptly notes, "at the very center of it all, unavoidably, was Marie Antoinette. It was her transformation in public opinion from innocent victim to vindictive harpy, from Queen of France to the 'Austrian whore,' that damaged the legitimacy of the monarchy to an incalculable degree." See Schama, 205.

2. Imbert de Saint-Amand, *Marie Antoinette and the Downfall of Royalty*, 65–66.

3. The particulars of this encounter in the Grove of Venus appear in the testimonies of Rohan, Le Guay, the Comtesse de La Motte, and Cagliostro, all of them reprinted (without sequential pagination and often without chapter or section titles) in an unattributed collection called *Pamphlets de l'Affaire du Collier* (Paris: n.p., 1786), stored at Butler Library, Columbia University, call no. 92M33 Z. The details included here also appear in three of the fine books that have been written on the Diamond Necklace Affair: Émile Campardon, *Marie Antoinette et le procès du collier, d'après la procédure instruite devant le Parlement de Paris* (Paris: Plon, 1863); Funck-Brentano; and Frances Mossiker, *The Queen's Necklace* (New York: Simon & Schuster, 1961). Of these works, Mossiker's is perhaps the more useful because it excerpts, and weaves into an overarching, explanatory narrative, the enormous array of testimonies and trial briefs that the court proceedings generated. See also relevant chapters in the biographies by Asquith, Castelot, Dunlop, Fraser, Goncourt, Hearsey, Lever, Imbert de Saint-Amand, among others. Shorter, cogent summaries of the Diamond Necklace Affair appear in Schama, 203–210, and in Maza, *Private Lives and Public Affairs*, 167–211, and "The Diamond Necklace Affair Revisited (1785–1786): The Case of the Missing Queen," in Goodman (ed.), 73–97.

4. On this point, see especially the legal *mémoire* of Cagliostro's testimony, also reprinted in the *Pamphlets de l'Affaire du Collier*.

5. Lafont d'Aussonne, 91; Imbert de Saint-Amand, *Marie Antoinette and the Downfall of Royalty*, 67; Schama, 207.

6. Of all Marie Antoinette's biographers, it is perhaps Ian Dunlop who describes the necklace in the greatest detail: "a band of seventeen equally sized stones encircled the throat; from this depended one central festoon set between the two smaller ones, each enclosing a pendant. Below this, a long double chain of brilliants hung in the form of a capital M to which were attached two rather heavy tassels" (210).

7. Campan, 244.

8. Citations taken, respectively, from Sarah Maza, "The Diamond Necklace Affair Revisited," in Goodman (ed.), 81, and *Private Lives and Public Affairs*, 193. The latter work, in particular, provides many useful details on the "avalanche" of publications spawned by the scandal (190–192).

9. Schama, 205.

10. Maza, *Private Lives and Public Affairs*, 185.

11. Imbert de Saint-Amand, *Marie Antoinette and the Downfall of Royalty*, 104.

12. On this point see Maza, "The Diamond Necklace Affair Revisited," 87–88; and Pierre Saint-Amand, "Terrorizing Marie Antoinette," in Goodman (ed.), 264.

13. Cited in Mossiker, 313–314. Mossiker adds in a footnote that the police received explicit orders to "remove the portrait" from the *bonbonnière*. The *Mémoires secrets* made the story even more titillating by reporting that, at Marie Antoinette's request, La Motte had not just had *La Reine en gaulle* image painted on the little box's lid, but had also had an obscene, semi-nude portrait of the Queen painted on the inside. See Bachaumont, XXX, 29–30; also cited in Hervez, *Mémoires de la Comtesse de La Motte*, 263 n. 1.

14. Hervez, 262–264. Nevertheless, argued La Motte's lawyer Doillot, Rohan ought to have been able to tell the difference between lowborn Le Guay and "a queen who is both the daughter and the sister of emperors" just by the way she walked. In Doillot's logic, the Cardinal's failure to distinguish between the Queen's famously regal deportment and the necessarily inferior movements of her impersonator attested more to the "extravagance of the Cardinal's fantasies" for advancement at court than to La Motte's own duplicity. See Doillot, *Mémoire pour dame Jeanne de Saint-Rémy de Valois, épouse du Comte de La Motte*, cited in Campardon, 130.

15. Cited in Cornu, III [3²], plate 204. See also J. Blondel, *Mémoire pour la demoiselle Le Guay d'Oliva, contre M. le Procureur Général, accusateur*, in *Pamphlets de l'Affaire du Collier*, 16.

16. Lever, *Marie Antoinette: The Last Queen of France*, 178.

17. Fraser, 242.

18. S.P. Hardy (journal entry of Sept. 6, 1785), cited in Mossiker, 338. See also Varron, 893, and Reiset, I, 10.

19. The Abbé de Georgel cited in Mossiker, 339.

20. Campardon, 143; Schama, 208.

21. Mossiker, 338.

22. Dunlop, 233.

23. Besenval, 383.

24. Campan, 250.

25. Mossiker, 52; Dunlop, 233.

26. Campan, 500.

27. Fraser, 240.

28. Métra, *Correspondance secrète* (27 février 1785); also cited in Langlade, 168.

29. Oberkirch, 540.

30. Bessborough (ed.), 106.

31. Campan, 500; La Tour du Pin, 89.

32. La Tour du Pin, 89.

33. Cornu, III [3²], plate 207.

34. Erickson, 177.

35. About this outbreak of defamatory paternity rumors, in which Fersen was now included, see de Baecque, *The Body Politic,* 48.

36. Joseph Weber, 65–68; Lafont d'Aussonne, 76; Lever, *Marie Antoinette: The Last Queen of France,* 157.

37. Boyer and Halard, 62–66. Although it has never been proven that Marie Antoinette served as the model for the famous "breast cups" of the Hameau, the story has remained part of her legend. See Fleischmann, *Les Pamphlets libertins,* 64–65.

38. Castelot, *Marie Antoinette* (1989), 94. See also *Correspondance de Marie Antoinette,* II, 105, where she describes her children—and particularly her *chou d'amour,* Louis Charles—as her "only consolation."

39. Delpierre, 30.

40. On this scandal at the Salon, see Bachaumont, XXX, 189; *Le Mercure de France* (October 1, 1785); and Magnus Olausson (ed.), *Marie Antoinette: Porträtt av en drottning* (Stockholm: Nationalmuseum, 1989).

41. For more on the Queen's love for this song, and on the fashions it launched, see Bachaumont, XXI, 186; XXII, 149; and XXIII, 13, as well as C. Hirsch (ed.), *Correspondance d'Eulalie, ou Tableau du libertinage à Paris* (Paris: Fayard, 1986 [1785]), 159–160. In addition to a new style of "bonnets, ribbons, coiffures, and hats," the Queen's Marlborough obsession inspired a spate of plays, vaudevilles, and poems with "Marlborough" in the title, including a popular comedy by Beaumarchais. For reasons that remain obscure, when a man was described as being "à la Marlborough," this implied that he had homosexual proclivities; see Adamy (ed.), 364 n. 476.

42. Cornu, III [3¹], plates 178 and 187.

43. Blum, plate 53.

44. Adamy (ed.), 364. See also Métra (24 septembre 1783), XIV, 123.

45. Challamel, 172, 172; Adamy (ed.), 364.

46. Challamel, 174; for more on the "discovery" of the harpy, see Schama, 225–226; and de Baecque, *The Body Politic,* 166–167.

47. Cornu, III [3²], plates 239 and 240.

48. On this pamphlet, the "Description historique d'un monstre symbolique, pris sur les bords du Lac Fagua, près de Santa Fé . . ." ("Santa Fé et Paris": n.p., 1784), see Gruder, 283 n. 47; de Baecque, *The Body Politic,* 168; and Annie Duprat, *Le Roi décapité: essai sur les imaginaires politiques* (Paris: Cerf, 1992), 75—all of whom identify Provence as the pamphlet's sponsor, even perhaps its author, and Marie Antoinette as the "harpy" in the cartoon. The Queen-as-harpy image was later reprised by revolutionary caricaturists, as I discuss in Chapter 8.

49. Cited in Challamel, 175.

50. Nolhac, "La Garde-robe de Marie Antoinette," 853; Sapori, 77–78.

51. Sapori, 80; Varron, 903.

52. See the Comtesse d'Ossun, *État général des dépenses de la Garde-robe de la Reine,* in the Archives Nationales de France, O.1.3792–3798.

53. Nolhac, "La Garde-robe de Marie Antoinette," 853.

54. Varron, 893; Reiset, I, 10.

55. François Furet, *Revolutionary France 1770–1880,* trans. Antonia Nevill (Oxford: Blackwell, 1996 [1992]), 38.

56. Ségur, *Memoirs and Recollections,* 175. Because political unrest, and discontent with the monarchy's spendthrift, despotic ways, had simmered in France since Louis XV's (and indeed Louis XIV's) clashes with the *parlements,* Ségur perhaps over-

states the degree to which, before Necker published his report, the nation had been "a stranger to its own affairs." He is nevertheless right to insist that Necker's report catalyzed major additional discontent against the throne.

57. Schama, 93; and Hardman, *Louis XVI*, 58–59.

58. Schama, 92.

59. Furet, 39.

60. Schama, 235.

61. Ibid, 236.

62. May, 138.

63. Montjoie, 193. And according to Joan Haslip, the "general public in Paris . . . hummed [a] ditty" that directly "linked the Queen's name with that of Calonne": "It is not Calonne that I love/But rather his unstinting gold/When I find myself strapped for cash/Then I go straight to him/And my favorite [Polignac] does the same thing/And then we laugh to ourselves quietly, quietly." See Haslip, 172.

64. Stella Blum, plate 56. Significantly, this fashion plate pairs the *chapeau à la Calonne* with the Queen's signature dress, the white *chemise*.

65. Campan, 220–221.

66. Joan Haslip, *Madame Du Barry: The Wages of Beauty* (New York: Grove Weidenfeld, 1991), 128.

67. Asquith, 126. Marie Antoinette's presumed complicity in Calonne's excesses was later reprised in Anonymous, "Observations et précis sur le caractère et la conduite de Marie Antoinette d'Autriche" (Paris: n.p., 1793), 9–12.

68. Furet, 40. According to Simon Schama, Calonne's initial estimate for the current deficit was 80 million livres, a figure that he subsequently revised to 112 million.

69. Erickson, 180.

70. Lever, *Marie Antoinette: The Last Queen of France*, 185.

71. Reiset, I, 64.

72. See Chapter 5.

73. Haslip, *Marie Antoinette*, 172.

74. Lever, *Marie Antoinette: La dernière reine*, 72.

75. Mayer, 164.

76. On the "effective collapse" that the King underwent at this time, see Fraser, 454.

77. Delorme, 205.

78. See, for instance, Delorme, 208.

79. According to Madame Campan, Marie Antoinette had received "written proof" of Calonne's involvement in the publication of La Motte's memoirs. See Campan, 315–316, as well as Campardon, 180. For the memoirs themselves, see Jean Hervez, *Mémoires de La Comtesse de La Motte–Valois . . . d'après les mémoires justificatifs de la Comtesse de La Motte, les mémoires du comte de La Motte, etc.* (Paris: Bibliothèque des Curieux, 1911).

80. Bibliothèque Nationale de France, Ms. Français 6686.

81. Langlade, 201–202.

82. Oberkirch, 187. Interestingly enough, Oberkirch herself was not above relying on credit to spend far more than she could afford (or at least far more than she was willing to pay): according to Michelle Sapori, the Baronne figured on the list of the *marchand de modes* Beaulard's list of "dubious debtors"—people unexpected to pay him back—in 1789. See Sapori, 289. Bertin kept similar lists that revealed how far her aristocratic clients were willing to go in abusing their credit with her; by 1820, there were still 1,300 clients who had not settled their accounts with the *marchande de modes*, and who, due to the ravages of the revolutionary era, were unlikely ever to make good on their debts. See Sapori, 296 n. 180.

83. Hardy cited in Langlade, 198, and Crowston, 92.

84. Varron, 893; Blum, 79; Contini, 196.

85. Archives Nationales de France, O.1.3798.
86. Reiset, I, 59.
87. Ibid.
88. Ibid, 40, 54,
89. Haslip, *Madame Du Barry*, 128.
90. Langlade, 200.
91. Haslip, *Marie Antoinette*, 176. In his harpy pamphlet, the Comte de Provence had already alluded to this nickname by satirizing his rapacious heroine as "Madame Laspicit"; see de Baecque, *The Body Politic*, 168.
92. Reiset, I, 15.
93. Ibid.
94. Langlade, 204.
95. Campan, 122.
96. Lever, *Marie Antoinette: The Last Queen of France*, 187.
97. Cited in Haslip, *Marie Antoinette*, 167.
98. Langlade, 204.
99. For more on *Le Magasin des modes* and the emergence of fashion journals in France, see Fukai, in Fayolle and Davray-Piekoek (eds.), 113–117; Varron, 911; and, most important, three definitive works by Kleinert: *Die frühen Modejournale in Frankreich*; *Le "Journal des dames et des modes"*; and "La Mode, miroir de la Révolution française," in Join-Dieterle and Delpierre (eds.), 59–81. (In the second of these three texts [13 n. 10], Kleinert also outlines the development of the fashion press in England, starting in 1792, and in Germany, beginning in 1786.) As both Kleinert and Fukai point out, the French fashion journals mentioned here are to be distinguished from fashion plates, almanacs, and print coverage in newspapers such as *Le Mercure Galant* (1677–1730) and the *Courier de la nouveauté* (1758). As such, these fashion journals had only one noteworthy French predecessor: the short-lived *Courier de la mode ou journal du goût* of 1768 (see Fukai, 113, and Kleinert, *Le "Journal des dames et des modes,"* 13 n. 3). Indeed, it was with *Le Cabinet* and *Le Magasin des modes* that the fashion journal (suspended for a brief period during the Reign of Terror) became a lasting institution in France.
100. Aileen Ribeiro, *The Art of Dress: Fashions in England and France 1750 to 1820* (New Haven and London: Yale University Press, 1995), 76.
101. *Le Magasin des modes nouvelles françaises et anglaises* (20 novembre 1786), Cahier I, 1. Women's widespread adoption in 1786 of "men's clothes," especially "redingotes and flat-heeled shoes," also received mention in the highbrow *Correspondance littéraire*; see Bluche, 137.
102. See Reiset, I, 144 and plate 35.
103. *Le Magasin des modes nouvelles françaises et anglaises* (30 avril 1787), Cahier XVII, 133. This claim about the primacy of the *pouf* was not altogether true, as this fashion journal's own plates attested. By the late 1780s, wildly oversized hats—not so much towering as massively round and wide—emerged alongside *poufs* as head-dresses of choice and were amply documented in *Le Magasin des modes*. Although no surviving records link Marie Antoinette to this trend in hats, many of them were named for characters from Beaumarchais plays, which despite their incendiary political implications the Queen actively supported, and even performed at the Petit Trianon.
104. Ribeiro, *Fashion in the French Revolution*, 33–34; *Le Magasin des modes nouvelles françaises et anglaises* (20 janvier 1787), Cahier VII, 49. On Marie Antoinette's and Georgiana's shared love of fashion, see Foreman, *Georgiana, Duchess of Devonshire*, 39.
105. *Le Magasin des modes nouvelles françaises et anglaises* (20 novembre 1786), Cahier I, 3–4; (10 décembre 1786), Cahier III, 19.

106. *Le Magasin des modes nouvelles françaises et anglaises* (20 juin 1787), Cahier XXII, 170. This issue is notable because it calls "masculine" redingotes and white dresses—two of the Queen's best-known innovations—*the* two styles of the era.

107. Montjoie, 101. See also Reiset, I, 48. To explain this paradox, Pierre Saint-Amand has suggestively hypothesized that by presenting "herself as an object to be looked at, an object of desire," the Queen exposed herself to widespread "rivalry and imitation," which in turn were fostered as much by envy as by admiration, as much by a desire to surpass and destroy her as by a desire to resemble her. See "Adorning Marie Antoinette," 25.

108. Langlade, 211.

109. Timothy Tackett, *When the King Took Flight* (Cambridge, Mass.: Harvard University Press, 2002), 35. See also Fraser, 454.

110. Tackett, 36.

111. Campan, 255–256.

112. Jacques Necker, *Éloge de Colbert* (1773); cited in Schama, 89.

113. *Correspondance de Marie Antoinette*, II, 16.

114. Lever, *Marie Antoinette: The Last Queen of France*, 200.

115. As Keith Michael Baker, among others, has noted, the question of an ancient constitution that already—or had once—subtended the French political order had been a subject of intense debate for at least four decades before Necker's triumphant return to Paris. As the Estates General drew nigh, the urgent question was framed as follows: "Was the French constitution to be fixed by 'strengthening' an ancient constitution or by 'establishing' a new one?"—with the latter notion coming to the fore in the summer of 1789. See Keith Michael Baker, *Inventing the French Revolution: Essays on French Political Culture in the Eighteenth Century* (Cambridge, Eng.: Cambridge University Press, 1990), 252–305. See also Marina Valensise, "La Constitution française," in Keith Michael Baker (ed.), *The French Revolution and the Creation of Modern Political Culture*, 4 vols. (Oxford and New York: Pergamon Press, 1987), I, 441–468. As Valensise points out, the idea of a preexisting constitution was rooted in sixteenth- and seventeeth-century theories of sovereignty, whereas the idea of a new constitution drew its strength from the political philosophy of the Enlightenment (447).

116. In fact, Loménie de Brienne had already urged the King to take this step earlier in the summer.

117. *Cahier de doléances* of the *baillage* of Fenestrange; excerpted in Hardman, *The French Revolution Sourcebook*, 76–77.

118. See Hardman, *Louis XVI*, 90–92, 95; and Karmel, 55.

119. In the end, the double representation did not advance the Third Estate's voting power since votes in the Estates General were eventually decreed to be counted "by order," not "by head." But as Madame Campan recalled, the doubling of the number of deputies from this Estate "preoccupied all politically minded people" in the months leading up to the convocation. This issue also introduced a rift between Marie Antoinette, who favored the double representation, and the Comte d'Artois, who actively opposed it. See Campan, 258.

120. François-Emmanuel Guignard, Comte de Saint-Priest, *Mémoires: Règnes de Louis XV et Louis XVI*, ed. Baron de Barante, 2 vols. (Paris: Calmann-Lévy, 1929), II, 77–83; Campan, 224; Tackett, 36; and Karmel, 54–55. According to Madame Campan, Marie Antoinette's deep-seated royalism had also made her disapprove thoroughly of France's involvement in the American Revolution, for "she could not understand how a sovereign could be persuaded to contribute to England's abasement, by helping a people to organize a republican constitution." See Campan, 254.

121. Campan, 258. Fraser notes that this was also the view of the Queen's former protégé Loménie de Brienne; see Fraser, 261–262.

122. Fraser, 272–273.

123. Mercier describes the legendary Sancy diamond in "Diamants," I, 273.

124. Fraser, 273.

125. Haslip, *Marie Antoinette,* 186.

126. Ibid; Langlade, 210; Zweig, 212.

127. Claude Manceron, *Blood of the Bastille 1787–1789,* trans. Nancy Amphoux (New York: Touchstone/Simon & Schuster, 1989), 457; Ribeiro, *Fashion in the French Revolution,* 45, and *The Art of Dress,* 83; and Jean Starobinski, *1789, les emblèmes de la raison* (Paris: Flammarion, 1973), 12.

128. Rabaut Saint-Étienne, *Précis historique de la Révolution française* (Paris: Didot, [1792]), 68. In a more indignant vein, the progressive British writer Mary Wollstonecraft fulminated that "the nobility were gaudily caparisoned for the show, whilst the commons were stupidly commanded to wear that black mantle." See Mary Wollstonecraft, *A Vindication of the Rights of Woman* (London: n.p., 1792), 437.

129. Emmanuel Joseph, Abbé Sieyès, *Qu'est-ce que le Tiers état?* (Paris: 1788).

130. Saint-Étienne, 68–69.

131. Starobinski, 12, and Batterberry, 192. As the Batterberrys go on to note: "Outraged by [this] form of sartorial humiliation, [the Third Estate] banded together mutinously against all the class distinctions that had been crystallized in repressive rules of dress. The era of the sumptuary law had long passed, and it was a sad comment on the King's lack of awareness that he should have thought otherwise."

132. La Tour du Pin, 111.

133. Campan, 261.

134. Ibid, 259.

135. Bombelles, II, 305.

136. Duquesnoy, cited in Manceron, 462.

137. Castelot, *Marie Antoinette* (1989), 119.

138. As Jean Starobinski has written, the people's disdain for the higher orders' splendid attire represented a turning point in French history, for it was the moment when the court's lavish "spending [ceased to] inspire respectful astonishment." See Starobinski, 12.

139. Duquesnoy, in Manceron, 462.

140. Zweig, 212. As John Hardman explains, Mirabeau was in fact legally classified as a member of the Third Estate, because of the relative newness of his family's claims to nobility. Thus, although he could and would posture as an aristocratic supporter of "the people," Mirabeau was in some sense pushed into this position by a legal designation that provoked, in Hardman's terms, "considerable resentment" in himself and other recently ennobled men consigned to the Third Estate. See Hardman, *Louis XVI,* 89.

CHAPTER EIGHT: REVOLUTIONARY REDRESS

1. Ribeiro, 46.

2. Mayer, 172–173.

3. La Tour du Pin, 117.

4. Gouverneur Morris, *A Diary of the French Revolution,* ed. Beatrix Cary Davenport, 2 vols. (Boston: Houghton Mifflin, 1939), I, 66.

5. Mayer, 173. This said, I recognize that an enormous amount of research has been done on the difficult and deeply important question of when and how "the Revolution" began, and I cannot even begin to enter into that polemic in a work that proposes to concentrate primarily on "what Marie Antoinette wore to the Revolution." This complex issue receives especially persuasive and subtle treatment in the work of Keith Michael Baker, cited above. I should add that although his focus and sources are vastly different from mine, Baker's perspective has been helpful to me insofar as he maintains that:

Politics . . . depends on the existence of cultural representations that define the relationships among political actors, thereby allowing individuals and groups to press claims upon one another and upon the whole. Such claims can be made intelligible and binding only to the extent that political actors deploy symbolic resources held in common by members of the political society, thereby refining and redefining the implications of these resources. . . . Political contestation therefore takes the form of competing efforts to mobilize and control the possibilities of political and social discourse, efforts through which that discourse is extended, recast, and—on occasion—even radically transformed [33].

It is my thesis in these later chapters that the revolutionaries, like Marie Antoinette, recognized clothing as a "symbolic resource" or "cultural representation" that could help to "press claims upon one another" and their foes.

6. Cited in Jacques Godechot, *La Révolution française: chronologie commentée 1789–1799* (Paris: Perrin, 1988), 59.

7. For a fuller account of the Tennis Court Oath, see Baker, 252–264.

8. Lever, *Marie Antoinette: The Last Queen of France,* 209.

9. Ibid.

10. Lamothe-Langon, *Souvenirs sur Marie Antoinette,* III, 170–175; John Hardman, *The French Revolution Sourcebook* (London: Arnold, 1999), 97.

11. Cited in Evelyne Lever, *Louis XVI* (Paris: Fayard, 1985), 146.

12. Godechot, 61; G. Lenôtre and André Castelot, *L'Agonie de la royauté* (Paris: Perrin, 1962), 88.

13. Godechot, 61.

14. As Vivian Gruder has observed, the practice of wearing a cockade to signal one's political loyalties actually preceded the Revolution. In her forthcoming work, *The Notables and the Nation: The Political Schooling of the French, 1787–1788,* she recounts how *cocardes* were worn to show enthusiasm for Louis XVI's decision to recall his *parlementaires* from exile in the fall of 1787. Furthermore, she notes, these *cocardes* were tricolor in emulation of the King's blue, white, and red livery. As many other historians have shown, however, the tricolor cockade did not become a ubiquitous political accessory until after July 1789, at which point it assumed a quite different political valence. For the most exhaustive treatment of this topic, see Richard Wrigley, *The Politics of Appearances: Representations of Dress in Revolutionary France* (Oxford and New York: Berg, 2002), Chapter 3, "Cockades: Badge Culture and its Discontents," 97–134.

15. See Wrigley, 98–99; Lynn Hunt, *Politics, Culture, and Class in the French Revolution* (Berkeley: University of California Press, 1984), 57; and Jack Censer and Lynn Hunt (eds.), *Liberty, Equality, Fraternity: Exploring the French Revolution* (University Park: Pennsylvania State University Press, 2001).

16. Reiset, II, 159.

17. Again, see Wrigley's indispensable chapter on the cockade, 97–134.

18. Mayer, 180.

19. Jean-Marc Devocelle, "D'un costume politique à une politique du costume," in Join-Dieterle and Delpierre (eds.), 83–104, 85; and Lynn Hunt, "Freedom of Dress in Revolutionary France," in Sara E. Melzer and Kathryn Norberg (eds.), *From the Royal to the Republican Body: Incorporating the Political in Seventeenth- and Eighteenth-Century France* (Berkeley: University of California Press, 1988), 11. See also "Cockades: Badge Culture and Its Discontents," in Wrigley, 97–134. On the more general subject of how clothes became politicized during the French Revolution, see also Hunt, *Politics, Culture, and Class;* Wrigley; Ribeiro, *Dress in the French Revolution;* and most of the articles in Fayolle and Davray-Piekolek (eds.) and Join-Dieterle and Delpierre (eds.).

20. Devocelle, 85.

21. Reiset, I, 351.

22. De Baecque, *The Body Politic*, 162.

23. Thomas Carlyle, *The French Revolution*, 3 vols. (London: Methuen & Co., 1902), I, 305–306. This passage refers specifically to a series of episodes on October 4, 1789, but the more prolonged persecution of men wearing black cockades is described in Lamothe-Langon, *Souvenirs sur Marie Antoinette*, IV, 248.

24. Carlyle, I, 306.

25. [François-Marie Arouet] Voltaire, *La Henriade*, Ch. IV, line 456.

26. Lenôtre and Castelot, 95–96, 100.

27. Hardman, *The French Revolution Sourcebook*, 106–107.

28. Cited in Haslip, 199.

29. A detailed and well-documented account of this incident appears in Reiset, II, 159.

30. Dorinda Outram, "Review of Richard Wrigley, *The Politics of Appearances: Representations of Dress in Revolutionary France*," in *H-France*, an electronic publication of the Society for French Historical Studies (January 2004): http://www3 .uakron.edu/hfrance/reviews/outram.html.

31. Cited in Haslip, 199.

32. Cited in Jacques Godechot, *La Prise de la Bastille: 14 Juillet 1789* (Paris: Gallimard, 1985), 418.

33. Reiset, II, 159.

34. For a more nuanced treatment of the different Assemblée members' political views in the summer of 1789, see Schama, 441–445.

35. It bears noting that, like Desmoulins's adoption of a green leaf "cockade" on July 12, La Fayette's ostensible invention of the tricolor cockade is attested to above all by his own writings and has been disputed by subsequent commentators—for example, Michel Pastoureau, *Dictionnaire des couleurs de notre temps* (Paris: Bonneton, 1992), 34. Whatever its origins, the national cockade's tricolor palette also, of course, became the basis for the French flag, as it still exists today. Unlike the *cocarde tricolore*, however, the tricolor flag was not adopted until September 21, 1790.

36. Boigne, 95. On the significance of "the national colors' triumph over the royal white," see also Roche, *The Culture of Clothing*, 254.

37. After October 6, 1789, Marie Antoinette apparently instructed one National Guardsman never to appear before her in his uniform on the grounds that "it reminds me of all the misfortunes my family has suffered." Cited in Castelot, *Marie Antoinette* (1962), 471.

38. Campan, 276.

39. Haslip, 199.

40. Louis-Sébastien Mercier, *Le Nouveau Paris*, ed. Jean-Claude Bonnet (Paris: Mercure de France, 1994), 282.

41. Evelyne Lever, *Philippe-Égalité* (Paris: Fayard, 1996), 346; J. Hammond, *A Keeper of Royal Secrets, Being the Private and Political Life of Madame de Genlis* (London: 1912), 191.

42. Reiset, I, 373, 380.

43. Ibid, 380, 423, 438–439. Despite Vivian Gruder's astute observation about the brief emergence of a promonarchist tricolor cockade in the provinces in 1787, none of these aristocrats had ever ordered *tricolore* accessories from Madame Éloffe before the Bastille fell.

44. Reiset, I, 432.

45. *Journal de la cour et de la ville* (avril 1791); see also Langlade, 216.

46. For more on the modishness of the ensembles that the Revolution inspired, see especially Annemarie Kleinert, "La Mode, miroir de la Révolution française," in Join-

Dieterle and Delpierre (eds.), 59–82. On the apolitical orientation of many of the women who adopted the tricolor cockade in this first phase of the Revolution, see Langlade, 216.

47. On Madame de Genlis's locket, see Hammond, 191. On Bertin's confection of *cocardes nationales,* see Delpierre, "Rose Bertin, les marchandes de modes et la Révolution," in Join-Dieterle and Delpierre (eds.), 22; and Langlade, 219. As Langlade points out, Bertin was a "royalist by conviction and out of self-interest" and seems to have restricted her pro-revolutionary offerings to the *cocarde* alone. Indeed Michelle Sapori maintains that like Marie Antoinette, Bertin was repelled by such styles as "dresses *à l'égalité* and *à la Constitution*" and refused to offer them in her store. See Sapori, 145–146.

48. Varron, 897.

49. Helen Maria Williams, *Letters Written in France, in the Summer of 1790, to a Friend in England; Containing Various Anecdotes Relative to the French Revolution,* ed. Neil Fraistat and Susan S. Lanser (Toronto: Broadview Literary Texts, 2001), 14.

50. *Le Magasin des modes nouvelles françaises et anglaises* (1 décembre 1789), Cahier XXXIV, 267.

51. Haslip, *Marie Antoinette,* 196.

52. Erickson, 235.

53. Ibid.

54. La Tour du Pin, 131.

55. Erickson, 235.

56. This was a premise that a revolutionary feminist named Olympe de Gouges articulated in her Declaration of the Rights of Woman in 1791. Although Gouges did not make women's dress a focal point of her manifesto (which was intended as a corrective to women's exclusion from the Declaration of the Rights of Man), she did dedicate it to Marie Antoinette.

57. *Le Magasin des modes nouvelles françaises et anglaises* (21 septembre 1789), Cahier XXXIV, 228.

58. Ibid.

59. Ibid, 227.

60. Ibid, 228.

61. A year later, in fact, the fashion journals of the day would promote *bonnets à la paysanne* ("peasant girl's bonnets") and several other white gauze and muslin caps trimmed, precisely, in the pomegranate flowers (*fleurs de grenadier*) of the *ancien régime* Grenada hat. See *Le Journal de la mode et du goût* (15 mars 1790), Cahier III, 2.

62. Indeed, although neoclassical and pastoral aesthetics (in literature, philosophy, etc.) both predated Marie Antoinette, it was during her reign—and in emulation of her Trianon costumes—that they fused at the level of costume to provide the draped, flowing silhouette of the *gaulle,* which became even more attenuated and togalike as the Revolution progressed.

63. Moitte herself published two pamphlets inciting French women to patriotic generosity. These are Adélaïde-Marie-Anne Moitte, *L'Âme des Romaines dans les femmes françaises* (Paris: Gueffier le jeune, 1789) and *Suite de L'Âme des Romaines dans les femmes françaises* (Paris: Knapen fils, 1789). Another contemporary source that chronicles the episode is Johann Georg Wille, *Mémoires et journal de Jean-Georges Wille, graveur du roi,* 2 vols. (Paris: J. Renouard, 1857), II, 219–223. For a more detailed treatment of this incident, see Auricchio, 18–30.

64. Williams, 86.

65. Moitte, *L'Âme des Romaines,* 5–6.

66. Ribeiro, *Fashion in the French Revolution,* 98; Lenôtre and Castelot, 142.

67. Moitte, *L'Âme des Romaines,* 5.

68. Auricchio, 24. Auricchio also notes that "the white garments of the *donatrices* . . . added another layer of significance" to their generous action (21). For

more on the Lesueur brothers' role in shaping the visual culture of the Revolution, see Philippe de Carbonnières, *Lesueur: Gouaches révolutionnaires. Collection du Musée Carnavalet* (Paris: Nicolas Chaudun, 2005).

69. Cited in Roche, "Apparences révolutionnaires ou révolution des apparences," in Join-Dieterle and Delpierre (eds.), 193–201, 197.

70. This, again, is not to deny that both the pastoral and the neoclassical tastes of late eighteenth-century France had other important antecedents and avatars, as discussed at the beginning of Chapter 6. But in the specific domain of dress, no one was a more conspicuous or widely recognized partisan of the "Trianon" look than Marie Antoinette herself.

71. Ribeiro, *The Art of Dress*, 86. On the political ambiguity of the color white in the revolutionary era, see Roche, *The Culture of Clothing*, 245.

72. *Le Journal de la mode et du goût* (15 avril 1790), Cahier XIV, 2–3; Ribeiro, *Fashion in the French Revolution*, 58.

73. Akiko Fukai, "Le vêtement rococo et néoclassique," in Fayolle and Davray-Piekolek (eds.), 109–117, 115.

74. Reiset, II, plate 74.

75. Ribeiro, *Fashion in the French Revolution*, 88.

76. On misogyny in French revolutionary politics, see especially Lynn Hunt, *The Family Romance of the French Revolution*, and Joan B. Landes, *Women and the Public Sphere in the Age of the French Revolution* (Ithaca, N.Y., and London: Cornell University Press, 1988).

77. *Le Journal de la mode et du goût* (25 août 1790), Cahier XIX, 2, plate II.

78. Hunt, *The Family Romance of the French Revolution*, 104.

79. Colwill, "Pass as a Woman, Act Like a Man," in Goodman (ed.), 145. See also Duprat, 58.

80. Thomas, 108. Colwill makes the same point as Chantal Thomas in her article on revolutionary pamphlets describing Marie Antoinette's supposed lesbianism: "What was revolutionary about the charges of the Queen's sexual deviance was, in part, their growing audience and their potential for political mobilization." See Colwill, "Pass as a Woman, Act Like a Man," in Goodman (ed.), 145.

81. Hunt, *The Family Romance of the French Revolution*, 105. See also Hunt, "The Many Bodies of Marie Antoinette." I should point out here that Hunt makes a distinction between prerevolutionary and revolutionary pornography, insofar as the former was often placed in the service of a broader philosophical program, whereas the latter was "devoted almost exclusively to the depiction of pleasure in and of itself." Perhaps the more important distinction in the case of Marie Antoinette, though, is the one that Elizabeth Colwill insists upon when she notes that in the philosophical pornography of the *ancien régime*, "bodies were interchangeable," whereas "the pornography of the Revolution specified precisely which bodies were doing what" and paid particular attention to the body of the Queen. See Colwill, "Pass as a Woman, Act Like a Man," in Goodman (ed.), 147.

82. As Antoine de Baecque has shown, the pamphlet literature of the Revolution portrayed many high-placed members of the nobility as depraved monsters, descendants of Judas Iscariot (whose last name stood as an imperfect acronym for "aristocrat"), and betrayers of France. As de Baecque also shows, at least one revolutionary pamphlet described Marie Antoinette as this horrible Iscariot's mother, thus locating her at the root of the corruption that was seen as laying waste to the nation. See de Baecque, *The Body Politic*, 161–163. Interestingly for the purposes of my analysis, de Baecque notes how Marie Antoinette's hairstyle links her to this monstrous personage, both through its "tresses of snakes" and through the "red hair [that] connotes the 'Royal Redhead'" (162).

83. See Anonymous, "Les Fureurs utérines de Marie Antoinette" (n.p., [1791]).

84. Anonymous, "La Messaline française" (Tribaldis [*sic*]: De l'imprimerie Priape, 1789); reproduced in Fleischmann, *Les Maîtresses de Marie Antoinette*, 190.

85. Ibid.

86. "Le Godmiché royal" (Paris: n.p., 1789); reprinted and translated in Thomas, 191–201. For corroboration of the putative identities of "Juno" and "Hebe" in this text, see Hunt, *The Family Romance of the French Revolution*, 104.

87. On this notion, see also the pamphlet by Keralio, 447.

88. Thomas, 107.

89. For more on the "Austrian conspiracy" of October 1789 and its coverage in the revolutionary press, see de Baecque, *The Body Politic*, 157.

90. See my discussion of this headdress in Chapter 5. Perhaps not incidentally, at least one prerevolutionary fashion caricature showed the bottom half of a fashionable woman's body transformed into that of a hen by the cropped and ruffled hem of her *polonaise*. This image was entitled *La Poule polonaise* (The Polish Hen) and is reprinted in Langlade, 128. The resemblance between the two images confirms that the revolutionary caricaturist of *La Poule d'Autry/uche* was drawing on the visual vocabulary of fashion to make his scathing point against the Queen.

91. On the revolutionary press's frequent description of the Queen as a monster, see de Baecque, 168–173; Duprat, 79; Saint-Amand, "Terrorizing Marie Antoinette," in Goodman (ed.), 265; and Ernest F. Henderson, *Symbol and Satire in the French Revolution* (New York and London: G. P. Putnam's Sons, 1912), 161.

92. For the precise dating of this image, which was reprinted numerous times throughout the revolutionary period, I am relying on de Baecque, *The Body Politic*, 169.

93. Anonymous, "Memoirs of Marie Antoinette," 51.

94. See, for instance, Anonymous, *Petit journal du Palais Royal* (Paris: n.p., 1789), in the Bibliothèque Nationale, m.2344(1), no. 4; cited in de Baecque, 169.

95. Anonymous, "L'Iscariote de la France, ou le député autrichien" (Paris: n.p., September 1789), 5, 16.

96. Hearsey, 115.

97. Carlyle, 195–196.

98. Fraser, 292.

99. Campan, 277–278; La Tour du Pin, 133–134; and Marie-Louise-Victoire de Donnissan, Marquise de La Rochejaquelein, *Mémoires de la Marquise de La Rochejaquelein,* ed. André Sarazin (Paris: Mercure de France, 1984 [1814]), 78. Admittedly, these women's monarchist loyalties allow for the possibility that they lied, but their account has been almost universally accepted by historians discussing the incident. I have not yet found a biography of Marie Antoinette that claims she distributed white cockades at this banquet.

100. La Tour du Pin, 134. Neither Campan nor La Rochejaquelein alludes to this moment, but their accounts of the evening generally confirm La Tour du Pin's version.

101. Schama, 460.

102. The Comte de Saint-Priest, cited in Dunlop, 266.

103. According to Joan Landes, cross-dressed male rioters in October 1789 and earlier *ancien régime* uprisings "drew on the sexual power and energy of unruly women . . . to defend the community's interests and standards, and to tell the truth about unjust rule." See Landes, 234. In making this argument, Landes cites Natalie Zemon Davis, *Society and Culture in Early Modern France* (Palo Alto, Calif.: Stanford University Press, 1975), 147–150. At the same time, Landes identifies the antifeminist bias that inheres in accounts of this episode (like Mary Wollstonecraft's, cited below) that attach undue weight to the role played by the cross-dressed men and their ostensible male ringleaders. See Landes, 149–150.

104. Lamothe-Langon, *Souvenirs sur Marie Antoinette,* IV, 248. See also Mary Wollstonecraft, *An Historical and Moral View of the Origin and Progress of the*

French Revolution and the Effect It Has Produced in Europe (New York: Scholars' Facsimiles, 1975 [1794]), 430–458.

105. Schama, 462. Although, according to Wille, the working-class men in the group "for the most part wore vests, leather aprons, or dilapidated coats," contemporary prints depict several such men in drag. See Wille, II, 225.

106. Much more detailed accounts of this episode appear in Jules Michelet, *Histoire de la Révolution française* (Paris: Laffont, 1979), Book II, Chapters 8 and 9; and La Tour du Pin, 134–144. According to eyewitness accounts cited by Thomas Carlyle, the total number of the guards who rallied to defend Versailles did not exceed 2,800. See Carlyle, 318.

107. Campan, 295.

108. Testimonies of Messieurs de Frondeville, Brayer, de La Serre, and Jobert, in *Procédure criminelle instruite au Châtelet de Paris*, 3 vols. (1790), II, 13–15, 71, 83, 125–126. See also La Tour du Pin, 145.

109. Campan, 292.

110. Reiset, I, 445.

111. These clothing details appear in Campan, 293; Castelot, *Marie Antoinette* (1962), 327; and Lever, *Marie Antoinette: The Last Queen of France,* 228, 232.

112. Léonard, II, 2.

113. Schama, 468.

114. Louise Élisabeth Félicité, Duchesse de Tourzel, *Memoirs of the Duchesse de Tourzel, Governess to the Children of France,* ed. the Duc des Cars, 2 vols. (London: Remington and Co., 1886), I, 38.

115. Hézècques, 149.

116. La Tour du Pin, 136; Lever, *Marie Antoinette: The Last Queen of France,* 231.

117. Wille, II, 227.

118. Hézècques, 150.

119. Along with the Comte d'Hézècques's account of this incident, see those of Campan, 296–297; and Bertrand de Molleville, according to whom the hairdressers were found in Sens, not Sèvres.

120. G. Touchard-Lafosse (ed.), *Chroniques pittoresques et critiques de l'Oeil-de-Boeuf, sous Louis XIV, la Régence, Louis XV et Louis XVI,* 4 vols. (Paris: Gustave Barba, 1845), IV, 539. Because Touchard-Lafosse describes himself as the "editor" of this work, I have been unable to uncover any information—much less to determine the possible political affiliations—of the "eyewitness" to this particular episode, or indeed even to establish its veracity. An alternative, somewhat less convincing etiology of the term *sans-culotte* traces it to an eighteenth-century study of Indian culture, which introduced French readers to a trouserless deity called Camaltzèque; see Roussel d'Épinal, 281 n. 1.

121. Wrigley, 190.

122. Touchard-Lafosse, IV, 539. On *sans-culottisme* as a sartorial as well as political phenomenon, see especially Wrigley, Chapter 5, "*Sans-culottes*: The Formation, Currency, and Representation of a Vestimentary Stereotype," 187–227.

123. As Daniel Roche has noted, though without any reference to Marie Antoinette, "the sans-culottes' way of dressing [came to] symbolize a political ideal and a commitment to definitive social change." See Roche, "Apparences révolutionnaires ou révolution des apparences," in Join-Dieterle and Delpierre (eds.), 193. Similarly, Albert Soboul has written that "the sans-culotte is outwardly characterized by his costume and in that way opposes himself to the most exalted social categories: the *pantalon* is the distinctive sign of the people, the culotte of the aristocracy. . . . [His] social costume is accompanied by a certain social comportment; [and] in this domain too, the sans-culotte affirms himself by opposition." See Soboul, *Les Sans-culottes en l'An II: Mouvement populaire et gouvernement révolutionnaire* (Paris: Seuil, 1968), 22.

124. Tourzel, I, 43.

125. Wille, II, 227.

126. Tourzel, I, 44.

127. *Correspondance de Marie Antoinette*, II, 30.

128. Reiset, I, 431.

129. Pellegrin, 118. By contrast, the *cocardes* worn at this time by the ladies of Versailles cost anywhere between 7 and 9 livres in Bertin's shop.

130. Campan, 299.

131. Gérard Walter (ed.), *Actes du Tribunal révolutionnaire* (Paris: Mercure de France, 1968), 48.

132. Ibid.

133. Ibid, 49.

134. At the Tuileries the royal family was, as Montjoie has written, "guarded like criminals; all [their] actions and movements were under surveillance" (249). In addition, Anne Forray-Carlier specifies that as at Versailles, "all decently dressed people were admitted to the Tuileries gardens." See Forray-Carlier, "La Famille royale aux Tuileries," in Léri and Tulard (eds.), 17–51, 27.

135. See for instance *Correspondance de Marie Antoinette*, II, 32, 35.

136. See Anonymous, *Premier hommage des habitants de Paris à la famille royale, 7 octobre 1789* (1789), in the Musée Carnavalet; reproduced in Jean-Marc Léri and Jean Tulard (eds.), plate 16, 14.

137. *Correspondance de Marie Antoinette*, II, 30; Reiset, I, 432.

138. *Correspondance de Marie Antoinette*, II, 169.

139. On the conveyance of the royal family's possessions (especially their furniture) from Versailles to the Tuileries, see Forray-Carlier, "La Famille royale aux Tuileries," in Léri and Tulard (eds.), 26.

140. Reiset, II, 88–89. It was Joseph II's successor and Marie Antoinette's brother, Leopold, who notified her in February of the older emperor's passing.

141. *Le Journal de la mode et du goût* (25 mars 1790), Cahier IV, 7–8. French mourning practices are discussed at greater length in Chapter 9, below.

142. See Reiset, II, 6–185.

143. For more on the "patriotic" clothing of 1790, see *Le Journal de la mode et du goût*, Cahiers I–XXXV.

144. Campan, 323; Ribeiro, *Fashion in the French Revolution*, 58.

145. On the King's tactical error in refusing to wear the uniform of the National Guard at this and other appearances during the Revolution, see Mansel, 72–73.

146. On the public's positive reception of the Queen, see Tourzel, I, 166; and Anonymous, *Détails de tout ce qui s'est passé au Champ de Mars, à la Cérémonie de la Fédération le 14 juillet: anecdote sur la Reine* (Marseille: Jean Mossy, 1790), 5–6. On the cult of the "good mother" in revolutionary discourse, see especially Lynn Hunt, *The Family Romance of the French Revolution*, Chapter 6, "Rehabilitating the Family," 151–191.

147. Tourzel, I, 166.

CHAPTER NINE: TRUE COLORS

1. Ribeiro, *Fashion in the French Revolution*, 58.

2. *Correspondance de Marie Antoinette*, II, 87.

3. Haslip, *Marie Antoinette*, 227.

4. For more on the Queen's antirevolutionary sentiment at this time, see especially *Correspondance de Marie Antoinette*, II, 169, 180. In the second of these two citations, she disparages the leaders of the Assemblée as a "mass of scoundrels, madmen, and beasts."

5. For a good overview of the King's and Queen's attitude toward the Constitution at this time, see Price, 218–221.

6. On this much observed contrast, see for example Tackett, 36: "Unlike Louis,

the Queen was not plagued by indecision and uncertainty. She never doubted for a moment that the reforms being proposed by 'patriots' and liberal ministers were anathema to everything she believed in." By the same token, as Munro Price points out in documenting the degree to which Marie Antoinette "played a leading role" in the royal family's political machinations, "it is easier to trace [her political] views than the King's," because much of "her most intimate political correspondence has survived, whereas almost none of Louis's has." See Price, 217.

7. Comte de Mirabeau, *Notes pour la cour* (20 juin 1790); cited in Imbert de Saint-Amand, *Marie Antoinette at the Tuileries*, trans. Elizabeth Gilbert Martin (New York: Scribner's, 1891), 54; and in Lever, *Marie Antoinette: The Last Queen of France*, 239–240.

8. *Journal de la cour et de la ville* (5 mai 1790); also cited in Hunt, *Family Romance of the French Revolution*, 115.

9. Anonymous, "Memoirs of Marie-Antoinette," 35. For more on the people's (converse) view of Louis XVI as a "Restorer of Liberty," see Karmel, 167.

10. Anonymous, "Louis XVI et Antoinette, traités comme ils le méritent" (Paris: Imprimerie des Amis de la Constitution, 1791), 5–6.

11. Anonymous, "Le Rêve d'un Parisien, ou, Ce qui n'a point été, ce qui devroit être, et ce qui ne sera peut être pas" (Paris: L. M. Cellot, 1789 [?]), 3.

12. Campan, 329.

13. Albert Mousset, *Un témoin ignoré de la Révolution: le comte Fernan Nuñez, ambassadeur d'Espagne à Paris* (Paris: 1924), 244.

14. Campan, 323. See also Antoine François, Marquis de Bertrand de Molleville, *Mémoires secrets pour servir à l'histoire de la dernière année du règne de Louis XVI*, 3 vols. (London: Strahan, 1797), II, 295.

15. On the plans for the Queen's divorce, see especially Fraser, 317, and Lever, *Marie Antoinette: The Last Queen of France*, 244.

16. For brevity's sake, I have condensed this account of the royals' escape attempt, which receives much more thorough treatment by Lenôtre, Price, Tackett, and Schama, and most recently, by Mona Ozouf in her *Varennes: la mort de la royauté 21 juin 1791* (Paris: Gallimard, 2005), as well as in contemporary accounts like that of the Duc de Choiseul–Stainville, all cited throughout this section. As these authors rightly point out, the tensions preceding the Bourbons' flight were substantially exacerbated by two factors I do not address in detail here: mounting tension between the King and the revolutionaries over the Civil Constitution of the Clergy (to which Louis XVI did not want his clergy to swear allegiance), and Mesdames the Aunts' controversial emigration to Rome in February 1791.

17. Noëlle Destremau, *Les Évasions manquées de la reine Marie Antoinette* (Paris: n.p., 1990), Chapter 1, "Les premiers projets d'évasion." (Destremau's short monograph does not contain page numbers, but her summary of Mirabeau's suggestion of escape appears on the last page of this chapter.)

18. For an investigation of the still somewhat obscure question of "what Louis XVI and Marie Antoinette intend[ed] to do once they had reached Montmédy and what political plan, if any, they had to end the Revolution," see Price, 192–205. As Price points out, there were competing escape plans under consideration in the month before the flight, and these envisioned quite different outcomes.

19. O. G. de Heidenstam (ed.), *The Letters of Marie Antoinette, Fersen, and Barnave*, trans. Winifred Stephens and Mrs. Wilfrid Jackson (London: John Lane, 1926), 63. On the crucial notion that "the Revolution not only depended upon but *was* a language, a language of consensus through which men and women spoke" and—I might add—dressed, see Christie McDonald, "Words of Change: August 12, 1789," in Petrey (ed.), 33–46, 39.

20. Indeed, the three major orders she placed with Éloffe during the spring of 1791 were for work on blue court dresses; at least one of these three, a "blue *habit* for spring, embroidered with small bouquets," seems to have been worn with a white "English fichu." See Reiset, II, 506. On March 19, she also had repairs done on two of her spring-weight redingotes—one of them blue and white, one of them "striped with blue"—and ordered 12 *aunes* of blue ribbon. See Reiset, II, 203.

21. Pierre Saint-Amand makes this observation in a more general way when he points out that "Marie Antoinette's long march to the scaffold will take her from a deliberate ignorance of the pamphlets . . . to the point at which she comes to embody these utterances, conforming to the image created of her. Marie Antoinette becomes the image projected by her persecutors, the incarnation of their hatred." See Pierre Saint-Amand, "Terrorizing Marie Antoinette," in Goodman (ed.), 266. Later in this passage, Saint-Amand cites a similar, and similarly insightful, observation by Chantal Thomas: "The words of the pamphlets had become flesh, and this flesh was her very self." See Thomas, 72.

22. Louis-Marie Prudhomme, "Reproche véritable par la majesté du peuple à l'épouse du roi sur ses torts" (Paris: Imprimerie des Révolutions de France, 1790), 6.

23. Mercier made much the same point when he noted that Parisians objected to seeing their Queen use her son as though he were a "prop in a tragedy." See Mercier, *Le Nouveau Paris*, III, 416.

24. Although already in March she began to order a limited number of clothes and accessories in green and violet—one redingote and 14 *aunes* of ribbon in each color (see Reiset, II, 203)—this color scheme only became truly prominent in the large clothing orders she placed with Éloffe just before leaving: on June 1, June 10, and June 16, 1791 (see Reiset, II, 230–235). The same colors began to assume pride of place as well in the work for which she enlisted Rose Bertin in the months leading up to her departure: January 14 (a green satin *robe*), April 24 (a white satin court gown), May 1 (a white gauze skirt and a "violet stripes on violet" overdress), June 12 (trim for a violet taffeta court gown), and June 18 (trim for a black-and-blue-striped *robe à la turque*). For these records, see Fonds Jacques Doucet, Dossier 596.

25. Campan, 338.

26. One probably apocryphal offshoot of this episode holds that La Fayette himself received advance notice of the royal family's escape plans and that he confronted Rose Bertin directly about her role in assisting them. To prove that he knew something was afoot, he brandished fabric swatches from the family's traveling costumes in Bertin's face. At this, Bertin allegedly ran straight to the Queen and warned her that "some unfaithful person" in the Tuileries (i.e., the revolutionary wardrobe woman) had given La Fayette incriminating details about "the dresses Your Majesties are to wear on the day of your departure." See Léonard, II, 60–65.

27. Campan, 289–290; Claude-Antoine-Gabriel, Duc de Choiseul-Stainville, *Relation du départ de Louis XVI, le 20 juin 1791* (Paris: Badouin Frères, 1822), 50–52.

28. Hyde, 302.

29. Anonymous, "Memoirs of Marie Antoinette," 23.

30. Camille Desmoulins, *Les Révolutions de France et de Brabant* (31 janvier 1791), no. 62.

31. Campan, 338.

32. For the complete list of the names the royal family used and the costumes they wore on their journey, see Reiset, II, 239–240; and Alcide de Beauchesne, *Louis XVIII: His Life, His Suffering, His Death: The Captivity of the Royal Family in the Temple,* trans. and ed. W. Hazlitt, 4 vols. (New York: Harper & Bros., 1853), 68–70. Beauchesne was a dyed-in-the-wool royalist, but as far as I have been able to determine, his account of the royals' costumes for the escape bears no obvious marks of idealization or fabrication. The fact that even his more politically fraught accounts of how

Louis Charles was later treated in prison are supported by testimonies from people on the opposite end of the political spectrum (for example, revolutionary prison guards) would seem to make him a reliable commentator, as Ian Dunlop has pointed out. See Dunlop, 368.

33. Beauchesne, III, 68.

34. Neither Rose Bertin's nor Madame Éloffe's ledgers seem to make mention of the dress or the bonnet the Queen reportedly wore on the flight to Varennes. However, on May 18, 1791 she commissioned Bertin to make a plain black shawl, which may have been the one she donned for her escape. See the Archives Nationales de France, O1 3792. Her large black hat and other aspects of the royal family's Varennes costumes receive mention in Choiseul-Stainville, *Relation du départ de Louis XVI*, 261.

35. Many commentators have pointed out that even unencumbered by so much cargo, the *berline* Fersen commissioned for the royals was far too luxurious and conspicuous to serve as an effective escape vehicle. See Reiset, II, 241.

36. This manicure set is in the permanent collection of the Musée Carnavalet in Paris.

37. For a firsthand account of these delays and mishaps, see Tourzel, I, 326–328.

38. Haslip, *Marie Antoinette*, 232. See also Tackett, 59.

39. Choiseul-Stainville, *Relation du départ de Louis XVI*, 80–84; G. Lenôtre, *The Flight of Marie Antoinette*, trans. Mrs. Rodolph Stawell (Philadelphia: J. B. Lippincott Co., 1908), 229–231; Tackett, 71.

40. See Lenôtre, *The Flight of Marie Antoinette*, 232; and Michelet, 552. This detail was reported in Métra's *Correspondance secrète* as early as June 30, 1791.

41. Tackett, 72. Revolutionary legend held that Louis XVI got out of his carriage at Sainte-Menehould to sample the local delicacy of pigs' feet, and that that is how Drouet spotted him. As Tackett and others have shown, however, this story is apocryphal.

42. Tackett, 75–76.

43. Price, 181.

44. Although Bouillé and his troops failed to appear, Choiseul-Stainville had managed to enter town with a cavalry of hussars, and he offered to help the royal family escape Varennes by force. Louis XVI, however, rejected this plan on the grounds that "in this unequal combat a musket shot might kill the Queen, or my daughter, or my son, or my sister." See Choiseul-Stainville, *Relation du départ de Louis XVI*, 93–94.

45. Lever, *Marie Antoinette: The Last Queen of France*, 259; Price, 184.

46. Imbert de Saint-Amand, *Marie Antoinette at the Tuileries*, 183.

47. Lever, *Marie Antoinette: The Last Queen of France*, 261.

48. Tackett, 81.

49. Hearsey, 158.

50. Hézècques, 179.

51. Tourzel, I, 360.

52. Campan, 348.

53. Ibid, 349.

54. See *Le Patriote français* (22 juin 1792), no. 683.

55. On the pivotal role of the Club des Cordeliers in the republican opposition that emerged after Varennes, see especially Tackett, 111–116.

56. Marie-Jeanne Philippon, Madame Roland, *Lettres de Madame Roland*, ed. Claude Perrould, 2 vols. (Paris: 1902), II, 316.

57. At his coronation at Reims, the King had been anointed as "God's lieutenant on earth," an exceptional figure among mortals and the intercessor between France and Heaven. See Hézècques, iv.

58. Campan, 360–362; Price, 219.

59. Schama, 573.

60. Campan, 360.

61. The King, too, was virulently attacked for his participation in the escape, which more or less definitively destroyed the French people's early idea of Louis XVI as a pro-revolutionary "Restorer of French Liberty." For a more comprehensive account of the public's irate reaction to the flight to Varennes, see Tackett, 88–150. For an in-depth analysis of the political caricatures of both the King and Queen that proliferated in response to Varennes, see Duprat, 58–209.

62. Anonymous, "Memoirs of Marie Antoinette," 51, 62. In her study of caricatures deploring the flight to Varennes, Annie Duprat notes that "the visual codes" used to designate the Queen include above all "coiffures featuring serpents and peacock or ostrich feathers. . . . It is the Queen's hair that transforms her into a figure of discord, [and] it is her clothing that forms the basis of the [cartoonists'] criticism, as befitting a woman whose taste for expensive fashions is well known!" See Duprat, 69.

63. Anonymous, "Nouvelle scène tragicomique et nullement héroique entre M. Louis Bourbon, maître serrurier, et Madame Marie Antoinette, sa femme" (Paris: Imprimerie de Tremblay, 1792 [?]), 6.

64. Both the blue trim on the Queen's fichu and the blue ribbon wrapped around her hat evoke the blue sash and feathers of *La Reine en gaulle*—a fact that attests to the persistence of the scandal that canvas provoked.

65. Hearsey, 155.

66. Campan, 341.

67. All these elements are perhaps implicit in one commentator's suggestive claim that "the flight of the French royal family was [ultimately] frustrated by Marie Antoinette's devotion to fashion." See Varron, 912.

68. Reiset, II, 245. See also Tackett, 98, who reports on the destruction these invaders wrought "in the Queen's room" but does not mention her clothing in particular.

69. For further discussion of how this bad trade not only substituted "coiffure" for "crown" but "humiliation" for "authority," see Duprat, 70.

70. Like several Varennes cartoons, this one mocked the Queen for masquerading as "la Baronne de Korff," though it was Madame de Tourzel who had assumed this identity, while Marie Antoinette tried to pass as the Baronne's governess. In all likelihood, the cartoonists' mistake was a function of the Germanic sound of the Baronne's surname, which thus functioned as further proof that Marie Antoinette had been operating as a nefarious agent of Austria, not a patriotic Queen of France.

71. Lenôtre, *The Flight of Marie Antoinette*, 231.

72. In this regard it is perhaps telling that between the return from Varennes and her death two years later, Marie Antoinette only placed one more order for *rubans à la Nation*, on January 4, 1792. Otherwise, it seems that she dropped the tricolor motif from her wardrobe altogether. See Reiset, II, 506.

73. Louis Prudhomme, "Réponse aux reproches qu'on nous a faits de n'avoir rien dit à Marie Antoinette pour l'année 1792," in *Les Révolutions de Paris*, no. 131, 152. This publication was founded by Élysée Loustalot, who died in 1790, leaving Prudhomme to take it over thereafter. See Schama, 445.

74. Campan, 346.

75. For the Éloffe orders, see Reiset, II, 238–250. For the Bertin orders, see Fonds Jacques Doucet, Dossier 596; as well as Langlade, 221.

76. *Correspondance de Marie Antoinette*, II, 136.

77. Fraser, 358. See also Girault de Coursac, 199–237; and Schama, 585.

78. Heidenstam, 112.

79. Fonds Jacques Doucet, Dossier 596.

80. Anonymous "Vie de Marie Antoinette, reine de France, femme de Louis XVI, roi des Français" (Paris: May 1791), 130–132; cited and translated in Thomas, 59.

81. Cited in Castelot, *Marie Antoinette* (1962), 331.

82. Heidenstam, 189.

83. This piece of fabric, a creamy white satin embroidered with a dove-gray wreath pattern, is in the permanent collection of the Musée Carnavalet in Paris.

84. *Correspondance de Marie Antoinette*, II, 180. It is André Castelot who hypothesizes that "powerful" is the illegible word in this letter of the Queen's. See Castelot, *Marie Antoinette* (1962), 412.

85. Fraser, 356.

86. *Correspondance de Marie Antoinette*, II, 171–173.

87. Erickson, 300.

88. Langlade, 215–216.

89. Williams, I, 143.

90. Alfred Pizard, *La France en 1789* (Paris: n.d.), 33.

91. The hat is mentioned in Léonard, II, 72; the dog in Fraser, 361.

92. This is not to say that Louis XVI utterly failed to take any political initiatives during this period, for as Munro Price, among others, has pointed out, his commitment to the monarchist cause was deep-seated and absolute. (See Price, 5, 192–205). It is rather to say that he was far from seeing eye to eye with his wife about how—and with how much speed and force—they ought to react to the revolutionary threat. As a result, Price likewise notes (224–226), Louis XVI was viewed by many even in his own government as woefully dissociated from the problems that faced his rule. As his foreign minister, Montmorin, told Mercy's friend the Comte de La Marck in January 1791, when the King "spoke about his affairs and his position, it seemed as though he were talking about matters concerning the Emperor of China." See A. de Baucourt (ed.), *Correspondance entre le Comte de Mirabeau et le Comte de La Marck,* 3 vols. (Paris: 1851), III, 30.

93. Castelot, *Marie Antoinette* (1962), 402.

94. *Correspondance de Marie Antoinette*, II, 178.

95. For a good cursory account of Le Brun's politics, see Annemarie Kleinert, "La Mode, miroir de la Révolution française," in Join-Dieterle and Delpierre (eds.), 70–71. See also Françoise Tétart-Vittu, "Presse et diffusion des modes françaises," in Join-Dieterle and Delpierre (eds.), 129–136, 134.

96. See Pierre Arizzoli-Clémentel (ed.), *Soieries de Lyon: Commandes royales du XVIIIe siècle* (Lyon: Sézanne, 1989), 90–93.

97. *Le Journal de la mode et du goût* (15 février 1791), Cahier XXXVI, 1; and (15 mars 1791), Cahier III, 1–2.

98. On the exodus of fashion merchants from Paris, see, among others, Morris, I, 368; cited in Ribeiro, *Fashion in the French Revolution*, 75.

99. Mansel, 71; see also Roche, *The Culture of Clothing*, 315.

100. Edmond and Jules de Goncourt, *Histoire de la société française pendant la Révolution* (Paris: Boucher, 2002), 9. On the displacement of Parisian by provincial fashion merchants during this period, see also Morris, I, 368.

101. Goncourt, *L'Histoire de la société française*, 12.

102. Delpierre, "Rose Bertin, les marchandes de modes et la Révolution," in Join-Dieterle and Delpierre (eds.), 22.

103. *Journal de la cour et de la ville* (1 avril 1790), 12.

104. *Le Journal de la mode et du goût* (25 juin 1790), Cahier XIII, 1.

105. Ibid (15 mai 1791), Cahier IX, 2. This would remain one of Le Brun's favorite hairstyles, resurfacing in his journal as soon as October 25, 1791, and as late as August 1, 1792, not long before the magazine folded.

106. *Le Journal de la mode et du goût* (25 mai 1791), Cahier X, 2.

107. Goncourt, *Histoire de la société française*, Chapter V. See also Ribeiro, *Fashion and the French Revolution*, 75–76.

108. *Le Journal de la mode et du goût* (25 juin 1791), Cahier XIII, 1; (5 juillet 1791), Cahier XIV, 1–2; and (15 jullet 1791), Cahier XV, 2.

109. *Le Journal de la mode et du goût* (5 août 1791), Cahier XVII, 1; (15 août 1791), 2; (5 septembre 1791), Cahier XX, 2; (25 septembre 1791), Cahier XXII, 2; (15 novembre 1791), Cahier XXX, 2; (25 décembre 1791), Cahier XXXI, 2.

110. Lever, *Marie Antoinette: The Last Queen of France*, 277.

111. Léonard, II, 68; Langlade, 227.

112. Léonard, II, 68.

113. Lafont d'Aussonne, 569.

114. Baron R. M. de Klinckowström (Fersen's nephew), *Le Comte de Fersen et la cour de France*, 2 vols. (Paris: Firmin-Didot, 1877–1888), II, 219. See also Tourzel, II, 109.

115. La Rochetière, II, 339.

116. Reiset, II, 300.

117. F. de Barghon Fort-Rion (ed.), *Mémoires de Madame Élisabeth, sœur de Louis XVI* (Paris: Auguste Vaton, 1860), 401.

118. At this time, Louis XVI also vetoed a measure outlining severe punishments for priests who refused to swear an oath to the Civil Constitution of the Clergy. He did, however, accept a contemporaneous decree that called for the disbanding of the royal guard at the Tuileries. For a cogent overview of the start of the war and the nature and effects of these vetoes, see La Rochetière, II, 317–323; as well as A. Aulard, *The French Revolution: A Political History, 1789–1804*, trans. and ed. Bernard Mall (New York: Scribners, 1910), II, 31–33.

119. For more on the "liberty bonnet" and the *bonnet rouge* (which were themselves prone to subtle distinctions), see Wrigley, 152–158.

120. Montjoie, 322.

121. Hearsey, 169; Montjoie, 322; Mansel, 156.

122. Mansel, 72. See also Duc de Lévis-Mirepoix, *Aventures d'une famille française* (Paris: 1949), 279.

123. Marie Antoinette did, however, allow the Dauphin to be coiffed with the cap, after the mobsters began to scream menacingly: "If you love the Nation, set the red cap on your son's head!" See Imbert de Saint-Amand, *Marie Antoinette and the Downfall of Royalty*, 213.

124. Roussel d'Épinal, 279.

125. This claim about "Ça ira" coming from a tune Marie Antoinette had been known to play on the clavichord appears in Reiset, II, 130–131. This translation of the title and refrain "Ça ira" comes from Williams, I, 143 n. 6.

126. Which is not to say that Danton and Robespierre began their careers as radical republicans; Danton and the Cordeliers had only assumed that stance after Varennes, and Robespierre (who condemned the Cordeliers' June 1791 call for republicanism as untimely) reversed his own, constitutional-monarchist position several months afterward. See Karmel, 77–79.

127. *Le Père Duchesne*, no. 123. It bears noting that despite the "republican" sentiment that emerged after the flight to Varennes in June 1791, and despite his own involvement in and exploitation of that shift, Hébert was quite cautious about endorsing "republicanism" as such until the fall of 1792, when the publication of Louis XVI's hidden state papers further dramatically "deroyalized"—in Hébert's parlance—public opinion. On this point, see Aulard, II, 94–95.

128. Tourzel, II, 204; Castelot, *Marie Antoinette* (1966), 428.

129. Campan, 399. Louis XVI, by contrast, donned a bulletproof metal cuirass when appearing before potentially hostile crowds at the 1792 Fête de la Fédération. See Lever, *Marie Antoinette: The Last Queen of France*, 277.

130. Imbert de Saint-Amand, *Marie Antoinette and the Downfall of Royalty*, 263–264.

131. Marie Antoinette herself noted as much when she wrote to Fersen on July 15, 1792: "Paris is in a great agitation; everyone is waiting for some big event, which each party hopes to turn to its advantage, but of which I can scarcely conceive. . . ." Nine days later, she sent him another letter to inform him that "the lives of the King and Queen are in the greatest danger; that a delay of even one day could lead to incalculable misery; that we are awaiting [the allies] with extreme impatience; . . . [and that] the troop of assassins is growing unstoppably." See *Correspondance de Marie Antoinette*, II, 243, 246.

132. Lever, *Marie Antoinette: The Last Queen of France*, 279.

133. Archives Nationales de France, AN C192: depositions of Calley, Larchey, Topet, Frenot; also cited in Mansel, 74.

134. *Correspondance de Marie Antoinette*, II, 248.

135. François Huë, *Dernières années du règne et de la vie de Louis XVI par l'un des officiers de la chambre du roi, appelé par ce prince, après la journée du 10 août, à l'honneur de rester auprès de lui et de la famille royale*, with a bibliographical notice by René du Menil de Maricourt (Paris: Henri Plon, 1860 [1814]), 328. It is worth noting that Huë's memoir was published before the Restoration, and thus cannot be (and has not been) dismissed as royalist propaganda designed to curry favor with the new Bourbon government.

136. This shoe was salvaged and today forms part of the permanent collection at the Musée Carnavalet in Paris.

137. Hearsey, 180.

138. Huë, 339; "Relation de Dufour," in G. Lenôtre (ed.), *La Captivité et la mort de Marie Antoinette, d'après des relations de témoins oculaires et des documents inédits* (Paris: Perrin, 1928), 10; Cléry, *Journal de ce qui s'est passé à la tour du Temple pendant la captivité de Louis XVI, roi de France, au Temple* (Paris: Mercure de France, 1987 [1798]), 45, 206 n. 1. Like Huë's, Cléry's memoir was published before the Restoration and thus can be exempted from charges of politically expedient royalism.

139. "Relation de Dufour," in Lenôtre (ed.), 13.

140. Huë, 338.

141. Roussel d'Épinal, 168.

142. J. G. Millingen, *Recollections of Republican France from 1790 to 1801* (London: n.p., 1848), 120.

143. Roussel d'Épinal, 168. Another account maintains that "the hats, caps, bonnets, and other articles of female attire were placed on the parts of [the] degraded carcasses" that lay on the palace floors. See Hyde, 303.

144. Roussel d'Épinal, 168–169. On the Vigée-Lebrun paintings that survived the sacking of Marie Antoinette's wardrobe, see Roussel d'Épinal, 362.

145. Pierre Saint-Amand, "Adorning Marie Antoinette," 29. Saint-Amand's wonderful term for this process, coined to describe the fallen queen's increasingly restricted and shabby prison wardrobe, is "[the] gradual denarcissization of Marie Antoinette." See Saint-Amand, "Terrorizing Marie Antoinette," 266.

146. Roussel d'Épinal, 92–93, 114–115.

147. At the auction of the royals' possessions, Marie Antoinette's clothing elicited far more excited bidding than did her husband's. (One of the King's most insanely luxurious court outfits, which "was embroidered with a thousand flowers" and had cost 30,000 livres to make, fetched only 110 livres, for instance.) These auctions began in the summer of 1793 and lasted six months, but yielded disappointing profits for the Nation. See Langlade, 225–226; and Fraser, 420. According to Roussel d'Épinal, the crown and the scepter that Louis XVI had received at his coronation were sent to the mint and melted down for their gold (369 n. 2).

148. On the "widespread, collective dissemination of items of royal dress" after August 10, see Wrigley, 21. As Wrigley points out, on August 13, the Convention ordered that all items stolen from the Tuileries be returned and placed in the Archives Nationales, but this decree does not seem to have been strictly obeyed where Marie Antoinette's clothing was concerned.

149. On the transformation of the royals' abandoned personal effects into monarchist relics, see Wrigley, 18–25. For longer discussion of how clothes functioned, in the early modern period, as "materials of memory," see Ann Rosalind Jones and Peter Stallybrass, *Renaissance Clothing and the Materials of Memory* (New York: Cambridge University Press, 2000). Although this book focuses on Renaissance England, its central thesis that memory, which at the dawn of the early modern period was understood to be located in clothing, gradually became "vagrant and subject to restless change" is a fascinating one. It could be most useful in a more in-depth consideration of how royalist relics functioned in the wake of the sovereigns' execution, when the revolutionaries, as a matter of state policy, tried to place the royals' memory under erasure.

150. The order for this *pouf* survives in the Archives Nationales de France, F4 1311, and is reproduced in Langlade, 225.

151. On this point, see Soboul, 22; Ribeiro, *Fashion in the French Revolution,* 67–70; and Roche, "Apparences révolutionnaires ou révolution des apparences," in Join-Dieterle and Delpierre (eds.), 193.

152. Williams, II, 193. As is well known, Maximilien Robespierre presented an unusual exception to this rule, preferring to retain the powdered hairstyle, tailored silk jackets, and impeccable ruffled cravats of the *ancien régime,* despite his radical politics. As Helen Maria Williams remarked of the Jacobin leader, he "always appeared not only dressed with neatness, but with elegance, and while he called himself the leader of the sans-culottes, he never adopted the costume of his band" (I, 194). For more on the shabbiness of the sans-culottes, see Roussel d'Épinal, 267. In point of fact, many of these men were far more prosperous than their grubby uniform revealed—a prime example being the successful brewer Santerre, who had participated in the storming of the Bastille and helped to lead the attack on the Tuileries of June 20, 1792. As Simon Schama has observed, Santerre and some of the other leading sans-culottes "were not merely comfortable, but rich"; their adoption of working-men's pants, in particular, thus betrayed a "romanticization of the [humble] world of craft shops," despite their own origins in "the better off strata of the artisanal trades and professions." See Schama, 602–603. The nineteenth-century author Alexandre Dumas, *père,* pokes fun of this contradiction when he writes in *Le Chevalier de Maison-Rouge*—an historical novel based on the Carnation Affair (discussed below)—that "Santerre's patriotism was visible to all in the grease-stains on his jacket." See Dumas, *Le Chevalier de Maison-Rouge,* ed. Gilbert Sigaux (Lausanne: Rencontre, 1967), 170.

153. F. Hervé (ed.), *Madame Tussaud's Memoirs and Reminiscences of France* (London, 1838), 177.

154. On this point, see also Dr. John Moore, *A Journal During a Residence in France, from the Beginning of August to the Middle of December, 1792,* 2 vols. (London, 1793), II, 430; cited in Ribeiro, *Fashion in the French Revolution,* 70, in the context of her larger discussion of how during this phase of the Revolution, "functional simplicity . . . was sometimes carried to extremes in a determination to indicate a sympathy with republicanism." The suspicion with which Orléans was looked upon became altogether apparent when he was arrested and executed as a counterrevolutionary suspect in 1793, but even his election to the new Convention Nationale in the fall of 1792 attested to his diminished public popularity. As A. Aulard has noted, Orléans received fewer votes than any other deputy from Paris. See Aulard, II, 122.

CHAPTER TEN: BLACK

1. Zweig, 367.
2. Tourzel, II, 347.
3. Huë, 343.
4. Lever, *Marie Antoinette: The Last Queen of France,* 282.
5. Huë, 348.
6. Ibid, 347.
7. Castelot, *Marie Antoinette* (1962), 444.
8. A little wooden horse and buggy that the Dauphin played with in the Tower survives to this day; a photograph of it appears in Castelot, *Marie Antoinette* (1989), 196.
9. Fraser, 384. In her text, Fraser refers to this dog by its nickname, Mignon ["Cute"]. I, however, have retained the name the Princesse de Lamballe originally gave it, Thisbée—in part because that happens to be my own dog's name, and in part because it is a name that, in Ovid's *Metamorphoses,* signifies faithfulness to the death, a quality that Lamballe demonstrated in spades. Interestingly enough, the novelist Alexandre Dumas, *père,* renames this animal "Black" when narrating Marie Antoinette's captivity, and imagines Black, "exhausted, scrawny, broken-down," howling disconsolately on a Parisian street corner as his mistress is led to the guillotine. In this scene, Black himself becomes—like Marie Antoinette's black widow's weeds and her friend Lamballe's black beaver hat—a figure for inextinguishable royalist loyalty and (nonverbalized) mourning. See Dumas, *Le Chevalier de Maison-Rouge,* 492.
10. Cléry, 63.
11. The most detailed—though, one might say, suspiciously, gloatingly so—account of Marie Antoinette's physical transformation is offered by Walter in his introductory materials to the documents from the Queen's trial. See Walter, 57.
12. Cited in Castelot, *Marie Antoinette* (1962), 448.
13. "Relation de Goret," in Lenôtre (ed.), 129 n. 1.
14. Cléry, 45.
15. Madeleine Delpierre has described the Bourbons' Temple outfits as betraying an "expressive . . . mélange of simplicity and the remnants of grandeur." See Delpierre, "La Garde-robe de la famille royale au Temple," in Delpierre and Join-Dieterle (eds.), 27–30, 30.
16. "Relation de Moelle," in Lenôtre (ed.), 204–205 n. 1. Like most of the narratives published in Lenôtre's collection, Moelle's was first published during the Restoration. See Moelle, *Six journées passées au Temple et autres details sur la famille royale qui y a été détenu* (Paris: Dentu, 1820).
17. On the Bertin order of May 1, 1791, see Archives Nationales, O1 3792; and Langlade, 221. On the orders she placed with Bertin at the start of her confinement, see Archives Nationales, F4 1311; and Langlade, 240. On the orders she placed with Éloffe at this time, see Reiset, II, 347–350. On the orders she placed with sundry other fashion purveyors while in the Temple, see Asquith, 194–195.
18. Langlade, 255; Archives Nationales de France, F4 1311.
19. Reiset, II, 507. The brown, floral-embroidered dress she also wore in the Temple is mentioned in the "Relation de Moelle," in Lenôtre (ed.), 206, as is the taffeta *chemise*-dress, 206 n. 1. On the conveniently modish practicality of "Paris mud," see Reiset, II, 342. Even this drab color appears to have remained part of Marie Antoinette's fashion legend, as a journalist writing for *The New York Times Magazine* recently predicted that "next season, [fashion will] probably [drop] a collective curtsey to Rose Bertin, Marie Antoinette's designer, who created a shade of brown based on the color of mud in the Paris gutters." See Horacio Silva, "Belles de Jour," *The New York Times Magazine* (February 26, 2006): 80. Mentioned in the afterword, the drab-toned "Marie Antoinette" dress Rocahs unveiled in December 2005 anticipated this forecast.

20. According to Huë, she did have three *femmes de chambre* in her service, but none of them, it seems, was qualified or willing to assist with the Queen's *toilette*. Cléry, for his part, reports that he himself was conscripted to do Marie Antoinette's hair; see Cléry, 63.

21. Such a concern would be consistent with Marie Antoinette's exactingly "German" preoccupation with good hygiene, remarked upon by women who waited on her at Versailles, like Madame Campan, and in her later prison at the Conciergerie, like Rosalie Lamorlière (cited below).

22. "Relation de Moelle," in Lenôtre (ed.), 206–207.

23. One report penned during the Terror claimed that Léonard had been guillotined, presumably for his suspect ties to the Queen; but that report was later proven to be false, as Léonard somehow eluded the authorities and survived into the next century. (His brother may have been executed in his place.) See Lenôtre, *The Flight of Marie Antoinette*, 232–237.

24. Though he was commonly called Cléry, the valet's full name was Jean-Baptiste Cathaney. As Simone Bertière notes, it was because Cléry had "proven his patriotism in 1789" that Pétion accepted his offer to enter the royals' service in the Temple. See Bertière, 603.

25. Between 1785 and 1788, Léonard received between 1,574 and 4,063 livres per year for his services to the Queen. See Archives Nationales de France, O1. 3792.

26. In a somewhat different vein, Carrolly Erickson has hypothesized that "it may have given Antoinette a small measure of satisfaction to spend the Commune's [money] on finery . . . believing as she did that any day the Austrian and Prussian soldiers would be in Paris." See Erickson, 320–321.

27. Madame Campan relates that Marie Antoinette's affection for Louis XVI had been steadily growing for over a decade before their imprisonment—and that although her feelings never assumed the form of a grand romantic passion, the Queen felt a powerful "enthusiasm and tenderness for the goodness of his character." See Campan, 211.

28. Castelot, *Marie Antoinette* (1962), 447.

29. Bertière, 609.

30. M. Cléry, *Journal de ce qui s'est passé à la tour du Temple, suivi de "Dernières heures de Louis XVI," par l'abbé Edgeworth de Firmont, et de "Mémoire" écrit par Madame Royale de France,* ed. Jacques Brosse (Paris: Mercure de France, 1987), 42.

31. Cléry, 41.

32. Ibid, 40.

33. *La Chronique de Paris* (21 août 1792); also cited in de Baecque, *Glory and Terror,* 221.

34. Cléry, 63; Huë, 351–352.

35. Cléry, 69.

36. Zweig, 370; Bertière, 610–611.

37. Fraser, 386. But as Madame Royale recorded, she and her family were occasionally allowed to read newspapers written by revolutionary journalists reporting on the Nation's victories against the allies, and on the continuing exodus of French aristocrats to destinations outside France. These sporadic exceptions to the no-newspaper rule seem to have been designed to demoralize the prisoners. See Madame Royale de France, *Mémoire sur la captivité des princes et princesses ses parents depuis le 10 août 1792 jusqu'à la mort de son frère,* in Cléry, 131–183, 141.

38. Huë, 366–367; Cléry, 51–52.

39. On this point, see Fraser, 409; as well as note 172, below.

40. Already in the days leading up to the August 10 uprising, the Parisians had formally demanded that the monarchy be overthrown, a demand that the members of the Assemblée failed to address in time to dissuade the people from violence.

41. Schama, 627; Aulard, II, 109.

42. *Chronique de Paris* (19 septembre 1792); cited in Aulard, II, 107.

43. Reiset, II, 361.

44. Campan, 306. André Sarazin notes that over time, white cockades became ubiquitous, too, among the counterrevolutionary insurgents in the Vendée; see La Rochejaquelein, xxx.

45. The original Dumont portrait is alternatively dated 1791 (by Marguerite Jallut) and 1792 (by the Comte de Reiset); it is Reiset who claims that she gave miniature versions of it to Madame de Tourzel and the Duchesse de Fitz-James sometime in the summer of 1792. See Reiset, II, 287. Jallut, by contrast, attributes these miniatures to the Polish painter Alexandre Kucharski (who executed an unfinished portrait of Marie Antoinette, wearing quite a different outfit, during the summer of 1792). Jallut suggests that the Dumont image belonged to Louis XVI himself and was later copied by an engraver named Tardieu. See Jallut, 58.

46. *Le Journal de la mode et du goût* (20 septembre 1792), 2. In fact, Le Brun had conveyed a similar message in his journal on the first anniversary of the flight to Varennes. In this issue, he also featured a black and yellow *pouf à la contre-Révolution* and wrote of its color scheme: "This is entirely symbolic and women of distinction know perfectly well how to interpret it." See *Le Journal de la mode et du goût* (20 juin 1792), Cahier XIX, 3.

47. Aulard, II, 91.

48. Erickson, 305.

49. Campan, 306. Similarly, Mark Wrigley has documented the acts of violence that these "signs of disorder"—the Bourbon rosettes—elicited at this time. See Wrigley, 102–103.

50. Cléry, 46. Madame Élisabeth, too, was forced to help unstitch the royal monograms.

51. Thomas, 103. According to Annie Duprat, Hébert was particularly vigilant about maintaining the plainness of his prisoners' wardrobes, construing this as part of a larger project of "de-royalizing" the republic. See Duprat, 208.

52. Godechot, 113. As Godechot points out, Jean-Paul Marat was particularly instrumental in fueling public fears that counterrevolution was brewing among the aristocratic prisoners of Paris.

53. Madame Royale, 138.

54. Cited in Hearsey, 192. Additional, corroborating accounts of this episode are cited in Wrigley, 115. According to Madame Campan, the same tactic had been used to protect the royal family during their brief stay in the Feuillants convent after August 10. See Campan, 409.

55. de Baecque, *Glory and Terror,* 78. Antonia Fraser, by contrast, argues that the story of Lamballe's hair being dressed after her murder is "plausible" on the grounds that "the Princesse's original coiffure could hardly have survived the assault of the hammers outside La Force, even if she had managed to preserve it during her fortnight inside" and that it was the blond hairdo that made her head "instantly recognizable" to the inhabitants of the Tower.

56. Cited in de Baecque, *Glory and Terror,* 79; and in M. de Lescure, *La Princesse de Lamballe* (Paris: H. Plon, 1864), 421.

57. Cited in Beauchesne, 364–365; and in de Baecque, *Glory and Terror,* 79.

58. In this reading, I part company somewhat from Antoine de Baecque, who notes that Lamballe's recoiffing was "intend[ed] to show, in contrast with the gushing blood, . . . the refinement in which the princess wanted to live. [Her] delicate, finely worked, frivolous appearance designates the past and the caste to which the victim belongs: the *ancien régime*, the court." See de Baecque, *Glory and Terror,* 80. While this

observation is suggestive, it fails to recognize that in fact Lamballe's "finely worked, frivolous appearance" identified her specifically with the Queen, whom she resembled both in her appearance and in her clothing tastes, and not just generally with the court.

59. de Baecque, *Glory and Terror,* 80.

60. Nicolas Rétif de la Bretonne, *Les Nuits révolutionnaires: 1789–1793,* preface by Charles Brabant (Paris: Éditions de Paris, 1989), 103. Like other supposed eyewitnesses, Rétif insists that Lamballe's murderers decided to "wash and curl" her hair before carrying her head to the Temple (103).

61. The phrase is de Baecque's (*Glory and Terror,* 80), though he reads these qualities merely as a generalized "sign of scandalous femininity," without insisting on the degree to which they underscore the two friends' specific, shared (and "scandalous") involvement in fashion.

62. Madame Royale, 138.

63. Ibid.

64. Fraser, 389.

65. Madame Royale, 138; Moore, 183.

66. Chevalier Nicolas de Maistre, *Marie Antoinette, Archiduchesse d'Autriche, Reine de France (1793),* ed. Paul de Perugia (Mayenne: Yves Floch, 1993 [1793]), 23.

67. Anonymous, *La Famille royale préservée au Temple par la garde nationale de Paris et surtout par la conduite énergique d'un officier municipal, secondé par les commissaires de services, le 3 septembre 1792,* cited in de Baecque, *Glory and Terror,* 62; and in Georges Bertin, *Madame de Lamballe d'après des documents inédits* (Paris: Bureaux de la Revue retrospective, 1888), 323–326.

68. Fraser, 387; Godechot, 114.

69. "Vie de Marie Antoinette d'Autriche," 124; cited and translated in Thomas, 124. Like the "Essai historique," the "Vie de Marie Antoinette" was printed in several releases and expanded each time to include references to the latest current events and scandalous allegations. The version cited here thus alludes to Lamballe's imprisonment (August 1792) and the prison massacres (September 1792), even though an earlier version was published in the summer of 1791.

70. Perhaps not incidentally, this trope of red markings on white skin also surfaces in at least one description of the punishment—branding with the letter "V," for *voleuse* (thief)—that Madame de La Motte received for her role in the Diamond Necklace Affair. The memoirs of Léonard allude to the throbbing red "V" standing out beautifully on La Motte's "skin white as satin" (II, 108).

71. "Vie de Marie Antoinette," 78; cited and translated in Thomas, 134.

72. As Antoine de Baecque has pointed out, the Convention never officially "proclaim[ed] the foundation of a new regime. The historian can look: nowhere will he unearth an official decree in the archives installing the first French republic. He will only find, dated September 21, 1792, a suggestion from Camus, responsible for the National Archives, henceforth to date [all] administrative documents from the 'Year I of the French Republic'" (*Glory and Terror,* 87). September 21 is nevertheless the date that is generally given for the abolition of the royalty and the foundation of the Republic, though sometimes September 22 is mentioned instead, as a date on which a decree reiterating Camus's notion of "Year I," effective immediately, was published. See Godechot, 121.

73. Reported the following day in *Le Moniteur universel,* no. 266 (22 septembre 1792). As Aulard points out, the Assemblée had declared on August 14 that the King's name should be stricken from the list of public officials and removed from all government documents. Similarly, the Commune decreed the destruction of all heraldic and royal emblems on August 21, 1792—although, in fact, many such emblems had already been destroyed after Varennes in June 1791. See Aulard, II, 85–86, 92.

74. David P. Jordan, *The King's Trial: The French Revolution versus Louis XVI* (Berkeley: University of California Press, 1979), 57–58.

75. Jordan, 58.

76. On the legal and political complexities of trying the King, see Jordan, 56–207, as well as Michael Walzer's excellent, lengthy introduction to his anthology, *Regicide and Revolution: Speeches at the Trial of Louis XVI,* trans. Marian Rothstein (New York: Columbia University Press, 1992), especially 8–68.

77. Walzer, 123–124; italics original.

78. Godechot, 123; Erickson, 323–324.

79. Aulard, II, 83.

80. Walzer, 138.

81. Ibid. Robespierre's fellow deputy Maihle pointed out, however, that as a mere consort, whose role was circumscribed by Salic Law, Marie Antoinette's case did not merit the special consideration that her husband's necessarily demanded: "By what right could her case be treated like that of Louis XVI? Have the heads of those women who bore the name of Queen of France ever been any more inviolable or more sacred than the heads of the mob of rebels and conspirators? When you come to consider her case, you will decide if there are grounds for bringing charges against her, and it is only to ordinary tribunals that those charges can be sent." See Walzer, 108.

82. This change in nomenclature may have been designed not just to strip Louis XVI of his royal title but also to remind him, as Michael Walzer points out, that "kings were once elected," as evidenced by the fact that "in France, the ruling family itself dated its authority from the choice of Hugues Capet, whose father was no king, who was himself no conqueror" (47). Nevertheless, Louis XVI himself objected strenuously to this designation; see Cléry, 74.

83. Cléry, who helped the King dress for his appearance at the Convention, confirms that he wore "his hat and his redingote" (74). That the redingote in question was the "riding-coat colored *cheveux de la Reine*" that he ordered for his captivity is apparent from the reference to his "yellowish coat" in the *Grand détail exact de l'interrogatoire de Louis Capet à la barre de la Convention nationale* (Paris: 1792), cited in de Baecque, *Glory and Terror,* 90.

84. Cléry, 77.

85. Godechot, 125.

86. Ibid, 126. See also the *Décrets de la Convention nationale des 15, 16, 17, 19 et 20 janvier,* Article I. The death penalty is stipulated in Article II.

87. Cléry, 104–105.

88. "Relation de Goret," in Lenôtre (ed.), 148.

89. Lever, *Marie Antoinette: The Last Queen of France,* 288; "Relation de Turgy," in Lenôtre (ed.), 102. According to Bertrand de Molleville, Louis XVI had worn his redingote—colored *cheveux de la Reine*—to the scaffold. See Molleville, III, 219.

90. Lenôtre (ed.), "Relation de Goret," 149, and "Relation de Turgy," 129. Although this incident is commonly reported in biographies of the Queen, I should note here that Antonia Fraser has challenged its plausibility, on the grounds that it was not recorded by Madame Royale, "the prime witness" to her mother's reactions on that day, and that "open recognition of the boy as King would have been an astonishingly dangerous act" so soon after Louis XVI's execution (404–405).

91. Schama, 673.

92. *Correspondance de Marie Antoinette,* II, 180.

93. *Correspondance de Marie Antoinette,* II, 236.

94. Fraser, 404; Madame Royale, 147.

95. "Relation de Goret," in Lenôtre (ed.), 149. This account is corroborated by Madame Royale, 147.

96. Antonia Fraser makes a similar point when she asserts that "as the widow of a King of France, she attached much symbolic importance" to her mourning garb (378).

97. "Relation de Goret," in Lenôtre (ed.), *La Captivité et la mort de Marie Antoinette*, 149. See also *Demandes de Marie Antoinette à la Commune de Paris, avec les arrêts que la Commune a pris sur ces demandes (23 janvier 1793)*, in the Archives Nationales de France, N. L641.489.

98. Where Fraser identifies Pion as the woman who made the clothes, Haslip describes her as "a servingwoman formerly attached to [Madame Royale's] household," who was simply brought in to "do the alterations" on badly fitting clothing procured from another, unnamed source. Dunlop, for his part, identifies Pion as "one of Madame de Tourzel's women" and merely notes that she was asked "to prepare the clothes" for the mourning royals. See Fraser, 378; Haslip, *Marie Antoinette*, 278; and Dunlop, 363.

99. Dunlop, 363–364.

100. "Relation de Lepitre," in Lenôtre (ed.), 172; Delpierre, "La Garde-robe de la famille royale au Temple," in Delpierre and Join-Dieterle (eds.), 29; F. de Vyré, *Marie Antoinette: Sa vie, sa mort* (Paris: Plon, 1889); and the Archives Nationales de France, F4.1314, miscellaneous *mémoires* dated January 26 and 27, 1793.

101. Archives Nationales de France, AF II 3, plate 14; reproduced in Sapori, ill. 57. The itemized bill from Bertin is reproduced in Sapori, ill. 58.

102. See note 100, above; as well as Delpierre, "La Garde-robe de la famille royale au Temple," in Delpierre and Join-Dieterle (eds.), 29.

103. Sapori, 231.

104. Abby Zanger, "Making Sweat: Sex and the Gender of National Reproduction in the Marriage of Louis XIII," in Françoise Jaouën and Ben Semple, *Corps mystique, corps sacré: Textual Transfigurations of the Body from the Middle Ages to the Seventeenth Century*, a special issue of *Yale French Studies*, no. 86 (New Haven and London: Yale University Press, 1994): 187–205, 188. For the six-month mourning period, see Reiset, II, 224.

105. Jacques de Norvins, *Mémorial*, 2 vols. (Paris: 1896), I, 56. See also Mercier, "De l'habit noir," in *Tableau de Paris*, I, 200–201.

106. Castelot, *Queen of France: A Biography of Marie Antoinette*, trans. Denise Folliot (New York: Harper & Brothers, 1957), 76. See also Erickson, 95–96.

107. The subtleties of early modern French mourning are quite difficult to track with precision, as sources contradict one another as to what constituted appropriate apparel, for whom, and at what stage of the mourning process. However, some useful information on the subject appears in Reiset, II, 223–225; Roussel d'Épinal, 308–309; Kraatz, "Marie Antoinette: la passion des étoffes," 76–77; and Pellegrin, 71–73. The explanation of French royal mourning under Louis XV offered in Erickson, 95–96, closely resembles the one provided in Castelot, *Queen of France* (1957), 76.

108. *Le Journal de la mode et du goût* (25 mars 1790), Cahier IV, 7–8.

109. Pellegrin, 72.

110. For an account of a man who was arrested for wearing black buttons and a black collar construed as signs of mourning for the King's death, see Pellegrin, 49.

111. Molleville, III, 220; Erickson, 329; Schama, 670.

112. In 1815, at the start of the Restoration that brought Louis XVIII, erstwhile Comte de Provence, to the throne, Louis XVI's and Marie Antoinette's remains were dug up and reburied at Saint-Denis. Perhaps the most haunting account of their exhumation appears in René de Chateaubriand, *Mémoires d'Outre-Tombe*, 2 vols. (Paris: Gallimard/

Plëiade, 1955 [1803–1841]), I, 906. In this memoir, Chateaubriand claimed to recognize Marie Antoinette's once-enchanting smile in her disinterred jawbone.

113. Perhaps the best-known contemporary image of the decapitated king, this engraving is reproduced in Caroline Weber, *Terror and Its Discontents*, 67–68. It can also be found in the Bibliothèque Nationale de France, Département des Estampes, Qb1 M101 880. I should note here that "fields" is a loose translation for the French *sillons*, a more precise but somewhat stranger-sounding rendition for which would be "furrows in the land." Similar images were disseminated in Prudhomme's newspaper, *Les Révolutions de Paris*.

114. Cited in Haslip, *Marie Antoinette*, 277. For more on the British response to Louis XVI's death, see Dunlop, 362; and David Bindman, *In the Shadow of the Guillotine: Britain and the French Revolution* (London: British Museum Publications, 1989).

115. Haslip, *Marie Antoinette*, 277; Fraser, 412.

116. On the profusion of black accessories among royalists at this time, see Léonard, II, 287.

117. Mercier, "Collets noirs," in *Le Nouveau Paris*, II, 206.

118. On the violence that the royalists' black emblems, in particular, triggered, see Pellegrin, 49–50. This violence was already evident before August 10, as for instance when the mob attacked the royal guard who dared to wear mourning for Leopold II. On the degree to which royalists were forced underground in this period, see Aulard, II, 119.

119. The issue of royal mourning remained so politicized, in fact, that when Madame Du Barry was hauled before the Revolutionary Tribunal in November 1793, one of the charges leveled against her was that she had "worn mourning for Capet." As it so happened, Du Barry had returned to France from England (where she had lived awhile in exile) dressed in black, but this was in tribute to a recently deceased lover, not to her former lover's grandson Louis XVI. This part of the transcript from her trial is cited in H. Noel Williams, *Memoirs of Madame Dubarry of the Court of Louis XV* (New York: P. F. Collier & Son, 1910), 370–371.

120. As Edgar Quinet, one of the great nineteenth-century historians of the Revolution, has remarked, "once the King was dead, [republicans] thought they saw the rebirth of royalty everywhere they looked: people seemed to carry it or wear it [*la porter*] within themselves." See Edgar Quinet, *La Révolution française*, preface by Claude Lefort (Paris: Belin, 1989), 356.

121. Cited in Wrigley, 116; taken from the *Archives Parlementaires*, no. 59 (8 mars 1793), 712.

122. The republicans' anxiety about how citizens dressed, and about the possibility that uncontrolled costumes could lead to political chaos, eventually led the *conventionnel*, propagandist, and artist Jacques-Louis David to begin sketching proposed national costumes for the French people. This issue also sparked the publication of Claude-François-Xavier Mercier de Compiègne, *Comment m'habillerai-je? Réflexions politiques et philosophiques sur l'habillement françois et sur la necessité d'un costume national* (Paris: 1793). In this text, Mercier de Compiègne criticized the old régime habit of "immortalizing heroic deeds through bonnets," such as the *bonnet à la Grenade*, and pointed out that in Roman times, heroes were commemorated through public monuments (4, 8–10).

123. Ironically, this "patriotic" embargo on silk did just what Marie Antoinette's detractors had accused her of doing by (unpatriotically) wearing foreign fabrics like muslin, which was to lay waste to the French silk industry. Whereas, in 1786, there were twelve thousand silk looms in operation in Lyon, by 1793, this number had dropped to five thousand. See Mansel, 71, 74–75.

124. Wrigley, 104. As Wrigley also notes, by April 1793 the Convention was reviewing proposals that legislated precisely how the cockade should be worn: its size, its position on the hat, and so on (105).

125. Schama, 735.

126. As Roussel d'Épinal has pointed out, this strategy sometimes worked, for instance saving the life of the persecuted publisher of the royalist *Journal de la cour et de la ville*. The royal prisoners themselves, in fact, might have benefited from such a tactic; as one of the never-realized plots to rescue the Queen and her family would have involved her children dressing in the "battered and ragged trousers" of their enemies. See Fraser, 409.

127. Interestingly, Edgar Allan Poe's 1845 story, "The Purloined Letter," is set in Paris, and the eponymous letter is stolen from a French queen by a treacherous minister who wishes to blackmail or disgrace her. To conceal this letter—Poe's ingenious detective, Dupin, discovers—"the minister had resorted to the comprehensive and sagacious experiment of not attempting to conceal it at all" and had placed it "immediately beneath the nose of the whole world, by way of best preventing any portion of that world from even perceiving it." Perhaps it was this strategy that Marie Antoinette, who after all was used to leading her life "before the whole world [*devant tout le monde*]," hit upon when asking for a mourning dress. With this ensemble, she made her royalism invisible to her captors precisely by displaying it "immediately beneath the nose of the whole world." The classic psychoanalytic reading of Poe's story appears in Jacques Lacan, "Séminaire sur la 'Lettre volée,'" in *Écrits*, 2 vols. (Paris: Seuil, 1966–1967), I, 19–75.

128. "Relation de Goret," Lenôtre (ed.), 149.

129. Pellegrin, 71.

130. Fraser, 408.

131. See Anonymous, "Les Fureurs utérines de Marie Antoinette" (n.p., [1791]).

132. On Kucharski's visits to the Temple and, later, the Conciergerie, see Jallut, 64–65. An inscription on one of Kucharski's depictions of the Queen from this period notes that he took great pains to "recreate, down to the slightest detail, her mourning costume"; cited in Jallut, 67.

133. As Madame Royale remembered of her mother at this time, "living and dying had become all the same to her." See Madame Royale, 147.

134. The jailers' tolerance of the Queen's clothing choices is further supported by records of the prisoners' expenses during the first four months of 1793. These records reveal Marie Antoinette and her family were allowed to spend almost 2,000 livres for the repair and laundering of their mourning ensembles. See Archives Nationales de France, F4.1314.

135. Fraser, 408.

136. "Relation de Moelle," in Lenôtre (ed.), 213. Fraser surmises that the Queen herself shared this hope, supported by the fact that not long after her conversation with Moelle, Marie Antoinette sent Fersen the imprint from a signet ring or seal bearing the words, *Tutto a te mi guida* ("Everything leads me to you"), along with a note that read "never has this motto been more true." See Fraser, 410. For the remark about the guards, see Madame Royale, 147.

137. The complexities of the Vendée insurrections necessarily fall outside the scope of the present work. For more thorough treatment of this issue, see André Sarazin's introduction to Rochejaquelein, 9–30.

138. *Le Moniteur* (27 mars 1793), 816.

139. *Procès de Marie Antoinette, ci-devant reine des français, ou, recueil exact de tous ses Interrogatoires, réponses, dépositions des témoins* (Paris: Chez les Principaux Libraires, 1793), 87. On the importance of this symbol for counterrevolutionary agitators, see Reiset, II, 361.

140. This much is evident in the prosecution's discussion of this piece of fabric in Marie Antoinette's trial in October 1793. See *Procès de Marie Antoinette*, 43, 86–87, 136.

141. *Procès de Marie Antoinette*, 104. In his testimony, Jobert specifies that he showed some of his medallions to "the widow Capet and her daughter" (104).

142. *Procès de Marie Antoinette*, 104.

143. Ibid. I should add that this assertion about the discovery of the Medea medallion is not a republican fabrication: at her trial, Marie Antoinette herself acknowledged that she had owned such a cameo while in the Temple. See *Procès de Marie Antoinette*, 97.

144. For a discussion of how "the Revolution continually manipulate[d] the Queen's name" and calumniated her by constantly equating her with other monstrous and notorious beings, see Pierre Saint-Amand, "Terrorizing Marie Antoinette," in Goodman (ed.), 265.

145. Anonymous pamphlet published as a preface to *Procès criminel de Marie Antoinette de Lorraine, archiduchesse d'Autriche* (Paris: Chez Denné, Chez la citoyenne Toubon, Chez Courdier, 1793), 7.

146. Her mourning outfit may in fact have stood as a rallying cry to loyalists who received copies of Kucharski's portrait of her dressed in black, for the Polish artist disseminated replicas widely among émigrés abroad. See Jallut, 66–68.

147. Cited in Delorme, 300.

148. Lever, *Marie Antoinette: The Last Queen of France*, 290.

149. Cited in Delorme, 301.

150. Madame Royale, 154.

151. It is Madame Royale who tells us that Marie Antoinette's "desolation reached its peak when she learned that Simon, the cobbler, whom she had seen before, had been charged with caring for her poor child"; see Madame Royale, 154. On the decisive role the Commune—and particularly its Procurer-General, Chaumette—played in devising and implementing Louis Charles's "patriotic reeducation," see Jacques Hamann, "Louis XVII et l'enfant du Temple," in Léri and Tulard (eds.), 70–72; and Fraser, 413. Fraser cites Chaumette as saying of the boy: "I wish to give him some education. I will take him from his family to make him lose the idea of his rank."

152. Madame Royale de France, 157. On the black clothing that Louis Charles received after his father's death, see the bill from his tailor, Bosquet, dated January 26, 1793, in the Archives Nationales de France, F.1314.

153. Madame Royale, 157.

154. Ibid, 155.

155. The allied forces had just won a crucial victory at Valenciennes, which left the route to Paris dangerously open; and the *conventionnels* seem to have thought that threatening to bring Marie Antoinette to trial would give them some leverage with their enemies. See André Castelot, *Le Procès de Marie Antoinette* (Paris: Perrin, 1993), 106–107. Moreover, as Antonia Fraser emphasizes, the Convention came under tremendous pressure from the militant sans-culottes to deal harshly with the captive widow. See Fraser, 424–425.

156. Madame Royale, 156.

157. Castelot, *Marie Antoinette* (1962), 471.

158. Madame Royale, 156.

159. Ibid; Pierre Sipriot, *Les Soixante derniers jours de Marie Antoinette* (Paris: Plon, 1993), 18.

160. "Relation de Rosalie Lamorlière," in Lenôtre (ed.), 238.

161. For a complete inventory of the belongings Philippe-Égalité was permitted to keep in the Conciergerie, see Reiset, II. This list presents a striking contrast to the pitifully short inventory of Marie Antoinette's possessions in the Conciergerie, provided in Reiset, II, 423 n. 1.

162. Pierre Saint-Amand, "Terrorizing Marie Antoinette," 266; and "Adorning Marie Antoinette," 30–32.

163. "Relation de Rosalie Lamorlière," in Lenôtre (ed.), 257.

164. It bears noting that although the "Relation de Lamorlière" cited in these pages was first published during the Restoration, a subsequent interview with Lamorlière was conducted in 1836, six years after the Restoration came to an end, and thus at a time when it would have been less politically advantageous for the former maid to sing the late Queen's praises. Yet the interview and the earlier "Relation" contain strikingly similar versions of all the salient facts of Marie Antoinette's captivity; Lenôtre, who publishes both of them in his anthology, remarks in an editor's preface that this mutual corroboration attests to both texts' reliability. On the reliability of the memoirs of Lamorlière—and also of one Madame Bault (cited below)—see also Lord Ronald Gower, *Last Days of Marie Antoinette* (Boston: Roberts Brothers, 1886), 56–57.

165. "Relation de Rosalie Lamorlière," in Lenôtre (ed.), 239.

166. "Souvenirs de Mademoiselle Fouché," in Lenôtre (ed.), 314.

167. "Relation de Rosalie Lamorlière," in Lenôtre (ed.), 239. Lamorlière notes here that she entrusted the widow's bonnet to the prison concierge's wife, Madame Richard, to do the necessary cutting and restitching.

168. As Pierre Saint-Amand comments, it was a supreme irony that "the woman who had insisted on bringing her own seamstress [i.e., Bertin] to Versailles" now had to mend her shabby garments herself, deprived even of the use of sewing scissors. See "Adorning Marie Antoinette," 30.

169. "Relation de Rosalie Lamorlière" and "Relation de la femme Bault," in Lenôtre (ed.), 232, 282. See also Castelot, *Le Procès de Marie Antoinette*, 111–112. These women were Madame Larivière, the elderly mother of the prison turnkey; Madame Harel, whose husband worked for the police; and, after a change in the directorship of the prison on September 13, Mademoiselle Bault, the new concierge's daughter.

170. As Madame Bault, the wife of the concierge who replaced Monsieur Richard in mid-September, observed: "Her black dress was falling to pieces and her shoes were completely worn out." See "Relation de la femme Bault," in Lenôtre (ed.), 282.

171. Axel von Fersen, *Save the Queen: A Diary of the French Revolution, 1789–1793* (London: G. Bell & Sons, 1971), 197.

172. In trying to persuade Europe's other monarchs (especially Austria's) to help the Queen, Fersen was fighting a losing battle, as they all had their own political reasons for staying out of the matter. Apparently, when approached by another loyalist seeking his assistance in freeing Marie Antoinette from prison, the Austrian Emperor replied coldly: "Well, sir, I know the strength of my aunt's character; she will know how to die." See Lafont d'Aussonne, 417.

173. Lamorlière remarked upon the "discomfort that the heat waves of the month of August caused the Queen"; see "Relation de Rosalie Lamorlière," in Lenôtre (ed.), 249.

174. Lamorlière describes the hanging of the watch as one of the Queen's first actions upon taking in the "horrible nudity of her new cell." See "Relation de Rosalie Lamorlière," in Lenôtre (ed.), 230.

175. "Relation de Madame Simon-Vouet," in Lenôtre (ed.), 271. See also Gower, 27.

176. "Relation de Rosalie Lamorlière," in Lenôtre (ed.), 239.

177. "Relation de la femme Bault," in Lenôtre (ed.), 287–288.

178. The causes and timing of young Louis XVII's death remain obscure: he was not officially declared dead until June 8, 1795, and historians continue to debate what really happened to the child and when. However, as Madeleine Delpierre and Édouard Dupland have both pointed out, surviving bills from the laundress who cleaned his clothes while he was in the Temple (again, clothes telling the story) persuasively suggest that he died on or around January 4, 1794. See Delpierre, "La Garde-robe de la famille royale au Temple," 30; and Édouard Dupland, *Vie et mort de Louis XVII* (Paris: 1987), 87.

179. André Castelot, *Madame Royale* (Paris: Perrin, 1962), 111.

180. Cited in Castelot, *Marie Antoinette* (1967), 470.

181. "Relation de Rosalie Lamorlière," in Lenôtre (ed.), 238. This account is corroborated by the list of garments inventoried after Marie Antoinette's execution; see Reiset, II, 423 n. 1.

182. "Relation de Rosalie Lamorlière," in Lenôtre (ed.), 239, 243.

183. Gower, 68.

184. "Relation de Rosalie Lamorlière," in Lenôtre (ed.), 243, 244.

185. Ibid.

186. Ibid, 237.

187. The Conciergerie was full of prisoners awaiting judgment by the Revolutionary Tribunal, but also of people whose comings and goings were connected to that court, which happened to be housed within the prison complex. In this busy setting, Fraser notes, and "with the connivance of good-natured jailers, intent on pleasing the public where possible (for money), Marie Antoinette became one of the sights of the Conciergerie" (416). On this point, see also Gower, 12–13. In addition, certain officials paid regular visits to her cell: Fouquier-Tinville, the fearsome prosecutor of the Revolutionary Tribunal, stopped by her room every night after work to keep tabs on her. See "Relation de Rosalie Lamorlière" and "Relation de la femme Bault," in Lenôtre (ed.), 237, 281.

188. The Carnation Affair is somewhat complex and receives more detailed treatment elsewhere, as in Fraser, 418, 423–424, 429–430; and Destremau, "L'Affaire de l'oeillet" (no pagination in Destremau's monograph). I should mention that this was not the first escape plot with which loyalists had presented Marie Antoinette; while she was in the Temple, she had been offered a few suggestions for escape, but had rejected all of them, largely because they would have required her to leave her children. Once she was in the Conciergerie, this was of course no longer a consideration.

189. On the often overlooked fact that the decision to try Marie Antoinette predated the discovery of the Carnation Affair, see Fraser, 424–425.

190. "Relation de Rosalie Lamorlière" and "Enquête de Madame Simon-Vouet," in Lenôtre (ed.), *La Captivité et la mort de Marie Antoinette*, 245, 275.

191. "Relation de Rosalie Lamorlière," in Lenôtre (ed.), 237.

192. Ibid, 246.

193. Ibid, 245; see also the "Relation de la femme Bault," 282–283.

194. Ibid, 246.

195. On this point, see especially Gower, 75–77, 85–88, 104–105.

196. These charges appear in *Procès de Marie Antoinette*, on the following pages: 18–19, 21, 96 (depleting the national treasury and channeling funds to Austria); 31 (her precipitation of nationwide famine); 94–95 (the costs of the Petit Trianon); 24 (her selection of "perverse" government ministers); 102 (her ability to "make the *ci-devant* King do whatever [she] wanted"); 28 (her support of Calonne); 95 (her involvement with La Motte); 20, 32–34, 60, 65, 128 (the distribution of white cockades and the trampling of the *tricolore* at the Flanders banquet); 50, 87 (the costumes she ordered for Varennes); 43, 86–87, 130 (the Sacred Heart fabric); 97, 104 (the Medea medaillon).

197. *Procès de Marie Antoinette*, 65.

198. Ibid, 18.

199. Variations on this expression appear with striking frequency in the transcript of the trial proceedings; see *Procès de Marie Antoinette*, 21, 23, 24, 27, 35, 57, 121.

200. This proverb appears as one of the definitions for "noir" ("black") in at least three eighteenth-century French dictionaries: the *Dictionnaire de l'Académie française*,

4th ed. (1762) and 5th ed. (1798); and Jean-François Feraud (ed.), *Dictionnaire de la langue française* (1787–1788). All these dictionaries have been scanned into the University of Chicago's ARTFL database: http://humanities.uchicago.edu/orgs/ARTFL.

201. Lever, *Marie Antoinette: The Last Queen of France*, 301.

202. Hunt, *The Family Romance of the French Revolution*, 95. Lynn Hunt makes this point apropos of the prosecution's frequent references to the pornographic and sexual accusations that had been leveled against the Queen long before she was brought to trial.

203. "Petition from the Section des Piques," cited in Castelot, *Le Procès de Marie Antoinette*, 130.

204. Already in her prison, the contrast between Marie Antoinette's horribly ragged clothing and her calm, dignified behavior had reportedly moved numerous passersby to outbursts of passionate reverence. According to Madame Bault, "several people insistently asked for" shreds of the border that her daughter had replaced on the Widow Capet's black gown ("Relation de la femme Bault," 282). Similarly, Rosalie Lamorlière recounts that whenever she and a kindly prison guard tried to scrape the grime off the royal prisoner's footwear, both prisoners and visitors begged to be allowed to kiss it ("Relation de Rosalie Lamorlière," in Lenôtre [ed.], 240–241).

205. "Relation de Larivière," in Lenôtre (ed.), 355. Louis Larivière's mother was one of the women in the Conciergerie who helped to mend Marie Antoinette's black dress.

206. On this point, see, again, the horrifying physical description of the Queen in Walter (ed.), 57; the haunting portrait that Kucharski painted of her in her widow's weeds; and Fersen's notes in his diary about the emaciated, ravaged state to which he had heard the Queen had been reduced. Of course, none of these accounts can be accepted as objectively or empirically "true," but taken together, they paint a picture of a woman whose beauty had long since left her and whose travails had exacted a severe physical toll.

207. Antonia Fraser supports this notion when she writes: "Marie Antoinette's appearance caused an immediate sensation in the crowded courtroom. . . . The *ci-devant* Queen looked ghastly. . . . Her haggard appearance contrasted bizarrely with the mental image that most of the spectators had of the accused. . . . She was [patently neither] the ostrich with the harpy's face of the caricatures, [nor] the glittering Queen with her diamonds and her nodding plumes. . . . As *Le Moniteur* admitted, [the Widow] Capet was 'prodigiously changed' " (429).

208. *Procès de Marie Antoinette*, 48–49.

209. "Relation de Chauveau-Lagarde," in Lenôtre (ed.), 343. Similarly, Madame Bault speculated that Marie Antoinette would be found innocent because "she answered like an angel." See "Relation de la femme Bault," in Lenôtre (ed.), 348; for La Rochetière, see 343–344 n. 2. Lenôtre explains that the audience at the trial seems to have been a mix of militant revolutionaries, curiosity-seekers, and royalists in disguise.

210. Gower, 89. A similar account appears in Castelot, *Marie Antoinette* (1989), 211.

211. Gower, 104–105; and Fraser, 429. Gower notes that along with Herman and Fouquier-Tinville, "the tribunal which judged the Queen was composed of . . . four judges, the chief registrar, and fifteen jurymen. . . . The witnesses, over forty in number, consisted of all classes. [These people] appear to have been selected as much as possible from among those who were known or thought to be enemies of the Queen" (85).

212. *Procès de Marie Antoinette*, 125–126.

213. "Relation de Rosalie Lamorlière," in Lenôtre (ed.), 274.

CHAPTER ELEVEN: WHITE

1. This letter, which Madame Élisabeth never received and which was found among Fouquier-Tinville's belongings when he was arrested during the Thermidor coup of the following summer, is in the Archives Nationales de France. It is reproduced in full in Gower, 122–123.

2. "Relation de Rosalie Lamorlière," in Lenôtre (ed.), 252.

3. "Relation de Rosalie Lamorlière" and "Enquête de Madame Simon-Vouet," in Lenôtre (ed.), 252–253, 272–273.

4. "Enquête de Madame Simon-Vouet," in Lenôtre (ed.), 274–275.

5. "Relation de Rosalie Lamolière," in Lenôtre (ed.), 274.

6. "Relation de Rosalie Lamolière" and "Enquête de Madame Simon-Vouet," in Lenôtre (ed.), 253, 274. Identical details of the Queen's last outfit appear in the ostensible eyewitness account given by the Vicomte Charles Desfossés, "Récit de Charles Desfossés," in Lenôtre (ed.), 374.

7. The Queen's severe blood loss is remarked upon in "Relation de Rosalie Lamorlière," in Lenôtre (ed.), 252. Two of the purported witnesses to the Queen's death make mention of her extreme pallor: see "Récit de Desessartis" and "Récit de Charles Desfossés," in Lenôtre (ed.), 372, 373–374.

8. Although black, violet, and blue were the dominant colors of eighteenth-century royal mourning, Fraser points out that "no one remembered that in the past, white had been the mourning of the Queens of France." See Fraser, 438. I have not, however, emphasized this aspect of Marie Antoinette's ensemble here, for I have been unable to determine with any specificity when, exactly, darker shades replaced white in princely mourning gear. Conversely, a fashion curator of my acquaintance has suggested that white was temporarily revived as a principal mourning color at the end of the seventeenth century, during a brief vogue for black in stylish (non-mourning) clothes, but I have found no published sources to back up this claim. Indeed, in August 1789, Le Magasin des modes nouvelles categorically maintained that under the ancien régime, "mourning and even half-mourning were only ever worn in black," and that only with the onset of the new era—that of the Revolution—would people be able to "substitute white and colors" for this long-standing, aristocratic tradition. See Le Magasin des modes nouvelles françaises et anglaises (1 août 1789), 194.

9. See for instance "Relation du Gendarme Léger," "Récit de Desessartis," and "Récit de Charles Desfossés," in Lenôtre (ed.), 371, 374. The French newspaper Le Moniteur also made note of her white costume, a detail that so struck Goethe, who had toured her pavillon de remise twenty-three years earlier, that he chose a white dress as the costume in which his heroine, Mary, Queen of Scots, goes to her death in his play Maria Stuart. I am thankful to Liliane Weissberg for apprising me of this fascinating literary-historical anecdote.

10. Perhaps the best two narratives of the public's unexpectedly muted reaction to Marie Antoinette's passage appear in Gower, 145–146; and Horace de Viel-Castel, Marie Antoinette et la Révolution française (Paris: J. Techener, 1859), 351. Both Gower and Viel-Castel describe how a militant revolutionary actor named Grammont rode alongside Marie Antoinette's cart and tried to incite the people to insult her—an effort that was largely unsuccessful until he encountered small groups of rowdy, drunken market-women in front of the Saint-Roch Church and the Club des Jacobins. But apart from these limited outbursts, which apparently Grammont had organized in advance by telling the market-women where to stand and plying them liberally with wine, the crowds were above all "stricken and stupefied" (Viel-Castel, 351) at the sight of their former queen in her death-cart. Interestingly, Gower attributes this reaction to the onlookers' "amaze[ment]" at seeing this white-robed figure, so simple and

yet so grand in its forlornness" (145)—as if her outfit itself caused the crowds to fall silent.

11. Pierre Saint-Amand, "Adorning Marie Antoinette," 32.

12. Pierre Saint-Amand eloquently describes this drawing as "the final and definitive signature of the process of denarcissization" that the revolutionaries perpetrated on their royal victim's body. In the David sketch, he continues, "Marie Antoinette is already dead, drained, effaced, emptied." See Pierre Saint-Amand, "Terrorizing Marie Antoinette," in Goodman (ed.), 267.

13. The executioner's name was Sanson, and the claim that Marie Antoinette saw him pocket a lock of her hair appears in "Relation de Larivière," in Lenôtre (ed.), 363. Interestingly enough, the executioner's practice of shearing his victims' hair before they went to the guillotine was known as "the final *toilette*." As at her previous *toilettes*, Marie Antoinette thus found her hair a subject of politicized and ceremonial attention: according to Larivière, the piece of hair that Sanson purloined was ritually burned in a vestibule at the Conciergerie (363). Viel-Castel, however, asserts that the lock of hair later surfaced in an 1854 estate-sale of the belongings of an erstwhile *conventionnel*'s son. See Viel-Castel, *Marie Antoinette et la Revolution française*, 345.

Afterword: Fashion Victim

1. Cited in Batterberry, 145.

2. Interestingly enough, Walter Benjamin makes a similar point when comparing the selective memory of the French revolutionaries themselves—who tried to overwrite France's monarchical past by reinventing the polity as a revived version of a Roman republic—to the mechanics of fashion. See Walter Benjamin, *Illuminations*, ed. Hannah Arendt (New York: Schocken, 1968), 261.

3. Much ink has been spilled on these women's celebrated "style," a topic that exceeds the boundaries of the current project. I would, however, like to mention one book that I found most inspiring in its creative and intelligent analysis of Jacqueline Kennedy Onassis's relationship to fashion. That book is Wayne Koestenbaum, *Jackie Under My Skin: Interpreting an Icon* (New York: Farrar, Straus and Giroux, 1995).

4. Horace de Viel-Castel, *Collection de costumes, armes et meubles, pour servir à l'histoire de la Révolution Française et l'Empire* (Paris: Treuttel and Wurtz, 1834), 10.

5. Of course, in both psychoanalytic and Marxist terms, "fetishism" is the term for precisely this uneasy coexistence of memory and forgetting; and in another essay, I would welcome the opportunity to consider further the fetishistic mechanisms both of Marie Antoinette's relationship to fashion and of the contemporary fashion world's relationship to Marie Antoinette. I am especially intrigued by the philosopher Jacques Derrida's observation that commodity culture turns both commodities and consumers into ghosts—flickering traces on the cusp between past and present, materiality and abstraction, being and nothingness. The story of Marie Antoinette's *afterlife in fashion* has yet to be written—how her clothes were destroyed, redistributed, preserved, indeed fetishized, after her death, and how her image has since, in the words of contemporary fashion journalist Alix Browne (cited below), "officially become a brand." As the critic Thomas Keenan has pointed out, "in the rigor of the abstraction" by which a person, say, becomes a brand, "only ghosts survive" (168). It is no understatement to assert that Marie Antoinette haunts today's fashion scene, and in being haunted by her, we ourselves slide into a liminal position, neither fully acknowledging nor entirely forgetting her "material" existence. Key references for such an investigation would be Jacques Derrida, *Specters of Marx: The State of Debt, the Work of Mourning, and the New International*, trans. Peggy Kamuf (New York and London: Routledge, 1994), Chapter 5, "Apparition of the Inapparent," 125–176; and Thomas Keenan, "The Point

is to (Ex)change It: Reading *Capital,* Rhetorically," in Emily Apter and William Pietz (eds.), *Fetishism as Cultural Discourse* (Ithaca, N.Y.: Cornell University Press, 1993): 152–185.

6. Alix Browne, "Let Them Wear Couture," *The New York Times Magazine* (February 26, 2006): 64.

7. Browne, "Let Them Wear Couture," 64.

· SELECTED BIBLIOGRAPHY ·

CORRESPONDENCE, MEMOIRS, CHRONICLES, TESTIMONIALS

Adamy, Paul (ed.). *Recueil de lettres secrètes: année 1783.* Lausanne: Droz, 1997.

Amiguet, Philippe (ed.). *Lettres de Louis XV à son petit-fils Ferdinand de Parme.* Paris: B. Grasset, 1938.

Argenson, Marquis d'. *Journal et mémoires du marquis d'Argenson.* Ed. E.J.B. Ratherty. 9 vols. Paris: J. Renouard, 1839.

[Bachaumont, Louis Petit de.] *Mémoires secrets pour servir à l'histoire de la république des lettres en France.* London: Gregg International, 1970.

Baucourt, A. de (ed.). *Correspondance entre le Comte de Mirabeau et le Comte de La Marck.* 3 vols. Paris: n.p., 1851.

Baudeau, Abbé. *Chronique secrète de Paris sous Louis XVI,* reproduced in *Revue rétrospective du bibliothèque historique.* Ed. Jules-Antoine Taschereau. Paris: H. Fournier, 1833–1838.

Bernier, Olivier (ed.). *Secrets of Marie Antoinette.* New York: Fromm, 1986.

Besenval, Pierre-Victor, Baron de. *Mémoires sur la Cour de France.* Ed. Ghislain de Diesbach. Paris: Mercure de France, 1987 [1805].

Boigne, Adèle d'Osmond, Comtesse de. *Mémoires de la Comtesse de Boigne, née d'Osmond: récits d'une tante. I. Du règne de Louis XVI à 1820.* Ed. Jean-Claude Berchet. Paris: Mercure de France, 1999 [c. 1837].

Bombelles, Marc Marie, Marquis de. *Journal (1744–1822).* Ed. Frans Durif and Jean Grassion. Geneva: Droz, 1977–1982.

Bretonne, Nicolas Rétif de la. *Les Nuits révolutionnaires: 1789–1793.* Paris: Éditions de Paris, 1989.

Burke, Edmund. *Reflections on the Revolution in France.* Ed. Conor Cruise O'Brien. Baltimore: Penguin, 1969 [1790].

Campan, Jeanne-Louise-Henriette. *Mémoires de Madame Campan: première femme de chambre de Marie Antoinette.* Ed. Jean Chalon. Paris: Mercure de France, 1988 [1822].

Caraman, Comte de. *Mémoires.* Paris: Revue de France, 1935.

Chateaubriand, René de. *Mémoires d'Outre-Tombe.* 2 vols. Paris: Gallimard/Pléiade, 1955 [1803–1841].

Choiseul, Étienne-François de Stainville, Duc de. *Mémoires.* Ed. Jean-Pierre Giucciardi and Philippe Bonnet. Paris: Mercure de France, 1982 [1790].

Choiseul-Stainville, Claude-Antoine-Gabriel, Duc de. *Relation du départ de Louis XVI, le 20 juin 1791.* Paris: Badouin Frères, 1822.

Christoph, Paul. *Maria Theresia und Marie Antoinette: ihr geheimer briefwechsel.* Vienna: Cesam, 1952.

Cléry, Jean-Baptiste. *Journal de ce qui s'est passé à la tour du Temple pendant la captivité de Louis XVI, roi de France, au Temple.* Paris: Mercure de France, 1987 [1798].

Croÿ, Emmanuel, Duc de. *Journal inédit du Duc de Croÿ (1718–1784).* Ed. Paul Cottin and the Vicomte de Grouchy. 4 vols. Paris: Flammarion, 1907.

Dangeau, Philippe de Courcillon, Marquis de. *Journal du Marquis de Dangeau.* Eds. MM. Soulié, Dussieux, de Chennevières, Mantz, and de Montaiglon. 19 vols. Paris: Firmin-Didot, 1854–1860.

Deffand, Madame du. *Lettres de la Marquise du Deffand à Horace Walpole (1766–1780).* Ed. Mrs. Paget Toynbee. 3 vols. London: Methuen, 1912.

Delille, Abbé Jacques. *De l'imagination.* Paris: Guiget et Michaud, 1806.

Demandes de Marie Antoinette à la Commune de Paris, avec les arrêts que la Commune a pris sur ces demandes (23 janvier 1793). Archives Nationales de France (N. L641.489).

Devonshire, Georgiana, Duchess of. *Extracts from the Correspondence of Georgiana, Duchess of Devonshire.* Ed. Earl of Bessborough. London: Murray, 1955.

Diderot, Denis, and Jean Le Rond d'Alembert (eds.) *Encyclopédie, ou dictionnaire raisonné des sciences, des arts et des métiers par une société de gens de lettres.* Lausanne/Berne: Chez les Sociétés Typographiques, 1779.

Feraud. *Dictionnaire critique de la langue française,* 3ᵉ edition. Marseille: Mossey, 1787–1788.

Fersen, Axel von. *Save the Queen: A Diary of the French Revolution, 1789–1793.* London: G. Bell & Sons, 1971.

Frénilly, Auguste-François, Baron de. *Mémoires 1768–1828: Souvenirs d'un ultra-royaliste.* Ed. Frédéric d'Agay. Paris: Perrin, 1987.

Genlis, Stéphanie Félicité, Comtesse de. *De l'esprit des étiquettes.* Paris: Mercure de France, 1996.

———. *Mémoires inédits de la Comtesse de Genlis.* 10 vols. Paris: L'Advocat, 1825.

Girard, George (ed.). *Correspondance entre Marie-Thérèse et Marie Antoinette.* Paris: Grasset, 1931.

Goethe, Johann Wolfgang von. *Mémoires.* Trans. Baronne de Carlowitz. 2 vols. Paris: Charpentier & Fasquelle, 1855.

Grand détail exact de l'interrogatoire de Louis Capet à la barre de la Convention Nationale. Paris: n.p., 1792.

Griffet, Pierre. *Mémoires pour servir à l'histoire de Louis Dauphin.*

Grimm, Friedrich-Melchior et al. *Correspondance littéraire, philosophique et critique.* Ed. Maurice Tourneux. Paris: Garnier Frères, 1877–1882.

Hardy, S.-P. *Mes loisirs ou journal d'évènments tels qu'ils parviennent à ma connaissance de 1764 à 1790.* Paris: n.d.

Heidenstam, O. G. de (ed.). *The Letters of Marie Antoinette, Fersen, and Barnave.* Trans. Winifred Stephens and Mrs. Wilfrid Jackson. London: John Lane, 1926.

Hervé, F. (ed.). *Madame Tussaud's Memoires and Reminiscences of France.* London: n.p., 1838.

Heinzmann, Johann Georg. *Voyage d'un Allemand à Paris.* Lausanne, 1800.

Hézècques, Félix, Comte d'. *Page à la cour de Louis XVI: Mémoires du Comte d'Hézècques.* Ed. Emmanuel Bourassin. Paris: Tallandier, 1987 [1804].

Huë, François. *Dernières années du règne et de la vie de Louis XVI par l'un des officiers de la chambre du roi, appelé par ce prince, après la journée du 10 août, à l'honneur de rester auprès de lui et de la famille royale.* Foreword by René du Menil de Maricourt. Paris: Henri Plon, 1860 [1814].

Khevenhüller-Metsch, Rudolf, and Hans Schlitter (eds.). *Aus der Zeit Maria Theresias: Tagebuch des Fürsten Johann Joseph Khevenhüller-Metsch.* 8 vols. Vienna: Hozhausen, 1972 [1907–1925].

Klinckowström, Baron R. M. de. *Le Comte de Fersen et la cour de France.* 2 vols. Paris: Firmin-Didot, 1877–1888.

La Rochejaquelein, Marie-Louise-Victoire de Donnissan, Marquise de. *Mémoires de la Marquise de La Rochejaquelein.* Ed. André Sarazin. Paris: Mercure de France, 1984.

La Rochetière, Maxime de, and the Marquis de Beaucourt (eds.). *Lettres de Marie Antoinette.* 2 vols. Paris: A. Picard et fils, 1895–1896.

La Tour du Pin de Gouvernet, Henriette-Lucie Séraphin Dillon, Marquise de. *Mémoires: Journal d'une femme de cinquante ans (1778–1815).* Ed. Christian de Liedekerke Beaufort. Paris: Mercure de France, 1989 [1907].

Lauzun, Armand-Louis de Gontaut-Biron, Duc de. *Mémoires du Duc de Lauzun.* Ed. Georges d'Heylli. Paris: Édouard Rouveyre, 1880 [1858].

[Léonard, Jean-François Authier or Autié.] *The Souvenirs of Léonard, Hairdresser to Queen Marie Antoinette.* Trans. A. Teixeira de Mattos. 2 vols. London: n.p., 1897.

Lescure, Mathurin de (ed.). *Correspondance secrète inédite sur Louis XVI, Marie Antoinette, la cour et la ville de 1777 à 1792.* Paris: Henri Plon, 1866.

Lévis-Mirepoix, Duc de. *Aventures d'une famille française.* Paris: n.p., 1949.

Ligne, Charles-Joseph Lamoral, Prince de. *Mémoires du Prince de Ligne.* Pref. Chantal Thomas. Paris: Mercure de France, 2004 [1809].

Lough, John (ed.). *France on the Eve of Revolution: British Travellers' Observations, 1763–1788.* London: Croom Helm, 1987.

Madame Élisabeth de France. *Mémoires de Madame Élisabeth.* Ed. F. de Barghon Fort-Rion. Paris: Auguste Vaton, 1860.

Madame Royale de France. *Mémoire sur la captivité des princes et princesses ses parents depuis le 10 août 1792 jusqu'à la mort de son frère arrivé le 9 juin 1795,* in Cléry, *Journal de ce qui s'est passé à la tour du Temple pendant la captivité de Louis XVI, roi de France, au Temple.*

Marie Antoinette de France et de Lorraine. *Correspondance de Marie-Antoinette.* 2 vols. Clermont-Ferrand: Paléo, 2004.

———, Marie-Thérèse d' Autriche, and le Comte de Mercy-Argenteau. *Correspondance secrète.* Ed. Alfred von Arneth and Mathieu Auguste Geoffroy. 3 vols. Paris: Firmin-Didot, 1875.

Mercier, Louis Sébastien. *Le Nouveau Paris.* Ed. Jean-Claude Bonnet. 2 vols. Paris: Mercure de France, 1994.

———, *Tableau de Paris.* Ed. Jean-Claude Bonnet. 2 vols. Paris: Mercure de France, 1994.

Mercier de Compiègne, Claude-François-Xavier, *Comment m'habillerai-je? Réflexions politiques et philosophiques sur l'habillement françois et sur la nécessité d'un costume national.* Paris, 1793.

Métra, François. *Correspondance secrète.* 18 vols. London: John Adamson, 1787–1790.

Mirecourt, Mademoiselle de. *L'Autrichienne: Mémoires inédits de Mademoiselle de Mirecourt sur la reine Marie Antoinette et les prodromes de la Révolution.* Paris: Albin Michel, 1966.

Moitte, Adélaïde-Marie-Anne. *L'Âme des Romaines dans les femmes françaises.* Paris: Gueffier le jeune, 1789.

————. *Suite de L'Âme des Romaines dans les femmes françaises*. Paris: Knapen fils, 1789.

Molleville, Antoine François, Marquis de Bertrand de. *Mémoires secrets pour servir à l'histoire de la dernière année du règne de Louis XVI*. 3 vols. London: Strahan, 1797.

Moore, Dr. John. *A Journal During a Residence in France, from the Beginning of August to the Middle of December, 1792*. 2 vols. London: n.p., 1793.

Morris, Gouverneur. *A Diary of the French Revolution*. Ed. Beatrix Cary Davenport. 2 vols. Boston: Houghton Mifflin, 1939.

Mousset, Albert. *Un Témoin ignoré de la Révolution: le comte Fernan Nuñez, Ambassadeur d'Espagne à Paris*. Paris: n.p., 1924.

Northumberland, Elizabeth Seymour Percy, Duchess of. *The Diaries of a Duchess*. London: Hodder and Stoughton, 1926.

Norvins, Jacques de. *Mémorial*. 2 vols. Paris: n.p., 1896.

Oberkirch, Henriette-Louise de Waldner de Freudenstein, Baronne d'. *Mémoires de la Baronne d'Oberkirch sur la cour de Louis XVI et la société française avant 1789*. Ed. Suzanne Burkard. Paris: Mercure de France, 1970 [1853].

Ossun, Comtesse d'. *État général des dépenses de la Garde-robe de la Reine*. Archives Nationales de France (O.1.3792–3798).

Procédure criminelle instruite au Châtelet de Paris. 3 vols. Paris: Chez Baudouin, 1790.

Procès criminel de Marie Antoinette de Lorraine, archiduchesse d'Autriche. Paris: Chez Denné, Chez la citoyenne Toubon, Chez Courdier, 1793.

Procès de Marie Antoinette, ci-devant reine des français, ou, recueil exact de tous ses Interrogatoires, réponses, depositions des Témoins. Paris: Chez les Principaux Libraires, 1793.

Prudhomme, Louis-Marie. "Réponse aux reproches qu'on nous a faits de n'avoir rien dit à Marie Antoinette pour l'année 1792." *Révolutions de Paris*, 131, 152.

————. *Reproche véritable par la majesté du peuple à l'épouse du roi sur ses torts*. Paris: Imprimerie des Révolutions de France, 1790.

Raunié, Emile. *Chansonnier historique du XVIIIᵉ siecle*. Paris: A. Quantin, 1879–1884.

Recueil général des costumes et modes contenant les différens habillemens et les coëffures les plus élégantes. Paris: Chez Desnos, 1780.

Roland, Marie-Jeanne Philippon. *Lettres de Madame Roland*. Ed. Claude Perrould. 2 vols. Paris: n.p., 1902.

Roussel d'Épinal, Pierre Joseph Alexis. *Le Château des Tuileries*. Paris: Lerouge, 1802.

Saint-Priest, François-Emmanuel Guignard, Comte de. *Mémoires: Règnes de Louis XV et Louis XVI*. Ed. Baron de Barante. 2 vols. Paris: Calmann-Lévy, 1929.

Ségur, Louis Philippe, Comte de. *Memoirs and Recollections of Count Ségur*. Boston: Wells & Lilly, 1825.

Sieyès, Emmanuel Joseph, Abbé. *Qu'est-ce que le Tiers état?* Paris: n.p., 1788.

Soulavie, Jean-Louis (l'aîné). *Mémoires historiques et politiques du règne de Louis XVI*. 6 vols. Paris: Treuttel & Würtz, An X.

Smythe, Lillian C. (ed.). *The Guardian of Marie Antoinette: Letters from the Comte de Mercy-Argenteau, Austrian Ambassador to the Court of Versailles, to Marie Thérèse, Empress of Austria (1770–1780)*. 2 vols. New York: Dodd, Mead, 1902.

Tilly, Alexandre, Comte de. *Mémoires du comte Alexandre de Tilly, pour servir à l'histoire des moeurs de la fin du XVIIIᵉ siècle*. Ed. Christian Melchior-Bonnet. Paris: Mercure de France, 1986 [1804–1806].

Touchard-Lafosse, G. (ed.). *Chroniques pittoresques et critiques de l'Oeil-de-Boeuf, sous Louis XIV, la Régence, Louis XV, et Louis XVI*. 4 vols. Paris: Gustave Barba, 1845.

Tourzel, Louise Élisabeth Félicité, Duchesse de. *Memoirs of the Duchesse de Tourzel, Governess to the Children of France*. Ed. Duc des Cars. 2 vols. London: Remington & Co., 1886.

Véri, Joseph-Alphonse, Abbé de. *Journal de l'Abbé de Véri.* Ed. Baron Jehan de Witte. 2 vols. Paris: Jules Tallandier, 1928.

Vigée-Lebrun, Élisabeth. *The Memoirs of Élisabeth Vigée-Lebrun.* Trans. Siân Evans. Bloomington and Indianapolis: Indiana University Press, 1989 [1835].

Voltaire [Francois-Marie Arouet]. *Siècle de Louis XIV.* 2 vols. Paris: Garnier-Flammarion, 1966.

Walpole, Horace. *Correspondence.* Ed. W. S. Lewis. New Haven and London: Yale University Press, 1965.

———. *Letters of Horace Walpole.* Ed. P. Cunninghan. 9 vols. London: n.p., 1891.

Walter, Gérard (ed.). *Actes du Tribunal révolutionnaire.* Paris: Mercure de France, 1968.

Weber, Joseph. *Mémoires de Joseph Weber concernant Marie-Antoinette, archiduchesse d'Autriche et reine de France et de Navarre.* Ed. MM. Berville and Barrière. 3 vols. Paris: Baudouin Frères, 1822.

Wille, Johann Georg. *Mémoires et journal de Jean-Georges Wille, graveur du roi.* 2 vols. Paris: J. Renouard, 1857.

Williams, Helen Maria. *Letters Written in France, in the Summer of 1790, to a Friend in England; Containing Various Anecdotes Relative to the French Revolution.* Ed. Neil Fraistat and Susan S. Lanser. Toronto: Broadview Literary Texts, 2001.

Wollstonecraft, Mary. *An Historical and Moral View of the Origin and Progress of the French Revolution and the Effect It Has Produced in Europe.* New York: Scholars' Facsimiles, 1975 [1794].

———. *A Vindication of the Rights of Woman.* London: n.p., 1792.

Contemporary Pamphlet Literature

Unless otherwise noted, these sources are anonymous.

"Description historique d'un monstre symbolique, pris sur les bords du Lac Fagua, près de Santa Fé" . . . "Santa Fé & Paris": n.p., 1784.

"Détails de tout ce qui s'est passé au Champ de Mars, à la Cérémonie de la Fédération le 14 juillet: anecdote sur la Reine." Marseille: Jean Mossy, 1790.

"Essai historique sur la vie de Marie Antoinette d'Autriche, reine de France." Paris: Chez la Montensior, 1789.

"Les Fastes de Louis XV, de ses ministres, généraux, et autres notables Personages de son règne." Villefranche: chez la Veuve Liberté, 1782.

"Les Fureurs utérines de Marie Antoinette." n.p., [1791].

"Le Godmiché royal." Paris: n.p., 1789.

"L'Iscariote de la France, ou le député autrichien." Paris: n.p., September 1789.

[Keralio, Louise de.] "Les Crimes des reines de France." Paris: Chez Prudhomme, 1791.

[Lebois, R.-F.] "Grand complot découvert, de mettre Paris à feu et à sang à l'époque du 10 août jusqu'au 15 août, de faire assassiner les patriots par des femmes, et par des calotins déguisés en femmes; Marie Antoinette d'Autriche d'infernale mémoire, sur la scélette. . . ." Paris: De l'Imprimerie de l'Ami des sans-culottes, [1792].

"Louis XVI et Antoinette, traités comme ils le méritent." Paris: Imprimerie des Amis de la Constitution, 1791.

"Memoirs of Marie Antoinette, ci-devant Queen of France." Paris: n.p. [translated and reprinted in the U.S.], 1794.

"La Messaline française." Tribaldis [*sic*]: De l'imprimerie Priape, 1789.

[Morande, Charles Théveneau de.] "Le gazetier cuirassé ou anecdotes scandaleuses de la cour de France." Imprimé à 100 lieues de la Bastille [*sic*]: 1783.

[La Motte, Jeanne de Saint-Rémy de Valois, Comtesse de.] *Mémoires de la Comtesse de La Motte-Valois . . . d'après les mémoires justicatifs de la Comtesse de La Motte,* les mémoires du comte de La Motte, etc. Ed. Jean Hervez. Paris: Bibliothèque des Curieux, 1911.

"Nouvelle scène tragicomique et nullement héroïque entre M. Louis Bourbon, maître serrurier, et Madame Marie Antoinette, sa femme." Paris: Imprimerie de Tremblay, [1792].

"Observations et précis sur le caractère de la conduite de Marie Antoinette d'Autriche." Paris: n.p., 1793.

Pamphlets de l'Affaire du Collier. Paris: n.p., 1786.

"Petit journal du Palais Royal." Paris: n.p., 1789.

"Portefeuille d'un talon rouge." Paris: Imprimerie du Comte de Paradès, 178 . . . [sic].

"Le Rêve d'un Parisien, ou, ce qui n'a point été, ce qui devroit être, & ce qui ne sera peut-être pas." Paris: Imprimerie de L. M. Cellot, [1789].

"Vie de Marie Antoinette, reine de France, femme de Louis XVI, roi des Français." Paris: n.p., 1791.

Archival Sources

AN = Archives Nationales de France
BNE = Bibliothèque Nationale de France, Département des Estampes
FJD = Fonds Jacques Doucet
BV = Bibliothèque de Versailles

AEI 6 no. 2	[AN]
AF II 3, pl. 14	[AN]
AN C192	[AN]
Dossier 596	[FJD]
F4.1311	[AN]
F4.1314	[AN]
K 1017(1) (bobine 539)	[AN]
Portraits de Marie Antoinette (t. I, vol. 1181, D 205801)	[BNE]
Ms. 402 (254F)	[BV]
Ms. Français 6686	[BNE]
Ms. 8157 and 8158	[BNE]
N.L641.489	[AN]
O1. 3792–3798	[AN]
Qb_1778 (cotes 46.B.2139, 67.A.16387, 80C 103422)	[BNE]
Qb1 M101 880	[BNE]

Contemporary Journals and Periodicals

L'Ami du peuple
Le Cabinet des modes
Chronique de Paris
Journal de la cour et de la ville
Le Journal de la mode et du goût
Le Magasin des modes nouvelles françaises et anglaises
Le Mercure de France
Le Moniteur universel
Nouveau jeu des modes françoises
Le Patriote français
Le Père Duchesne
Les Révolutions de France et de Brabant
Les Révolutions de Paris

MARIE ANTOINETTE BIOGRAPHIES AND BIBLIOGRAPHY

Armaillé, la Comtesse d'. *Marie-Thérèse et Marie Antoinette*. Paris: Didier & Cie., 1870.

Asquith, Annunziata. *Marie Antoinette*. London: Weidenfeld & Nicolson, 1974.

Bertière, Simone. *Les Reines de France au temps des Bourbons: Marie Antoinette, l'insoumise*. Paris: Fallois, 2002.

Campardon, Émile. *Marie Antoinette et le procès du collier*. Paris: Plon, 1863.

Castelot, André. *Marie Antoinette*. Paris: Perrin, 1962.

———. *Marie Antoinette*. Paris: Hachette, 1967.

———. *Marie Antoinette d'après des documents inédits*. Paris: Perrin, 1989.

———. *Le Procès de Marie Antoinette*. Paris: Perrin, 1993.

———. *Queen of France: A Biography of Marie Antoinette*. Trans. Denise Folliot. New York: Harper & Brothers, 1957.

Chalon, Jean. *Chère Marie Antoinette*. Paris: Perrin, 1988.

Delorme, Philippe. *Marie Antoinette: Épouse de Louis XVI, mère de Louis XVII*. Paris: Pygmalion/Gérard Watelet, 1999.

Dunlop, Ian. *Marie Antoinette: A Portrait*. London: Sinclair Stevenson, 1993.

Erickson, Carolly. *To the Scaffold: The Life of Marie-Antoinette*. New York: William Morrow, 1991.

Fraser, Antonia. *Marie Antoinette: The Journey*. New York: Doubleday/Nan A. Talese, 2001.

Goncourt, Edmond and Jules de. *Histoire de Marie-Antoinette*. Ed. Robert Kopp. Paris: Bourin, 1990 [1858].

Gower, Lord Ronald. *Last Days of Marie Antoinette*. Boston: Roberts Brothers, 1886.

Haslip, Joan. *Marie Antoinette*. New York: Weidenfeld & Nicolson, 1987.

Hearsey, John E. N. *Marie Antoinette*. New York: E. P. Dutton & Co., 1973.

Imbert de Saint-Amand, Arthur-Léon, Baron. *Marie Antoinette and the Downfall of Royalty*. Trans. Elizabeth Gilbert Martin. New York: Charles Scribner's Sons, 1895.

———. *Marie Antoinette and the Fall of the Old Régime*. Trans. Thomas Sergeant Perry. New York: Charles Scribner's Sons, 1891.

———. *Marie Antoinette at the Tuileries*. Trans. Elizabeth Gilbert Martin. New York: Charles Scribner's Sons, 1891.

Lafont d'Aussone, N. Abbé. *Mémoires secrets et universels des malheurs et de la mort de la reine de France*. Paris: A. Philippe, 1836.

Lever, Evelyne. *Marie Antoinette: la dernière reine*. Paris: Fayard, 1991.

———. *Marie-Antoinette: The Last Queen of France*. Trans. Catherine Temerson. New York: Farrar, Straus and Giroux, 2000.

Maistre, Chevalier Nicolas de. *Marie Antoinette, archiduchesse d'Autriche, reine de France (1793)*. Ed. Paul del Perugia. Mayenne: Yves Floch, 1993 [1793].

Mayer, Dorothy Moulton. *Marie Antoinette: The Tragic Queen*. New York: Coward-McCann, 1968.

Montjoie, Félix Christophe Louis de. *Histoire de Marie Antoinette Josèphe Jeanne de Lorraine, Archiduchesse d'Autriche, Reine de France*. Paris: H. L. Perronneau, 1797.

Palache, John Garbor. *Marie Antoinette, the Player Queen*. New York: Longmans, Green & Co., 1929.

Ségur, Marquis de. *Marie Antoinette*. New York: E. P. Dutton, 1929.

Sipriot, Pierre. *Les Soixante derniers jours de Marie Antoinette*. Paris: Plon, 1993.

Tourneux, Maurice. *Marie Antoinette devant l'histoire: essai bibliographique*. Paris: Henri Leclerc, 1901.

Viel-Castel, Horace de. *Marie Antoinette et la Révolution française*. Paris: J. Techener, 1859.

Vyré, F. de. *Marie Antoinette: sa vie, sa mort*. Paris: Plon, 1889.

Younghusband, Helen Augusta, Lady. *Marie Antoinette: Her Early Youth 1770–1774*. London: MacMillan & Co., 1912.

Zweig, Stefan. *Marie Antoinette: The Portrait of an Average Woman*. New York: Harmony Books, 1984.

ADDITIONAL SOURCES

American Research on the Treasury of the French Language. http://humanities.uchicago.edu/orgs/ARTFL/.

Apostolidès, Jean. *Le Roi-machine: Spectacle et politique au temps de Louis XIV*. Paris: Minuit, 1981.

Appiah, Anthony. "Tolerable Falsehoods: Agency and the Interests of Theory," in *Consequences of Theory: Selected Papers from the English Institute 1987–88*. Ed. Jonathan Arac and Barbara Johnson. Baltimore and London: The Johns Hopkins University Press, 1991, 63–90.

Apter, Emily, and William Pietz (eds.). *Fetishism as Cultural Discourse*. Ithaca, N.Y.: Cornell University Press, 1993.

Arrizioli-Clémentel, Pierre (ed.). *Soieries de Lyon: Commandes royales du XVIIIe siècle (1730–1800)*. Lyon: Sézanne, 1989.

Aspden, Peter. "Gilt Verdict." *Financial Times*, 26 November 2005.

Assailly, Gisèle d'. *Les Quinze Révolutions de la mode*. Paris: Hachette, 1968.

Aulard, A. *The French Revolution: A Political History, 1789–1804*. Trans. and ed. Bernard Mall. New York: Charles Scribner's Sons, 1910.

Auricchio, Laura. "Portraits of Impropriety: Adélaïde Labille-Guiard and the Careers of Women Artists in Late Eighteenth-Century Paris." Ph.D. Diss. Columbia University, 2000.

Baecque, Antoine de. *The Body Politic: Corporeal Metaphor in Revolutionary France, 1770–1800*. Trans. Charlotte Mandell. Palo Alto, Calif.: Stanford University Press, 1997.

———. *Glory and Terror: Seven Deaths under the French Revolution*. Trans. Charlotte Mandell. New York and London: Routledge, 2001.

Baker, Keith Michael. *Inventing the French Revolution: Essays on French Political Culture in the Eighteenth Century*. Cambridge, Eng.: Cambridge University Press, 1990.

Batterberry, Michael and Arianne. *Mirror Mirror: A Social History of Fashion*. New York: Holt, Rinehart & Winston, 1977.

Beales, Derek. *Joseph II: In the Shadow of Maria Theresa*. Cambridge, Eng.: Cambridge University Press, 1987.

Beauchesne, Alcide de. *Louis XVII: His Life, His Suffering, His Death: The Captivity of the Royal Family in the Temple*. Trans. and ed. W. Hazlitt. 4 vols. New York: Harper & Bros., 1853.

Beaumont, C. W. *Three French Dancers of the Eighteenth Century: Camargo, Sallé, Guimard*. London: n.p., 1934.

Benjamin, Walter. *Illuminations*. Ed. Hannah Arendt. Trans. Harry Zohn. New York: Schocken Books, 1968.

Berg, Maxine, and Elizabeth Eger (eds.). *Luxury in the Eighteenth Century: Debates, Desires, and Delectable Goods*. London: Palgrave Macmillan, 2003.

Berlanstein, Léonard. *Daughters of Eve: A Cultural History of French Theater Women*. Cambridge, Mass.: Harvard University Press, 2001.

Bernier, Olivier. *The Eighteenth-Century Woman*. New York: Doubleday, 1981.

———. *Pleasure and Privilege: Life in France, Naples, and America 1770–1790*. New York: Doubleday, 1981.

Bertelli, Sergio, Franco Cardini, and Elvira Garbeo Zorzi. *Italian Renaissance Courts*. New York: Sidgwick & Jackson, 1986.

Bertin, Georges. *Madame de Lamballe d'après des documents inédits*. Paris: Bureaux de la Revue retrospective, 1888.

Bimbenet-Privat, Michèle. "L'art et le commerce au service de la reine: une mosaïque d'archives," in Yves Carlier et al. (eds.), *Les Atours de la Reine: Centre historique des Archives nationales (26 février–14 mai 2001)*. Paris: RMN, 2001: 5–12.

Bindman, David. *The Shadow of the Guillotine: Britain and the French Revolution*. London: British Museum Publications, 1989.

Black, T. Anderson, and Madge Garlan. *A History of Fashion*. New York: William Morrow, 1980.

Bluche, François. *La Vie quotidienne au temps de Louis XVI*. Paris: Hachette, 1980.

Blum, André. *Histoire du costume: les modes au XVIIe et au XVIIIe siècle*. Paris: Hachette, 1928.

Blum, Stella (ed.). *Eighteenth-Century French Fashions*. New York: Dover Publications, 1982.

Boucher, François. *20,000 Years of Fashion: The History of Costume and Personal Adornment*. New York: Harry N. Abrams, 1987 [1965].

Bouchot, Henri. "Marie Antoinette et ses peintres." *Les Lettres et les arts*, no. 1 (1887): 45–48.

Boutry, Maurice. *Autour de Marie Antoinette*. Paris: Emile-Paul, 1908.

———. *Le Mariage de Marie Antoinette*. Paris: n.p., 1904.

Boyer, Marie-Françoise. *The Private Realm of Marie Antoinette*. New York: Thames & Hudson, 1996.

Broglie, Gabriel de. *Madame de Genlis*. Paris: Perrin, 1985.

Brooks, Peter. "The Opening of the Depths," in Sandy Petrey (ed.), *The French Revolution: Two Hundred Years of Rethinking*. Lubbock: Texas Tech University Press, 1989: 113–122.

Browne, Alix. "Let Them Wear Couture." *The New York Times Magazine* (February 26, 2006): 63–71.

Burke, Peter. *The Fabrication of Louis XIV*. New Haven and London: Yale University Press, 1992.

Cabanès, Auguste. *Mœurs intimes du passé*. 11 vols. Geneva: Farnot, 1976.

Carbonnières, Philippe de. *Lesueur: Gouaches révolutionnaires. Collections du musée Carnavalet*. Paris: Nicolas Chaudun, 2005.

Carlier, Yves, Stéphane Castellucio, Anne Kraatz, and Françoise Tétart-Vittu (eds.). *Les Atours de la Reine*. Paris: Centre Historique des Archives Nationales, 2001.

Carlyle, Thomas. *The French Revolution*. 3 vols. London: Methuen & Co., 1902.

Castelot, André, and G. Lenôtre [Théodore Gosselin]. *L'Agonie de la royauté*. Paris: Perrin, 1962.

Censer, Jack. "Remembering the *Mémoires secrets*." *Eighteenth-Century Studies* 35:1 (2002): 291–295.

———, and Lynn Hunt (eds.). *Liberty, Equality, Fraternity: Exploring the French Revolution*. University Park: Pennsylvania State University Press, 2001.

———, and Jeremy Popkin (eds.). *Press and Politics in Pre-revolutionary France*. Berkeley and London: University of California Press, 1987.

Challamel, Augustin. *The History of Fashion in France; or, the Dress of Women from the Gallo-Roman Period to the Present Time*. Trans. Mrs. Frances Cahsel Hoey and John Lillie. London: Sampson Low, Marston, Searle, & Rivington, 1882.

Chartier, Roger. *The Cultural Origins of the French Revolution*. Trans. Lydia G. Cochrane. Durham, N.C.: Duke University Press, 1991.

Colwill, Elizabeth. "Pass as a Woman, Act Like a Man: Marie Antoinette as Tribade in the Pornography of the French Revolution," in Dena Goodman, ed., *Marie-Antoinette: Writings on the Body of a Queen*. New York and London: Routledge, 2003: 139–169.

Contini, Mila. *Fashion from Ancient Egypt to the Present Day*. Foreword by Count Emilio Pucci. New York: Crescent Books, 1965.

Cornu, Paul (ed.). *Galerie des modes et costumes français: 1778–1787*. 4 vols. Paris: Émile Lévy, 1912.

Corson, Richard. *Fabulous Hair: The First Five Thousand Years*. London: Peter Owen, 1980 [1965].

———. *Fashions in Make-Up from Ancient to Modern Times*. London: Peter Owen 2003 [1972].

Crawford, Katherine. *Perilous Performances: Gender and Regency in Early Modern France*. Cambridge, Mass.: Harvard University Press, 2004.

Crow, Thomas E. *Painters and Public Life in Eighteenth-Century France*. New Haven and London: Yale University Press, 1985.

Crown, Patricia. "Sporting with Clothes: John Collet's Prints in the 1770's." *Eighteenth-Century Life* 26:1 (2002): 119–136.

Crowston, Clare Haru. "The Queen and Her 'Minister of Fashion': Gender, Credit, and Politics in Pre-revolutionary France." *Gender & History* 14:1 (2002): 92–116.

———. *The Seamstresses of Old Régime France. 1675–1791*. Durham, N.C.: Duke University Press, 2001.

Cuisenier, Jean. *Mille ans de costume français*. Ed. Gérard Klopp. Thionville: Klopp S.A., 1991.

Cunnington, Phillis, and C. Willett. *Handbook of English Costume in the Eighteenth Century*. Philadelphia: Dufour, 1957.

Darnton, Robert. *The Corpus of Clandestine Literature in France 1769–1789*. New York: W.W. Norton, 1995.

———. *The Forbidden Best-Sellers of Pre-revolutionary France*. New York: W.W. Norton, 1995.

———. *The Literary Underground of the Old Régime*. Cambridge, Mass., and New York: Harvard University Press, 1982.

Daudet, Ernest (ed.). *Dans le palais des rois: récits d'histoire d'après des documents in-édits*. Paris: Hachette, 1914.

Davis, Natalie Zemon. *Society and Culture in Early Modern France*. Palo Alto, Calif.: Stanford University Press, 1975.

Dejean, Joan. *The Essence of Style: How the French Invented High Fashion, Fast Food, Chic Cafés, Style, Sophistication, and Glamour!* New York: Free Press, 2005.

Dekker, Rudolf M., and Lotte C. van de Pol. *The Tradition of Female Transvestism in Early Modern Europe*. New York: St. Martin's Press, 1989.

Delpierre, Madeleine. *Dress in France in the Eighteenth Century*. Trans. Caroline Beamish. New Haven and London: Yale University Press, 1997.

———. "La Garde-robe de la famille royale au Temple," in *Modes et Révolutions: Musée de la mode et du costume (8 février–7 mai 1989)*. Eds. Catherine Join-Dieterle and Madeleine Delpierre. Paris: Éditions Paris-Musées, 1989: 27–34.

———. "Rose Bertin, les marchandes de modes et la Révolution," in *Modes et Révolutions: Musée de la mode et du costume (8 février–7 mai 1989)*. Eds. Catherine Join-Dieterle and Madeleine Delpierre. Paris: Éditions Paris-Musées, 1989: 21–26.

Derrida, Jacques. *Specters of Marx: The State of Debt, the Work of Mourning, and the New International*. Trans. Peggy Kamuf. New York and London: Routledge, 1994.

Destremau, Noëlle. *Les Évasions manquées de la reine Marie Antoinette*. Paris: n.p., 1990.

Devocelle, Jean-Marc. "D'un costume politique à une politique du costume," in Catherine Join-Dieterle and Madeleine Delpierre, eds., *Modes et Révolutions: Musée de la mode et du costume (8 février–7 mai 1989)*. Paris: Éditions Paris-Musées, 1989: 83–104.

Drew, Katherine Fischer (trans. and ed.). *The Laws of the Salian Franks*. Philadelphia: University of Pennsylvania Press, 1991.

Duindam, Jeroen. *Vienna and Versailles: The Courts of Europe's Dynastic Rivals 1550–1780*. Cambridge, Eng.: Cambridge University Press, 2003.

Dumas, Alexandre, *père*. *Le Chevalier de Maison-Rouge*. Ed. Gilbert Sigaux. Lausanne: Rencontre, 1967.

Dupland, Édouard. *Vie et mort de Louis XVII*. Paris: O. Orban, 1987.

Duprat, Annie. *Le Roi décapité: essai sur les imaginaires politiques*. Paris: Cerf, 1992.

Eckhardt, Karl. *Lex Salica*. Hanover: Hahn, 1969.

Elias, Norbert. *La Société de cour*. Trans. Pierre Kamnitzer and Jean Etoré. Paris: Flammarion, 1985.

Farr, Evelyn. *Marie Antoinette and Count Fersen*. London and Chester Springs, Pa.: Peter Owen, 1995.

Fayolle, Rose-Marie, and Renée Davray-Piekolek (eds.). *La Mode en France 1715–1815: de Louis XV à Napoléon 1er*. Paris: Bibliothèque des Arts, 1990.

Feydeau, Élisabeth. *Jean-Louis Fargeon, Marie Antoinette's Perfumer*. Trans. Jane Lizzop. Paris: Perrin, 2004.

Fleischmann, Hector. *Les Maîtresses de Marie Antoinette*. Paris: Editions du Bibliophile, 1910.

———. *Les Pamphlets libertins contre Marie Antoinette, d'après des documents nouveaux et des pamphlets tirés de l'Enfer de la Bibliothèque nationale*. Paris: Publications Modernes, 1911.

Fontaine, Laurence. "The Circulation of Luxury Goods in Eighteenth-Century Paris Social Redistribution and an Alternative Currency," in Maxine Berg and Elizabeth Eger, eds., *Luxury in the Eighteenth Century: Debates, Desires, and Delectable Goods*. London: Palgrave Macmillan, 2003: 89–102.

Foreman, Amanda. *Georgiana, Duchess of Devonshire*. New York: Random House, 1999.

Forray-Carlier, Anne. "La Famille royale aux Tuileries," in Jean-Marc Léri and Jean Tulard, eds., *La Famille royale à Paris: De l'histoire à la légende: Musée Carnavalet, 16 octobre 1993–9 janvier 1994*. Paris: Paris-Musées, 1993: 17–51.

Fournier-Sarlovèze. *Louis-Auguste Brun, peintre de Marie Antoinette*. Paris: Goupil, 1911.

Franck, André. *D'Éon: Chevalier et chevalière*. Paris: Amiot-Dumont, 1953.

Frasko, Mary. *Daring Do's: A History of Extraordinary Hair*. Paris and New York: Flammarion, 1994.

Freida, Leonie. *Catherine de Medici: Renaissance Queen of France*. New York: Fourth Estate/HarperCollins, 2003.

Fukai, Akiko. "Le vêtement rococo et néoclassique," in Rose-Marie Fayolle and Renée Davray-Piekolek (eds.), *La Mode en France 1715–1815: de Louis XV à Napoléon 1er*. Paris: Bibliothèque des Arts, 1990.

———. (ed.). *Fashion from the Eighteenth to the Twentieth Century*. Cologne: Taschen, 2004.

Funck-Brentano, Frantz. *L'Affaire du collier*. Paris: Hachette, 1903.

Furet, François. *Revolutionary France 1770–1880*. Trans. Antonia Nevill. Oxford, Eng.: Blackwell, 1996 [1992].

Galerie des modes et des costumes français, dessinés d'après nature. 16 vols. Paris: Chez les Sieurs Esnauts & Rapilly, 1778–1787.

Garber, Marjorie. *Vested Interests: Cross-dressing and Cultural Anxiety*. New York and London: Routledge, 1992.

Gay, Peter. *The Enlightenment: An Interpretation—The Rise of Modern Paganism*. New York: Knopf, 1966.

Gelbart, Nina Rattner. *Feminine and Opposition Journalism in Old Régime France: Le Journal des dames*. Berkeley and London: University of California Press, 1987.

————. "The *Journal des dames* and Its Female Editors: Politics, Censorship, and Feminism in the Old Régime Press," in Jack R. Censer and Jeremy Popkin (eds.), *Press and Politics in Pre-revolutionary France*. Berkeley and London: University of California Press, 1987.

Girault de Coursac, Paul and Pierrette. *Le Secret de la Reine*. Paris: F. X. de Guibert, 1996.

Godechot, Jacques. *La Prise de la Bastille: 14 juillet 1789*. Paris: Gallimard, 1965.

————. *La Révolution française: chronologie commentée 1789–1799*. Paris: Perrin, 1988.

Goncourt, Edmond and Jules de. *La femme au XVIIIᵉ siècle*. Paris: Flammarion, 1982.

————. *Histoire de la société française pendant la Révolution*. Paris: Boucher, 2002.

————. *Les Maîtresses de Louis XV et autres portraits de femmes*. Ed. Robert Kopp. Paris: Robert Laffont, 2003.

Goodman, Dena (ed.). *Marie-Antoinette: Writings on the Body of a Queen*. New York and London: Routledge, 2003.

Gruder, Vivian. *The Notables and the Nation: The Political Schooling of the French, 1787–1788* [unpublished manuscript].

————. "The Question of Marie Antoinette: The Queen and Public Opinion Before the Revolution." *French History* 16:3 (2002): 269–298.

Guillaumot, A. Étienne. *Costumes du XVIIIᵉ siècle*. Paris: Roquette, 1874.

Gutwirth, Madelyn. *Twilight of the Goddesses: Women and Representation in the French Revolutionary Era*. New Brunswick, N.J.: Rutgers University Press, 1992.

Haigh, Christopher. *Elizabeth I*. New York: Longmans, 1998.

Hamann, Jacques. "Louis XVII et l'enfant du Temple," in Jean-Marc Léri and Jean Tulard (eds.), *La Famille royale à Paris: De l'histoire à la légende: Musée Carnavalet, 16 octobre 1993–9 janvier 1994*. Paris: Paris-Musées, 1993.

Hammond, J. *A Keeper of Royal Secrets, Being the Private and Political Life of Madame de Genlis*. London: n.p., 1912.

Hampson, Norman. *A Cultural History of the Enlightenment*. New York: Pantheon, 1968.

Hardman, John. *The French Revolution Sourcebook*. London: Arnold, 1999.

————. *Louis XVI*. New Haven: Yale University Press, 1993.

Haslip, Joan. *Madame Du Barry: The Wages of Beauty*. New York: Grove Weidenfeld, 1991.

Henderson, Ernest F. *Symbol and Satire in the French Revolution*. New York and London: G. P. Putnam's Sons, 1912.

Hibbert, Christopher et al. *Versailles*. New York: Newsweek Book Division, 1972.

Hirsch, Charles (ed.). *Correspondance d'Eulalie, ou Tableau du libertinage à Paris*. Paris: Fayard, 1986 [1785].

Hosford, Desmond. "The Queen's Hair: Marie Antoinette, Politics, and DNA." *Eighteenth-Century Studies* 38:1 (autumn 2004): 183–200.

Huet, Marie-Hélène. *Mourning Glory: The Will of the French Revolution*. Philadelphia: University of Pennsylvania Press, 1997.

Hundert, Edward. "Mandeville, Rousseau, and the Political Economy of Fantasy," in Maxine Berg and Elizabeth Eger (eds.), *Luxury in the Eighteenth Century: Debates, Desires, and Delectable Goods*. London: Palgrave Macmillan, 2003: 28–40.

Hunt, Lynn. *The Family Romance of the French Revolution*. Berkeley: University of California Press, 1992.

————. "Freedom of Dress in Revolutionary France," in Sara E. Melzer and Kathryn Norberg (eds.), *From the Royal to the Republican Body: Incorporating the Political in Seventeenth- and Eighteenth-Century France*. Berkeley: University of California Press, 1988.

————. "History as Gesture, or the Scandal of History," in *Consequences of Theory: Selected Papers from the English Institute 1987–88*: 91–107.

————. "The Many Bodies of Marie Antoinette," in Dena Goodman (ed.), *Marie-Antoinette: Writings on the Body of a Queen*. New York and London: Routledge, 2003: 117–138.

————. "The Many Bodies of Marie Antoinette," in Lynn Hunt (ed.), *Eroticism and the Body Politic*. Baltimore: The Johns Hopkins University Press, 1991: 108–130.

————. *Politics, Culture, and Class in the French Revolution*. Berkeley: University of California Press, 1984.

Hurt, John J. *Louis XIV and the Parlements: The Assertion of Royal Authority*. Manchester and New York: Manchester University Press, 2002.

Hyde, Catherine [Marquise de Gouvion Broglie Scolari] (ed.). *Secret Memoirs of Princess Lamballe, Being her Journals, Letters, and Conversations During her Confidential Relations with Marie Antoinette*. Washington and London: M. Walter Dunne, 1901.

Jallut, Marguerite. *Marie Antoinette et ses peintres*. Paris: A. Noyer, 1955.

James-Sarazin, Ariane. "Le Miroir de la reine: Marie Antoinette et ses portraitistes," in Yves Carlier, Stéphane Castellucio, Anne Kraatz, and Françoise Tétart-Vittu (eds.), *Les Atours de la Reine*. Paris: Centre Historique des Archives Nationales, 2001: 13–24.

Join-Dieterle, Catherine, and Madeleine Delpierre (eds.). *Modes et Révolutions: Musée de la mode et du costume* (8 février–7 mai 1989). Paris: Éditions-Musées, 1989.

Jones, Ann Rosalind, and Peter Stallybrass. *Renaissance Clothing and the Materials of Memory*. New York: Cambridge University Press, 2000.

Jordan, David P. *The King's Trial: The French Revolution versus Louis XVI*. Berkeley: University of California Press, 1979.

Jourdain, Annie. *Monuments de la Révolution 1770–1804: Une histoire de répresentation*. Paris: Champion, 1997.

Kaiser, Thomas E. "Ambiguous Identities: Marie Antoinette and the House of Lorraine from the Affair of the Minuet to Lambesc's College," in Dena Goodman (ed.), *Marie-Antoinette: Writings on the Body of a Queen*. New York and London: Routledge, 2003: 171–198.

Karmel, Alex. *Guillotine in the Wings: A New Look at the French Revolution and Its Relevance to America Today*. New York: McGraw-Hill, 1972.

Kates, Gary. *Monsieur d'Éon Is a Woman: A Tale of Political Intrigue and Sexual Masquerade*. New York: Basic Books, 1995.

Keenan, Thomas. "The Point Is to (Ex)change It: Reading *Capital*, Rhetorically," in Emily Apter and William Pietz (eds.), *Fetishism as Cultural Discourse*. Ithaca, N.Y.: Cornell University Press, 1993: 152–185.

Kleinert, Annemarie. *Die-frühen Modejournale in Frankreich: Studien zur Literatur der Mode von den Anfängen bis 1848*. Berlin: Eric Schmidt Verlag, 1980.

————. *Le "Journal des dames et des modes": ou la conquête de l'Europe féminine*. Stuttgart: J. Thorbecke, 2001.

————. "La Mode, miroir de la Révolution française," in Catherine Join-Dieterle and Madeleine Delpierre, eds., *Modes et Révolutions: Musée de la mode et du costume (8 février–7 mai 1989)*. Paris: Editions Paris-Musées, 1989: 59–82.

Kopplin, Monika (ed.). *Les Laques du Japon: Collections de Marie Antoinette*. Paris: Réunion des Musées Nationaux, 2002.

Kraatz, Anne. "La 'Gazette des atours' de Marie Antoinette," in Yves Carlier, Stéphane Castellucio, Anne Kraatz, and Françoise Tétart-Vittu (eds.), *Les Atours de la Reine*. Paris: Centre Historique des Archives Nationales, 2001: 25–38.

————. "Marie Antoinette: la passion des étoffes." *L'Objet d'art* no. 357 (April 2001): 73–82.

Kunstler, Charles. *La Vie privée de Marie Antoinette*. Paris: Hachette, 1938.

————. *La Vie quotidienne sous Louis XVI*. Paris: Hachette, 1950.

La Bruyère, Jean de. *Les Caractères, ou les moeurs de ce siècle*. Ed. Robert Garapon. Paris: Garnier Frères, 1962 [1688].

Lacan, Jacques. *Écrits*. 2 vols. Paris: Seuil, 1966–1967.

Lamothe-Langon, Étienne-Léon, Baron de. *Memoirs of Madame Du Barri*. New York: Stokes & Co., 1930.

———. *Souvenirs sur Marie-Antoinette et la Cour de Versailles*. Ed. L. Mame. 4 vols. Paris: Bourgogne et Martinet, 1836.

Landes, Joan B. *Women and the Public Sphere in the Age of the French Revolution*. Ithaca, N.Y.: Cornell University Press, 1988.

Langlade, Émile. *La Marchande de modes de Marie-Antoinette: Rose Bertin*. Paris: Albin Michel, 1911.

Laurent, Rachel. "Marie Antoinette: le caprice et le style." *Art-Presse* (1988): 113–115.

Leclercq, Jean-Paul. "Sur la Garde-robe de Marie Leczinska et de Marie Antoinette." *L'Oeil: Magazine international d'art*, no. 478 (January–February 1996): 30–39.

Lenôtre, G. [Théodore Gosselin] (ed.). *La Captivité et la mort de Marie Antoinette*. Paris: Perrin et Cie., 1897.

———. *The Flight of Marie Antoinette*. Trans. Mrs. Rodolph Stawell. Philadelphia: J. B. Lippincott, 1908.

———. *Versailles au temps des rois*. Paris: Bernard Grasset, 1934.

Léri, Jean-Marc, and Jean Tulard (eds.), *La Famille royale à Paris: De l'histoire à la légende (Musée Carnavalet 16 octobre 1993–9 janvier 1994)*. Paris: Éditions Paris-Musées, 1994.

Lescure, Mathurin de. *La Princesse de Lamballe*. Paris: H. Plon, 1864.

Lesniewicz, Paul. *The World of Bonsai*. London: Blanford, 1990.

Lever, Evelyne. *Louis XVI*. Paris: Fayard, 1985.

———. *Philippe-Égalité*. Paris: Fayard, 1996.

Levin, Carole. *"The Heart and Stomach of a King": Elizabeth I and the Politics of Sex and Power*. Philadelphia: University of Pennsylvania Press, 1994.

Levin, Harry. *The Myth of the Golden Age in the Renaissance*. Bloomington and London: Indiana University Press, 1969.

Lewis, W. H. *The Splendid Century*. New York: Sloane, 1953.

Manceron, Claude. *Blood of the Bastille 1787–1789*. Trans. Nancy Amphoux. New York: Touchstone/Simon & Schuster, 1989.

Mansel, Philip. *Dressed to Rule: Royal and Court Costume from Louis XIV to Elizabeth II*. New Haven and London: Yale University Press, 2005.

Marie Antoinette, Archiduchesse, Dauphine et Reine: Exposition au château de Versailles 16 mai–2 novembre 1955. Paris: Éditions des Musées Nationaux, 1955.

Marin, Louis. *Le Portrait du roi*. Paris: Minuit, 1981.

Martin, Henri. *Histoire de France, depuis les temps les plus reculés jusqu'en 1787*. Paris: Furne, 1865.

May, Gita. *Élisabeth Vigée Le Brun: The Odyssey of an Artist in an Age of Revolution*. New Haven and London: Yale University Press, 2005.

Maza, Sarah. "The Diamond Necklace Affair Revisited (1785–1786): The Case of the Missing Queen," in Dena Goodman (ed.), *Marie-Antoinette: Writings on the Body of a Queen*. New York and London: Routledge, 2003: 73–97.

———. *Private Lives and Public Affairs: The Causes Célèbres of Pre-revolutionary France*. Berkeley: University of California Press, 1993.

McDonald, Christie. "Words of Change: August 12, 1789," in Sandy Petrey (ed.), *The French Revolution 1789–1989: Two Hundred Years of Rethinking*. Lubbock: Texas Tech University Press, 1989: 33–46.

Michelet, Jules, *Histoire de la Révolution française*. Paris: Laffont, 1979.

Millingen, J. G. *Recollections of Republican France from 1790 to 1801*. London: H. Colburn, 1848.

Mossiker, Frances. *The Queen's Necklace*. New York: Simon & Schuster, 1961.

Naginski, Erica. "The Object of Contempt." *Fragments of Revolution*, a special issue of *Yale French Studies*, no. 101. Eds. Caroline Weber and Howard G. Lay. Yale University Press, 2002: 32–53.

Néret, Gilles. *Erotica Universalis*. Cologne: Taschen, 1994.

Nolhac, Pierre de. *Autour de la Reine*. Paris: Tallendier, 1929.

———. *La Dauphine Marie Antoinette*. Paris: Nelson, 1896.

———. "La Garde-Robe de Marie Antoinette." *Le Correspondant* (25 September 1925): 840–859.

———. *The Trianon of Marie Antoinette*. Trans. F. Mabel Robinson. London: T. F. Unwin, 1925.

Olausson, Magnus (ed.). *Marie Antoinette: Porträtt av en drottning*. Stockholm: Nationalmuseum, 1989.

Ondaatje, Michael. *The Collected Works of Billy the Kid*. New York: W. W. Norton, 1974.

Outram, Dorinda. "Review of Richard Wrigley, *The Politics of Appearances: Representations of Dress in Revolutionary France*." *H-France* (January 2004): http://www3.uakron.edu/hfrance/reviews/outram.html.

Ozouf, Mona. *Varennes: la mort de la royauté, 21 juin 1791*. Paris: Gallimard, 2005.

Padover, Saul K. *The Life and Death of Louis XVI*. New York and London: D. Appleton-Century, 1939.

Pastoureau, Michel. *Dictionnaire des couleurs de notre temps*. Paris: Bonneton, 1992.

Payne, Blanche. *A History of Costume*. New York: Harper & Row, 1965.

Pellegrin, Nicole. *Vêtements de la liberté: abécédaire de pratiques vestimentaires en France de 1780 à 1800*. Aix-en-Provence: Alinéa, 1989.

Pizard, Alfred. *La France en 1789*. Paris: n.p., n.d.

Popkin, Jeremy. "Pamphlet Journalism at the End of the Old Régime." *Eighteenth-Century Studies* 22 (1982): 351–67.

Pernod, Régine, and Marie-Véronique Clin. *Joan of Arc: Her Story*. Ed. Bonnie Wheeler. Trans. Jeremy du Quesnay Adams. New York: St. Martin's Press, 1998.

Price, Munro. *The Road from Versailles: Louis XVI, Marie-Antoinette, and the Fall of the French Monarchy*. New York: St. Martin's Press, 2002.

Quicherat, Jules Etienne Joseph. *Histoire du costume en France depuis les temps les plus reculés jusqu'à la fin du XVIIIᵉ siècle*. Paris: Hachette, 1875.

Quinet, Edgar. *La Révolution française*. Paris: Belin, 1989.

Reiset, Gustave-Armand-Henry, Comte de. *Modes et usages au temps de Marie Antoinette: Livre-journal de Madame Éloffe*. 2 vols. Paris: Firmin-Didot, 1885.

Revel, Jacques. "Marie Antoinette and Her Fictions: The Staging of Hatred," in Bernadette Ford (ed.), *Fictions of the French Revolution*. Evanston, Ill.: Northwestern University Press, 1991.

Ribeiro, Aileen. *The Art of Dress: Fashions in England and France 1750 to 1820*. New Haven and London: Yale University Press, 1995.

———. *Dress in Eighteenth-Century Europe: 1715–1789*. New Haven and London: Yale University Press, 2002.

———. *Fashion in the French Revolution*. New York: Holmes & Meier, 1988.

Rimbault, Caroline. "La Presse féminine de langue française au XVIIIᵉ siècle." Diss. Université de Paris, 1981.

Roche, Daniel. "Apparences révolutionnaires ou révolution des apparences," in Catherine Join-Dieterle and Madeleine Delpierre, eds., *Modes et Révolutions: Musée de la mode et du costume (8 février–7 mai 1989).* Paris: Éditions Paris-Musées, 1989: 193–210.

———. *The Culture of Clothing: Dress and Fashion in the Ancien Régime.* Trans. Jean Birrell. Cambridge, Eng.: Cambridge University Press, 1994.

———. *Histoire des choses banales.* Paris: Fayard, 1997.

Rousseau, Jean-Jacques. *The Collected Writings of Jean-Jacques Rousseau.* Ed. and trans. by Roger Masters and Christopher Kelly. 4 vols. Hanover, N.H.: University Press of New England for Dartmouth College, 1990–1992.

———. *La Nouvelle Héloïse: Julie, or the New Heloise.* Trans. Judith H. McDowell. University Park: Pennsylvania State University Press, 1968.

Saint-Amand, Pierre. "Adorning Marie Antoinette." *Eighteenth-Century Life* 15:3 (1991): 19–34.

———. "Terrorizing Marie-Antoinette," in Dena Goodman, ed., *Marie-Antoinette: Writings on the Body of a Queen.* New York and London: Routledge, 2003: 253–272.

Saint-Étienne, Rabaut. *Précis historique de la Révolution française.* Paris: Didot, [1792].

Sainte-Beuve, C. A. *Portraits of the Eighteenth Century, Historic and Literary.* Trans. Katherine P. Wormeley. 2 vols. New York: Ungar, 1964.

Salvadori, Philippe. *La Chasse sous l'ancien régime.* Paris: Fayard, 1996.

Sapori, Michelle. *Rose Bertin: Ministre des modes de Marie Antoinette.* Paris: Éditions de l'Institut Français de la Mode, 2003.

Schama, Simon. *Citizens: A Chronicle of the French Revolution.* New York: Vintage, 1989.

Semmens, Richard. *The Bals Publics at the Paris Opéra in the Eighteenth Century.* Hillsdale, N.J.: Pendragon Press, 2004.

Sheriff, Mary. "The Portrait of the Queen," in Dena Goodman, ed., *Marie-Antoinette: Writings on the Body of a Queen.* New York and London: Routledge, 2003.

———. "Woman? Hermaphrodite? History Painter? On the Self-Imaging of Élisabeth Vigée-Lebrun." *The Eighteenth Century* 35:1 (1994): 3–27.

Shevelow, Kathryn. *Charlotte: Being a True Account of an Actress's Flamboyant Adventures in Eighteenth-Century London's Wild and Wicked Theatrical World.* New York: Henry Holt, 2005.

Soboul, Albert. *Les Sans-culottes en l'An II: Mouvement populaire et gouvernement révolutionnaire.* Paris: Seuil, 1968.

Starobinski, Jean. *1789, les emblèmes de la raison.* Paris: Flammarion, 1973.

Steele, Valerie. *The Corset: A Cultural History.* New Haven and London: Yale University Press, 2001.

Tackett, Timothy. *When the King Took Flight.* Cambridge, Mass.: Harvard University Press, 2002.

Tapié, Victor Lucien. *L'Europe de Marie-Thérèse: du baroque aux lumières.* Paris: Fayard, 1973.

Tétart-Vittu, Françoise. "1780–1804 ou Vingt ans de 'Révolution des têtes françaises,'" in Catherine Join-Dieterle and Madeleine Delpierre, eds., *Modes et Révolutions: Musée de la mode et du costume (8 février–7 mai 1989).* Paris: Éditions Paris-Musées, 1989: 41–58.

———. "La Garde-robe de Marie Antoinette et le regard des historiens," in Yves Carlier, Stephane Castellucio, Anne Kraatz, and Françoise Tétart-Vittu (eds.), *Les Atours de la Reine.* Paris: Centre Historique des Archives Nationales, 2001: 39–44.

———. "Presse et diffusion des modes françaises," in Catherine Join-Dieterle and Madeleine Delpierre, eds., *Modes et Révolutions: Musée de la mode et du costume (8 février–7 mai 1989).* Paris: Editions Paris-Musées, 1989: 129–136.

Thomas, Chantal. *The Wicked Queen: The Origins of the Myth of Marie Antoinette.* Trans. Julie Rose. New York: Zone Books, 1999.

Valensise, Marina. "La Constitution française," in Keith Michael Baker, ed., *Revolution and the Creation of Modern Political Culture.* 4 vols. Oxford and New York: Pergamon Press, 1987.

Van Dijk, Suzanna. *Traces des femmes: Présence feminine dans le journalisme du XVIIe siècle.* Amsterdam and Maarssen: Holland University Press, 1988.

Van Elslande, Jean-Pierre. *L'Imaginaire pastoral du XVIIe siècle: 1600–1650.* Paris: Presses Universitaires de France, 1999.

Varron, A. *Paris Fashion Artists of the Eighteenth Century.* Special issue of *Ciba Review*, no. 25 (1939): 878–912.

Viel-Castel, Horace de. *Collection de costumes, armes et meubles pour servir à l'histoire de la Révolution française et l'Empire.* Paris: Treuttel and Wurtz, 1834.

Villers, Chevalier de. *Essai historique sur la mode et la toilette française.* Paris: 1824.

Walzer, Michael. *Regicide and Revolution: Speeches at the Trial of Louis XVI.* Trans. Marian Rothstein. New York: Columbia University Press, 1992.

Weber, Caroline. *Terror and Its Discontents: Suspect Words in Revolutionary France.* Minneapolis: University of Minnesota Press, 2003.

Wilcox, R. Turner. *The Mode in Costume.* New York: Charles Scribner's Sons, 1958.

Williams, H. Noel. *Memoirs of Madame Dubarry of the Court of Louis XV.* New York: P. F. Collier & Son, 1910.

Wrigley, Richard. *The Politics of Appearances: Representations of Dress in Revolutionary France.* Oxford, Eng., and New York: Berg, 2002.

Zanger, Abby. "Making Sweat: Sex and the Gender of National Reproduction in the Marriage of Louis XIII." *Corps mystique, corps sacré: Textual Transfigurations of the Body from the Middle Ages to the Seventeenth Century*, a special issue of *Yale French Studies*, no. 86. Eds. Benjamin Semple and Françoise Jaouën. Yale University Press, 1994: 187–205.

· ACKNOWLEDGMENTS ·

It is safe to say that I would never have managed to complete this project without the wit, wisdom, and tireless efforts of my agent, Rob McQuilkin, and my editor, George Hodgman. As they both know all too well, there were many days when working on this book felt more like a trip to the guillotine than an afternoon at the Petit Trianon. I could not, however, have asked for two more gifted readers or patient morale-boosters than Rob and George. Indeed, nothing would make me happier than for us to work as a trio again—and again and again. In the meantime, I am looking for a stylist who will make me a *pouf au sentiment* bearing their likenesses, framed by the pages of brilliant edits with which they helped me to make an argument and tell a story.

At Henry Holt, John Sterling, Sara Bershtel, Jennifer Barth, Supurna Banerjee, Erica Gelbard, Raquel Jaramillo, Richard Rhorer, Kenn Russell, and Kelly Too all gave my project more enthusiastic support than I could ever have hoped to expect. As copy editor and proofreader, respectively, Jolanta Benal worked miracles. At Lippincott Massie McQuilkin, Maria Massie deftly guided me through the foreign rights process, while Will Lippincott stepped in at a key moment during the initial marketing phase. Arabella Stein worked wonders with the sale of this book in Great Britain. My research assistant, Sara Phenix, deserves special notice for her indefatigable willingness to track down elusive images and inscrutable facts; I was enormously lucky to have her as a partner in historical sleuthing.

I also owe a tremendous debt of gratitude to those colleagues and friends who agreed to read bits and pieces of this manuscript before its publication. Faith Beasley and Darrin McMahon provided encouraging early feedback. Along with a kind invitation to present pieces of this manuscript at University College London,

Jann Matlock gave me one of the most rigorous, thought-provoking, and scrupulously detailed critiques I have ever received, and I hope these pages are the better for it. Other invaluable guidance came from Dan Edelstein, Maurie Samuels, Claire Goldstein, Jean-Vincent Blanchard, and Kate Norberg. Pierre Saint-Amand and Tom Kaiser, both of whom have published brilliantly on Marie Antoinette, were extremely generous with their time and their insights. I am likewise most grateful for the magnanimous input of Chantal Thomas, whose identification of Marie Antoinette as a "queen of fashion" first inspired me to explore the subject further.

Thanks also to my colleagues Peter Connor, Serge Gavronsky, Anne Boyman, Rachel Mesch, Brian O'Keeffe, Antoine Compagnon, Pierre Force, Elisabeth Ladenson, James Helgeson, Joanna Stalnaker, Sarah Sasson, and Priya Wadhera for making the French departments at Barnard and Columbia such collegial and rewarding places to work; to the members of the Columbia Early Modern Salon for ongoing intellectual stimulation; and to Tracy Hazas, the departmental administrator at Barnard, for cheerfully resolving any number of logistical and technical crises.

My friend and mentor, Larry Kritzman, thoughtfully invited me to present a portion of this work at the Dartmouth Institute for French Cultural Studies; his and the other seminar members' illuminating feedback remained with me for a long time after I left Hanover. I am likewise grateful to Wendy Steiner for inviting me to begin this project under the auspices of the Penn Humanities Forum's yearlong seminar on "Style" in 2000, and to students of my "Mythes de Marie Antoinette" courses at the University of Pennsylvania for their infectious enthusiasm for the subject.

I am thankful to Laura Auricchio, Judith Dolkart, Vivian Gruder, Gita May, Daniel Rosenberg, and Downing Thomas for sharing their expertise on matters ranging from *donatrices patriotiques* to tricolor cockades to Opéra girls. Amanda Foreman, Simon Schama, and Antonia Fraser all graciously made time for someone who had previously only admired their writings from afar; I feel privileged to have met each of them. Gridley McKim Smith became an inspiring interlocutor about the pleasures and challenges of writing about costume. Meg O'Rourke has been an infinitely sagacious sounding board about all manner of writerly issues, from the two-page-a-day rule to the irresolvable tension between *anomie* and lip gloss. Unsung authorities on the treacherous social culture of Versailles, Joan Dejean, Elena Russo, and Julia Douthwaite afforded me a heightened understanding of the complex dynamic between Marie Antoinette and Mesdames the Aunts.

In France, I have benefited from the knowledgeable guidance of numerous librarians, curators, and cultural officials. Foremost among these are Camille Boisseau at the Musée de l'Histoire de France; Anne Bonnardel in the Département des Estampes at the Bibliothèque Nationale; and the extraordinary Cécile Coutin, who is both a librarian at the Bibliothèque Nationale and a leading light of the Association Marie Antoinette. Ariane James-Sarazin and Michèle Bimbenet at the Archives

Nationales de France made it possible for me to consult firsthand Marie Antoinette's surviving *gazettes des atours:* an unforgettable experience for which I shall always be thankful. In England, Emmajane Lawrence included me in an exciting Marie Antoinette study day at the Wallace Collection. Here in New York, I received wonderful support from the Rare Books and Prints curators at the New York Public Library and from Will Russell, George McNeely, Will Strafford, Kate Swan, and Marissa Wilcox at Christie's. In the fashion world, I am deeply grateful to Anna Wintour and Valerie Steiker for excerpting this book in *Vogue,* and to Marc Jacobs for his efforts to get my manuscript into the right hands.

Directly or indirectly, this project has also benefited from the kindness and generosity of the following individuals: Elizabeth Amman, Ulrich Baer, Betsy Bradley, Dan Brewer, Peter Brooks, Tayyibe Gülek Domaç, Ginna Foster, Michael Friedman, Christine Harper, Anne Hayes, Eve Herzog, Elisabeth Hodges, Ömer Koç, Paul Kopperl, Natasha Lee, Claude Mosséri-Marlio, Alain Nerot and David Selikowitz, Rulonna Neilson, Alexandra Pelosi, Ruth Powell, Gerry Prince, Jean-Michel Rabaté, Michèle Richman, Tory Robbins, Sheryl Sandberg and Dave Goldberg, Valerie Schweitzer, Laura Silverstein, Claudia Solacini, Jacob Soll, Teresa Teague, Gillian Thomas, and Liliane Weissberg. My husband's parents and siblings—Jack, Lois, Sally, and Bill Stegeman—have been admirably patient with me despite the constraints this project has placed on my availability for family gatherings. Even more prodigal with their compassion, my own parents and brother—Jack, Carol, and Jonathan Weber—remain three of the most important people in my life. Not only have they spent over three decades enduring my own unpredictable fashion statements; they have offered me nothing but unconditional love and support ever since I declared my intention to write about someone else's.

Last, but certainly not least, I would like to thank Tom Stegeman, my husband, my knight in shining armor, and my *grand amour.* He read an early iteration of this manuscript two years ago in a deer-blind, and he has gracefully withstood living with Marie Antoinette ever since. More than that, he has taken care of me in ways that I cannot begin to enumerate, and for which no words can adequately express my appreciation. Like its author, this book is dedicated to him.

· ILLUSTRATION ACKNOWLEDGMENTS ·

Plate 1. John Galliano for Christian Dior, "Masquerade and Bondage" (2000) (*Women's Wear Daily*)

Plate 2. Georg Weikert after Martin Mytens, *"The Triumph of Love": A Ballet Performed by the Archdukes and Archduchesses of Austria on the Occasion of Joseph II's Marriage* [detail] (1765) (Réunion des Musées Nationaux/Art Resource, NY)

Plate 3. Joseph Ducreux, *Marie Antoinette, Archduchess of Austria* (1769) (Réunion des Musées Nationaux/Art Resource, NY)

Plate 4. Unknown, *Louis XIV as Apollo in the Ballet, "La Nuit"* (17th century) (Réunion des Musées Nationaux/Art Resource, NY)

Plate 5. French School, *Marie Antoinette Arriving at Versailles* (1770) (Réunion des Musées Nationaux/Art Resource, NY)

Plate 6. Louis-Auguste Brun, *Marie Antoinette on Horseback* (1781–1782) (Réunion des Musées Nationaux/Art Resource, NY)

Plate 7. René-Antoine Houasse, *Louis XIV on Horseback* (1679–1690) (Réunion des Musées Nationaux/Art Resource, NY)

Plate 8. French School, *Marie Antoinette of Austria, Queen of France* (c. 1778)

Plate 9. French fashion caricature: *Coiffure à l'Indépendance or the Triumph of Liberty* (c. 1778) (Réunion des Musées Nationaux/Art Resource, NY)

Plate 10. A corset belonging to Marie Antoinette (The Picture Gallery at the New York Public Library)

Plate 11. Jean-Baptiste Gautier-Dagoty, *Marie Antoinette Wearing Court Dress* (1775) (Réunion des Musées Nationaux/Art Resource, NY)

Plate 12.   Plate from *Galerie des modes: Robe à la polonaise* (1778) (The Picture Gallery at the New York Public Library)

Plate 13.   Vicenza Benzi-Bastéris, *Marie Antoinette, Archduchess of Austria, Queen of France* (late 18th century) (Réunion des Musées Nationaux/Art Resource, NY)

Plate 14.   Plate from *Galerie des modes: Redingote à l'Allemande* (1787) (The Picture Gallery at the New York Public Library)

Plate 15.   Élisabeth Vigée-Lebrun, *The Comtesse Du Barry* (1781) (Philadelphia Museum of Art/Art Resource, NY)

Plate 16.   Joseph Boze, *Marie Thérèse Louise de Savoige Carignan, Princesse de* Lamballe (late 18th century) (Réunion des Musées Nationaux/Art Resource, NY)

Plate 17.   Plate from *Galerie des modes:* Milkmaid's bonnet and apron (c. 1780) (The Picture Gallery at the New York Public Library)

Plate 18.   Unknown, *Marie Antoinette of Austria* (c. 1780s) (Bibliothèque Nationale de France, Paris)

Plate 19.   Eugène Battaille, after Adolf Ulrik von Wertmüller, *Marie Antoinette at the Petit Trianon* (19th-century copy of the 1785 painting) (Réunion des Musées Nationaux/Art Resource, NY)

Plate 20.   Fashion engraving: *Coiffure à la redoute and Coiffure à la Nation* (1790) (The Picture Gallery at the New York Public Library)

Plate 21.   Plate from *Le Journal de la mode et du goût:* "A Woman Patriot in Her New Uniform" (1790) (Bibliothèque Nationale de France, Paris)

Plate 22.   Anonymous, *Marie Antoinette as a Harpy* (c. 1789) (Snark/Art Resource, NY)

Plate 23.   Pierre-Étienne Lesueur, *Arrest of Louis XVI at Varennes* (c. 1791) (Erich Lessing/Art Resource, NY)

Plate 24.   The Marquise de Bréhan, *Marie Antoinette Imprisoned in the Conciergerie* (c. 1793–1795) (Erich Lessing/Art Resource, NY)

Plate 25.   William Hamilton, *Marie Antoinette Taken to the Guillotine* (1794) (Réunion des Musées Nationaux/Art Resource, NY)

Plate 26.   Jacques Louis David, *Marie Antoinette on Her Way to the Scaffold* (1793) (Giraudon/Art Resource, NY)

ABOUT THE AUTHOR

Caroline Weber is an associate professor of French at Barnard College, Columbia University. A specialist in eighteenth-century French literature, culture, and history, she has also taught at the University of Pennsylvania and Yale University. Her other publications include a book on the Reign of Terror, an edited volume of *Yale French Studies,* numerous academic essays, and articles for *Vogue* and *The New York Times.* She lives with her husband in New York City.